The Writer's Handbook

Edited by
SYLVIA K. BURACK
Editor, *The Writer*

Publishers　　　　THE WRITER, INC.　　　　Boston

808.02
W956
1986

"Guidelines for the Beginning Playwright," Copyright © 1981
by Louis E. Catron

"The Editor's Side," by Olga Litowinsky, is reprinted by permission from *Publishers Weekly*. Copyright © 1985 Xerox Corporation.

"One Clue at a Time," by P. D. James, is reprinted by permission. Copyright © 1983 The New York Times Company.

"Writing Poetry for Children," Copyright © 1977 by Myra Cohn Livingston

"Putting Science into Science Fiction," by Gregory Benford.
Copyright © 1983 by Abbenford Associates.

"Creating Television Stories and Characters," from *Writing for Film and Television*, by Stewart Bronfeld (Prentice-Hall, Inc.). Copyright © 1981 by Stewart Bronfeld. A Book-of-the-Month Club Quality Paperback selection.

"Notes for a Young Writer," from *Come Along With Me*, by Shirley Jackson. Copyright © 1968 by Stanley Edgar Hyman. Reprinted by permission of Viking Penguin Inc.

"How to Sell Your Television Script" is reprinted by permission of the author from *Television Writing: From Concept to Contract*, by Richard A. Blum. 1st edition copyright © 1980 by Richard A. Blum. Revised edition © 1984, published by Focal Press/Butterworth Publishers, 80 Montvale Avenue, Stoneham, MA.

Library of Congress Catalog Card Number: 36-28596
ISBN: 0-87116-145-1

Printed in The United States of America

CONTENTS

PART I—BACKGROUND FOR WRITERS

PART II—HOW TO WRITE: TECHNIQUES

GENERAL FICTION

SPECIALIZED FICTION

NONFICTION: ARTICLES AND BOOKS

PART III—EDITORS, AGENTS, AND BUSINESS

PART IV—WHERE TO SELL

THE WRITER'S HANDBOOK

1

THE WILL TO WRITE

By Rumer Godden

"WHAT is needed is constant work, day and night; constant reading, study, will. . . . Every hour is precious for it. You must drop your vanity. You are not a child. It is time."

That is what Chekhov said, perhaps some two hundred years ago, to a young writer who wanted advice, but if he had said it now, probably the young writer would have laughed: He knows quicker, easier, more competent ways—he, but not all young writers. More and more of these gifted young people seem to be falling out of love with the short-cut mechanical methods and are trying to get back to the old traditions, which, I suspect, is why the Editors of *The Writer* have asked me to describe my own Chekhovian and tortoise ways. These are not, I hasten to add, "dictates"—all authors are different—but ways that I have found rewarding for myself.

When I was a young novelist, I, and almost all the serious writers of that time—I smile now when I remember how intensely serious we were—wanted one thing above all for our novels: that they would last. Not as long as Chekhov—I do not think any of us dared to aspire to that—but at least for a worthwhile span. We wanted success, too—what writer does not?—but, even if we achieved a splash (as I did with *Black Narcissus*), in spite of the notices, the invitations, the big advances and extravagant "rights," we had an innate recognition that this would be just a brief hour in the limelight, and that the only success worth having meant building it book by book, usually slowly, laboriously, by that "constant work day and night." This sounds an impossible dictum, but "constant" does not merely mean "perpetual": its larger meaning is faithfulness, firmness of purpose, resolution.

The word, though, that jumps out from Chekhov's axiom is "will," the will to write. I have never understood why "hard work" is supposed

3

to be pitiable. True, some work is soul-destroying when it is done against the grain, but when it is part of a "making" how can you grudge it? You get tired, of course, often in despair, but the struggle, the feeling of being extended as you never thought you could be, is fulfilling and deeply, deeply satisfying. Yet, sadly, most young writers nowadays seem not to know what hard work is. How can they? It has never been required of them in those important formulative years of their literary career. Instead, they are encouraged to "express themselves" before they have learned to use their language; they take "creative writing" courses, never dreaming that "creation" is the acme, not the beginning.

No one else can teach a writer how to write or how to use imagination; only life and experience can teach that, but he or she can and should be taught technique. In this I was lucky. When I was at the last of the several schools from which I was not expelled, but "asked to be removed"—I was an abominable girl—the teacher of English, herself a writer, suggested I should be taken out of class and the school curriculum and work alone under her. "Aha!" I thought. "Now I can write my stories, my poems"—and what did I do? For a whole term I had to reduce, every day, the leader in our *Times* newspaper to fourteen lines; I know well what Thoreau meant when he said, "It's a short book but it takes a long time to make it short!" I did write poetry, but always in set forms: sonnets, rondels, triolets, Anglo-Saxon riddles, haiku. I spent weeks comparing Milton's use of consonants to achieve the melancholy of "Il Penseroso," the gaiety of "L'Allegro." It was grammar, grammar, grammar: tracing the roots of words, writing a story without a single adjective or adverb. My teacher told me long afterwards she often wondered how much more I would take but, rebellious and opinionated as I was, miraculously I had the wit to understand what she was arming me with, and I would not have changed her for the world.

When I left that school, peaceably this time, in no way did she try to influence me except to advise me to do something quite different for two or three years—I did dancing for ten—and when, at last, I began to write freely, she would not even look at what I was doing. I quickly learned not to let anyone else look either, nor even talk about it, but I am sure it was the discipline she gave me, the instilled patience, tenacity and, yes, courage—it takes a lot of courage to be a writer—that made me follow the lonely secret way in which I so much believe and which has, in a measure, been justified: The books I have written have lasted surprisingly long.*

I hope that does not seem like boasting. There is no room for that in a writer's career. "Drop your vanity," said Chekhov, and I know that as soon as I approach a new book or story, humility is bound, willy-nilly, to appear. How can I do it, I wonder? How start? Worse, how go on? I have to try again and again—and I am not alone: Rebecca West, doyenne of fine writers, once told me she wrote a certain chapter twenty-six times. Oddly enough, so did Turgenev.

Some writers make blueprints of their books with the chapters drafted out, what is to go into each, what part each chapter will play. This strikes me as fearfully clever and fearfully dull—"fearfully" because it must be limiting. It is far more exciting to let the book take almost its own path, but I have one shibboleth which, as far as I have discovered is peculiar to me and must seem extremely peculiar to any sensible person: If I am writing a story, set in a place or about a way of life unfamiliar to me—such as the enclosed Benedictine Abbey of *In This House of Brede,* or the Italian setting of *The Battle of the Villa Fiorita*— I write the story first and research the place and way of life afterwards. I have, of course, to alter, correct, fill in, but I have a novel, not a documentary. With my characters, again, I let them grow; if characters are forced to illustrate a purpose they seem to remain cardboard. Readers tell me mine are alive: if so, it is only because I give them time to make themselves known to me. I put it like that because, given that time, they seem presently to assert a character of their own, sometimes even contradicting my original conception—and causing endless trouble! It must also be person to person, as it were; even to talk about a character to anyone is an interference. Names, too, are important; I cannot begin to know a character until I have found a name that fits.

"Names" bring me to words. I have a passion for words and am always glad to think my great-grandfather was a Professor of Philology. It is a realm of wonders. Who has ever come to the end of the riches— and of surprise—of Shakespeare's words? Of how Dylan Thomas, for instance, new-minted his? In any writer of imagination there must be a hidden poet because, through every good book, there runs a rhythm

*Black Narcissus, written in 1938, has never been out of print.

that is its writer's style, and if that is interfered with, the flavor, the individuality is lost. You have, in the deepest meaning of the old cliché, to choose your words, brood over them, listen to them, and that takes time. Well, why not? Once we wrote with a quill pen: We had to pause to sharpen and shape it, which gave time for thought; most of us know how doing something with our hands releases thought. (It is said that one poet whittled away his whole quill because he was so deep in thought.) Then we had dip pens; at least we had to dip, change nibs. Then came fountain pens which had to be filled; then, of course type-writers, dictaphones (It is remarkable that, as soon as any author uses a dictaphone, he becomes prolix; think of Henry James.) Now word processors have arrived to beguile us, and some authors use computers. They save time and trouble, which is true, but a book *needs* time and trouble, and there is something else these mechanics prevent—an intangible thing that perhaps only true artists know: There is a mystique between the brain, the hand and the pen or brush. That may sound exaggerated, but you will read of it again and again, in the accounts and memoirs of the Chinese and Japanese calligraphers. The West seems largely to have lost this, but any artist who uses a beloved tool—a pen, an exactly sharpened pencil, a brush that fits its purpose—knows that sometimes a flow is established between it and him, rhythmic and bringing strange power. I know you can have a flow on a typewriter—at times it seems to run away from you—but I distrust it because it is too quick, and can you love a typewriter as you love a pen or tool?

That mystique is needed because, no matter how experienced you are, how thorough your technique, the book can still fail. Then an author's best friend is the wastepaper basket or the fire. If my trusted publishers feel it better not to publish a book of mine, that is where it will go; I would never ask my agent to offer it anywhere else. There is, too, something wonderfully prodigal in watching a year's—maybe two years'—work go up in flames, but I have one more "trick" before the book reaches that.

There comes a time when, though there is still discontent, I know I have done my best, such as it is, and the need for secrecy is over, so I find some poor victim and read the book aloud, not for anyone else's reactions but for my own, as nothing shows more clearly where the story flows or drags, loses interest. The worst indictment, of course, would be if the victim went to sleep! It hasn't happened so far. Afterwards, I cut, "considering faithfully," as Kipling counseled, "every paragraph, sentence and word." I wish I could cut as he did, instead of using a mundane blue pencil and scissors. His way was to "take well-ground Indian Ink, as much as suffices and a camel hair brush, and black out where requisite: re-read and you will find it will bear a second shortening. Think it over and a shade more brushwork may impose itself. If not, praise Allah, and let it go."

Let it go. It is at this point that wise, sensitive editors can help, as indeed they do; but unless what they say strikes an inner chord of conviction—as it usually does—you have to stand out against even this counsel. I have had to fight for a book and, over and over again, for a title, because this curious writing integrity that has been given me said, "No."

When my last novel was published, I received from the publicity department one of those biographical questionnaires sent to authors these days. Some of the questions were impertinent, especially, I thought, the last: "What makes you feel your books are different from other peoples'?" I did not have to ponder over this because there is really only one answer: "What makes my books different? They are written by me."

Every author ought to be able to say that.

2

DON'T THINK: WRITE!

By Madeleine L'Engle

WHEN we write, for whom do we write? Or, as we would be more likely to ask, whom do we write for?

It sounds like an easy question to answer, and in some ways it is. But when it is applied to the matter of fiction, the logical answer—that we write for a specific audience—does not work. At least not for me.

Each year I teach at one or more writers workshops. I enjoy them for many reasons, not the least of which is the opportunity to meet other workshop leaders, often writers whose work I have long admired. Writing is a solitary profession, and a writers conference gives us a chance to get together. Another reason I enjoy the workshops is that I am forced to articulate what I have learned about the techniques of the craft of fiction writing; it is easy to get forgetful and sloppy. Having to explain imagery, simile, metaphor, point of view, is a way to continue to teach myself as well as the people who have come to the workshop.

At one workshop, I talked, as usual, about all the hard work that precedes the writing of fiction. Often there is research to be done. For my Time Trilogy I had to immerse myself in the new physics: first, Einstein's theories of relativity and Planck's quantum theory for *A Wrinkle in Time;* then cellular biology and particle physics for *A Wind in the Door;* and astrophysics and non-linear theories of time for *A Swiftly Tilting Planet.* For *The Love Letters* I had to learn a great deal more about seventeenth-century Portuguese history than I needed or wanted to know, so that the small amount needed for the book would be accurate. Before, during, and after research, the writer needs to be thinking constantly about the characters, and the direction in which the novel seems to be moving.

Does the story have the Aristotelian beginning, middle, and end? How do the events of the novel relate to me, personally, in my own journey through life? What are my own particular concerns at the time of writing, and how should they affect—or not affect—the story? When I actually sit down to write, I stop thinking. While I am writing, I am listening to the story; I am not listening to myself.

"But," a young woman in the class said in a horrified tone of voice, "my creative writing teacher says that we must keep the audience in mind at all times."

That is undoubtedly true for the scientist writing an article that is expected to be understood by people who have little or no scientific background. The writer will have to keep simplifying scientific language, explaining technical terms. Keeping the audience in mind is probably valuable for reporting in newspapers and magazines. The reporter is writing for the average reader; language should be neither so bland as to be insulting, nor so technical as to demand special knowledge.

As for lawyers, I assume they have each other in mind at all times as they write. Certainly they don't have most of us in mind. Their grandiosity appalls me. In a movie contract, I was asked to grant the right to my book to the producers, in perpetuity, throughout the universe. When I wrote in, "With the exception of Sagittarius and the Andromeda galaxy," it was accepted. Evidently the lawyers, who are writing to avoid litigation in a litigious world, did not anticipate a lawsuit from Sagittarius.

Of course I am being grossly unfair to many lawyers; I come from a family of fine lawyers. But the language used in a will or a contract is indeed a special language, and it is not aimed at the reader who enjoys stories, the reader of fiction.

Whom, then, does the writer of fiction write for? It is only a partial truth to say that I write for myself, out of my own need, asking, whether I realize it or not, the questions I am asking in my own life.

A truer answer is that I write for the book.

"But why do you write for children?" I am often asked.

And I answer truthfully that I don't. I haven't been a child for a long time, and if what I write doesn't appeal to me, at my age, it isn't likely to appeal to a child. I hope I will never lose the child within me, who has not lost her sense of wonder, of awe, of laughter. But I am not a child; I am a grown woman, learning about maturity as I move on in chronology.

A teacher, in introducing me to a class of seventh graders, said,

"Miss L'Engle has made it in the children's field, and she is now trying to break into the adult market."

I felt that I had better not explain to this teacher that I had no desire to break into the adult market and see my fiction in "adult bookstores." I am not interested in writing pornography. I did explain that my first several books were regular trade novels, which means that they were marketed for a general audience, not for children. And I explained that when I have a book that I think will be too difficult for a general audience, then we will market it as a juvenile book. It is a great mistake to think that children are not capable of understanding difficult concepts in science or philosophy.

A book that has a young protagonist will likely be marketed as a children's book, regardless of content. Since adolescents are usually more willing than their elders to ask difficult questions, and to accept the fact that the questions don't have nice, tidy answers but lead on to more difficult questions, approximately half of my books have young protagonists. But while I am writing, I am not thinking of any audience at all. I am not even thinking about myself. I am thinking about the book.

This does not imply anything esoteric. I do not pick up the pen and expect it to guide my hand, or put my fingers on the keyboard of the typewriter and expect the work to be done automatically. It is work. But it is focused work, and the focus is on the story, not on anything else.

An example of the kind of focus I mean is a good doctor. The good doctor listens to the patient, truly listens, to what the patient says, does not say, is afraid to say, to body language, to everything that may give a clue as to what is wrong. The good doctor is so fully focused on the patient that personal self-consciousness has vanished. Such focused listening does not make the doctor—or any of the rest of us—less ourselves. In fact, such focused listening makes us more ourselves.

The same thing is true in listening to a story as we write it. It does not make us any less writers, this strange fact that we do not think about writing as we are writing; it makes us more writers.

Then, of course, there is all the revising to be done. We do not always listen well. We do not always have our full attention on the story. Some scenes will need to be written and rewritten a dozen or more times before they work. We do have to revise with attention to infelicities of rhythm, flaw of syntax; there is, indeed, a great deal of conscious work to be done. But still, the writer is paying attention to the work itself, not the potential audience. I have, it is true, toned down scenes when the decision has been made to market a book as a "young adult" novel, because I know that young adult novels are read as often by nine- and ten-year-olds as by young adults. But such revisions are done long after the story has been listened to as attentively as possible, and cannot mutilate or betray the intent or integrity of the story.

It would be very inhibiting for me to have to keep an audience in mind. It would take a large piece of my mind off the story as it is unfolding, and I want all of my mind to be where it belongs: on the writing.

Have I had an audience in mind while I have been writing this piece? Not particularly. I'm telling myself things I need to remember. Nobody but someone interested in the writing of fiction is going to want to read this, so I am also writing for people who share my own concerns.

So, gentle reader (the Victorians seems to assume that all readers are gentle), give yourself the pleasure of forgetting earnestly to remember your audience at all times, and give yourself the fun of plunging deeply into your story, and having your mind focused on that, and nothing else. If the story that comes from this way of writing is a better story than the forcedly audience-centered story (and I am convinced it will be), it will have a wider audience. And isn't that what we hope for?—to reach as many people as possible, because we believe that what the story has to say is worth saying.

3

THREE ESSENTIALS FOR A
SUCCESSFUL WRITING CAREER

By John Jakes

To succeed, any writer must master the tools of his trade. A fiction writer, for example, must learn plot construction; how to characterize by showing instead of telling; how to write dialogue that is functional and natural at the same time; and so on.

Those are matters of craft, and fairly technical. But they are by no means the whole story. Over the years, I've become convinced that three less technical, but no less important, factors play a vital part, not to say a crucial one, in determining the long-term course of a writing career.

Since I am primarily a fiction writer, I have thought about the three factors from that point of view. But all three can apply just as easily to the writing of nonfiction, plays, or even poetry. When I speak to writers' groups, I call these factors "the three P's." By any name, I believe they spell the difference between failure and success in making the great leap from amateur ambition to a career as a part-time or full-time professional.

I. PRACTICE

Some writers prefer to have outsiders think of writing not as a skill but as some form of sorcery, forever incomprehensible to the "layman." And it's true that you can never reduce the work of a Dickens, a Zola, a Faulkner to a formula, or a list of technical do's and don'ts. There are certain forever-indefinable attitudes and abilities that set the genius apart from those of us of lesser literary ability.

Genius aside, however, the literary protectionist is wrong; writing is in part a skill, and certain technical aspects of it can be learned by any reasonably intelligent person.

Even more fundamental to success is practice. There is nothing mysterious about it, either. Writing is a lot like playing golf, or the piano. To lift yourself out of the amateur class, you must do more than dabble; and once launched, you cannot, I believe, sustain a professional career without a continuing commitment to practice.

Top golfers on the pro tour continue to practice, no matter how much money they've won. A Broadway actress with a role in a hit play continues to take acting and voice lessons in her spare time because she knows you can never do too much of what you do best. It's the same with a writer. Whether you're a beginner or a selling professional, you should write so much material, on a set schedule, every day, or every week, almost without fail.

These thoughts are by no means original. They are, in fact, re-statements of the old writing adage about the seat of the pants and the seat of the chair. To me, however, the word practice expresses that idea in a simpler and more meaningful way, because implicit in the word is an added benefit: IMPROVEMENT.

Consider golf and piano playing again. The more you do of either one, however poorly at first, the better you become. Sometimes you are not even aware of this improvement, but it's there. Thus, for a writer, practice does much more than guarantee that you will produce a certain amount of material every week or every month. It actually helps you get better at what you're doing.

Admittedly, such practice isn't always pleasant. Many times you'd probably rather be doing other, less taxing things. During the years in which our children were growing up, I set a writing schedule of 2½ to 3 hours, three nights a week. I tried to stick to that schedule regardless of the demands of my full-time job in advertising, sometimes even the demands of my family—and to do it no matter how tired I was at 7 o'clock in the evening.

Of course, if there was an important school program one night, or if someone in the family was sick, or I absolutely had to go back to the office for a couple of hours, no writing got done. But I always tried to make up for it at another time during the week.

Unless you have the determination to practice, which would improve your work consciously and through the sheer act of repetition, you do not really want to be a writer. Rather, you probably just want to be *known* as a writer. There's a vast difference between the two, and you would be better off doing something else.

II. PERSISTENCE

Beginning writers who are too easily discouraged will never achieve the big breakthrough to the professional ranks. I've known would-be writers who gave up after the third or fourth rejection of a story, never dreaming that factors *outside the material itself* sometimes influence a decision to accept or not.

This first dawned on me some years ago, when my then-agent requested a new, clean copy of a detective story I had all but forgotten. I wrote to ask what had happened to the first manuscript. Too grubby and dog-eared for further submissions, was the answer. "But we'll keep trying it at market; there's always a buyer somewhere for a salable story."

And there was. Ultimately the story wound up in a cheap pulp-paper men's magazine—just about what it deserved—and I was paid $30. The point is, I would have retired the manuscript long before the agent did. He knew the realities of publishing better than I.

Editorial tastes change, sometimes with incomprehensible rapidity; *editors* change, sometimes with even greater rapidity. Editor "A" may take an instant and illogical dislike to your material and never buy anything from you, no matter how expertly your manuscripts are put together. Then editor "A" moves on to another job, and editor "B" snaps up your first offering—the same piece editor "A" rejected twice!

That is, editor "B" snaps it up if you haven't given up on that particular publisher—even on writing itself—and have resubmitted the manuscript after noting in a writers' magazine that the name on the editorial door has changed.

You must always be dispassionate enough to understand that your material *probably* fails to click because it isn't up to professional standards—but confident enough to realize that other factors could be playing a part.

How to strike that balance? It isn't easy, and there are no rules anyone can give you. It's something you must feel. I failed again and again with given stories and novels—still do—yet I always believed the fault was in the specific piece and my handling of it; the rejection never signaled to me that I had no business trying to be a writer.

True enough, I came close to feeling that way many times; discouragement is part of every writer's emotional baggage. Offsetting that is belief in your own ability, a belief that pushes you ahead. My shorthand term for this state of constant forward movement is persistence.

Alas, the lesson of persistence is lost on many beginning writers—if indeed they ever hear it at all. If beginners did not give up so easily, the writing trade would be far more crowded and competitive than it is. That is a professional secret you should never forget.

So keep your faith in yourself, and don't retire a script after five rejections. Refuse to settle for anything less than six to twelve and realize even then that the sale might not come until submission number thirteen.

A final, purely personal aside. Keep your self-confidence internal, silent. Too many amateur writers (too many professionals, I might add) are basically insecure people; this inclines them toward conversation almost exclusively centered around themselves and their work. I dislike socializing with most writers because their talk tends to be little more than a tiresome variation on one theme: "I."

Avoid that sort of thing. Let others pay you the compliments. People will like you better for it, and the compliments will have some meaning.

III. PROFESSIONALISM

This is not a "do" or "don't" as much as a state of mind, an attitude toward your work.

For me, the true professional is exemplified by the playwright. Typically, in the thick of rehearsals for a new show, he is forced to edit, refocus, often completely destroy and rebuild his script because it is failing its ultimate test: It is not working on stage, and the actors, the director, and the tryout audiences keep telling him so.

In such a situation, the writer can't hide from the truth about his work. Unless he wishes to withdraw the script, he is forced to search for and confront its weaknesses, then struggle to shore them up, or eliminate them. He is professional when he chooses to do this, rather than withdraw and sulk.

Narrative writing, too, either "works" or it doesn't. The difference is, the writer of narrative material is far removed from his audience; he is cushioned from the shock of watching his material fail. This distance makes it easier for the writer to find scapegoats: The editor gave the book a bad title. The cover was terrrible. The publisher's salesmen didn't push the book hard enough. All of which may be perfectly true—or, alternatively, such excuses may represent the writer's understandable, but unprofessional, protection of his own ego.

15

About the only time a writer of narrative prose confronts an uncompromising "audience" is when he submits his manuscript to an editor. And if the editor expresses dissatisfaction with some or all of it, that lone opinion is more easily overridden by the writer's rationalization than are the scowls of the playwright's cast, or the snickers and coughs of his disapproving audience.

Hence, since it's easier for a narrative writer to dodge the truth, he must work twice as hard to develop a professional attitude.

I have known a lot of writers who will never realize their full potential because they haven't made the effort. Although they sell material, I wouldn't consider any of them professionals in the fullest and best sense. Most of these writers, not surprisingly, belong to the "Don't-touch-a-comma-of-mine" school.

Such an attitude is a protective device, and to some extent understandable. Publishing is a business like any other; not all people who hold jobs in it are competent. I have sat in enough publishing and advertising meetings to know that even highly intelligent, apparently reasonable men and women can come up with a great many silly, stupid, or downright harmful ideas, given the right circumstances and enough time to deliberate.

I am not suggesting that you surrender your work and your principles to any and every criticism. On the other hand, without a willingness to accept—indeed, to seek—competent advice, you are not professional. But if you are, you will usually find yourself asking silent questions about a finished piece: "What's wrong with it? How can I fix it?"

Because of the writer's inevitable psychic closeness to his work, answering the first question is often hard, if not downright impossible. Hence the professional usually asks a third question as well: "Since I feel something's wrong, but I can't find the flaw, who can?"

I've always believed that you should at all costs avoid "criticism" from well-meaning amateurs such as friends or relatives. Aunt Nell may be able to tell you that your story "doesn't interest me"—but is it because there's no narrative hook? No sympathetic protagonist? No dramatic irony? No suspense?

Aunt Nell doesn't know, and what's more, she probably couldn't care less. You're no better off than you were before you showed her the manuscript. Seek help from those qualified to give it. A good teacher.

An agent. Or, most often, an editor whose judgment you trust—and who is looking for material.

On the Kent family novels, I was blessed with two such editors, both of whom spotted numerous weak points in the manuscripts and suggested (but never dictated) ways in which these might be eliminated, with a resulting improvement of the final product. The specifics of this repair work they left to me—assuming, I imagine, that I knew the materials and techniques needed to effect them.

You begin to mature as a writer, and to deserve the name, when you not only sense something wrong in your work, but can figure out how to fix it. This didn't happen to me until I was about thirty-five—or some sixteen years after I made my first sale.

Many times during those first sixteen years, when an editor would ask for changes in a script, I panicked because I wasn't sure I knew how to bring off the requested improvements. Now I know how to strengthen motivation, develop more sympathy for a protagonist, alter the style of a character's dialogue, underplay a scene, and so on.

I don't mean I do it perfectly; I mean I am usually confident that I know how to approach a repair job, and can bring it off. Parenthetically, I might note that this is the sort of technical control you acquire through practice.

Moreover, I'm usually anxious to do the fixing. I have learned a simple lesson that eluded me for too many years. The better the writer makes his material, the better his rewards.

So cultivate an objective attitude. Ruthlessly examine your own work for deficiencies. Study acknowledged masters, or contemporaries whose writing you admire, to see how they achieve their effects.

Welcome—encourage—comments from an experienced critic whose opinions you respect, and do this no matter how painful the criticism may be. Reflect on each suggestion, weigh its merits (I have seldom if ever turned down a suggestion from a good editor), then make your plan for reworking the material, and carry it out with all the technical skills at your command.

All of this can be called professionalism. But the core of it is the objective attitude about yourself and your work. When you achieve that, you have left the ranks of the amateur forever, and you stand an excellent chance of success in your writing career.

17

4

THE PROLIFIC WRITER

By Isaac Asimov

THERE are grave disadvantages to being a prolific writer and if you are seriously interested in writing, it may very well be that prolificity is the last thing you want.

To be prolific means that you must be able to write quickly, facilely, and without much concern as to what improvements you might possibly introduce if you took enough time. That is precisely what you *don't* want to do if your interest is in writing well.

To write quickly and to write well are usually incompatible attributes, and if you must choose one or the other, you should choose quality over speed every time.

But suppose you do write pretty well. Isn't it possible to write quickly and easily, *too?* Surely, it is legitimate to dream of that. Any writer who has perspired his way through some bit of creation, who has worked his way through endless crossing-outs and crumplings, and who has ended uncertainly with something whose virtues seem to dim perceptibly as he gives it a final reading, must wonder what it might feel like to dash something off between yawns, so to speak, and have it read perfectly well.

Not only will a mind-wrenching job then become simple, but you will be able to turn out many more items, charge for each one, and improve your bank balance enormously.

What do you need to achieve that?

1) You have to like to write.

Without that, everything else falls to the ground, and you will have to seek other daydreams. Prolificity isn't for you.

Mind you, I don't say you must have the urge to write or the deep ambition to write. That is not enough. Everyone who tries to write must obviously have the urge and the ambition to do so, and everyone would just love to have a finished manuscript on the desk.

18

What about the in-between, though? What about the actual mechanical process of scribbling on paper, or beating on typewriter keys, or speaking into a mouthpiece? If that is just an agonizing intermediate between the original urge and the final ecstasy, then you may be a good writer, you may even be a writer of genius — but you will never be a prolific writer. No one could stand that much agony.

No, the very act of turning it out must be actively pleasurable.

2) You must not like much of anything else *but* writing.

After all, most of us are constantly torn between desires, but for the writer who wants to be prolific, there should be no room for doubt. It's writing you must want to be doing, not anything else.

If you look out at one of those perfect days, when all nature is smiling and calling to you to get out there and enjoy life, and you say, "Oh, hell, I'll write tomorrow," then abandon all dreams of prolificity.

If you can look out at such a day and feel a sudden pang of apprehension that some loved one is going to come over and say, "What a perfect time for a pleasant walk" or "What a perfect time to go out and do thusand-so!" then there's hope for you. (Frankly, what I do is keep the shades down at all times and pretend there's a blizzard outside.)

3) You have to have self-assurance.

If your sentences never seem perfect to you and if you are never happy unless you have revised and revised and revised until the sentence disappears altogether under the weight of erasures and interlineations, or until you have restored it full-circle to what it was originally, then how can you hope to be prolific?

You may ask, "But what if the sentence isn't good? I can't just leave it, can I?"

Of course not, but the assumption here is that you're a reasonably good writer to begin with and that it's your dream to be prolific, also. As a reasonably good writer, you have undoubtedly written a reasonably good sentence, so let it go. Once you are finished with the piece, you can go over it and change anything that really *needs* changing, and then type the whole thing to get clean copy. But then, that's it.

Remember, change only what *needs* changing. You must cultivate an active dislike for changing and never do it without a sigh of regret.

Undoubtedly, you have read over and over again that there is no such thing as writing, only rewriting; that it's the polish that does it. Sure, but that's if you want to be a *great* writer. We're talking prolific here.

4) Never lose time.

You can replace money, if you lose a wallet. You can buy a new type-writer, if your apartment is ransacked. You can marry again, if a divorce overtakes you. But that minute that has vanished unnecessarily will never come back, and what's more, it was the best minute you will ever have, for all future minutes will come when you are older and more nearly worn out.

There are a variety of ways of saving time and every prolific writer chooses his own. Some become completely asocial, tearing the phone out of the wall and never answering mail. Some establish a family member as dragon to stand between themselves and the world. Some turn off their senses and learn to write while activity swirls all about them.

My own system is to do everything myself. I have no assistants, no secretaries, no typists, no researchers, no agents, no business managers. My theory is that all such people waste your time. In the time it takes to explain what you want, to check what they do, to point out where they did it wrong — you can do at least three times as much by yourself.

So there you are. If you want to be a prolific writer, you have to be a single-minded, driven, nonstop person. — Sounds horrible, doesn't it?

Well, then, concentrate on being a *good* writer, and leave prolific for those poor souls who can't help it.

5

SHOULD YOU COLLABORATE?

By Marcia Muller and Bill Pronzini

WHEN we mentioned to a fellow mystery writer that we had written a collaborative novel, he shook his head wonderingly. "And you're still *friends*?" he asked.

Indeed we are. In fact, we've since written a nonfiction book together, and are contemplating a second novel; and we've also done collaborative short stories, as well as co-edited several anthologies. It should be emphasized, however, that literary collaboration is *not* everyone's cup of tea. Most writers prefer to work alone. Of those who experiment with collaboration, many find it unsuccessful; a few have even suffered the loss of friendship because of it. It is not something to be entered into lightly.

But when a collaboration works, it can be highly rewarding for both partners, and in terms of their literary product. A successful collaboration is a work of fiction or nonfiction which is better than either party could have written alone. It is not the voice of one or the other, but a *third* voice created by the blending of two styles and visions.

There are other advantages to collaboration, as well. Writing, as we all know, is a lonely profession; working with a partner certainly alleviates some of that loneliness. (A warning, though: Any good collaboration is not half the work, as one might think, but usually *twice* the work.) Another advantage is the obvious one that two heads are better than one: Developing a fictional plot, for instance, can be a much easier chore for two people than for one.

There are various kinds of joint projects. One is ghostwriting. This is a partnership between a writer and a nonwriter who has special expertise, an unusual experience, or a specific story he wants to tell. The work may be fiction or nonfiction, and the nonwriter, rather than the writer, receives credit on the work. Closely akin to ghostwriting is celebrity collaboration in which the writer and the celebrity work together to produce an account of the celebrity's life or experiences. Both receive credit; one or both may do the writing. (Ghostwriting and celebrity collaboration are areas open only to professionals.)

The third type is the two-author collaboration—our area of expertise and the type we'll confine ourselves to here. This type may take various forms, and may of course be fiction or nonfiction. In most cases, both writers' names appear on the work, although some teams may prefer a single pseudonym. And depending on the individual writer's strong points and abilities, the workload is broken up in various ways. In collaborating on a novel, one popular method is for the person who plots best to create the basic storyline, while the other does most of the actual writing. Another—which we use—is joint plotting and joint writing.

Our recent mystery novel, *Double,* which features Muller's Sharon McCone and Pronzini's "Nameless Detective," was a joint project in every way. The plot, which had to be complex in order to accommodate the skills of both series sleuths, was developed during many hours of discussion and planning. At first we considered setting it in San Francisco, the city in which both our characters live and work; but then we realized the dramatic possibilities inherent in using a different locale, one with which Sharon was familiar but "Nameless" was not. We settled on San Diego, her hometown and the place where her family still lives. How to get both of them to San Diego at the same time? They attended a private investigators' convention at a posh beach hotel, where an old friend of Sharon's is head of security. Once we had this basic premise, the various intrigues and relationships that make up the plot began to suggest themselves. But that was still only the beginning of our work. We then had to structure the book so that each of us (and each of our detectives) would share more or less equal worktime.

Because there were two of us on the project, the first draft was written rather quickly and easily—but the fact must be stressed that we did no writing at all until our plot was established and each of our characters was sharply delineated. Starting a collaborative project prematurely, before the authors have a clear idea of the direction the book will take, can produce disastrous results.

Before *any* work is done on a collaborative project, two vital elements must be present in the partnership. The first of these is *trust.* By this we mean that each person must have faith in the other's commitment to the project, writing abilities, and professionalism in following the work through to completion. In a way it is an implied contract. You know your collaborator will put his best efforts into the project, will support you whenever you need reassurance or help, and vice versa. This doesn't mean that every collaboration is a complete 50-50 sharing of the workload; often circumstances such as other commitments or differences in ability prevent that. But each partner must trust that the other will contribute a fair share throughout.

How do you know if you can trust your collaborator? It's the same as in any other personal or business arrangement. You make certain assumptions about how your collaborator will work and live up to responsibilities. If you know the person well enough, these assumptions will usually prove correct. In our case, we had been reading each other's works-in-progress for years; each of us knew how the other approached the craft of writing. Because we have similar styles and outlooks, each was able to offer helpful suggestions to the other. If you do not know your proposed partner well, if you cannot proceed on a firm basis of faith and trust, *do not* enter into a collaboration. Mutual enthusiasm for an idea is not enough on which to base weeks or months of difficult physical and mental labor.

The second essential element is *willingness to compromise*. Disputes will inevitably arise: one partner's dazzling plot twist may seem hopelessly contrived to the other; one's stylistic flourishes may seem embarrassingly purplish to his collaborator. The only useful method of settling such disputes is to discuss them rationally and to effect some sort of compromise satisfactory to both parties.

In the writing of *Double,* for instance, a problem arose with the plot: The "Nameless Detective" simply did not have enough to do. Muller yielded to Pronzini's judgment on this matter, even though it meant more work for her (sections had to be restructured and rewritten in order to integrate "Nameless" more fully into the story), because "Nameless" is Pronzini's creation and because Pronzini has more experience in plotting than Muller. Another dispute concerned fictionalizing and shifting a bit of San Diego geography, which also necessitated restructuring and rewriting. Pronzini yielded to Muller because she once lived in San Diego and had strong feelings on how to fictionalize that setting in a realistically acceptable way.

As we move on to the various methods of collaboration and the additional problems that may arise, we think you'll see how strongly the presence—or lack—of trust and the willingness to compromise can affect the quality of the final product. Indeed, how they can determine whether or not there *is* a final product.

The question we're most often asked is: *"How* do you collaborate?" There is no easy answer, for we have written together and with others in a variety of ways. It depends on the nature of the project—novel, short story, nonfiction book, anthology, article such as this one; and it also depends on the partners themselves. Pronzini has collaborated with some ten different writers over the past fifteen years, and each method of working was at least somewhat different. (And yes, Pronzini is still friendly with all ten of those authors.)

One of the easiest methods—the one we used in *Double*—is for each person to write alternate chapters. We were fortunate in that we were using two series detectives who were well-established and who had distinct first-person voices; it wasn't necessary to blend our styles, only to maintain a consistency throughout in Sharon's and "Nameless's" dealings with each other and with the various other characters. This method also works well for nonfiction and for non-series, third-person novels in which multiple viewpoint is employed (such as in Pronzini's recent collaboration with John Lutz, *The Eye*).

A variation on the above method is for each person to write alternate sections, rather than single chapters or scenes. This method worked well in another meeting of San Francisco sleuths, *Twospot*, in which Collin Wilcox's Lieutenant Frank Hastings and Pronzini's "Nameless" joined forces. *Twospot* is divided into four sections of some seven chapters each, the first section narrated by "Nameless," the second by Hastings, and so on. This is an advantageous approach in a novel whose plot requires a number of scenes involving one character before another character can be introduced.

A third method is for both collaborators to write from the point of view of the same character, or about the same things, dividing the work as they see fit, and then in a subsequent draft to rewrite each other's material in order to create a smooth flow—the "third voice" we spoke of earlier. Again, Pronzini has had success with this method in his several collaborations with Barry N. Malzberg. Muller and Pronzini have also used it successfully on a short story and on nonfiction projects, one of them being this article.

A few words should be said here about work habits. In any collaboration in which both parties do the actual writing, it is important that both maintain a steady output; and for both to read and discuss regularly what each has written. It is much easier to mediate a dispute and effect a compromise early on in a project, while it is in its first-draft stage. Waiting until a book or story is finished and then arguing about it does neither the collaborators nor the work any good.

No matter how confident you feel when you set out on a collaborative project, problems of one kind or another will surely develop. Some will be easily solved, others not so easily. But you should be aware of the pitfalls at the outset.

Ego. It is natural to have pride in your work; it is also natural to bristle when a collaborator says, "That scene doesn't work," or "That's a terrible metaphor; we'll have to cut it." But keep in mind that as often as not the collaborator is right. We are not always the best judge of our own work. Therefore your ego *must,* in many instances, yield to trust and compromise. If it doesn't, if it becomes a major stumbling block once a project has begun, the project should probably be abandoned. No decent collaborative work ever emerges from a battle of wills.

Snags. These usually concern work habits, and they come in all sizes and shapes. A common one is that elusive malady called "writer's block." One collaborator comes down with it and is unable to proceed, while the other remains as productive as ever. Another snag may occur when one person writes more quickly than the other and gets too far ahead. Still another is the interference of outside commitments, such as a bread-and-butter job or other, nonliterary projects. As soon as any kind of snag occurs, you should try to work out an immediate solution or compromise. Perhaps the partner not suffering writer's block can offer strong moral support, or take on some of his collaborator's workload. Perhaps the faster writer can regulate his pace to that of the other's. Perhaps the one without commitments can alter or adapt this schedule to accommodate his partner's.

Major snags. These concern such elements as the central premise of the work, important plot points, thematic statements. When they confront you, it can seem as if the entire project is doomed to failure. But they, too, can usually be remedied with enough discussion and compromise. We were not immune on *Double:* We had a draft finished, we liked it, we felt it worked well, and yet . . . there was a solution to one of several crimes that didn't seem to be well-motivated. The only alternative solution we could come up with required extensive rewriting, the addition of scenes and chapters. How did we deal with this? By going back to our typewriters, of course, and revising accordingly. When such snags develop, you'll find that your collaborator's willingness to undertake greater amounts of work is in direct proportion to his commitment to the project. And we were both 100% committed.

Collaboration is a unique opportunity for two writers to create something better than either could have accomplished alone. But this is only true if the partners remain in sync with each other on all fronts. Otherwise, each would be much advised to pursue individual literary careers.

Remember: No collaboration is worth the loss of a friend.

6

WRITER'S BLOCK

BY ROGER CARAS

IF YOU have never suffered from "writer's block," I suspect you have never been a writer. I have not seen anything about the disease in medical literature (but, then, I have never seen anything about love or spring fever there either, and they certainly have a lot to do with how we live and perhaps how long we live), but the "block" is an affliction as surely as diabetes and athlete's foot are.

Exactly what is "writer's block"? To quote Tevia in *Fiddler on the Roof,* "Well, I'll tell ya, I don't know." It is a cross between writer's cramp, self-pity, an intellectual hangnail, the vapors, and paranoia. How do you know when you have it? That is easy to answer. If you start to put the smaller size paper clips on one part of the clip holder on your desk and the larger size in another, you are showing signs of the early stages of the disease. The next symptom usually is mailbox-oriented. All that third-class junk mail you usually throw out unopened you now read. Then you start writing letters that don't have to be written. It can get expensive when you start ordering stuff from catalogues you don't really need. You phone friends you haven't seen in a long time (often with good purpose), and then uncertainty sets in. You are suddenly frightened that the secret is going to get out. All the editors in the world are going to find out at the same time: You can't write! The bubble has burst. It has been a fluke. You have been faking it, or you've been plain lucky. It is coming, there is no way you can stop it from happening, your cover is blown. You are a closet non-writer.

The nice thing about writer's block is that if you can stay away from window ledges and medicine chests, it will go away. There is proof of that in everything you read because every writer whose work you admire has had it, too. (Except Isaac Asimov.)

Therein lies the first step to recovery, the awareness that you are not alone. In studies, studios, attics and garages across the world other writers are writhing even as you writhe, washing already clean cars, mowing lawns that already have a crew cut and walking dogs whose legs are almost worn to nubs from the sudden spurts of exercise they are being subjected to. Bookshelves are being rearranged all across America, and spouses are suddenly amazed as their loved ones, the ones who sometimes used to write, offer to do things they have never offered to do before.

Writer's block made me into a pretty good cook, good enough to have recipes in at least a half a dozen cook books. COOK BOOKS! For crying out loud, I am a naturalist, an adventurer, a world traveler, not a cook! But I offered to cook lots of times, and that is the secret of the cure. Do something else creative besides write. Paint, sculpt, whittle, compose, garden, sketch, do ceramics, sing, dance, bake, write terrible poetry, rearrange pictures, write anything, but ease your way back into the real project, the one that has you hung up and panting with an identity crisis. Ease back into the creative mode. If that doesn't work, jog. There is nothing like worrying about chest pains to get you back in front of your desk.

Now, there is one very important point to all this: It is possible for a writer to be just bone lazy and not have a real writer's block at all. The disease can be an excuse. There are lots of times when house painters don't feel like painting houses, plastic surgeons don't feel like lifting faces, and lawyers would rather play golf than get some snarling couple divorced, and there are times when writers don't feel like meeting a deadline. You have to be able to tell when you are being a sloth and when you are truly beset by that unique writer's malady. If you are being slothful, give yourself no quarter. Place yourself in front of your typewriter, try to forget about the unanswered mail, unperused catalogues (you don't need a reproduction cast-iron stove or a machine that rolls *The New York Times* into fireplace logs, anyway) and start writing. You will get into the swing of it.

If on the other hand you have really been suffering from the block, think positively about your craft, consider the readers who are out there waiting for you to finish, think of how pleased and proud of you your editor will be, finish up in the kitchen, chuck the catalogues, vow to open no more third-class mail, and face the fact that the time has come to force the issue. Slowly at first, then with gathering speed, ease, and glee, write.

7

OWED TO THE PUBLIC LIBRARY

By Lesley Conger

YESTERDAY I fell in love with the public library all over again.

It was a mild, sweet day, not bright, not gloomy; faintly misty, but not wet. A perfect day, really. And because I had had an errand elsewhere, I approached the library from a direction I don't ordinarily use. It was like seeing a familiar, beloved face in a new and enchanting light. WALK, the traffic signal commanded me, but I stood bemused on the curb, just looking, until I found myself disobeying WAIT and loping across as the red turned green.

It's a middle-aged building, our library, rose brick and gray stone, built in a style that reminds me of some children's blocks I must have had when I was small, the kind that came with doors and windows and chimneys and arches. Georgian, Colonial? I don't know enough about architecture to tell you. But it's a lovely building, with tall windows arched at their tops, and broad stone steps leading up to the doors.

I usually take those steps two at a time. But yesterday I hesitated, and then I walked around the block. There are large elms lining the street, and on the inner edge of the sidewalk, a low concrete balustrade with a rail of the perfect width for young wall-walkers. Between the balustrade and the building grow rhododendron and other greenery, but along the walk concrete benches are set at intervals, each with a name chiseled upon its backrest: Henry Fielding, George Eliot, William Makepeace Thackeray. . . . On Henry Fielding an old man dozes, knobby hands resting on top of his knobby cane. Behind George Eliot, inside the balustrade, a young man sits on the grass reading. Charles Dickens, Charlotte Brontë, Victor Hugo. . . . There is a girl in a long patchwork skirt sitting on Victor Hugo; she looks at me through great, round, violet sunglasses, which she doesn't really need. Edgar Allan Poe, Mark Twain, Bret Harte . . . I wonder, do people always notice whose lap they are occupying? Is the girl with the violet glasses waiting for someone, and did she say she'd meet him at the Victor Hugo bench? Oliver Wendell Holmes, Robert Louis Stevenson. . . . Can you remain utterly indifferent to Charlotte Brontë once you've sat leaning against her, eating an apple, feeling the spring sunshine?

Dumas, Hawthorne, Irving. Trollope, Sterne, Austen. . . . There are over twenty benches—twenty-two, I think. Sir Walter Scott, Charles Kingsley, James Fenimore Cooper. And if you approach from the southwest corner, the first two benches you see are Charles Reade and George Borrow. . . . Reade and Borrow, borrow and read. Yes, of course, that's what I'm here for!—and I stop to tie my shoe on Borrow's knee.

On the building itself there are more names, clusters of names, engraved large and clear high up on the gray blocks of the frieze. Not only writers, there, but inventors, musicians, explorers, scientists, painters, religious leaders. Palestrina, Aeschylus, Zoroaster, Copernicus, Raphael. I am dizzy, but less from looking up than from thinking of them: all of them, inside the library, waiting for me—all mine, all just for the asking!

Someone once wrote me to comment on my knowledge of literature. *Enviously.* But there is nothing to envy. The truth is that I never studied literature, certainly not in college, where for some mysterious reason I spent half my time grubbing about in exotic languages, most of which I haven't used since. My college education stands me in no good stead when it comes to writing this chapter—or anything else, for that matter.

Let me confess something—though, indeed, it's not a confession if confessing means admitting to something I'd rather conceal. When I write about books and writers, I am a great deal of the time writing about books and writers I have myself just that moment encountered, and the greatest part of my enthusiasm is the joy of recent discovery.

For finding out is the most delightful part of knowing. And fresh knowledge, even be it concerning things old to others, is my favorite commodity.

Not long ago I pointed out that writing is an occupation with free entry. You need no diploma, no union card, no previous experience. It doesn't matter who you are; everyone's eligible.

Well, unlike most colleges and universities, the public library doesn't care who you are, either. Victor Hugo doesn't care. Jane Austen doesn't care. Euripides doesn't care, and he is waiting there for you as much as he waits for me. To those who have asked me what kind of education a writer should have, and to those who have bemoaned their lack of an education, let me say that the best of *my* education has come from the public library—and still does, week after week. My tuition fee is bus fare and once in a while, five cents a day for an overdue book.

But despite the engraved names and despite the emotions they inspire in me, the library is not a pantheon, not some kind of temple dedicated to these gods of intellect and achievement, not a sterile memorial or a musty tomb. It holds not dry bones but still viable thoughts that can leap from a mind long dead to yours, through the agency of the printed page. And more—because of course it isn't Euripides that I seek out every time, or Thackeray, or Brontë or Poe. Last week it turned out to be Barbara Pym, Russell Baker, and John Updike; next week, who knows? Henry James, Jean Auel, and Shirley MacLaine? Or how about *The Cloister and the Hearth* (that's Reade) and *The Romany Rye* (that's Borrow)?

I rounded the block. Oh, it's a beautiful building, warm and mellow in the sunshine. For the sun is out now, and the girl with the violet glasses needs them after all. I look up at the frieze once more—Molière, Voltaire!—and I take the steps by twos and push my way through the heavy doors.

You don't need to know very much at all to start with, if you know the way to the public library.

8

FORMULA FOR SUCCESS

By Marjorie Holmes

WHENEVER I teach a class in writing I insist on a blackboard where I put the following formula:

IF YOU HAVE THESE	AND WILL DO THESE
Talent	Write every day
Belief in your own ability	Keep a notebook
Patience, persistence	Study your writers' magazine
Self-discipline	Send your work out

YOU CANNOT FAIL!

I am absolutely convinced from personal experience that this hypothesis is true. You can become a selling writer, *if you first have certain essentials,* and *if you will then proceed to do certain things.*

Let's examine the basic qualifications:

First and foremost, *Talent.* The talent for writing is a must. It includes imagination and originality, plus an inborn ability to use words gracefully and effectively in written form. Talent is a gift—and this is true of music, painting, any of the arts. It is something that can't be acquired; and although talent can and must be developed through study and practice, it can't be taught.

Talent, especially for writing, usually shows up in childhood, and seldom goes unnoticed. The neighbor kids are an eager audience for your incessantly scribbled stories. Parents and teachers are impressed. While the others in the room worriedly chew their pencils, you are already halfway through a writing assignment. Yours is the paper read before the class. This continues through college, if you go; and if there is a campus magazine your work appears in it. People tell you (as if you didn't know) you should be a writer, you have talent!

Even talent, however, must be backed up by: *A burning belief in your own ability.* The deep inner conviction that you can and will do it.

A force that will drive you to the typewriter come hell or high water, no matter how many people interrupt you, discourage you, or more commonly, simply don't care. Because, alas, the hallelujah chorus about your talent is silent once you are out of school. Swept into marriage and/or a job, the mere *time* to write is scarce, and when you try, the rejections are often quick and cruel. This is a time when your own faith can be seriously threatened, but it is *not the time to quit.*

I was lucky. My college writing instructor made us send our stuff out. This confirmed the fact that I should not quit, by way of a few small checks (the first, $7.00 from *Weird Tales* Magazine for a poem). I married right after graduation, in the depths of the Depression; but again the gods smiled. Two weeks before our first child was born, I sold my first story (the $200.00 paid for the baby). Two weeks later, I sold another. World, here I come! Then, seemingly, it was all over. I was to "beat my knuckles bloody against the wall," as Thomas Wolfe said, before I sold again.

These are the times that wring a writer's soul. *To know you can do it,* and yet fail. Why, why, why? Even so, it never occurred to me *not* to do it. And however brutal the pain of failing, you never *really* fail at something until you stop trying. For me, to abandon my gift would be unthinkable. The guilt would be intolerable. . . . "Defeat new-forges the chosen among men," wrote Romain Rolland in *Jean Christophe.* "It sorts out the people. It winnows out those who are purest and strongest and makes them purer and stronger." I make no claims to be pure, but in periods like this, a writer soon finds out whether or not he or she is strong.

Patience and persistence. If you have enough faith in yourself, these will follow. You will refuse to give up, you will keep trying. Through sheer stubborn persistence, I gradually broke into the magazines, first the small ones, then the more prestigious, meanwhile working on a novel. When stories and articles came back I revised and retyped them, if necessary, and sent them out again. Eventually most of them landed somewhere, sometimes after numerous rejections. One piece had been rejected so often (17 times!) I was on the verge of offering it to a local paper for five dollars when, to my amazement, it was accepted by *Nation's Business* for $150.00.

As for that first novel, *World by the Tail,* it was revised and rejected repeatedly over a period of at least ten years. We were finally using the manuscript as a perch for our little girl at the breakfast table, when a few pages fell out one day. I picked them up, started reading and decided it had to have one more chance. After one more revision, following the advice of a professional critic, it sold to Lippincott, on condition that I revise *again*. More months of patient persistent work before publication. The book enjoyed marvelous reviews, but modest sales, then was out of print so long I almost neglected to renew the copyright. But lo, after all those years along came Bantam, who brought it back to life in paperback with a first printing of 250,000 copies! Later the in-print figure approached a million. . . .

Another novel, *Two From Galilee*, written long after I'd become an "established writer" (which means only that you've published enough to feel more secure), took six years to sell. It was turned down by practically every publisher extant, including the firm for whom I'd already written two best sellers. In fact, they had the distinction of rejecting it twice! Yet when Fleming H. Revell finally took the gamble, it made *The New York Times* best seller list and was listed by *Publishers Weekly* as one of the ten best sellers of 1972.

You've got to believe in yourself and your own ideas. If the project is valid, the writing good, and you are patient and persistent, it will succeed.

Self-discipline. The will to work, whether you feel like it or not. Making a schedule and sticking to it. The courage to say, "No!" to temptations—coffee klatches, luncheons, bridge parties, or to the dozens of civic duties other people are always trying to get you to perform. The only duties that should take precedence over your writing are duties to your family. And make sure even these are not simply your own excuses to procrastinate.

I was lucky enough to have four children. Yes, lucky, although it didn't always seem so at the time. Children are the perfect excuse *not* to leave home for the presumed freedom of "working." I'd had that, in law offices while working my way through college. After years of pounding somebody else's typewriter, it was almost an indulgence to pound my own. Also, kids have to be bathed, fed and gotten off to school pretty much on schedule. This gives you a framework into which to fit your writing. Time was too precious to waste; I raced to accomplish as much as possible before they woke up or got home.

People with plenty of time on their hands seldom feel this urgent need to get *at* it. This I found true of several childless friends who were always talking about writing; yet they took jobs, joined clubs, chaired committees, held office—did everything else but write. In short, they *invented* interruptions to keep from it. I think when life itself provides the interruptions you are far more likely to make the effort to overcome them.

So you have the basic qualifications, some of which will, by their very nature, guide you in getting the audience a talented writer's work should have. But what are the specific steps to take?

First, *Write every day*. This, of course, is part of discipline; but here are some things that have helped me:

Have your own place where you do nothing else but write. The psychology of having your own writing desk or table and going to it at the same time every day will help you develop the habit. And once you get there don't sit waiting for ideas; get something *down—write!*

That's almost a direct quote from a lecture I heard years ago by Ruth Suckow, an Iowa novelist I very much admired. The advice was invaluable. During the Depression my husband and I moved a lot. My "place" was indeed often only a card table in a bedroom corner, but it was sacrosanct to my writing, and I went there, insofar as humanly possible, at the same time every day. Later, we always managed a proper well-equipped study. This, too, encourages the attitude of self-confidence and determination so important to a writer. You're not simply playing at a hobby; you are a professional writer.

Write at least two hours or more. But let no day pass without writing *something*. If only a page, a paragraph, or even a sentence on your current project. Incredibly, and however slowly, words add up to finished articles and stories, even books. If you just stay with something long enough, the day will come when you finish it! That this is important should be obvious. One completed piece of work, however dissatisfied you may be with it, is better than ten or twenty dazzling starts. Remember, there is no earthly way to publish anything, no matter how good, unless it's done.

Keep a notebook. I echo every word. A notebook is a valuable treasure house wherein to store ideas, bits of dialogue, characters observed, scenes from life you may not need right now but simply can't bear not to record. My own notebook began with daily assignments to "write a paragraph or two about anything you want to express." How glorious, this freedom to write as you please about whatever you please! This too helps develop the writing habit; while sheer immediacy and spontaneity will accumulate priceless material, and bring forth some of your best writing.

My notebook, begun when I was a college freshman, was to be the inspiration and chief source of material for the column I began years later for the *Washington (D.C.) Star.* One day, poring over that bulging notebook, wondering if there weren't *some* way to utilize its many scenes of family life, I decided to try them as a column. The result, *Love and Laughter,* not only appeared for twenty-five years, there were spin-offs by way of books: A collection called *Love and Laughter* (Doubleday), *To Treasure our Days* (Hallmark), and two from EPM Publications, *As Tall as My Heart* and *Beauty in Your Own Backyard.* I also drew on the notebook for many stories and articles.

Send your work out. As the old but true saying goes, "Nothing ever sold in a desk drawer!" If you will write and rewrite and polish, bringing to every piece of work, however small, your finest artistry; if you will follow the rules of submission (a clean, double-spaced, easy-to read manuscript, accompanied by a stamped, self-addressed envelope); and if you market intelligently, choosing publications appropriate to your material, then, other things being equal, the time will come when you will succeed.

In short, if you first have the qualifications for becoming a writer and will do the things I've stated, *you cannot fail!*

9

CREATIVE TRUST

By John D. MacDonald

THE writer and the reader are involved in a creative relationship. The writer must provide the materials with which the reader will construct bright pictures in his head. The reader will use those materials as a partial guide and will finish the pictures with the stuff from his own life experience.

I do not intend to patronize the reader with this analogy: The writer is like a person trying to entertain a listless child on a rainy afternoon.

You set up a card table, and you lay out pieces of cardboard, construction paper, scissors, paste, crayons. You draw a rectangle and you construct a very colorful little fowl and stick it in the foreground, and you say, "This is a chicken." You cut out a red square and put it in the background and say, "This is a barn." You construct a bright yellow truck and put it in the background on the other side of the frame and say, "This is a speeding truck. Is the chicken going to get out of the way in time? Now you finish the picture."

If the child has become involved, he will get into the whole cut-and-paste thing, adding trees, a house, a fence, a roof on the barn. He will crayon a road from the truck to the chicken. You didn't say a word about trees, fences, houses, cows, roofs. The kid puts them in because he knows they are the furniture of farms. He is joining in the creative act, enhancing the tensions of the story by adding his uniquely personal concepts of the items you did not mention, but which have to be there.

Or the child could cross the room, turn a dial and see detailed pictures on the television tube. What are the ways you can lose him?

You can lose him by putting in too much of the scene. That turns him into a spectator. "This is a chicken. This is a fence. This is an apple tree. This is a tractor." He knows those things have to be there. He yawns. And pretty soon, while you are cutting and pasting and explaining, you hear the gunfire of an old western.

You can lose him by putting in too little. "This is a chicken," you say, and leave him to his own devices. Maybe he will put the chicken in a forest, or in a supermarket. Maybe the child will invent the onrushing truck, or a chicken hawk. Too much choice is as boring as too little. Attention is diffused, undirected.

You can put in the appropriate amount of detail and still lose him by the way you treat the chicken, the truck, and the barn. Each must have presence. Each must be unique. *The* chicken. Not *a* chicken. He is eleven weeks old. He is a rooster named Melvin who stands proud and glossy in the sunlight, but tends to be nervous, insecure and hesitant. His legs are exceptionally long, and in full flight he has a stride you wouldn't believe.

If you cannot make the chicken, the truck, and the barn totally specific, then it is as if you were using dingy gray paper for those three ingredients, and the child will not want to use his own bright treasure to complete the picture you have begun.

We are analogizing here the semantics of image, of course. The pace and tension and readability of fiction are as dependent upon your control and understanding of these phenomena as they are upon story structure and characterization.

Here is a sample: The air conditioning unit in the motel room had a final fraction of its name left, an "aire" in silver plastic, so loose that when it resonated to the coughing thud of the compressor, it would blur. A rusty water stain on the green wall under the unit was shaped like the bottom half of Texas. From the stained grid, the air conditioner exhaled its stale and icy breath into the room, redolent of chemicals and of someone burning garbage far, far away.

Have you not already constructed the rest of the motel room? Can you not see and describe the bed, the carpeting, the shower? O.K., if you see them already, I need not describe them for you. If I try to do so, I become a bore. And the pictures you have com-

38

posed in your head are more vivid than the ones I would try to describe.

No two readers will see exactly the same motel room. No two children will construct the same farm. But the exercise of the need to create gives both ownership and involvement to the motel room and the farm, to the air conditioner and to the chicken and to their environments.

Sometimes, of course, it is useful to go into exhaustive detail. That is when a different end is sought. In one of the Franny and Zooey stories, Salinger describes the contents of a medicine cabinet shelf by shelf in such infinite detail that finally a curious monumentality is achieved, reminiscent somehow of that iron sculpture by David Smith called "The Letter."

Here is a sample of what happens when you cut the images out of gray paper: "The air conditioning unit in the motel room window was old and somewhat noisy."

See? Because the air conditioning unit has lost its specificity, its unique and solitary identity, the room has blurred also. You cannot see it as clearly. It is less real.

AND WHEN THE ENVIRONMENT IS LESS REAL, THE PEOPLE YOU PUT INTO THAT ENVIRONMENT BECOME LESS BELIEVABLE, AND LESS INTERESTING.

I hate to come across a whole sentence in caps when I am reading something. But here, it is of such importance, and so frequently misunderstood and neglected, I inflict caps upon you with no apology. The environment can seem real only when the reader has helped construct it. Then he has an ownership share in it. If the air conditioner is unique, then the room is unique, and the person in it is real.

What item to pick? There is no rule. Sometimes you can use a little sprinkling of realities, a listing of little items which make a room unique among all rooms in the world: A long living room with one long wall painted the hard blue of Alpine sky and kept clear of prints and paintings, with a carved blonde behemoth piano, its German knees half-bent under its oaken weight, and with a white Parsons table covered by a vivid collection of French glass paperweights.

I trust the reader to finish the rest of that room in his head, without making any conscious effort to do so. The furnishings will be appropriate to his past observations.

How to make an object unique? (Or where do I find the colored paper for the rooster?) Vocabulary is one half the game, and that can come only from constant, omnivorous reading, beginning very early in life. If you do not have that background, forget all about trying to write fiction. You'll save yourself brutal disappointment. The second half of the game is input. All the receptors must be wide open. You must go through the world at all times looking at the things around you. Texture, shape, style, color, pattern, movement. You must be alert to the smell, taste, sound of everything you see, and alert to the relationships between the aspects of objects, and of people. Tricks and traits and habits, deceptive and revelatory.

There are people who have eyes and cannot see. I have driven friends through country they have never seen before and have had them pay only the most cursory attention to the look of the world. Trees are trees, houses are houses, hills are hills—to them. Their inputs are all turned inward, the receptors concerned only with Self. Self is to them the only reality, the only uniqueness. Jung defines these people in terms of the "I" and the "Not I." The "I" person conceives of the world as being a stage setting for Self, to the point where he cannot believe other people are truly alive and active when they are not sharing that stage with Self. Thus nothing is real unless it has a direct and specific bearing on Self.

The writer must be a Not-I, a person who can see the independence of all realities and know that the validity of object or person can be appraised and used by different people in different ways. The writer must be the observer, the questioner. And that is why the writer should be wary of adopting planned eccentricities of appearance and behavior, since, by making himself the observed rather than the observer, he dwarfs the volume of input he must have to keep his work fresh.

Now we will assume you have the vocabulary, the trait of constant observation plus retention of the telling detail. And at this moment—if I am not taking too much credit—you have a new appraisal of the creative relationship of writer and reader. You want to begin to use it.

The most instructive thing you can do is to go back over past work, published or unpublished, and find the places where you described something at length, in an effort to make it unique and special, but somehow you did not bring it off. (I do this with my own work oftener than you might suppose.)

Now take out the subjective words. For example, I did not label the air conditioner as old, or noisy, or battered, or cheap. Those are evaluations the reader should make. Tell how a thing looks, not your evaluation of what it is from the way it looks. Do not say a man looks seedy. That is a judgment, not a description. All over the world, millions of men look seedy, each one in his own fashion. Describe a cracked lens on his glasses, a bow fixed with stained tape, tufts of hair growing out of his nostrils, an odor of old laundry.

This is a man. His name is Melvin. You built him out of scraps of bright construction paper and put him in front of the yellow oncoming truck.

The semantics of image is a special discipline. Through it you achieve a reality which not only makes the people more real, it makes the situation believable, and compounds the tension.

If a vague gray truck hits a vague gray man, his blood on gray pavement will be without color or meaning.

When a real yellow truck hits Melvin, man or rooster, we feel that mortal thud deep in some visceral place where dwells our knowledge of our own oncoming death.

You have taken the judgment words out of old descriptions and replaced them with the objective words of true description. You have taken out the things the reader can be trusted to construct for himself.

Read it over. Is there too much left, or too little? When in doubt, opt for less rather than more.

We all know about the clumsiness the beginning writer shows when he tries to move his people around, how he gets them into motion without meaning. We all did it in the beginning. Tom is in an office on one side of the city, and Mary is in an apartment on the other side. So we walked him into the elevator, out through the foyer, into a cab, all the way across town, into another foyer, up in the elevator, down the corridor to Mary's door. Because it was motion without meaning, we tried desperately to create interest with some kind of ongoing interior monologue. Later we learned that as soon as the decision to go see Mary comes to Tom, we need merely skip three spaces and have him knocking at Mary's door. The reader knows how people get across cities, and get in and out of buildings. The reader will make the instantaneous jump.

So it is with description. The reader knows a great deal. He has taste and wisdom, or he wouldn't be reading. Give him some of the vivid and specific details which you see, and you can trust him to build all the rest of the environment. Having built it himself, he will be that much more involved in what is happening, and he will cherish and relish you the more for having trusted him to share in the creative act of telling a story.

10

THE RIGHT TITLE FOR YOUR BOOK

By Patricia Tompkins

AT LAST you've finished writing, revising, and typing your manuscript. You have reworked your opening paragraphs several times and agonized over your first sentence. Your work is almost done. But the first words your readers will see must get the same attention. An editor—your first reader—will look for early signs that your manuscript is worth reading, and your title is a leading indicator. An appealing title can persuade readers to select a particular book from all of those on the library or bookstore shelves. If your title is awkward, confusing, difficult to pronounce, it is working against you.

It's important to know the difference between a good title and a bad one. The following suggestions apply to titles for most manuscripts, with some special distinctions that you should be aware of between fiction and nonfiction titles. But the essentials are the same: know your market; catch the reader's attention; for nonfiction, describe the book accurately.

First, let's consider titles for novels. You can draw on a wide range of sources in composing an appropriate title for a novel, from poetry, to the Bible, to puns, and clever reversals of famous sayings, to name only a few. By consulting several reference books in the public library, you can also show editors that you are familiar with what has been recently published or is still in print, so that you don't repeat or come too close to the competition.

Start with the latest edition of *Books in Print,* an annual compilation that consists of three volumes arranged alphabetically by title, author, and subject—over 5,000 pages. Check to see whether the titles you have in mind are the same as those you find in these volumes. You might, for example, discover that four recently published books share the name, *Fallen Angel.* Such duplication is possible because titles are not protected by copyright laws. In *theory,* therefore, you are free to use any title you wish, including *Fallen Angel* or *Gone with the Wind.* But it would be inadvisable. Not only would it indicate a lack of familiarity with what is in print and invite comparisons between your book and those previously published, but using well-known titles may confuse the public. For that reason, a court may enjoin such duplication of a title, which would appear to trade on the popularity of the earlier work and confuse the buyer.

Part of knowing your market is being aware of a publisher's list, so that you would not submit a book with a title that is the same as one he has already published, even if it is in a different field. Keep in mind that your first task is to please an editor so that you can reach a wider audience of readers through publication.

To keep up to date with the newest book titles, consult *Publishers Weekly,* the most important journal for the publishing trade. In it you will find weekly forecasts of forthcoming books, lists of hardcover and paperback bestsellers, and book advertising for most major and specialty publishers. In this way, you'll get a sense of the prevailing tastes and trends in book titles. The fall and spring announcement issues are particularly useful, and you can find these in most public libraries.

You should also read regularly *The New York Times Book Review,* published as part of the Sunday *Times* and available in most libraries.

Some of the titles may strike you as unimaginative or silly, certainly not memorable. In genre fiction—romances, historical and contemporary; westerns; mysteries—titles are as predictable as the cover art, because their purpose is to identify the *category* or *series* rather than distinguish one book from another. Well-established authors can rely on their names to attract buyers and readers, who will ask for the latest Dick Francis or Louis L'Amour or Janet Dailey. James Michener's titles are almost code words—*Poland, Space, Centennial*—and he could probably use letters of the alphabet *(P, S, C)* without losing readers. A new writer has to work harder to come up with inviting titles.

Another important source of title possibilities is a book of quotations like *Bartlett's Familiar Quotations,* or Burton Stevenson's *Home Book of Proverbs, Maxims and Familiar Phrases,* or *The Oxford Dictionary of Quotations*—all available in most library reference rooms. Entries are arranged variously—chronologically, by subject, or by author, but the indexes, arranged alphabetically by key words in the quotations, will help you narrow down the quotations most appropriate for your book. If, for example, you take the word *hand, power,* or *green,* you'll find listings of notable quotations using each of those words, with the context and source of the line. Almost every line in these volumes has good title possibilities.

During your next visit to a bookstore, do some casual research by looking at the new titles on display. What makes you pick up one book rather than another? You are, essentially, judging the books by their covers. Except for those by best-selling authors whose names take up most of the front of the book's jacket, the title is the prominent feature.

In addition to sifting through masses of mediocre titles, consider proven successes. Most of us recognize certain titles although we may not have read the books. A few titles of novels have become part of our language: *Catch-22, Babbitt, 1984, A Burnt-Out Case, Brave New World* (words Aldous Huxley borrowed from Shakespeare). Some titles share the names of their main characters: *Madame Bovary, Jude the Obscure, Lolita.* Pairs and dichotomies are often effective: *Pride and Prejudice, The Naked and the Dead, The Beautiful and the Damned.* There are descriptive titles—*Around the World in 80 Days* and *Portrait of the Artist as a Young Man*—and titles that express attitudes—*Of Human Bondage* and *Invisible Man.* Some titles only make sense in retrospect; you must read a novel to understand its name—*To Kill a Mockingbird,* for example. (And although I've read it and know what the title refers to, *Watership Down* reminds me of submarines, not a rural rabbit homeland.)

If you're beginning to think the best titles have already been used, remember that John Steinbeck and F. Scott Fitzgerald are among those authors who struggled with titles. *Of Mice and Men* was originally *Something That Happened.* Steinbeck (perhaps with the help of his editor) learned to use simple names *(The Red Pony, Cannery Row)* and to borrow evocative phrases *(In Dubious Battle, East of Eden).* Fitzgerald tried half a dozen awful concoctions, including *Trimalchio on the Road to West Egg,* before settling on *The Great Gatsby.* Winesburg, Ohio started with *The Book of the Grotesque* as its title; *Look Homeward, Angel* was *O Lost* originally. You can learn from the mistakes of others.

Poets have supplied novelists with many titles—*For Whom the Bell Tolls, The Winter of Our Discontent;* other popular sources include the

Bible and nursery rhymes—*Song of Solomon, All the King's Men.* You can twist a familiar phrase—*Loser Takes All, The Little Drummer Girl*—or create a word—*Utopia* (from the Greek word for *no place*) and *Erewhon* (a scrambling of *nowhere*).

Just as an effective title won't get a poor novel published, a lack of talent for creating a title won't be fatal to your writing career, but you can avoid greeting readers with a graceless or hackneyed one. Your title should reflect the style, as well as the content, of your material. For example, the title *The Old Man and the Sea*—common monosyllabic words—matches its spare text. *An American Tragedy* fits the novel's scope and subject, while *The Restaurant at the End of the Universe* indicates the off-beat. As in your prose, don't strain to be clever, literary, or cute in your title.

Subtitles, popular with such novelists as Thomas Hardy and Herman Melville, are rarely used in fiction today, but you may find one useful in clarifying your main title. For example, *Brideshead Revisited* is less obscure with its subtitle: *The Sacred and Profane Memoirs of Captain Charles Ryder.* Like a main title, a subtitle should say something important about the work (a point so obvious it's sometimes forgotten). Generally, publishers add the words "A Novel By" on the front of the jacket to help distinguish works of fiction from nonfiction. "A Novel of Japan" was useful in introducing James Clavell's *Shōgun,* before the book became a bestseller. *Shōgun* illustrates another exception to a general rule: in titling your books, stick to English. Unlike many foreign words, *Shōgun* works because it is easy to pronounce and is included in English-language dictionaries.

In nonfiction, an informative title is almost essential, and subtitles often provide concrete information. Literary allusions in titles generally don't mix with books of plain facts. An editor should turn from your title page to your text with a sense of anticipation rather than in search of an answer to the question, "What is this manuscript about?" If your title is clear, readers won't need to ask the question.

A straightforward title does not mean you should settle for something bland and artless. You could, for example, refer to another work, but don't follow a crowd of imitators. *The Rise and Fall of the Third Reich* gains authority by alluding to Gibbon's classic history—*The Decline and Fall of the Roman Empire. Walden Two* is another type of deliberate borrowing. You can change a mundane how-to title into a memorable one by adding a single word. Perhaps you have compiled a guide to California wineries. Is it comprehensive or selective? Does it evaluate wines or simply list what is produced? Whom is it written for? As a title, "A Guide to California Wines" does not answer these basic questions; a few added words could indicate what makes your guidebook unique.

What about *Bury My Heart at Wounded Knee?* That title suggests a novel, but the book is nonfiction. It demonstrates two points: (1) there are exceptions to any guidelines, and (2) some types of nonfiction can benefit from literary titles, especially those that offer interpretation—for example, some history *(A Distant Mirror: The Calamitous 14th Century)* and biography *(The Dark Side of Genius: The Life of Alfred Hitchcock).* Note how subtitles help identify the topic, as in this title—*American Caesar: Douglas MacArthur, 1880–1964.* The main title expresses a concept, the subtitle names the subject, and the dates indicate the book's scope.

A subtitle is secondary, but two recent nonfiction bestsellers demonstrate how subtitles effectively strengthen their main titles. *In Search of Excellence* suggests a quest for the best, but the best what? The subtitle explains: *Lessons from America's Best-Run Companies.* A title like "The Best-Run Companies in America" is more direct but also duller. *Megatrends: Ten New Directions Transforming Our Lives* uses two devices—a popular new word from the field of economics and a subtitle to explain it. when a more conventional word serves as a title—*Passages,* for example—a subtitle could define the word in terms of its specific contents.

If the title you want to use for your nonfiction book is already being used, analyze your work and determine how it differs from the book in print and incorporate that difference into a subtitle or a twist on the title you had intended to use. You may decide to abandon your first choice of title and rework it to your advantage or with an original touch that fits your book more specifically.

Every book category, fiction or nonfiction—mysteries, romances, travel, self-help, politics, or whatever—has some conventions for its titles. Study the genre you are writing for, and keeping in mind the purpose of a book title—to distinguish and describe what you have written in an appealing and attention-getting way—see how original and appropriate you can make your title.

11

STRINGS THAT TOUCH THE SKY

BY JANE YOLEN

I COME from a family of string savers and kite fliers. It is an easy connection: kites/strings. Taking what is left over and used up and making it touch the sky is a good metaphor for writing.

If I were a scientist, I would remind myself that matter can never be lost. If I were a gardener, I would call it the great recycle of life. If I had a religious vocation, I would call it the second coming. But I am a writer from a family of string savers and kite fliers, so I see my writing in terms of a series of loops. What you have researched and written about once, you can use again and again in brand new ways. Loop upon loop. A veritable cat's cradle of ideas. Let me give you an example.

I wrote a book about the Quakers, a biography of the founding father of the religion, entitled *Friend: The Story of George Fox.* And because it was successful, another publisher asked me to do a book about the history of the Shakers, for they were a bizarre and radical outgrowth of the Society of Friends.

Loop 1. Simple Gifts, the Shaker book, was built upon some of the history I had already researched for the Quaker book. The earlier work had also prepared me to understand the group religious mind as well as persecuted religious minorities and their behavior. However, as I researched this particular nonfiction book project, I kept thinking that there were surely many stories in that history. I had already found dozens of them in the journals of believers and apostates. One that interested me especially (probably because my then fourteen-year-old daughter was beginning to get interested in boys) was a Romeo and Juliet story set in a Shaker community, made more interesting by the central fact that Shakers were celibate! This led me to write a novel.

Loop 2. The Gift of Sarah Barker was that novel. Sarah greatly resembled my daughter in both looks and character: headstrong, passionate, self-doubting, but always questioning authority. Set *that* girl down in a community of would-be angels in nineteenth century Massachusetts, and there's bound to be an interesting explosion.

Loop 3. For that Shaker novel about Sarah, I used the great round barn of Hancock Shaker Village as the central meeting place for her and the boy Abel Church. I loved that barn and had spent many quiet moments meditating there when I was doing my research. I longed to make use of that peculiar, fascinating barn again. But how? I didn't want to write another Shaker book. For the moment, two were enough. But a year later, when I was in the midst of writing a science fiction novel, *Dragon's Blood,* the Shaker material surfaced again. *Dragon's Blood* takes place in the 24th century on an ex-penal colony planet called Austar IV. The dragon farm on which my young hero worked as a bond slave quite naturally began to resemble a Shaker farm community—*without* the celibacy. And the stud barn where the great cock dragons were kept was, not surprisingly, built around a round central mow. The description of the steam rising from the stored grasses in that mow comes directly from a period description of the Hancock barn.

Loop 4. Dragon's Blood grew into a trilogy. *Heart's Blood* is the second book. I'm currently writing the third, tentatively called *Dragon's Eyes.* I am thinking about new ways to transform all that I have learned in the writing of this particular series of loops, all involving Shakers in some way. Another novel about religious communities—this time the millennial kind who sit on mountain tops waiting for the predicted end of the world—is already beginning to take shape in my mind.

Loops within loops within loops.

Nothing is lost in research or writing, though it may take years before any one idea is rediscovered, disinterred. This is personal literary archeology.

English teachers in school writing classes always caution their students to "write about what you know." They always neglect to add (indeed they may not realize) that there are many ways to "know" something. By looping and re-looping, an author gets to know a lot of characters and settings in a very deep way. To reuse them, melting them down in the furnace of the heart and mind, then reshaping them

49

into something new, is what writing is all about. We are, after all, craftspeople, and the heart-metal is tempered by that cooling process between books and stories.

Whether you call it crafting or the great recycle or the second coming or the fact that matter cannot be lost, it is the same. All writers are savers of string, and the best writers know instinctively that pieces of string tied together can make a line long enough, eventually, to touch the sky.

12

ON BEING A GOOD BOSS

By Katherine Paterson

RECENTLY I had lunch with a young writer whom I admire extravagantly. She has the kind of vision that can see exquisite, telling details which even Eudora Welty might miss and a voice whose clarity E.B. White would admire. Someday hers will be a name all of you will recognize. I'd be consumed with envy except for one thing. I don't think I could stand to work for her boss.

But, you say, that is ridiculous. If she is a free-lance writer, she is her own boss. Exactly. I do not believe for a minute that I am a better writer than my friend, but I know I have a better boss.

Now I haven't always had a good boss. When I started writing twenty years ago, I had an overcritical, demanding, sneering ogre at my elbow. But over the years, as I've learned more about how to write, I've also learned better how to manage my one employee. After all, if the writer is not working well, the whole company is in serious trouble. For those of you with poor labor/management relations, here are a few things I've discovered.

1. A good boss expects her worker to do the best she can and never compares her to someone else. Any boss who compares you to Leo Tolstoy would be laughed at, but how many of your bosses make snide comparisons between you and so-and-so who just got a $15,000 advance on *her* first novel?

2. A good boss sets realistic goals. Part of the job description for a manager is goal setting. Any goals set should, however, be attainable by work on the writer's part and not depend on the caprice of prize juries and even the decision of editors. It is all right, therefore, for the boss to say that the first draft of the novel will be mailed by October 3rd. It is not all right for the boss to say that it will be bought by November 3rd, published by June 3rd, and receive the Pulitzer Prize by the following

spring. In my company, the boss breaks up big goals into lots of little ones. On the calendar are dates when each chapter should be written (or revised) as well as the momentous day on which a project should be mailed. Also, because she is such an understanding manager, she builds in a cushion. Then if I have dental surgery or a sick child, I can still make the mailing deadline, and if nothing untoward occurs, I have the genuine delight of beating the targeted date by two weeks.

3. A good boss is understanding without being wishy-washy. She knows that there are days that you absolutely cannot get to the type-writer. But in all proper companies, sick leave and personal leave are carefully restricted. No good boss allows an employee simply to work whenever "inspired." A good boss know that a writer who writes only when she is inspired will work three or four days a year. Books do not get written in three or four days a year. On those terrible occasions when the writer is blocked, a good boss will not berate, but will gently insist that the writer go to work as usual. The last time I suffered one of these spells, my boss told me to write two pages before getting up from the typewriter and giving up for the day. On a number of days, the margins were suspiciously wide, but I continued to produce two mal-nourished pages each day, until, just as my boss had hoped, the log jam broke up, and the words began to flow normally.

4. A good boss reserves criticism for appropriate times. She knows that no one can work creatively and critically at the same moment. She never peers over your shoulder while you're on a first draft. In fact my boss doesn't come to work much while I'm on a first draft. I call her in for consultation, only after I've gotten through the whole story once. I have respect for her critical ability, but if I allow her to make remarks on my work when it is still tentative and fragile, she is likely to kill something before it has a chance to breathe properly. Later on, I don't mind how ruthless she becomes. She's a stickler, for example, on checking for accuracy, but if she makes me stop and do it in the middle of a thought, I may lose what I'm trying to say.

5. A good boss provides working conditions that are as congenial as she can possibly make them. She knows that if she does not take your work seriously, no one will. She regards your privacy as important, doesn't fuss when you don't clean up after yourself every day, and tries to keep up with supplies so that you don't run out of paper or need a new ribbon in the middle of a hard morning's work. A good boss doesn't

try to make you feel guilty about spending money that she knows will pay in the long run. My boss, for example, no longer insists that all first drafts be written on the back of Christmas letters, notices from school, and first drafts of earlier novels. She found that I work better on clean paper, even if it is only the first draft.

And finally, 6. A good boss makes the worker feel good about her work. My boss, in the old days, never missed a chance to sneeringly tell me how far short I fell of her vision. Now she knows that only makes me discouraged and reluctant to try again. So when I say, "How can I write another book? I don't even know where to begin," she says to me, "Sweetie, you can begin anywhere you want to. Just try something. Anything. It's not going to be engraved in stone. You can always throw it out tomorrow."

Sometimes my boss will pick up a book I wrote long ago and read a particularly felicitous passage. "Nice, huh?" It makes me glow all over. These days, she hardly ever goes back to point out the other less cheering examples. "What's the use?" she says. "It's too late to change it." Formerly, when reviews were painful, my boss would say, "See, they've caught on to you. That's just the fatal flaw I was telling you about. Whatever made you think you could write a book?" These days she just sighs and says, "Sweetie, haven't I told you never to read reviews? Good or bad, they just take your mind off the work you're doing now. And that is what's important. After all, *this* is going to be the best book we've ever written." See why I'm not about to trade the old girl in?

13

TESTAMENT TO PERSEVERANCE

By Carol Amen

MANY writers agonize over talent, when a more logical area for concern, it seems to me, might be an evaluation of the capacity for persistence. In my own case, I've had a number of projects I cared about deeply—not brilliant writing, I'm sure, but nevertheless important to me—even though editors did not agree at first.

I'd like to tell you about two of these.

The inspiration for one came about four o'clock on a January morning in 1969. I woke from a sound sleep with a strange sensation. I knew who I was and where I was, but in some puzzling way, I also identified with another person—a fictional wife and mother in an isolated northern community after a series of nuclear explosions.

The woman and others in the town think at first they are "the lucky ones." They've survived the initial blasts which leveled San Francisco and other U.S. cities. They distribute bottled water and canned food. But later, as neighbors begin to die, they fear they all will succumb to radiation sickness. Inexplicably, I saw myself as both observer and participant in the town's events, and when the two-hour waking dream ended, I felt a tremendous urgency to communicate the story.

On a pad I always keep on my bedside table, I was able to record a few details and hold the rest in my mind until I had time to get to my typewriter. For about five hours I wrote, and not once did I have to stop to think up some plot device, some bit of conflict to make the tale more interesting. It was as if I were merely recording. I had the viewpoint character use a journal to try to hold onto her sanity, and she sees that diary as a record to leave for any possible survivors—something like a last will and testament, hence the story's title, "Last Testament."

While the story was infinitely sad because of the implied probability that no survivors would remain to read the journal, it was at the same time a quiet testament to human love. People in the town didn't resort to animal behavior, didn't give up. They were neighbors in the best sense of the word. They died with dignity.

For several months I polished the story, and then I began sending it out. At that time, I'd had a number of art-of-living, family pieces published, but not much fiction. I sent "Last Testament" first to women's slicks, then to denominational/religious magazines, finally to college or literary quarterlies.

Nobody wanted it.

The closest I came to any interest was with *Today,* a United Methodist family magazine whose editor thought the story deserved a chance. If I hadn't succeeded in placing it in about a year, the *Today* editor suggested I resubmit it to him. Then *Today* suspended publication. I tried to *give* "Last Testament" to a peace group. They informed me they weren't in the publishing business.

After about two-and-one-half years of fruitless effort, I put the manuscript in a drawer and didn't submit it again until a few months after the Soviet invasion of Afghanistan.

In early 1980, I read it in a manuscript workshop, then sought reactions from two friends whose fiction sensibility I admire. I removed a hint or two of preachiness, tightened it, and sent the result to *St. Anthony Messenger.* They published it in September 1980. After eleven years of frustration, I finally saw the story in print in a magazine with a circulation of 350,000, but for some reason I wasn't content. And so, I started all over again.

Because *St. Anthony Messenger* had purchased first rights only, I was free to offer the published story as a reprint. I took tear sheets and began another assault on the marketplace. In some cases, I set aside the strict protocol free lancers are taught to observe: I implored certain publications to take a look. "Please," I remember saying in cover letters, "this is important. Will you give it a careful reading?"

To date at least twenty-five magazines and newspapers have reprinted "Last Testament." Besides those publications to which I'd submitted it, many others wrote to ask permission to run it. It has been published in Canada, New Zealand, and Australia; broadcast in various parts of the United States and four times in West Berlin. A mime and street theater group took it on tour. In two separate states, families bought space in their local newspapers at *advertising rates* and ran the story.

One of the places I sent tear sheets of "Last Testament" was *Ms.* Magazine. They published it in August 1981, and then movie producers started phoning. Of four who approached me, I signed a contract with Lynne Littman, an independent film maker, because her fervor for the basic story was as intense as mine.

She originally produced and directed the movie, called *Testament,* for Public Broadcasting's "American Playhouse," and after enthusiastic reactions at film festivals, it was picked up by Paramount Pictures and released in movie theaters here and abroad. Jane Alexander's performance was praised by critics (she was nominated for a 1983 Best Actress Academy Award), while the film itself made a number of "Best of 1983" lists. It is also available on video cassettes for home use.

What explains such a turn of events after so many years of frustration? A story I couldn't *give away* in the early '70s has been presented again and again in the '80s to many different kinds of audiences. Because of the subject matter—end-of-the-world by nuclear means—*timing* certainly played a significant part, but, I am convinced, so did persistence.

Another piece of my fiction—"Ritual in the Goldfish Bowl"—is proof of the effectiveness of persistence. I submitted that story sixty-three times over a period of almost nineteen years before it was published. It, too, started as a dream.

In 1965, our family was concerned about a grandmother who had had surgery and was in poor health. One night I dreamed Grandma had died and our family was gathered in her Iowa farm home following the funeral. Sideboards and buffets groaned under the dishes of food brought by neighbors and friends. Somehow, though, to me there was a false note. Instead of the warmth and fellowship one might reasonably expect at such a gathering, I detected an exaggerated preoccupation with *ritual,* and especially with food. Everyone seemed to have forgotten the reason for this get-together—the death of a loved one.

When I awoke, my grandmother was still alive (and, indeed, she lived for several more years), but I immediately did a "what if" exercise. What if there were a family in which something unfortunate happens— an estrangement resulting from some breakdown in family relations— and an important event, presumably a wedding, brings Reenie Martingale, daughter and viewpoint character, home. And what if—after the careful planting of clues and double meanings—it is revealed at the very end of the story that the event that brought Reenie home is not her brother Randy's wedding, but his funeral? Aren't some of the ritual elements of weddings and funerals very much alike?

The first draft of "Ritual in the Goldfish Bowl" went together fairly easily, and from the day in July 1965 I first submitted it, I had a lot of faith in it. My initial target was *Redbook,* and over the years, I resubmitted it three more times to that magazine. I reasoned that in such a long time, editors would have moved on, or, if the same ones were still on the staff, they would certainly not remember my story out of all the others they read.

On an August morning in 1981, my newspaper horoscope informed me it was a good day for submitting manuscripts, so I sent "Ritual" to *Redbook* once more. They didn't buy it, but the fiction editor wrote, "Your writing continues to interest us, and we hope you'll show us other stories." (The same editor subsequently commented encouragingly on four or five other stories submitted.)

Some editors found the ending of "Ritual" gimmicky. "O. Henry is out," I was informed. And several observed that my characterization of the mother was not convincing.

In the first few versions, I admit, Mrs. Martingale was stereotypical of all manipulative, controlling matriarchs—a cardboard figure. In nineteen years and I don't know how many rewrites, however, she became real—at least for me. She had a past, and she had reasons—if not excuses—for the way she had behaved toward her children. In a scene late in the story, Mrs. Martingale stiffly tells her daughter why appearances have always been more important to her than any expression of affection.

This was not a story ahead of its time; nor did it offer any particular revelation except perhaps a small one about human nature. Why, then, did I persist so long with something sixty-two editors had deemed unpublishable?

I'm not entirely sure. Had this been nonfiction, I'd have assumed automatically that the fault was mine. But I felt somehow that fiction was different, and I tried not to let doubts deter me. I told myself that the story just hadn't yet hit the right editor's desk at precisely the right time. And I continued to search for that "right" editor.

In the fall of 1982, when *Campus Life,* a Christian magazine for high school and college age readers, published another short story of mine, the editor and I spoke on the phone several times. Then he saw the movie, *Testament,* and ran a review of it in his magazine. As an editor, he was interested in the considerable lag time between my writing the story that inspired the film and its first appearance in print. "If you have any other 'sleepers' in your files," he said, "please give us a look at them."

In December, 1983, I prepared a clean copy of "Ritual" and sent it to him. About a month later, he phoned with some excitement, I thought, saying he was buying the story. I have seldom been as pleased. ("Ritual" appeared in the June 1984 issue of *Campus Life,* titled "Under Mom's Thumb.")

I daydream sometimes about selling a story on its first trip out. A number of my articles have clicked immediately, but that almost never happens for me with short fiction, except to obscure or lower-paying markets. I fantasize, too, about seeing my byline on fiction in a top slick or literary magazine. *Ms.* qualifies, but that was a reprint, so it isn't quite the same.

In the meantime, I have tacked above my desk a sentence from May Sarton's *A World of Light.* "I understand that a talent is something given," Sarton wrote, "that it opens like a flower, but without exceptional energy, discipline, and persistence will never bear fruit."

Some days that reminder really helps. As I address the inevitable manila envelope for some challenging-to-place story, I am grateful that whatever writing talents I have, I also possess a good supply of energy, a tad of discipline, and a *lot* of persistence.

When I'm in a particularly candid frame of mind, I admit I've written many stories that don't deserve to be published. I've penned some real losers, stories I've never sent out in the mail even *once,* let alone sixty-three times. But when I write something I deep down believe in, I never give up.

14

THE MAGICAL WORLD OF THE NOVELIST

By Sidney Sheldon

One of the questions I am frequently asked is, "How does one write a best seller?" My answer is that I don't know. If someone deliberately sets out to write a best seller, what he is really saying is that he is going to try to write a book that will appeal to everyone. In essence, he is looking for the lowest common denominator. I believe when you try to appeal to everyone, the result is that you end up appealing to almost no one. Every good writer that I know writes to please himself, not to please others. He starts with an idea that excites him, develops characters that interest him, and then writes his story as skillfully as he knows how. If one worries about quality rather than success, success is much more likely to follow.

How does one get started as a writer? The best advice I ever heard of came from Sinclair Lewis. After his Pulitzer Prize for *Main Street,* he was besieged by requests to speak to writing classes at various universities. He turned them all down until one day, after frantic importuning from an Ivy League college, he consented to speak. At the appointed time the auditorium was packed with eager would-be writers, waiting to hear words of wisdom from the master. Sinclair Lewis strode out on the stage and gazed upon his audience. He stood there for sixty seconds of absolute silence, and then said, "Why aren't you home writing?" And he turned and walked off the stage.

I started as a script reader in Hollywood when I was seventeen, then went on to write motion picture scenarios, Broadway plays and television series.

I was a producer at Columbia Studios when I got the idea for *The Naked Face,* my first novel. I contemplated writing it as a motion picture or a Broadway play, but hesitated because the plot called for a great deal of introspection on the part of the protagonist. Because so much of the story was cerebral, there seemed to be no way to let the audience know what the character was thinking. Then it occurred to me that if I wrote it as a novel I could do exactly that. Every morning from nine to twelve I dictated the book to one secretary, while another kept the outside world at bay. At twelve o'clock, I put on my producer's hat and worked on other projects until the following morning. The book was finished a year later. Irving Wallace sent me to his agent, who liked the book and sold it to William Morrow. Most of the reviews on *The Naked Face* were excellent, but the sales were minor. Since I had turned down other projects while writing the book, it proved to be an expensive experiment for me. It would have been easy to have returned to the dramatic rather than the narrative form of writing; but I was hooked. I immediately began another novel with no expectation that it would be any more rewarding financially than was *The Naked Face*. But I was not looking for financial reward. I had found something better: Freedom.

When you are writing for television, theatre or motion pictures, you have a hundred collaborators. There is the star who complains, "I can't read those lines. You'll have to change them"; the director who says, "That scene you wrote in the tea room—let's change it to having them climb the Matterhorn"; the cameraman who filters your story through his lens; the musicians who will finally create moods for your words with their music. I had been used to working with such collaborators all my professional life. It is part of the system. When a writer is under contract to a studio and he's told to change something, he changes it. He is an employee who receives a weekly check, just like the grips and the hairdressers.

Now, with my first novel, I had a taste of freedom—complete and total freedom. No one was looking over my shoulder, no one was telling me how or what to write, no one was second-guessing me. It was an exhilarating experience. I knew that what I wrote might fail, but at least it would be *my* failure.

My second novel was *The Other Side of Midnight,* and it turned out to be one of the ten best-selling novels of the past decade. *Turned out to be.* I did not set out to write a best seller. It began as an idea that I liked, and I went to work on it. Two and a half years later I turned it over to a publisher.

When I begin a book, I start out with a character. I have no plot in mind. The character begets other characters, and soon they begin to take over the novel and chart their own destinies.

A caveat: Even though it works for me, I strongly advise beginning writers not to write without an outline. Writing without some kind of blueprint can lead to too many blind alleys. (While writing *Bloodline*, I found that the character of old Samuel was taking over the book, and since he was not a major character, I had to throw 250 pages into the wastebasket to bring the story back into perspective.)

I dictate the first draft of my novels to a secretary. When the first draft is typed—and it usually runs between 1,000 and 1,200 pages—I go back to page one and start a rewrite. Not a polish—a complete rewrite. I will often throw away a hundred pages at a time, get rid of half a dozen characters and add new ones. Along the way, I constantly refine and tighten. When I get to the end of the book again, I go back to page one. I repeat this process as many as a dozen times, spending anywhere from a year to a year and a half rewriting and finally polishing, until the manuscript is as good as I know how to make it. When I have done my final polish, instead of sending it to the publisher, I start out at the beginning once more and cut ten out of every hundred pages so that the book will read ten percent faster.

The only one beside my secretary who sees my work while it is in progress is my wife, who is a brilliant editor. She reads the second drafts of my books, and I incorporate her comments into the following drafts. When the finished manuscript is ready, my editor and I meet to discuss any changes. He makes suggestions, but he emphasizes that they are *only* suggestions. If there is a difference of opinion, mine is allowed to prevail. Try that at MGM!

I think it is important to set up a disciplined schedule. If you write only when the muse sits on your shoulder, it is unlikely that your project will ever get completed. I work five or six days a week from ten in the morning to six in the evening, with a short break for lunch. I live with my characters, as they live with me.

There are two kinds of writers: Those who want to write and those who have to write. *Wanting* to write is not enough, for it is a painfully difficult profession filled with rejections, disappointments, frustrations. *Having* to be a writer is something else again. If that is the case with you, then I pity you and I envy you. I pity you because you are without a choice. There is no way for you to escape from the agonies and despair of creation, for you will find that what you write will never be good enough to satisfy you. You will always be striving to reach that impossible perfection. You will be Orpheus, using the music of your words to try to reach the unattainable Eurydice.

I envy you because you are going to reach heights that you never dreamed possible. You will create your own exciting worlds and people them with your own wonderful creatures. You will burden them with sorrows and disasters, fill them with joy, give them love, destroy them. What a fantastic and awesome thing it is to play God!

Perhaps, in this, is the clue to writing successfully. Make your characters live, make them real. If your readers do not empathize with your characters, your story, no matter how clever, must surely fail. Make them love your characters or hate them. Let the reader be envious of them or repelled or fascinated; but make the reader *believe*. There is only one way to do that: *You* must believe.

And when you have created that magic world, with characters that move and breathe and feel joy and sorrow, as you feel joy and sorrow, then, ah, then, you will have come as close as any mortal can to reaching out and touching the stars.

15

BEING THERE

BY GRAHAM MASTERTON

IF I HAVE any kind of describable technique, it is the technique of "being there."

Whenever I sit down at my typewriter to create a novel, I gradually build up in my mind's eye the places, the water, the noises, the smells, the people, until the typewriter vanishes as if it were nothing more than a mirage, and I am walking around inside my imaginary world, treading those imaginary streets, and talking to my imaginary characters in the same way that I talk to real people.

I never "write" in the sense that I am conscious of sentence construction or grammar or even the words I use. I simply describe what I can see, hear, smell, and feel, and that is why my books are much more conversational than literary.

I will often be inspired to write a novel by a painting or a photograph, something visual. I have recently completed an historical romance called *Silver*, based on the lives of H. A. W. Tabor, the Colorado silver baron, and his beautiful mistress Baby Doe. That book grew out of a photograph I found of Baby Doe in the ermine robes which Horace Tabor bought for her—a sad and haunting photograph of a lovely dark-eyed girl, now long dead.

In creating this novel, I sought the assistance of the Colorado Historical Society and several picture libraries in London, and gradually collected engravings and photographs of Leadville and Denver in the period I wanted to write about, the 1870s, as well as photographs of all the leading characters in the story.

Then, with all these visual aids around me, I simply imagined myself to be there, and told my story. It begins:

In the second week of January, when the snow was falling as thick as a thousand burst-open pillows, and the thermometer had dropped fifteen degrees below freezing, a boy came into the lobby of the Imperial Hotel with a bright red nose and a message in a snow-blotched envelope.

I believe in directness, in simplicity, in telling my story with total conviction, no matter how farfetched some of the incidents may seem; to "be there" is a tremendous help in achieving this conviction. It enables me to pare down descriptive passages to the very minimum, because all I have to do is describe the few key features in any particular room or garden or landscape that strike me the most, just as if I were really there.

"Know this hotel, do you?" asked Mr. Cutforth, pacing around, inspecting the crimson flock wallpaper with its spreading damp patches, and the half-collapsed horsehair sofas. He lifted the wilting leaf of a potted aspidistra, and said, "This could do with some water." He wrung out his wet gloves, one after the other, over the dried-up soil.

A great many of my scenes and the way in which I develop and describe them are cinematic. The tremendous advantage of writing over cinematography, however, is that the writer not only can use all of the cinema's techniques, such as slow-motion, fade-out, close-ups, and so forth, but can introduce a whole range of other sensations at the same time. Here is a short passage that you could describe as a "pullback" scene, in which the mind's eye draws away from the central characters like a telescopic movie camera, but which includes observations and emotions which the movie camera would have difficulty in putting across.

She leaned forward and kissed him. Her lips parting made a click like a cricket. Behind her, the engraved-glass oil-lamp softly flickered, and Jesus sadly looked down from the bedroom wall. *I am the way, the truth, and the life: no man cometh unto the Father, but by me.* He kissed Nina back, and held her shoulder; and the wild flowers fell as slowly as a memory on Doris's grave; and Alby Monihan looked up from his lunch; and the train rattled across the southern shore of Lake Michigan, still in darkness, although dawn was very near now, and the lights of America's homesteads glimmered pale. Milking time, dreaming time, time for open eyes.

Particularly when I am writing an historical novel, I create in my mind an entire historical world, not just a small, carefully researched stage set in which each of my individual scenes takes place. I like to feel that my characters could at any moment disobey the edicts of the plot

64

line and walk out of the door and go do something completely different, and that the real world would be out there waiting for them, just as meticulously imagined as the scene in which they are really supposed to be acting out their fictitious destiny. I undertake an enormous amount of research that I never use; in fact I use as *little* of my historical research as possible. I am not out to impress my readers that I have spent hours studying old maps and drawings. All I want to be able to do is convey my historical world with the confidence of somebody who happens to know what kind of calendar might be hanging on the wall, what kind of boots that old man sitting in the corner might be wearing, and how much he paid for them.

When it comes to people, I try not only to picture them but to imagine what they *sound* like, what they *smell* like, how they act. What they *feel* like, too. Here's a lady tightrope dancer with whom our hero has just gone to bed:

Soft skin, the color of blanched almonds, thin wrists, delicate limbs. But no superfluous flesh whatsoever, a body light and fit, with a ribcage like a shuttlecock.

Just as I try to imagine a whole world going on outside of my novels' central stage, I also remember that secondary characters are still walking around and doing things when the main characters are speaking and acting. And I remember, too, that my characters' expressions and gestures are just as important as what they say.

Whenever my characters are speaking, and particularly when they are arguing, I act out the scene as if I am rehearsing it for a play or a movie. The cartoonist Ward Kimball, who used to draw Donald Duck for Walt Disney, caught the duck's expressions by pulling faces in a mirror. I do that, too.

I find dialogue one of the greatest challenges of all, because real-sounding dialogue is exceptionally difficult, especially when you are using it to explain your character's feelings and motivations and also to move your story along. I detest reading novels in which characters "explain" themselves. People just don't do that. Their conversation is fractured, tangential, abstruse, emotional, inaccurate, repetitive. Yet if I ever attempted to write verbatim dialogue, it would be unbearably tedious to read. What I spend a great deal of my time doing is trying to perfect speech that reads as if it's authentic, and yet still conveys all the information I want my character to put across.

Here's a scene from my novel *Maiden Voyage*. Our heroine is meeting Baroness Zawisza for the first time, in the swimming pool of a luxury liner:

"Well," replied the baroness tartly, "just because I can remember Poland before the War, that doesn't actually make me a certifiable antique. Krysia! My cape, I think I'll swim. Sabran, go to the bar and order champagne. I *hate* champagne," she confided in Catriona, "but unless you drink it all the time, and very conspicuously, people begin to suspect your heritage. Such a nuisance. Will you swim with me?"

In these few plain lines of dialogue, I have attempted to convey the baroness's approximate age, her national origins, something about her class and her background, a suggestion of the way she dresses, her relationship to the two people with whom she appears (Krysia and Sabran), and the general style and sound of her speech.

Timing is one of the most interesting skills in writing authentic-sounding dialogue. If you act out your dialogue scenes, as I do, it is far easier to control the timing of your characters' conversations. Sometimes they should respond to each other's questions and comments quickly and directly. At other times, they should pause, hesitate, demur. Sometimes my characters don't answer at all, even when it would be a great deal more convenient for my story line if they did.

In this scene from *Silver*, the hero is offering Baby Doe the role of Ophelia in one of his stage productions:

"You're awfully direct, Mr. Roberts," she said. "I scarcely even know you, for all of your attentions."

Henry rested his hand against the lintel and watched her in amusement and appreciation. "In that case, I shall do everything I can to make sure that you do. Especially since you're going to be my Ophelia."

She looked up at him with those slanting, hypnotic eyes. "You *assume* that I'm going to be your Ophelia."

"Why shouldn't you? Whatever Murray Holman offers you, I'll offer you double."

"Murray Holman's furious. I mean he's really, really furious. He kicked a newsboy on the way out of the restaurant."

"Then I shall pay the newsboy double, too."

"You're funny."

Henry shook his head. "No, I'm not funny. I just appreciate a jewel when I see it, and want to have it for myself."

"Are you drunk?" she asked.

"Not even slightly. You will be my Ophelia, won't you?"

"Do you know what kind of girl Ophelia was?"

The rhythm of this conversation is vital in conveying the awkwardness between them, the way in which they are testing each other, teasing each other, and trying to establish the relationship that will carry them on through the remainder of the novel.

In real life, people use conversation to display themselves, not to advance the "plot" of their human destiny. To me, one of the most important ingredients of this display is humor. Listen to any conversation between friends, or between people who are trying to impress one another, and you will hear a joke or a wry remark. Yet I read so many novels, especially thrillers, in which nobody has any sense of humor at all. With my occult thriller *The Manitou*, in which an Indian medicine man returns from the dead to wreak a grisly revenge on the white man, I believe that I succeeded in putting over what could easily have seemed like a pretty preposterous story by making the hero flippant and funny. Most of us react to fear by trying to make light of it, and the more humorous this hero's reaction was, the greater the fear appeared to be.

By "being there" when I write, by trying my best to convey a sense of reality both in the people and the places about which I am telling a story, I find that I can be much more economical in the words I use to describe scenes of high drama.

Some of my more conventional readers have protested about scenes of sex and violence in some of my novels. Yet I take a great deal of care not to overindulge in either, and to use only a few telling words instead of a welter of graphic language. In a scene in *Ikon*, a recent thriller of mine, a police chief is dynamited in his car:

He began to feel cold. His head began to droop. He looked down and saw that somebody had been inconsiderate enough to leave yards and yards of fire-extinguisher hose in his lap. Yards and yards of it, glistening and wet. You would have thought that they might have treated a shocked man with more care than that.

That was one of the most violent scenes in the book. And yet the language itself is very simple, very reserved. The same technique can be used in scenes of sexual passion, of excitement, of tragedy, of joy. If you can hit exactly the right emphasis, the key which unlocks the true significance of the whole scene, then you can convey volumes of thought and pictures and ideas, all in a few simple sentences.

If you are actually "there" in your mind, you will avoid the mistake of overdescribing scenes in an attempt to get them to come alive. The scenes will be alive already, and you will find that you are conveying their atmosphere quite unconsciously. If your characters are there too, real people who have real backgrounds and real likes and dislikes—even if you never mention their backgrounds, even if you never describe their tastes—you will find that they act more realistically, speak more convincingly, and you will also avoid the pitfall of pontificating about them and what they think. They will speak for themselves.

The only advice that I can give to anyone who wants to embark on a novel about anything at all is—forget about the page in front of you, let your pad or your typewriter melt away into transparency. Go to the place you want to tell your readers about, and simply describe it as it is.

Here is a short scene from *Corroboree*, a novel I wrote about explorers in the Australian outback in the 1840s:

The ground dropped steeply away below their feet into a deep-layered gorge, scoured out of the limestone over thousands and thousands of years by a rushing array of waterfalls. The reddish crags on either side were in darkness now that night had fallen; but their terraces and balconies and water-hewn pulpits were sparkling with hundreds of cooking-fires and torches, so that the gorge had taken on the appearance of the grandest of civilized theatres, La Scalla in the middle of the Australian outback, with chandeliers and footlights and carriage-lamps.

Now you'll have to excuse me. I'm just off to China in the 1930s, to live and walk and converse and eat with all those people who are about to shape my newest historical novel. If I've put on weight by the next time you see me, please forgive me. I've always adored Chinese food.

16

BECOMING THE CHARACTERS IN YOUR NOVEL

By Gail Godwin

THE frontiers of my writing life expanded remarkably when I discovered what good writers before me always knew: I could be anybody—if I was willing to work hard and be patient and trust my intuitions and disregard my fears.

Paradoxically, it was a knowledge I had as a child writer, but I had to re-learn it as an adult. At the age of nine, of twelve, I took it for granted I could enter the mind of any character I wanted to. I did not hesitate. I sat down and wrote a story about a henpecked husband, about a rich and lonely little boy who lived behind an ornate fence, about a dog on holiday, written from the dog's point of view.

Then I entered the age of self-consciousness and self-doubt and lost my innocent confidence. The writing teachers of the moment were preaching Write About What You Know, and I cringed at my childhood folly (What did I know about husbands, about being rich, about being a little boy, about being a *dog?*) and obediently shrank my horizons. I wrote about a girl like myself, and then I wrote about a woman like myself; and though I discovered some interesting insights and techniques in the process, I often raged against the fence I had built around myself and wondered how I could tear it down.

It was not easy, because the Spirit of the Time was trumpeting "consciousness" and self-consciousness and, above all, the self. And, as every literary historian knows, the Spirit of the Time shapes the style and the content of its Literature. Out of style were the old Victorians with their baggy monsters of novels and their devout assumptions that it was their *duty* to create a world and populate it with multiple and varied characters. The new rule was: Keep a chaste point of view and explore one's own inner processes; don't go populating worlds!

Now you can do a lot with a single point of view, provided you make your central character intelligent, sensitive, and compassionate, capable of having fascinating thoughts and meeting a fascinating array of other people. I stretched each heroine as far as I could: made her travel far from home, get involved with complex or unusual people, made her suffer, think and grow.

But something in me was longing to leap that point-of-view barrier and be more than one person at a time.

The turning point came with my novel, *A Mother and Two Daughters*. Its subject matter—three strong and different women bound in the closest of ties—demanded three points of view, if I were to show the subjective reality of each character, complete with her history, her style of behavior and speech and thought, the important people in her life, and—most crucial, perhaps—the mysterious way in which she had shaped and been shaped by the other two heroines.

I wanted the reader to identify equally with each of the three characters. I wanted to strike such an authentic and distinctive tone with each protagonist that a reader could open any page of the novel at random and know whose point of view was being expressed.

I myself was none of these women—nor was my mother or my sister. (The idea for the novel had come from a friend who told about a disastrous vacation she and her sister and her mother had taken six months after the father's death. There was a fight, and the sisters did not speak for two years afterwards.) So I would have to work hard to imagine myself into them, without the props of personal experience or memory. I would have to create *their* experiences, *their* memories, *their* social worlds.

As I wrote this novel, two unexpected things happened: first, I realized that, though none of the women was based on me, I could be any of them. When we as writers create characters, we are in the process stretching our own identities. We begin each new character with the warm clay of sympathy, some feeling in common, and, before we know it, we are that character. Concerning Nell, the mother, I did not know what it is like to be 63, or to be a widow, or even to have daughters of my own, but I did know what it feels like to be an ironic personality, always a little apart from my surroundings—as Nell is, by nature; and I knew, as Nell knows, what it is like to be lonely and yet to treasure one's aloneness for the freedom it allows you to be "nobody," just an awareness committed to the universe of which you are a part.

Concerning Cate, the older daughter, I knew what it feels like to rail against complacency and rebel against the status quo; I have never been particularly brave, or even very much of a rebel, but I could start Cate on her way to being one, with the basis of those feelings rooted in my own experience. Concerning Lydia, the proper younger daughter, so nervous with her sense of responsibility, so aching with her need to accomplish something for herself, I could bond myself to her with those shared feelings and set her on her course of cautious, but ardent, self-emancipation.

The second unexpected revelation that came to me as I wrote this novel was that I was not only telling the story of these three women, I was also creating a society. And, as the book grew thicker with characters, each with a need to express himself or herself, I discovered what I wish for every developing writer to discover: I discovered that I knew more than I thought I knew, about a great variety of people.

Ironically, I often came to this knowledge by listing all the things I *didn't* know about a certain character. I knew that Cate was going to meet a man who would tempt her spirit of independence as it had never been tempted before. But what would that man be like?

The intuition that flashed upon my mind was: Cate enjoys conflict; so this man would do something Cate would disapprove of. What would she disapprove of? Well, she mistrusts people with a great deal of money. So, make my man a millionaire. How did he make those millions? My intuition flashed again: pesticides. Those would certainly be out of favor with an idealist like Cate, who championed fair distribution, whether in economy or biology.

And so I began to see Roger Jernigan. First I had to research pesticides, about which I knew next to nothing. Furthermore, I had to research them *from their positive side,* as a man like Jernigan would see them. Thus I could speak from inside him when he tells Cate at their first dinner together, "When I started my business, it was considered a safeguard industry. We were the saviors; now we're the villains. But I've never made a product thinking, Let's hope this wipes out all the robins." Jernigan is sincere. He believes in what he does. And, in spite of herself, Cate is attracted to his authenticity.

But I had to learn who he was before I could make him authentic.

"Who are they?" Turgenev used to ask himself this about his characters before starting a story or novel. His second question was: *"What can I make them do that will show them completely?"*

71

During the writing of this novel, I often asked about a new character who had just walked onstage, What can I show this person doing, how can I describe this person, so his or her essence, or function, is immediately evident to the reader?

For instance, in the first chapter, which describes a party, there is a very minor character, Lucy Bell, who has made it her function in life to grease the wheels of society so events can run smoothly. What quick vision can I give of Lucy as she enters the party with her belligerent, alcoholic husband? I chose to personify Lucy Bell *as her function:* "Latrobe Bell was preceded into the room by the plucky Lucy, who was smiling and blinking rapidly, like one of those small cars with flashers that escort an oversized vehicle which might prove dangerous on its own."

Don't be afraid if some of your characters come to you shadowed in their own mysteries. Don't retreat, saying, "Maybe I'd better imagine somebody closer to home." Be courageous. Say, it is my job as a fiction writer to bring them out. Your impetus for wanting to write about just these characters may be that their mystery attracts you. Don't you often walk down the street and feel perfectly free to imagine the lives of all kinds of people who pass by? You do it naturally, without thinking. But, in writing, we often lose confidence because we draw ourselves up suddenly and say: "What right have I to imagine what is in that person's mind or heart? Of course I can't know." Maybe you don't know *exactly,* but people reveal worlds in their gestures, their clothes, the set of their mouths, the words they speak, the way they live, the friends (and enemies) they choose.

If you find yourself going blank about a character, don't think it a waste of time to sit down with a notepad and ask questions about him. This process often yields more than you'll be able to use in your story. But that's not a waste, either. What you know and don't tell will often be evident in a kind of richness of texture that envelops that character.

Start anywhere. How does _____ speak? In long, rambling sentences or in short, decisive ones? What does that tell you about _____? Is there a note of apology? Irony? What about pet expressions? (If a character prefaces his remarks habitually with, "I wouldn't lie to you about this," what could that mean?) Does the way _____ speaks tell you anything about his deepest beliefs? If you listen carefully enough, it will.

How does _____ look? Not so much whether the eyes are brown

or blue or the hair blonde or red, but what does that character's appearance tell you about his or her mode of life?

How does _____ feel about the other people in this scene? What kind of things does _____ notice or fail to notice?

During the writing of *A Mother and Two Daughters,* I also kept a special notebook with a page for each character's chronology. When born. When married. Important dates. Characters are influenced by their times, just as we are. If a character is born into the Great Depression, that may influence his subjective reality as well as his objective fortunes.

These are some of the techniques that helped me escape that terribly limiting enclosure of one point of view. And every time I succeeded in entering the special reality of another character, it expanded my vision of human life. After all, Point of View remains the eminent domain of fiction: no other medium has succeeded quite as well at getting into the minds of its characters. As writers, we ought to explore and exploit our privileged territory for all it is worth. Dickens did not hesitate to describe the viewpoint of a dog—or of a lamp post!—and I was on the right track with those childhood stories of other realities. So remember: You know more about those others than you think. Bond yourself to each mysterious new character with compassion, and then cling to him with all the tentacles of your curiosity. Pretty soon you'll surprise yourself by looking at the world through his eyes.

17

IMAGERY AND THE THIRD EYE

By Stephen King

SOME CRITICS have accused me—and it always comes out sounding like an accusation—of writing for the movies. It's not true, but I suppose there's some justification for the idea; all of my novels to date have been sold to the movies. The assumption seems to be that you can't do that sort of thing without trying, but as some of you out there will testify, it's the sort of thing you very rarely can do by consciously trying.

So, you're saying, why is this guy talking about movies when he's supposed to be talking about writing? I'll tell you why. I'm talking about movies because the most important thing that film and fiction share is an interest in the image—the bright picture that glows in the physical eye or in the mind's eye. I'm suggesting that my novels have sold to the movies not because they were written for the movies, but simply because they contain elements of vivid image that appeal to those who make films—to those for whom it is often more important to see than it is to think.

Novels are more than imagery—they are thought, plot, style, tone, characterization, and a score of other things—but it is the imagery that makes the book "stand out" somehow; to come alive; to glow with its own light. I'm fond of telling my writing classes that all the sophistries of fiction must follow story, that simple caveman invention ("I was walking through the forest when the tiger leaped down on me . . .") that held his audience spellbound around a fire at night—and perhaps he even got an extra piece of meat for his efforts if the story was a good one, the first writer's royalty! But I also believe that story springs from image: that vividness of place and time and *texture*. And here the writer is always two steps ahead of the film director, who may have to wait for the right weather, the right shadows, or the right lens (and when the real world gives way, as it so often does in my books, he must then turn to the special effects man).

Where does good imagery come from? Rather than that tiresome question, *What does it mean?* that always seems to come up when an image is presented, a better and more profitable question might be, *What does it make you think of?*

Sometimes would-be writers will say to me, "I know what I mean but I don't know how to describe it." What this usually means is, "I can't describe it because I can't quite see it."

An example: A beginning writer may put down, "It was a spooky old house," and let it go at that, knowing it doesn't convey any real punch or immediacy, but not knowing what to do about it. The writer has a sense that "It was a spooky old house" is somehow wrong, but he or she doesn't quite . . . know why. It's like that maddening itch in the middle of your back that you just can't scratch. Well, I'll tell you what's wrong with "It was a spooky old house." It isn't an image; it's an idea. Ideas have no emotional temperature gradient; they are neutral. But try this, from the early going in my novel, *'Salem's Lot:*

> The house itself looked toward town. It was huge and rambling and sagging, its windows haphazardly boarded shut, giving it that sinister look of all old houses that have been empty for a long time. The paint had been weathered away, giving the house a uniform gray look. Windstorms had ripped many of the shingles off, and a heavy snowfall had punched in the west corner of the main roof, giving it a slumped, hunched look. A tattered no-trespassing sign was nailed to the right-hand newel post.

Nowhere in the paragraph does it say the house being described is "spooky"; the closest I come is the use of the word "sinister" to describe the boarded-up windows. If I've succeeded, readers will not need me to supply the adjective "spooky"; they will come to that decision on their own.

Now you might think of some details the above description (and I'm using that word, not "image," quite deliberately—come along with me for another couple of minutes and I think you'll see why) does *not* supply. What sort of a walk leads up to this house? Any? How many storeys does it have? What style is it—Jacobean? Victorian? Is there a driveway? A garage? A weather vane on the roof? None of these details is here; that is what the reader brings to it.

The point is, I think, that imagery is not achieved by overdescription—a Roget's full of adjectives by your typewriter may not be the answer to your problems with imagery. A good artist may be able to impress you with a young girl's beauty in a line sketch that takes only minutes to do—a curve of cheek, a wavy S-curve indicating the fall of hair, the tilt of a single eye. A painting that the artist labors over for weeks or months may be able to achieve no more—and may achieve much less because the artist has overkilled his subject.

If I can say anything important to writers who are still learning the craft of fiction, it's this: imagery does not occur on the writer's page; it occurs in the reader's mind. To describe everything is to supply a photograph in words; to indicate the points which seem the most vivid and important to you, the writer, is to allow the reader to flesh out your sketch into a portrait. Since 'Salem's Lot was originally published several years ago, I've seen maybe three dozen different pictures of the Marsten House, all based on the description I gave in that short paragraph quoted above; no two are the same, and none of them is quite the picture I had in my own mind—and I wouldn't have it any other way.

Good description produces imagery, then. The next question that always comes is, "How do I know what details to include and which to leave out?" The answer to the question is simply stated but more difficult to apply: Leave in the details that impress you the most strongly; leave in the details you see the most clearly; leave everything else out.

Our eyes convey images to our brains; if we are to convey images to our readers, then we must see with a kind of third eye—the eye of imagination and memory. Writers who describe poorly or not at all see poorly with this eye; others open it, but not all the way. Here is a paragraph from The Shining that I still like pretty well (it's funny how books recede from you, like people you once shared long and not particularly comfortable journeys with; you promise you'll stay in touch but somehow never do. And yet, from every book I've ever written, there are a few passages with which I'm still on friendly terms, and this is one of those):

His father would sweep him into his arms and Jacky would be propelled deliriously upward, so fast it seemed he could feel air pressure settling against his skull like a cap made out of lead, up and up, both of them crying 'Elevator! Elevator'; and there had been nights when his father in his drunkenness had not stopped the upward lift of his slabmuscled arms soon enough and Jacky had gone right over his father's flattopped head like a human projectile to crash-land on the hall floor behind his dad. But on other nights his father would only sweep him into a giggling ecstasy, through the zone of air where beer hung around his father's face like a mist of raindrops, to be twisted and turned and shaken like a laughing rag, and finally to be set down on his feet, hiccuping with reaction.

I saw this scene played in my own head; I saw it with that third eye as clearly as I now see this dark green typewriter I sit before, with its black keys and its bright white letters. I saw it as image; translated as much as I felt I needed to into description; and then turned it over to the reader. The details that impressed me the most strongly as I imagined the scene were: 1) that peculiar sensation of weight on the boy's head as he is swept up (not air-pressure, of course, but gravitational pull); 2) the father's huge arms (fair skin, fine fair hairs, and freckles, although none of those are in the description); 3) the father's short haircut; 4) that smell of beer, which is, in its own way, as unmistakable as the smell of lemon or vinegar or roses. And of all of them, the two that seemed to fill the image up for me best were the smell of beer and the boy *looking down from above* on his father's crewcut, seeing the white scalp through the bristly hairs.

I left out the fair skin, the freckles, the hallway where the Elevator game always took place, the fact that there was an umbrella stand there—a brass one that used to be a shell casing—because none of them seemed to make the image stronger. The reader may have seen different furnishings: a light fixture casting shadows of father and son on the wall; the sound of a television or radio in the other room. But the idea of imagery is not to set the picture by giving everything (that is for photographers, not writers), but to give enough to suggest a texture and a feel. And the writer must be confident enough in his or her own imaging ability to stop when it's time to stop, because as we all know, the joy of reading novels, which no movie can equal, is the joy of seeing in the mind, feeling the fantasy flower in the way that is unique to each individual reader. The reader has his or her own third eye; the job of the writer is only to provide a spectacle for it.

Too many beginning writers feel that they have to assume the entire burden of imagery; to become the reader's seeing-eye dog. That is simply not the case. Use vivid verbs. Avoid the passive voice. Avoid the cliché. Be specific. Be precise. Be elegant. Omit needless words. Most of these rules—and the four hundred I haven't quoted—will take care of themselves almost automatically if you will, from this point on, take two pledges: First, not to insult your reader's interior vision; and second, to see everything before you write it.

The latter may mean you'll find yourself writing more slowly than you've been accustomed to doing if you've been passing ideas ("It was a spooky old house") off as imagery. The former may mean more careful rewriting if you've been hedging your bets by overdescription; you're going to have to pick up those old pruning shears, like it or not, and start cutting back to the essentials.

Let's say you want to describe (and thereby create an image of) a rainy day in a big city; and further, let us say that the mood you want to pass along to the reader is one of dreariness. When you finish this sentence, lean back—I mean physically lean back—and see that city, that rain, that mood.

You opened your eyes too soon. Close them and try again—give yourself thirty seconds, maybe even a minute. O.K. Go ahead.

How widely did your eye see? Did you see a skyline? Many buildings? An aerial view? Was the sky white or dark? Did you see people? Men holding their hats, bending forward a little, the wind belling out the backs of their coats? Women with umbrellas? Taxis splashing water? All of these are good; they offer a sort of description that bears the fruit of imagery. But now suppose you sharpen your focus; suppose I ask you to see *one street corner* in that gray, rainy, dismal city. It's three o'clock in the afternoon and now that rain is really coming down—look at it! And it's Monday, too; what a bummer. Now, close your eyes again, this time for a full minute, and see what's happening on that corner. And if you peek before the minute's up, you lose your Writers Guild card. O.K. Do it now.

Did you see it? The bus that droned by and splashed the women, driving them back? The faces looking out indifferently or tucked away behind newspapers? There was an ad for jeans on the back of the bus—it showed a girl bending over and the slogan, blurry with rain, read: THE ENDS JUSTIFY THE JEANS. Did you see the awning of the small grocery store across the way running with rivulets of water? Could you hear water gushing into the sewer gratings? And when the cars braked for the light, could you see their tail lights reflected up from the pavement in long scarlet streaks? Did you see the man with the newspaper on his head?

Some of them, maybe. Probably not all. You maybe saw other things, just as interesting; perhaps you even caught the tag end of a story in the image—a man running through the rain, looking back over his shoulder, or a child in a yellow slicker being pulled abruptly into a car with DPL plates—or perhaps you just saw the image itself. But, believe this: if you saw the image, you can put it on paper. If you doubt it, go to your typewriter *this minute* and write down what you saw. You know the feeling: to write is to re-experience, and as you write, that image will grow brighter and brighter, becoming something that is very nearly beautiful in its clarity. Do a paragraph; do two. And then give someone a rainy Monday afternoon in the city. Or, if you caught that tantalizing tag of story, chase it before it gets away. Follow the running man or get into that car and see what's in there; see who grabbed the child, and try to find out why. You can do it, if you care to open that inner eye just as wide as it will go.

Last word: Don't ever become totally transported with imagery. The eye sees everything, but the mind behind the eye must make the judgments on what to keep and what to throw away. "Always leave the table while there's still a little edge on your hunger," my mother used to say, "and you'll never have to worry about making a glutton of yourself, Stevie." The same is true of imagery. Once you've trained that third eye to see well, the hand itches to write down everything. If you're writing fiction, you don't want to drown your reader in textures; remember that image leads to story, and story leads to everything else. But also remember that a writer's greatest pleasure is in seeing, and seeing well.

What that third eye—that inner eye—can see is infinite. It's a little bit like having a whole amusement park in your head, where all the rides are free.

18

WHAT MAKES A FICTION WRITER?

By B. J. Chute

THE other day, an interviewer asked me, "What makes a fiction writer?" and I could only answer, "I have no idea." It is a time-honored and shopworn question, and there are as many answers to it as there are writers, because all writers are different.

The interviewer, being neither time-honored nor shopworn but, on the contrary, young and lively, changed her question to "What makes *you* a fiction writer?" I felt I could answer that question reasonably well, and I did so by offering such (time-honored and shopworn) reasons as a natural bent for storytelling, a life-long habit of reading, a love of words, and all the etcetera of halfway answers which I hope were useful to her but which really did not satisfy me.

Thinking now about her question, I have been turning it over and over in my mind until I arrived, like Alice, at my looking-glass destination by walking away from it. I do not believe I know what makes me a fiction writer, but I do believe that there are four qualities without which one cannot write fiction at all.

The first, of course, is *imagination.* Imagination is as necessary to a novelist or short-story writer as the spinning of webs is to a spider and just as mysterious. It defies analysis (either one is a spider, or one isn't), and it has been quite properly called "the creative impulse." It has also been called the Muse, and, when the Muse vanishes, that yawning void she leaves behind her is known as "writer's block."

Imagination cannot be created, but it can be fostered, and this fostering is part of the writer's duty. It is not enough to congratulate oneself on having been gifted (lovely word!) with imagination, though it is certainly a major cause for rejoicing. The imagination, like the intellect, has to be used, and a creative writer ought to exercise it all the time. There is no idea, however insignificant or vague it may be, that the imagination cannot touch to new beginnings, turning it around and around in different lights, playing with it, *listening* to it. One of the most marvelous things about spiders (and writers) is the way they will launch themselves into space on a filament so infinitely slender as to be nearly invisible, and, lo, there is suddenly a bridge flung over the chasm, across which any fly (or any reader) can walk with perfect confidence.

The second quality I believe to be essential for writing fiction is *empathy,* which the dictionary properly defines as "mental entering into the feeling or spirit of a person or thing." As with imagination, one is to a degree born with empathy; but, like imagination, it can be fostered. Writers of fiction write from inside themselves, but they also write from inside other people, and, again, this is a kind of gift. It is what produces strong and believable characterization. *Madame Bovary* was written from the inside out. Flaubert seems to know not only the passion, the boredom, the despair and the terrible loneliness of that pitiful woman, but he also seems to know the most trivial light or shadow that falls across her mind. Imagination could create her, and her world, and the people around her, but it is Flaubert's empathy that makes his unhappy Emma not just credible but totally real. This is Melville's "subterranean miner that works in us all," and, although we cannot expect to be Melvilles or Flauberts, we can mine what we have. And if we do that, with honesty and intensity, who knows what lode of treasure we may strike?

The third quality is *style.* In its simplest form, style in writing can be defined as the way in which a thing is said. It is a much abused word, and it sometimes seems to me that it is woefully misunderstood by writers and readers alike. Style does not exist apart from the story, and, if five people tell an identical story, each one will tell it in a different style. The best style will produce the best story, and the listeners will turn to it even if they do not know why they turn. Style is a great preservative of writing, and no writer ought ever to think that a really good style is beyond his reach. But many writers do think so, and too many settle for second best when, in fact, they ought to be working all the time against any such preposterous limitation of their own capacities.

Once I ran across a description of style as applied to architecture, which is just as true of writing—"What is style? Clear thinking, really; the ability to use your head before you do anything with your hands." Sloppy thinking will produce sloppy style, and I am certain there is not a writer among us who has not stared hopelessly at the written page which reflects the muddy results. What to do? Go back, of course. Find out what you are trying to say, and, having found it, select the words that will make the reader see what you are seeing. Selection is vital to style. Because English is an incredibly rich language, there are many bad ways of saying something, and many good ways, but there is usually only one right way. This right way will be the writer's *own* way—in short, his style, or what Proust called "the underlying tune" which distinguishes one writer from another. This should represent the very best the writer has to offer. "Second best" will not do.

Take, as an example, a description from Nathaniel Hawthorne. He is introducing a minister, and all he wishes to say about him is that he is a serious person, wears a beard, and is dressed in the kind of dark clothes and tall hat that would have been affected by a clergyman of his time. There are perhaps a hundred ways of putting all these details together so that the reader can visualize the character sharply, and most such descriptions would probably take a paragraph, certainly several sentences. Hawthorne does it in seven words; his minister is "grave, bearded, sable-cloaked and steeple-crowned."

This is perfectly beautiful writing, and it is as exact as it is beautiful. The picture is instantaneous and vivid, and the tone is faultless. I do not know whether Hawthorne got those seven words right the first time, or whether he labored over them in rewrite after rewrite. Even successive drafts of his manuscript would tell us nothing, because the majority of a writer's work goes on in his mind. What matters is that every word in Hawthorne's description is the right one: *grave,* with its sonorous double meaning; *bearded,* just the simple piece of information to balance the poetic images that follow; *sable-cloaked,* concealing, mysterious, and darker than darkness itself; and, finally, the triumph of *steeple-crowned,* which makes us see not only the minister in his tall hat, but Church, Authority and Heaven as well.

It is true that the average writer is not a Nathaniel Hawthorne, but it is also true that none of these seven words is in the least obscure or recondite or self-conscious; each one would be available to any writer who was craftsman enough to persist in finding it. If a writer is willing to work all the time and in everything he writes to achieve the best style of which he is capable, the words will be there for him as they were for Hawthorne.

And this brings us, inevitably, to the fourth quality, which is *patience*.

Patience in a writer is many things, but most of all, I think, it is characterized by concern for the words on the page. The aim of this concern is "to see the thing and throw the loop of creation around it," as Joyce Cary said. (And notice how riveting the phrasing of that statement is; there's style for you!) What Cary calls "the thing" is the idea, the initial impulse, the product of imagination and empathy. The "loop of creation" is the finding of the right words that will make it possible for the reader to share the writer's special vision, and such words can be very evasive, very slow to come.

At rare and wonderful intervals, the stars in their courses do seem to join together, and the writer finds himself writing so effortlessly and with such precision that it almost seems as if he were taking dictation. These are the best of times, but they are certainly not ordinary. In ordinary times, the words on the page are merely adequate: they move the story along; the second draft will be easier; experience lends hopefulness. The worst of times are when the words will not come at all, and the writer feels as if he were floundering in a swamp or gasping for air in a desert. This can be really frightening, and it is here—in swamp or desert—that the quality of patience will spell the difference between disaster and survival.

In the dictionary, the second definition for the word *patience* is "calmness in waiting." I like this definition very much indeed, because there is a steadiness about it and a good deal of faith, and any writer needs both.

When the final draft of a manuscript is on paper, the words are all that really matter. Money, status, and fame are by-products; nice to have, but nothing permanent. If that statement seems idealistic, of course it is. It is meant to be. To call upon the dictionary once more, idealism is "the cherishing or pursuing of ideals, as for attainment." For the writer of fiction, the pursuit is through imagination and empathy, the cherishing is through style, and the attainment is through patience.

Excellence is simply idealism in action, and so high an aim is bound to fall short of the mark many times. I call to your attention the words of John Adams, written in February of 1776—"We cannot ensure success, but we can deserve it."

19

THE FACTS ABOUT FICTION
A Written Interview

WITH IRVING WALLACE

Q. *We've read somewhere that you draw your ideas for topical novels from the headlines. Is that true? If so, explain.*

A: What you've read is absolutely untrue. It must have been written by a journalist or critic who knows nothing about the making of books. Generally, if an author were to base his novels on daily headlines, he would write and publish books that were terribly dated, almost historical.

Let us presume you decide to base a book on today's major headline because you want to write about a current event. How would you do it? The headline has given you an idea for a theme, subject, background. You begin to develop it in your mind as a novel and you make notes. You evolve some fictional characters, decide where they came from, what they are going through, and where they are headed. Out of these characters and the overall theme you begin to develop a story line or plot. Once you have that, you begin to research the subject of your headline, read all you can about it, interview experts on it, even travel to the sites of the story to guarantee authenticity and get a feel for the background. In my case, this process takes six months to a year.

Now you are ready. You begin writing the first draft of the novel. For me, this creative part may take a half year of writing, writing daily—even Saturdays, Sundays, Mother's Day—at least five or six hours a day. With the first draft completed, you begin to rewrite and revise it, to delete scenes that do not work, to write new scenes that work better, to strengthen a character, to improve sentence structure. For my novel, *The Almighty,* I did six rewrites after I had a first draft. I don't mean I completely rewrote every page each time. But on every go-through I revised at least half the pages.

O.K. Now you have a finished book ready for submission to a publisher. Your literary agent reads it and comments. A publisher reads it, likes it, buys it, and prepares it for publication. Your editor will want some more revisions (because your novel may need revisions, or perhaps the editor must justify his or her job, or simply wishes to impose his or her point of view on the manuscript). With this done there follows copyediting (inconsistencies are spotted, semicolons inserted). Next, your book goes to the printer, and back come the first galley proofs, which your publisher and you collaborate on correcting, even revising some more. Finally, page proofs, which most writers don't see. To the printer, to the bindery, to the reviewers, to the bookstores, and certainly a bound copy to you. Publishers like to say this process takes eight months.

Remember, you wrote a topical book based on a headline. But here it is possibly two-and-a-half years since you saw that headline. Your topical book about a current event is no longer topical or current. No, that is definitely not the way to develop a topical book.

Q. *Well, if not from headlines, how do you get book ideas on subjects that will be current when the novel appears?*

A: By finding a subject of continuing and ongoing interest—a good example, *Space,* by James Michener. Another example, my novel *The Prize,* which deals in fiction with the behind-the-scenes story of Nobel Prize judges and Nobel Prize winners. The subject is in the news annually. It never dates. The other approach: By selecting a subject you sense and anticipate will be in the news and much on readers' minds three or four years from now.

Instinctively, I've used both approaches. A subject that is always news? The so-called Kinsey Report came out. Most people bought it but did not read it. It was too dense, too academic. People read *about* it. Some time after, I read another sex survey and was inspired to look into the subject. I learned there had been many sex surveys before Kinsey made them news. And there have been almost countless ones since. I wondered how a sex survey really worked, what kind of humans were involved in conducting it, why ordinary persons cooperated by giving personal answers, and how these answers affected them. So I researched the subject in depth. Along the way, I developed fictional characters. I blended facts with imagined fiction. The result was my novel, *The Chapman Report,* fortunately an international best seller. The central subject of the novel remains in the news constantly. Sex surveys are always news. More important, love and sex, the relationship between men and women, the emotions of the characters, remain timeless.

As to anticipating the news, can that really be done? I can only say that I have done it (and I can't say I'm psychic, although my daughter Amy—the co-author of *The Psychic Healing Book*—is). I don't know how you anticipate what readers will be interested in three or six or ten years from now. If you write about human emotions and problems, you are surely safe and will write a timely book. But we are discussing subject matter. Well, it has to do with reading, listening, thinking, imagining, above all *sensing* what you might be interested in and what future readers might be interested in some years from now.

When I published *The Man* in 1964, many persons, even in my publishing house, thought I was crazy. A black man who becomes President of the United States, even accidentally? Really crazy. I wrote the book because I had strong feelings about racism in America, and I felt such a novel could dramatize for millions of white readers what they were doing to the black minority. But I also sensed—anticipated—this would be an even more newsworthy or topical subject through the 1970's and 1980's and after.

I had the same instinct when I wrote *The Word,* published in 1972. It seemed to me that religion, faith, belief in a Supreme Being would be of growing interest in a confused world in the years to come. I guessed that my story, centered on the discovery of a previously unknown fifth gospel that might be added to the New Testament, could be an overall subject of continuing interest to me, as well as—hopefully—future readers. This proved to be true. The Born Agains are only one manifestation of the public's non-ending need for order, belief in something, belief in anything.

Q. *In your novel,* The Almighty, *you seem to have reached straight into the current news about terrorists for the subject. True, it is a continuously topical subject, but it was also a contemporary news subject. What do you say about that?*

A: *The Almighty* is not about terrorism. It is about the way the media misuse and manipulate the day-to-day news, and thus keep the reading public misinformed. I employ terrorists in the story largely to make my point and because this means of telling the story had a good dramatic feel to it.

Let me tell you how I got the inspiration for *The Almighty*. One evening, some years ago, I was watching the national network news on television. The anchorman was reporting some event concerning a subject upon which I was well informed at first hand. I realized that the news he was reporting was being utterly distorted, sensationalized, warped, to grab viewers and ratings. I was dismayed by the false picture of the world this was giving viewers. Then I thought about the hundreds of press interviews I had given this past decade in cities across the country, and how reporters who had interviewed me had exaggerated, omitted, rearranged statements I had made in order to produce more attention-getting features. More distortions. Immediately, I saw the subject for a new novel. The new publisher of a floundering Manhattan daily wants to top his competitors, wants to headline exclusive beats that no one else has. So he does the ultimate thing in manipulating the news: He invents it. He hires a terrorist gang to create front-page stories only for him. Until a woman reporter he has employed gets onto his trail. So you can see. My novel is not about terrorists. It is about the manipulation of events by the media. It was a statement I had to make. It was also a challenging drama to plot and write.

Q. *All right, let's talk about the use a novelist can make of fact in fiction. Several of your works of fiction have been called factions, because of the way you blend fact with make-believe. Why do you do it? How do you do it? How did you do it in* The Prize?

A: Novelists have always blended fact and fiction. Some were better at it than others. Charles Dickens was a past master. Leo Tolstoi and Stendhal were good at it, also. When I came to write novels, my experience as a writer had been largely in nonfiction. When I turned to fiction, I became fascinated by the technique of intermingling factual material with imagined material. It was, indeed, a technique. To thread fact through fiction was one more means of making the fiction absolutely believable, and even more colorful and interesting, as long as the use of facts did not obstruct the flow of story narrative. In *The Chapman Report* the members of the Chapman sex-survey team discuss their fictional findings, but they also compare their findings to earlier real-life sex surveys I had researched and studied. In *The Prize* two fictional Nobel laureates from different countries, sharing the same scientific discovery, are at odds, antagonists, because one believes that the other has stolen his work and does not deserve to share the honor. I worried that readers might not accept this conflict as possible in real life, so to enable readers to suspend disbelief I had a wise Swedish official, who sensed the antagonism, relate to the pair some historical disputes and disagreements between famous Nobel laureates who did not like sharing the prize.

Actually, *The Prize* grew out of a visit I had made to Stockholm to write some articles on advances in Swedish science—and when one Swedish scientist, Dr. Sven Hedin, told me he was a judge on three different Nobel Prize committees, I was astounded. The reason I was astounded was that Dr. Hedin was not only pro-Nazi and pro-Hitler, but he was highly political, prejudiced, and utterly uninformed in certain areas in which he voted. (Since he was a judge for the literature award, I asked him whether James Joyce's name had ever come up as a contender for the Nobel Prize. Dr. Hedin said to me, "James Joyce? Joyce? Who's he?") This encounter led me to further research, interviews with other Nobel judges and even prizewinners, and they taught me about the human element in the annual prize-giving. That inspired me to write a work of fiction, *The Prize,* about the awards. It took me fifteen years before I found out how to write it, but write it I did, weaving incredible factual information with my fiction throughout. I even wrote a documentary book about how I wrote this work of fiction. It is called *The Writing of One Novel* and recounts in detail the whole process of how I used facts to underline and accent my fiction. Needless to say, in *The Word,* employing factual material I had obtained in interviews with clergymen, theologians, biblical scholars, I helped clarify and heighten the fiction I had written.

Q. *If, as many novelists believe, truth is too strange for fiction, how do you modify it to make it believable, real, true?*

A: You don't modify facts, you never tamper with them. A fact is a fact. Fiction *is* fiction. But the twain does meet, can meet. You use facts as support for your fiction, when helpful, when necessary. But you don't distort the facts. As my one-time agent, Paul R. Reynolds, used to say, "If truth is too unusual and strange, don't use it in fiction; use it only in nonfiction, where you can authenticate it with more facts."

Q. *Do you feel factual research is necessary for the writing of a novel?*

A: Of course not. We've been discussing fact in relation to a certain kind of novel. Most novels, some of the very best, require no research at all. The characters and plot come out of the author's own personal experiences, observations, readings, feelings. The trap here—in writing only about what you know or have experienced in your life—is that after a while, after many books, you can run out of first-hand material. You might tend to repeat yourself. You also limit yourself. I know one published author who always wanted to write a novel about an attorney, but he told me he simply couldn't because he wasn't an attorney and had never known one well. I told him that was no excuse. I told him to do some research on attorneys, meet some and interview them, find out about their professional and personal lives. I told him to research and broaden his horizon.

I remember when I was preparing my novel *The Seven Minutes*. It was about an attorney and an obscenity trial. I happened to know quite a few lawyers, and I questioned them closely about their lives and obscenity law and censorship. But I didn't know a thing about how an obscenity trial was conducted—this was to be the climax of my novel—and there were no trials in progress I could observe. So what I did was track down a copy of the transcript of the last great obscenity trial held in Los Angeles. It dealt with a Henry Miller book then banned. All transcripts had been destroyed save one, still in the hands of a court clerk at that trial. I rented his transcript and Xeroxed it. It came to twenty thick manuscript volumes, and I spent months studying these volumes to learn obscenity trial procedure. Several renowned attorneys, among them F. Lee Bailey, told me my resultant novel was the best trial book of its kind ever written and one without a single inaccuracy.

Another important value of factual research is that it gives you ideas for your fictional plotting. For *The Almighty,* I planned a fictional heist at the Dead Sea scrolls museum. I went to Jerusalem twice to research the scene and the scrolls. Just as I was leaving the museum on the second visit, I said casually to the expert who had been guiding me,

"Well, I guess this is just about the most valuable collection of authentic ancient documents on earth." And he said to me, "Not quite. The scrolls here aren't all authentic. One of them, the main one, is a phoney." This information was a stunner, and I was able to use it twice in *The Almighty.*

I had my protagonist write a feature story about the scrolls after he visits the museum:

> With reluctance Ramsey attended to his job, made notes for his story, noted everything from the fact that the museum's interior architecture was in the form of the cave in which the scrolls had been found to the fact that the scrolls were enshrined behind thick glass in ten display cases to the fact that the fragments of the main scroll, the Isaiah, were not the originals but clever photocopies, since the fragile real fragments might be destroyed by exposure to light in the building.

Later, when this tidbit is passed on to a terrorist leader on his way to attack and rob the museum, the leader instructs his cohorts:

> After the entrance hall and souvenir area in the museum, there's a tunnel with its lighted glass showcases. Ignore those. Don't bother with them . . . Those are not the great treasures. Go on past them into the main circular central hall. Avoid the elevated pedestal in the center of the room. It contains leaves of the Isaiah scroll, but these are photocopies, fakes, not the original. Go for the ten showcases around the room.

Q. *Is there one piece of advice you can give to an aspiring writer, one who wants to write but is finding it difficult to do so?*

A: There are many things I could say, but there is one thing I must say. The most difficult, even frightening, step for an aspiring writer is transforming the marvelous creative imaginings in his head into words on a blank sheet of paper. Somehow, the imagined words become clumsy and awkward when written down. Yet, writing them down is what writing is basically all about—putting black on white, as de Maupassant used to say it. The best way to ease into that is to keep a daily journal. I've kept a daily journal, one page a day, for many, many years. My children, David and Amy, used to watch me fill that journal. Eventually, both of them started keeping daily journals in their own manner. It was wonderful practice for them. It got them used to setting their thoughts down on paper. It made them comfortable about working with words. When it came to writing actual books, neither of them was blocked. To date, David has published more than ten books, and Amy has published more than six. Go thou and do likewise.

20

DON'T LET YOUR MOTHER LOOK OVER YOUR SHOULDER

By Nancy Thayer

The best advice about writing that I was ever given is also the advice that I still and continually find the hardest to follow: "You'll never be a good writer until you learn to write without your mother looking over your shoulder."

I was told that in 1968, at the University of Iowa, when I was finishing my masters in English literature and taking a course in creative writing from C. D. B. Bryan (who had then published *P.S. Wilkinson* and has since published *Friendly Fire* and *Beautiful Women, Ugly Scenes,* among other books).

I have always been grateful for that advice and tried to keep it in mind, because it reminds me of my greatest problem, and in just repeating that sentence to myself, I help set myself free from that problem.

I like to write from the first-person point of view. I like the use of "I". It provides an immediacy and an intensity that the third person does not give. I like to write about contemporary women, women like me. Because of this, I run the risk of having every novel I write thought of as autobiographical. This gives me trouble at both ends of the novel-writing process.

At one end, the final stage, when the novel is published and read, I have to face the reaction of my friends and neighbors—and my mother—who assume that I have done all those things my characters did.

Part of this I have brought on myself, because *Stepping,* my first novel, was partly autobiographical. I was married when I was twenty, to a man sixteen years older than I; I did become a stepmother to his two young daughters; I did later have two children of my own; I did anguish over the difficulties of trying to combine home, family, and career.

But *Stepping* is not an autobiography. Zelda, the heroine, does a lot of things I haven't done, and—thank heavens—I've done a lot of things she doesn't do. But readers often don't believe or understand this.

For example, Zelda manages to stay happily married, in spite of the fact that she is pursued by a handsome professor named Stephen. I am now happily divorced, and for reasons that had absolutely nothing to do with "another man." But when *Stepping* was published, the same year I was divorced, I received a scathing letter from one of my oldest friends. She said she had read *Stepping,* and now she knew why I was getting a divorce, and how could I do that to my husband, have an affair with Stephen, run off with another man. . . . She wanted nothing more to do with me!

I wrote back to her that *Stepping* was fiction, and that I had added Stephen to the novel to try to add more dramatic tension, and also because I was trying to write a novel about the challenges women face in this day and age and one of those challenges was faithfulness in a world of easy infidelity. And after all, in my novel, Zelda had not actually had the affair with Stephen; she had remained faithful to her husband. I tried to impress upon my friend that she was mixing my fiction with my life. But, unfortunately, she remained certain that what I had written was what I had lived.

Long before *Stepping* was published, I had run into a similar problem with a short story. I had been experimenting with point of view and had written a short story entitled "The Genius," which was written from the point of view of a schizophrenic woman. The point of view alternated from first person to third person and back again. It was great fun to write. It turned out to be rather humorous and also to capture the frightening zaniness of a crazy woman. It was published in a Canadian journal, *The Capilano Review,* and I sent off copies to my family.

Shortly thereafter, my mother called my sister in alarm. Mother was afraid I was going crazy, or had gone crazy, and she didn't know what to do, and was too worried about my mental health to risk even asking me about it. I called Mother and tried to convince her that I was sane and that the story had been only a piece of fiction, but it was a long time before she stopped worrying.

My second novel, *Three Women at the Waters' Edge,* was about a mother of fifty and her two grown daughters, who are going through various crises: having babies, getting divorced, falling in love, trying to balance the desire to nurture others with the desire to nurture oneself. People often asked me: which of the three women is *you*? I had to answer, not any one of them, and yet that there were parts of all of them in me. Several women wrote to me, or came up to me when I gave a talk, to tell me how angry they were at Margaret, the mother, who finally chooses to please herself rather than forever be at the beck and call of her daughters. These women didn't see how I could write about such a selfish mother, and they were genuinely upset with me.

Dealing with the reactions of friends, readers, and relatives when a novel is finally published can be troublesome—but the worst trouble it can bring is at the beginning stage of the novel-writing process. Fear of negative reactions from readers can hamper, diminish, and even halt creativity. "What will people think?" can be the most limiting and destructive thought a writer ever has to deal with.

When I wrote my third novel, *Bodies and Souls,* I set myself a challenge. I didn't want to write only about contemporary women and their children and their loves, although that subject will always be dearest to my heart and will be endlessly fascinating to me. I wanted to stretch myself, to reach. I live in Williamstown, Massachusetts, the home of the Clark Art Museum, which houses a magnificent collection of impressionist art. I find those paintings a continual source of inspiration, and because of them, I decided that in my own way I wanted to paint on a broader canvas.

So I wrote *Bodies and Souls* from the point of view of many different people: a troubled minister, a beautiful vamp who seduces a young man, a lesbian mother, an elderly man who runs a dry cleaning establishment, a bachelor professor who does not care for people or desire to touch flesh, a young girl in love, a woman concerned with appearances and perfection to the point of obsession. I wanted to stretch myself, to write from many different points of view. Most of the characters I wrote in third person, but two of them just "came" to me in first person. When I sat down to write them, I found myself writing, "I . . ." I cannot explain just why. I think it had something to do with the personality of those two characters. Liza Howard, the beautiful vamp, is an intense, vital woman, impatient and passionate, who demanded to be written in the immediate first person. Mandy Findly, the young girl, is just falling in love, and she wants to be an artist. She is innocent and vulnerable, and the reserve and slight barrier inherent in the third person did not seem right for her.

I also set myself the challenge in *Bodies and Souls* of writing rather explicitly about sex. Because I was writing about bodies and souls, sex was a natural part of the book. Also, it was, for me, a challenge of craft. I did worry about what my mother would say. She is an intelligent woman who reads constantly, but she is still my *mother*. I was delighted when she called me after reading the book, to say she loved it. I hesitantly asked, "But what did you think about . . . the sex?" She laughed and said, "Oh, heavens, I know about *all that!*"

Before I could be daring in the creation of my characters, I had to decide first what I would do when the book was published and people asked: "Which character are you? Did you do all that?" I decided I would not try to explain the idea of fiction to people anymore. Instead, I would only smile and say, "I did it *all.*"

Still, whenever a new novel of mine comes out, I am tempted to go around this small town I live in, to the grocery store and the school meetings and the dry cleaners, wearing a t-shirt that says, "It's FIC-TION!"

Deciding on which point of view to use is a difficult task.

I find it easier to describe a character when I am writing in third person. For example, I can write, "She was beautiful," or "He was an unusually kind man," when I would not be able to write, "I am beautiful," or "I am an unusually kind man." Readers tend to identify with the "I" in a story, and they don't want to identify with conceited people. Any time a person speaks from the first-person point of view, the meaning of the sentence is weighted with the significance of that person's self-knowledge. Consider, for example, the difference between the statements, "He is a genius," and "I am a genius." The first sentence (third person) is factual, while the second (first person) seems loaded with conceit.

Because it is so much simpler to comment on the looks or character of a person when writing from the third-person point of view, I tend to choose that if my main concern in a story is with plot development.

However, if my main concern is with character development, I usually choose first person. This requires more work, and, in a way, the writer must be a little sneaky, devious, a sort of mystery writer, giving the reader clues about a character without making that character seem too self-analytical or vain or blunt. It is then that the old dictum, "show, don't tell," comes to mind. Showing takes more work, more subtlety. A writer cannot have a character say, "I am beautiful," or "I am insane." Instead, he must set up a series of events that show the reader that the character is beautiful or insane, while letting the "I" remain relatively unenlightened.

The first-person point of view takes more subtlety; but it also has more immediacy. Many first novels or short stories are partly auto-biographical and are easier for the writer when written in first person. It's almost like writing a diary. The danger, there, of course, is in including irrelevant material because it "really" happened. The writer might stray from the fictional truth to the factual truth when writing in first person.

One of the best ways to decide on point of view is to write five or six pages of the story from both points of view, and then compare. Which "comes" most easily? Which provides the effects you want? Which makes you forget your own life and gives the novel and the characters lives of their own? After a few pages, it's usually clear which technique will serve you best.

At the end of her award-winning novel, *The Color Purple,* Alice Walker says, "I thank everybody in this book for coming. A. W. author and medium." This is the strongest statement I have seen of a writer being taken over by her characters, of a writer feeling that she is only the means by which real people express themselves. And for a novel to be good, it must be genuine; the readers and writers must believe that those characters are real, that they do actually live and breathe.

In the 4th series of the *Paris Review Interviews, Writers at Work* (which is a helpful and fascinating collection for writers), John Updike is asked about the resemblance between his family and himself and the characters in his books. He says, "Once I've coined a name . . . I feel utterly hidden behind that mask, and what I remember and what I imagine become indistinguishable."

It is this fusion of memory and fantasy that makes fiction. It is this amazing and frightening and wonderful leap into the body and mind of another person—an imaginary person—that a writer must make in order to write at all. To take that first step into the world of imagination, it is necessary first to drop the barricades set up by the fear of the opinion of others.

When I sit down to write, I have to forget, for example, that my next-door neighbor, who happens to be the superintendent of the grade-school my children attend, might read a book of mine in which a character has sex or sobs all night in despair or yells horrid threats at her children or even steals or kills.

It's often hard to liberate oneself from the thought of the critical parent, lover, neighbor, or friend. But when you write, you are entering a world of your own. Be sure no one is looking over your shoulder, blocking your light. Try not to carry the weight of a real person with you. Then you'll have the freedom to range as far and wide into your imagination as you can go.

21

THEME AND PLOT: THE DELICATE RELATIONSHIP

By Josephine Jacobsen

OFTEN, in fact usually, the short story is spoken of as though it were monolithic, as though certain principles applied to all kinds of short stories, excluding, of course, the specific genre stories such as fantasy or science fiction. As the writer well knows, there are short stories with quite different purposes. Aside from the fantasy and science fiction genres, there are primarily two other kinds of short stories, each difficult to accomplish with distinction, and each with a definite purpose and value, but grounded in different assumptions and produced by different techniques.

There is the story written purely as entertainment—and anyone who relegates such work to a level of inferiority is naïvely unaware of the true, urgent necessity for release into Once-Upon-A-Time. Entertainment is not only one of the universal joys, but at its best, it is not produced by the easy formulas many people assume are ready at hand.

But there is also another kind of short story, a story that appeals to a smaller audience, is more difficult to place, and does not necessarily leave the reader more refreshed and relaxed. Why is it written? Why read?

It is usually written because its writer has an irresistible desire to communicate a deeply-felt experience, one of those epiphanies which in some way, however minute, change the reader's own experience; and it is because of that tiny enlargement of true experience that it is read.

Stories of this kind are so diverse as to preclude any kind of generalization, but there are a few characteristics that are apt to be constant. The story will end, not according to the wishes of the reader, but according to the nature of the characters. It will neither begin nor end on the page; the reader will truly understand that these people have had lives before they appeared in the story. And the "end" of the story will be really the end of a particular section of that life: an incident, an action that will in some way permanently affect their minds, emotions and their future.

I like to believe that when the last word of my story has been read, the reader has been given choices for speculation, as in the lives of actual people, and can say, among the choices, "I think that things will now go this way."

This certainly does not mean that the story's plot can be a vague, shapeless section of the characters' time or circumstances. On the contrary, every single word must make its own contribution toward the climax the story will reach. Every move, by every character, must give to the reader an added knowledge of that character's implicit nature.

One of the fascinating aspects of this kind of story is that of the relation of theme and story line. Any theme worth its salt will be applicable to a great number of people—the enduring themes lie under everything. But whatever the theme—justice, loneliness, betrayal, fear, or the nature of power—it can be illustrated and given body by the most diverse plots. No one can possibly set out to produce a good story by determining to illustrate a theme, any more than one can fall in love upon an order.

I believe that what happens in most cases (certainly in mine) is that one becomes at some period haunted by a theme that knocks about in the consciousness or the unconscious for perhaps months; maybe even for a year or more. Then suddenly something unforeseen—a face, a gesture, an incident, a situation—turns out to have that theme as its very core, and you are off and running. Interestingly, the theme may be incarnated in a large or small subject, yet retain its own scale, untouched.

In a recent story of mine about whether a very attractive and endearing boy did or did not steal a wristwatch from a self-righteous stuffed shirt, the story line is small scale. Nothing here deals with matters of life or death. Practically speaking, the question involved is a single, minor, often-encountered situation.

In a second story, which takes up the thorny problem of how the sincere beliefs of an all-out pacifist can result in injury to others to whom such an attitude is inexplicable, the story line is large: A marriage, the nature of trust, and a young boy's entire future life are at stake.

It is the theme that gives the story its resonance, because in some fashion, the theme will apply to the reader as the plot may never do; it is the theme that leaves its echo on the reader's nerve. But the development of the plot is the very flesh and lifeblood of the story, and unless that carries conviction and interest, the theme will remain as cold and stiff as an admonition or a rule. Indeed, I feel that the theme should not be fully apparent until the end of the story—a discovery the reader makes with a shock of recognition, not by carefully-placed signposts that distinguish it en route.

An intriguing, and incidentally very useful, exercise for someone who hasn't yet consciously explored the relationship of plot and theme, is to take a dozen really fine short stories—preferably personal favorites—and separate theme from plot, as carefully and surely as one can separate whites from yolks. It will almost certainly be found that the size and weight of the plot may differ greatly from the size and weight of the theme. Then take one of the denuded themes, and locate it in other stories, where it is hidden in utterly different subject matter.

Certain rare writers (Tennessee Williams and Flannery O'Connor would be prime examples) are able to perform the miraculous juggling act of producing hilarity and pity or terror simultaneously. Humor—which is always based on a strict sense of proportion (how can it be distorted until it has been established?)—can carry a theme somber indeed. We need only think of Eudora Welty's "The Petrified Man," or Flannery O'Connor's "Revelation," or—in drama—Blanche DuBois's birthday dinner (in *A Streetcar Named Desire*), to see how possible this is, though one wrong movement would bring every ball to earth in disorder.

I think that a profound sense of reality (not necessarily a reality with which we are ourselves familiar) is the short story's basic necessity—even those details that don't enter the story verbally must be visible and familiar to the writer. If the writer sees, feels the weather, the setting, the time of day, the objects visible to the characters at that moment, those details will somehow infiltrate the story with a sense of actuality.

In a story of mine recently published, much of the dialogue takes place between two men of antipathetic temperaments, sitting over the enforced intimacy of pre-dinner drinks on the concrete porch of a small Caribbean boardinghouse. Before them is a garden in which a man is working, and behind him is a fence, and behind that is the cabin where he lives with his wife and child; his goat is tethered to a peripatetic stake. All these details are important to the story; but also present to me as I wrote were the clothes the two men were wearing, the variety of blooms in the garden, the quavering bleats of the goat, the shimmer of Caribbean heat. I know what sort of chairs the men were sitting on, what color of shorts the gardener wore, where the sun was, over the sea. And these last things, which in the story are not mentioned at all, are as important to the feel and taste and shape of the story as those details which are specified.

What all this really means is that the writer must, in her or his imagination, have actually lived through the story that is being told: There is no substitute for that identification.

The second great rule is that the story must grow out of the characters themselves, their reactions to each other, to the situation they are encountering. The story cannot be imposed upon them so that they lie, lopped, on a Procrustes bed. That is why the writer of this sort of short story often has the exciting experience of having a character move unexpectedly, right under the pen; assume an importance, show a side, which was never expected. In my story of two boys and the wristwatch, I had that happen. That confrontation, of natures and backgrounds, *was* the basis of the story; yet perhaps the most significant and lingering note turned out to be the conduct of the master who had to deal with the problem.

Any advice from writer to writer is at best so conditional, and should be so modest, that perhaps the summing-up of this piece on the "serious" short story (which can often be the hilarious short story of serious intent) would be three simple things, standing like warning guardians by the desk. Remember that the people are real enough to have previous or subsequent lives, and let your story offer valid glimpses of how their mind-sets or emotions may be altered by what has happened.

Live with and in your characters, so that you not only see what they see, hear what they hear, but are aware of all the peripheral surrounding life that forms part of their consciousness. And remember that if this is the sort of story you choose and need to write, you cannot aim it at a market as though it were a commodity, but must struggle to bring it to its own most complete life—and then let it take its chance on reaching out to human beings who recognize and believe in the validity of its existence. When it does so, it will be a friend to them and to you for a long time.

Stories of this kind are more difficult to place than more conventional work; they earn less money. But on them, as they are published, their author builds a reputation for a quality of work, and this effect is durable. Such stories have their widest welcome in the university quarterlies and in the more stable and respected of the "little" magazines, though they are encountered, like unexpected travelers, in publications generally given over to "pure entertainment." They are, obviously, in some ways, a lonely venture; but the obverse of this is the sense of intimacy shared with their congenial readers, and it is surprising how many an unexpected letter comes in to say what such a story has meant to one of its readers, or how such a story's crucial incident will be brought up, sometimes years later, in a strange place, by a stranger.

22

BUILDING TENSION IN
THE SHORT STORY

By Joyce Carol Oates

THE most important aspect of writing is characterization—does a character come alive, is he memorable in some way? But the means of disclosing character is also important, for if a story lacks a strong narrative line, an editor or reader might not be patient enough to discover even the most stunning of fictional characters.

Novels are complex matters; the density of interest has to go up and down. Short stories, however, are generally based on one gradual upward swing toward a climax or "epiphany"—moment of recognition. A good chapter in a novel should probably be based on the same rhythmic structure as a short story. The novel, of course, can be leisurely while the average short story must be economical. Certain modern stories are so economical that single words or phrases are used to reveal the story's meaning—for instance, John Collier's "The Chaser," which ends with the words "au revoir" and not "goodbye."

While I think the best kind of contemporary story is much more rich and complex and daring than the Chekhovian-type stories so fashionable a few decades ago, still the writer must be careful to limit the range of his "secondary" material—descriptions, background. If he succeeds in winning the reader's attention by dramatic means, then the more important aspects of his story will be appreciated. We have all written wonderful little stories that are "hidden" somewhere in overlong, awkward, unsatisfactory masses of words.

Here are two examples of short story beginnings, each leading into a different kind of story:

1) "Let me tell you something about the Busbys," the old gentleman said to me. "The Busbys don't wash themselves—not adequately. And especially not as they grow older."

2) Just around the turn, the road was alive. First to assault the eye was a profusion of heads, black-haired, bobbing, and a number of straw hats that looked oddly professional—

The stories following these beginnings are to be found in *Prize Stories 1965: The O. Henry Awards,* edited by Richard Poirier and William Abrahams. The first story, "There," by Peter Taylor, invites the reader to listen in on a confidential, gossipy conversation: the words "Let me tell you" are intriguing enough, but the surprise comes in the second line. And we are introduced to a strange little town, "There," where each family seems to have a peculiar trait all its own—not washing properly, eating too much, narrow-minded complacency—and dying. Peter Taylor, the author of many excellent short stories of a rich, complex type, builds tension in a highly refined manner. We listen in on this old man's monologue, amused by his portraits of people back "there," and gradually we become emotionally involved in the pathos of his love for a girl who belonged to a family with a secret common trait—and then we find out, along with the narrator, that this common trait is dying. The girl has died young; the lover, now an aged man, has married someone else; there is no tragedy here, everything is muted and understated. But the story is unforgettable because Taylor has built so very gradually and unobtrusively the tension that arises out of the girl's impending death. Everything is past tense, but vitally alive.

The second beginning is from a story of mine, "First Views of the Enemy." Beginning with a near-accident, this story relies on tension building up within the main character's mind. A bus carrying migrant fruit pickers has broken down at the roadside, and when a young mother with her child drives by, one of the Mexican children darts in front of the car to frighten her. The tension between the young, American, rather materialistic woman and the socially-marginal people is the theme of this story. The woman arrives home safely, but she carries the image of this "enemy" with her into her expensive home, which now seems to her vulnerable. Her realization that she could lose everything she owns drives her to an orgy of selfishness as she locks things up, closes her drapes, even picks her most beautiful flowers and forces food upon her child. The tension is psychological, not active; the "enemy" does not appear after the first

104

encounter. We see that the true "enemy" is the woman's hysterical selfishness, which she is forcing upon her child also.

Franz Kafka's classic, "The Metamorphosis," begins like this:

> As Gregor Samsa awoke one morning from uneasy dreams he found himself transformed in his bed into a gigantic insect.

Incredible, of course. Unbelievable. But Kafka's mild-mannered prose proceeds on as if an event of no great dimensions has taken place. You, the reader, find out about Gregor's metamorphosis at the same time he does. You are surprised, yes, but so is Gregor—a quite ordinary young man, devoted to his family and his work. This surrealistic story is much more "realistic" in its ability to convince and emotionally involve than most slick fiction with its easily-recognizable people. But Kafka thrives on tension. He builds it from his first sentence on. Kafka is always asking, "What happens next?" and then he asks, "After that, what happens?" Like Simenon, he drives his characters to extremes and tests them. "The Metamorphosis" is beautifully constructed in three sections, each dealing with the tense relationship between the stricken Gregor and his family, until Gregor dies in order to release his loved ones. Tension is achieved on the literal level—what is going to happen to the insect-man?—and on the symbolic level—what will be the outcome of the "love" between members of a family when one of them is mysteriously stricken and is no longer "human"?

These three stories, widely differing in technique, build up tension through an accumulation of detail. If violence erupts in fiction, it should be the outcome of tension; it should not come first, nor should it be accidental. Action stories are of interest to certain audiences, but quality stories usually refine action onto a psychological level. There is "action"—movement—but it takes place in a person's mind or in a conversation. If someone finally kills someone else, it is simply the climax of a rhythmic building of tension that lasts long enough to be convincing but is short enough to be interesting.

Remember that tension created for its own sake is cheap; no one will read your story more than once. The tension is part of your technique but technique is only a means to an end; it is never the end itself. That is why the French "new novel" is so boring—it has no capacity to move us—while older, stormy works like *Wuthering*

105

Heights (which could only be "camp" to today's *avant-garde*) will be interesting to all imaginable future generations. I think the stress placed today on technique is misleading. A writer should imagine his scenes dramatically, as if they were to take place on the stage. There, empty, wordy passages are found out at once. It isn't "words" or "style" that make a scene, but the content behind the words, and the increase of tension as characters come into conflict with one another. "Words" themselves are relatively unimportant, since there are countless ways of saying the same thing.

A final suggestion: be daring, take on anything. Don't labor over little cameo works in which every word is to be perfect. Technique holds a reader from sentence to sentence, but only content will stay in his mind.

23

THE WILLING SUSPENSION OF DISBELIEF

By Elizabeth Peters

ALTHOUGH Coleridge coined the useful phrase, "the willing suspension of disbelief," it has been the goal of storytellers since the pre-literate dawn of time and of writers since fiction began. Writers of suspense fiction particularly depend upon this gesture of good will on the part of the reader, but successful achievement of that goal depends upon the writer as well as the reader. Presumably, the reader of thrillers or novels of suspense starts each book in the proper mood of suspended disbelief, but he cannot sustain this mood if the author taxes his intelligence too much. How, then, does the writer of suspense fiction create an aura of plausibility which will allow readers to accept his creation, "for the moment," as Coleridge adds?

The so-called Gothic novel is a sub-category of the novel of suspense. In most cases, the term "Gothic" is a misnomer, for the romantic, "damsel-in-distress" thrillers which publishers label "modern Gothics" are not Gothics at all. Their ancestors are not Mrs. Ann Radcliffe's *The Mysteries of Udolpho* or Horace Walpole's *The Castle of Otranto*, but Wilkie Collins' *The Moonstone* and Charlotte Brontë's *Jane Eyre*. The true Gothic novel requires an atmosphere of brooding supernatural horror and a setting that includes ruined castles and desolate moors. I don't consider my books to be true Gothics, but it would be pedantic of me to object to the term, which is certainly more succinct than more accurate designations. I may then be forgiven if I refer henceforth to this form of fiction as "Gothic."

The most important thing for a writer of Gothics to recognize is that the genre is inherently incredible, almost as unlikely as a fantasy novel. Personally, I find it as easy to believe in the green Martians of Barsoom as I do in the adventures of Gothic heroines. Some writers of Gothics seem to feel that because their plots are fantastic, they need not be logical. The converse is true. The more fantastic the plot, the more important are those factors that invite belief, or, at least, the suspension of disbelief.

What are these factors? Some may be seen in the three elements of plot, character and setting.

The plot of a Gothic novel must be tight, consistent, and logical —within the given framework. Like the fantasy novel, which starts with a single fantastic premise, the Gothic begins with what I like to call an "initiating coincidence." The heroine happens to overhear a conversation between two people who are planning a murder; or she happens to accept a job as governess in an isolated household whose inhabitants all suffer from severe neuroses. None of these situations is very likely, but we can admit one such fortuitous occurrence in order to get our plot moving. From that point on, however—no coincidences, no lucky accidents. If the hero is walking down Main Street at the moment when the heroine, cornered by the villain, screams for help, the hero must have a reason for being on Main Street at that vital moment. It will not suffice to explain that he keeps in shape by jogging down Main Street every fine afternoon. If the heroine is to be rescued—and Gothic heroines always are—the rescuer must be brought to the spot by hard work and/or logical deductions.

Plausibility of character is as important as consistency of plot. The two are related, of course. A stupid heroine's foolish behavior can lead to plot complications. Indeed, the plots of the poorer Gothics seem to depend wholly on the heroine's incredible naïveté, as she falls into one pitfall after another. But it is difficult for the reader to identify, or even sympathize, with heroines of such consummate imbecility. Admittedly, Gothic heroines have a propensity for getting into trouble. It is one of the important elements of the Gothic plot, but it can also be one of the great weaknesses of the genre. Critics justifiably jeer at the dim-witted girls who take nocturnal strolls around grim old mansions. If you must get your heroine out of her nice, safe, locked room in the middle of the night, after two murders have already been committed, do give her a good reason for leaving that security. (I cannot think of anything that would induce me to leave my room under those circumstances, except perhaps the voices of my children screaming for help.) Your heroine must have an equally pressing motive. Better yet, have her stay in her room and get into trouble in some less conventional manner. And no mysterious notes asking for a midnight rendezvous in the castle crypt, please. Critics sneer at that one, too. A heroine ought to have sufficient intelligence to check with the hero to make sure he actually sent the note before she ventures into a crypt.

The characters of Gothic novels are not profound or complex; in two-hundred-odd pages we do not have space for such luxuries, since we must spend a good deal of verbiage on plot and atmosphere. But if our characters are cardboard, they need not be absurd. They must not exhibit flagrant personality aberrations, or behave so idiotically that the reader begins to hope they will be murdered in the crypt, as they deserve to be.

Of course, the more fully developed and realistic your characters, the more plausible their actions will seem. One of the classics in the field, Daphne du Maurier's *Rebecca*, has a heroine who has always exasperated me by her timidity and docility; but she is believable, because she behaves in a way that is consistent with her background and her personality.

Atmosphere and setting are particularly important to thrillers of this type, and the same rule applies: the more unusual or exotic the setting, the harder you must work to give it an appearance of authenticity. In these days of jets and travel books, Samarkand is no more exotic than Paris or Rome. But you must make sure that your descriptions of these cities are accurate, and that you include enough details to convince the reader of the reality of the setting in which your heroine's wild adventures are to take place. I do not subscribe to the theory that a writer can write only about things he or she has personally experienced. I have personally visited all the cities and countries I have used in my books; but I could not have written about them without the aid of maps, photographs, and detailed notes taken on the spot. Perhaps a conscientious writer can do this with a city he or she has never seen—but it will require a great deal of work.

The rule holds even when you are inventing a setting. In one of my books, the action takes place in Rothenburg, a small German town I know fairly well, but for various reasons I decided to add an imaginary castle to that city instead of using an existing structure. I did almost as much research on the castle as I did on the city, reading about medieval castles and Franconian architecture, so that the description of my imaginary castle would agree with details of real structures of that period. If your characters do a lot of running around, draw floor plans. Readers love to spot discrepancies, and will write irritated letters if you have your heroine descend a staircase where no staircase can conceivably exist.

One useful trick to make sure that the reader will accept your devices of plot or of setting is to prepare him for them well in advance. A strategically located doorway, through which the hero gains entrance to the conference room—a secret passage whereby your characters can escape when danger threatens—these, and other devices, will seem more plausible if they are mentioned before you actually need them. Again, the more unusual the prop, the more carefully you must explain its presence. A secret passage in a medieval castle needs only a sentence or two of description, since the reader knows that medieval castles abound in such conveniences. A secret passage in a modern split-level house requires considerable explanation—and perhaps a brief character sketch of the eccentric individual who had it built.

Plot props require the same advance preparation. If the heroine's knowledge of Urdu is going to save her from a fate worse than death, or expose the master criminal, you must tell the reader early in the book that she is an expert in this abstruse language. If you do not, she will resemble Superwoman when she comes up with the information. And for pity's sake, if she or the hero is to be an expert in ichthyology or Egyptology, learn something about those subjects before you talk about them. I was once put off an otherwise readable Gothic because it involved a reincarnated Egyptian princess named Cha-cha-boom, or something equally absurd. No reincarnated Egyptian, fake or genuine, would have such a name, and the repetition of the inane syllables grated on me so strongly that I never finished the book. The author could easily have found an authentic ancient Egyptian name in the encyclopedia. I remember another book I never finished reading because the villain, a German sea captain, kept shouting "Grüss Gott!" in frenzied moments. If you do not know that "Grüss Gott" is a friendly greeting in southern Germany, have your villain stick to English.

You may think that few readers have much knowledge of Egyptology or other abstruse subjects. This would be a dangerous assumption. Archaeology is a popular field, and for some odd reason, which I mean to investigate one day, archaeology buffs seem to be especially addicted to thrillers. But that is not the important thing. The important thing is that plausibility depends upon the accumulation of consistent, accurate details. They really do add verisimilitude to an otherwise bald and unconvincing narrative. The reader may not consciously note all your errors; but a series of careless inconsistencies will tax the reader's willingness to accept your imaginary world, and a single glaring error may be enough to snap that fragile thread on which the suspension of disbelief depends.

Of course, you are bound to slip up occasionally, no matter how conscientiously you research your book. As I work through revision after revision, I come across howlers I can't believe I missed the first and second times. To my chagrin, a few of them escape me even in the third and fourth revisions and get into print, despite the additional efforts of my intelligent editors. In one of my books, written under another name, an integral plot prop was an old family Bible. Long after the book was published, a reader wrote to me inquiring how the Bible happened to survive the conflagration that had destroyed the equally ancient family mansion and most of its contents. "I can imagine several possible solutions," she added charitably, "but I do think you ought to have *told* us."

She was absolutely correct. I should have told her. And I would have done so, if I had noticed the discrepancy. However, errors of this sort are not in the same category as careless mistakes or poorly developed characters. An occasional gap in the plot or an error of fact will not be serious if the rest of the plot is as tight as you can make it, and if the other facts have been checked and rechecked.

I could go on, giving examples of the basic rule, but if you read many Gothics, you will spot plenty of other cases, of success and of failure. Of course there are some writers who seem to be able to break all the rules and get away with it. Don't bother writing to tell me about them. I know about them. I only wish I knew how they do it.

111

24

WHERE CHARACTERS COME FROM

By Colby Rodowsky

THE one question that I'm asked most frequently—aside from "How old were you when you wrote your first book?"—is, "Where do your characters come from?"

For a while I tended to shrug, scuff my feet, and change the subject—which satisfied no one, including me. Then I came upon a quote by William Faulkner that seemed to sum up what I had been doing all along, without even knowing it. "It begins with a character, and once he stands up on his own feet and begins to move, all I can do is trot along behind him with a paper and a pencil trying to keep up long enough to put down what he says and does."

In the course of writing seven published novels, several failed efforts and false starts, I've done a lot of trotting along behind. But it's the character's initial standing up on his own two feet that I'd like to consider here. And as for the question, "Where do your characters come from?" I have come up with an answer that, if not profound, is at least obvious.

Characters—mine, at least—come from *anywhere* and *everywhere* and, at times, *nowhere*.

They come from a face in a crowd, a picture on a wall, an older brother I wish I'd had. They come from a story in a newspaper, a name in a book, a need to balance other characters already there, and from the deepest, innermost parts of myself.

And once they're here—standing on their own two feet, as it were—they frequently set off with an independence that astounds me, so that from time to time I have to catch up with them before I can determine where some of these people who stepped unbidden into my mind and my books came from.

There was the time, six or seven years ago, when I was at the beach. It

112

was a cold, cloudy day and I was reading in a downstairs room that had a sliding glass door opening onto a small boardwalk with a pier jutting out into the water. At the end of the pier a young boy was working on a boat. I thought at the time that he seemed to be puttering rather than working, as if shielding himself from something. His shoulders were hunched, and I'm sure his eyes, if I could have seen them, would have been what novelists call "hooded."

A neighbor went by and called to another neighbor on an upstairs porch, "Did you see in the paper that so and so was indicted today?"

There then followed much gesturing and mouthing of words so that I finally figured out that the boy working on his boat was the son of the man in the newspaper.

Now obviously that boy must have known he was the butt of all the pointing and whispering. This worried me, and for a long time afterwards I wondered how he felt about himself, about his father, and about the world in general.

Thadeus St. Clair, the boy I wrote about in *A Summer's Worth of Shame,* wasn't the boy on the pier. I don't even remember that boy's name. I didn't know him. But over the months I was working on the book I came to know Thad—and to know him very well.

Another time and another summer. A woman I met briefly was talking about her powers of ESP. She gave examples of things she had known, not always things she wanted to know. Because at the time this woman was taking care of her grandchild, I began to wonder what it would be like for a child living with a grandmother with extrasensory perception. This seemed to be a natural extension of my memory of an old woman—certifiably crazy—who wandered the streets of my grandmother's town picking things out of the trash and storing them away in her hodgepodge of a house until she was hauled off to the state asylum in Williamsburg.

The character of Gussie that I wrote about in *Evy-Ivy-Over* was not the old woman who roamed the streets of that small Virginia town. My Gussie—and Slug's Gussie, because how could she have a granddaughter named anything but Slug October?—did indeed have ESP. She did prowl the town garbage cans, not because she was crazy, but because she was searching for treasures for her son Brian, an artist who lived in the city and made collages.

There was another element in the character of Gussie: To me she was the quintessential grandmother. I myself was blessed with two special grandmothers, and Gussie embodied all that was good in those relationships. The way Gussie felt about Slug—and Slug felt about Gussie—was the way my grandmothers and I felt about each other, though I've often thought that it would be difficult for those two very proper women to see themselves in a character who delighted in finding an empty milk of magnesia bottle or who knew how yellow felt all the way through.

As for Slug October, that points-and-angles child with the knobby knees and elbows, I don't know where she came from. I only know that she nags at me so that having written a book about her, I then gave her a cameo appearance in *H, My Name Is Henley,* and fully expect her to turn up again, older, changed the way we all change with the years, and ready to fill me in on what has happened to her since we last met.

Now, Nelson Trimper is another story. Nelson popped onto the scene because I needed a repulsive child, and there, from my childhood, was an odious red-haired boy whose mother had been a friend of my mother's. In the frequently misguided way of grown-ups, it was decided that this child and I should be friends. We weren't. In fact, he stuck pins in my best doll. So Nelson Trimper in *Evy-Ivy-Over* is, in a sense, my way of giving that other child his comeuppance.

Mrs. Prather, Slug's mean-spirited and wretched teacher, is indeed every mean-spirited and wretched teacher I, or any of my children, ever had. But if Mrs. Prather was a composite of the bad teachers, so Guntzie, the art teacher in *What About Me?,* was all the good, mind-broadening, imagination-stretching teachers I ever had, or wanted to have.

My husband and I have had different approaches when it comes to visiting museums. He is insatiable, moving from gallery to gallery, reading the cards, seeing, remembering. I, on the other hand, have a short attention span when confronted with what seem to be endless rooms of art. It is as if it were all suddenly too much, and I find that I wander aimlessly around until I come upon something special. Then I look, drift away, come back to look again, finally giving up and heading for the museum shop to get a postcard of the treasures I have found.

Several years ago at the National Gallery in London, I discovered a Murillo painting called "Peasant Boy Leaning on a Sill." I stopped and stared, moved on, then came back again, saying, "His name is Mudge and I'm going to write a book about him."

114

His name wasn't Mudge in the painting—but only in my mind, and later in *The Gathering Room,* the book I did write about him. There was, of course, nothing of that 17th-century peasant boy in my present-day book about a boy living with his parents in the gatehouse of a cemetery, but nevertheless, that painting had triggered something in me.

And the other characters in the book? There was Ned, Mudge's father, a psychologically bruised man, the result of the events that had threatened him and sent him fleeing to the security of that gatehouse. Serena, the mother, became the special laid-back kind of person it took to put up with that whole scene, and a passing fishing boat I saw one summer at the beach with *Serena* across the stern gave me, at least, her name.

Mudge's friends came as a result of my wanderings through cemeteries, both in person and in books. A bronze butterfly yielded The Butterfly Lady, though I am unable to explain her propensity for reciting the poems of Edgar Allan Poe. A newspaper article about unusual grave markers gave me Little Dorro, while the epitaph, "After Life's Fitful Fever She Sleeps Well," produced Frieda.

Two wordy and somewhat pompous eighteenth-century inscriptions produced The Captain and his aide-de-camp Jenkins, who, with a slight adjustment in time, became veterans of the War of 1812. The words, "He was a just judge and an honest man," resulted in the Judge.

Aunt Ernestus, who is somehow the catalyst for all that happens in the book, started out to be modeled after someone I knew—someone not known for her imagination or her flights of fancy. But Ernestus Stokes wouldn't hold still for that. Or maybe my own imagination wasn't big enough to create someone completely without any.

When *H, My Name Is Henley* came out, a friend wrote me about a book, closing with the questions, "Where *do* your characters come from?"

Sometimes the answer to that isn't clear, even to me, and it took a bit of thinking to sort it out. Booshie, I found, came from a woman I observed once in church during a long and boring sermon. She had the same spongy bosom; the blue-white mottled legs; the squishy arms that made me think, as Henley did in the book, that if I poked them my finger would disappear.

Aunt Mercy was an admirable character indeed, and something like one of my grandmothers. She was so admirable, in fact, that she caused my editor much grief, and as each new character trait emerged in the writing of the book, he would strike his brow, sigh, and say, "All this and she plays Chopin too."

The characters in *Keeping Time,* my most recent book, are a varied lot: a group of present-day street performers. There are Drew Wakeman and his father Gunther, his sister Betina, old Nicholas who juggles, and Kate, who lives and sings with them. And from another time, there is Symon Ives, an apprentice to a London wait in 16th-century England.

I'm still not sure where they all came from. They're too new, too raw, untried, though I do seem to remember Drew looking out at me from a group I saw singing one night down by the waterfront. I only know that while I was working on the book I went to London and walked the streets that Drew and Symon walked: along Cheapside, up to St. Paul's, onto Milk Street where Symon lived with Master Robert Baker. And it felt right to be there. Almost as if I might come upon them at any minute.

But I should be used to that by now. My characters have a way of intruding when I least expect it. Take my great-aunt Mildred's funeral, for example.

Several years ago, when she died at the age of ninety-four, we went to the funeral. It was in an old cemetery in the middle of the city—*my* cemetery. The one I had renamed Edgemount and wrote about in *The Gathering Room.*

It was a hot summer day. A lulling kind of day. The priest droned on, and I started to look around, casting quick surreptitious glances behind this angel, that vault or marble lamb. I knew, somehow, that they were all there. Mudge and his friends: Little Dorro, Frieda, The Butterfly Lady, the Captain and Jenkins. And of course Aunt Ernestus.

That's how real they are to me.

How real I try to make them to my readers.

25

BOOKS THAT ENCHANT AND ENLIGHTEN

By Ken Follett

WHY are good books so boring?

We wondered about this as students, plodding through Henry James or Virginia Woolf while we longed to get back to *My Gun Is Quick*. Perhaps we were afraid to ask, for fear of seeming naive. As writers I think we should be asking the question still. It could turn out to be the most important question around.

Literature wasn't always so dull: this is a truism. *Oliver Twist* was a magazine serial. I read somewhere that one episode ended as Bill Sikes began to beat up Nancy; and when the ship carrying the next issue of the magazine arrived in New York, there was a crowd on the quay waiting to find out if Nancy died. The story may be apocryphal, but it makes a point: the greatest novelist in the English language used melodrama as liberally as any writer of soap opera.

Nowadays melodrama is unfashionable. Or is it? The literary phenomenon of the decade is the romantic-historical blockbuster — the kind of book my English agent calls a Sweet Savage Hysterical. There's melodrama — but it doesn't get reviewed in the *New York Times*. All right, I know — Kathleen Woodiwiss isn't in the Dickens class. Actually, that's the point. Nobody that good writes melodrama any more. Nobody that good writes mass-market fiction any more. This is a catastrophe. How did it happen?

In England the Education Act of 1870 made everyone go to school. No doubt something similar happened in the USA. Anyway, soon there was a literate population and a mass market for fiction. Publishers, writers and readers then divided into two camps: the elite, who until then had been the only readers, turned to increasingly rarefied intellectual fiction; and the newly literate mass went for sensation. The highbrows read Henry James while the rest of us devoured Tarzan. This is history. What I want to say is that both camps suffered because of the dichotomy.

117

First, character became the only permissible subject for a serious novel. (This was new: *Robinson Crusoe* was no more about *character* than *Raise the Titanic.*) Second, after the publication in 1922 of James Joyce's *Ulysses,* introspection became the paramount literary technique. Today the tail end of that movement is in a bad way (which is what people mean when they say the novel is dead). Although occasionally capable of touching an exposed nerve — as did *Fear of Flying,* for example — the light-comic approach of intellectual fiction today generally can't cope with much more than the trivia of middle-class life. Revolution, tragedy, passion, power, death: Thomas Hardy and Emily Brontë could write about these, but Kingsley Amis and John Updike can't; and when Gore Vidal writes about the end of the world he does it as a comedy. This, I think, is why friends of mine who like their novels deep at all costs read nineteenth-century stuff all the time. Serious fiction today is up a blind alley and banging its head against the wall.

I realize all this is not too terrifically scholarly: I'm just saying how it looks to me as a working storyteller.

While the intellectuals were plodding through Evelyn Waugh the rest of us were gasping with Mickey Spillane and swooning with Daphne du Maurier. And, just as they had to eat an awful lot of pudding to get at the plums, so we found — didn't we? — that cotton candy may be sweet but it nourishes not at all.

What went wrong (stick with it, now, I'm getting to the point) was that both fiction markets set themselves low standards. So long as they gave us thrilling tales the great mass-market writers, from Edgar Rice Burroughs to Dennis Wheatley, were permitted cardboard characters, sloppy writing, and texture as bland as Formica. The elite, who could get away with none of that, were allowed to dispense with plot, story, excitement, sensation, and the world outside the mind, so long as they were deep.

Well, what's to be done? I hope it's clear by now that this isn't going to be another plea for thrillers to be treated with critical seriousness: most of them, mine included, don't merit it because they aren't good enough (and it's small consolation that most serious novels aren't either). But our profession won't produce too many great writers while we continue to opt either for exciting trash or thoughtful tedium.

Will the intellectuals learn to enchant as well as enlighten us? It *can* be done. *One Flew Over the Cuckoo's Nest* satisfies the intellect without

118

boring the pants off us. There are a few others: *The Grapes of Wrath, 1984, Lord of the Flies.* They're all mavericks, though: freaks, offshoots from the literary mainstream; each of them is about something more than character, and none of the authors produced a body of mass-market hits. Being an intellectual usually involves belonging to a social sub-group of intellectuals, and we get our standards of excellence from our social peers. Anyone who swallows the idea that character is all there is to write about starts the race with one leg in a plaster cast.

For the writer of popular fiction it's different: and here's where I get around to technique, which is what I was asked to discuss.

Yes, people will sometimes buy a weepy romance or an exciting thriller even if it's as shallow as Mickey Mouse and written like a Maoist press release. But our readers don't actually *prefer* trashy writing. On the contrary.

Look: the underwater knife fight is more exciting, not less, if it's described in graceful, powerful prose; the plot has more drama if it depends on character development as much as external events; the romance is more thrilling if the tall, dark hero nurses a genuine, credible sadness behind that handsome-but-cruel smile.

Some examples. There are lots of fine police procedurals, but Ed McBain's 87th Precinct mysteries stand out, not because of their authen-ticity or ingenuity, but because Steve Carella and Meyer Meyer and Bert Kling are funny and worried and clever and brave and *real. The Spy Who Came in from the Cold* hasn't got a terrific plot, but it is written with such grace, insight and conviction that it was the thriller of the decade. Stephen King's *Salem's Lot* keeps us awake at night, not because of the vampires in the story — Vampires? Is he kidding? — but because we believe in and care for the small town where they strike. There have been many Mafia novels, but only one made us feel how it is to be part of the Family; only one explained how murder and Catholicism can be recon-ciled in the prayer of the Mafia wives.

Take note: these four examples have virtues we expect of serious fiction — and those virtues gave them mass-market success.

What's more, serious novels which (perhaps accidentally) have the merits of pulp fiction are often both critical and commercial hits: *The Forsyte Saga* is a soap opera, *Fear of Flying* is an old romance in radical-feminist clothes, *Sons and Lovers* is a family saga, *Intruder in the Dust* is a detective story.

119

So here comes the message. I don't, as you've guessed, want us all to start writing heavy stuff: God forbid. Let's concentrate on the need to thrill readers, move them, and scare them half to death. When we need a standard by which to measure our plots, we'll look to Robert Ludlum, not Saul Bellow. For construction we'll emulate *The Day of the Jackal* rather than *Nicholas Nickleby*. We'll learn how to make people cry by reading *Love Story*, not *Women in Love*.

But let's learn other things from the intellectuals. Watch how Faulkner creates a rural community, and forget *Peyton Place*. We know how Agatha Christie creates suspense on stage, but what is Harold Pinter's trick? If there's an adolescent in the story, compare him with the boy in *Catcher in the Rye*, not the girl in *The Exorcist*.

I know, it's a depressing experience. It tells us how shallow our work is. But it also tells us how good fiction *can* be. Writing successful fiction is a matter of getting lots of different things right (which is why there's no formula for a best seller) and the way to get better, I suspect, is to discover new things to get right.

O.K., let's get something practical out of all this theorizing. The hero of your thriller has a streak of ruthlessness. They generally do: perhaps they have to, to be thriller heroes. But let's not leave it at that. What were the events, who were the people, who shaped his personality? Why did he, as a sixteen-year-old, decide that the thing to be is *tough,* when others were picking *clever* or *sexy* or *rich?*

Your passionate melodrama is set in eighteenth-century England, and all the main characters are wealthy. You think this means you don't have to worry about where their money comes from. Worry about it. Do they own land? Then they need to know the price of corn. Are they in politics? Then which party, and why do they get elected? Are they merchants? Are they richer or poorer than they were a generation ago? Why? These things aren't as important as their gowns and their manners and their weddings, but you should know about both.

The spymaster has a mentally retarded son. You put this in to make him more human: good idea. Now, what happens to a family when a child like this is born? If you don't know, find out. You went to the trouble to research the gun he carries and the unbreakable book code he uses to communicate with the double agent; now think about his home life. And when you've developed that idea so well that it's beginning to get in the way of that tricksy little plot you've got all figured out, then you know you're writing a better book.

120

Writers have something of a responsibility. People get an awful lot of their ideas about life from fiction. Like it or not, one or two of us will probably change the way our contemporaries think — and it's mass-market stuff that does this. My generation learned about Nazi Germany from the TV show "Holocaust." The popular view of life under communism comes from George Orwell's *1984,* not *The Gulag Archipelago.* British people never understood Watergate until we saw the movie *All the President's Men.* And then there's *Roots.*

It's often said that a romance or a mystery can't be well characterized, true to life and beautifully written because everything has to be subordinate to the plot. I think that's like saying verse will never have the impact of prose because the choice of words is constrained by metre and rhyme. In fact the rules of formal poetry give the words *more* impact. Plot ought to do the same for character.

"When that spymaster's everyday life begins to make the plot implausible, which do you sacrifice — story or realism?"

Sorry, you don't get off the hook that easily. The object is to have a plot and a character that fit together like ball and socket. It is terribly difficult to write beautiful rhyming verse, because the rules are so restricting. Similarly, the need for a happy ending, a violent climax, a ludicrously ambitious theft, or a love interest for the hero — all of these make it harder to write real people and credible events and sensitive prose. Anyone can write: it's writing *well* that is so tough.

But then, who told you it was easy?

26

MIDDLE-OF-THE-BOOK BLUES

Ten Ways to Get Your Novel Back on the Track

By Phyllis A. Whitney

MIDDLE-of-the-book blues! I get them every time, and sometimes more than once along the way. The enthusiasm with which I started out has evaporated. The excitement of discovering and developing a new set of characters, a new setting and situations, lies in the past, and freshness is gone. Boredom is a dreadful state for any writer, and it must be dealt with promptly.

Nevertheless, forcing oneself to write is not the answer. Boredom is usually a warning that all is not well, so that the creative part of the brain is balking. Fortunately, I've been adrift on these becalmed waters before, so it's not as frightening as it was the first few times it happened. Now I pay attention to the warning and take several specific steps to turn myself around and rekindle interest in my work. You may develop a different set of steps for yourself, or adapt some of these for your own use.

1. When I find myself stopped, it is often because I'm not clear about where I am going next, or because I'm taking a mistaken direction, and my unconscious is alerting me. The first thing I do is to talk to myself on paper—whether in pencil or on the typewriter. I discuss the problems with myself, looking for leads that will help me understand what is wrong, and how I can start my imagination working again.

I jot down every stray idea that occurs to me that might be used in future action. I find that the mere act of setting something on paper can stir up the creative juices. Since this isn't really writing-for-keeps, there's no strain. At this point I take care not to be critical of any notion that comes my way. The sorting out, the judging can come later. Being critical too early may stop the flow.

2. Next I re-examine each character in turn, testing for ways in which

unforeseen action can be produced. Is there some hidden relationship between this character and that one—something I haven't thought of before? In one novel it suddenly developed that one of my important characters had been married years before to a secondary character in the story. Like me, my main character knew nothing of this marriage. The moment I discovered this, all sorts of possibilities opened up. My imagination stopped balking and went into action—because I had fed it something intriguing to work on.

Conflict and interest can grow endlessly out of our characters. I always keep in mind Brian Garfield's advice to "jolt the reader." Our characters are full of surprises if we give them half a chance. So I try to open up those past lives and develop new and unexpected turns for my plot.

3. Settings, interior and exterior, are always good sources for new plot possibilities. Each background is different and individual, and the setting itself will provide endless story material.

When I went to Sedona, Arizona, for the background of *Vermilion,* one of my first impressions of that stunning Red Rock country was of a line of tall rocks that reminded me of Egyptian statues. Some seemed to have faces carved into them by nature. I saw such "statues" in the red rocks a number of times, and I took color pictures of them. Later, when I studied these snapshots at home, the mystical possibilities began to stir in my imagination until I had part of the main theme of my story.

Exploring your setting again when you reach a static period can furnish new material that will make you eager to get back to your writing. Out of just such feeding of the imagination does inspiration grow.

Whenever I travel to find a new background for a novel, I am on the lookout for anything mysterious, any setting in which something nefarious might happen. West Martello Tower is an old Civil War fortress in Key West that I roamed through and knew that I would want to use in a novel at some point. It is now the home of the Key West Garden Club, and a variety of tropical plants and trees have been planted within the fort's enclosure. The fort is built against a hill, so that it is partly underground, and there are vaulted brick passageways and ceilings—all perfect for scenes of mystery! The setting itself was a challenge to my imagination.

4. It is important for my characters to interact with my settings. In

Vermilion my heroine is haunted by the faces in the rock. The mystical elements provided by the imaginary character, "Vermilion," are brought out all the more by the setting itself. Until setting *integrates* with character, I have only a travelogue.

When I was writing *Domino,* set in the Colorado Rockies, I wanted to use a tiny ghost town that was blowing away to dust. In the plotting, I devised ways in which this little town could affect the heroine's life and become so forceful a part of the story that the book could carry the town's name in the title.

For me, one of the most stimulating preparations for writing is this deliberate examination of character and setting, to find the ties that chain them together.

5. Of course, in the process of collecting background material, the real people I meet who live in a particular place are endlessly fascinating. I talk to everyone who will talk to me, though I'm not looking for *their* stories: I like to make up my own. Encounters with strangers provide take-off points for story ideas, though these may not come to me until later. For example, I saw a woman on a pier in Key West flying a spectacular kite, and I was able to use her to pick up a scene that was lagging.

In Carmel, California, an elderly sculptor whom I met in the Monterey Library invited me to see his beautiful home. Of course I jumped at the chance, since I always need to discover how people live in the setting I'm visiting and will want to write about later on.

All these elements make a rich stew of material and later, just going through pictures and brochures and reading the notes I've taken can set me off on interesting story trails.

However, not being able to travel doesn't mean that I can't write. When I had knee surgery, I had to forgo a trip to Newport, but I wrote a book about it anyway, leaning heavily on photographs and research material and finding someone who would check my manuscript for mistakes.

Wherever one lives, there are interesting corners, villages, city streets. When I couldn't take a long trip, I wrote about the place where I live, Cold Spring Harbor on Long Island, which became the background for my novel *Rainsong.*

6. In the planning stages, I always look for ways in which to make my main character's situation intolerable. Putting on emotional pres-

sure leads to conflict, explosions, action. In the opening of *Rainsong,* my heroine's husband—a famous pop singer—has died under mysterious circumstances. To escape the furor of the media, she accepts an invitation to an old Gold Coast mansion on Long Island. In the quiet of this huge house, she hopes to recover her talent for song writing. I asked myself how I could jolt my heroine and make her situation even more unbearable and frightening. One night she hears music playing in the supposedly empty house. Her dead husband's voice drifts up to her, singing the "rainsong" she had written for him. There are chills aplenty here, and the pressure is on.

Since *Jane Eyre,* the character hidden away and kept secret from the heroine is always fascinating, and possible variations for developing plots from this situation are endless. I never mind if a story idea or character has been used before, as long as I can give it a new twist. In *Poinciana,* my heroine becomes aware of the old woman living in a cottage on the grounds of her husband's Palm Beach house. By doling out a little information at a time, I fed the heroine's curiosity (and the reader's), until the confrontation scene between the old woman and the young one could furnish real jolts, and bring about the realization that the situation was intolerable for both my heroine and the old woman.

7. Since none of our characters leaps into existence full blown but must grow out of the events that have shaped them, it pays to look into past happenings, which may have a tremendous effect on the present. Of course, I do some of this in the plotting stages for my novel, but I can do so even more effectively when I know my story people and have seen them in action.

Characters who are dead before the story starts can be almost as important in the action as the live characters. There are always secrets in the past that still influence and affect the present and make a splendid source of new action. (*Rebecca* is an outstanding example.)

In writing *Dream of Orchids,* I found that the second wife of the heroine's father—dead a year before the novel begins—was still very much alive in the memories of the other characters, because of events she had set in motion. Jolts and surprises again—and a rich source of story action to pull me back on the track.

Force your characters to make decisions, for this always results in action. If you find that your main character is drifting along without much drive, you may have found one source for your lagging interest.

125

Not only the main characters, but other characters as well, need to make choices. Such decisions force characters to plan and act—often against one another.

8. Research in books and libraries can be an endless source of exciting ideas. When I started work on my Key West novel, *Dream of Orchids,* I had no suspicion that I would become interested in the subject of orchids, or in action that involved diving to a sunken Spanish galleon. I am not an orchid fancier, nor have I ever done any scuba diving. But after bringing home ten books on raising orchids, I could write about them with some assurance, and the orchids themselves gave me all sorts of plot material, including attempted murder. My research included a visit to an orchid greenhouse in my own locality— with a list of questions in hand.

My agent had suggested wreck diving as a subject I might use for the Key West background. I resisted at first, feeling that it had all been done too many times before, and I didn't know anything about scuba diving and wasn't interested anyway. She paid no attention to such nonsense and mailed me four issues of *National Geographic* with accounts of treasure brought up in recent years from Caribbean wrecks. Eventually, I was able to write those diving scenes with confidence. I was under water in my imagination, while my typewriter stayed dry.

A rule learned long ago: *If you don't know, find out.* Once you have your facts right, your imagination can take you anywhere you want to go.

9. I like to be specific about the questions I must find answers for before I begin to write. Very early in my plotting phase, I jot down all those questions for which I have no answers.

When I feel becalmed, I take out the list, cross off those that have been answered, and add others to the list. Since I never throw away any of my plotting material, but keep it all in labeled envelopes, I can give you examples of some questions that I wrote down when I was in the middle of writing *Emerald.* They will mean nothing to anyone else, but may give you a glimpse of the method I have found worked for me.

What action does Linda take to protect Monica from suspicion in Saxon's death?

What does Carol learn from Henry Arlen, without realizing until later what he has told her?

What about Linda's quarrel with Saxon? When? Where?

126

These go on and on, and when nothing else works, I turn to my question list and pick one of them to *think* about *at that moment*. This is the time for thinking, not writing. When the answers begin to come, my interest grows and I can push ahead.

10. Somewhere during this time, I may search back into my own life and emotions. What have I felt deeply about? What has angered me? What has made me happy? Parallels between our own emotions and those of our characters are always important. We can pull those feelings out of memory and apply them to the people in our stories.

Discouragement need never be permanent. It only feels that way while you are going through it. Stir up your imagination. Put in new combinations, new energy—open all those closed doors! Once you see what's out there, you won't be able to resist stepping through to make the novel in your typewriter even better.

27

THE LISTENING EAR

By Anne Chamberlain

"DUMB!" The unseen woman in the next booth exclaimed, "about as dumb as a coon in a tree, that's my opinion, and who knows better'n me?"

"You're the one as knows," an eager girlish voice supplied.

"More brains than you can shake a stick at, and turns them all the wrong way, that's my opinion. Why, let me tell you now what she done last Wednesday afternoon, nobody home, and in she snaked and I think she got into my parlor table drawer, read my postcards—my bills too, electric and the gas, she read, and that weren't the worst of it. Let me tell you . . ." The narrative slipped into a tantalizing whisper, incoherent to the casual listener. I was that listener, a traveler, enjoying a quick stopover meal at the village restaurant. Not having previously noticed the two women, I now realized that I probably wouldn't catch a good look if I left before they did. Fascinated, I lingered for a few minutes, and was rewarded with the suddenly loud, dramatic final line: "And then she ate the *whole* watermelon!"

Over the mountainous miles of the homeward drive, over the years since, this delectable tidbit remains one of the small treasures in my memory. A "treasure" it can be justly termed, for, with the intimate village atmosphere, the rural idiom and emphasis of the narrator, the avid (perhaps fawning?) attendance of her companion, this fragment limns a scene, hints at characterization, suggests numerous stories. What a sneaky, spiteful, absurd act, eating somebody's watermelon! And why would the marauder, obviously well known to the victim, indulge in so barbaric a feast? Were they feuding neighbors, rivals in quilting club contests, jealous sisters-in-law, or simply harborers of a longtime natural animosity? A humorous situation, certainly, which—as always with comedy—would be seasoned with sound psychological undertones. Over the countless possibilities, the listener/writer can muse, fantasize, and, in due time, select that which seems most suitable to his particular talents.

For me as an author, cultivating an astute ear for dialogue is a lifelong process. Having grappled with the task of presenting dramatic scenes on paper, of distilling ordinary speech for extraordinary effects, yet of preserving the tones and rhythm of natural talk, I have become a student, a collector, and a connoisseur. Mine is not a calculated eavesdropping. The phrases, fragments of discussion, and sometimes complete anecdotes that reach my ears by chance are tossed into the air wherever people gather and talk, free to any and all who pay attention. They are often delightfully unexpected, and in afterthought, may lend themselves to fascinating interpretations.

In restaurants, airports, stores, hotel lobbies, elevators, the listener finds rich fields to explore. Settings for arrivals and departures may be especially fruitful:

"Please," a woman clutches at the arm of her escort; they are standing in line at the airport, he with a gleaming briefcase, she—apparently—about to say goodbye: "I ask you once more, Arthur, please . . ." He does not answer, nor does he look at her. Her fingers tighten on his sleeve. "Arthur, I'm asking," she murmurs, her voice sinking into a whisper.

For what is she pleading? That he phone at the customary time tonight, forgetting this morning's argument? That he look up the wayward son, who in the city of the father's destination, has recently moved in with an objectionable girl friend? That he think more carefully before he accepts the promotion that will take them from the home and neighborhood she has learned to love? Is he usually "Arthur" to her or, in more relaxed moments, "Art"? Does he remain silent because he is angry, or merely bored?

The listener knows only that she is serious about something, that he is adamant. An alert ear learns the importance of inflection. How many dozens of ways there are of saying "please"! Politely, as a vocal punctuation, urgently, sardonically, savagely, humbly, sometimes a mixture of emotions pour into the single syllable. "It isn't what he said, it's the way he said it," is the frequent plaintive tagline of an anecdote, when the narrator remembers the direct quote but realizes that—in itself—this fails to capture the impact. It is the desperate, last-minute quality of the airport woman's utterance, the breathlessness, the sleeve-clutching, the fading into a whisper that dramatizes her words. Were the writer to develop a story line from this episode, he would use the verbs, adjectives, and action detail to present the dialogue within its emotional context.

Perhaps Arthur is indeed expecting to be offered a promotion, his acceptance of which will take them and their children to a much larger city, a strange and—to Millicent, his wife—a frightening environment. It means transplanting their two youngsters, in sensitive early teen years, to more urban schools and (she suspects) more hazardous temptations. Ashamed as she is to admit it, she hates leaving the house she has cherished for years, the garden she has lovingly tended, the church and the women's clubs; oh, she loves him far more than any *place*, he surely knows this, but isn't she human, doesn't her own life, don't the lives of the children count? The present action, which seems to have evolved easily from Millicent's point of view, could be unfolded within the airport setting, as they arrive, check in, wait, continue the discussion that may have previously waxed into an argument, softened into mutual understanding, flared again into anger. Brief flashbacks, dramatizing the tensions, could be woven into the immediate scene, which builds to the last few minutes, as they stand in line. At this point, even though the situation may have been artfully developed, it would be temptingly easy to overwrite:

"Please," she begged wistfully, clutching at his sleeve, pouring her heart into this last minute entreaty, "I ask you once more, Arthur, please . . ."

Stone-faced, stubbornly silent, he stood, refusing to look at her.

"Arthur," tears surged into her voice. Her fingers tightened on his sleeve, as though she would hold him, draw him to her, fold him into her arms, "I'm asking . . ." Her voice sank into a whisper, a strangled sob.

He stared coldly and mutely into space.

This has too much trimming. Overembellishment is a weakness common to the writing of dialogue. If the author astutely employs other techniques, descriptions of characters and of setting, perhaps subjective delineation of the unspoken feelings of one or more of those concerned, the actual spoken exchange should need little adornment. Knowing Millicent and Arthur, through their airport wait and through the thoughts and the flashback episodes that have illuminated their tensions, the reader understands much of what is not spoken at their parting. Seeing him board the plane, Millicent knows that some day she and the children will be boarding with him. Or she realizes, only dimly yet, as she turns from waving goodbye, that this time he is truly leaving, she is going home. One story possibility; airports bustle with them.

The listening author discriminates. It would impossible to hear, much less to heed, the countless words that may be spoken around one in the course of a crowded day. As a fiction writer, I have a built-in tape recorder, which, for my purposes, is more convenient and dependable than its mechanical counterpart. It receives constantly; it erases the superfluous; it may splice; it will store what seems worth keeping.

"I went downtown this morning—oh the loveliest day, I just can't tell you! Sunshine and breeze and spring everywhere, I danced, danced on my toes all the way, and right at the corner by the mailbox, you can't imagine who I saw, I ran right into her, I hadn't seen her for—you can't imagine how long!— centuries! And you'll never guess what she told me, she came right out with it—" the young woman babbles merrily to her hairdresser, a captive but not uninterested audience, "on the street, on the corner by the mailbox, I'll have you know, she told me, might have been saying, 'it's a nice day,' she was that nonchalant, she came right out with it—"

An individual's speech is as unique as his handwriting, his manner of dress, his voice, walk, gestures, his smile and his eyes. This woman talks in hyperbole, loves to prattle, and contrives through suspenseful hints to keep her audience attentive:

"She was divorced, that's what she said, cool as a cucumber, and then before I got over *that,* I mean I'd barely begun to digest it, she goes right on to say she's married again. Can you imagine! And all within five minutes, well no more than ten, and here I am, my jaw just dropping and she says, 'I thought you knew, didn't you know,' and I said no I didn't know, how could I, hadn't seen, hadn't heard a word about her in centuries and—" to a murmured question from the beautician, "didn't I tell you *who* she is? Well-l-l . . ." Into a genealogical chart she spins, spilling names, father, grandfather, uncle, aunts, first husband and, "a Hardquist, of course, and you do, well maybe you don't know the Hardquists but he, number one husband I mean, he was a chip off the old block, his father Jedson, *the* Jedson, and what I couldn't tell you, my dear, about Jedson Hardquist—"

Seated two chairs away in the beauty salon, I reflect that shocking news, delivered bluntly by a mailbox, might—for a minute or two— silence the babbler's torrential monologue. And I ponder over that woman, "as cool as a cucumber," with the mixed-up marital history. And what about Jedson? I will be hearing more, for I, too, am a captive audience.

In dramatizing the speech mannerisms of the babbler, who can rapidly become a loquacious bore, the writer must aim to convey her effect on others without producing a similar tedium in the reader. One quoted paragraph, like that above, can characterize her compulsive gushiness, and additional phrases will suggest all that is not on paper. While the incessant talker is particularly difficult to harness in dialogue, the need for pruning and culling applies to the speech of all characters.

"No, I didn't know about the Hardquists," the beautician interposes pointedly. She is tired of the monologue. Perhaps she dislikes scurrilous gossip; too much of it whirls around her shop. And is there, in the weary but gentle rebuke of her tone, a distaste for the whole carefree society, the smug, prosperous, much-married and divorced people about whom she hears so much? A story, a hundred or more stories could be written from the point of view of a skilled and patient beautician.

In contrast with the fluent monologuist, the terse speaker, who favors a form of verbal shorthand, poses a different challenge to the writer. Often his reticence can be dramatized through the speeches addressed to him. In the hotel lobby, I notice the young wife greeting her husband enthusiastically:

"How was your morning?"
"Same as ever." He kisses her amiably and takes her arm, steering her to the dining room.

She has come into town from suburbia. They will lunch together, and I reflect that she is hungry for excitement and news.

"Same?" She pouts, teasing him. "Oh, you, it's always the same, same, same," and pats his arm, "but what about Chalmers? Anything happen?"
He motions toward the hostess, they are conducted to a table, sit down, order cocktails.

From this overheard exchange, I spin an imaginative continuation, just enough to suggest more:

"You haven't told me about Chalmers. . . ."

"Fired," he lights a cigarette.

"Oh no! Oh how terrible, was he upset, how did he take it? Oh poor Lydia—"

He has opened the menu. "Think I'll have the steak."

"Did he come in? Did you see him? What did he *do?*"

"Yes," he smiles to the waitress, as she places the cocktails before them, "I think we'll order now."

With this taciturn man, who may have excellent reasons for not wanting to tell his wife about Chalmers, the problem is to convey what he does not choose to say; much can be achieved through action detail.

Fine stories have been written without a scrap of dialogue; others have consisted entirely of spoken words. Most authors use direct quotes at high dramatic points, emphasizing and advancing the narrative. Often, I become so absorbed with other aspects of the story that I do not give enough consideration to the question: Would this character say this in this way? By cultivating the listening ear, I am more aware of natural speech and more alert to those weaknesses that may be distilled into direct quotes.

I have learned to be wary of the overly structured sentence, the too complete and well-rounded paragraph. It is not inconceivable (in writing, nothing is!) for the anguished husband, leaving his wife, suitcase packed and hand on doorknob, to address her: "Much as I love you and always will, our marriage has become totally incompatible, is beyond the help of counselors, and is mutually erosive to our respective personalities." Not inconceivable, as this husband may be a person addicted to eloquence; one does imagine that, if he used such terms, his wife willingly opened the door for him. It is more likely that he would speak briefly, might shout, mumble, lunge out of the house. Under intense emotional pressure, a character's talk is usually jagged, sentences incomplete, feelings too deep for balanced, measured phrases.

A vehement discussion may go on for thousands of words, lasting a whole evening, and to report it literally would not only cover dozens of pages but would bury the story in the process. I am, therefore, aware that I must delete and, if I listen as an author may, I find myself deleting swiftly, editing what I hear, saving what is worthwhile.

"I told him in no uncertain terms," said the portly man at the bus stop, "that his attitude was depressing. demoralizing, and disappointing." He paused,

133

groped for another alliterative adjective, exploded triumphantly, "destructive." He bit at his cigar. "Yes," I told him—"destructive!"

His companion nodded sagely and stroked his drooping moustache. "You
told him off, Fred, you surely did. I wish I had your gift for language. But
what'd he say? Fred, what *did* he say?"

The bus arrived, they climbed on together, still talking. . . .

The listening bystander will not know what he said. Or how he
managed to be all of those adjectives, rolled into one, or were these
faults pure imaginings of a pompous fellow worker? Was our denoun-
cer guilty of the very accusations he so relished? A distinct possibility.
A story? I muse.

Cultivating the listening ear is an educational process that helps me
write dialogue I have never heard until I imagine the characters and
what they are saying; it is also a rich source, an inexhaustible mine of
material. Of perhaps a thousand tidbits that I overhear and speculate
about, only one or two may combine within the ever mysterious creative self to produce a story. Constant entertainment is at my command.
I can turn on that tape recorder which, in the depths of memory, is
always waiting, brimming with ideas.

How did matters finally work out for Arthur and Millicent? Maybe
he wasn't considering a promotion, after all. She might have been
pleading because, in the city of his destination, there lived that former
secretary, the golden-haired and lynx-eyed, the sly and determined,
with whom Arthur was still in touch. He had said it would be stupid,
plain unfriendly not to look her up, at least to telephone; why, she and
Millicent had been on good terms, hadn't they? She had made the
mistake of protesting and had lighted the match—or had the fire been
simmering already? Another story.

The babbler in the beauty shop prates on. In the next chair may be
Old Jedson Hardquist's third wife, young, sharp-eared, new to town,
rapidly absorbing important information. Or the patient beautician,
scissoring deftly, may have had, as her last client, the carefree "cool as
a cucumber" woman who had met the babbler at the mailbox. Anything
can happen; the listener can pick and choose.

How did poor Chalmers react to being fired? Will the eager wife ever
learn details from her cautious husband? Was the portly man's unknown target actually "depressing, demoralizing, disappointing, and
destructive"? Delectable, that phrasing, in its pompous smugness.

Come to think of it, how big was that watermelon?

28

HANDLING TIME IN FICTION

By Jonathan Penner

"BEGIN at the beginning," the King of Hearts commanded the White Rabbit in *Alice in Wonderland*. "Go on till you come to the end. Then stop."

In fiction, the arrangement of time is rarely so simple. Odd as it seems, not all stories stop at the chronological end. Some have circular patterns, concluding in the middle of the events they narrate. One or two even run backwards, starting with the final event and ending with the first.

But it's the beginnings of stories that present the most nettlesome problems. The very notion of a "beginning" is not philosophically secure. Everything comes *from* something, which in turn comes from something else. The selection of any starting point is a more or less violent imposition of order upon the flux of events.

A more practical problem is that once you've selected what feels like a beginning—someone waking up in the morning, or someone getting sick with the flu, or someone's first day on the job—you may find that it's dull stuff. And the start of a story is where you *must* be interesting. Though wonderful scenes may follow, the reader won't get to them if the opening is a bore.

Fortunately, what occurs first *chronologically* needn't come first *narratively*. You can begin your story partway through its chain of events, choosing material that's vivid, suggestive, amusing, tense. You can introduce your central character, and provide at least a thread-end of plot.

The opening is a huckster, a harlot. Engage the reader, charm him, seduce him, until he surrenders to your cause—until the critic in him concedes that he is going to finish this story. Then you can go back in time for relatively dull but indispensable background information.

135

In a few stories, of course, the handling of time presents no problem. These stories usually comprise a single scene, with little need for background. They may deal with a span of time no greater than that required to read them: perhaps ten minutes in a character's life.

But usually the author must choose where to launch into the river of events. And though his journey is with the current, at some point he must portage upstream to inspect the watersheds from which his story springs.

How far should you carry your story's first forward rush before providing a flashback? How long should the flashback continue before you return to the main story?

Each story will dictate its own rhythms. But a fair principle, albeit one easier to state than to apply, is to continue forward from your opening point until the reader's curiosity about the past outweighs his curiosity about the future.

You won't, in general, insert a flashback right in the middle of fascinating action. That merely frustrates the reader, who is trying to find out what happens next—not what happened a long time ago.

But at a certain moment he will *want* a flashback. He'll want to know how things got like this, what makes these people the way they are. He may require orientation: time, place, relationships. This is the moment—when the story has completed its first advance—to direct the reader's attention to such anterior matters.

Now: how do you move back and forth between the two time periods—the one that's *narratively* first (which we're calling, for convenience, the "main" time period) and the one that's *chronologically* first (the flashback material)?

The technique chiefly involves the use of appropriate verb tenses—complemented by indicators such as "now" and "back then"—to let readers know where they are in time.

A detailed example follows. At the start of our story, fifteen-year-old Cameron Pearl is going to have his hair cut. But we also want to include a flashback, dealing with Cameron's barbershop experiences when he was a little boy.

We begin in the *simple past* tense. (Yes, some stories are told in the present tense, and require slightly different mechanics.) Verbs in the simple past tense are *italicized*.

(1) One morning soon after his fifteenth birthday, Cameron Pearl *entered* Willy's Barber Shop, sliding around the half-open door as though he *hoped* nobody would notice his arrival. But the place *was* empty except for Willy himself, slowly pushing a broom. He *welcomed* Cameron with a toothy grin. "Into the chair, young fella." In no time at all, the familiar laundry-smelling sheet *was* around Cameron's neck, and he *heard* the rapid snip-snip-snip of the approaching scissors.

Suppose we insert our flashback right here. To let the reader know what's happening, we switch from the simple past tense to the PAST PERFECT tense (the "had" tense). Verbs in the past perfect tense are CAPITALIZED.

(2A) Cameron HAD BEEN coming to Willy for haircuts ever since first grade. In the early years he HAD ENJOYED it.

If that's enough flashback, and we want to return to the main story, we let the reader know it by returning to the simple past tense:

But now, staring at the eternally half-filled bottles aligned on the shelf below Willy's mirror, all he *felt* was boredom and irritation. "Leave it long in back," he *sighed*.

Smooth enough. But suppose we want a longer flashback? Won't page after page of the past perfect tense—"had done," "had said," "had thought," and so on—become a nuisance? It will indeed. A more graceful technique is to ease into the simple past as soon as we've gone far enough with the past perfect to establish that this is indeed a flashback.

Here's an example. In all that follows, verbs in the simple past are *italicized* and verbs in the past perfect are CAPITALIZED. Please reread paragraph (1) above. Then continue on with the following, and watch for the switch.

(2B) Cameron HAD BEEN coming to Willy for haircuts ever since first grade. In the early years he HAD ENJOYED it—paging through magazines while he *waited*, climbing into the throne-like chair, the tickle of the shears, the hot lather, and finally the cool air on his awakened neck when he *left* the shop. Because there *were* busy streets to cross, he always *came* with his father, who in those days *had* a full head of silver-blond hair. Cameron *thought* it so handsome that he *hated* to see the first locks of it fall to the floor.

His father always *entered* the chair first, and Cameron would pretend

(Note this "would" tense, which is often useful in flashbacks. It indicates habitual activity in the past.)

to read *Esquire* or the *Police Gazette* while he *listened* to the conversation of the men. Regulars, most of them: men like Mr. Hastings, from the candy store, and Dr. Albrecht, and Mr. Kutzko, who *owned* the shoe store. When they *talked* politics, Cameron *felt* proud—his father *knew* more than anyone, and they all *listened* with respect. But when the discussion *turned* to sports, Cameron *sat* in dread. His father's unconcerned ignorance about baseball *was* shocking—Cameron himself *knew* more—and he *prayed* silently that his father would say nothing at all.

See? We've finessed our way out of that awkward "had" tense and are now narrating the flashback in the simple past tense. We can stay in the simple past for the rest of the flashback—though if it were extremely long we'd look for ways to remind the reader, every so often, that it *is* a flashback, not the main story. That would prevent a jolt when the flashback ends.

Now, let's prepare to end our flashback, to get on with the story of fifteen-year-old Cameron and toothily grinning Willy. Can we go straight back to the simple past tense with which we began the story?

No—because we've just been giving the flashback, too, in the simple past tense. The reader wouldn't know where one ended and the other began. So we unobtrusively return to the past perfect tense to finish the flashback. Again, watch for the switch.

Fortunately, his father never *did*—he only *nodded* gravely at the recitations of statistics, the predictions and postmortems. And gradually Cameron HAD COME to understand that this *was* all that wisdom *was*—knowing what you *knew* and what you *didn't*. It *was* a discouraging insight, and once he HAD HAD it, he *lost* a degree of respect for his father. And it *was* then that he HAD STARTED enjoying his visits to the barber less.

By returning to the past perfect tense, we've reminded the reader that this is a flashback. Next we'll signal, with a shift from the past perfect tense to the simple past (and with the extremely useful word "now"), our return to the main story.

Now, staring at the eternally half-filled bottles aligned on the shelf below

138

Willy's mirror, all he *felt* was boredom and irritation. "Leave it long in back," he *sighed*.

From this point, the story will continue forward in the simple past tense to its conclusion—or until the next flashback.

I should like to make one more point about flashbacks, a point also illustrated by our tale of Cameron Pearl. Many writers are under the impression that, in order to go back in time, you have to have your central character *remember* past events.

This is emphatically not so. In fact, few devices of fiction are cornier or phonier than forcing bouts of nostalgia upon your central character.

Yes, people do sometimes remember things—but seldom with the coherence and completeness that flashbacks require. Yet many a character in fiction is made to relive the past regardless of psychological plausibility, regardless of what would more likely occupy his mind at the moment. Character is falsified for the sake of the reader's education. "Stanley stared out the window, letting his mind drift back—back—back to the time when . . ."

But if you keep that glassy stare out of Stanley's eyes, how will you enter the flashback?

The answer is that you simply *tell* us what happened in the past. No need for Stanley or anyone else to glaze over and remember. Just tell us. Telling is narration: as used here, the words are synonyms. This is one of the things narration, or narrative, is for.

I think there are two reasons many writers are uncomfortable with narrative—with telling. The first is that they were raised on movies and television, in which almost nothing *can* be told. In a visual medium, everything must be dramatized—shown.

The other reason is that some writing teacher, perhaps in high school, issued a commandment: "*Show,* don't tell." Misapplication of this excellent advice has caused incalculable mischief.

What the aphorism *does* mean is that you shouldn't (for example) tell us "Cameron's father was prudent" and expect us to believe it. Instead, you've got to present Cameron's father in such a way—for instance, by having him stay within his area of expertise when shooting the bull in the barbershop—that the reader himself comes to the conclusion that the man was prudent.

"Show, don't tell," does *not* mean that you can't narrate your story! Notice that we didn't make Cameron sit there in the barber chair remembering his childhood. Fidelity to point of view requires that the flashback be limited to what Cameron *could* remember—it can't deal with material unknown to him—but not that he actually do the remembering.

We simply *told* the reader, "Cameron had been coming to Willy for haircuts ever since first grade." And our flashback continued from there.

29

THE PRACTICE AND THE PASSION

By Elisabeth Ogilvie

THERE are three gifts which you already have if you are a writer, either established or on the way. But they may need to be developed; it's not enough to be born with perfect pitch and an acute musical ear: We have to learn music as our second language, and the technique of our chosen instrument.

The three gifts are: the *power of observation*, a *free-roving imagination*, and a *passionate love affair with words*.

The three are absolutely essential for any aspect of creative writing, but I am going to talk specifically about using them to create background, a background that will be far more than the mere platform for the story, but an inescapable and *alive* part of the story. I have often called background the most important character, because my people act and react in response to their environment. They are its creatures, whether they want to be or not. It either blesses or betters them.

Though I didn't set out at the age of five or six to be a writer (it was a choice then between a cowboy or a mother), I know now that I was in training. I had such an infatuation with words, the looks and sounds of them, that even now I can taste that lovely one, "ibex." *I is for Ibex*, I read, and was smitten like stout Cortez upon his peak in Darien.

Certain lines of poetry retain for me the original glory with which they burst upon a child. "What was he doing, the Great God Pan, down in the reeds by the river?" And there's "October's bright blue weather." There were the asters by the brookside that made asters in the brook; every September the drifts of wild lavender-blue asters shock me with the same delight I knew then, when I first saw poetry become reality, and vice versa. It's as fresh and strong as ever. I was absolutely enraptured with lines from the Psalms: "And he shall be like a tree planted by the rivers of water, that bringeth forth his fruit in his season." What did

141

it mean? At six I didn't really know, but I did know that it was rich and beautiful.

You know what it's like. Our memory banks are stuffed with ravishing treasures collected by our five senses.

Remembering those schoolroom adventures, try two schoolroom exercises; they work well, no matter how old you are. Examine a picture that is new to you. It doesn't matter whether it's a photograph, a reproduction of a painting, a scene on a calendar or a postcard— anything will do as long as it's fairly complicated. First write a quick survey of instant impressions—what immediately hits you—and then do a detailed description, not missing the smallest thing. The more you look, the more you'll find. Try for different ways to describe colors and shapes. Make your word picture as lively as possible. Not only did I do this in the second grade, but I do it now. I've never walked high on a mountain anywhere, let alone in the Highlands of Scotland, but I can describe what a camera or an artist sees from up there. I have seen for myself the shapes of mountains against the sky, and their white skeins of waterfalls, but the rest has to come from somewhere else.

That's observation of what someone else has recorded. Now for the first-hand side of it. Did you ever have to write paragraphs describing something you'd seen? I did, and I have a school notebook of my mother's, dating from the early 1890's. Every day the children were required to write for ten minutes about something they had observed the day before.

Wherever you are, town or country, you're surrounded by wealth. Take a bit of it each day and describe it in detail. People, place. Sounds, smells. Search out the tiniest particulars; don't dismiss anything as trivia. Try to make the vignette come alive for someone who hasn't the slightest conception of the reality.

Spending at least a half-hour a day on this—faithfully—will show you great results in a week—assuming that you have the passion to commit yourself to it. Minute observation will become second nature to you in time, like any other skill which, as you become expert, doesn't require a conscious, labored effort.

The effort comes at the beginning, and I can't overemphasize the need for concentration and fidelity. You know when is the best time of day for you to write, when your mind is sharpest and the words come easiest. (I'm supposing that you're trying to squeeze out time before or after your day's work, whether that's at home or outside.) Early in the morning is best for me, before the world gets at me. But some people do better when everything quiets down for the night.

The important thing is to do something *every* day, whether in practice or in execution, until you can't kick the habit, and a day without writing at least a paragraph will seem a day wasted. If you find the words coming hard, try something else, as long as you keep writing. If you don't see anything around you that appeals, write from memory and get a little exercise for those muscles. And don't throw anything away even if you don't think it's much good. Put it out of sight for a week. It may look a lot better to you then, or worthy of revision, which will give you another good exercise.

Now that you're getting pretty good at this observation business, you're ready to work on your imagination. Going back to my mountain-side, I have collected all the available facts, but it's my imagination that will put me there, to hear the rushing streams and breathe the pure cold air, watch an eagle or a ptarmigan. I am now in my character's skin, discovering how she responds to her present environment and to the circumstances that have put her there.

Make yourself the principal actor in one of your scenes. Be someone who is either frightened, depressed, guilty, hopeful, haunted, or joyful. How does your setting affect this version of *You?* Does it terrify or exhilarate? Does everyone and everything look wonderful to you, or awful? If it's quiet, does this unnerve you or do you savor it? If it's noisy, do you want to explode, run from the noise, or go with it?

One of these exercise sessions could develop into a story or even a novel for you. It has happened for me. I keep doing these things because I need the practice, and once in a while something takes root. If I don't do anything with it now, it's in a safe place, quietly growing in the dark, and one day I'll bring it out into the light to blossom.

Let us suppose that one of these plot seedlings is rooted in a land-scape you must imagine from pictures and maps. So you need to do some research. I equate research with passion, because you have to really *care* (and I split that infinitive on purpose) to go digging for material and to keep at it. But let me caution you about getting bogged down in it. My own system is to work out the action, to be sure it moves right along, placed against the sketchiest of backgrounds. If I keep stopping the forward movement to look something up, I'll lose the flow.

So this first draft is full of handwritten marginal notes, or messages typed in capitals and starred with red ink. DON'T FORGET IT'S RAINING. CHECK BIRDS. FIGURE OUT TERRAINS FOR THIS SCENE. FIX!!!

Meanwhile I have done or am still doing my required reading at periods kept well apart from writing time. After I reach a good stopping place in my very messy first draft, I settle down to put the mish-mash into shape. This is the real writing, when each scene is treated as a separate entity and done with as much color and detail and emotion as possible, using the notes from my research. My thesaurus too, I should add.

In writing *Jennie About to Be,* though I knew much Scottish history and have been to Scotland, there was plenty I didn't know. So I had to find out what flora and fauna my people could expect to find on their long walk through the Highlands, what surprises the weather could come up with, and what mysterious phenomena might occur, like the Great Grey Man, and so forth. (He was suspected of being a ghost.)

Through guidebooks and maps I traced out a rough route for the walkers, though I didn't use actual place names until they reached their destination, which was and is a real town. By keeping the mountains and lochs anonymous, or inventing names for them, I allowed myself freedom for my imagination and kept myself from making glaring errors of ignorance. And then there were those paintings and photographs, into which I had thought myself so completely.

When I sat down to flesh out the bones of the story, I was there. To make this background come alive and show how Jennie was emotionally involved with it, I had to be passionate about its creation from the start until it was in its final version on the printed page.

Whether you are using a time and a place you know well, or a locale and period for which you have to mine the information, your characters' love or loathing for their environment will be an integral part of them if you can convey through your words their visceral reaction to what there is to love or loathe. Your gift of observation will make you instinctively add those seemingly insignificant touches that add up to authenticity. Your imagination will put you on the scene in your protagonist's skin; *your* senses will be taking in everything, *your* heart will be thudding in suspense, because *your* passion had taken charge.

30

HOW TO BE YOUR OWN CRITIC

By Margaret Chittenden

ONE of our most difficult tasks as writers is to be objective about our own work. It's not easy to convince ourselves once a novel is finished that this is not necessarily the greatest story ever told. But we have to be honest with ourselves. We have to learn to criticize our manuscripts *constructively,* one step at a time. What should we look for?

From time to time, as I've read novel manuscripts by unpublished authors, I've discovered three main flaws that occur over and over again: the *beginning* is too slow, the *middle* is padded with irrelevant action, and the *ending* is either too long, or too unbelievable, or both.

Beginnings

The beginning of a novel should introduce your main characters, show where the story is taking place, and hint at the conflict. But none of these things should be revealed under static conditions. The story should get under way with the first word on the first page. The reader does not want to wade through a whole river of information and description of the characters before the story gets moving.

Yet many novel manuscripts that I've read either start out with long, long passages of exposition, or else they start with a paragraph of action and *then* go into long passages of exposition. It is not necessary to tell the reader everything about the main characters in the first chapter; you should hold back some of that information. Often, you can leave some of it out altogether. As the writer, you need to know everything there is to know about the main characters before you start writing the book, but you don't need to tell the reader right off about their parents, grandparents, ex-lovers, degrees they've earned in college, every happening in their lives that took place before the start of the story.

Usually, it's best to begin a novel with some kind of action going on, but not necessarily with the protagonist in an airplane circling the airport just before landing—a very popular opening that gives the main character lots of time for soul-searching. Instead, show the main character doing something, going somewhere, talking to someone. Make the opening *intriguing* and then continue with your characters in action, introducing *short* pieces of information that are essential. Later, you can weave in other essential acts through dialogue and in short quotes from the main character's thoughts. Be sure your reader can tell *where* the story is taking place. Don't open with pages of dialogue without giving at least a hint of the setting and who these characters are. Don't give the impression that the story is set in a drawing room and have it turn out to be in a car or an airplane.

Middles

The middle is the place where the novel should *develop*. Here again, writers often put in too much introspection on the part of the main character. Let your reader know what your main character has on his or her mind, but keep it brief. Also, when you write your original synopsis, make sure that enough *action* takes place in the middle section. Frequently, novel synopses by beginning writers have long beginnings and long endings, but the reader would have to take a giant leap between the two. The story doesn't grab the reader at the start and take him or her *suspensefully* to the end.

In plotting the middle, apply the law of cause and effect. Instead of simply asking, what comes next, ask yourself, what would happen as a *result* of this? When the synopsis is finished, go through and check for the *cause-and-effect*.

Here is an example from the synopsis of my novel, *This Dark Enchantment*. Karin has come to Quebec City to assist Charles in writing an architectural history of the city. *Because* of this she meets Doctor Paul Dufresne, whom she first sees being solicited by a seedy young man who looks as though he's on drugs. *Because* of what she sees, Karin suspects that Paul might be involved in drug dealing. *Because* of this, she is not receptive to his advances, and *because* of this . . . and so on. I don't write the synopsis this straightforwardly, but I do check to make sure it could read that way. Cause and effect—two much neglected, often forgotten words in novel writing.

Endings

If you have your causes and effects in proper sequence, the ending will be logical, though not too predictable. I try to sustain suspense in the main plot while tying up any loose ends in the sub-plots, so that the reader will want to stay with me till THE END. But once I've reached the end, when resolutions or solutions are arrived at, I try to exit as rapidly as possible.

It's also necessary to strive for *believability* in the ending. For example, if you've had your hero being really nasty to the heroine in the beginning—which seems to be a popular thing to do—you can't suddenly have him be sweet and lovable at the end, unless you've shown cause and effect in the middle. Some of the manuscripts I've read in which the hero and heroine ended up at the altar would not convince the reader that any sane woman would want this man, or even want to speak to him again.

Now that you've checked the beginning, middle and end of your novel manuscript, it's time to look at it page by page, word by word.

Try going backwards through the manuscript, one page at a time, so you don't get caught up in the flow of the story. Look first for too many *wells, justs* and *verys,* and cross out most of them. Then check spelling and grammar, looking especially for mistakes in syntax. (In a recent novel manuscript, I read the following: "Her shoulders squared and left the room.")

Check to make sure the nouns are specific, that you have written, "the weeping willow" rather than "the tree," the "cocker spaniel" rather than "the dog."

Scrutinize verbs. Try to replace passive verbs with active verbs. "David hugged Joanna" is stronger than "Joanna was hugged by David."

Cut out as many adjectives and adverbs as you can, and check punctuation. (I have a tendency to forget commas.)

Once all this nit-picking is done, make yourself very comfortable, preferably in a recliner, then read the book from beginning to end, pretending it was written by a writer whose work you don't particularly enjoy. If you find yourself going to sleep, take a long, hard look at the passage that brought on your fatigue. Try to read straight through, as a reader would, making brief notes in the margins of anything obviously wrong—sections that seem slow or dull or unbelievable or trite. Mark scenes that don't seem *visual* enough, transitions that are too abrupt.

Once you've finished this initial reading, revise all the things you've marked. Then read the whole manuscript again. Check the movement of the characters, so that you haven't had a character go off on a week's trip and then be present in a scene that takes place the next day. Check characterization. Have these invented people come to life? Can you see them—not just at the beginning, but all the way through? Do you *care* about them?

I try to check diligently to make sure my heroine has *acted,* not just reacted. I don't care for timid heroines. I want to be sure my young woman has done something for herself and not waited for the hero to initiate all the action. Has *your* heroine come through as a real, caring, compassionate, intelligent woman? If this is a romance novel, is she *worth* loving?

Take a close look at your hero. Is he a real human being with admirable qualities, or is he just an ad for jockey shorts?

Next, check on viewpoint. If the entire novel is told from the heroine's point of view, all of the action must be filtered through her point of view. The reader should not see, hear, learn or observe anything that the heroine cannot see, hear, learn or observe. Some editors have told me they don't mind seeing the viewpoint character from the outside occasionally, but I'm a purist about viewpoint. I try never to write, "Tears rolled down her beautifully sculptured cheeks." One: This sort of thing makes the heroine sound conceited. Two: Such a description jars the reader into looking at the heroine from the outside, instead of looking at everything through her eyes. When in doubt, I change the sentence temporarily into first person. I wouldn't write, "Tears rolled down *my* beautifully sculptured cheeks." So when I'm writing in her viewpoint, my heroine can *feel* her tears, but she can't *see* them. She can *look* at people, but she doesn't look at them with her "sparkling amethyst eyes."

If the writer presents the story from the main character's viewpoint, it's difficult to describe her completely, without using the trite device of having her look in the mirror, but it can be done. In my book *Song of Desire,* for example, Vicki's aunt tells her it's O.K. for her to look like an ad for sunshine and vitamins. Vicki herself complains that when people look at her they say, "Ah, a California Girl," and expect her to run around with a surfboard under her arm and not a thought in her head. Maintaining one viewpoint assures greater reader identification. It also gives unity to the emotions.

However, if your novel is written in multiple viewpoint, you still need to check to be sure that you haven't bounced in and out of several characters' minds in a short space of time. Viewpoint-hopping can be very confusing to a reader.

Once you are sure the viewpoint is consistent, make certain all the characters' actions have been properly motivated, so no one does anything without having a reason. Then ask yourself if any of the dialogue sounds stilted. Do the young people talk as young people do, or do they sound like senior citizens? "That's exceedingly kind of you," for instance, is not something a young person would usually say today.

Next, try to unravel the various threads in your story to make sure you haven't dropped any halfway through the novel, and that they are all tied up at the end. In *Song of Desire,* for example, one thread dealt with the hero's acting career, another with the heroine's career as an interior designer. A third thread dealt with the hero's young sister and her adventures, and a fourth with thefts from a hotel. In a multi-layered novel, it's easy to lose track of one of the threads, so this aspect of the manuscript must be carefully checked.

After all these questions have been answered and all necessary revisions are completed, read the whole manuscript again. By now you should be thoroughly sick of it, so if it still holds *your* interest, it should hold an editor's and a reader's. After this final reading, put the manuscript aside and think the story through, making sure you haven't missed anything significant.

Your aim in all this self-criticism is to produce the best book you can possibly produce. Before you send a completed manuscript to an agent or an editor, it should be the best work you can do. This is the writer's responsibility, the writer's task, the writer's joy.

31

LET YOUR DIALOGUE SPEAK FOR ITSELF

By Randall Silvis

LET US ASSUME that you know how to write good dialogue. This might be a dangerous assumption, but it is a necessary one; no one can train a tone-deaf writer to have a sharp ear for the rhythms and patterns of natural-sounding speech, for the infinitely rich music of the human language. Either you can carry that particular tune or you cannot. It is what is called talent, and talent, like blue eyes or a freckled nose, is a gift. Such gifts are not rare among us. What is rare is the drive to perfect the talent, the tenacity and compulsion that seem to grow stronger with each rejection.

What can and must be learned, then, is how to use your gift effectively to create realistic dialogue, how to make your characters' words an integral part of the story, so they serve a purpose other than padding or diversion—a mere fattening up of the story's physical dimensions.

Dialogue, like every other component of the successful piece of fiction, performs a function. It *does* something; that is why it is there. Dialogue can be used, in fact, to perform several functions—sometimes singly, often three or four simultaneously. But if too much of your dialogue goes nowhere, if your characters talk a lot but say nothing, your fiction is destined to hit a sour note.

One of the most important functions of dialogue is characterization. Through his own words, a character comes alive. You might have described him vigorously, or painted a wonderfully telling portrait of him, but not until that character speaks will he step off the flat page and into the multi-dimensional arena of the reader's imagination. Through his own words, a character defines himself and reveals who he is, whether he is trustworthy or deceitful, whether naturally ebullient or chronically depressed. His speech pattern will identify him as erudite or obtuse, an Okie or a New Englander, a stuffed-shirt or a clown. A

150

few lines of well-chosen dialogue provide the perfect application of Hemingway's admonition that a writer must *show, not tell.*

In my novella, *The Luckiest Man in the World,* an adolescent Mexican revolutionary, Emiliano Fortunato, has returned to his mountain village as the only surviving member of an ill-fated regiment. Emiliano tells his mother:

"You will never know, mama, how horrible it was for me. You will never know how bravely I fought. And all to no avail. I sometimes wish that I had not been successful in keeping myself alive."

Because it has already been established through a brief description of the one-sided battle that Emiliano survived not through heroics but through his own negligence, the reader immediately gains an insight into the boy's basic nature. How much better it is to allow Emiliano to reveal his true character in this way than to intrude with a mechanistic pronouncement such as: "Emiliano Fortunato was a liar and a braggart, and very often displayed a tendency toward self-pity." By employing dialogue I have *shown, not told* the reader what kind of person Emiliano is. Emiliano Fortunato will be a fuller, more believable creation because of it.

At the same time that dialogue is delineating character, it can be establishing the tone or mood of a particular scene. The manner in which characters address one another, for example—answering a question with another question; engaging in lighthearted repartee; exchanging caustic, guarded remarks—can draw a reader into the scene by making him "feel" its electricity and excitement, its dynamism. A long passage of dialogue, if handled skillfully, can keep the reader enthusiastically flipping the pages, because in his mind he smells the burning fuse that signals the inevitable explosion of accumulating tensions. Even a relatively brief passage can do much to invigorate a scene, just as a loud exclamation can in an instant silence and electrify a crowded room.

In this example from my story "Trash Man," Warren Schimmel, a trash collector, and his wife Sharon are about to begin the morning run. What we already know, through exposition, is that Sharon is driving the garbage truck today because Warren's helper has been accidentally injured, and that Warren holds himself responsible for the accident.

What we do not yet know is how Warren's sense of guilt has affected his relationship with his wife. In this scene, as Warren stands on the running board and clings to the side of the truck, Sharon asks him to sit in the cab until they reach the first pick-up point. Warren declines.

"What's the sense in freezing yourself to death?" she asked.
"Just drive," he said.
"You'd better get a hold of yourself."
"Just *drive,*" he said.
"You've acting like a baby."
"For Christ's sake, Sharon," he said, leaning back wearily against the barrel-shaped hull, "can't you just shut up and drive?"

This simple and unexceptional exchange of remarks accomplishes two things: First, it contrasts Sharon's no-nonsense, practical nature with her husband's laconic, preoccupied attitude (i.e., it delineates character); secondly, by creating a tension between the two characters, it helps to establish the mood. The reader senses without being told that a resolution of one kind or another, either showdown or surrender, is inevitable.

If a passage of dialogue succeeds in animating a story, in making it come alive with a sense of imminent conflict, that dialogue also advances the plot and hones an edge on the tension, thereby bringing the reader more quickly to the story's climax. And the advancement of plot is a third function of dialogue.

It would not be difficult for a writer to tell his entire story through narrative alone. It would not be difficult, but it would not be very entertaining, either. Consider Hemingway's *A Farewell to Arms.* Instead of the teasing banter between Rinaldi and Frederick Henry, instead of the lovely, bittersweet, understated conversations between Henry and Catherine Barkley, the author could have condensed each passage into a few informative words:

After Catherine Barkley met Frederic Henry, she decided she liked him better than she liked Rinaldi.

Or this:

After rowing across the lake to Switzerland, Catherine and Frederick had breakfast at a small café. The café had no rolls. Catherine said she did not mind. Then they were arrested.

152

Fortunately, such uninspired summarization is not the task of the fiction writer. Fiction must live and breathe. Characters and situations must be made so vivid, so compelling, that for a short while the reader is able to ignore the growl of the neighbor's lawnmower, the children arguing, the nagging, bothersome banalities of his daily life. The reader immerses himself as beguiled spectator in a larger-than-life scenario, and it is the task of the fiction writer to keep him beguiled until the story achieves its natural end.

Although straight narrative can advance a plot faster and less circuitously, dialogue often does it more interestingly. Dialogue allows the reader to eavesdrop and observe. It is the difference between experiencing a summer lightning storm firsthand and having it described for you by someone else. Dialogue might slow down the pace of a story, but it also draws the reader closer to the action, *intensifying* it, letting the reader be surprised by the sudden flash of illumination and then instantly anticipate the crack of thunder, the scent of ozone. In other words, it allows him that vicarious pleasure of "being there," without which a story is mere journalese.

These two functions of dialogue—the advancement of plot and the changing of a story's pace—are quite often separate and yet inseparable. While it is possible to advance plot through dialogue without breaking an established stride, every sentence, whether used to quicken or retard the pace, must bring the reader that much closer to the story's resolution.

In the following two examples from *The Luckiest Man in the World*, dialogue is used to accomplish similar goals, but by different means. Although in both cases the spoken word advances the plot, one does so by speeding up the action, the other by slowing it down.

"Maria is having her baby!" Emiliano cried, breathless and redfaced, his hazel eyes wide with worry.

"Hurry, please!" Emiliano urged the doctor.

Sevilla smiled calmly. "Why?" he asked.

"Why? Sweet Jesus, I told you, Maria is having her baby!"

"So?" Sevilla said.

"What do you mean, so? Aren't you coming? She needs you!"

"The midwife can attend to her."

"I don't want that old witch near Maria! Please, doctor, I know you're angry with me, but can't you forget about it for now? I'm sorry I said what I did. Won't you please come? Maria needs you!"

"You're sorry?" Sevilla asked.
"Yes, truly, a hundred times!"

In the pages preceding this passage, the pace was leisurely, almost lethargic. But a few lines of dialogue can set the story off on a run again, imbuing it with a sense of urgency. Compare that effect to the following:

"Maria's crazy," Emiliano whispered to Rosarita, as though imparting a secret. "Her mind has been all stirred up like a sopa seca. We'll find another place for your mother to live, and then I'll move in with you. We will be the king and queen of Torrentino, guapa. You'll be the first mother, and I will be papacito grande."
Stretched out beside Rosarita, Emiliano nuzzled her neck and stroked her huge belly.
"You don't need to worry about our baby," he told her. "It's going to be a strong and healthy boy. You wait and see. It was only because of Maria and her stupidity that we lost the first one. But I've been lucky all my life and I can feel in my bones that this baby is going to be fine. He'll grow up to be just as handsome and brave as his father."

Besides adding evidence to what we already know about Emiliano—that he has a conceited, distorted opinion of himself; that he is guileful and hopelessly dishonest—this piece of dialogue provides the opening into a scene that is used as an interlude, a breather between two other scenes of rather frenetic activity. Interludes such as this, if not extended over too many pages, can actually *heighten* the pre-established tension by hinting at the climax, and then holding that climax in abeyance.

To sum up: It is not enough that your dialogue rings true, that it echoes the resonance and rhythms of actual speech, though this is a necessary beginning. But when that task is accomplished, you must ask yourself this: Does each passage of dialogue define or at least contribute to the delineation of character? Does it invigorate the scene with a tangible sense of mood, an enlivening tone of immediacy? Does it provide a change of pace where a change of pace is warranted, and in so doing, continue to advance the plot? If you can answer yes to at least one of these criteria, and preferably to two or more, give yourself a pat on the back. You are writing now with authority, with control. The "fictive dream," as John Gardner called it, has come alive; incorporeal characters have taken on bulk and density; they speak, they interact, they argue and laugh and make love as convincingly, as comically, as tragically as do the rest of us; and in so doing they have become more interesting, more *real* than reality itself.

In this manner, each passage of dialogue must justify its existence. When it has done so, there remains but one thing for you, the writer, to do. The advice is three hundred years old, but the truth of it ageless: *Trust on,* John Dryden said, *and think tomorrow will repay.*

32

THE NOVEL SYNOPSIS
Your Best Selling Tool

By Serita Deborah Stevens

One of the most difficult problems in writing a novel may be preparing the synopsis, knowing just what it involves and what makes it different from a query, an outline, or a summary. Writing a good synopsis is a skill every novelist today must master.

Most editors, if interested in your novel on the basis of your query, will ask for your synopsis and opening chapters, often called a "partial." If that passes muster, you will then be asked for the complete manuscript. Established writers may be offered a contract on the basis of a partial, but a not-yet-published author will usually be required to submit the complete manuscript first.

The query

The query letter should indicate time, setting, and type of novel—especially if the company publishes more than one genre—and describe the major characters, their problems, their relationship to the other characters, and how the problems are resolved. The query should also include your qualifications and a summary of any special research you have done in preparing to write this novel. Indicate if the book is historical or contemporary. The query letter should be no more than two pages long.

Here is an example:

Dear Editor:
Enclosed find my partial of *Tame the Wild Heart,* a romance novel of about 85,000 words, which takes place in James II's court of Ireland.
Roxanna Alden, 19, niece of the great Irish general Patrick Sarsfield, hates James for what he did to her mother and vows her revenge in the only way she knows how—spying. She knows it would hurt her uncle, who supports James, if he found out, but she cannot let a man like James rule her beloved Ireland.

To her horror, she finds her assignment is to spy on Sebastian Steele, 30, her uncle's aide-de-camp.

Despite her own misgivings she is attracted to Sebastian. With the political intrigues of the day swirling about them, Roxanna must decide if she will betray the memory of her mother, or betray her heart.

In researching this book, I spent time in Ireland and at the British Museum in London.

My previous books are *This Bitter Ecstasy* and *A Dream Forever*.

Sincerely,

Sometimes you can use one or two sentences that sum up the story. For *Torrid January* I wrote: Will the D.A. prosecute the man she loves or will she first prove his innocence?

Also in your query tell the editor about your previous writing experience, whether, for instance, you've worked as a copywriter or done articles for a local newspaper, or related work. Also describe special knowledge that qualifies you to write about the subject. If your heroine is a dancer and you are, too—say so.

A query letter like the one above was my entrée to the Tapestry (Pocket Books) line. The editor then asked to see my partial, then my detailed synopsis.

Often "outline" and "synopsis" are used interchangeably, but they really mean two different things. The outline is only the barest of bones and is often used by the author in plotting the synopsis. I consider the outline for the author's use only; it states the facts but seldom gets into the emotional aspects of the story.

Here is a sample:

Chapter One: Roxanna learns of her new duty. Meets Sebastian as they both go into the castle together. He sees mud on her dress. Does he know where she has been? Will he tell her uncle?

Chapter Two: Attracting the eye of the King, she must fend him off. Sebastian helps her. She should be grateful, but she's angry he had to help her. She becomes ill at the ball. Uncle Patrick asks Sebastian to see her safely home to the manor.

Chapter Three: Waking after the fourth day of illness, she realizes Sebastian has been there taking care of her all the time. Has she said anything? She also realizes today is the day she must meet her contact. Can she ride back to Dublin in her ill state? She must.

Chapter Four: Sebastian finds her trying to leave and locks her in the room. She manages to get out and rides the following night.

This type of outline could go on for twelve chapters, or could be in

A.B.C. Roman numeral style. While writing, keep in front of you as a guide an outline listing each chapter and the scenes to go in it. But you must do a synopsis as well, and it is the synopsis of the full narrative that is sent to the editors.

The synopsis

The synopsis is often the first thing the editor reads, and it must be of sufficient interest to persuade her to read your first chapter.

Most beginning writers have trouble with the synopsis because they don't understand the necessity for immediacy, for action, for drawing the editor into a story. Instead, they philosophize for pages about the worthwhile objectives of their novel and the goals of their characters—without really touching the heart of the story.

Remember: The synopsis is your selling tool. It must hook your reader/editor just as your first chapter must in the next stage. The synopsis should show your writing at its best and prove to the editor that you know how to construct a fast-paced story. I know of several cases in which novels were bought or rejected, solely on the synopsis.

The hook I used in my synopsis of *Bloodstone Inheritance* follows:

After the sudden accidental death of her mother, Elizabeth Ann Larabee discovers a letter indicating someone other than Zebulon Larabee had fathered her. Who? Beset by curiosity, forced to sell off what she and her mother had, Elizabeth journeys to the thriving river town of Aberdeen, Illinois, to her mother's old home. She feels here she will find a clue to her natural father.

For *Spanish Heartland:*

Jersey Jordon couldn't believe her luck. Professor Tomas Ramirez, one of Spain's leading historical experts, had agreed to let her come study with him for the year, and to live with a Spanish noble family in Seville.

And for *Tame the Wild Heart:*

May, 1689, Dublin, Ireland:

Hating the English Catholic King James II and his court for what they did to her mother, Roxanna Alden has become a spy for the forces of William III. Being the niece of the Earl of Lucan, Patrick Sarsfield, a man highly regarded by James, Roxanna has no difficulty in getting information to pass on. The difficulty she does have is in keeping her feminine identity a secret from her contact and in coping with the nosey Sebastian Steele, Lord Bristol, her uncle's trusted aide.

On a misty, damp night, Roxanna is waiting for her contact on the bridge. There had been no time to change since she had to go straight to the ball that James was giving. She detests these parties as much as she detests James, but she does get good gossip there. . . .

In the beginning of all my synopses, I indicate who the heroine is and something of what the major problem will be, as well as the place and setting. To hook the reader (editor), think of the most crucial point of the story. This is usually where your novel starts (but not always); it comes at a point at which the heroine or hero is up against some problem or anxiously awaiting the outcome of a crucially important situation.

When the novel manuscript is first being considered by a publisher, the synopsis alone may be sent to several different people in a publishing house who decide if they want to read the whole manuscript. Seldom does a single editor have say over purchase of a book. The editor usually uses the synopsis in the sales meeting when she is trying to push for the acceptance of your book. It is the synopsis that is sent to the cover artists and blurb writers.

The synopsis is the outline with meat on it—just enough meat to give your skeleton form, but not enough to flesh it out fully. Making your synopsis too detailed will sometimes lead to a rejection. In one case, I made the mistake of mentioning in the synopsis that the heroine crossed herself at a crisis moment (since she was a good Irish Catholic). Immediately, I had a call from the editor. "We don't want religious books." The fact was, there was no religion in the book, but mentioning this incident in the synopsis made it seem so.

The synopsis should be in narrative form, usually in present tense (though some writers prefer past), including the premise of the story, and a bit about the characters. You want to get across not only who your characters are but their motives, emotions, and reactions. In these few pages, show the conflict that will develop between the characters, as well as the conflict that starts the novel moving. This building of tension is what will hook the editor. You should also include major turning points of your plot, as well as beginning, middle, and end. If the book is sexy, then sex should be mentioned in the synopsis.

Sometimes, I find it necessary to throw in a bit of dialogue or description, especially if I'm doing a historical novel. This will illuminate the character and her desires and will also give background for the story.

Editors have complained of writers ending their synopsis with: "Read the rest of this exciting novel to see what happens." I can almost guarantee you that this kind of come-on for an undisclosed ending will get your story rejected immediately. It's the mark of a novice. Editors want to know that all the loose ends are tied up and the story is brought to a satisfactory and satisfying conclusion.

Although the synopsis doesn't need to reveal all your secret twists and turns, include enough to catch the reader's interest. Don't be coy and cutesy, but do pack as much excitement and drama into these few pages as you can.

Not only must the synopsis open with a hook, but secondary characters who will be important to your story must be described and the viewpoint revealed. Give enough background about your characters to make them believable. If you're writing a suspense novel, requiring foreshadowing, mention the clues and indicate which are followed up and how. Action must be well spaced throughout the story. Because it is not necessary to put every scene into the synopsis, what you give the editor may not necessarily follow the chronological progression of events—but you should be clear on where each part of the story comes and how each scene fits, leading to a logical conclusion.

Some writers prefer to present their synopsis chapter by chapter—similar to what I did with the outline, only in much more depth. If so, write about four or five paragraphs per chapter—one for each major scene. Writers also sometimes complete the first three chapters and then synopsize the last part of the book in two or three pages.

I have found that this last method is not acceptable to most editors because, as I have said, they will usually read the synopsis first and send the synopsis around to other editorial readers. Doing a straight narrative rather than a chapter-by-chapter synopsis helps the story flow. If you want to do a chapter-by-chapter synopsis first, then by all means do so. You may then find it easier to make the synopsis tighter when you do it in narrative form.

In the sample one-page synopsis for my novel *For Love Betrayed* (see page 162), much of the first part describes events that had happened before the book opens, but are necessary to explain the story background and indicate what is happening to Montana McCormick, my heroine, *now*. Then I mention the major characters and two minor ones as well as three of the major turning points.

A lot happens in between those points, but I gave the editor only enough to hook her—enough, it turned out, to have her ask for the first few chapters and a more detailed synopsis.

The "mechanics"

As for "mechanics" of presentation, the majority of my synopses are single-spaced (since editors do no editing here), but I double-space between paragraphs. However, if you have elite type and the margins are small, you can double-space the entire synopsis for readability.

My synopsis can be as short as three pages or as long as twenty. There is no rule that applies to novels. Generally, the shorter your synopsis, the better. The average length for an 80,000-word book is six pages (single-spaced). As a guideline, I would say:

    55–65,000—3–4 pages
    75–90,000—5–6 pages
    100–125,000—8–10 pages
    150,000 + —10–14 pages

Before you write your synopsis, it's important to have your plot worked out fairly well. That doesn't mean that in writing the novel you have to stick exactly to the synopsis. Often, as I start writing, the story changes because the characters take over, but if the editor has bought your novel on the basis of the synopsis, you're going to want to discuss any major changes with her. There are writers who can write super synopses but fail when it comes to writing the book, just as there are authors who can write great books but fail when it comes to doing a tantalizing synopsis. Professional writers must do both well.

Sample Synopsis. . . .

FOR LOVE BETRAYED

Montana McCormick is in love again but she is also scared. Her first marriage was a tragedy—more so than anyone knows. Shane Hunter tries to convince her to let go, to love him but he doesn't know the past that plagues her.

Having moved from a small Southern California town to the West Hollywood area, where she had hoped to "get lost," Montana found that she could not forget what had happened and the death of her husband. An abused wife, she had longed many times to take a gun to him but had not. Only when his mistreatment makes her lose her longed-for child, does Montana verbalize her threat—overheard by others.

Not wanting his property (wife) to leave, he comes after her with his gun. In self defense, Montana hits him with the fire stoker. He is knocked out. The stress and injury he had caused her make her faint.

She wakes in the hospital to learn that she is accused of her husband's death. Had she really killed him? She doesn't think so but he is dead and with his rich family, she is sure that she will be found guilty.

Escaping from the hospital, she goes to L.A. where she changes her name and finds herself falling in love with Shane. She wants to trust him with her past but doesn't know if he will love her or if he will treat her in the same way.

Shane's sister, who does not like Montana, finds out about the past. She tells Shane. He is shocked and wishes that she would have confided in him but wants to know what happened and wants her to know that he thinks she's innocent.

Going to her home, he finds that she has fled back to the town. Montana has decided that she cannot be free of the past until she learns what has happened. The house had not yet been sold so she goes there as she tries to reconstruct the events of that night.

She is surprised to find her brother-in-law, Holt, there. Holt has longed for her secretly for some time and admits that he had killed his brother because he could not stand what was happening to her. He wanted to follow her but could not find her. This is the first Montana has known of his love.

Shane comes and realizes what is happening. Holt realizes that Montana will not be his and tries to make her come with him by force. She cannot testify if she is married to him. Either that or he shoots her. If he cannot have her, no one can. Shane attacks him. In the struggle, the gun goes off and Holt is stunned. Shane goes to Montana to comfort her. Holt regains consciousness and gets the gun—but turns it on himself. He would rather die than face the charges of killing his brother and tells Montana how he loves her.

Shane and Montana return to L.A. to get married.

33

MOTIVATE YOUR CHARACTERS

By Jean L. Backus

Every story is someone's story, but someone's motives are not always everyone's motives. Two or twenty people will respond in two or twenty different ways to the same stimulus, depending on age, experience, beliefs, sex, or whatever else distinguishes them as individuals. It's not what makes Peter run, but what makes Peter run up bills he cannot pay, or steal a car for a joy ride, or starve rather than accept charity. It's what makes Janet want to work even if she doesn't have to, work efficiently or inefficiently if she has to, or remain a contented housewife. It's what makes every person different from all others in the world, and in the beginning, it's what makes the writer provide reasonable and logical causes for imaginary people to react to. It's called motivation.

What if the writer does not understand the principle of causes and reactions? Only too often a character, for no apparent reason, will act in a manner contrary to normal expectations, either because the writer acted on a whim, or because he wished to alter the dramatic action artificially. If the uncharacteristic behavior is not required by your plot (or is not explained as the story progresses), you should omit it. If such an action represents a significant change in the plot line, you must have it occur for an acceptable reason. Otherwise, the plot contrivance will destroy the emotional effect you are working to achieve.

Motives are logical and realistic reasons for the behavior of your characters and their reactions to other characters and to the situations in the story. You find them in your material when you are planning the dramatic action. It is your prerogative to choose how your characters will behave and react in any instance, provided you choose consistently for them, or account reasonably for an inconsistency thereafter. Most readers will tolerate any kind of behavior, sympathetic or not, if you make it clear that the character has an acceptable reason for his action, has no choice in the matter, cannot control or avoid events, or cannot take responsibility for his actions.

Unless you have a good reason for not telling the reader, you should show the ultimate effect of a decision—a change of heart, or other uncharacteristic action. After a quarrel, for example, does the couple in your story make up or make war? Are there bruises or black eyes? If one is hurt, does he jog as usual the next morning, or go to see his lawyer? Who else may be affected? Does the family, work, or social situation change? If you show a husband and wife quarreling bitterly at night and have them go about their business as usual the next morning, you leave the reader bewildered and unconvinced. There must be evidence—either of lingering resentment or an attempt, however slight, at a reconciliation.

Uncharacteristic behavior that does not vitally change the plot may be explained, through either past or present action, in one of the following ways (or you may find another method better suited to the particular situation in your story):

The character says, "What happened just now [or the other day or whenever] made me change my mind."

A symbolic act reverses the initial emotional effect or impact. "After the lovers quarreled, they kissed and made up."

Other characters comment on an unusual action or its absence. "They didn't weep at the child's funeral, and nobody's seen them since."

The writer presents a mental reaction to a stimulus in the character's viewpoint. "John thought about the charges. A woman suing him? To establish the paternity of her child? Thank God, thirty years ago he'd had that vasectomy."

To alter the plot line of a story often requires the character to behave uncharacteristically or inconsistently in response to an unexpected crisis. For example, a selfish person dies while trying to save another, and a family's future (and the plot) takes a different turn. Or the change in behavior is not apparent until a will is read or a secret revealed, or another unexpected event occurs. To make such dramatic effects fit smoothly into the overall structure, you must work out short but explicit transitions. "When papa died, he cut me off, so there was no money for school. I went to work where I met my future wife and assumed adult responsibilities, although I was only seventeen." Transitions of this nature, indicating changes of locale, time, mood, or whatever, are easily inserted after the manuscript is completed. Unfortunately, some writers forget to put them in at all.

What happens after a person behaves in an uncharacteristic way may be proportionately too great for the cause. If Edward forgets to bring home the magazine his wife asked him to buy, and because of this her family starts a row that leads to divorce, the reader, quite naturally, will doubt the writer's perspective and sense of proportion. But if you have Edward kill Joanne in a fight over their child, her family would be guilty of criminal neglect if they failed to sue for custody of the grandchild. In that case, the effect would be *insufficient for the cause*. If you provide an extreme cause for an extreme effect, and a lesser cause for a lesser effect, you can be confident that the emotional impact made on your reader will be strong and credible.

To create *full and deep characterization,* use a basic, universal situation: the fight for survival, search for a mate, parental protection or instinct, etc., characters in conflict with one another, or conflict within one character or against another person as a result of the dramatic action. The fight for survival can be set in opposition to the maternal urge, for example, in a childless forty-five-year-old woman who knows childbirth will kill her. You must give her extremely strong reasons for persisting in a pregnancy. In a catastrophe, a man may or may not choose to save other people if the cost will be his own life. Consider his state of mind as he swims in icy waters or fights to get out of a burning room. What conceivable reason can he have for trying to save someone else rather than himself? Some people are instinctively noble in a crisis; we often hear about them in the news.

But newspaper, radio and television commentators don't have to give reasons for the noble actions they report; a fiction writer does. If he has led the reader to respect Smith as a man who loves people and is honorable in all dealings, and Smith dies while saving another person, the reader will be satisfied that this was a characteristic act, even as he grieves over Smith's death. If, on the contrary, Smith has been presented as shallow, self-centered, and ungenerous, either the reader will not be satisfied by his sacrifice, much less grieve for him, or the writer must have shown, *before the tragedy,* that on rare occasions, Smith was capable of grand gestures and noble sacrifices. This same principle must apply if you have shown that the character has a weakness or physical disability—a fear of heights or of animals, for example, or a hatred of snakes. In other words, before a character performs hero-ically, you must reveal that he has overcome that weakness.

While the main plot elements advance toward the climax of a story or novel, in elaborating, explaining or complicating the character's actions, you must be aware of the *false conflict*. Suppose all her life, the middle-aged woman had wanted a child, but now she is dying of an inheritable disease. Should she continue the pregnancy and possibly leave a re-tarded or handicapped child? Or suppose the man in the icy water was forced to choose between saving his wife or his child? Each of these is a genuine *major* conflict. If, however, the woman wants merely to spite someone, or if the man must choose between saving a child or a puppy, the conflicts won't seem real to the reader. Unless you have carefully prepared for an unusual response to such illogical choices this behavior or action will be unconvincing and will destroy your characterizations.

Now suppose you wish to present a believable character who *would* sacrifice his own life to save a puppy. To convince the reader, you must exaggerate the characterization, emphasize an inordinately strong love of animals in general and puppies in particular (possibly going back to a traumatic childhood incident), and in every way possible present his character so positively that the reader will accept this sacrifice as a characteristic act.

The *all-good* or *all-bad character* is naturally unbelievable. Although most readers prefer the protagonist to be good, and the antagonist to be bad, heroes and heroines must have human failings, and villains have some good in them. In writing fiction, you should first show your hero's weaknesses, and then gradually reveal his better qualities until, at the end of the story or novel, the good outweighs the bad. Conversely, show the villain's good traits early and then let the reader see his bad side. A Robin Hood, for example, is always shown first at his worst, and only gradually does the reader see him as a benefactor and defender of the poor and oppressed. An author's cleverness and skill (or lack of either) can be measured by his ability to disguise the truth about such a character until the last possible moment—and still make the revelation convincing and believable to the reader.

Since it is no longer acceptable to treat the motivation of women in fiction superficially or to ignore it totally, many writers now attribute contemporary feminist attitudes and beliefs to historical heroines. This kind of anachronism destroys the credibility of the characterization and of the writer. Few women in history were "liberated" and able to leave home and husband, for any reason. Few consciously expressed a desire to do so, because their entire training as women was to be domestically submissive. Yet no one can question the reality of female *yearnings* for freedom over the ages. In her novel. *The Mists of Avalon,* set in King Arthur's England, Marion Zimmer Bradley and her women often dream and argue among themselves about being independent, being equal to men, and being allowed to help make decisions that would affect their lives and their children. At the time of King Arthur and for centuries thereafter, most women could do no more. Their frustrations continued unrelieved, their desires unsatisfied.

In general, make your *major* characters as deeply motivated as possible within the framework and form of your narrative. The motivation of *secondary* characters should also be more than superficial, except in short fiction, or in an introspective story written entirely from the viewpoint of the main character, when deep motivation may or may not be necessary. Motivation of *minor* characters is often less complex or deep, but should be clearly though briefly shown. The motives of *background* characters can be implied; that is, a postman simply delivers the mail and a cook prepares a meal—unless either is supposed to influence the dramatic action in some way. For example, if a cook serves a meal, and nothing happens as a result of the food, she need not be characterized, although a bit of description is customary. If, on the other hand, the cook overhears the head of the house say he is going to fire the cook, and he is the only one served a portion of poisoned fish, then the reader has to be told through action and dialogue that the cook has a motive for murder, even though she will later be proved innocent.

The need for clear, logical, consistent, and realistic motivation seems self-evident, yet one of the most common weaknesses in the work of novice—and some professional—writers is creating characters who are puppets rather than people a reader can believe are real.

If as a writer you feel free to move your characters around at random, either on a whim or as a simple, quick way of altering the course of the story, you do your talent and your craft a disservice. Remember, it is vital for you to provide convincing motivation for all the actions and reactions of your characters and to make that motivation clear and persuasive, so that the fictional people you create may step off the printed page right into the living memory of your reader.

34

DESCRIPTIVE DETAIL IN YOUR SHORT STORY

BY JINGER HOOP GRISWOLD

DESCRIPTION, I used to think, was easy to write. The difficulties came with point of view, conflict, tone. These were new to me, but I'd been writing descriptive essays since junior high. Nothing could be simpler. You had a living room, you wrote down what it looked like, and—bingo!—description.

But then I had problems. As I became more skillful at writing fiction—and more critical of my work—I noticed that my descriptive passages were often the weakest in my stories. They stopped the action; they were boring, or inconsequential, or, horror of horrors, trite. So I began a brief period of writing descriptionless stories—lean and fast, all dialogue and action. But eventually I tired of those skinny stories and, with new respect for description, began to incorporate it into my fiction again, this time with my eyes open.

What I've learned is that even though description may be the simplest of the rhetorical modes, it's also the easiest to underestimate. We agonize over plot, making sure every event is convincing. We give our characters full and complex motivations; we work hard to avoid jarring the reader with a violation of point of view. Yet we spend little energy on the one thing—descriptive detail—that can particularize a story, make it visual and realistic, the thing, in short, that allows a reader to believe our story "really happened."

For an example of what I mean, let's suppose you're writing a short story in which the climax occurs out of doors, at a picnic, say, where your heroine and her lover begin the argument that will destroy their relationship. Think about the kind of setting you'd create for such a scene. In particular, what kind of *weather* would you be apt to choose?

Would you describe a storm—dark clouds that gather on the horizon, a sudden chill wind? If so, you may be fond of using symbolic description. Such detail would work thematically in the story: The scene is climactic, so it's only logical that a storm should be brewing. But while details of this kind are good for reinforcing theme, they're absolute flops when it comes to adding realism. An astute reader (and who writes for any other kind?) will easily recognize the description for what it is—a device. For this reason, I've learned scrupulously to avoid detail that obviously underscores the action.

All right, you say, let's describe the weather as perfection itself—warm and clear, birds singing, cotton candy clouds and all the rest. A description like this does seem more realistic than the storm—but it too smacks of the device. In this case, the effect is ironic, as if you want to heighten the conflict by contrasting it with the placid weather. There's nothing wrong with irony, of course, except that ironic details like this are a snap to create (merely choose the opposite of what one would expect) and are often overdone. A story dripping with irony is less painful to read but no more realistic than a story dripping with sentimentality.

What kind of weather, then, *would* add realism? Simply put, any kind that doesn't appear tied to the action of the story. A warm day, perhaps, with the wind a bit gusty. While the other two examples carry strong emotional connotations—the first is "bad" weather, the second "good"—a warm, gusty day is refreshingly free of them. *It is the most convincing of the choices, because it is more description than symbol.* We are not, after all, used to having real weather make a comment, ironic or otherwise, upon our lives; and, while fiction should order and interpret experience, good fiction never loses the surface ambiguity of real life.

The same principle applies to the description of character. Suppose, for example, that one of your characters is a rich man, and you wish to add a minor detail to flesh him out. At first you might be tempted to give your character a habit like rubbing his palms together, or you might decide to dress him in threadbare clothes and give him a ten-year-old car to drive. But neither of these details is truly realistic, since both are overworked—palms rubbed together often signifies greed; old clothes on a wealthy man adds heavy-handed irony. The miser and the greedy tycoon—both are too close to cliché to be believable.

But virtually any detail that doesn't relate directly to the character's primary characteristic—his wealth—will work. He might have a

169

smoker's cough, a penchant for the color yellow (but not green or gold, please), or a craving for salty food.

Creating this kind of descriptive detail is relatively easy, once you learn to question your first impulses, and it exercises the imagination in a way most writers love. Best of all, realistic detail can transform even a contrived story into something that begins to approach the fascinating ambiguity of real life.

Once you get caught up in the fun of creating realistic description you'll probably encounter another problem, that of *degree*. You may find yourself spending far too many words describing the irrelevant and far too few on the truly significant. I overcame this difficulty when I finally realized that in most cases everything I wished to describe had to be filtered through my protagonist's consciousness. (This is especially clear with a first-person narrator, but it holds true for third-person point of view as well.) Since I was describing what my protagonist saw, heard, and felt, I only needed to use the amount of detail such a character would perceive.

For example, in a minor scene in one of my stories, my protagonist, Anne, looks distractedly out her window to see a "German shepherd" walk slowly up the street. Even with this insignificant bit of description, I had several choices. For instance, I wrote "German shepherd" when I could have easily substituted a more general term like "dog." Then, too, I could have been much more specific, perhaps calling the dog a "mangy German shepherd wearing a silver collar."

I made my choice on the basis of what I knew about my protagonist. Anne is not very interested in what she sees and doesn't examine the dog closely enough to distinguish much about it. There is no reason, then, to describe the dog in much detail. On the other hand, I decided to use the specific "German shepherd" in place of "dog," since Anne could be expected to recognize such a common breed at a glance.

The key here is that it is the *protagonist's* interest and experience that count, not the author's. A long or detailed description of the dog would improperly suggest that Anne is greatly interested in it. In the same way, calling the dog a "member of the genus *Canis*" would suggest she has specialized knowledge inappropriate to her character.

Actually placing description in your story presents its own problems. The awful truth is that your reader probably hates description. You and I know description's good for him because it helps him visualize the action, but he'll surely balk if you try to serve it up in big chunks. You've got to sneak your description past the reader, inserting details one at a time throughout each scene—a sentence here, another there. If you find that you cannot work in all of the information you'd like—drop the rest, no matter how it pains you to do so. Use only what you can incorporate so smoothly that the reader absorbs the information without being uncomfortably aware of it.

The same technique is also useful when describing character. Since your reader usually gets to know real people slowly and gradually, he'll feel comfortable learning about your characters in the same way. Don't rush to tell everything about them; in many wonderful stories, character is not fully revealed until the last sentence.

You can also add a few descriptive details wherever your story's pace seems too hurried. A few sentences of description here and there can subtly slow the action. Notice how the one-sentence description in the following exchange of dialogue suggests the passage of time.

"I'm tired of talking," Matthew said.
"No, sit back down," Molly said. "I've got something else to say."
The chair Matthew sat in was rickety; whenever he shifted his weight, he swayed for a moment and felt on the verge of falling.
"Are you listening to me?" Molly said.

Finally, beginning writers often write such spare dialogue that one gets the sense of little more than disembodied voices. Adding a few details—describing the characters' gestures and the setting perhaps—can make such a dialogue-filled scene suddenly become visual.

I hope I've shown that description is a powerful tool; like any it can be overused. It's easy to forget that sometimes the best word is actually the vaguest. One such instance is in dialogue. Real people often speak in the most general of terms, and, unless you're striving for a comic effect, you had best let your hero tell the heroine, "You look nice" instead of the highly descriptive but highly improbable:

"You look fresh, Gina, and radiant somehow. Your hair is all shot through with golden lights and it looks soft the way it's tousled across your brow."

That's an exaggeration, I admit, but even a little of that kind of thing can make your character sound like a lousy actor in a shampoo commercial. Remember that it's *your* job to describe Gina's hair. Let your hero tell her she looks good in his own vague way.

Another time to avoid description is when the subject is something most readers can already visualize. If your scene takes place in a high school classroom, don't describe the kind of desk the students sit at. Most readers are familiar with them and will imagine them quite readily without your help. The same holds true for easily visualized actions—when two characters kiss, for example. Don't get caught up trying to describe who turns to the right and who to the left. Tell your reader they kiss, and leave it at that unless there is something truly unusual in the way they go about it. The rule here is to describe only what is necessary, and then get out of the way of your reader's imagination.

There is no denying the problems using too much description can cause. But in your zeal to avoid overusing detail, don't prune it from your story completely. A story lacking in description is inhospitable somehow, full of faceless people talking in empty rooms. But in the hands of a careful and patient writer, description can give even a wholly imaginary tale the living "reality" of the very best fiction.

35

PLOTTING SHORT STORIES

By Dan J. Marlowe

AFTER thirty years of plotting mystery/suspense short stories, a writer knows what has worked; more important, he knows what hasn't. The fact remains, however, that current trends in magazine fiction should induce the writer to re-examine the building blocks of his plotting structure.

With markets contracting and writers increasing, it's difficult to send an editor a short story sufficiently unique or unusual to encourage him to consider publishing it. The first idea that comes to mind may not be good enough. The second, third, or fourth may not be, either.

Some editors send guidelines that state what they are looking for. Unfortunately, guidelines are generalizations that can confuse as much as they can help. Also, despite such guidelines, an editor doesn't really know what he or she wants to buy or will buy until he has it in hand.

Plot lines can come from a number of places. Reading, of course. How many times have we finished reading a story and said to ourselves, "Now, if that ending were changed and that character eliminated, and that background changed . . . why, it would be a different story. A better story." And we rush to the typewriter.

Conversations, either direct or overheard from two tables away, can be helpful. Conversations are tricky, though. Unlike reading it in a story, how much of a plot twist heard in conversations can be retained? If you don't have a notebook and pencil with you, trying to recall conversations later can be frustrating, since they fade away quickly, no matter how good a writer's memory.

Television shows can provide a plot line; radio can, too, although that's less likely nowadays. But probably the most helpful aid of all in putting backspin on a story idea is the most available medium of all, the daily newspaper.

Hardly a day goes by without having something appear in the paper that will lend itself to fictional conversation. A file of newspaper clippings can go a long way to jog laggard inspiration when the plotting well runs dry, as it occasionally must for all of us.

What type of newspaper item produces story ideas?

Almost anything.

It can be a headline.

It can be the lead story of the day, a sidebar item, or a blind classified ad.

The following ad appeared recently: "A highly qualified chauffeur is needed to drive for a leading company. The right candidate will have a background in law enforcement, business driving experience, and will be articulate and well-groomed. Excellent references and the ability to work flexible hours are also required. Duties other than driving may be assigned in the corporate offices, depending upon experience and background."

The plotting mind leaps immediately into action. The company is looking for an ex-cop or ex-private eye (perhaps both in the same package). A bodyguard? The wording suggests more than that. There's a taste of something not quite aboveboard. Something a bit shady.

So the writer can take an ex-cop, ex-private eye character and send him to the company of the writer's choice to apply for the job. The character can be a burnt-out case on his current job and be looking for a change. He applies, is accepted, and at once finds himself deeper in the manure pile than he had been formerly.

It doesn't matter what the writer gives the character to do. It's sufficient that the writer has found an offbeat situation into which to insert his character. "The right candidate will be articulate and well-groomed." Hm-m-m . . . could the corporate employer be a woman? The writer's imagination has no restrictions upon it.

Sometimes a newspaper item will develop over a period of time into one or more plot twists, not immediately apparent to the writer. The story may take a direction impossible to discern at the beginning.

Recently, a salesman 75 miles from home came out of his motel room one morning, and when he got into his car, it exploded. The roof and both doors were blown away. Amazingly, the salesman walked away from the blast, his major injury a seriously scorched rear end.

The police at first concluded the car-bombing was gangland connected. Extensive checking proved this to be incorrect. A parallel thought was that the salesman might have staged the bombing for his own purposes. The discovery of an unexploded pipe bomb under the car's front seat ruined that theory. One pipe bomb had gone off, one hadn't. No one could depend upon that kind of freakish incident to further a plot of one's own devising.

Time passed. Three months later the police arrested two men for the bombing, one of them a good friend of the salesman's wife. The friend insisted the wife had encouraged his activity in connection with her husband. The wife denied it. The salesman loyally supported his wife's statements.

More time passed while the police dug more deeply. The next public announcement was to the effect that the police were theorizing that the wife's friend might have done the dirty deed without the wife's knowledge to further his own relationship with her.

This was followed a week later by the police charging the wife with instigating the entire affair. She was indicted, and her boy friend and his companion agreed to testify against her. The wife protested her innocence and said that whatever her boy friend had done he had done without her knowledge. The salesman still supported his wife.

The next time the veil was lifted the wife was in court pleading no contest to a charge of attempted murder. In the eyes of the law, a no contest plea is the same as a guilty plea except it allows the judge more leniency in sentencing. During the wife's plea, the salesman was in court; unbelievably, he was still supporting her. The wife comes up for sentencing in three months.

That's the end of the newspaper story, but examine the possibilities it opens up for the fiction writer. It can be written fictionally as it happened, of course, but that's only the beginning of the options. It's true that as it happened it's bizarre enough to attract an editor's attention, but some of the possible spin-offs would be almost as attractive.

1) Instead of appearing as an innocent fool, the salesman could take the bit in his teeth and do some digging himself, which places the key information in the hands of the police. The tale can be a story of revenge.

2) Instead of the bloody and would-be bloodier circumstances of the situation, the story line could be lightened up all along the way without

the factual grimness. The story can be treated as a farce which—except for the participants—it was.

With an example like the foregoing, writers can't complain that newspapers aren't writing their stories for them. Day after day some odd item in the newspaper can be clipped and added to a writer's file. Sometimes two items can be combined to make a better fictional whole.

Sometimes the truth itself is better than fiction. An almost illiterate man served three years in jail for a warehouse robbery he insisted he didn't commit. His defense was that he was a mile away in a shopping plaza, but he had no witnesses.

Eventually, he interested a lawyer in his case, and the lawyer did some checking on his own. The man serving time had furnished a passionately detailed description of the shopping plaza where he claimed he had been, right down to a description of a pie truck, which had blocked his exit when he wanted to leave. The lawyer determined that no store in the plaza handled pies and lost his interest in the matter.

Some time later while the prisoner was watching television in the prison rec room, a commercial came on. "There!" the prisoner screamed to his befuddled fellow prisoners. He was pointing at the television screen. "There's the truck!" On the screen, an 18-wheeled behemoth was disappearing into the distance. Its rear doors were labeled "P.I.E." In smaller letters underneath, additional lettering said "Pacific Intermountain Express," a well-known trucking company.

The prisoner got in touch with the lawyer, who re-opened his inquiry. Pacific Intermountain Express log books confirmed that one of their company trucks had indeed made a call at that particular plaza at the time claimed by the prisoner. With that hinge to hang further questions on, the lawyer developed additional facts that enabled him to go back to court and ask for his client's freedom, which was granted. The "pie truck" story became a staple of prison lore and can still be heard from time to time today.

But can you imagine an editor accepting it as fiction? The editor would think it too strange, too incredible. And the offer of proof would not be likely to satisfy him. After all, having lived as long as he has, he knows the difference between truth and fiction, doesn't he?

Occasionally fact and fiction can be worst enemies.

One final note about the plotting of mystery/suspense short stories. Editorial attitudes change and must be taken into consideration. Have you as a writer ever given thought to the steadily increasing number of women editors in the magazine world? And that at least some of these women editors look with disfavor upon stories told from a male chauvinist viewpoint? It's a factor that should be seriously considered today in your plotting to increase your chances of getting your story published.

But for a beginning, start a file of newspaper clippings of the odd and bizarre of life's happenings, which, allowed to marinate, may well produce a salable story.

36

WHY DID MY STORY GET REJECTED?

By Marion Zimmer Bradley

One of the hardest things a young writer—one who has made maybe two or three sales, but cannot sell *regularly*—must cope with, is to distinguish between the story which sells first time out, and the other story he or she has written, which is "just as good" but for one reason or another does not sell.

A story may be bad in all kinds of ways, and still be salable, if it has some things the editor finds important (because he knows from experience that this is what his readers want). But a story may be good in all kinds of ways, excellently written, with warm, lovable characters and wonderful style, plus a philosophical outlook, and it is still going to get rejected if it doesn't give the editor those few things the editor wants and needs.

When I was editing two recent anthologies, I tried very hard to analyze the "gut feelings" I had about why one story worked and another one didn't. In general, I rejected stories for one or more of the following reasons, and this had nothing to do with how well written the stories were.

1. The pace was wrong. 2. The story was not complete in itself. 3. Main character was not identifiable. 4. Editor could not get interested in the characters. 5. Nothing happened in the story. 6. Character did not have a serious enough problem. 7. The story was just too grim. 8. The story was offensive, or the editor thought it was offensive.

Nine out of ten stories that are rejected fall into one or another of these eight categories; there is some big hole in the plotting of your story; or it is told in a way which is unclear, confusing, or offensive to your editor's idea of his preferred reader. But there is always the tenth story, which has absolutely nothing wrong with it, but gets rejected anyway. You can say it isn't your fault, but in a very serious way it *is* your fault, because all of the following "no-fault rejections" are *preventable*.

1. *The editor couldn't read your story* because it was typed on a dim ribbon, was a sloppy unreadable Xerox, or because your spelling was so bad he didn't want to be bothered figuring out what you meant. Or the editor never got a chance to read your story because you didn't address it right, or because the label fell off and it went to the dead letter office. Or he read it, and loved it, but he never got a chance to tell you so because you hadn't put your name and address on the story, only on the envelope, and the envelope got thrown away in the mail room. Or he couldn't write you and tell you about it because you didn't send enough postage and his magazine has a firm policy not to answer any manuscripts not accompanied by return postage.

2. *The story was a perfectly good, well-plotted story,* but this particular editor doesn't buy sword and sorcery, or high-technology space opera, or post-doomsday stories, or horror stories. Next time, *read the market requirements.*

3. *The story was a pretty good story,* but the editor just didn't happen to like the end, and he wasn't enthusiastic enough about it to write and ask if you would mind if he changed it.

4. *The story was a pretty good story,* but your opening was a little slow and the editor got bored before he could find out how good it was and ask you to change the first page a little.

5. *The story was a perfectly good story,* but something about this story pushed one of the editor's personal buttons—maybe he is a devout Roman Catholic and the story spoke favorably of abortion, or he is a dedicated environmentalist and the story dealt with something which hit one of his personal fears, neuroses or emotional convictions. It's even possible that you had a character in the story who reminded the editor of his hated stepmother, or the college professor who flunked him out of Integral Calculus and wrecked his chances of getting into grad school. Try another editor.

179

6. *The story was a perfectly good story,* but the editor was going to press tonight and needed a story exactly 7,500 words long to fill a spot vacated by an ad that cancelled or a column that missed its deadline, and your story was 8,500 words long. Or he needed a story 10,000 words long and yours was only 7,500.

7. *The story was a perfectly good story,* but the editor had just bought another story on the same theme by Harlan Ellison, Ben Bova, or Ursula K. LeGuin. Tough luck, and that's the breaks.

It is all too easy, when the editor sends back your story, to flatter yourself that your story is really pretty good, and that it was rejected for one of these no-fault reasons. In general, your first dozen or three dozen rejections will be for cause: Your story just isn't well enough plotted, the characters are too tangled, the plot doesn't make sense, there is something wrong with the end or the beginning, or for some reason, the editor just can't care enough about your characters.

The difference between the amateur and the professional is that the professional *assumes* that the editor knows his job, and if his story is rejected, he must have done something wrong. (And once an editor respects you as a professional and assumes *you* know your job, he will *tell* you if it's not your fault: "Dear Joe—sorry, this is too long for me," or "I'm overbought," or . . .

Try your story again if it's rejected. But if it's rejected *everywhere,* assume there was some reason nobody liked it, and try another story. . . . And listen to that sneaking little voice that tries to tell you where that first one really fell apart.

37

VISUALIZING FICTION ON PAPER

By Dorothy Uhnak

WRITING began so far back in childhood that I literally cannot remember a time when I was *not* writing. I spent fourteen years of my adult life as a police officer in New York City. During all that time, I wrote continually, drawing on everything around me: the unique, exciting situations, the deadly boredom, the brutality, sadness, pain, humor (often macabre), the courage, cowardice, intelligence, stupidity, greed, anger, danger, and intense loyalty which characterize the working life of a police officer.

I was a capable police officer: I was promoted three times and awarded medals twice. I worked hard, was dedicated and earnest and concerned. Yet all the time, the writer in me was compiling events, feelings, atmosphere, emotions, situations for future use. *Policewoman*, semi-autobiographical, semi-fictional, was published during my tenure as a police officer and was my first attempt to set forth some things I had observed, learned, experienced, been a part of.

My first novel, *The Bait*, was published after I resigned from police work in order to devote myself more fully to writing and to continue my education. It was awarded the Edgar for the Best First Mystery of 1968, which I felt was somewhat ironic, for I never considered myself a "mystery writer." People are my main concern as a writer, and the task I set myself is to dig into the "mystery" of human behavior in given circumstances.

I have used the police world in all my books to date in order to explore certain events occurring between people, rather than to tell a "cop story" per se.

The Bait dealt with a sex murderer. On a deeper level, it explored the tormented world of a tragically demented man and his impact on a bright, sensitive young policewoman.

181

The Witness, second in my trilogy set in the Manhattan District Attorney's Squad, was a straightforward story about black organized crime and corruption. It was also a story about youthful idealism, hopes and energies that were misused and betrayed. It was part of the education-in-life of young Detective Christie Opara.

The Ledger, third in the trilogy, could be described as the story of the beautiful mistress of a crime lord. It was also a character study of two apparently opposite young women: one the worldly mistress, the other the idealistic Christie Opara. It was a probing of the painful, hidden truths each girl had to face about herself.

When I undertook my latest novel, *Law and Order,* I realized it was a radical departure from anything I had previously attempted. It was to span three generations, through four decades which have seen more social, political, moral upheaval than most of the rest of our history all put together. For one solid year, I did nothing but research. I probed back more than a hundred years to gain a fuller understanding of the immigrants who came to populate New York City, to lead and dominate not only the Police Department but the political and religious structure of the city for so many years. While the main characters are Irish, I also had to study all the important ethnic groups who comprise New York, to understand their aspirations, backgrounds, influences, self-image. I immersed myself in reading and discussion not only about politics, religious and ethnic history and folklore, but in economics and the effects of the Great Depression, World War II, the post-war world, the Korean War, Vietnam, the youth movement, generation gap, emergence of the drug culture.

I spent three weeks in Ireland wandering at random through that lovely tortured country: spoke to people, listened to them, read as much Irish writing as I could absorb until I could *feel* the rhythm of Irish thought and emotion. I allowed myself to get caught up and carried by the Irish idiom.

My characters grew out of the research. Certain strong characters began to dominate the other members of their family. And it was a "family" that grew into the story. They were at the hub and center of all the changing times of their city and their world. Through the three generations of O'Malleys, my aim was to present some of the social and moral questions with which we are confronted in these complex times. My hero, Brian O'Malley, is first introduced as a young, inexperienced boy of eighteen, faced with the sudden responsibility of caring for his mother, grandmother, brothers and sisters on the violent death of his policeman-father. The book ends when Brian is a fifty-two-year-old Deputy Chief Inspector in the New York City Police Department, dealing as best he can with forces of corruption, coming to terms with his own policeman son, a Vietnam veteran, trying to live in a rapidly changing and always puzzling world.

One of the most exciting things about writing *Law and Order* was when the characters "took off" on their own. This hasn't happened to me as a writer very often. It is a rare, exciting, heady, exhilarating experience and occurs only when the characters are so well known, so well loved, that they can be trusted to act and react instinctively true to themselves.

The worst moment came when the manuscript was totally completed—all polished and ready to be set in galleys. I experienced the most dreadful sense of loss imaginable. All those warm, exciting, wildly active, strong and familiar people with whom I had shared my life for so long were suddenly taken from me, to be thrust out into the large and critical world.

The solution to this feeling of loss, for me at any rate, was to let a little time go by, enjoy the fruits of my labor, involve myself in other facets of the work, i.e., promotion and publicity—to relax, enjoy, take a deep breath, and begin the whole process all over again.

It must be admitted that no matter how many books I've written, how many characters created and lived with and let go, when I put the blank white paper in my machine, it is no easier for me to begin the written word than it ever has been. Publicity tours and best-seller lists, and book club and movie and TV sales are all very exciting and rewarding and lucrative. However, at the beginning of the day I am a pauper before the blank white paper. The trick is, I guess, just to keep at it from ground zero and to build on it during each session at the machine. Happily, it has started again for me; tentatively, fragilely, hopefully, I've begun a new book. Thankfully.

Since I've always been curious about other writers' work habits,

I will set down some of my own with hopes that my example will warn others to adopt other methods. Sometimes I wonder how in the world I've ever accomplished *any* body of work: I never seem to do all those things I'm positive a writer *should* do.

I've never kept notebooks filled with valuable phrases, impressions, observations. Oh, I've stacks of notebooks of all kinds—spiral ones with businesslike brown covers and spiral ones with pretty flowers on the cover. Somber little black looseleaf notebooks that fit into the palm of my hand and large ones that fill up my lap. They are all filled with empty pages, because I've never really known what to put in them. Once or twice, I've jotted down phrases which I conjured in the middle of the night, or en route somewhere on the subway, but somehow that never seemed pertinent to anything, and I spent too much time wondering what in the world I had in mind when I wrote them down in the first place. There are also pencil sketches of advertisements and some interesting doodles, not one of which is helpful.

A long time ago, I came to a strange conclusion relative to me and note-taking. Mysteriously, it has worked for me, but I do not recommend it to anyone else, merely report on it. If the thought, impression, idea, phrase, situation, or whatever is important enough for me to remember and use somewhere in my writing, I will retain it in cell x-y-or-z of my brain. If it isn't worth using, I will forget it. I don't remember how many flashing, brilliant thoughts might have been retained had they been jotted down. I do know that many conversations between characters in my stories give me a strong sense of *déjà vu*, because they were carried on in my head at some unconnected time in the past.

Another thing I don't do and feel I should: I don't have any work schedule. I mean, *I don't have any work schedule at all.* For a person who spent so many years in a structured work-situation, this leaves much room for feelings of guilt. I know I *should* sit at the machine and accomplish at least *that* much work each day, but I don't. I frankly don't know *when* I work. Sometimes, I leap out of bed at six in the morning, jump into my clothes, gulp my cup of tea and hammer out scene after scene after scene. Then, for days at a time, I avoid the top floor, which is where I work. At about three in the afternoon, the urge might hit again, and I hammer away at the next scene. I will point out that no matter how remiss I am about regulating my work schedule, at least this much is structured: I work a scene through, beginning to end, whether it runs for four pages or forty, whether it takes twenty-three minutes or six hours. Maybe it's those six-hour binges that get the job done for me.

In between actually sitting and pounding the keys, the story does go on inside my head, regardless of what else I am, physically, doing. I rake the leaves, play with the dogs, feed the cats, forget to defrost the supper, stare at daytime television (which is a horrible admission, I realize). The saving grace is that the story process continues, sometimes in some subterranean, unknown manner, because solutions to story problems sometimes take place when least expected. For example: in the shower, riding in a car at night, folding laundry, dusting the furniture, painting a wall.

When I'm well into a manuscript—in fact, during all stages of the manuscript—I rarely if ever rewrite. Probably because I wait so long before actually sitting down to the task, forming sentences in the air before I form them on paper, by the time I actually *do* sit down to work (whenever that is!), the phrases are ready and generally come out the way I want them to. Not always, but more often than not.

Generally, I am amazed at the way the pages of a manuscript pile up, given a particular period of time, because although I complain continuously about working too hard, when it's all over, I have very little remembrance of having worked *at all*.

Given one magic wish as a writer, I would want to be gifted with some kind of power to transform the scene in my head immediately into a bound, printed form without the ever-present struggle to find the words to frame and form the thought. My constant struggle as a writer is to zero in on the exact words that will enable my reader to see, feel, experience a particular scene with as much concern and intensity as I experience while visualizing and writing it.

I don't know what advice to offer young writers. I'm not even sure anyone should presume to offer any advice beyond that one tormenting, beautiful, obvious, obscure, demanding, torturous ecstasy: WRITE. Don't talk about it, whine about it, rap about it, agonize over it, dissect, analyze, study or anything else: Just do it. WRITE.

185

38

ABOUT THAT NOVEL

By Evan Hunter

STARTING: If you haven't got an idea for one, forget it. If you haven't got an idea you want to express on paper, in words, forget it. If you prefer putting paint on canvas, or rolls on your pianola or in your oven, forget it. You're going to be with this novel for a long, long time, so you'd better have *thought* about it before you start writing it. When it's ready to be written, you'll know. You'll know because you can't get it out of your mind. It'll be with you literally day and night. You'll even *dream* about it, but don't get up and rush to your typewriter. Go back to sleep. Only in movies do writers get up in the middle of the night with an inspiration. The time to go to the typewriter is when you're fresh and ready to do battle. There *will* be a battle, no question, a siege that will seemingly go on forever. So sit down, make yourself comfortable, and begin.

No outline at first, except the loose one in your head, draped casually around the idea. The thing you are trying to find is the voice. This is the single most important thing in any novel. The voice. How it will *sound*. Who is telling the story? Why is he telling it? If you're sixty years old and writing in the first person singular about a sixteen-year-old high school student, beware of the voice. It may be your own, and that is wrong. If you're writing in the third person, you can change the *tone* of the voice each time you switch to another character, but the *voice* itself must remain consistent throughout. The voice is your style. Except in my mystery series, I try to change my style to suit the subject matter of any novel I'm writing. I've come a hundred pages into a novel using the wrong voice, and I've thrown those pages away and started a new search for the right voice. Don't worry about spending days or weeks trying to find a voice. It will be time well spent. You'll know when you hit upon it. Things will suddenly *feel* right.

Once you've found the voice, write your first chapter or your first scene. Test the water. Does it still feel right? Good. *Now* make your outline. First of all, determine how long the book will be. The average mystery novel runs about 200 pages in manuscript, but a straight novel can be something as slim as *Love Story* or as thick as *Gone With the Wind*. You are the only person who knows in advance what your story is about. You are the only one who can figure how many pages you will need to tell this story. Take out your calculator. Are you writing a 300-page novel? O.K., how many chapters will you need? The length of each chapter will be determined by how much you have to *say* in that chapter. If you're depicting the Battle of Waterloo, it might be a trifle difficult to compress it into ten pages. If you're writing about a man putting out the garbage, you probably have only a scene, and you'll need additional scenes to make a full chapter.

Outline the novel in your own way, never mind freshman high-school English courses. I've outlined a forty-page chapter with just the words "Father-son confrontation." The outline is you, talking to yourself on paper. Get friendly with yourself. Tell yourself what you, as the writer, want to accomplish in any given chapter. "O.K., now we want a big explosion in the garage, and we want to see all these goddamn flames, and smell the smoke, and we want neighbors running over with garden hoses. Bring the little girl in at the end of the scene, shocked by what she's done." Got it? *Talk* to yourself. You don't have to outline the whole book. Just take the outline as far as your invention will carry it. Later, when you've written all the chapters you've already outlined, you can make another outline of the *next* several chapters. If a chapter is needed between something that has happened before and something that will happen later, and you don't know what to put between those two slices of bread, just type in the words, SCENE MISSING. You'll come back to it later. You're going to be here awhile.

MOVING: Set yourself a definite goal each day. Tack it on the wall. Ten pages? Five pages? Two pages? Two paragraphs? It doesn't matter. *Set* the goal, make it realistic, and *meet* it. If you're writing a planned 400-page novel, it will seem impossible ever to get it finished.

400 pages may be a year away. But your daily goal is here and now, and it's important to set that goal and meet it so that you'll have a sense of immediate reward. At the end of each week, on your calendar, jot down the number of pages you've already written. Store your kernels. Watch the cache grow. Keep the thing moving. If it bogs down, if you're supposed to write a tender love scene and you've just had a fight with your accountant, put the anger to good use. Jump ahead and write the Battle of Waterloo chapter. *Don't stop writing!* It's easier to go fishing or skiing—but sit at that damn typewriter, and look at the four walls all day long if you have to. There is nothing more boring than looking at the walls. Eventually, if only to relieve the boredom, and because you've made a deal with yourself not to get out of that chair, you'll start writing again. At the end of the day, read over what you've written. If you think it's lousy, don't throw it away. Read it again in the morning. If it still looks lousy, do it over again. Or if it's still bothering you, and you don't know why, move on. Keep it *moving.* The nice thing about writing, unlike public speaking, is that you can correct all your mistakes later.

CHANGING: The only true creative aspect of writing is the first draft. That's when it's coming straight from your head and your heart, a direct tapping of the unconscious. The rest is donkey work. It is, however, donkey work that must be done. Whether you rewrite as you go along—taking that bad chapter from the night before and putting it through the machine again from the top—or whether you rewrite everything only after you've completed the book, you *must* rewrite. But be careful. You can hone and polish something until it glows like a diamond, but you may end up with something hard and glittering and totally without the interior spark that was the result of your first commitment to paper. You're only a virgin once, but try to bring to each rereading of your own material the same innocence you brought to it the first time around. You will be rereading it *twenty* times before you're finished. Each time, ask yourself what you intended. Do you want me to cry when I read this scene? Well, are *you* crying? If you're not, why aren't you? Find out why you aren't. Did someone say something that broke the mood of the scene? Is that field of daffodils too cheerful for the tone of the scene? Has your heroine stamped her foot when she should be tearing out her hair? Work it, rework it. When you yourself begin crying, you've got it.

ENDING: How do you know when you're finished? You're finished when you're satisfied. If a scene is right the first time around, leave it alone. Tell yourself, "Terrific, pal," and leave it alone. You'll know you're getting to the end because you'll suddenly slow down. When that happens, set smaller goals for yourself. Instead of those five pages today, make it three. Your pace is slower because you don't want to let go of this thing. You've been living together for a long, long time, you've let this smelly beast into your tent, and you've grown to love it, and now you're reluctant to have it gallop out over the sands and out of your life forever. The temptation is to keep it with you forever, constantly bathe it and scent it, groom it and curry it, tweeze its lashes and tie a bow on its tail. *Recognize* the temptation and recognize too that everything eventually grows up and leaves home. When you've done the best you can possibly do at this time (there *will* be other books, you know) put it in a box, give it a farewell kiss, and send it out into that great big hostile world.

SENDING: Where do you send it? Be exceedingly careful in choosing your agent or your publisher. Don't send the book to anyone who charges a fee for reading it or publishing it. In the real world of publishing, people pay *you* for your work. The Society of Authors' Representatives (if you decide to go the agent route) will send you on request a list of reputable agents in the United States. The address is P.O. Box 650, Old Chelsea Station, New York, NY 10113. Just write and ask, enclosing a self-addressed, stamped envelope. If you decide to submit your manuscript directly to a publisher instead, a long list of publishers looking for various kinds of novels appears in *The Writer* Magazine, or in the market list in Part IV of this volume. Although some book publishers today have given up reading unsolicited manuscripts, many others still maintain reading staffs, and their sole purpose is to search for publishing possibilities. Send the novel manuscript out. One publisher at a time. Multiple submissions are frowned upon except when an agent is conducting a huge auction, and then the publishers are made aware beforehand that the book is being submitted simultaneously all over the field. Choose a publisher who has previously published your sort of book. Don't shotgun it around blindly. If your novel espouses atheism, don't send it to a religious publisher.

WAITING: So now your monster is out roaming the countryside, trying to earn a living. No, there it is in the mailbox. Damn thing. Wish you hadn't given it life at all. Tear open the package. Nice little noncommittal note. Thanks a lot, but no thanks. Despair. Chin up, kiddo, send it out again. But here it is *back* again. And *again.* And *yet* again. Plenty of publishers in the world, just keep trying. Pack it, send it, wait again. Why? Why wait? Why set up a vigil at the mailbox? Why hang around the post office looking like someone on the Wanted posters? You should be *thinking* instead. You should be mulling a new idea. *Don't* wait. What you *should* be doing is—

STARTING: If you haven't got an idea for one, forget it. If you haven't got an idea you want to express on paper, in words, forget it. If you prefer putting paint on canvas, or rolls on your pianola or in your oven, forget it. You're going to be with this novel for a long, long time, so you'd better have *thought* about it before you start writing it. When it's ready to be written, you'll know.

Write it.

39

POINT OF VIEW: EXPERIMENT IN LIVING

By Marjorie Franco

A few years ago I walked into a New York office, gave my name to the receptionist and sat down. The receptionist, a young girl, turned to me and inquired, "Are you an actress?" "No," I said, disappointing her, "I'm a fiction writer." I had the feeling she wanted me to be an actress—it's more glamorous, I suppose—and to make amends I said, "Inside many a writer lives an actor." Nodding agreeably, but clearly dissatisfied, the girl returned to her work. Had she been interested I could have explained that writing, like acting, is an experiment in living, and that the writer (and the actor), by lifting himself out of his own particular life, looks at life from another point of view.

What is point of view, and what does it have to do with writing, or acting, or the persons behind either of these creative arts? The dictionary says point of view is a "position from which something is considered or evaluated." All right; that seems clear. The writer takes up a position from which to tell a story. What position? A reader might say, "That's simple; he tells a story in either the first or third person." It might seem simple, but for the writer it is not.

There are at least six third-person viewpoints and five first-person viewpoints, some rarely used. To discuss all of these or to discuss technique without a story to hang it on can be confusing. Even though the writer has an intellectual mastery of viewpoint techniques, he may not create a good viewpoint character. Writers learn by doing. Did Chekhov sit down and ask himself, "Should I adopt the position of concealed narrator and third-person protagonist narrator restricted, or what?" Or did he simply write "The Kiss"?

This is not to say that it is unimportant to learn technique, for a writer needs to learn as much as he can about the tools of his craft. But tools are only a means to something more, and a preoccupation with them can lead to mechanical writing. Viewpoint, then, is not a matter of manipulation, of attaching oneself, willy-nilly, to a position, to a character, and then telling the story through that character's mind and feelings. Viewpoint is organic, and writers have in common with the actor the method to make it work.

An actor trained in the Stanislavski method knows the psychology of his character; he knows *how* he does things because first he knows *why*. The actor tries to put himself in his character's place, to enter his world, live his life, master his actions, his thoughts and feelings. His truth. It is not enough merely to think of an emotion. Abstract emotions don't come across, or they fall into clichés. It is better to imagine what a character might think or do in a *certain situation*. Then the emotion comes of itself.

A writer uses a similar method of organic viewpoint. He puts himself in his character's place, enters his world, indeed creates his world, suffers his pains and celebrates his joys. If a writer has never laughed or cried at his typewriter, then I doubt if he has ever been deeply inside a character.

Before a writer takes up a viewpoint position he might do well to consider his own temperament and personality and the limitations these impose on his choices. Fiction is personal, as personal as the writer's imagination and emotional experience. New writers are often told, "Write what you know." I would broaden that by saying, "Write what you know emotionally." Love, hate, anger, joy, fear—these are universal. They become unique when they are connected to experience. Our emotional experiences are stored within us. Filtered through memory and a well-developed imagination, they can be called up, made fresh and organized into the work at hand. Creative imagination is the writer's valuable gift, and even though it is somewhat limited by his experience, within that sphere of experience it is unlimited in variety and combination. Hopefully the writer is always enlarging his sphere, adding to his storehouse with outward experience in reality.

Out of the sphere of my emotional experience I wrote "The Poet of Evolution Avenue" (*Redbook*), the story of a young wife and mother who was, also, a bad poet. She believed her creative gift was being hampered by the intrusion of her family. She had neither the time nor the privacy to write a real poem. Time and privacy are practically forced on her in the form of a vacation alone in her father's California apartment, but it isn't until she is ready to go home that she is able to write a real poem, and then only because she doesn't want to go home empty-handed.

This story is based on the old Ivory Tower idea: a poet is more productive when isolated from the world. My poet discovered that she had been making excuses for herself, that her world was her stimulus, and that she had trouble producing poetry without it.

The idea for that story came out of my own emotional experience. Some years earlier I had gone to California to be near my father while he was in the hospital undergoing surgery. For three weeks I lived alone in his apartment, a large, tight-security building in which I rarely saw the other residents. I had brought my typewriter, thinking I would turn out a volume or two between hospital visits. It didn't work. I was accustomed to working with people around. Interruptions. Interruptions can be marvelous. They take the place of pacing, a necessary activity of some writers. I learned that I am not an Ivory Tower writer, ideal as that may seem; I need the stimulus of family and friends.

Every writer has his own voice, and it is up to him to find it and use it with authority. That voice comes through as male or female, child or adult, humorous or serious, but behind it, within it, is the author's brooding presence, his vision of life. He describes the world from his point of view. He is on intimate terms with his viewpoint characters. Henry James could imagine what his focal character (he is never named) in *The Aspern Papers* might think and do when he is forced to admit to the woman who loves him that he has been using her for his personal gain. But I doubt if James could have lived inside Bigger, as Richard Wright did in *Native Son*, and chased and killed the huge rat in a Chicago tenement. Who is to say one view is better or worse than another? Each is different, unique.

Recognizing his limitations, an author adopts a viewpoint position he can understand emotionally as well as intellectually. My story, "Miss Dillon's Secret" (*Redbook*), is about a teacher. I have never been a teacher, but teaching is within the sphere of my emotional experience. I have been a student, of course, and my husband, now a principal, was once a teacher. His experiences have rubbed off on me. I believe that a natural teacher is born, not made, that the qualities in such a person work together to make learning exciting. The title character in my story, Miss Dillon, is drawn from a real person, an experienced teacher whose students come back to visit her with their husbands and wives and children and grandchildren.

I adopted the viewpoint position of a young teacher who had worked with Miss Dillon. There were more decisions for me to make. Will I place myself inside or outside the viewpoint character? And how far inside or outside? This can be a difficult choice, for each character has its own limitations, and the author, to keep his voice appropriate to the viewpoint, puts limits on his "knowledge" accordingly. He seems to know less than he does. Consider, for example, Hemingway's camera-eye view which limits his "knowledge" to what can be seen from the outside. Or, at the other extreme, Joyce's deep internalizing, which limits him in the other direction.

For my viewpoint character I adopted a position somewhere in between. With the story told in the third person, my character's problems are external, but her discovery of Miss Dillon's secret is internal, brought about by an emotional experience with one of her former students.

We might ask ourselves certain questions concerning viewpoint: 1) Who will be the narrator? author, in first or third person? character, in first person? or nobody (omniscient narrator)? 2) From what angle does the narrator tell the story? Above, center, front, periphery, shifting? 3) Where does the author place the reader? Near, far, shifting?

Sometimes an author adopts a viewpoint position instinctively, and all goes well. The voice flows from a stable position. At other times an author finds himself tangled in clumsy sentences and tedious explanations, surrendering his surprises too early, battling predictability, placing his best scenes offstage. When this happens, the problem could very well be the viewpoint he chose. He may be looking from the wrong angle. Usually I can tell by the way it "feels" if I'm in a good or poor viewpoint. But not always. Four years ago I wrote a short story called "The Boy Who Cooked." The title character, Benny, was the antagonist, and the viewpoint character was a woman protagonist whose name changed with each of the many versions I wrote. I couldn't sell the story. But I continued writing it, on and off, for four years, always keeping the boy, but frequently changing the characters around him, including the viewpoint character. The total number of pages devoted to that story runs into several hundred, which is some indication of my devotion to a character. But finally I gave up and put the story away.

Meanwhile, I had written and sold a story called, "No Such Thing as a Happy Marriage" (*Redbook*), in which the viewpoint character was a wife and mother named Jenny. Six months after that story was published, my editor, in a letter to me, mentioned Benny, the boy who cooked. Even before I had finished reading the letter, Benny, like Lazarus, rose from the dead. Why couldn't I write a new story for Benny? And why couldn't I surround him with the same cast of characters I had used in "No Such Thing as a Happy Marriage," with Jenny as the viewpoint character? I could, and I did. This time the viewpoint felt right; the voice flowed clearly from a stable position, and I wrote the story in a matter of hours. After four years of roaming through my typewriter, Benny had found his place, and his story, "The Boy Who Cooked," was published in *Redbook*.

The author's attitude toward a character (and his desire to create a similar attitude in the reader) can help determine the angle from which he views him. If the character is obviously sympathetic, the reader will identify. With some characters, however, the reader may feel only a tentative sympathy, until he is shocked into understanding by some revelation which allows him to feel complete sympathy. Sometimes, reader and character start out with a great distance between them. Perhaps their worlds are totally different. The author gradually pulls the reader into the character's world, and the reader ends by feeling sympathy. (I have this experience, as a reader, when I read Jean Genêt, for example.) A difficult relationship for an author to achieve is one in which the reader is forced to identify, perhaps unconsciously, with a character he dislikes. He is left wondering what there was about the story that fascinated him. What he may not realize is that, being human, we all

195

have our share of unattractive qualities, and seeing them in someone else stirs our recognition. Playwright Harold Pinter frequently achieves this kind of relationship.

In my story, "An Uncompromising Girl" (*Redbook*), my aim was for tentative sympathy and eventual complete sympathy. As the author (concealed narrator), I speak in the third person through the focal character. The channels of information between author and reader are a combination of the author's words, thoughts, and perceptions, and the character's words, actions, thoughts, perceptions and feelings. I used the angle of the character attempting to see herself from the outside, but erring in her vision—a position which placed limits on my "knowledge" of the character.

Earlier I spoke of the writer's voice, which I related to his vision of life and which includes his entire personality. Now, to that voice I would add two more voices: the story voice, which is the pace, the music, the tone of the story; and the voice of the viewpoint character, since it is through his eyes that we see everything that happens. Actually, it is impossible to separate all these voices, fused as they are into a creation that has passed through a maturing process in the author's mind and found its way to the page, either in harmony or dissonance. But for the sake of clarity, let us for a moment consider the voice of the viewpoint character.

If a story is told in the first person through a character (and not the author), then that character's voice is ever-present, and the writer, like the method actor, must know the character's every thought, act, feeling and desire. He must know his truth, his conscious and unconscious life, what he wants, or thinks he wants, and the difference between the two. My story "Don't Call Me Darling" (*Redbook*), was written from such a viewpoint. I had to know my character's attitude toward herself as a woman pursuing a career. I had to know how she felt about women's rights in general. And how she felt about friendship and human communication. I had to understand her intellect, her ambitions, her habits, and her insights. When she spoke, she revealed herself as a careful individual, and this voice had to remain consistent throughout the story, even though some of her attitudes were undergoing a change.

When an author knows the details of action and speech in a

character, he is in control of his material. He can become more familiar with his character by spending time with him, engaging him in conversation or argument, as if he were a living entity. He may even want to get up from his typewriter to act out a detail, a gesture, or an entire scene, in order to visualize it more clearly in his mind. Creating characters, seeing them come to life, is an exciting experience.

The entire experience of a story, from start to finish—and it may cover a period of several years—is an exciting one, in spite of the hard work, frustration and failures. Not a small portion of that excitement lies in the discoveries that are made, for in any work of creative imagination one looks for insights. What does the story have to say? Does it reinforce a shallow view of life? Or does it open up new insights for the viewpoint character? When I write a story about a character who seems very real to me, am I not at the same time making a discovery about myself? Writing, like acting, is an experiment in living. It is looking at life from another viewpoint. And life can be exciting wherever it is lived, or re-created—on the stage, or on the page.

40

TWENTY QUESTIONS TO ASK A CHARACTER

By Winifred Madison

Dig deeper! How many times does an author hear this advice? Characters are the life and breath of a story. Get your reader to care about what happens to them and you have won him over. But how do you do this?

First, most important of all, the character must seem alive to you, so very much alive that you feel as though you were inside his skin. This may happen instantly as you pass someone on the street or meet someone at a party and immediately you know something instinctively about this person and you feel you must use him in one of your stories. It may be a matter of luck that has no logical explanation. It simply happens.

The source does not matter so much as the *depth* and *insight* you develop. I get to know and understand my characters the same way I discover those individuals who come into my life. It's a mixture of first impressions, concrete factual knowledge, that mysterious "knowing" that comes about when you spend time with a person. Time is the key word.

Make up a dossier for each of your principal characters, either before you write your story or after you've completed the first draft. The twenty questions that follow will help you "dig deep," to probe the depths of your characters so you will get to know them.

1. Pretend you are walking down the street and you see your character for the very first time. Quick now—what word or phrase leaps to your mind? It may be one word: tyrant, drudge, darling, dreamer, flirt, macho, slob . . . anything at all. It may be a phrase, a warning, such as "Watch out!" or "Me first!" It could be a foolish giggle or a friendly hello or a plaintive, "I really wouldn't know . . ." No matter how far-

fetched or illogical this initial impact may be, it may prove a valuable insight into the essence of that particular person.

One day a young woman came to my door—attractive, blonde, smiling easily. The first words that filled my mind were "California, country sun, remarkably good health in every way." I made her sixteen years old, a capable 4-H girl, and she became the heroine of my young adult novel, *Dance With Me*. As I wrote it, that first impression stayed in my mind.

Some authors, attracted by a photograph or illustration in a newspaper or magazine, will clip it and use it as a model. A good idea.

2. Quickly following the initial impact will be the general physical impression of the person. Again, do not try to think of the words you may ultimately use when you write the story; let them come freely to your mind: "a burly block of a man," "a sunbeam," "a weed," "a wisp," "a full-blown cabbage rose about to shed its petals." The posture, the stance, the stride and rhythm of movement, possibly some body gestures, as well as the bulk and density of the physical build, will immediately give you clues to your character.

3. Are you reminded of an animal or an object? If a comparison happens to come to mind, explore it. Some people definitely resemble birds, cats, rodents, or monkeys, and in the case of inanimate objects such disparate things as a bus, or a feather duster, or a fragile wine glass. Be careful about clichés, the too frequent "birdlike woman" or the "China doll heroine."

4. Can you sense a color in your character, something beyond skin color or purely physical features? Certain psychics claim to see colors emanating from personalities. We cannot always go that far, but we may have the impression of an insistent color, a "brown personality," or a radiant red-gold, or a dismal blue-gray. One person may make you think of bright primary colors, while a subtle shifting of gray tones characterizes another.

5. What kinds of clothes does your character wear? Here is an important key to his psyche. Often people dress to conform to what they

believe is their social status: We all wear uniforms. However, we may be fooled, as individuals sometimes dress according to their fantasies and unconscious or unfulfilled desires—interesting and worthwhile for a fiction writer to explore. And use. For example, the middle-aged woman who wears too much makeup and designer jeans meant for her daughter or even for her granddaughter, may be saying she doesn't want anyone to know her age, or that she has a real dread of getting old and unattractive to young people (young men?), or that she wants to relive her youthful, romantic experiences. A businessman who wears western boots, shirt, and string tie and carries his attaché case to his big-city office is saying something important about himself and his dreams. It can be a defiance of convention or a yearning for a carefree youth he never had.

6. The person's voice is also revealing. Can you describe its tonal quality in one word, such as, soft, soothing, abrasive, enthusiastic, energetic, etc.? Does your character speak with an accent, a lisp, a certain eccentricity? How does he use words? What does he say, and what does he leave unsaid? As you learn more about this man, you should be able to imitate him, the quality of voice, the expression, suggest the very words he would use. Become an actor or actress as you write, saying out loud your character's speeches until you are convinced that is exactly how they must sound.

7. Where does your character live during the course of the story? How much of his immediate environment is forced on him and how much of it does he control? Does he like it? What does it mean to him? Is it possible he wants to leave it and if so, why?

You will not need and should not include in your story or novel every detail of your hero or heroine's life, but the more you know about it, the more you will understand some of the reasons for his or her actions.

8. Where and when was he born? Where did he live during his childhood? What country? What environment, i.e., a city, a small town, a rural area, mountains, the coast? How has this background shaped his personality? Was anything in particular happening historically?

9. What were the earliest and theoretically the most important influences? What of his parents, his siblings, relatives, friends, teachers, early loves? Here is where you will find many keys to the personality you are studying.

10. Every decade has new problems, changing standards, different moods. The forties are not like the fifties, nor are the fifties like the sixties, and so on. Does the one in which your hero formed his personality influence him in his actions and philosophy? Does he accept the standards of his time or does he rebel?

We have progressed beyond our first impression, although it should always stay with us. Can you imitate your character, walk like him, talk as he would, know exactly what he would think and how he would react to almost anything at all? If so, he is taking physical shape. Now try to get inside him. Know him better than he knows himself.

11. What is most important to him? What does he want more than anything else? Do you know his fantasies, his daydreams?

12. What is his conflict? If he has no problem, chances are he won't be interesting. Is his conflict imposed by circumstances, or does it emanate from within him? Suppose, for example, he is a young man who detests war and yet wishes to defend his country, a common dilemma for many young people today.

What of a woman who wants to get out and live by herself and yet fears she will lose her family if she does so?

Do you want your character to settle his conflict by himself, or will fate or circumstances do it for him?

13. How far will he go to get what he wants? Will he steal, commit a crime or perform an immoral act to achieve his goal? You may hook your reader by getting him to wonder about it along with you.

14. Here is a most telling question: What does your character fear the most? Does this keep him from achieving his ends?

15. More revealing areas. Cards, money, love. How much does winning matter to your character? How does he handle competition?

16. How does he react to children, and animals, foreigners, old people? How do you know? Would he kick his wife's dog if she weren't there to defend it? Would he carry a spider outside rather than kill it when it had crept into his bedroom? Would this woman refuse to rent a room to an oriental or a black or to someone who had children?

17. How does your character shape the plot? How does the plot shape him or her? Does he grow or change during the course of the story? If by any chance he remains the same, which should be unlikely, can you explain that?

18. How does this character interact with other members of the cast? Who acts as his foil? Who contrasts or complements your hero or heroine? Who or what threatens him?

19. By this time you've made quite a study of this character. Do you like him or her? What is undesirable or negative about him? What, no faults? Then such a character is likely to be b-o-o-ring. And not quite human. The same theory will hold for the villains of the piece. A person who is completely bad is only slightly less boring than one who is entirely good. Rembrandt used to advise mixing a little darkness in the light areas and a little light in the dark sections of a drawing. The same principle will make your characters more interesting.

20. Finally, what is there in your character that will make the reader care about what happens to him? Whether you are writing "the great American novel" or something more modest, your reader must be touched by your hero or heroine, or you have lost him. And what about you? Do you find yourself so involved that you hate to make your characters suffer? (Although you will have to do it anyway, because without suffering there is no story.)

A human being can be endlessly complicated. Twenty questions are only the first of many questions you will want to ask your character. What does he do on a stormy day? Does he cheat on his income tax? What does he like to eat? Where would he go on a vacation if he had a free choice and didn't have to think about money?

"Digging deeper" means living with your character day and night. It's one way of meeting interesting people!

41

FIRST PERSON SINGULAR

By Donald Hamilton

LET US now consider the case of Ethelbert Hackworthy, one of the country's foremost producers of unpublished novels. With unquenchable optimism, Ethelbert is commencing a new book. In the opening scene, carefully planned to seize the reader's attention in a grip of iron, he brings his proud but impecunious young hero, John Pennywhistle, into the music room of rich old Senator Silverbuck's mansion, where pretty Mary Silverbuck is seated at the piano.

Ethelbert is going strong now; he's right in the groove. He has John look at Mary and think she's quite a dish. He describes Mary, tenderly, down to the last ruffle on her fashionable gown and the last freckle on her piquantly upturned nose. So far, so good. But now Bert realizes that something is missing. Great Heavens, he hasn't described John yet! Well, that's easy to fix; and he has Mary look up from her music. She sees John in the doorway, and thinks him a fine tall figure of a man, which leads naturally to a detailed description of John. . . .

Do you like this? Do you feel free to jump from character to character and from viewpoint to viewpoint whenever the fancy takes you? Well, I suppose that's your privilege. Certainly you have lots of company. Many very good, or at least very successful, writers operate in just this way; and after all, it's the way most movie and television scripts are constructed, isn't it, with the cameras cutting freely from one character to another? So what, if anything, is wrong with it?

As far as I'm concerned, everything is wrong with it. The typewriter—or word processor, if you're modernized to that extent—is not a camera, capable of recording only the surface of things, and people. Why throw away your ability to penetrate character and personality by using it as a mere photographic instrument? As a matter of fact, I hate this floating-viewpoint technique; in treating the reader to brief glimpses of all the people in a novel, it really presents a good look at none of them.

As a writer, I disapprove of it, which is O.K., since nobody's forcing me to use it. But more important, as an omnivorous reader, I detest it, because it cheats me out of a great deal of literary entertainment. Why? Just as I'm getting interested in a certain character, male or female, the fickle author switches his attention—and tries to switch mine—to a different character, female or male. As far as I'm concerned, this kind of jumpy writing (we might call it kangaroo writing, considering the way the viewpoint leaps around) is strictly expendable.

The corny scene with which I opened this article is one I actually wrote years ago to illustrate a literary piece I never managed to sell. At that time, I was naive enough to think that everybody shared my prejudice against writers who flitted from viewpoint to viewpoint. I took for granted that every sensible reader much preferred writers who stuck to one character through thick and thin. But the years have brought resignation, if not humility. I'm now hardened to the fact that a lot of readers and editors actually *like* the wandering viewpoint, and that a lot of fairly skillful writers employ it profitably. I will even admit that a truly good writer can get away with it, even with a cantankerous reader like me. But then, a truly good writer can get away with anything.

Even if you think it's perfectly fine to switch protagonists as the fancy moves you, you should be aware of the fact that there is another school of writing that's been around for quite a while. I seem to recall that Fielding stuck pretty tightly to Tom Jones; and Daniel Defoe concentrated on Mr. Crusoe, and didn't bother us much with Mr. Friday's intimate hopes and aspirations. So let's consider the alternative to the omniscient spy-in-the-sky kind of viewpoint treatment that's so popular today.

Some years ago I was very flattered when, reviewing several mysteries for a rather highbrow publication, Jacques Barzun referred to one of my early suspense novels as a first-person story. It wasn't, but the fact that he'd come away from the book thinking that it was showed that I'd achieved my goal. I'd put the reader into the mind of my character— one character—so firmly that the reviewer had laid the book down at the end with the impression that it had been narrated by that character, not by me. Which was exactly the effect I'd been striving for. Now I understand that many writers consider other techniques of viewpoint perfectly proper. I understand; but I don't necessarily agree.

But enough of my literary preferences. Let's just consider the problems of a single-viewpoint novel, as opposed to one written from multiple viewpoints. The basic problem is discipline. As you write about your single character, treating the rest of the cast as peripheral to him, or her, you'll be subjected to continual temptations. The plotting can be tough, if everything has to be filtered through the consciousness of one individual.

You'll hear seductive little voices whispering that the creative life would be much less laborious if, instead of sticking grimly to the thoughts and experiences of "he," for example, you just slipped next door for a minute and let the reader know what "she" or "they" were thinking and doing. Resist! Stay with it, work it out from the hero's viewpoint, if that's what you started with, and figure out how to tell him, and the reader, what the heroine or the villains were up to, while he was struggling desperately to free himself from the cruel bonds securing him to the rusty ringbolts in the wall of the secret cavern soon to be flooded by the rising tide. You know nothing that the hero doesn't know, you see nothing he doesn't see, you feel nothing that he doesn't feel.

The reward for such authorial self-discipline can be great: a kind of hypnotic intensity that leads the reader to identify himself completely with your character; an identification that can never be achieved if you spend two pages on this gent in Moscow followed by a couple of paragraphs about this lady in Washington followed by a whole chapter about this married couple—viewpoint shifting constantly between him and her, of course—in London.

There is a simple substitute for this difficult discipline: Just write your novel in the first person, and you won't be tempted to let the viewpoint wander. If your hero or heroine is "I" instead of "he" or "she," you'll never find yourself slipping into any other viewpoint accidentally, just because it makes the plot work out more easily. You're locked into one character for good or ill.

Many years ago when I asked an editor about the salability problem, I got the following answer: "I'd say there is no prejudice against first-person stories, but in general, first-person viewpoint is difficult to use successfully." The notion that first-person writing is tough in some mysterious way is held by many writers and editors, and that puzzles me tremendously. To me, it seems a very simple technique. It's self-policing. With only one viewpoint available to you, how can you goof? Of course, I've used it for well over twenty novels, so I should have mastered it by now; but I can't recall having any trouble with it even at the first.

There are just two hurdles to be surmounted when using first-person narrative. The first is the plotting, which, as I've already said, can be demanding whenever you stick to a single protagonist—whether you write in the first person or the third. Since your lone hero or heroine can't be everywhere, many things have to happen off stage, so to speak, and you have to avoid getting your book cluttered up with too many messages or messengers of doom, as your protagonist learns of dramatic disasters occurring elsewhere. But I've never found this a great handicap, and I don't see why you should.

More difficult to overcome for some writers is a second obstacle: If the story is to be narrated by the chief character in the novel, he or she has to be a fairly compelling character. An interesting author can write an interesting third-person novel about a dull character, enlivening the text with his own comments and observations; but a boring character is almost bound to tell a boring first-person story about himself. So consider your protagonist very carefully before you commit yourself to writing a whole book as told by or through him or her: Is he, or she, good enough, strong enough, intriguing enough, exciting enough, to carry it off?

Please understand, I'm quite aware that the multiple-viewpoint technique has a place in the literary scheme of things: Tolstoy would have played hell trying to write *War and Peace* through the eyes of a single character. For a truly big book, a panorama novel, it's obviously the way to go. But my feeling is that a lot of lazy writers use it, not because their books are so tremendous in scope, but simply because they can't be bothered to work out how to tell the story from a single point of view. For these writers, and for the beginner learning how to master the tools of the trade, planning and writing a whole novel about *one* character should be a valuable exercise, teaching the student many new things about the profession of writing.

I have a hunch that a novel so written might well turn out to be the best thing that author ever wrote. Of course I'm prejudiced.

42

CREATING A SERIES CHARACTER

By Robert B. Parker

WHILE I have ventured outside the form upon occasion *(Three Weeks in Spring, Wilderness, Love and Glory),* it is the chronicle of a series character named Spenser that puts bread and Promise margarine on the table at my house.

Writing about a protagonist who has appeared before and will appear again presents some specialized problems. For instance, you have to find exposition tricks that will inform people who are reading you for the first time, without boring people who have read all your books in sequence. And, while both the writer and the reader are aware that the hero of a series is very unlikely to die, the hero doesn't know it. One has to be careful to render him as a man no less mortal than the rest of us.

But if there are problems in a series, there are also opportunities. If you create a character in one book that you like (Hawk, for instance, in *Promised Land*), you can use him again. And if you didn't get him right the first time, you have another chance, and another. Moreover, you have the chance to develop your hero over a sequence of books and during a span of real time. Thus Spenser, who first appeared when I was 41, can grow, as I have.

There are, then, a few things that are uncommon about writing a series of novels. But there is much more that is common to the craft. In each instance, series or not, I begin with what Henry James called a "treatment," a brief statement of story and locale and major characters. The treatment is normally about two pages in longhand. Don't be misled. This is the hard part. The treatment may take a month of sitting, several hours each day, thinking (my wife says thinking has always been especially trying for me, but one should pay her little mind. She once described me as looking like a Mississippi state cop). I didn't have to think up the protagonist when I set out on my first novel *(The Godwulf Manuscript).* Spenser sprang fully conceived from my imagination where he had been lurking since I wrote my age in single figures. Because I don't have to imagine the hero, I always start with the scene, i.e., the place, the circumstances, the people that I can write about, the academic scene, for instance, or the book-tour-talk-show scene.

From the treatment, I develop a chapter outline, still in longhand, that lays out the sequence. It's not very fancy (a chapter might be outlined in a sentence, "Spenser drives to Smithfield and talks with the police chief"), and it partakes of none of those insistent curlicues that you learned in school (if there's an A, there has to be a B, etc.). The whole novel gets outlined in five or six pages. It is primarily for my emotional well-being. It saves me from rolling a piece of white paper into the typewriter and then staring blankly not knowing what to write. The outline is there, Linus; I need only look. Sometimes I don't look at all. The outline to *The Judas Goat* was there beside me on the desk every writing day, and I never so much as glanced at it. Sometimes I follow it closely, sometimes I stop mid-book and re-outline something I haven't been able to get right. But I always know pretty much what the story is when I begin to write it.

Then, the outline completed, I have only to write the book. I'm not being cute. Once the story is conceived, the hard part is over. If you have the ability, then executing the book is merely a matter of sustained (though hardly exhausting) effort. Discipline (though hardly of monastic intensity) is required.

If you have the talent without discipline, you'll have thirty pages of a swell novel in your desk for the rest of your life and you'll publish a couple of good short poems somewhere. If you have the discipline without talent you'll have ten unpublished novels in your closet. There's a third possibility, I suppose. You could have discipline, no talent, and a knack, and be Harold Robbins. Ideally, perhaps, all three would be best. But of one thing I am certain. Writers write, and one is not a writer until one has written.

I set myself a minimum number of pages, as a way to get from beginning, through middle, to end. The number of pages varies with circumstance. I have never set the limit lower than two pages a day, or higher than five. Unless I'm on a roll, I stop when I've written my quota. If there is time left in my writing day, I'll turn to something else, but by writing my quota I have fulfilled my responsibility to the book that day.

Since my typescript tends to equate one-to-one to the printed page, five pages a day will give me a two-hundred-page book in forty days of writing. That sounds mechanical, and it is. It is a large task broken down into many small ones. When I can, I try to follow Hemingway's advice to stop while you're hot so it will be easy to start up next day. But sometimes I'm not hot for weeks on end and then I just do my quota. If you wait to be hot you'll accomplish that thirty-page novel mentioned above.

I am not compulsive about writing. I don't work weekends. I don't work nights. If one of my sons is performing, I go and watch. If my wife will take a trip with me, I'll travel. I don't bring a typewriter. If my novel comes out three days later, or two weeks later, it makes small difference. Writing is my livelihood, not my life. And while I can't conceive of not writing at all, I'm not compelled to do it every day.

On the other hand, I do have to do it regularly. I would assume most writers who succeed in publishing any quantity of work do it regularly.

I have always been more interested in the protagonist than in the plot, which is, I suppose, one reason I write largely in the first person. If you're in doubt, I'd urge you to try first-person narration. It's the natural storytelling mode ("You shoulda seen what happened to me at Hampton Beach last night"), and it helps prevent inflated narrative language. If you tell your story in the first person, it is very handy to invent some people who can help you interpret your hero by offering some objective comment. In *The Great Gatsby,* Fitzgerald took that technique to the extreme by having Gatsby's story told to us by Nick Carraway. It is, of course, part of Gatsby's tragedy that he doesn't understand what happened to him. He couldn't have explained it. Carraway had to.

Spenser talks of himself, but for the parts he can't or won't speak of, Susan Silverman serves. She helps us understand him. She helps him understand himself. Hawk too helps illuminate Spenser. The ways in which Hawk and Spenser are alike, and the ways in which they are not alike, are crucial in imagining Spenser.

An interesting story about dull people may be possible, but I can't think of one. For me, the plot is in large part a frame, a series of occasions in which Spenser is able to demonstrate what he is, to enact himself. But to speak of the two, plot and character, as if they were separable is misleading. "What is character," James said, "but the determination of incident? What is incident but the illustration of character?"

The best books are always about more than the plot anyway. They have echoes and implications. They are informed by a sense of how life is, or ought to be. George Higgins wrote about cops and robbers. But his books are also about the thinness of the line between them, and about the way a man should behave, and about the relationships among men in groups. In *True Confessions,* John Gregory Dunne wrote about a murder investigation. But he also wrote about brothers, and hierarchy and autonomy and Catholicism, and Irish-ness. "The only reason for the existence of the novel," James said, "is that it does attempt to represent life." Aspiring writers should give their days and nights to Henry James (and me).

Writing isn't as hard as writers lead you to think it is, but it does not lend itself to shortcuts. Clichés are shortcuts; avoid them like the plague. But there are other more subtle temptations to cut across the field. I remember a manuscript in which the author used one description for two people, something to the effect that they were both huge and bald and menacing. That's a shortcut. The novelist attempting in some way "to represent life" must recognize that rarely in life are two people identical, even if they are minor characters.

A writer does that not because he's lazy, but because he's impatient. He wants to get on with it. It takes some understanding and some self-control to come to terms with the fact that the careful representation of life *is* getting on with it.

I have sometimes made the remark that I don't think writing very teachable. But if you are going to pursue writing instruction despite that admonition (no one has ever lost money rejecting my advice), be certain that your teacher has done what he/she/it teaches. Many people understand reading, but only writers understand writing. An intelligent reader can often say what's good or bad about a piece of writing, and there are critics who have helped me understand my own work better. But only a writer can tell you how (if it can be told): a writer who publishes; for money. I believe that there are very few good novels that don't get published. In fact I believe there are none.

210

There are, however, good novels that don't get finished. There is no one right way. Each of us finds a way that works for him. But there is a wrong way. The wrong way is to finish your writing day with no more words on paper than when you began. Writers write.

43

THE HISTORICAL NOVEL: BLENDING FACT
AND FICTION

By Thomas Fleming

First the good news. Writing an historical novel fuses factual research and the creative imagination in a way that is both exciting and meaningful.

Now the bad news. Making an historical novel work is the most difficult kind of writing I have ever attempted. As someone who has written formal history books, biographies, and contemporary novels, I think I can qualify as the voice of experience.

When I emphasize the difficulty, I presume a writer will take both fiction and history seriously. Taking fiction seriously means you have to have believable characters, whose motivations are intensely personal, whose individual lives are significant enough to make readers care.

Most of the characters in a serious historical novel are a blend of the writer's unconscious and his research. In my novel, *Liberty Tavern,* for instance, I discovered that before the American Revolution not a few British officers retired to the American colonies and went into business. Some bought taverns, a very lucrative operation in those days. Jonathan Gifford, one of the main characters in the novel, began to take shape in my mind. But his personal characteristics were formed by my enduring interest in conflict between strong taciturn fathers and idealistic sons—a conflict rooted in my own life experience.

The general ideas for my historical novels have always emerged from digging into the gritty, confusing tumultuous world of the past. There is simply no such thing as a dull era, if you get into the daily lives people led in other times, the things that worried them, obsessed them. But discovering the inner life of another time is not easy. You have to make an often mind-bending effort to grasp the way men and women felt about the large and small events that swept through their lives. I can assure you that nine times out of ten, it is not the way the formal history books tell it.

Take the Civil War, for instance. A crusade to free the slaves? Or at least to preserve the Union? Only about 50% true. Millions of northerners loathed the war and violently opposed it. To discover these forgotten voices in the past takes hours of reading diaries and letters, staring blearily at old newspapers on microfilm, plowing through articles in historical journals, devouring 700- and 800-page memoirs of politicians and pundits.

Here we come to an important principle in writing the historical novel. It should offer a fresh point of view about an historical experience, even a new interpretation of it, that says something significant to modern readers. My novel, *Liberty Tavern,* published in 1976, was set in the American Revolution—a long distance from our computerized, electrified, modern world. Yet it spoke to the concerns of post-Vietnam America. It portrayed the Revolution, as it was fought in New York and New Jersey, as a civil war that often pitted brother against sister, father against son, wife against husband. To a nation divided by the upheavals of the 1960's, riven by bitter conflicts between the generations about the meaning of America, *Liberty Tavern* reminded readers that even in the primary experience of the country's birth, Americans had had to deal with similar traumas.

Not all historical novels have to be set in the distant past. I considered my 1981 novel, *The Officers' Wives,* an historical novel because when I began it in 1979 it required the same techniques of massive research to exhume the attitudes and opinions of the 1950's when the book begins. I got the idea for this book while writing a history of West Point. In my four years of toil at the Military Academy, I got to know a lot of officers and their wives. I also read about the often grisly adventures of Army wives in other eras. Suddenly it occurred to me that no one had ever written a novel about the U.S. Army from a woman's point of view. Here was the new interpretation I feel is so important in an historical novel. I blended it with the twin agonies of Korea and Vietnam to give readers a picture of the post-World War II army from the inside.

Both these books offer other insights into technical aspects of the historical novel. *Liberty Tavern* dealt with the guerilla war side of the Revolution in New York and New Jersey—with experience that was too scattered, undocumented, erratic, to appeal to the systematic mind of the historian. Guerilla encounters are minor events in history books, if they are mentioned at all. But they were not minor to the men who fought and died in them. More important, they were ideal material for me as a novelist, because they gave my literary imagination room to invent characters and events out of my knowledge of the period.

Similarly, in *The Officers' Wives,* by focusing on the women's experience in the Army, I instantly achieved the freedom to explore a world that official and formal histories never even mention. But it was (and is) a world intimately and intensely attached to the larger world of battles and policies in which the officers move. The oblique approach is highly recommended in writing historical novels. Coming at the big history from an unexpected angle can be the secret of a novel's success.

In these two novels, major historical figures—Douglas MacArthur in *The Officers' Wives,* George Washington in *Liberty Tavern*—appear on only one or two pages. The main stories are told almost entirely through the lives and passions of the imaginary characters. I know historical novels are written about great men and women (Gore Vidal's *Lincoln* is a recent example), but I have always felt uncomfortable about converting famous names into important fictional characters, inventing scenes and dialogue for them at length. To me this bespeaks either an indifference to the facts of history or a naïveté unbecoming to the serious historical novelist. Even moderately educated readers know too much about these people to give the literary imagination room to invent without blundering into outright distortion of the historical truth. The novelist should never confuse himself with the biographer.

Similarly I have never seen much point in historical novels that recreate the battles of Yorktown or Gettysburg or Midway. The novelist may make us feel these events with more intensity, but we learn nothing new from an historical point of view. These vast collisions can be—and have been—reported in exhaustive detail from known historical facts. I wrote a 320-page book, *Beat the Last Drum,* on the battle of Yorktown, without inventing a single character or line of dialogue.

Whether a book deals with major or minor events, one of the fundamental problems of the historical novel is the question of how much the writer can alter history as his research reveals it to him. In a brilliant discussion of the difference between fiction and the so-called new journalism, John Hersey laid down the principle that the fiction writer has a duty to invent while the nonfiction writer must never invent. This is a sound proposition, but it does not work for the historical novelist because he is consciously blending fact and fiction, telling a story set in another time, which has considerable historical importance (otherwise it's not worth telling) yet is invented. The historical novel exists in a border area between fiction and fact. This puts added strains on the artistic process and requires more than ordinary judgment from the writer.

Some writers have decided that this lack of clear-cut rules gives them the license to do almost anything with the historical facts. I disagree. If the historical novel is to be taken seriously as history—and I believe it can and should be—there are certain ground rules that should be observed. Major figures or events should never be altered in absurd or extreme ways. For instance, it would be ridiculous to portray George Washington as a homosexual, or tell your readers that the South won the battle of Gettysburg.

It is, on the other hand, perfectly permissible to have a jaundiced historical character of the second rank, such as Aaron Burr, portray Washington as an idiot, as the fictional Burr does in Gore Vidal's novel.

Remember, the imagination can invent anything. This is a boon if you are writing a novel set in the year 3500. But an historical novel requires the writer to anchor his imagination in a reality with discernible boundaries.

At the same time, the historical novelist should have the freedom to simplify certain aspects of the story he is telling. History is simply too confusing, too cluttered with extraneous characters saying or doing similar things, to be told exactly as it happened.

In my recent novel, *The Spoils of War,* one of the major characters becomes deeply involved in stealing the presidential election of 1876. This was a very complicated operation, involving at least two dozen people. I simplified it by focusing on two or three of the more interesting participants—my imaginary main character, Jonathan Stapleton, John C. Reid, the managing editor of *The New York Times,* and James Garfield, the future president of the United States.

Although the personal story must remain the primary focus, one of the chief reasons for writing an historical novel is to show the power, the impact of major events on peoples' lives. Here is where the novelist and the historian, artistry and research, should unite. It is too

215

humdrum, too obvious, merely to show your characters getting thrown into the maelstrom of a war or a political upheaval. There has to be a personal dimension visible in their reaction to these major events.

In *The Spoils of War,* Jonathan Stapleton's son, Rawdon, is violently antagonistic to his father for the part he plays in the Civil War. Rawdon shares the feelings of the majority of the family, who opposed the war. It is also a neurotic wound, caused by the misery his father's participation in the war inflicted on his mother. In 1877 America was swept by stupendous strikes and riots. Many people feared it was the beginning of a revolution. Rawdon exultantly joined this radical upheaval, because he was eager to undo the status quo that his father and the men of his generation had established after Appomattox.

But Rawdon's wife, Genevieve, cannot join him because she has been wounded by history in another way. She lived in New York during the three nightmare days of the Draft Riots in 1863—a proto-revolution that was suppressed by Union troops, including a regiment commanded by her father. She cannot bear the thought of encouraging the mob to run wild in the city's streets again. She denounces Rawdon's recklessness, inflicting a wound on their marriage from which it never recovers.

I think—or at least hope—that readers watching these characters struggling with this blend of the personal and the historical will feel their personal anguish and simultaneously think and learn about the historical experience.

That is what makes the historical novel so exciting and so challenging—this need to appeal to both the reader's head and heart. For me, fiction makes history live with an intensity and reality usually lacking in the analytic prose of the modern historian. At the same time, history adds dimension to fiction. It makes the literary imagination more ambitious, more profound.

44

INSIDE THE MYSTERY NOVEL

By Stanley Ellin

To THE author, plot is one of the most important elements of his mystery novel. To the reader, it is one of the least important.

If that sounds like too glittering a generalization, sit down with pencil and paper, consider any mystery novel that has made an imprint on you, then try to outline its plot in fair detail. I do not exclude even that mystery you read yesterday; in fact, it's the one whose plot may now seem to be most opaque.

What you will have remembered with some clarity is what Alfred Hitchcock has labeled The McGuffin, that element which provides purpose for the events in the story. The plan to blow up the city, the search for the lost heir, the pursuit of a vendetta, the million-dollar jewel heist: these are McGuffins and can be summed up in a line. It is only after they have been developed into a dramatic sequence of events leading to the climactic disposition of the case that they may be properly called plots.

Plot is to the mystery novel what the skeleton is to the human body. It must be there to provide form and dimension to the body, but it is not something we are inclined to take notice of. What we are affected by in our view of the body is its fleshy covering. We assume the skeleton is there, all parts in proper conjunction, but, unless we are medical doctors or representational artists, we don't give it any thought at all.

The relevance of this to the mystery novelist is both obvious and paradoxical: He must provide a plot for his story that makes dramatic sense, but if he achieves this, he will not be judged by it. If, however, he totally fails to construct a sound plot, he will be judged by it in very unkind terms.

Not that plotting requires such perfection that failure to achieve it will put the author on the rack. A good many mysteries have plots that are not all that logical or convincing or fair to the reader and yet they have been highly successful. No one put it better than Nora Charles, in Hammett's *The Thin Man,* who, after husband Nick has explained to her his solution of the mystery, says as the last line in the book: "That may be, but it's all pretty unsatisfactory."

So it was, both mystery and solution, each being helped over hard places by the author's nudging, and it took a mordant, objective self-critic like Hammett to make a joke about that in his curtain line for the tale. But in no way did this flawed plot bear on the public reception of the book, either in published form or movie dramatization, because the vastly talented Hammett provided a covering for his skeleton that glossed over all flaws. He created a compatible marriage between two attractive, clever, and articulate people, plunged them into the intellectual and social high life of New York City, A.D. 1932, and presented them in a narrative style so precise and jazzily rhythmical that it is a pleasure to read, line by line. Nick and Nora became immortal as the epitome of what marriage could be when the partners in it really enjoyed each other's company, out of bed as well as in. Such plot as the story displays simply gives them room for that enjoyment.

Hammett could get away with it. And Raymond Chandler, who sometimes scrambled his plots so wildly that he could barely find his own way through them, could get away with it. And so, at times, could Conan Doyle and Agatha Christie and Rex Stout and others of that distinguished ilk. They earned the right to occasional faulty plotting, one might say, by their sheer skill in potent characterization, vivid ambience, and scenes that so satisfy the reader that he, although now and then aware of a little bump on the rails, still takes pleasure in the trip.

The writer who has not yet earned that license, however, must take heed. For his story he has to provide a goal to be attained and a sequence of events that moves the protagonist, plausibly and with dramatic interest, toward that goal. How narrowly this course is to be charted is up to the writer. One may outline each chapter in detail; another may prefer to jot down several giant steps along the way and then depend on inspiration during the writing to fill in the gaps between. But logic must always prevail, and dramatic interest, and, not to be forgotten, the necessity to play fair with the reader.

That last pretty well defines the most difficult plotting problem for the mystery novelist to solve. In a proper mystery, the author must withhold information from the reader or else there is very little mystery. A mystery written from the omniscient viewpoint, where the private thoughts of every character are exposed, cannot fairly obscure the thoughts of any one of them, and that is bound to give away the works very soon, if only by process of elimination. If the writer does try to get away with this, it will eventually become clear that he is manipulating the reader just to sustain the mystery, and in that lies failure of the work as a whole.

Long ago, to get around this, the Comparatively Close Associate was invented: friend or partner or whatever of the protagonist, close enough to him to share in events, not close enough to know his unspoken thoughts. Thus it wasn't the author who was arbitrarily concealing vital information from the reader, it was the limitations of the Comparatively Close Associate that were responsible. Holmes's Watson is, of course, the prime example of this, and it is worth noting that it is the superb, life-like drawing of Watson in his limitations that makes the device work.

But every literary device grows thin with time and usage; this one grew thin, too, and nowadays there is much more reliance on having the reader identify directly with the protagonist rather than through an intermediary. This may be done through first-person or third-person narrative, first person offering instant empathy with the protagonist but demanding that the author manage always to express himself exactly as the protagonist-narrator logically would; third person freeing the author from this obligation but sacrificing instant empathy in the process.

In either case, the vital elements in putting the story across are the characterization of the protagonist—demonstrated in his pursuit of his goal—and the ambience of the locales through which he moves. These, after the brief gratification of finding out how the mystery is solved, are what the reader takes away with him. And, though the reader himself may not be aware of it, these elements are what will make him look forward to the next book featuring that protagonist. It was not Conan Doyle's plotting that won him his audience; it was Sherlock Holmes and the vivid evocation of Victorian and Edwardian London that did it. The persona of Holmes, larger than life yet wholly convincing and sympathetic, is the magic. The same applies to the following generations of private eyes drawn by such writers as Hammett and Chandler where there was an effort to present a more realistic protagonist. Willy-nilly, Sam Spade and Philip Marlowe became commanding and magnetic presences, and the corrupt world they inhabited, a source of endless fascination.

Beyond these presences must be others in any compelling narrative. The characters with whom the protagonist interplays are born out of the need of the story's plot. But once born, they must be given the same intense life as the protagonist. Detailed descriptive writing is a dull instrument in achieving this. Seen from the protagonist's viewpoint, the secondary character reveals himself or herself through speech and action. Handled properly, the secondary character on introduction will reveal the outlines of an identity ready to be developed into a full-fleshed image as the story progresses.

In turn, these lesser characters will, occasionally to the writer's surprise, reveal facets of themselves along the way the novelist had not anticipated. They may then affect the course of the plot, give it twists not considered in the preparation of the story line. All to the good, if the writer remains in command and can properly judge whether to explore these unexpected developments or to reject them.

Finally, in terms of reader appeal, the well-written mystery novel provides an acute and graphic sense of place. The room, the building, the street, the neighborhood, an entire area must be more than a stage setting. True, they must be as relevant to the story as a stage setting is to a play; the difference is that the novelist's presentation of locale and setting must reflect the protagonist's view of them. In this way, the author is given an excellent device for digging that much deeper into his protagonist and providing us with unstated insights into his nature. His sensitivity and powers of observation, perhaps his cynicism, his nose for corruption, his sense of hidden menace—all can be suggested by a view of locale he would reflect.

Any description of place, no matter how nicely worded, that goes beyond what the protagonist might make of it instantly suggests the author's hand at work, and there will be a break in the narrative at that point. The one way of avoiding this pitfall is for the writer to know his protagonist so well that he is fully aware of his capabilities and limitations from the start.

Plot is the skeleton, characterization the flesh, everything else the clothing.

Thus, in the long run, the mystery novel devotee who innocently believes he is drawn to certain authors because of their clever plotting is very much mistaken in this.

It is not a mistake that the author himself can afford to make.

45

ONE CLUE AT A TIME

By P.D. James

FOR ME one of the keenest pleasures of rereading my favorite mysteries is their power to transport me instantly into a familiar world of people, places and objects, a world in which I feel at once comfortably at home.

With what mixture of excitement, anticipation and reassurance we enter that old brownstone in Manhattan, that gentle spinster's cottage in St. Mary Mead (never fully described by Agatha Christie but so well imagined), that bachelor flat in London's Piccadilly where Bunter deferentially pours the vintage port [for Lord Peter Wimsey], that cozy Victorian sitting room on Baker Street.

A sense of place, creating as it does that vivid illusion of reality, is a necessary tool of any successful novelist. But it is particularly important to the fabricator of the mystery: the setting of the crime and the use of commonplace objects help to heighten by contrast the intruding horror of murder. The bizarre and the terrifying are rooted in comforting reality, making murder more believable.

There is probably no room in crime fiction that we enter with a keener sense of instant recognition than the claustrophobic upstairs sitting room at 221B Baker Street. Baker Street is now one of the dullest of London's main thoroughfares, and it is difficult, walking these wide pavements, to picture those foggy Victorian evenings with the inevitable veiled lady alighting from her hansom cab outside the door of the celebrated Sherlock Holmes.

But we can see every detail of the room into which Mrs. Hudson will usher her: the sofa on which Holmes reclines during his periods of meditation; the violin case propped against the wall; the shelves of scrapbooks; the bullet marks in the wall; the two broad windows overlooking the street; the twin armchairs on each side of the fireplace; the bottle of 7-percent-cocaine solution on the mantel shelf; the desk with the locked drawer containing Holmes's confidential records; the central table with "its white cloth and glimmer of china and metal" waiting for Mrs. Hudson to clear away.

The mental scene has, of course, been reinforced countless times in films and on television, but what is remarkable is that so vivid a picture should be produced by so few actual facts. Paradoxically, I can find no passage in the books that describes the room at length and in detail. Instead, Sir Arthur Conan Doyle builds up the scene through a series of stories object by object, and the complete picture is one that the reader himself creates and furnishes in his own imagination from this accumulation of small details.

Few things reveal the essential self more surely than the rooms in which we live, the objects with which we choose to surround ourselves, the books we place on our shelves, all those small household goods that help reaffirm identity and provide comfort and a sense of security. But the description in crime fiction of domestic interiors, furnishings and possessions does more than denote character; it creates mood and atmosphere, enhances suspense and is often crucial to the plot.

In Agatha Christie, for example, we can be confident that almost any domestic article mentioned, however commonplace, will provide a clue, either true or false. A loose door number hanging on its nail; flowers that have died because no one watered them; an extra coffee spoon in a saucer; a picture postcard lying casually on the desk. In *Funerals Are Fatal,* we do well to note the bouquet of wax flowers on the malachite table. In *Murder at the Vicarage,* we can be sure that the tall stand with a plant pot standing in front of the window isn't there for nothing.

And in *The Murder of Roger Ackroyd,* we shouldn't be so intrigued by the corpse that we fail to notice how one chair has been strangely pulled out from its place by the wall.

All writers of mystery fiction use such devices, but few with such deceptive cunning. It is one of the paradoxes of the genre that it deals with that great absolute, death, yet deploys the trivia of ordinary life as the frail but powerful instruments of justice.

Because in a Christie mystery the puzzle is more important than either the characterization or the setting, she seldom describes a room in great detail. Hers is the art of the literary conjurer. How very different is the loving care and meticulous eye with which a novelist such as Margery Allingham creates for us her highly individual domestic interiors.

In *More Work for the Undertaker,* how brilliantly she describes every room of the eccentric Palinode family, so that the house itself is central to the plot, its atmosphere pervades the novel, and we feel that we know every secret and sinister corner.

But my favorite Allingham rooms are in *The Tiger in the Smoke,* with its opposing characters of the saintly Canon Avril and the psychopathic killer Jack Havoc. How simply described and how absolutely right is the Canon's sitting room. "It was the room he had brought his bride to 30 years before, and since then . . . nothing in it had ever been changed. It had become a little worn in the interim, but the good things in it, the walnut bookcase with the ivory chessmen displayed, the bureau with 13 panes in each glass door, the Queen Anne chair with the 7-foot back, the Persian rug which had been a wedding present from his younger sister, Mr. Campion's mother, had all mellowed just as he had with care and use and quiet living."

Right, too, in its very different style, is the sitting room of his dress-designer daughter, Meg, littered with its sketches of dresses and strewn with swaths of material and samples of braids and beads. "Between the demasked grey walls and the deep gold carpet there ranged every permissible tint and texture from bronze velvet to scarlet linen, pinpointed and enlivened with draining touches of Bristol blue."

This is a highly individual room in the grand manner but without pretentiousness, and I'm not in the least surprised that after a dubious sidelong glance, Chief Inspector Luke decided that he liked it very much indeed.

A room I like very much indeed is Lord Peter Wimsey's sitting room in his flat at 110A Piccadilly. We see it most clearly through the eyes of Miss Murchison in Dorothy L. Sayers's *Strong Poison.* She is shown by Bunter into a glowing, book-lined room "with fine prints on the walls, an Aubusson carpet, a grand piano, a vast chesterfield and a number of deep, cozy armchairs upholstered in brown leather."

"The curtains were drawn, a wood fire blazed on the hearth, and before it stood a table with a silver tea service whose lovely lines were a delight to the eye." No wonder Miss Murchison was impressed.

After his marriage, of course, Lord Peter honeymooned with his

Harriet at Talboys, an Elizabethan farmhouse in Hertfordshire that Lord Peter bought as their country retreat, complete with inglenooked fireplace, ancient beams, tall Elizabethan chimneys, erratic plumbing and the inevitable corpse in the cellar. Meanwhile, the dowager Duchess of Denver was busying herself collecting the chandeliers and tapestries for the Wimseys' town house in Audley Square and congratulating herself that the bride "was ready to prefer 18th-century elegance to chromium tubes." I am myself partial to 18th-century elegance, but I still feel more at home in that bachelor flat at 110A Piccadilly.

Incidently, Talboys was modernized and completely refurnished, including the installation of electricity and the provision of additional bedrooms, before the murderer of its previous owner had been executed—in England a matter then of only a couple of months. That was remarkably speedy even for the 1930's. Today I am doubtful whether even the son of a Duke would be able to command such speedy service.

I myself work in the tradition of Margery Allingham and share her fascination with architecture and domestic interiors; indeed, it is often the setting rather than a particular character or a new method of murder that sparks my creative imagination and gives rise to a novel.

In my last book, *The Skull Beneath the Skin,* the setting is a restored Victorian castle on a lonely offshore island. Here the owner, obsessed with violent death, has created his own private chamber of horrors, a study decorated with old woodcuts of execution scenes, Staffordshire figures of Victorian murderers, mourning regalia and the artifacts of murder.

Here I have used the setting to fulfill all the functions of place in detective fiction; to illustrate character, create atmosphere, provide the physical clues to the crime and to enhance that sense of unease, of the familiar and ordinary made strange and terrible, which is at the heart of detective fiction.

And it is surely the power to create this sense of place and to make it as real to the reader as is his own living room—and then to people it with characters who are suffering men and women, not stereotypes to be knocked down like dummies in the final chapter—that gives any mystery writer the claim to be regarded as a serious novelist.

46

WRITING THE SUSPENSE-ADVENTURE NOVEL

By Clive Cussler

I HATE to write.

Quite frankly, I see nothing blasphemous in admitting it. There are thousands of writers who find scribbling words on paper a colossal drag. Writing is a damned tough way to make a buck, at least to most people. I seethe internally when I hear or read about those Pollyannas who merrily peck away at their typewriters, whistling while they create, morning, noon and night, tossing off 20,000 words between coffee breaks.

I hate them, too.

On a good day of total effort, beginning at nine o'clock and ending at five (an old routine carried over from my advertising agency days), I'm lucky if I turn out four finished pages or 1,000 words. And then I have to take a long walk, indulge in a martini and take a snooze prior to dinner, before I'm mentally rejuvenated enough to return to the land of the living.

When I finally type THE END to a novel, the clouds part and the sun bursts through, flowers blossom across the land, angels sing along to harp music, and I deflate like an old balloon whose elastic is shot.

Therefore, because writing is so exhausting, to me at any rate, I plan and research each project thoroughly before hitting the proper keys to spell out CHAPTER ONE. My problem is that I can visualize my characters, backgrounds, and events as though I were standing in the middle of the action, so the difficult part is turning all these wonderful sights and sounds into mere words that place the reader amid the action, too.

To me the readers come above all else. I look upon them as guests who have gone out of their way to spend time and expense to indulge in whatever small enjoyment I can provide. My particular genre is suspense-adventure, so in order to get off the mark quickly, I must find a concept that grabs the reader's fancy before he turns past the title page. Within the realm of adventure there are thousands of subjects and tales that have great appeal. One of the trends in fashion at present is for novelists to write fiction based loosely on a non-fiction event. This often revolves around a "what if" principle. For instance, one day I asked myself, what if they raise the *Titanic*? The next question that entered my mind was why? Obviously the cost of salvaging the great liner from two and one-half miles down in the abysmal depths would be enormous. What reason would justify the effort and expense? Out of this pre-examination a plot was born.

Without a concept hook to hang your plot on, you have nothing. The swashbuckler of yesterday who chopped up the moustached villains and did little else but carry the insipid heroine off into the sunset at the finish won't cut the mustard today. The idea of having a blimp bomb the Superbowl as in *Black Sunday* was a good hook for a "what if" adventure. *Airport* and of course *Jaws* are other successful stories that embraced this principle.

More than ever, the reader who shells out for your novel is looking for an escape. It's a fact of life, that if you don't aim your talents at the market, you won't sell. If the reader isn't presold by an author's past reputation, or by word-of-mouth recommendation, or a blitz publicity campaign, he has no other reason to select your masterpiece except for one hell of an intriguing concept.

Assuming that you have the story the world is waiting to devour, you should now turn your energies to the next step in the adventure novel—structure.

Gotcha! I'll bet you thought I was going to say plot or perhaps characterization. Not so. Next to a mind-boggling concept, structure is the most important foundation for a novel. Whether you intend to write it in the first person or the third is elementary. You should take the path that makes you comfortable. First person allows you to probe the hero or heroine's mind in depth; you see only what they see. The third-person narration, on the other hand, gives a wider range of freedom to travel into areas the first person cannot follow. Seeing the action from the central character's eyes limits the writer to what I call the "Formula-A Structure." You travel with the narrator from prologue to epilogue, seeing only what he sees. This is a common practice among new writers because of its basic simplicity.

However, I do not mean to suggest that Formula A is mundane. Hardly. It has been used with great success by writers since man first scratched in the sand. The classical love stories, mysteries and, yes, horror stories, too, have taken advantage of its storytelling smoothness. Formula A also makes for a tight tale that involves the readers as closely in the action as though they were the parrot on Long John Silver's shoulder.

For writers who turn on to intricate plotting and a cast of hundreds, Formula B is the only way to fly. Here the third-person viewpoint throws open the floodgates of creativity, and you can pull the reader through a labyrinth of subplots, "sideplots," and "twistplots." You have the opportunity of setting the scene in a jet over the Arctic in one chapter and suddenly switching to a camel caravan crossing the Sahara in the next.

Leon Uris, Robert Ludlum, and Harry Patterson alias Jack Higgins are all masters of the complex structure. Instead of studying flowery prose and in-depth characterization as most writers are prone to do, you should examine quite closely the organization and precision the authors mentioned above weave throughout their stories. Harold Robbins, for example, used the epilogue as the prologue in *The Adventurers,* and then went on to slip his hero deftly in and out of first- and third-person narration.

Do you intend to utilize the advantages of a prologue to set up future conflicts? Will you need an epilogue to tie the ends together? Have you the guts to combine several plots into one? Have you considered dividing your novel into different parts? This is what we mean by structure.

There are no hard-and-fast rules for structuring the modern adventure novel. In Formula A, you must keep your hero believable and the action moving to keep readers turning the pages. With Formula B, the trick is to keep them second guessing and so involved with who's-doing-what-to-whom they can't put the book down. This is achieved by alternating your characters and their personal conflicts so that in the beginning there seems to be no comprehensible connection. Then as the plot unfolds, they're all irresistibly drawn together into an ever-heightening climax. I call this threading the needle. You've got to sew all your characters into the same pocket and thereby give your reader a satisfying conclusion.

A satisfying conclusion can never be stressed too strongly. How many books have you read that began like gangbusters and then fell to pieces in the end? The sad result is that you forget them damned quickly while a tale that has a smash ending stays with you.

All too often a writer will sit down with a blockbuster concept and barrel through the first half of the story only to fall off a cliff because he had no idea where he was going in the first place. You have to know what you're aiming at in the last chapter and then backtrack and work toward it. That's why planning your structure is so important. Creative blueprinting can't turn a bad book into a good one, but it sure helps.

When it comes to plotting, so much has been written by renowned authorities of mystery and adventure writing, I see no reason simply to repeat most of their well-known rules. I plot as I go. Many novelists write an outline that has almost as many pages as their ultimate book. Others knock out a brief synopsis. Again, do what is comfortable: If you have to plot out every move your characters make, so be it. Just make sure there is a plausible purpose behind their machinations. A good reader can smell a phony plot a block away.

In modern adventure writing, the trend seems to be to sacrifice great gobs of character-probing in favor of fast-paced action. Sad to say, most critics are still hung up on finely tuned character definition. but then critics only concern themselves with how well a book is written. The guy who actually lays down the cash for it is more interested in how well it reads.

Alistair MacLean, perhaps one of the finest adventure writers of the last several decades, favors rapid pace over character psychiatry. His people are sharply defined in their looks and mannerisms and come across very well, without pages of historical background.

The hero in my series is usually described through the eyes of other characters. These observations, usually in small doses, occur only when they appropriately add to a particular scene or action.

They don't make good heroes these days. The anti-hero seems to be currently in vogue, especially in detective and spy novels. But pure adventure is something else again. A Casper Milquetoast just won't do. Men readers want to identify with the shrewd, devil-may-care hero who surmounts every obstacle put up by the opposition and emerges victorious in the end. Likewise, women, in spite of the current hoopla about equality, still secretly yearn for the rugged he-man to sweep them off their feet. If you doubt this last statement, simply take a look at the staggering sales figures of the romantic novels by Rosemary Rogers and several other astute women writers.

In most dramatic genres, the reader likes to identify with the characters and to experience what they see and feel. In adventure, the reader runs along the sidelines, cheering everyone on—a prime reason for your characters to be bigger than life, but still believable. That's what's called walking the tightrope. On one hand, you run the risk of making some characters too ordinary. On the other, you don't dare allow them to become comic book Supermen or Wonderwomen.

If your hero must save the world, at least let him act human while he goes about it. He should still put his pants on one leg at a time, sneeze occasionally, blow his nose, and feel the urge to go to the bathroom. What man can identify with another who does none of these? Same with women. I like my girls to zing in a few four-letter words when they're angry or frustrated. Show me one who doesn't at least say "Damn!" after ramming a painted toenail through a pair of new pantyhose.

There is an old saying in the advertising business: "See what your competitors are doing, then do just the opposite." That's the whole idea of writing a book: You're telling a story no one else has told before.

When I decided to develop a series hero, I looked around the field and studied everyone from Sherlock Holmes to James Bond to Travis McGee. I figured the last thing the adventure arena needed was another private detective, spy or CIA agent. So I created a guy by the name of Dirk Pitt who is the Special Projects Director for NUMA (the National Underwater & Marine Agency). Fortunately, I stumbled onto a good thing. The mysteries that can be expanded upon in and around water are as boundless as the oceans themselves. I might mention that I chose the name Pitt partly because it is one syllable, thus making it easy to say, "Pitt did this, and Pitt did that," etc.

My final suggestion relates to what I said earlier about treating the reader as an honored guest. Every so often I'll stop and ask myself, what would the reader like to see at this particular moment in the story? Then I'll try my best to give it to him. I figure that since my reader paid good money or took the time and trouble to check out my efforts from the library, the least I can do is place his interests above mine.

I don't cotton to writers who engrave on marble what *they* think should be read. My work is geared strictly to provide a few hours of enjoyable escape. I don't believe in imparting personal philosophy, social commentary, or hidden meanings between the lines. Some writers prefer to be called novelists, some storytellers, others spokesmen for the masses.

Me: I'm an entertainer, no more, no less.

47

ON WRITING SCIENCE FICTION

By Ursula K. Le Guin

I LOOK over my typewriter, out the study window, forty miles north to the mountain called "The Lady"—Mount St. Helens. Since the May 18, 1980 eruption and the May 25 ash-fall, people keep saying to me, "You're a science fiction writer—you should write a story about the volcano!" And I can only stare, and whimper, "But—But—"

I could attempt to describe what the eruption looked like from my study window. I could research and write up a history of the volcano. I could tell the true story of the old man who wouldn't leave his home at Spirit Lake (but that's been better done already in a country song). I could write poetry that has the volcano in it somewhere, some day. There's a great deal any writer could write about the eruption, and the ash-fall, and the people involved. But the one thing no writer could make of it, now, is a science fiction story. Science fiction is about what hasn't happened, but might; or what never will happen, but this is what it might be like if it did.

St. Helens happened. The Lady blew. Having seen that pillar of darkness towering seventy thousand feet above my city, I know that the most and best any artist could do with it is to try—and fail—to describe it.

Before May 18, a major eruption of St. Helens was an *idea*. Since then, it's an *event*. Science fiction works with ideas. It is basically an intellectual form of literature—with all the limitations, and all the potentialities, that go with the dominance of intellect.

I hear a polite mutter in my mind's ear: "The woman is nuts. Brainless heroes bashing brawny villains to rescue bronze-bra'd princesses while boring through Hyperspace towards Beta Bunthi, home of the Bug-Eyed Yrogs—this is intellectual?"

Well, no. But it isn't science fiction, either. It's space opera. Let me define my terms. As far as I can make out, "science fiction" and "speculative fiction" are the same thing—and so henceforth I'll call them SF, which nicely includes both. "Fantasy" covers all imaginative fiction, but may be used as a category including all imaginative fiction *except* SF and horror stories. It also includes "science fantasy." As for "space opera," in print or on the screen, it is to SF what "sword and sorcery" is to fantasy: the stuff produced for mass sales. Not steak, not hamburger, just baloney. Mindless, macho, and miserably imitative; but with a thirty-million-dollar budget it can be lots of fun and very pretty.

Space opera not only borrows hardware and gimmicks from SF, but also filches the great imaginative themes, such as space travel, time travel, alien beings, other worlds. But instead of using them as metaphors of the human condition, as SF does, space opera makes them into meaningless decorations. They are not part of the structure of the work, but serve instead to disguise it. You peel off the space suits and the tentacles, and guess what? Howdy, podner! Welcome to Hyperspace, Texas!—And, frankly, I miss the horses.

A real SF story, book, or film is fundamentally different. It starts with an act of the mind, a step from *is* to *if,* a reach of the imagination into the nonexistent. But it is not a leap into the impossible or the absurd. Indeed, SF dreads absurdity and loves logic almost as much as Mr. Spock does. In SF, the risky act of imagination is controlled by the thinking mind, the intellect. And therefore the discipline it accepts most naturally and gracefully is that of science. Real science: a respect for fact, and a sympathy with the patient way science arrives at fact.

Fantasy makes its connection to ordinary-daylight-outside-the-book-cover-reality through the emotions and through ordinary physical perception. (I could go on about that, but this chapter's about SF, not fantasy!)

SF makes its connection with ordinary-day-light-etc.-reality through ideas—principally the evidence of science and the speculations of the thinking mind. In SF, there is a reason for what happens, and it is a rational reason. The events of the story make sense in a cause-and-effect system. No matter how wildly imaginative they are, they don't happen just because the author likes it that way, or thinks it "feels right." Fantasy admits such reasons unknown to Reason. But SF doesn't. In SF, the questions "Why?" and "How?"—asked at any point in the story—should be answerable.

This doesn't mean that an SF story is an educational lecture with some fictional sugar-coating. Anything but! The ideas are the seed, not the tree—the blueprint, not the building. An SF story that hasn't *grown from* its ideas, but just flatly states them, is dull stuff.

A very few SF writers are practicing scientists, in such various fields as psychology, anthropology, biology, astronomy. Most are not. My impression is that the knowledge of science used by most SF writers comes from self-education—reading books and articles on subjects that interest them. (As for myself, the total of my formal training in science is one semester of anthropology and one of geology.) The point is, what's wanted is not a great mass of technical knowledge, but an attitude towards knowledge—an attitude of curiosity, above all. If learning facts and finding how events connect together bores you, then you probably don't read much SF, and certainly wouldn't enjoy writing it.

Let me try to illustrate this apparently paradoxical situation. Let's take a typical crazy SF invention: A five-hundred-foot-tall woman lands on Earth. Now, first of all, does she walk up Main Street, mashing a Honda at every step, and sit down for a rest on the First National Bank building?

In fantasy, she could. In the space opera movie, she does. In SF, she doesn't, because she can't. If she's really a woman just like us only a hundred times taller, she's too heavy to stand up, let alone walk. Crushed by her own weight—the gravitational pull of the Earth—the poor thing is lying there dying of internal injuries. We know that beings of our general type and mass cannot exceed a certain size, under our local conditions. Brontosaurus was at the limit for a land animal, and he wasn't any five hundred feet tall. Even Bill Walton has problems. And we are following Delany's Law. S.R. Delany, a most innovative writer of SF, put it this way: "Science fiction must not contradict *what is known to be known.*" And we know that it is known that solid 500-foot ladies are impractical.

But what if she's a projection of a five-foot Alien who is staying up in her space ship above the Earth until she finds if it's safe to arrive in person? She meant to beam down a five-foot projection, but the beamer got the size wrong. The technology involved—perhaps using holographic images—is not known to be impossible. Or, what if she really is five hundred feet tall, but, since she comes from a giant gas planet like Jupiter, she is made of airy, gauzy stuff, with almost negligible weight and mass? Realizing that she got the size wrong, she compresses herself into the shape of a five-foot woman weighing 3½ pounds, and walks briskly into the First National Bank building, holding her breath. . . . Well, this is getting pretty hard to explain, but I'm not sure that we've contradicted anything that is known to be known. And so long as that rule is kept, SF is perfectly free to invent. It just has to make sure, as it goes along, that it doesn't contradict *itself*. The pieces must hang together.

Figuring out how it hangs together, all the where-why-what-and-whether, is half the fun of SF, for both the reader and the author. There's so much to know about our friend in the First National Bank Building—what life is like for someone as gauzy and compressible as a silk scarf, and what the weather is like on her home planet, and what kind of society her people might have, since they are all very fragile, very agile, and able to change size and shape at will. And what might have brought her here to Earth, and, as a matter of fact, what she's doing in the Bank. Madame, what are you up to in there?

"Prrswit frumbo rigpot thoom," she says into her Vox-Coder, which instantly prints out in English: * I * AM * GATHERING * MATERIAL * FOR * A * SEARINGLY * REALISTIC * STORY * ABOUT * BANK * TELLERS *

Fantasy and SF certainly overlap, but there is a real difference between them, and in general I believe they are best not muddled up together. A fantasy element—something rationally unexplainable—can be very annoying in an SF story, and often looks like what it is: a bit of laziness on the author's part, sloppy or wishful thinking. The reverse mix, SF intruding into fantasy, often occurs in books for young people by authors who are basically distrustful of the power of fantasy, and so try to explain away the whole thing—"But it was really all a dream!" That's a cheat, and the kids know it.

There is one more thing about SF that I feel I have to mention, but don't want to, because it is so undignified. In workshops I call it PSG. PSG stands for Pseudo-Scientific Garbage. It isn't meant as an insult, merely as a description. After all, the truth is that science fiction is not true. It isn't science. It's fiction. Although it starts from a known fact or an educated guess or at least a crazy but plausible hunch, and although it tries loyally not to contradict what is known to be known and not to stumble over its own internal logic—still, the whole thing is made up. And, especially if it's set in the future or on a different world, *all the details* have to be made up. Here's where the PSG comes in, and here's where the gift for SF may shine brightest.

For example: that Vox-Coder our Alien was using. I didn't explain that it's an instant translating machine, voice-activated. I didn't really have to. It's not a big step from the little hand-carried translator-computers we have right now. The Vox-Coder seems not only possible, but probable. Yet, the more you happen to know about language and translation, the less probable it may seem. Here evidence from one science (computer technology) contradicts evidence from another science (linguistic theory), and you have to take your choice. But your choice is warped by the fact that translators are so handy in SF. Without them, all the Aliens have to spend months learning English, or the Terrans have to painfully learn Voobish. So we gave our 3½-pound Alien a ¼-ounce Vox-Coder. And so I call it, with all due respect, a piece of PSG.

All interstellar space ships are PSG.

Much PSG is truly common property in SF. You learn it simply by reading SF. (Anybody who tries to write SF without having read it is wasting his time and ours.) There's a good deal of genuine sharing: the word "FTL," for example, meaning Faster Than Light. Anybody can fly an FTL ship. More often you don't borrow the name—Vox-Coder, phaser, pinlighter, etc.—but take the general idea and deck it out your own way. Of course you also are free to make up any gimmick or device you want or need, and this is fun. Much of the joyful inventiveness, the shock and beauty of SF is in its PSG. I think of Philip K. Dick's fully automated and highly verbose taxicabs, which tend to argue with their customers, sometimes becoming quite emotional. . . . Of Vonda McIntyre's gentle replacement of the hypodermic needle by the serpent's tooth. . . . Of H.G. Wells's lovely, shimmering Time Machine. . . . Of the pleasure I had trying to figure out what it would feel like to be a woman this month and a man next month and both/neither in between. . . . PSG, all of it. *Taxicabs don't talk!* Only if you're perfectly sure of that fact should you write a story about talking taxicabs.

In 1968 I wrote a book, *The Lathe of Heaven* (and in 1979 WNET/TV made a movie of it). At a climactic point of the book, Mount Hood erupts, and then the extinct volcano inside Portland city limits, Mount Tabor, erupts, and the whole Cascade Range goes off—except Mount St. Helens.

Why did I deliberately leave her out, knowing that she was in fact the likeliest to erupt? I can't explain. When I was writing the book I looked at her out the window, the "misty, blue-grey cone" which is in the story but not here in the real world any longer; and she must have whispered to me, "Sshh. Quiet. I have my own plans."

And I'm very glad I got it all wrong. My job's fiction. I'll leave the reality business to the Lady.

48

SUSPENSE WRITING

By Mary Higgins Clark

My publisher recently forwarded a letter to me from a man who had just read my suspense novels. It was brief and to the point. The reader also wanted to be a writer and he had a question for me: "About how many words and pages are required to turn out a best seller like your own?"

My immediate response was a smile, but it was quickly followed by a feeling of sadness. I don't think that particular aspiring writer will ever make it. And while his question is almost unbelievably naive, it's not the first time it's been asked.

For some reason, I find it difficult to put down advice in an organized manner. Telling someone how to turn out a marketable suspense novel is rather like dancing with an octopus. Which hand (or tentacle) do you reach for first?

However, I think that by attempting to answer the kinds of questions that pop up in my mail and by explaining how a story evolves for me, I might be able to pass along some useful suggestions.

Therefore, with the understanding between us that this will not be a precise blueprint or an annotated "how to," shall we begin?

Question: "I'm eager to write a mystery, but can't think of a plot. Where do you get your ideas?"

Obviously the plot, like the foundation of a house, is the structure on which all else is built. No matter how glib the writing, how enchanting the characters, if the plot doesn't work, or if it works only because of flagrant coincidence or seven-page explanations at the climax, I believe the book is a failure. But where to get the *idea?* Easy. Pick up your local newspaper. The odds are that on the first page or two it contains news of at least one homicide, an aggravated assault, a bank robbery, a mugging, a jailbreak. There also may be a recap on a criminal trial that merits national attention, an update on a series of unsolved murders, and an item about the child who has been missing six months. In other words, material for a dozen short stories or novels.

Now for your own plot. Select a case, one that for whatever reason sticks in your mind. Begin a file on it. Cut out every newspaper item that refers to it. *Know* that case. If a defendant is indicted, try to attend some of the trial sessions. And then—and here's the key—use that case as a nucleus for your story. You're a fiction writer; invent, go further, say to yourself, "What if?"

Several years ago I decided I wanted to try my hand at a suspense novel. Like everyone else, I was faced with the decision: What shall I write? At that time there was a celebrated case in New York in which a young mother was accused of murdering her two children. She stoutly denied her guilt. Two juries rejected her defense. The case fascinated me. I had five children, and the thought of losing any of them gave me nightmares. The thought of not only losing them but being accused of *murdering* them was beyond comprehension. A voice in my subconscious whispered, "And then suppose it happened again?" *Where Are the Children?* was in gestation. Let me reemphasize my point: *Where Are the Children?* was not based on the actual case. I took two ingredients: the young mother accused of infanticide; the frantic denials of guilt. With these in mind I began to build the story.

In my opinion time and place are essential contributors to a successful suspense novel. I chose to set *Where Are the Children?* on Cape Cod for a number of reasons. The Cape offers privacy. New Englanders and particularly "Capeys" do not intrude. The stranger who rents the big house off-season will not be the subject of idle scrutiny. The Cape has mists and fogs, churning surf, nor'easter storms, weatherbeaten captains' houses perched high on embankments above the sea. All these enhance the atmosphere of terror and gloom.

A Stranger Is Watching has as a principal location the bowels of Grand Central Station. Why? There you find dark, damp tunnels throbbing with the echo of rushing trains and groaning machinery; stray cats; underground people silently flitting by; abandoned storerooms, eerie with accumulated cobwebs and grime. I explored the area and knew it was right. And I loved the possibility of the juxtaposition of kidnap victims bound and gagged near a ticking time bomb while overhead thousands of commuters rush through the terminal.

Like the Greeks, I believe in the containment of time. *Oedipus Rex* starts in the morning with the king observing the problems of his stricken domain. It ends a few hours later with his wife a suicide, himself blinded, his world vanished. The swiftness of the action adds to the shock value.

I believe that if you write a book in which people are kidnapped and the villain plans to execute them at a specific time, the suspense is considerably greater than if the reader is only generally concerned about the victims' welfare. In *Where Are the Children?* the reader knows that the kidnapper is planning to throw the children into the rock-filled surf at high tide, seven P.M. In *A Stranger Is Watching,* the time bomb is set to go off at 11:30 A.M. Hopefully as zero hour approaches the reader is sharing the anxiety of the protagonists.

Question: "When I start to write, all my characters sound alike. What am I doing wrong?" That's another good inquiry and a valid problem. Through trial and error, I evolved something of a system that has helped me. The key phrase is *know your people.* Do a biography of them before you begin to write your story. Where were they born? Where did they go to school? What do they look like? What kind of clothes do they wear? Are they sophisticated, easy-going, observant? Are they married? Do they have children?

Think of someone you know or knew as a child who reminds you of the character you're trying to create. Remember the way that person talked, the expressions he or she used. When I was inventing Lally, the bag lady in *A Stranger Is Watching,* I combined two people from my childhood. One was our cleaning woman, who used to come up the street invariably singing "lalala"; the other the proprietor of a hole-in-the-wall candy store near my grammar school. She was one of the homeliest women I've ever known. The boys in my class always used to make jokes about calling her up for a date. Together the candy store proprietor and "Lala," as we nicknamed our cleaning woman, merged into Lally. But then to get the feeling of authenticity, I haunted Grand Central Station and chatted with real bag ladies. One of them became the prototype for Rosie, the other bag lady in *Stranger.*

There are hundreds of examples of fine books which contradict what I'm about to say, but here it is anyhow. I like to write about *very nice people* who are confronted by the forces of evil and who through their own courage and intelligence work their way through to deliverance. Personally, I'm not comfortable with the non-hero or non-heroine who is basically so bad-tempered or self-serving that in real life I would avoid him or her like the plague. I myself don't get emotional satisfaction out of a book in which the villain is so desperately attractive that I find my-

238

self rooting for him to beat the system. My villains are, and probably will continue to be, as evil, as frightening, as quietly vicious as I can dream them up. I know I'm on the right track if I'm writing at night and no one else is home and when the house makes a settling noise, I uneasily start looking over my own shoulder.

Another key element in creating characters is to *orchestrate* them. Within the framework of the plot try to have a variety of people in whom your readers will not only believe but with whom they can identify. Never, never throw away a minor character. Let your reader understand him, know what makes him tick. And make it a cardinal rule that every minor character must move the story forward. Suspense by its very nature suggests an express train or a roller coaster. Once on board, you cannot get off until the ride ends. I am committed to the belief that this kind of speedy action is essential to good suspense writing.

Question: "Do you do much research before you start writing?" Yes. Yes. Yes. And as I am working on the book I continue to research. My book, *The Cradle Will Fall,* is about an obstetrician who experiments on and sometimes murders his pregnant patients. I read everything I could get my hands on about artificial insemination, *in vitro* pregnancies, and fetal transplant experiments. I interviewed and picked the brains of a doctor friend who is a researcher in a pre-natal hospital laboratory. I proposed "what if" questions to obstetrician buddies. Then when the book was completed I gave a Xerox to one obstetrician friend. I was in New York. He was in Minneapolis. I was on a tight deadline: He stayed on the phone with me four hours. I had a list of all medical references in the book, e.g. page 2 top line, page 8 fourth paragraph, etc. Jack reviewed every one of them with me. On some he said, "That's fine." On others, he'd suggest changes. For example, near the climax of the book, a desperate search is going on for the gravely ill heroine. Jack said, "It's an emergency. Two doctors are talking. Don't have Richard say, 'She'll need a transfusion when we find her.' Put it this way, 'We'll hang a bottle of O-negative.' "

The Cradle Will Fall is set in New Jersey. The protagonist, Katie DeMaio, is a young assistant prosecutor. My daughter is an assistant prosecutor in New Jersey. She was my expert in police procedure. She went over every line that referred to the working of the court, the prosecutor's office, trials, witness statements, etc. For example, after a murder scene I had the homicide detective post a sign, CRIME AREA. POSITIVELY NO ADMITTANCE. I remembered having seen a sign like that somewhere. My daughter said, "No, that's wrong. In a suspicious death, we'd leave a cop guarding the premises until the apartment has been thoroughly searched." In another chapter, I had the prosecutor televise the interrogation of a witness. She corrected me. "In New York that's being done sometimes, but it's still not legal in New Jersey." The point is that authenticity of detail gives the ring of truth to a book.

Question: "How much rewriting do you do when you're working on a book?"

Plenty. But rewriting is a two-edged sword. I know too many people who've spent months working over the first chapter of the projected novel. That's wrong. Get it down. Bumble through it. Tell the story. Then when you have fifty or one hundred pages typed you've got something to work with. It may be at that point you'll start again from the beginning because the book has a fundamental flaw that has become obvious. I wrote fifty pages of *The Cradle Will Fall*. In that first version Katie DeMaio is the twenty-eight-year-old wife of a prominent judge. She is in a minor automobile accident while he is away, stays overnight in the hospital, and while sedated witnesses a crime.

I soon realized something was wrong. I couldn't get worried about Katie. The reason became obvious. Here she is married to an interesting, handsome man, a Superior Court judge. I just knew that when John DeMaio got home the next day, he'd make very sure that no one would hurt his Katie.

How to solve the problem? John had to go. Instead of the *wife,* Katie became the young *widow* of Judge John DeMaio. Immediately, she is infinitely more sympathetic—vulnerable and alone in the large secluded house she inherited from him. A great additional plus is that we now have room for a love interest. Doctor Richard Carroll, the provocative medical examiner, is very keen on Katie, and she has been holding him off. The reader, we hope, becomes emotionally involved in the potential romance and worries that Katie is sealing her fate because she does not let Richard know she is scheduled for minor surgery. The doctor who will operate on her is planning to kill her.

So there we have it. As I warned in the beginning I suspect this advice has a disjointed quality. I tend to offer writing hints the way an old

County Sligo cousin shared her recipe for Irish soda bread: "Take a handful of this, a fistful of that, a pinch of whatever . . . . Now taste it, love. Does it need more caraway seeds and raisins?"

Nevertheless if any of this advice helps anyone, I'm glad. There is surely no sweeter satisfaction to the suspense writer than to hear a heavy-eyed friend say accusingly, "You kept me up half the night reading your darn book!"

49

PLANNING AND PLOTTING THE DETECTIVE STORY

By Catherine Aird

A FULL-LENGTH detective story is made up of individual chapters. This much is obvious. It is the construction and organization of these individual chapters that, in my opinion, merit the attention of anyone writing a first detective story.

It hardly needs saying that the first and last chapters are among the most important in the detective novel—and probably in any story. Starting used to be easier: "Once upon a time. . . ." The old-fashioned storytellers may have had a stereotyped beginning to their tales, but at least the listener knew at once where he was: in the land of make-believe. The storyteller of today, who is writing fiction as opposed to recounting fact, has as one of his first tasks the creation of that make-believe. He hasn't got very long in which to do it, as his tale has to get underway as quickly as possible. Even the first sequence is important.

The modern writer isn't surrounded by a circle of eager listeners, hanging on his every word with no other entertainment in sight, so the fiction writer has to attract and sustain interest against competition a medieval troubador would not have begun to know about. In the writing of detective fiction, this quite often means having the body of the victim on page one. For many readers and writers, this is quite a good place for it to be. It is terribly tempting to establish an elaborate setting first, but this approach has its dangers. Of course the setting has to be established, but if possible, it should be done within the context of the action, rather than before it. I think this is very important.

If the body is not on page one, it certainly must appear no later than the end of chapter one. There are, of course, exceptional circumstances in which this rough-and-ready rule does not apply. There may be one or more missing persons; the plot may not concern bodies at all but, say, forgery or drugs; the whole story may be about fraud, and, if there is a murder, it may be only incidental. As a generalization, though, I think the main problem of the story should be apparent from reading the first chapter, whether it is who kidnapped the heiress, who robbed the bank, or "Who Killed Cock Robin?"

One of the advantages of having the body in chapter one is that the presence of a victim demands action, no matter what the setting is. This action may involve the full and detailed panoply of the police procedural story or a gifted amateur sleuth cooperating with the appropriate authorities. Either way, the activity engendered by the discovery of the body of the victim necessarily carries the reader into the next chapter.

The murderer should appear, in my view, no later than chapter two—or chapter three, if a particularly large amount of background writing is required—but he must, by hook or by crook, so to speak, be there as soon as possible, taking his place in the plot. It is a great temptation to have the murderer play a subordinate role in the story, but this, alas, will not do. This temptation arises because it is technically difficult to write about someone whom you—and you alone as the writer—know to be the murderer. But I cannot stress too strongly the importance of keeping him visible.

Time spent, therefore, in considering the role of the murderer within the story is not wasted. A conscious effort should be made from the very beginning to see that his function in the plot is significant enough so that you can keep him in front of the reader without obvious contrivance. This will also allow his villainy to be made increasingly clear in subtle ways throughout the book. It is obvious to all those who read and write detective fiction that for profound psychological reasons neither victim nor murderer is ever an entirely sympathetic character. Both are going to be lost, so to speak—one at the beginning of the book and one at the end—and by some long and deep-seated convention, the reader does not expect either loss to be too poignant.

By the time you come to chapter three, you may broaden the situation to indicate that *Things Are Not What They Seem*. In fact, in good detective stories they seldom are, and the experienced reader will expect something more. By chapter three or four, the author should be giving a slight twist to the problem outlined in chapter one. This is more subtle than simply presenting a complicated problem at the outset.

There is a school of thought that holds that most of the important clues to the correct solution of the detective mystery should be given in the first three chapters, albeit presented with great subtlety, and that all the clues really necessary should have appeared no later than chapter six, even though they are still well hidden. I try my hardest to subscribe to and follow this theory and can recommend a most useful exercise in connection with it.

Take your first three chapters and underline what you know to be the significant clues. Ask yourself whether—if you *knew* these were the factors that were important—you could solve the problem as outlined in chapter one. If so, then it should also be possible for a really astute reader of the genre to do so, too. Repeat the process when you have written six chapters and consider if an ordinary intelligent reader could have worked out who the murderer was, had he known what was significant as he was reading.

If the answer to both exercises is "No," you should go back and work in more clues. Remember, though, that it does not matter at this stage how well hidden they are; what is important is that they are there. If you haven't written your own first six chapters yet, I suggest that you take a detective story that you personally find satisfying and practice the exercise on it. The wisdom of hindsight will show you where—and how carefully—the author has given you the information that he or she wanted you to have, even though you were unaware of its significance at the time.

It is also important that all the main characters of the story are present no later than chapter three. Bringing them in later than, say, chapter four, smacks of contrivance. If, for example, the plot hinges on the long lost brother turning up from the mysterious East, then a clue to his existence should have been given before this point in the story. (On the subject of characters, a small point, but one that can save some time: Make sure that none of the names of your characters end in the letter s. Apostrophes need especially careful watching.)

Also, before the story advances too far, it is necessary to introduce the particular suspects with whom the detective is concerned. The reason for the popularity of the closed community (the country house, cruise ship, etc.) as a setting soon becomes apparent. Limiting the number of suspects to those characters at the house party or other confined setting is essential and one that devotees of the detective novel will quickly recognize.

Hoard your exciting chapter endings and try to space them so that those chapters finishing on a high note do not come one after the other. Spacing them out is better than having two cliff-hanger chapter endings in succession, followed by four more pedestrian ones. It is axiomatic that every single chapter in a detective story must have some action: Description and dialogue are not enough. Also, I believe that chapters should not exceed 3,500 to 4,000 words, but this decision is up to the individual writer. The ending of a chapter is a good point at which to change the venue of the scene, end a particular sequence of action, or bring in a new clue.

By chapter six some further important action is called for. Theoretically, the ideal is to have some minor excitement or discovery at the end of every third chapter and a more major event after chapters six and twelve. In fact, by chapter twelve you will, I think, feel the necessity for this yourself. It is really quite difficult to stop the plot from closing in on the author about two-thirds of the way through, and it is at this point that there is often a second murder. Real aficionados of the crime story know that it is by no means uncommon to have as the victim a character who, up to this particular point in the story, has been the chief suspect. This has the merit of opening up the story in more ways than one.

This juncture should be one of the two really high peaks in the story, as opposed to the climax which, of course, should be the highest peak of all. Another important point is that the denouement, although it comes of necessity after the climax, should not be anti-climactic. Detective stories, ironic as it may seem, usually do have at least satisfactory, if not happy, endings, and no small part of the readers' satisfaction comes from the knowledge that all—*all*—the loose ends in the plot have been neatly tied.

One factor that can contribute greatly to an effective climax and explanation is the clearing up of any points that can be cleared up in the third chapter from the end, leaving the last two chapters for the climax and, of course, the last part of the chapter for the explanation, a winding up of the action—a confession, a conviction, or what you will. There are always some small points, or perhaps even large red herrings, that can be disposed of effectively before the grand finale, sometimes even adding to its excitement. If you can get them out of the way before the climax and thus reduce the post-revelation explanation, so much the better.

245

I hope that what I have written does not read too much like a formula, because that is not what it is meant to be. Nor does it detail a pattern that I myself conscientiously follow in every book I write. What it does attempt to do is to save you at least some misplaced effort when you write your first detective story. Be strong-minded enough to ignore all well-meaning advice if you have better ideas. You could be right. But as will be apparent to anyone who has tried his hand at writing one, a detective story seldom springs—like Athena—fully formed from the author's forehead.

50

WESTERNS: FICTION'S LAST FRONTIER

By Loren D. Estleman

COUNTRY music and Stetsons are in; disco and headbands are out. On walls that once sported Degas and Cezanne originals, prints of round-ups and gunfights by Remington and Russell explode from frames made of weathered barnwood. Can Western novels be far behind in popularity?

As a matter of fact, they're way ahead. In recent years, Western sales, which can always be expected not to descend below a certain level, have risen steadily. Louis L'Amour, author of *Hondo* and heir to the poncho of such late great frontier fictioneers as Zane Grey and Luke Short, has sprung into national prominence after thirty years of writing about sun-parched deserts and whipsaw-lean cowpokes who roll their own, with one leg cocked over their saddle horns. Douglas C. Jones *(The Court-Martial of George Armstrong Custer, Arrest Sitting Bull)* is recognized by many of today's critics as a major force in contemporary literature.

As the author of six novels set in the Old West, I have one word of advice for the writer who wants to get in on the ground floor of this ranch-style renaissance: Authenticity. You may get published if you write of showdowns between Good and Evil at high noon on Main Street, but critical acclaim and sales will elude you. Describe a lawman waiting with a shotgun in a dark alley to blow the head off a feared killer as he walks past, and you'll be applauded for your realistic portrayal of the true Code of the West.

For a century—from the time of Buffalo Bill to John Wayne—popular fiction has built an entire mythology around tall, silent men with fast draws, who conformed to their own noble creed. Wild Bill Hickok, a professional gambler and sometime lawman who claimed a cut of every game in town, and Wyatt Earp, a political hack whose famed gunfight at the OK Corral in Tombstone represents the first recorded example of gang warfare in modern history, have been presented as "heroes" flawed only by their unwillingness to accept thanks for their humanitarian actions.

The result is that the truth about the West hasn't been scratched. A gold mine of characters and plots far more interesting than anything offered by Hollywood awaits the writer sharp enough to recognize them. Where else would one find someone as juicy as lovely Polly Bartlett, who in 1867 poisoned twenty-two men at the inn she and her father ran in Wyoming for what was in their pockets; or Sam Brown, a gunfighter who once demonstrated his mettle by carving out the heart of an innocent drifter in front of a saloon full of witnesses in California?

Matt Dillon never fascinated me as much as John "Liver-Eatin'" Johnson, a gigantic mountain man in Montana who slaughtered Sioux braves for sport, and who is said to have dined on his victims' entrails. I based the character of Bear Anderson in *The High Rocks* on Johnson, and described him as follows:

He was even bigger than I remembered him. Crouched though he was . . . he was nearly seven feet of solid muscle without an ounce of suet anywhere . . . The eyes beneath the rim of his fur hood were the clear blue of his Scandinavian ancestors, and his features, despite the leathery grain of his complexion, were even and handsome enough to turn the head of a mining camp's most hardened prostitute. His full beard, like his shoulder-length hair, was reddish and streaked with yellow. The only flaw was a jagged patch near the corner of his jaw on the left side where the whiskers grew sparsely over scar tissue—the remnant, I judged, of an old tomahawk wound.

Granted, the parts might prove difficult to cast in Studio City, but the most memorable characters are larger than life. Johnson himself was hardly less impressive.

Similarly, the narrator of that tale, Deputy U.S. Marshal Page Murdock, bears little resemblance to the popular image of the stalwart lawman. He's unscrupulous but likable—which is more than can be said for the type of peace officer represented by Hugh O'Brian on television twenty years ago. Because I'm more comfortable with Murdock than with the conventional Western hero, he's become the star of a series since his introduction in *The High Rocks*.

I departed from the norm in *The Hider,* my very first Western, when

I made buffalo hunter Jack Butterworth a garrulous old man instead of the taciturn Gary Cooper-type that crops up so often in formula yarns. In reality, after weeks on the prairie with only their horses to talk to, back in civilization these loners were more than eager to bend the ear of whoever would listen to them. It's the braggarts history remembers; nobody would even have heard of Pat Garrett or Bat Masterson had they been as reticent about their adventures as Ben Cartwright and the Lone Ranger. Consider Butterworth's recollection:

". . . Onliest time I was ever in bed past six was the day a twelve-pounder slipped its chocks at Antietam and rolled over my left leg. I was back on the field that next morning, and I brung three Yanks to ground afore a ball from a Colt Dragoon snapped my crutch in half and sent me back to the hospital to get my leg reset."

If not for his new friend's lack of humility concerning his past, narrator Jeff Curry would probably not have decided to accompany him on the hunt for the last surviving buffalo.

This is as good a place as any to discuss dialect. Avoid it wherever possible. Butterworth's speech rings of dropped g's and flatted o's, yet neither of these spelling aberrations appears in print. Once you get into phonetic spelling, comprehension suffers, and consistency is hard to maintain. Since there are quite as many rules to bad grammar as there are to good, don't complicate things. An occasional "brung," an "afore" here and there, one "betwixt" to two hundred lines of dialogue, will carry the illusion. Be very sparing with "I reckons" and "much obligeds," as too much use of Western idiom lends itself to caricature.

As might be expected, decades of distortion have obscured much of the truth. When I set out to write *Aces & Eights,* I was faced with the dilemma of whether to present Wild Bill Hickok as a hero or a villain, or something in between. At length I decided not to make the choice. The story, which opens with Hickok's murder, reveals the events of his life as his killer's trial unfolds, with witnesses for both sides presenting wildly conflicting accounts of his character. In the end, it's up to the readers to determine what kind of man he was.

Again, the watchword is authenticity, as in this passage:

The prosecutor half-turned to see United States Marshal Burdick standing thirty paces away, sideways, his long right arm extended at shoulder level, a big Navy Colt growing out of his hand and pointing at the drunk. A big man except when compared with such as the drunk and the bouncer, he still had his checked napkin thrust inside his high starched collar . . . Black-powder smoke swirled about him and a thin stream of plaster was leaking from a hole in the ornate tin ceiling above his head. In a single, fluid motion he had drawn the revolver from beneath his coat, fired a shot in the air, and pulled down on the drunk while the latter was still bringing his own cumbersome weapon into play.

Here, I've reconciled the fast draw of modern fiction with the calm, take-aim-and-fire stance of historical fact, and clothed them in a few words with the dress and architecture of the late Victorian period. Frontier action takes on a third dimension when rooted in contemporary reality.

The Time-Life series on the Old West is the finest guide I can recommend to the beginner in this field. Period photographs and tintypes, many of them never before published, and hundreds of out-of-the-way facts and fascinating anecdotes, open up a whole new world to the reader who thinks he knows everything there is to learn about the era from movies and television. The bibliography of each is an excellent reading list for those who would delve deeper. If these books don't inspire the tyro, Westerns aren't his meat.

But don't get carried away with authenticity at the story's expense. It must be remembered that between 1875 and 1900, there were fewer violent deaths in Dodge City than there were in any major American industrial center last year. The average westerner would have been as shocked to witness a gunfight as would today's urban dweller. Home was a sod hut on the treeless prairie or a tent on a street of soupy mud, entertainment a seat by the coal-oil lamp with Bible in hand. In order to make this life interesting to the reader, some telescoping of the more exciting events of the age is necessary. But then life itself is always in need of editing. Good luck, pardner!

51

PUTTING SCIENCE INTO SCIENCE FICTION

By Gregory Benford

PEOPLE don't read science fiction to learn science any more than others read historical novels to study history. There are easier ways to go about it.

Yet the fact remains that "hard" science fiction—the kind based on the physical sciences—remains the core of the field. The reading public persists in thinking of rockets, lasers and aliens as the central subject matter of science fiction (s-f). Writers like Robert A. Heinlein, Isaac Asimov, and Arthur C. Clarke—all classic "hard" s-f figures—now appear on the best-seller lists.

Similarly, most s-f magazines yearn for more stories with a thorough grounding in science. Such work is in short supply at the offices of *Analog, Omni, Isaac Asimov's Science Fiction Magazine, Amazing,* and even the *Magazine of Fantasy & Science Fiction.* Generally, it is easier to sell a short story with high scientific content than one which concentrates, for example, on social changes, or age-old conflicts in a futuristic setting.

The shortage is even more acute for book publishers. One s-f editor told me recently that at least two-thirds of the manuscripts he receives are fantasy, and many of the rest are only nominally science fiction.

Why is this so? Because science is daunting, complex, and hard to work into a story. Few writers have very much scientific training to build on, and the pace of research is so rapid that you can be outdated while you're working out a plot line. Many s-f stories of twenty years ago look antique now. One reason some published hard science fiction isn't very well written is that the editors can't get anything better.

For the enterprising writer, though, this represents a real opportunity. S-f is traditionally open to new talent and new ideas. The trouble with many beginning authors in the last decade was that their "new" idea often was simple doom-crying—tending to see problems rather than to think of their solutions. Stories built on simple recognition of the unforeseen side effects of technology have a sameness about them, a lack of inventiveness that bores readers.

This is an easy trap to fall into. It may be an unconscious choice; the current glut of fantasy novels (often trilogies) often comes from newer writers, who seem to share the anti-science sentiments of the middle 1970s. Of course, powerful yarns have been spun with this angle and will be again—but it is a high-risk avenue to take.

Admittedly, people with a background in science or engineering have an edge in writing hard s-f. But even if your degree is in linguistics or animal husbandry, and you're interested in science, you can use your training. The fundamental requirement, of course, is that you like "hard" s-f in the first place. Trying to write something you have no enthusiasm or "feel" for is a ticket to disaster. If you have read hard s-f for pleasure, and know the basic motifs, you have already served your apprenticeship.

There are several steps that can help you become a journeyman writer of science-based stories or novels. They aren't hard and fast, of course, but I use them every day.

1. *Do your homework.* Everybody laughs when s-f TV shows routinely mistake "solar system" for "galaxy," use light-year as a unit of time, and commit other howlers. Such blunders seem to pass right by the TV audience, but even one can easily cause immediate rejection among s-f editors.

Science is replete with such terminology (or, uncharitably, jargon). If you need it, be sure you consult a reference. I keep my set of the *Britannica* nearby, but more specialized books are invaluable. A brief list from my own shelf:

The Science in S-F, Peter Nicholls, Editor (Knopf). The best place to start. Covers everything, with many references to fictional treatments and nonfiction background.

Cambridge Encyclopedia of Astronomy, Simon Mitton, Editor (Crown). A good overview, technically accurate and well-written.

Isaac Asimov's Biographical Encyclopedia of Science & Technology (Avon). Tidbits of history and science.

The Quest for Extraterrestrial Life, Donald Goldsmith, Editor (University Science Books). A collection of readings with many speculative ideas.

Black Holes and Warped Spacetime, William Kaufmann (Freeman). The best book on the subject.

The Seven Mysteries of Life, Guy Murchie (Houghton Mifflin). Observations on many sciences. You can pick up many "bits of business" here that lend atmosphere to even the driest facts.

The S-F Encyclopedia, Peter Nicholls, Editor (Doubleday). A thorough listing of major treatments of major s-f ideas, plus much else of interest about the field.

This last entry is invaluable for trying out your newborn idea, to see if somebody used it in a famous story from 1938. Not that you can't reuse an idea, but you should know if you are; that affects how you treat it.

Don't pass up any chance to do some background reading, no matter how minor it seems. *Use* your natural curiosity.

I am working on a novel about archaeology, and I recently had a character remark in passing, "The ancients were building elegant domes when *our* ancestors were hunting mastodons." After I'd typed those words, I realized I had no idea when the mastodons disappeared. A few minutes' checking showed that while they had been hunted to extinction in Europe well before the Greeks, they lived on in North America until a few thousand years ago. I then used this fact later in the conversation, adding an insider's detail that an archaeologist might plausibly know, but the casual reader wouldn't.

2. *Organize!* Technical material needs to simmer in your unconscious. Good hard s-f demands not that you parrot material from an encyclopedia, but that you *think* about it. I let my unconscious do most of my idea-making. I even go to the extent of lying in bed each morning, mulling over the science and plot of my current project, seeing if any idea has surfaced in the night.

To keep myself open to fresh notions, I keep my material handy, so that I can review it whenever I want. That means accumulating clippings, photocopies, copious notes—and organizing them into quickly-findable form, using headings like *Starship, Alien Biology,* and *Techtalk.*

I was browsing through this material when it suddenly occurred to

253

me that an opening line in an already-written chapter could have two different meanings. The line was, "When he woke up he was dead." In the novel it meant one thing, but in the near future it could mean the man had his nervous system cut off. Why? How would he regain control?

Within a few minutes, the material I had filed under *Advanced Medical* fell into place. I used the idea for a separate short story, "Lazarus Rising," which sold for $400 to *Isaac Asimov's Science Fiction Magazine*. Then I incorporated some of this new material into the novel I had been working on, finding that this diversion had opened up new possibilities in the original situation! Simon & Schuster published the novel as *Across the Sea of Suns* in 1984.

3. *Counter-punch.* S-f is full of common assumptions that were once inventive but are now mere conventions. Time and again authors invoke faster-than-light travel so their characters can whiz around the galaxy, righting wrongs, with no more than a few weeks spent in travel. This is good for dramatic unity, but *not* using it can be an asset, if it leads you to a new angle. What would an empire be like if ships moved at a hundredth of light speed? How would it keep political unity? What conflicts would arise?

This policy of truly thinking through the ideas in s-f can lead to major projects. Years ago I started thinking about time travel, and asked myself—as a physicist—how scientists would proceed if they discovered a particle that could move backward in time. Would they send a man backward, as their first experiment? Of course not—too expensive, too dangerous.

So I spent years writing a novel called *Timescape,* in which physicists do nothing more dramatic than to try to send mere *messages* backward in time. This was more than enough to generate conflict and suspense, and I profited by not echoing the ideas of a thousand earlier stories. Asking how events might really happen, given the realities of our world, can always turn up unexplored avenues.

4. *Ask the next question.* This well-known motto, invented by Theodore Sturgeon, might well be the most important for any s-f work. New technology and science appear every day in newspapers and on TV. Much of it is obscure, or just another slight improvement of a particular

254

widget. But some changes can alter the lives of common people, and these are the most fertile fields for anticipating the unseen effects.

The easiest things to anticipate are problems, but this usually leads to downbeat, hopeless stories. There are two ways out.

First, you can go for the really unexpected side-effect. For example, the news coverage of Barney Clark's heroic use of an artificial heart stimulated my imagination. Would the public always applaud such exotic medical technology? What if for $250 million you could buy not merely a replacement heart, but virtual immortality? I wrote a story about a dying man who could not tolerate the sight of a millionaire buying a whole new life. With nothing left to lose, what would this man do? Pessimistic, in a way—but the story, titled "Immortal Night," sold immediately.

The less risky way around the pessimistic-story trap is to see an unexpected *positive* aspect of what looks at first pretty bleak. For example, the Coming of the Computer. Will its ability to save and check information lead to a "surveillance society" where we have no secrets from the government? Think of a way computers can help thwart the police state—and show it in action. So many people fear computers already, such a story could be very popular.

5. *Show the "tip of the iceberg."* The most dreaded beast in hard s-f is the Expository Lump. That's the long paragraph explaining how a new invention works, or what the ecology of a strange planet is like, or some other necessary but intrusive material. You have to explain a lot without slowing down the action.

Suppose your hero is on a low-gravity planet. Don't lecture your reader about it, throwing in the mass and size and atmospheric details of your world. Instead, let your hero notice *in passing* that many kinds of large animals have wings for gliding or flying, that life in trees is more abundant, etc. This one colorful detail allows the reader to fill in much of the background himself.

This can work even better in near-future stories. In my novel *Timescape*, I dealt extensively with a runaway biological disaster. The foreground is concerned with scientists and how they work, but I realized I hadn't shown how advanced knowledge of manipulating the genetic code would affect ordinary life. How could I fill this in without devoting much space to it? My solution was to let a character notice that a

255

road-filling job outside his laboratory was being done by apes. These animals had had their intelligence artificially enhanced until they could follow verbal orders and do manual labor. This, and one or two other quick touches, gave the background color I wanted.

Even if you're weak on science, you don't have to give up the hard s-f story. The most important role of science in s-f is establishing *setting*, and you can do that with reading or travel.

Years ago I sold a short story, but I couldn't put it out of my mind. Slowly I saw that it was the beginning of a novel—but the larger plot had to occur at the Jet Propulsion Laboratory in Pasadena. I didn't know anything about how working space scientists talked or thought. So I used my journalistic connections to find out. I had written articles for *Smithsonian* and *Natural History,* so I cited these credits to line up several visits to J.P.L. There I got to know several space scientists and picked up those little nuggets of detail I later used in *In the Ocean of Night.*

To the s-f reader, the "bits of business" incorporating the atmosphere of hard s-f are often enough to convince him you know what you're talking about. Then he will go along for your ride, to whatever strange and wonderful places you wish to take him.

52

ERMINE OR RABBIT SKIN

Authenticity in the Historical Novel

By Ursula Zilinsky

SEVERAL years ago, while I was out for my usual morning run, I met three little boys. Their names were Toby, David, and Felix. Felix was dark and slight, with his eyes a little too close together. He spoke English well, but with a German accent. The other two were English and fair. The one called David was dazzlingly good-looking; had he worn the costume of an earlier period, he could have stepped into a Gainsborough with no one the wiser.

For the next four years of my life, and the next twenty of theirs, I watched them, listened to their talk, read their letters, and peeked in their bedroom windows. There were times when I begged them to go away and leave me alone, and times when they did and I pleaded with them to come back. They took up an unconscionable amount of my time, paper, and typewriter ribbon, led me on many a wild goose chase, shouldered aside my friends and family, gave me insomnia and turned me into a monomaniacal bore. And all of you who are working on your own novels are now saying, "So what? That's what writing a novel is like."

Of course, you are absolutely right. But my little boys presented me with a special problem. When I met them, they were admiring a garden bed planted with lobelias, geraniums and daisies in the shape of a Union Jack to honor the coronation of Edward VII, who became king of England in 1901. After having written several contemporary novels, stories, and a play for children, I had willy-nilly, without plan, forethought, or qualification embarked on an historical novel.

My first notion was to write an authentic Edwardian novel, what is loosely referred to as the 19th-century novel: a cast of thousands, lots of

257

incident, weddings, parties, christenings, and of course a deathbed or two. I discovered almost at once that while historical accuracy was absolutely essential, authenticity was not possible. To write an Edwardian novel I could not afford to be Edwardian. I had to fake it.

A few years ago I saw an exhibit of the costumes used for the television series *The Wives of Henry VIII.* Anyone who saw that show on PBS will doubtlessly remember how sumptuous those velvets and ermines looked. Reality proved to be very different. Because the show had been filmed on a limited budget, the costume designer had contrived velvets of polyester, ermines of rabbit dipped in ink, jewels of rhinestones and colored glass. The great chains of office were toilet pull chains and plumbing washers. Yet it all somehow managed to look far more real than many recent American productions for which money was no object and fortunes were spent on "authenticity."

My own problem wasn't, of course, that I couldn't afford ermine and pearls for my characters. It is, after all, one of the chief pleasures of writing that generosity is so cheap. If you want your heroine to have a sable coat, you can give it to her and never be a penny the poorer. My problem was the reverse of that English costume designer's. In researching an exhaustively documented historical period, I could not give my characters the great wealth available to me or all the advantages of hindsight and modern sensibility.

Oh, those mountains of research. How fascinating it all was—that overripe, just-going-rotten time, which ended with its golden youth marching off to what was humorously referred to as the 4th Balkan War, until it disastrously grew into World War I. All those histories, letters, diaries, etiquette books, books on household management (bless Mrs. Beeton!), those newspapers and advertisements I'd studied. What did I get out of it? Accuracy of detail and a few telling incidents. Research, I discovered, is like fish spawn: Millions of eggs laid (or words read) and from this a few goldfish or, in a novel, what Conrad called "the accumulated verisimilitude of selected episode." Selected is the operative word.

I don't mean to speak slightingly of research. Titles, forms of address, the correct clothes and manner all matter. They matter a great deal. If they don't seem important, why bother with an historical setting? And you're bound to run into a reader who knows better. If I am that reader, you've lost me. Whenever I come across sloppy research in a novel, I can't help but conclude that the author didn't care, and if he didn't, why should I care to read his book?

But there is another reason that all those millions of eggs are necessary. The total immersion in another period, which comes with all that reading, allows us to write from the inside out rather than from the outside in.

This means that, having acquired all that knowledge, you have, in a manner of speaking, to disregard it. What was a matter of course to your characters can't continue to be a nine-days' wonder to the author, nor can their moral attitudes remain quaint or reprehensible simply because they seem so to us now. Edwardian views of women, the poor, and Jews frequently made me want to put one of my characters on a soapbox and tell everybody off, but since the people in my story were the kind who took such attitudes for granted (with the exception of a suffragette or two), I could not afford such luxury. And even if you do have a character who is at odds with his society, it is important not to have him express the author's view instead of his own. Suffragettes in the days before World War I, I found, had very little in common with the women's movement of the seventies; the anti-Semitism of the time, a pervasive but casual form of snobbery (more common in English writing than German, to my surprise), cannot be regarded in the same light in which we look upon anti-Semitism since the Holocaust.

My first setback in planning an authentic Edwardian novel came from my editor. Edwardian authors thought nothing of spreading themselves over 800 pages, and their readers would probably have been disappointed to get anything less. With the present cost of paper and printing, try to get an 800-page novel past your editor if your name does not happen to be James Michener!

Then there was the problem of authentic dialogue. Reading the popular fiction of the day, I discovered that it was totally unusable. English speech was florid enough ("The duke has most kindly offered to show me over the garden"), but German was so hedged with deference and politeness that it was nearly impenetrable. ("As the Herr Minister has had the condescension to remark, and if he will kindly permit me to agree with his ministership, it is a very nice day.")

I also had to cut back a good deal when dealing with forms of address and titles, most of which, if done authentically, would strike present-day readers as unbearably formal, or worse, humorous. Germans, especially, who think nothing of addressing someone in ordinary conversation as "Frau Lifeinsuranceactuarialistwidow," had all their lavish silks removed and were kept down to useful polyester instead.

It is easy enough to avoid the more obvious mistakes—letting your characters have "lifestyles" or "meaningful relationships"—using words that were not in existence then, or have since changed their meaning (square, gay), since such things can be looked up in Eric Partridge or the dictionary. What is more difficult is to judge just how much period slang to use. Characters in Edwardian novels tended to use a great deal of it, but I found that for me it worked best in small doses, mostly from children, servants and soldiers, who by Edwardian definition constituted an underclass.

As in real life, money and sex presented me with considerable difficulties. Had I stayed authentically in the minds of my characters, I would have mentioned merely what things cost and left it at that. But since I was dealing with foreign currencies (pre-inflationary ones at that), it would have been useless to say a character earned a hundred pounds a year. Was his employer a skinflint or incredibly generous? A present-day reader would have no way of knowing. I found it wisest not to be too specific unless the amount of money involved served to illustrate something about a character. When David gives five pounds to a soldier fallen on hard times to buy himself a civilian suit, and the soldier is shocked that there are people who actually spend as much as that on a suit, it tells both what five pounds would buy and that David tends to be careless about money. In present terms, that five pounds, incidentally, would be worth about $7.00. As Sylvia Townsend Warner remarked in regard to the price of gin then and now, it is a wonder any of us have the courage to write our memoirs.

As for sex, strictly speaking there shouldn't have been any. Of course, real Edwardians had a fair amount of it, some of it kinky enough to please the bluest noses, but in their books they had asterisks. I wasn't sorry to be able to avoid graphic sex scenes, which I hate writing in any case, since they always remind me of car repair manuals ("Push button Z, wind handle B. . . ."), but I realized I couldn't get away with pretending that all Edwardian babies were found under cabbages. I compromised by giving my characters some interesting kinks: one likes coachmen with high boots and whips; one likes little girls; one only fancies older women; and one is homosexual. But at crucial moments I resorted to Edwardian asterisks, plus the trappings of Edwardian romance: glades of bluebells, white lilac, snow on a skylight, and if not a nightingale, a cuckoo, since the marriage that results from that particular seduction breaks up over an accusation of cuckoldry.

On the whole I enjoyed all that patching and contriving. I loved the research. I found it restful to be able to write about characters who belong to an established class structure, but what I liked best of all was that in a novel set in the past, the writer can endow the characters with some old-fashioned virtues that in a contemporary novel would sound nauseatingly goody-goody. Before World War I, idealism was not yet considered square—indeed "square" was a term of praise—and my young men could value loyalty, friendship, courage and decent manners without being regarded as wimps. They were rich, mostly, but not pampered. English plumbing and six years in that upper-class hell, the English public school, saw to that. They had been brought up to detest self-pity, and though all three of them were of an age to serve in a fiendish war, they did not suffer from anomie, anhedonia, or cosmic angst. This made them enjoyable to live with. Now that I am done with them I miss them. And if on one of the morning runs I should meet with a knight in clanking armor or a shepherd speaking in Virgilian hexameters who didn't object to considerable patching and contriving on my part, I might easily be tempted to bring him home and give him my next four years.

53

CONSTRUCTING A SCIENCE FICTION NOVEL

By Roger Zelazny

THE LATE James Blish was once asked where he got his ideas for science fiction stories. He gave one of the usual general answers we all do—from observation, from reading, from the sum total of all his experiences, et cetera. Then someone asked him what he did if no ideas were forthcoming from these. He immediately replied, "I plagiarize myself."

He meant, of course, that he looked over his earlier works for roads unfollowed, trusting in the persistence of concerns and the renewal of old fascinations to stimulate some new ideas. And this works. I've tried it occasionally, and I usually find my mind flooded.

But I've been writing for over twenty years, and I know something about how my mind works when I am seeking a story or telling one. I did not always know the things that I know now, and much of my earlier writing involved groping—defining themes, deciding how I really felt about people and ideas. Consequently, much of this basic thinking accomplished, it is easier for me to fit myself into the driver's seat of a fresh new story than it once was. It may be the latest model, but the steering is similar, and once I locate the gearshift I know what to do with it.

For example: Settings. For me, science fiction has always represented the rational—the extension into a future or alien environment of that which is known now—whereas fantasy represented the metaphysical—the introduction of the unknown, usually into an alien environment. The distinctions are sometimes blurred, and sometimes it is fun to blur them. But on a practical, working level, this generally is how I distinguish the two. Either sort of story (I never tire of repeating) has the same requirements as a piece of general fiction, with the added necessity of introducing that exotic environment. Of the three basic elements of any fiction—plot, character and setting—it is the setting that requires extra attention in science fiction and fantasy. Here, as nowhere else, one walks a tightrope between overexplaining and overassuming, between boring the reader with too many details or losing the reader by not providing enough.

I found this difficult at first. I learned it by striving for economy of statement, by getting the story moving quickly and then introducing the background piecemeal. Somewhere along the line I realized that doing this properly could solve two problems: The simple exposition of the material could, if measured out in just the right doses, become an additional means of raising reader interest. I employed this technique to an extreme in the opening to my story "Unicorn Variation," in which I postponed for several pages describing the unusual creature passing through a strange locale.

A bizarrerie of fires, cunabulum of light, it moved with a deft, almost dainty deliberation, phasing into and out of existence like a storm-shot piece of evening; or perhaps the darkness between the flares was more akin to its truest nature—swirl of black ashes assembled in prancing cadence to the lowing note of desert wind down the arroyo behind buildings as empty yet filled as the pages of unread books or stillnesses between the notes of a song.

As you see, I was careful to tell just enough to keep the reader curious. By the time it became apparent that it was a unicorn in a New Mexico ghost town, I had already introduced another character and a conflict.

Characters are less of a problem for me than settings. People are usually still people in science fiction environments. Major figures tend to occur to me almost fully developed, and minor ones do not require much work. As for their physical descriptions, it is easy at first to overdescribe. But how much does the reader really need? How much can the mind take in at one gulp? See the character entirely but mention only three things, I decided. Then quit and get on with the story. If a fourth characteristic sneaks in easily, O.K. But leave it at that initially. No more. Trust that other features will occur as needed, so long as you know. "He was a tall, red-faced kid with one shoulder lower than the other." Were he a tall, red-faced kid with bright blue eyes (or large-knuckled hands or storms of freckles upon his cheeks) with one shoulder lower than the other, he would actually go out of focus a bit rather

263

than grow clearer in the mind's eye. Too much detail creates a sensory overload, impairing the reader's ability to visualize. If such additional details are really necessary for the story line itself, it would be better to provide another dose later on, after allowing time for the first to sink in. "Yeah," he replied, blue eyes flashing.

I've mentioned settings and characters as typical examples of the development of writing reflexes, because reflexes are what this sort of work becomes with practice—and then, after a time, it should become second nature and be dismissed from thought. For this is just apprentice work—tricks—things that everybody in the trade has to learn. It is not, I feel, what writing is all about.

The important thing for me is the development and refinement of one's perception of the world, the experimentation with viewpoints. This lies at the heart of storytelling, and all of the mechanical techniques one learns are merely tools. It is the writer's approach to material that makes a story unique.

For example, I have lived in the Southwest for nearly a decade now. At some point I became interested in Indians. I began attending festivals and dances, reading anthropology, attending lectures, visiting museums. I became acquainted with Indians. At first, my interest was governed only by the desire to know more than I did. Later, though, I began to feel that a story was taking shape at some lower level of my consciousness. I waited. I continued to acquire information and experience in the area.

One day my focus narrowed to the Navajo. Later, I realized that if I could determine why my interest had suddenly taken this direction I would have a story. This came about when I discovered the fact that the Navajo had developed their own words—several hundred of them—for naming the various parts of the internal combustion engine. It was not the same with other Indian tribes I knew of. When introduced to cars, other tribes had simply taken to using the Anglo words for carburetors, pistons, spark plugs, etc. But the Navajo had actually come up with new Navajo words for these items—a sign, as I saw it, of their independence and their adaptability.

I looked further. The Hopis and the Pueblo Indians, neighbors to the Navajo, had rain dances in their rituals. The Navajo made no great effort to control the weather in this fashion. Instead, they adapted to rain or drought.

Adaptability. That was it. It became the theme of my novel. Suppose, I asked myself, I were to take a contemporary Navajo and by means of the time-dilation effects of space travel coupled with life extension treatments, I saw to it that he was still alive and in fairly good shape, say, one hundred-seventy years from now? There would, of necessity, be gaps in his history during the time he was away, a period in which a lot of changes would have occurred here on Earth. That was how the idea for *Eye of Cat* came to me.

But an idea is not a science fiction novel. How do you turn it into one?

I asked myself why he would have been away so frequently. Suppose he'd been a really fine tracker and hunter? I wondered. Then he could have been a logical choice as a collector of alien-life specimens. That rang true, so I took it from there. A problem involving a nasty alien being could serve as a reason for bringing my Navajo character out of retirement and provide the basis for a conflict.

I also wanted something representing his past and the Navajo traditions, something more than just his wilderness abilities—some things he had turned his back on. Navajo legend provided me with the *chindi,* an evil spirit I could set to bedeviling him. It occurred to me then that this evil spirit could be made to correspond with some unusual creature he himself had brought to Earth a long time ago.

That was the rough idea. Though not a complete plot summary, this will show how the story took form, beginning with a simple observation and leading to the creation of a character and a situation. This small segment of the story would come under the heading of "inspiration"; most of the rest involved the application of reasoning to what the imagination had so far provided.

This required some tricky considerations. I firmly believe that I could write the same story—effectively—in dozens of different ways: as a comedy, as a tragedy, as something in between; from a minor character's point of view, in the first person, in the third, in a different tense, et cetera. But I also believe that for a particular piece of fiction, there is one way to proceed that is better than any of the others. I feel that the material should dictate the form. Making it do this properly is for me the most difficult and rewarding part of the storytelling act. It goes beyond all of the reflex tricks, into the area of esthetics.

So I had to determine what approach would best produce the tone

265

that I wished to achieve. This, of course, required clarifying my own feelings.

My protagonist Billy Blackhorse Singer, though born into a near-neolithic environment, later received an advanced formal education. That alone was enough to create some conflicts within him. One may reject one's past or try to accommodate to it. Bill rejected quite a bit. He was a very capable man, but he was overwhelmed. I decided to give him an opportunity to come to terms with everything in his life.

I saw that this was going to be a novel of character. Showing a character as complex as Billy's would require some doing. His early life was involved with the myths, legends, shamanism of his people, and since this background was still a strong element in his character, I tried to show this by interspersing in the narrative my paraphrases of different sections of the Navajo creation myth and other appropriate legendary material. I decided to do some of this as poetry, some original, some only loosely based on traditional materials. This, I hoped, would give the book some flavor as well as help to shape my character.

The problem of injecting the futuristic background material was heightened, because I was already burdening the narrative with the intermittent doses of Indian material. I needed to find a way to encapsulate and abbreviate, so I stole a trick from Dos Passos' *U.S.A.* trilogy. I introduced "Disk" sections, analogous to his "Newsreel" and "Camera Eye" sequences—a few pages here and there made up of headlines, news reports, snatches of popular songs, to give the flavor of the times. This device served to get in a lot of background without slowing the pace, and its odd format was almost certain to be sufficiently interesting visually to arouse the reader's curiosity.

The evolving plot required the introduction of a half-dozen secondary characters—and not just minor ones whom I might bring in as completely stock figures. Pausing to do full-scale portraits of each—by means of long flashbacks, say—could be fatal to the narrative, however, as they were scheduled to appear just as the story was picking up in pace. So I took a chance and broke a major writing rule.

Almost every book you read about writing will say, "Show. Don't tell." That is, you do not simply tell the reader what a character is like; you demonstrate it, because telling will generally produce a distancing effect and arouse a ho-hum response in the reader. There is little reader identification, little empathy created in merely telling about people.

I decided that not only was I going to tell the reader what each character was like, I was going to try to make it an interesting reading experience. In fact, I had to.

If you are going to break a rule, capitalize on it. Do it big. Exploit it. Turn it into a virtue.

I captioned a section with each character's name, followed the name with a comma and wrote one long, complex, character-describing sentence, breaking its various clauses and phrases into separate lines, so that it was strung out to give the appearance of a Whitmanesque piece of poetry. As with my "Disk" sections, I wanted to make this sufficiently interesting visually to pull the reader through what was, actually, straight exposition.

Another problem in the book arose when a number of telepaths used their unusual communicative abilities to form temporarily a composite or mass-mind. There were points at which I had to show this mind in operation. *Finnegans Wake* occurred to me as a good model for the stream of consciousness I wanted to use for this. And Anthony Burgess' *Joysprick,* which I'd recently read, had contained a section that could be taken as a primer for writing in this fashion. I followed.

Then, for purposes of achieving verisimilitude, I traveled through Canyon de Chelly with a Navajo guide. As I wrote the portions of the book set in the Canyon, I had before me, along with my memories, a map, my photographs and archaeological descriptions of the route Billy followed. This use of realism, I hoped, would help to achieve some balance against the impressionism and radical storytelling techniques I had employed elsewhere.

These were some of the problems I faced in writing *Eye of Cat* and some of the solutions I used to deal with them. Thematically, though, many of the questions I asked myself and many of the ideas I considered were things that had been with me all along; only the technical solutions and the story's resolution were different this time. In this respect, I was, at one level, still plagiarizing my earlier self. Nothing wrong with that, if some growth has occurred in the meantime.

From everything I've said, it may sound as if the novel was wildly experimental. It wasn't. The general theme was timeless—a consideration of change and adjustment, of growth. While science fiction often deals with the future and bears exotic trappings, its real, deep considerations involve human nature, which has been the same for a long time and which I believe will continue much as it is for an even longer time. So in one sense we constantly seek new ways to say old things. But human nature is a generality. The individual does change, does adapt, and this applies to the writer as well as to the characters. And it is in these changes—in self-consciousness, perception, sensibility—that I feel the strongest, most valid stories have their source, whatever the devices most suitable for their telling.

54

ELEMENTS OF THE POLICE PROCEDURAL NOVEL

BY REX BURNS

GIVEN the development of the writer's sense of which words live and which don't — a development that for me comes as much through reading as through writing — I think the areas most pertinent to a successful police procedural are four: research, setting, plot, and character.

These divisions are, of course, artificial. As in any "recipe," the elements blend and influence each other; and in any art such as cooking or writing, the whole is greater than the sum of its parts. But though each writer must discover for himself this sense of life or wholeness, some of the basic elements contributing to it can be distinguished. Let's begin with research.

The kind of research I favor is quite basic: my main source for information is the daily newspaper. I figure that if a newspaper article about a crime interests me, it will interest other readers. Naturally, the newspaper story must undergo a metamorphosis before it comes out as fiction. For one thing, there are the questions of libel and plagiarism; and, for another, too great a reliance on the facts as reported can cause a story to become quickly dated.

More important is the question of a good yarn — an interesting newspaper article is only a germ, a bud. It provides a sequence of events and an indication of setting for the full-grown fiction. For example, the following paragraph from a UPI newswire release was the nucleus of a chapter of a novel I was working on: "The raids in Cordoba began when a small airplane, circling the city to apparently coordinate the attacks, threw a bomb that exploded without causing injuries near a provincial bank about 11 A.M." In short, a newspaper article can provide a rich source of actual whats, wheres, and whens. The whys and the whos are the novelist's responsibility.

A second good source of information for the police procedural writer is court records. Affidavits, depositions, and transcripts — in addition to the writer's sitting in on court hearings — help provide not only events and incidental tidbits for a story, but also the language of narration. Increasingly, a cop, especially a senior officer such as a detective, must understand the technology of the law. Every technology has it jargon, and this can be found in legal records and in courtrooms.

Both newspaper stories and court records are as valuable for what they leave out as for what they offer. To get some of that which is left out, read the story with the questions "how?" and "why?" in mind. For instance, that favorite phrase of reporters, "police, acting on a tip from an informant . . ." gives rise to such questions as: Which policeman? Who was the informant? What incentive did he have for informing? What kind of communication — telephone, written, conversational? Who believed the informant? Who didn't? How much time passed between the tip and the raid? These and similar questions come up when the novelist begins creating the fictional world which will embody any actual events he chooses to use.

Though the writer's imagination furnishes the answers to such questions as those asked above, that imagination can be stimulated by a third kind of research which I've found to be most beneficial: interviewing. A policeman, like almost everyone else, enjoys talking about his work, and most municipalities have programs for bettering police-community relations. And a writer — despite what his neighbors may think — is a member of the community. In a larger town, check with the department's public information office. Departments in smaller towns tend to be less formal, and I think somewhat less accessible, perhaps because their manpower tends to be insufficient and the training less professional, generating a defensive attitude. The prosecutor's office and the sheriff's office are also worthwhile avenues of approach. For me, this interviewing tends to be quite casual and takes place during a duty watch; there's a lot of time for conversation during eight hours of riding in a patrol car.

Armed with some specific questions derived from reading newspapers and reports, the interviewer can start filling in those blanks found in the documents. The answers don't have to be related to the same cases read about — in fact, I like it better if they aren't. The novelist deals with probability, and patterns of common behavior offer more freedom for the invention of particulars than does the mere reporting of facts, which is where the journalist ends and the novelist begins. Unlike what takes place on most television talk shows, an interviewer-novelist should be a good listener and, speaking for myself, a copious but surreptitious notetaker. It also helps to train your eye for such minutiae as manufacturer's labels, model numbers, organization charts — in short, anything that gives quick specific detail for your story's setting. Interviewing also provides the latest slang and technical jargon.

The manner of introducing those technical terms into the narrative varies. If a character honestly might not know what a particular device or procedure is called, he can simply ask someone in the story. The character and the reader become informed together. I use this device sparingly, since my characters in the Gabe Wager books are generally professional and well-trained. (Moreover, as a reader, I get damned irritated when a story's development is continually interrupted by some idiot who needs everything explained to him.) Another means of introducing technical terms is to use the phrase in normal dialogue and let the descriptive passage carry the explanation: " 'Let me have the Kell-Kit,' said Wager. Sergeant Johnston handed him the small body transmitter. . . ." Or, for variation, the equation may be reversed: " 'Let me have the body transmitter,' said Wager. Sergeant Johnston handed him the small Kell-Kit." I'm not sure if police departments have yet surpassed the federal government in the use of acronyms and arcane initials, but these are an essential part of bureaucratic jargon. It is a rule of thumb in writing first to use the full phrase, then, in the next sentence or two, the more common initials: "Wager turned to his little book of Confidential Informants. The first C. I. was. . . ." No explanatory passage is needed, and the action moves without interruption.

Research, then, is the foundation for the police procedural, and on that foundation are built in setting, plot, and character. Setting is, of course, easiest to create if it's well known to the writer. For the Gabriel Wager stories, that means Denver. Ironically, my editors more than once pointed out that a street which I invented wasn't on their map of Denver, or an odd-numbered address should be on the north rather than south side of a particular avenue. But the familiarity I mean is as much in flavor as in fact, and its manner of presentation is — for me — impressionistic. The single well-chosen detail that captures the flavor of the setting and gives focus and life to an otherwise sketchy scene is part of the economy I associate with the "grittiness" of a police procedural. A gothic, a novel that explores states of mind, or a sci-fi fantasy may call

271

for more sweeping and panoramic descriptions to create a mood or sustain a romance. But I find harmony between a spare style and the realistic police story. Since this descriptive technique tends to emphasize action rather than setting, and since a police procedural is akin to a report — and a report is usually about "what happened" — the emphasis on concrete and concise detail feels right to me.

The concern with what happened brings us to plot. Plot is not just *what* takes place but *why* it takes place. The police procedural may or may not use the mystery as the basis of suspense. If the police do not know who the perpetrator is, then unraveling the mystery becomes the plot — i.e., the gradual revelation of motive and opportunity. But often, in life as well as in fiction, the police do know who the villain is, and the plot centers on gathering enough evidence for a viable court case. The manner of getting this evidence is quite tedious and even dull — questioning fifty or a hundred witnesses, long hours of surveillance, studying accounting records. The problem for the storyteller in the police procedural field becomes one of remaining true to reality without boring the reader. One technique that fits the police procedural is focusing attention on new methods of surveillance or on the ever-changing avenues of legal presentation. Here, research is indispensable. Another device is to give your detective more cases than one. This is by no means unrealistic, but a good story requires that the cases somehow work together toward a single conclusion. That's the old demand of art for unity, a unity seldom apparent in real life.

Another very familiar technique for maintaining interest is the foil — someone who offers byplay for the protagonist. A foil should serve a variety of purposes, all contributing toward the unity of the novel. The character used as a foil — a rookie, for instance — may be a device not only for explaining police procedure, but also for revealing the protagonist's character through his reaction to the foil's activities.

I try to make character as interesting as case. The strongest novels are those with living characters to whom the action is vital, and this holds true for any tale, even a plotless one. But whether it's a who-done-it or a how-to-prove-it, the police story is fundamentally an action story, and in it the development of character should not impede the action. Ideally, character development and action should coincide; but where they do not, I tip the balance in favor of action, possibly because I envision the Gabe Wager series as one long novel of perhaps fifteen volumes, and this view gives me plenty of room to let the character grow.

272

There are several other concrete devices that aid the quick presentation of character without interrupting the action. One device especially useful for creating secondary characters is the "signature" — a distinctive act, speech pattern, or habit of thought that identifies and distinguishes one character from another. This signature may be simple: one secondary figure from *The Alvarez Journal* smokes cigars, another has an old man's rumbling cough, a third speaks administrative jargon. Or, if the character is of more importance to the story, a combination of signatures may be used to flesh him out. At its worst, this device generates cliché characters — the western bad man with his black hat and sneer. At best, the signature makes the character become alive and individualized — the girth, thirst, and cowardice of Falstaff. The problem, of course, is to characterize without caricaturing — unless your aim is satire. The novelist's ability to create real characters can be improved by reading other writers who are very good at it: Shakespeare, Flaubert, Faulkner. Another means is "reading" friends and neighbors: What exactly is it that distinguishes one of your acquaintances from another? Given universal human qualities, what makes one individual different from another?

Minor and secondary characters, while absolutely necessary, do not give life to the action. Rarely can any story, police procedural or other, do without a protagonist. Again, because of the importance of action in police procedurals, the writer is faced with the need for an economical development of his main character. The technique I have chosen for my Gabe Wager series is by no means new: It's the familiar "recording consciousness" of Henry James, the restricted third-person point of view, in which every event and concept in the story is presented from the perspective of a single protagonist. I've found several advantages to this device: The action proceeds and the protagonist's character is revealed at the same time. The reader is faced with the same limitations of knowledge as the protagonist, and thus the element of suspense is heightened. Using third person rather than first person puts distance between the reader and the protagonist and offers another dimension to the story, which helps the reader through those necessary and authentic but often slow stages of a case's development.

This narrative technique also has shortcomings. The author can't give the reader any information that the protagonist does not have, thus leaving little chance for irony or depth. For this point of view to work, the

273

author must also have a total understanding of the protagonist. While it may not be relevant to the story, it is nonetheless necessary if the character's actions are to be consistent.

First-person narration achieves many of the same results but brings an even closer identification between author and character. Think of the popular image of Mickey Spillane, for example. I prefer third person because it enforces objectivity and quite possibly because, unlike Gabe Wager, I'm not a good cop.

Focusing all the action through Wager's perspective, then, contributes to a unity of action and characterization in which action dominates but character development follows quite closely and, I hope, unobtrusively. I try to achieve this by placing a heavy emphasis on dialogue. By its very nature, dialogue is dramatic — the characters are onstage talking rather than being talked about by a narrator. Again, the signature is very important, and I play a little game of trying to see how many lines of dialogue I can put together without having to state who is speaking. The idea is that each character's voice should be distinct enough to indicate the speaker.

I place the police procedural in the category of literary realism. The contemporary, the probable, the routine, determine my choice of a realistic subject. Once I select my subject, the elements of research, setting, plot, and character are indispensable, and, in my Gabe Wager police procedurals, all of these elements must contribute to the action.

55

TEN GUIDELINES FOR SALABLE CONFESSIONS

By Elvira Weaver

THE CONFESSION market is hungry for fresh, good stories, gobbling up approximately one hundred sixty of them every month. It is a "byline-less" market, where a beginner has an excellent chance of breaking in, but you must know the ropes. The following are guidelines I have devised in my four years of selling to this specialized field.

1. Begin with a positive-thinking, likable narrator with one staggering problem. In real life, if one thing goes wrong, everything seems to go wrong, but in confessions, the narrator has only *one* problem. I wrote a story in which the narrator was a young, pretty woman carpenter in danger of losing her job because the jealous wives of the other carpenters were making trouble for her. This was her *one* problem.

The heroine was also divorced, had two, preschool children, and was getting no financial help from her ex-husband. That was another problem, so I toned it down by showing that she was *glad* to be out of her bad marriage, and was managing financially, thanks to her well-paying, "man's" job. Carpentry was hard, physical work, so I showed her liking to work outdoors and adjusting to the strenuous labor. Her children were in a reliable preschool nursery during the day, and she was never tired or short-tempered with them at night. I went through my story, line by line, and took out even hinted-at problems. When I had finished, my main character's life wasn't a bowl of cherries, but she was coping with everything except one problem: The wives of the other carpenters wanted to get her fired!

Then I focused on this one problem to make it seem truly staggering. Every thought the narrator had, every action she took, every conversation, centered on that problem. There wasn't a moment that her problem was out of her mind. How was she going to keep her job, when the jealous wives were intent on getting her fired?

2. Have the narrator handle the one problem, inappropriately at first, but satisfactorily by the end of the story. A narrator is never passive. She will handle her problem, and because this is a confession (the narrator confessing something she did wrong), she will at first not handle it successfully, refusing to see that the wives might have a legitimate reason for their jealousy.

3. Keep reader sympathy for the narrator. This is probably the most important rule in confessions. Right off, the narrator has a strike against her because she is not handling her problem well, so you must give her at least three good reasons for doing what she does—one of which should go back to her past.

In this story, the reasons for the woman carpenter's blind refusal to see that the wives had any reason to be jealous were a) She didn't flirt with the male carpenters. Quite the opposite: she has to take their macho wise-cracking. b) She never needed much make-up, and she wore none. She dressed in work jeans and boots, never anything cool and sexy. c) (going back into her past) After her disastrous marriage, she didn't even like men much: she certainly wasn't out to "get" one of her co-workers.

Showing the motivation for the narrator's poor handling of her problem made her sympathetic and likable, but I didn't stop there: I never let the woman do anything else wrong for the rest of the story. To make sure, I went through the story again, line by line, and consciously made the narrator likable. When she spoke, she spoke softly; she was patient and loving with her children, never too tired to read them a story. (It is strictly taboo for mothers in confessions to put their children in front of the television.) In transitions, she baked cookies and was kind to animals. Everything she did was sweet and gentle, and love just dripped off those pages as my hurt and bewildered (not angry and vindictive) protagonist fought to keep her job. All she wanted was to work. She could see no reason for the wives to be jealous of her—until at the climax, when one married man who had been kind to her all through the story innocently put his arms around her to comfort her, and the natural attraction between a man and a woman took over. Then she could see the reason for the wives' jealousy, and resolved it satisfactorily by admitting she was not "one of the boys." This woman carpenter's story was my first sale, bringing a check from *Modern Romances* for $335.00!

4. Keep the story ordinary and believable. Confession readers don't want to read stories about terrible people who have horrible things happen to them. They want to read about normal people like themselves and think, "Heaven forbid, but this awful thing might have happened to me!"

In one story, my distraught protagonist's twelve-year-old daughter had suddenly become secretive and rebellious. The narrator handled the problem wrong by not communicating well with her daughter. At the climax of the story, when she discovered her thin, undeveloped little daughter was being coerced into posing nude for a child pornography magazine, she realized her noncommunicative attitude had kept her daughter from confiding in her. In order to carry off that lurid climax, I made the narrator and her family—even the villain and his family—as pleasant and normal as possible. This story sold—to *True Romance* for $200.00—because the reader could identify with the characters.

Reader identity is very important in confessions. Most readers are from blue-collar backgrounds, so give your protagonist a blue-collar background. Have her live in a small, neat house with a husband who works in a factory or a gas station or has some similar occupation, and give her one or two adorable children. If the narrator works, have her job be nothing too far up the economic ladder—a file clerk, a bank teller, a waitress.

5. Write in the warm, first-person confession style. I used to be embarrassed to buy a confession magazine, but you can't look down on a market when you want to write for it. Study the magazines. You'll find they don't deserve their bad reputation. Most are very moral. Absorb the confession style.

A confession story's heroine is a good person, not holding anything back, as she confides her deepest, darkest secret. The reader expects to know everything about her. Is her sex life good? Is she a good housekeeper and a good wife and mother? (She always is unless this is her story problem.) As she goes about her daily life in transitions, slip in lines showing these things. When the reader is finished with your story, she should feel she knows your narrator more intimately than she knows her own sister.

6. Write the story in scenes. Begin by presenting the problem in the opening scene. Always keep the story moving forward, with as little flashback as possible. Have the main character make a statement, then explain it. Don't have any limbo characters. Tell exactly where each one is.

> My roommate, Kathy, looked up from the sofa as I came into the living room. "Are you going out tonight?" she asked.
> "Yes," I answered. I raised my chin defiantly. "I'm meeting Tom downtown."
> Tom and I always met downtown. We'd have dinner at some romantic, out-of-the-way restaurant, then go to a nearby motel to make love. But it was only a temporary arrangement, until Tom felt able to tell his children about us. It wasn't cheap the way Kathy made it out to be!
> "I won't be late," I said, ignoring Kathy's disapproving look as I slipped out the door.

7. Make the writing strong, vivid and emotional. Use two-word descriptive phrases—"small, comfortable" living room; "quiet, reserved" mother-in-law; "sexy, blonde" neighbor. Be specific in your writing—two, little boys instead of two children; old, blue station wagon instead of car; handsome, sexy husband instead of husband.

8. Keep the writing tight. Cut out every character in the story who is not essential to it. If children are necessary, have two, not three. A sympathetic narrator would visit her mother or sister if they lived nearby, so if they're not essential to the story, have them live far away or be dead. Be explicit. Don't make the reader wonder about anything. If family members are dead, make it an ordinary death, but not a car crash or a heart attack. Those are overdone.

9. Write about things you know. My first sales were stories about: 1. a woman carpenter: when my husband started his remodeling business, I was the only help he could afford. 2. a mother-in-law: mine is extremely tidy and well-organized. 3. a teen-ager who searches for her birth mother: my two children are adopted.

Confession facts have to be accurate, and you feel much more confident when you write about things you are familiar with. What you don't know, research in the library. Don't lose valuable credibility with an editor—or your readers.

10. Find a fresh angle for every story. There is probably not a plot you can think of that hasn't already been written hundreds of times. A fresh angle is what will make your story stand out and sell.

In one story, my narrator was engaged to a man she had met while he was in the Navy. His family lived on a dairy farm in Wisconsin, and they had invited her to visit for a week so they could meet the "city girl who had stolen Cliff's heart."

My fresh angle was that Cliff's family farm was run by women—a widowed mother and two sisters, one divorced and the other married to a useless alcoholic. My heroine went, eager to assure these valiant women that she wouldn't take Cliff away from the farm after they were married. She would adjust to farm living. (Her overzealousness to please was her wrong handling of the situation.)

The modern, up-to-date farm women accepted the narrator immediately, showed her the dairy operation, and asked her help with the bookkeeping. She admired them tremendously and felt honored to be accepted. Then, in the climax, the truth about the women on the farm is revealed: They hadn't been strong women because of the weak men in their lives; they were strong-minded women who had made their men weak—and the narrator was becoming just like them, impatient with Cliff's gentle ways when that had been what had attracted her to him originally. This different twist made my farm story sell first time out, to *Modern Romances* for $375.00.

Confession editors need good, fresh material. Give them what they want, and you will sell.

56

TRICKS OF THE NONFICTION TRADE

By Donald M. Murray

UNDER the apprentice system still practiced in most crafts, a beginner has the opportunity to work beside an experienced worker and pick up small but significant tricks of the trade. Few of us, however, observe a writer at the workbench turning a phrase, cutting a line or reordering a paragraph so that a meaning runs easy and runs clear. Here are a few of the tricks I've picked up during more than forty years of trying to make writing look easy.

Before writing

An effective piece of writing is a dialogue between the writer and the reader, with the writer answering the reader's questions just before they are asked. Each piece usually has five or six questions that must be answered if the reader is to be satisfied.

I brainstorm and polish the questions first, then put them in the order the reader will ask them. For example, if I am doing a piece on diabetes, I list such questions as:

- What is diabetes?
- How can I tell if I have it?
- What's the latest treatment?
- Do I have to give myself shots?
- Where can I get that treatment?
- How dangerous is diabetes?

Then I reconsider, refine, and reorder the questions:

1. *Lead:* What's the latest treatment for diabetes?
2. How dangerous is diabetes?
3. What is diabetes?
4. How can I tell if I have it?

5. Do I have to give myself shots? No. New treatment.
6. Where can I get it?

As I write, I may have to reorder the questions if I "hear" the reader ask the question earlier than I expected, but that doesn't happen very often. It is also helpful to write these questions down before revising a draft—especially a confusing one. Just role-play a reader and put down the questions you would ask, combining them if necessary, and then put them in order. This trick will help you understand what readers want to know and when they want to know it.

Professional writers, however, don't wait until they have a completed draft to read what they have written. They learn to pay attention to lists, collections of information, partially drafted sentences and paragraphs, abandoned pages, notes, outlines, phrases, code words that constitute the kind of writing they do on the notebook page and in their heads before the first draft.

Reading those fragments, the writer discovers a revealing or organizing specific around which an article can be built, a pattern of action or argument on which a meaning may be hung, a voice that tells the writer what he or she feels about the subject and that may be used to communicate that feeling to the reader.

Many writers write everything at the same distance from the subject. It becomes an unconscious habit. Academic writers may stand too far back from the subject, so that the reader feels detached and really doesn't become involved with the content. Magazine writers usually move in close, many times getting too close, so that readers are lost in the details of a particular person and are not able to understand the significance of the piece.

The writer should use an imaginary zoom lens before writing the first draft and decide the proper distance for this particular article, the point from which the reader will see the piece clearly, understand its context, and care about the subject. The writer may stand back and put the winning play in the context of all Army-Navy football games or move in close and tell the story of the game in terms of the winning play itself, concentrating on the fifty seconds that made the difference.

Leads and endings

The first line, the first paragraph, the first ten lines of an article establish its direction, dimensions, voice, pace. "What's so hard about the first sentence is that you're stuck with it," says Joan Didion. "Everything else is going to flow out of that sentence. And by the time you've laid down the first *two* sentences, your options are all gone." It's worth taking time to get those sentences right.

The more complicated the subject the more time you may need to spend on the lead to make sure that you are giving the readers the information they need to become interested right away. You can't start too far back with background, and you can't plunge into the middle of the story so that the readers do not know what they are reading. You have to start at the right point in the right way, and the more time you spend drafting new leads, and then refining the leads you choose, the faster you will be able to write the whole piece. Most of the major problems in writing an article are solved when the right lead is found.

When I worked as writing coach at *The Boston Globe,* I found that the best writers usually knew where they would end. They had a quote, an anecdote, a scene, a specific detail with which they would close. It would sum up the piece by implication. The good writer has a sense of direction, a destination in mind. The best endings are rarely written to solve the problems of a piece that just trails off. The best endings are usually seen by the writer as waiting just ahead for the draft to take the writer and the reader there.

The right voice

Experienced writers rarely begin a first draft until they hear in their heads—or on the page—a voice that may be right. Voice is usually the key element in effective writing. It is what attracts the reader and communicates to the reader. It is that element that gives the illusion of speech. Voice carries the writer's intensity and glues together the information that the reader needs to know. It is the music in writing that makes meaning clear.

Writers keep rehearsing possible first lines, paragraphs, or endings, key scenes or statements that will reveal how what is to be said may be said best. The voice of a piece of writing is the writer's own voice, adapted in written language to the subject and audience. We speak differently at a funeral or a party, in church or in the locker room, at home or with strangers. We are experienced with using our individual voices for many purposes. We have to learn to do this same thing in writing, and to hear a voice in our head that may be polished and developed on the page.

The voice is not only rehearsed but practiced. We should hear what we're writing as we write it. I dictate most of my writing and monitor my voice as I'm speaking so that the pace, the rhythm, the tone support what I'm trying to say. Keep reading aloud as you draft and edit. To train yourself to do this, it may be helpful, if you use a word processor, to turn off the screen and write, listening to what you're saying as you're saying it. Later you can read it aloud and make the changes you need to develop a voice that the reader can hear.

Put your notes away before you begin a draft. What you remember is probably what should be remembered; what you forget is probably what should be forgotten. No matter; you'll have a chance to go back to your notes after the draft is completed. What is important is to achieve a draft which allows the writing to flow.

Planning allows the writer to write fast without interruptions, putting a space or TK (to come) in the text for the quote or the statistic that has to be looked up later. There are some writers who proceed slowly, but most of us learn the advantage of producing a draft at top speed when the velocity forces unexpected connections and makes language twist and spin and dance in ways we do not expect.

When you finish your daily stint or if you are interrupted during the fast writing, stop in the middle of a sentence so you can return to the text and start writing again at a point when you know what you have to say. It's always a good idea to stop each day before the well is drained dry, when you know what you'll try to deal with the next day. This is the best way to overcome the inertia we all suffer when returning to a draft. If we know how to finish a sentence, the chances are the next sentence will rise out of that one, and we'll be writing immediately.

Planning is important, but it isn't writing. You want to be free enough in writing a draft to say more than you expect to say. Writers do not write what they already know as much as they write to know. Edward Albee echoes many writers when he says, "I write to find out what I'm thinking about." Writing is an act of thinking, and the process of writing adds two and two and comes up with seven.

An effective article usually has one dominant theme or message; everything in it should advance that meaning. Other meanings collect around the dominant one, but in the process of revision, the writer must make sure that everything in the piece relates to the main idea, cutting what does not move the reader forward.

The inexperienced writer cuts a piece of writing by compression and produces a package of tight language that can be difficult to understand and is rarely a pleasure to read. The professional writer selects those parts that most efficiently and effectively advance the meaning and then develops them fully so that the reader understands the significance of the anecdote, the full strength of the argument.

Writing in which the meaning is not clear often occurs because writers bury the most important information. One way to make an article clear is to look at the most significant paragraphs and move the sections around so that the most important information is at the end of the paragraph, the next most important at the beginning, and the least most important in the center of the paragraph.

We need important information at the beginning to attract the reader, but what the reader remembers is usually at the end of the paragraph. This pattern doesn't work for every paragraph, and shouldn't. But it is a way of clarifying a complicated and significant paragraph, and the same rule may be applied to an entire piece of writing.

I find that I am a more efficient editor of my own draft if I read it three times and have a specific goal for each reading. *First,* I read it to see if I have all the information I need. Do I have the facts, statistics, quotations, anecdotes I need to construct an accurate, persuasive article? And do I understand that information? If I don't have the information or understand it I must stop my editing and deal with these problems.

Second, I read for organization. Does the article, as I have mentioned earlier, answer the readers' questions in the order they will ask them? Does the article flow naturally from beginning to end, with each part of the article fitting what has gone before and leading to what follows?

Third, I read the article line by line, listening both to what is said and how it is said, making sure, by reading it aloud, that my voice carries the meaning to the reader. I hope that my articles will be accurate and have the illusion of speech, the rhythm, music, and ease of an ideal conversation.

Those are a few of the tricks of the nonfiction trade. Try them out to see if they work for you. Collect others from your writer friends, and become aware of those devices that you have used to make your meaning clear, so that you will be able to call on them as you continue your lifelong course in learning how to write.

57

HEADING FOR YOUR FIRST ROUNDUP

By Susan Purdy

As a writer, I wear many hats, both imaginary and real. I've worn a hard hat to get a story about the construction of a movie studio, a cap with MAP CLUB emblazoned in red letters to interview a man who provides maps to the real estate industry, and a plastic rain hat to protect me from the elements as I did field research for a piece on dentistry. But my favorite head covering is the imaginary, ten-gallon cowboy hat I wear while writing roundup articles.

To write a successful roundup article, you have to corral a group of people with an occupation, hobby, or characteristic in common—celebrities, show people, politicians, musicians—and ask them to respond to an interesting question. The roundup format appears in many of the largest national magazines—*Cosmopolitan, McCall's, Good Housekeeping*— which have run roundup articles in the past year on the following: Celebrities were asked, "What's the One Thing You Couldn't Live Without?" Several of the world's great cooks were asked how they diet. And for a roundup piece I wrote for *Good Housekeeping,* I asked some of New York's most influential and powerful men to talk about their mothers.

Roundup articles also appear in most newspapers, regional publications, town shopping newspapers, and Sunday supplements, and provide an easy way for writers to break into print. Editors know that their readers are always interested in what people prominent in a particular field have to say, and by familiarizing yourself with the magazine or newspaper, you can pose a provocative question and sell a roundup article.

How do I come up with a provocative question that will capture an editor's attention? How do I find the right people to ask?

Let's tackle the "question" question first. What piques your interest?

If you had the opportunity to ask almost anyone one question—and as a writer, you do—what would it be? You could ask your local politicians to tell you about the most influential person in their lives, or go down to your community college and ask women who are returning to school after raising a family how it has affected their marriage. You can read your local paper and ask residents how they feel about the sewage plant that is under consideration for their area, or do a roundup of your local clergy. You can find good questions everywhere, if you start thinking like a roundup writer. *Psychology Today* ran an article on "Super Sellers," men and women who are tops in their sales field. Who are the super sellers in your area? Why are they so good? Would the editor of your local paper or regional magazine be interested in them? While shopping for summer clothes this year, I began thinking about what items I should buy in the fall to update my winter wardrobe. (Writers have a tendency to think ahead because of the long lead time required by magazines.) I decided to ask the experts and wrote a roundup article for *Good Housekeeping* last year that included advice from Halston, Geoffrey Beene, and Mary McFadden. Your family and friends are great sources to tap, as are letters to the editor in newspapers, and such advice columns as "Dear Abby."

At a writers conference I attended in Manhattan, editors from national and regional magazines said they were always looking for seasonal material. Holidays like Thanksgiving, Christmas, Valentine's Day lend themselves especially well to roundup articles. Such questions as, "Have you ever spent Thanksgiving (or Christmas) alone?" "What was it like?" and "How did you spend the day?" provide a good focus for an article. Or you might interview the residents in a local nursing home: Elderly people have wonderful—or sad—stories to tell, and you could ask them about the first Christmas they can recall, how they feel the celebration of a holiday has changed since they were young, and other questions that would evoke responses that would be of interest to readers: "How did you trim the Christmas tree?" "Did you make your own ornaments?"—and if so, would they describe how?

A roundup piece for Valentine's Day could include such questions as "What was the most romantic gift you ever received for Valentine's Day?" "Do you think a single rose is more romantic than a bouquet?"

Roundup questions may be serious as well as light, instructive as well as amusing. You might ask lawyers in your city or town, "Do you think a newly married couple should make out a will? Why?" Or a roundup article could deal with such serious questions as, "How did you react when you learned that a member of your family had cancer?" "How did your children react when you and your spouse told them that you were going to be divorced?" "Do you think that a single parent can raise a family successfully?"

Teen-agers are an excellent source of roundup material. Parents as well as pre-teens and young adults might well enjoy reading about problems like, "How do you avoid peer pressure involving drugs, sex, or alcohol?" "If you could change one thing about adults in the world today, what would it be?"

Now you have dozens of questions in mind, and you can't wait to get started. At this point the second HOW comes into play. How do you get to politicians, celebrities, and the experts? Begin in your own backyard. First, query the publications in your area about doing a roundup article of local politicians, singers, theater groups, or business executives on a topic you think will be of interest to local readers. For *Business Connections,* a local magazine, I decided I wanted to question top executives from the banking world, public relations, the aircraft industry, computer sales, real estate, entertainment, and local politicians for a roundup article titled, "Long Island Business People Look Into the Future."

I did not know any of those people personally, but I kept in mind that most people feel flattered when asked for their opinions on a particular subject. For that article, I interviewed the people I'd selected directly, either at their offices or by telephone. That is not always possible. Especially when dealing with celebrities, it is best to go through their public relations or press representatives. For my article on New Year's resolutions—"Promises, Promises"—which appeared in *Good Housekeeping,* I wanted to include some local TV personalities. I called the publicity office of the television station, and identifying myself and the publication I was writing for, I described the questions I wanted to pose for my roundup piece and asked who might be available. (For future reference, I made a note of the name of the publicity person.) From the list she gave me, I chose those celebrities that I thought most suitable for my article.

She took down the question, asked me the deadline (which I always cut by two or three weeks to give me enough time to check and follow up). I always ask for an in-person interview, but if that's not possible, I ask the PR person to mail me the responses, in this way providing me with written proof that the people queried were aware that their responses were for publication.

It sounds simple—and it is—because people in the public eye want to stay there, and writers are an excellent source of free publicity.

I follow the same procedure for political figures, governors or mayors, always dealing with their press secretaries or public relations representatives, who know the officials' schedules and can judge whether they are likely to want to participate in the roundup. When I'm turned down, which happens on occasion, I thank the person I've been in touch with and say I'll call at what may be a more convenient time, leaving the door open for another article.

Some basic information to keep in mind when doing the roundup article:

1. Always get photos of the people you interview. Most people in the entertainment field have "head-shots," glossy 8 × 10 pictures that are available in their press kits. Or, with their permission, you can take your own photos, black and white, to submit with your article.

2. First asking permission, tape the interview, whether in person or over the phone. (You can buy a handy little gadget that attaches to your tape recorder for phone interviews.)

3. Remember, the people you are interviewing do not get paid for their answers. . . . the free publicity is reward enough.

4. Make sure that the publication that runs the piece sends a copy to each person quoted in the article. I always include their names and addresses on a separate sheet of paper when mailing in my roundups and often follow them up with a personal thank-you note.

Now that you have come up with some fantastic questions, have queried the people you wish to include in your article, the only thing left is to write it. *Yes, a roundup is written.* It is not just a compilation of quotes. You need an opening paragraph to prepare the reader for what will follow; lead-ins to the various people interviewed, identifying them and their position; and in most cases, a closing paragraph.

My opening paragraph for "Sons and Mothers" (*Good Housekeeping*) set the mood for the famous sons I interviewed to talk about their mothers:

Ralph Waldo Emerson wrote, "Men are what their mothers made them," and some of New York's most powerful men concur. A mother can help her son attain success by providing nurturing love, guidance, and in many cases, a strong sense of purpose he can emulate. The following men, tops in their fields, have taken time from busy schedules to tell us about this influential person in their lives.

I then led off the piece with New York City Police Commissioner Benjamin Ward, by giving his name, title, the fact that he was one of eleven children, and that his mother Loretta Ward was a great source of inspiration to him. I had interviewed Commissioner Ward in person, so I had pages of quotes to edit before I decided which would be most pertinent to the article.

That's another area in which you "write" the roundup. You must go through each interview and select only the heart. With this roundup, I had interviewed a dozen men, so my space was limited. I wanted the essence of how their mothers had influenced their lives and not pages of uninteresting material. I did not end that roundup with a closing paragraph, because the Governor of New York Mario Cuomo had provided me with an excellent closing quote, and I like to leave my readers with something special to take away when they finish the article. I find this works in most instances, as there is always one quote that lends itself to tying up the piece.

It doesn't matter whether you live in a big city or a small town, the roundup article can be written anywhere about anyone or anything, if you keep in mind that people love to be asked their opinions and are as close to you as a phone call or letter.

58

WRITING PROPOSALS THAT GET BOOK CONTRACTS

By Samm Sinclair Baker

EVERY word of this brief chapter has just one focus: to help you put together a nonfiction book proposal that will get a publishing contract. I've cut every word that doesn't move to that objective.

I emphasize that point immediately, because it's exactly what you must do in shaping your proposal. Concentrate on presenting not why *you* think the book will sell (you're prejudiced), but *facts* to convince the editor and others at the publishing house to approve a contract. Eliminate everything else, no matter how charming or amusing or impressively "literary" you think your beloved words may be.

This may seem obvious, but practically every proposal draft by a beginning or experienced writer (including myself) I've seen has contained extraneous material. Such flab must be chopped out ruthlessly, or you'll lose the editor's attention and the contract opportunity. Eliminate any "look how good I am" and "see how beautifully I write" indulgences. Each word must move forward "why this book will sell."

Does the quality of the book proposal make a buy-or-reject difference? Before I became a co-author and prepared clear, orderly, convincing proposals, four of my books were turned down due primarily to inept, unfocused presentations. Since many other factors are involved in signing a book, a fine presentation doesn't guarantee getting a contract—but it sure helps.

My first two books were mystery novels that I offered as complete manuscripts. It's extremely difficult to sell a fiction book proposal unless you're a best-selling novelist, or unless you present at least three irresistible chapters.

On my nonfiction books, I've re-examined and analyzed the proposals carefully. All of them, from the first presentation I wrote as a beginner, through three blockbuster best sellers and others, follow the same contract-getting structure presented here for the first time anywhere. This is what has worked for me:

1. Book Title and Primary Sales Point(s)
   . . . presented as copy for jacket blurb
2. Market Potential
   . . . why this book will sell effectively
3. Personal Background Assets
   . . . biography, research, experience
4. Essentials, Uniqueness
5. Chapter Contents
   . . . chapter titles, main points in each
6. First Chapter of Book
   . . . preferably two or three finished chapters
7. Special Promotional Power
   . . . quick synopsis of unique features to project in interviews, all-media publicity
8. Cover Letter

I arrived at this structure in presenting my first nonfiction book for the general public—*Miracle Gardening*. I developed this solid sequence not out of the blue but based on hundreds of productive presentations for advertising campaigns during my 20-plus years in advertising agencies. I realized that the format that had been successful in selling ad campaigns amounting to millions of dollars should work in getting a book contract. It did.

Another tip from my Madison Avenue experience: Every word in the ad presentations was honed to convince the people who had to O.K. the campaign. I achieved the transference in my mind of becoming the advertiser reading, not the agency man writing. As you conceive your presentations, learn to channel your viewpoint to become the editor reading rather than the author writing.

1. Book Title and Primary Sales Point

As a beginning writer (as perhaps you are), I concentrated on boiling down the essence of the projected gardening book to one or two statements that would best attract book buyers. Therefore, it would appeal to the editor and publishing staff. My first page stated:

Gardening Book Proposal:
MIRACLE GARDENING
How to grow bigger, brighter flowers, thicker lawns, and huge mouth-watering vegetables, using the amazing new scientific miracle substances and methods.
Plus 1001 Tips
for Today's Gardener.
By Samm Sinclair Baker

292

That succinct, irresistible appeal to gardeners, who seek always to grow the best, hit home with the editor. She told me later, "Reading that powerful promise to gardeners, I had to continue—instead of stopping at the first page of a proposal as I usually do."

That opening page seems simple, easy to create. Not so. To arrive at those few compelling words, stated as an enticing reward for the reader, took me endless trying and revising. I kept changing titles, sequences, sentences innumerable times over a period of weeks. It still takes prolonged effort, no matter how many proposals I write. The extraordinary application to getting it exactly right is worth it in order to get that thrilling call or letter: "We want your book."

2. Market Potential

I've been told that most book proposals don't cover market potential, but I consider it an important element. To delineate the potential market for the book, I cite facts, not empty superlatives. I keep the data crisp, clear, sound, interesting. In the case of *Miracle Gardening,* I listed figures showing the impressive growth in the number of gardens and gardeners, and accelerating dollar sales of gardening products and supplies. All this grew from extensive research enabling me to quote authoritative statistics and sources—government agencies, trade journals, newspapers, associations.

The editor said, "This material helped me a lot. I was able to present the sales potential of the book factually to the marketing director and others who have to O.K. acceptance. Instead of saying, 'I think there are a lot of people who'll want this book,' your data gave me proof of the potential. You saved me a lot of digging in preparing *my* presentation."

3. Personal Background Assets

Of course it's helpful if you can show a list of successful published books. I couldn't. Instead, I stressed my background in gardening: "At age four, my father gave me some radish seeds. I planted and tended them. When I pulled up my first radish, I rubbed off the soil, bit into it—and it bit me back. I've been bit by the gardening bug ever since. By experience, I know how gardeners think, what they want and need . . ."

I detailed in few words my work on gardening accounts in advertising, how my copy built a mail order nursery from little one-inch ads to full pages in newspapers as a big national advertiser . . . "Sales proved that I know how to write to gardeners." I described my research for the proposed book, contacts with leading agricultural universities, scientists, experts, agricultural agents. Such digging is available in practically every field.

You don't need special magic or miracles in your background. If you haven't thorough knowledge of the subject, either through experience or research or other learning, you probably shouldn't be proposing a book. Of course you have the know-how or can get it—say so, backed by facts that prove your contention.

4. Essentials, Uniqueness, Superiorities

In the case of *Miracle Gardening,* I foresaw that the editor would be asking herself, "Why another gardening book?" So I asked that question in my proposal—and answered by naming specific modern garden aids. I listed fresh information, tips not covered by any other gardening book. I had studied the available books thoroughly, and provided explicit details.

Examples: I told about the new (at that time) water-soluble plant foods, how they had been developed in a noted university laboratory by top scientists, identified by name. I described and included in my presentation photos of tests using radioactive isotopes in specially prepared liquid fertilizer, checked with a Geiger counter. The fascinating tests proved that nutrients went from soil to top of a six-foot-high rose bush in minutes. Yes, I included in the proposal actual plant photos and drawings, charts and graphs—all obtained through research sources, with permissions to reproduce them in my proposed book. Again, proved facts, not self-serving, questionable claims.

Keep in mind that the editor is human, a reader, attracted by eye-catching visual material when available. So are members of the editorial and marketing committee who must approve the contract—all individuals saying "Show me."

The proposal for my book, *Reading Faces,* co-authored with Dr. Leopold Bellak, included a half-dozen photos of celebrities, with lines drawn on the faces according to the Bellak Zone System, the basis for the face-reading method to be taught in the book. I included compact instructions for reading faces.

Furthermore, instead of ignoring any competition, I named and described three other books published in the past ten years about reading faces. Then I explained exactly how our book would be entirely different and markedly superior. That negated any objections about competitive books which might block a contract. Our eventual editor told us, "I was fascinated, tried the Zone System on my own face in the mirror, then ran down the hall to try it on others. Soon the place was in an uproar, with everyone reading someone else's face. Your clear, simple demonstration in the proposal made this an easy sale."

5. Chapter Contents

I include in each presentation a listing of chapter titles, and a compact description of the content of each chapter. Sure, that's a lot of work because you're constructing the framework of the entire book. I consider that necessary because I'm asking a publisher to invest a lot of time and money in editing and producing my book.

Editors understand that proposed chapter titles and sequences are subject to change as you write the book. They can't ask for a contract, however, without clear delineation for the editorial and marketing board of what you're urging them to buy. For instance, in offering my first co-authored book, *Questions and Answers to Your Skin Problems,* I knew it wasn't enough to note one chapter heading as "Allergies." Here's the listing in the actual proposal:

Chapter 4. ALLERGIES AND RELATED PROBLEMS
Allergy Questionnaire. Allergy to Cosmetics. Food Allergy. Allergy to Drugs and Chemicals. Sensitivity to Detergents and Cleansers. Allergy to Various Materials. Allergy to Insect Bites. Miscellaneous Allergy Questions. Hives. Eczema. Poison Ivy.

Chapter listings and explanations convey two essential points to the editor and board: a) The scope of the book and that it will provide detailed information that readers need and want. b) The author knows the subject and will cover each facet fully. Some presentations require more chapter contents detail than others, as in the case of my book, *Your Key to Creative Thinking:*

Chapter 1. HOW THIS BOOK CAN MAKE YOU MORE CREATIVE
What is Creativity?
Proof that You Can Be More Creative.

C.Q. vs. I.Q. (Creative Quotient vs. Intelligence Quotient)
Why Your Participation is the Essential Element
Beware of Negative Thinking
How to Profit in Many Ways
Why the World Needs Creative Thinking and Ideas Now
Rewards like These are Great and Personal
Your First Practice Session:

AVOID-THE-OBVIOUS MENTAL-EXERCISE PUZZLERS

Since each chapter would include Practice Puzzlers of different types, I included some actual Puzzlers, some illustrated. My purpose was two-fold: to demonstrate exactly what a puzzler is, and to intrigue the editor as an individual. The presentation included a dozen actual puzzlers, of 82 planned for the book, such as this sample:

ANALYSIS PUZZLER: THE CASE OF THE MYSTERIOUS LETTER
The postmaster in a small town found this letter addressed with only these three words on the front:

WOOD
JOHN
MASS

What were the right name, city, state for delivery?
(Printed with other answers in back of book:)
ANSWER: The object is to analyze clearly why the three words were placed in that peculiar formation. Why is "JOHN" under "WOOD" and over "MASS."? Obviously:

JOHN UNDERWOOD
ANDOVER, MASS.

When the editor called to offer a contract, she said, "Those sample puzzlers helped sell us the book quickly. I tried them on my family. Their enjoyment clinched it for me." Proof that it pays to be innovative in your presentation. Just be sure that the attention-getting items make a pertinent point.

6. First chapter

The proof of the pudding is in the first chapter of your book. You can talk endlessly about the wonderful book you're *going* to write, but with a beginning writer in particular, the only validation for the publisher is the manuscript itself—one or more chapters. I usually present three chapters.

A would-be author complained to me, "That's an awful lot of work."

I agreed, "By the time I've listed chapter titles and contents, and written several chapters, about one-third of my work on the whole book is done. But I don't know whether the book will be worthy until I've done that much work. And if I don't believe in it enough to put in that extensive effort, how can I expect a publisher to have the faith to invest in my book?"

7. Special Promotional Power

Because of my background in business and advertising, I've always believed that it's up to me, along with the publisher, to promote my book. Therefore, I finish each book proposal with a short synopsis of my own special ability to promote the proposed book. I cite unique features which lend themselves to interviews on TV, radio, all media.

Get the evidence across in a few sentences, indicating that you're eager to help sell the book after it's published. Describe any visual material you can offer. You don't have to be an actress or a lecturer. If you have a background in teaching, that's a natural. Or mention speaking exposure as a club officer, active PTA member, salesperson, ability to instruct people verbally in your book subject.

Skip this section if you prefer—it's up to you. I've found it productive to include all the specific plusses embodied in the book project. They've definitely helped me get contracts.

8. The Covering Letter

In my experience, a book proposal must speak for itself—convincingly. No fancy binders. Just double-spaced loose pages, plus any exhibits, in a file folder. If your factual presentation doesn't confirm that your book is worth publishing, a ton of superlatives in a covering letter, or in your proposal, won't help, may turn off the editor. My covering letters are short and simple, for instance:

The proposal herewith for a new nonfiction book, *Reading Faces,* demonstrates its unique content and sales potential. Thank you for your kind attention and consideration. I trust that I may hear from you soon.

How long should a book proposal be? There is no set length. Keep it as short as you possibly can, making sure that every word is useful. Double-check to eliminate anything unnecessary. Include everything essential, holding the editor's attention by including only meaningful content.

This is all-important: You must grab and hook the editor's attention right in the first lines of your proposal. You do that by appealing to the editor's self-interest in finding a book that is a potential profit-maker or will benefit the publisher in specific ways. An example of an opening is the first paragraph of this article. I rewrote it repeatedly until I arrived at words that I believed would capture your self-interest and keep you reading.

Give the same essential attention and effort to the opening of the first paragraph of the first chapter of your book—which will be part of your presentation. I reworked again and again the opening lines of *The Complete Scarsdale Medical Diet* before submitting the proposal. It proved worthwhile—all part of formulating a blockbuster best seller. I compressed a long opening chapter to these few sentences (written in the person of the doctor):

I, personally, explain the Scarsdale Medical Diet's phenomenal popularity in two words: *"It works."* A slim, trim lady said to me recently, "Your diet is beautifully simple, and the results are simply beautiful." I just say, "It works."

After that grabber, do you think that an editor, or an overweight person, could stop reading?

The basic presentation structure I've set down here has worked repeatedly for me, and for others I've helped. My way is not the only way. If it doesn't suit your personal views, then do it your way, of course. You're an individual with your own ideas, your own focus, your own right to be yourself.

If your presentation is rejected, check it carefully again. If it appears right, submit it elsewhere. Even a superb presentation may be turned down by a particular publisher for reasons over which you have no control—such as not wanting *any* book on that subject. I kept resubmitting and writing, then sold some of my nonfiction books from complete manuscripts.

59

WRITING FOR SYNDICATES

By Valerie Bohigian

Jack Anderson, Erma Bombeck, Richard Simmons, Sylvia Porter, and Ann Landers are syndicated writers. They write regular columns familiar to much of newspaper reading America, and they are well rewarded financially for their efforts. For every one of these writers, there are dozens of unknowns also earning steady, though more modest, dollars writing for syndicates. Some of them will build up the kinds of followings that will result in big earnings, book contracts, television and radio spots and lucrative speaking engagements. Other columns will be dropped as national trends and interests change, creating new openings that can be filled by writers who understand how syndicates work and know how to approach this market correctly with fresh, timely ideas. With the right information and the right idea, you can write one of these new columns.

Writing for a syndicate is different from writing for a magazine. A syndicate is not a publication. It is an agency that purchases columns, articles, comic strips, cartoons, photographs, horoscopes, jokes, puzzles, fillers, etc., and sells them to newspapers all around the country and the world. Contributors are paid a percentage—usually 50%—of total sales. (Syndicates occasionally pay a set fee.) Basically, a syndicate seeks to provide first-rate material at reasonable prices to as many newspapers as possible, and tries to stock a little of everything so that if a particular paper calls and asks for a travel column, or an etiquette column, or a humor column, the syndicate has it on hand and can fill the request.

The more newspapers that purchase your column, the more money you earn. Though wide distribution and circulation are important, other factors are equally so: Who buys your column is important. A major metropolitan newspaper will pay $100 for a column, whereas a Peoria paper will pay only $5. This means that if your column appears in such large papers as *The Boston Globe, The New York Daily News,* and *The Los Angeles Times,* you'll earn more than if it appears in fifty small-town papers.

Having your column appear in a small list of large newspapers can be more lucrative than having it appear in a large list of small newspapers. Of course, the ideal situation is to have your column sell to a large list of large and small newspapers. Once you get rolling this can happen. There are about 1,700 newspapers in the United States, and columns like Ann Landers' are bought by about 900 of them on a daily basis. Assuming she were to earn only $5 per paper (and she undoubtedly earns more), that's $4,500 per day!

Most syndicated writers do not earn anywhere near $4,500 per day. Rare is the column that sells to 900 newspapers per day; and rare is the columnist whose columns appear daily. However, there are several beginning columnists whose columns appear once or twice a week in about fifty newspapers. These writers are netting between $200 and $400 per week—not the big time yet, but not bad at all. Who are these people and how can you become one of them?

You have the best chance of becoming syndicated if you are an expert on a subject that is currently popular, not glutted with too many knowledgeable writers, and one that is growing in appeal. Certainly, it doesn't hurt to have an easily recognized name, but it is not crucial: The subject is. Ten years ago, for example, a syndicated column on plant care would not have sold, but now that plants are widely used in homes and offices as major decorating accessories, there are a few successful syndicated columns about plants. Though the authors are not "household names," the information and help they provide is read and used in thousands of households all over the country.

Columns showing people how to cope with various problems are popular today, and they are often written by individuals who have successfully solved these problems, rather than by theorists. For example, there is a lot of current interest in helping the handicapped care for themselves. A recent column on the subject, written by an invalid of many years, is selling widely. The author of this column passes along to her readers useful self-help ideas that she has discovered over the years, and that other disabled people have passed on to her. The handicapped, families of the handicapped, and people in professions relating to the care of the disabled are avid readers of this column.

How-to-cope columns need not deal with disabilities or tragedies; if you're coping successfully with a situation of wide interest, you may have a potential column in your hands. One of the major syndicates just took on as a columnist a mail order specialist who has learned not only how to deal with inflation, unemployment, job security, etc., but more specifically, how to do so by becoming an expert in mail order selling. The problems, pitfalls, and profits awaiting novice entrepreneurs in this field will be covered in this column. Another major syndicate, reflecting the growing interest in religion, has taken on a religion column geared to readers concerned with what they consider a current spiritual crisis in our society.

How-to material is also in demand today. If you know how to do something that most people would like to learn how to do or how to do better, you may have a salable column. Do you have a lot of good information to pass along in the fields of home entertainment, computers, home construction projects, knitting and crocheting, entrepreneurship, animal care? Right now the syndicates are looking for and buying columns in these areas.

Assuming you have a good idea and a concise (columns are generally only a few hundred words each) and readable style, how best to proceed? Though it is not the only way, the best way to begin is to develop a column for your local newspaper. Try to get your local paper to run it for awhile and then submit tear sheets of your columns to the syndicates, either through your local editor or directly. Syndicates respond well to columns that have proven popular in local newspapers.

Whether you're submitting to your local newspaper or to a syndicate, the procedure is the same: Submit an outline of what you have in mind, with six to eight sample columns that will demonstrate to the editors that you have more than just three good shots in your bag. A syndicate's editor can love your column, but its sales force can give it the kiss of death. Make sure, therefore, that your column reveals that it can help many thousands of readers who do not have easy access to the information you can provide, since it is a syndicate's sales department that must ultimately be able to place your work.

Don't get discouraged if you don't have a "hot" item for a column, or if it gets a cold response from a syndicate's editor. The best route to syndicate sales is through a careful study of what the syndicates seem to be selling, new subjects they seem to be taking on, and the writing styles and formats used. Familiarize yourself with all the syndicated newspaper columns you can find. (There are out-of-town newspaper stands in many cities; they can also be found in libraries.) Keep an eye out for trends, and list the specialized information you have to offer and what new ideas syndicates are using. See page 750 for information on the current market needs and requirements of the various syndicates. Also, at a large public library, consult *The Editors and Publishers Syndicate Directory,* which lists all syndicated columns, and *Literary Market Place,* which has a listing of syndicates.

While you're waiting for the right column idea to come along, or for your column to find a home, you might consider trying to sell "one-shots" to the syndicates. One-shots are reportorial pieces that some syndicates buy because they can easily be placed in several newspapers on a one-time basis. One-shots often draw fairly high fees (20¢ to 50¢ per word), and can be on any timely topic ranging from acrophobia to acupuncture. They can also be spin-offs from your already published magazine articles. One-shots not only produce income, but when your big column idea does come along, the editors will know you, and your material will receive special attention. Even though that alone won't make editors buy an unsalable column from you, they will be more likely to comment personally on why your idea won't work or on what you can do to make it more marketable.

Though big syndicates stock a wide variety of material, at a particular time one syndicate may be overstocked with business and fashion-advice columns, or because a key contributor didn't renew his contract, they may have a need for a record/music column. Another syndicate may be very much in the market for a column dispensing fresh business advice or offering money-saving tips. How do you know? You don't. Things change daily and timing can be very important. Unless you have a lot of already produced sample material on hand, or reason to believe that a particular syndicate is in the market for the kind of material you would like to provide, your time is probably best spent sending out a few queries to different syndicates, pitching your idea (for a one-shot or column). When a syndicate expresses interest, you can then follow up with a finished manuscript or several sample columns demonstrating

302

your ability to produce quality with consistency. Always mention your specific qualifications.

The large syndicates sell material to hundreds of newspapers, large and small. There are also several smaller, more specialized syndicates you can try where you won't be competing with established professionals. Try them all, and don't be disheartened by rejections. Several widely syndicated features were turned down many times before being finally accepted. Yours may be, too.

60

SELLING ARTICLES SUCCESSFULLY
ON SPECULATION

By Linda R. Garvey

REAL writers don't work on speculation, right? Wrong. I think of myself as a real writer, and I've written—and sold—dozens of articles on speculation for magazines that include *American Legion, Money Maker, Consumers Digest* and *American Way.* Far from considering spec writing demeaning, I see it as a golden opportunity that is almost too good to pass up.

The willingness of most magazines to consider work produced on speculation gives all writers a potential key to editorial doors all across the country. On spec magazine writing offers writers a chance to show what they can do. Spec writing is, in fact, the great equalizer in the article writing field. If you can write a tantalizing query and are willing to work on speculation, you have as good a chance as anyone of getting a go-ahead to write for any market you set your sights on.

That doesn't mean, of course, that you can always sell the material on which you get a go-ahead. There are no guarantees in spec writing. If a piece doesn't work out, you're going to lose a lot of valuable research and writing time and not have a cent to show for your efforts.

Writing on speculation is indeed a gamble, but so are many other creative efforts. Most artists, for example, do not expect to sell their paintings or other art works sight unseen. Unless they are already well known, artists are in a sense creating all their works on speculation. While they naturally hope their works will find buyers, they also have no guarantees.

Writers working on speculation, in fact, have something of an edge in this creative gamble because they usually at least have an expression of interest in the work they are producing. An editor has said, "Yes, I might be interested in buying this piece," and that is much more encouragement than many other artists have while creating their works.

In most cases, a go-ahead on speculation is even more than simply encouragement from an editor because editors do not give go-aheads on speculation casually. With so many writers willing to work on spec, it would be relatively easy for an editor to give even marginal ideas a go-ahead. In my experience, most editors, however, will encourage a spec submission only if the idea has real potential.

This attitude is, of course, a tremendous boon for writers. It means that if you can interest an editor in an idea and deliver what you've promised in your query, you have a good chance of selling the article.

Still, isn't working on assignment a better deal for writers? Not necessarily. Having a contract to do a piece is nice, but you're still gambling that you're going to produce an article that an editor will buy. And, while a contract may guarantee you a "kill fee" if the piece doesn't work out, generally that kill fee is only a small percentage of what the editor would pay for the piece if he accepted it for publication. An editor might, for example, agree to pay a 15 per cent kill fee for an article that would normally bring $500. That means a writer would receive only $75 for a piece that doesn't work out, an amount that might cover just the phone expenses connected with the research the writer had to do.

A contract is, however, a kind of security blanket for many writers. It gives them a sense that they are authorized to write a particular piece. But I treat writing on spec as seriously as I do an assignment. The "contract" I feel that I have when doing an article on spec is a contract with myself to do the best and most professional work I'm capable of.

At this point in my career, I am able to sell nearly everything I write on speculation. Occasionally, however, a piece doesn't work out for one reason or another. But I am often able to sell the piece to another market, sometimes for more than I would have received from the magazine that turned it down.

Working on spec is a great opportunity for writers who are willing to gamble that the quality of their work will convince editors to buy what they write. And even though working on spec can be risky, there are a number of techniques that can help make writing on spec more successful for you.

1. Make the offer to write on spec in your query. While this may sound obvious, many writers just assume editors will suggest spec assignments to writers who are new to them. This is not necessarily the case, however. Unless you state your willingness to work on spec, many

editors will simply give a pass on your query. Once, as an experiment, I left the offer to work on speculation out of my queries to new editors. The resulting dearth of spec assignments convinced me I had to be explicit about my willingness to do spec work.

2. Get the go-ahead first. Although it may seem just as well to write the article since you're going to submit it on spec anyway, having an expression of interest from an editor greatly increases your chances of selling that piece. Also, having a go-ahead before you begin to write the article enables you to approach sources with more confidence. Even if you are writing on speculation, you can truthfully tell someone from whom you wish to get information that you are writing a piece on good dental care for, say, *Shopping Smart,* because that is exactly what you will be doing.

3. Select manageable topics. Don't, for example, offer to do on speculation a round-up piece on the latest advances in medicine. This kind of article simply requires too much research time to make it a good bet for on speculation writing. On the other hand, a profile, which might require just one or two interviews and some background research, is generally a good spec topic.

4. Aim for short articles. An 800–1,000-word piece frequently requires considerably less research and writing time than a 2,500-word article. In addition, many editors are much more willing to give unknown writers a chance at one of these shorter pieces. Many magazines have sections requiring a continuous supply of material under 1,000 words, and I have found these sections excellent outlets for my on speculation material that may not have sold to the original publication queried.

5. Build on past sales—or your own background. Once you've written an article on a topic, writing a second one requires very little additional research. Generally, your sources and background material are already lined up, which saves a lot of valuable research time. In addition, writing on topics with which you are already familiar is usually much easier—and quicker—than writing on topics for the first time.

Several years ago I wrote on assignment a piece on check fraud for a professional police magazine. It was a tough article to write as there was very little written on the topic at the time, and law enforcement professionals were reluctant to talk to a stranger about the ins and outs of the crime. After a lot of digging, however, I did manage to get the information I needed and wrote the piece.

After it was published, I offered to cover the topic again, this time on spec for *Kiwanis*. Though the focus of this article was naturally different—the problems of businesses that deal with check artists rather than with law enforcement officials tracking down criminals—I was able to use many of the same sources and much of the background information I'd uncovered for the first piece. And I wrote still another spec piece on the topic (with another angle) for a state business journal. In each case I was able to follow up my spec sales with other articles on assignment. This sort of pyramiding sales approach is open-ended for any writer willing to take advantage of it.

Even if you don't have a sales record to build on, you can still cut down on your research and writing time for spec writing by drawing on material with which you are already familiar. A baseball or football or soccer buff, for example, would have a wealth of valuable information that he could use as the basis of many sports-related articles.

6. Set a deadline. When I receive a go-ahead on spec, I generally try to drop the editor a note stating when the piece can be expected—and I always work hard to meet that self-imposed deadline. In addition to letting the editor know you're a professional who intends to follow through on your query, committing yourself to a deadline is a good way to make sure that the piece does, in fact, get written.

7. Try to keep your research expenses low. Editors rarely, if ever, make provision to cover a writer's expenses for spec pieces. While doing research by phone is generally faster and more convenient than doing it by mail, the post office usually is the cheapest way to obtain most information. Most sources, I have found, are willing to answer one or two questions on a topic by mail. Be sure, however, to keep your questions specific, or the person you are asking for information may feel that it's too much trouble or too time-consuming to respond. And don't forget to include a self-addressed, stamped return envelope for the response. Since gathering information by mail often takes several weeks, this kind of research takes some advance planning, but the money you save makes it worth the effort.

8. In the course of writing an on spec piece, it's often a good idea to send the editor an outline of your article about midway through your research. In this way you can be sure that the article is shaping up the

way the editor would like. If it's not, you can revise your writing strategy before losing more time on the wrong approach. To check in with an editor, I send a fairly detailed one-page outline, along with a self-addressed postcard for the editor's reply.

9. Beware of printed go-aheads. Some of the larger magazines use such forms when they give writers a go-ahead on speculation. Although some of these pieces may work out, I am leery of committing myself to do an article for an editor who does not send a personal go-ahead. Without even a name to whom you can address your manuscript, it is likely to end up buried in a pile of over-the-transom manuscripts.

10. Include a cover letter with your submission. Once an on spec piece is completed, mail it directly to the editor who sent you the go-ahead, with a cover letter reminding him or her of the original go-ahead. Also, I always offer to do any revisions that may be required. And while I hope not to get the manuscript back, I always include an SASE when submitting an on spec piece.

Writing on speculation may not be for everyone, but if you're confident of your writing skills and willing to take a calculated risk, on spec articles may be your entry to a long and lucrative writing career.

61

TRAVEL WRITING
FROM BOTH SIDES OF THE DESK

By Batya Moskowitz

Nothing sounds more enjoyable than traveling around the world visiting every exotic location you've ever dreamed of, returning home to write about it, seeing your words in print and receiving payment for it all. If it were only that easy. . . .

Travel writing requires hard work and a lot of time—researching, querying, waiting for a response from an editor, writing your article, and again waiting to see how the editor responds. There are ways to make the job simpler. If you know how to organize yourself and deal with your specialized editors, travel writing can be a warm wind if not a breeze. After 4½ years as an editor at *Travel & Leisure* Magazine, and now as a full-time free-lance writer, I have a viewpoint from both sides of the desk that I would like to share with you.

As a writer

There are a number of steps and procedures along the way for the beginning travel writer. First, you must familiarize yourself with the various types of travel articles you might write. The two most obvious are *destination-* and *establishment*-oriented. The former focuses on a particular place. It can be a town (Salem, Oregon), a city (San Francisco), a country (Bali), a museum (The Stephen Foster Center in Florida), a park (the San Diego Zoo), or similar places. *Establishment* pieces concentrate on one or more hotels, restaurants, cafés, sports arenas, nightclubs, antique shops, or other unusual shopping facilities. A new or renovated hotel would fit this category.

There are also *roundup* articles on such topics as the churches of Brooklyn or ethnic restaurants of Chicago. *How-to* articles can be about packing soft luggage, buying sweaters in Ireland, or choosing your berth on a cruise. *Fillers* and complete *service* articles are about specific new products, such as lightweight travel razors or magnetized games for children's travel. There are helpful and humorous *essays* (preferably upbeat) on reading maps or funny pieces on package tours. Any of these can address business, family, camping, adventure, foreign, domestic, upscale, budget, or other specific readership interests.

Also, familiarize yourself with the kinds of periodicals that publish travel articles. The trickiest part of travel writing, or any writing for that matter, consists of matching your idea to the needs of a publication. Study listings of magazines that specialize in travel and add general interest, regional, in-flight, business, men's, women's, and any other periodicals that have travel columns or special travel issues. Take a look at the markets that interest you most, and study the angles of the travel pieces they print. Remember that editorial policies change, so read recent issues.

How do you decide where to go? If you're just starting in the field, you'll have to reach your destination on your own and with your own money. Or you might start near your home or with vacation trips. Select a museum, a reconstructed landmark, a park with special hiking trails, an extraordinary restaurant or hotel, or a performing arts company. Local newspapers and magazines or even larger magazines that cover your region of the country might buy such a piece.

No matter how well you know a place, do some armchair travel and research it. Dig through your library and your travel agent's brochures. Keep track of references to local destinations in novels and stories, in biographies and news reports. Take notes on anything that strikes your fancy, even if it seems inconsequential. Often the smallest details are what make a travel article good reading.

After you've decided on your destination and the magazines that might publish your writing, send out a query letter. Some publications will give you a go-ahead for an article on spec; if you're willing to work on writing a piece with no guarantee of publication, these could be excellent markets for you. Beginners in the travel field should send proposals to those magazines, and later (after you've had some success) to those magazines that do make assignments.

What makes a good travel query? First, name the destination or establishment you want to write about. Second, the query should provide a feel for the location in fresh, lively language. Avoid clichés, overused adjectives, and superlatives. There is no *best* hotel, no *most wonderful* restaurant, no *most-amenities-for-the-money* resort.

The proposals that work well are those in which the first paragraphs could easily be expanded into an introduction for the article: They state the location, convey the ambience, and give evidence of your writing style.

Add to this the reason that *you* in particular should write the article for that particular magazine: give a little of your writing background; let the editor know if (and when) you visited the place, and describe what makes it special to you. If you've had any travel pieces published, include a few clips—two or three of your best will do. And if not travel articles, send tear sheets of any general nonfiction magazine pieces you've had published. Send only one or two proposals at a time, maximum of one to one-and-a-half pages each.

Get as much mileage from your travel as possible. Come up with as many angles as you can for as many publications as you can. Begin making notes of these before leaving for your trip, but remember to brainstorm as you travel. You might want to keep a separate page of your notebook just for ideas as you think of them.

While you shouldn't write different versions of the same story for competing magazines, you can use various topics from the same trip. For instance, you might write about a museum in Ibiza for *Signature*, the folkloric festival there for *Dance Magazine*, and three Balearic paella recipes for *Family Circle* or *Gourmet* (possibly as part of a feature travel piece).

Once you reach your destination, take as many notes as you can related to the ideas you already have. Also, jot down anything that intrigues you and might lead to an article in the future. I have an affinity for doll museums and always try to see at least one wherever I go. Someday, perhaps I'll write a roundup article.

I prefer to write as I go, making sure to get down on paper at least an outline of the relevant history and personalities, as well as legends and stories of the area. Dates and spellings (except for signposts) are often better taken from printed information than from someone's memory, even an expert's. But while it's important to get the facts down in your notebook, it is much more important to record your own impressions, observations, and reactions. You can always find a fact again, but if you didn't see the details of the Unicorn Tapestries at the Cloisters in New

York because you were too busy copying the descriptive tablets, your article will lack the personal touch that makes a travel writer successful.

Next point: Collect every scrap of paper, brochure, press kit, map, matchbook you can get your hands on, even if the topic of your article is right around the corner. Many magazines request these as checking backup. Facts and interesting items you missed can be gleaned from them. You should also get the names, addresses, and phone numbers of contact people—the general manager of a hotel, the shopkeeper (of antiques, special local items, or whatever), the education director of a museum, or whoever you think will enrich your material when you write it up later. On a long trip, I send a package of my papers, matchbooks, local newspapers, press materials, etc. (I usually hold on to my notes—they are irreplaceable) home to myself. This is a minor expense and saves me from carrying for a week or more the material I've collected.

You're now back home and ready to write. If you didn't submit proposals before you went, do it as soon after you return as possible, while you're still fresh and excited. Once you have the assignment or have decided to try a piece on speculation, read several issues of the magazine for which you're aiming. See if you can match the editorial focus of your piece to something already published there—something you like. Follow the style of that magazine. Don't use a lot of quotes if quotes are rare in the pieces you've read. Keep your article personal or formal, depending on the publication. What emphasis does the magazine seem to have? Some concentrate on people, some on scenery, some on history. Keep these priorities in mind for the particular article you're writing. And if you do have an assignment letter that spells out what the editor wants, try to follow it.

Many magazines require hard service information. They want addresses, phone numbers, costs, hours of operation, availability of transportation and schedules, reservation numbers, and the like. Contrary to popular opinion, such requirements were not created to torture writers but to help readers. If you have no patience for this sort of thing, be careful which publications you submit your ideas to. If not the most creative, it is actually the easiest part of the piece to write. Your sources will always give you directions, hours of operation, prices, and anything else you need. And try to keep it up to date.

When you have done the best possible job on your article and are ready to submit your manuscript, type it neatly, double- or triple-spaced. If you're working on a word processor, use a letter-quality printer. *This can't be restated enough.* Sloppy manuscripts not only cause editors eye strain, they also create a bad and lasting impression.

Editor's eye view

The first way to impress an editor is to address your query to the appropriate person *by name.* If you can't find a recent masthead, call the magazine. Most travel magazines divide editorial responsibilities geographically. Reaching the right person will save time and prove that you can do research.

For in-flight magazines (so named because they are distributed to travelers aboard the airlines that publish them), be sure to check the routing map (usually toward the back of the publication) before sending a proposal. In-flights cover only those destinations to which a particular airline flies.

Although editors are always looking for good new writers and fresh ideas, their publications have probably covered most locations in the world. Timely approaches and innovative views and angles are what catch their attention.

If the first two ideas you send don't bring a go-ahead from an editor, try another two. If you receive an encouraging rejection letter, keep trying. Go back and study the magazine again for contents, style, and focus. If, however, you've received three or more form rejections from a particular magazine, it might be a good idea to shift your efforts elsewhere. Not every writer fits every magazine. If *Northwest Orient* doesn't want your manuscript, you might try Delta's *Sky* or *National Geographic Traveler.*

Although you should look through the contents of your target periodical for the last six months or so, it is far more important to be familiar with its readership profile. While at *Travel & Leisure* (which reaches an upscale, service-oriented, mature audience), I received more than one proposal about traveling with children, RV vacationing, and "cheapest ways to get there." Not one of these was appropriate to *Travel & Leisure,* though if well written, any of these might have found publication in other periodicals. For example, *Camperways* publishes pieces on RV travel; *Chevron USA* zeroes in on family vacations; and

Travel Smart for Business concentrates on bargains for business travelers.

Let's assume the proper editor has your query and likes it. What happens next? At many magazines, the proposal is considered by a number of editors who give their suggestions, ideas, and comments. You might be asked to do the piece on speculation. Or the piece might be assigned in a different way from the one you presented. My best advice is to be flexible: The editor will appreciate your adaptability and be more willing to work with you in the future.

Whether you have a go-ahead on spec or a contractual assignment, read your letter from the editor carefully: You will be expected to produce what it asks for. I sent many first drafts back to authors asking them to give us what we had already asked for. If you are convinced the topic cannot be handled in the way the editor stipulated, drop him or her a note: Never assume that you can proceed with your version—or that the editor may not be persuaded to consider your approach.

Most travel magazines want you to entice their audiences to the destination, restaurant, hotel, or museum you write about. If problems exist, mention them in a light but honest manner. "The room becomes loud and lively at lunch hour, spacious and quiet after three," says the same thing as "Sheer havoc ensues during lunch." Warn readers about possible hardships: "The trail is steep and rocky; if you're not a dedicated hiker, take the bus to the other side."

Many major magazines prefer to have you concentrate on writing and leave the photography to them. If you're an accomplished photographer, however, you might want to click your shutters anyway. Fact checkers are known to appreciate photos (today's fact checkers are often tomorrow's editors), and even large magazines might need a picture of an out-of-the-way place. Smaller publications and newspapers, of course, are usually pleased to receive photographs to highlight your piece. (Send valuable photos registered mail; duplicate slides are safest.)

Finally, the most important thing a traveler can do is enjoy traveling. All the above is secondary. If you truly have a good time wherever you go, you'll be full of ideas, convincing in your proposals, and upbeat in your finished work. And fun, after all, is what travel is about!

62

GETTING STARTED IN BOOK REVIEWING

By Lynne Sharon Schwartz

I LIKE to think of a new book as a mysterious geological treasure, a rock never before handled. The delighted discoverer's first, most natural response is, What have we here? I hold the rock in the palm of my hand to examine it: what are its colors, its contours, its special beauty (or ugliness)? Is it like others I've seen, enough like them, even, to fit into a generic category? Is it more or less beautiful than those of its kind? Or is it, though it bears a surface family resemblance, distinguished by intriguing, individual markings?

The "what have we here" approach will yield a reviewer fruitful results. Every book deserves this careful attention; every one is unique— though some uniquely bad—and demands to be judged for its intrinsic, living qualities. The opposite approach might be labeled "negative criticism." The negative critic appraises a book on the basis of what it has failed to accomplish, with the failings usually derived from the critic's own notion of how he or she would have handled the subject. Not only unfair but misleading, too. For a critic's job is to leave aside his own musings and try temporarily to share the author's view. What has the author set out to do? is the crucial question. (If you believe, however, that what the author has set out to do is not worth doing, better pass up that book. It deserves a fighting chance, and you as critic deserve a more worthwhile application of your talents.)

Now, it is far easier to be explicit about the goals of nonfiction than of fiction. When I reviewed a biography of Margaret Sanger, it was not difficult to decide whether or not the book gave an accurate, coherent, inclusive account of Sanger's life. (The larger question of how well it does so, compared to other efforts, is more complex.) Again, in *Visions of Glory,* Barbara Grizzuti Harrison set out to detail the history of the Jehovah's Witnesses and of her experiences among them. I became convinced of her thoroughness and accuracy and said so in my review. But it is far harder to be unequivocal about fiction, since fiction at its best does not set out to prove or to do anything. To say that *Anna Karenina* "shows" what happens to an upper class nineteenth-century Russian woman who commits adultery would be literary blasphemy. Fiction is the working out of an inner vision; it is impossible to "judge" anyone's vision, and quite a delicate matter to evaluate its metamorphosis into words.

Still, books must be brought to the attention of readers, and a paid reviewer has certain obligations to an audience which sound exceedingly obvious yet are too often ignored. First, to tell the reader specifically what is in the book: to return to the rock analogy, describe its size, shape, color, texture and distinctive marks; the category it belongs to, its antecedents, its relative standing among others of its kind. If nonfiction, the premises on which it is based and the conclusions it reaches, the major issues and points raised along the way, the extent to which they are covered. If it is fiction, the themes, the areas and vicissitudes of life the author is preoccupied with. Plot summaries, as we all remember from school, should be minimal. But a dash of the reporter's standard questions—where, what, when, how, and why—will prove helpful. Above all, a discussion of the nature and interaction of the characters as they grow from the novel's inception through its development and close, is essential.

Secondly, an evaluation of style. Books, our fact-oriented age tends to forget, are made of words, in the best instances deftly laced together to create a texture that mirrors or complements its subject. Everyone, in the privacy of his brain, spins theories and fantasies. Only a writer labors to put the theories or fantasies into words. It is precisely for this labor with words, as much as for the quality of the content, that a book should be assessed. What is the flavor of the author's special idiom? Does the style aid or hinder the emergence of the themes? An even larger question, does the use of words enhance or detract from the richness and capacity of our common inherited language?

Finally—and here is what frightens many new reviewers—a personal judgment. In book reviewing, as in so much else, there is no way out of accountability for one's views. Certainly, don't review a book unless you have the courage and authority to state your convictions honestly. But once you do, don't shrink from the truth, pleasant or not; it is, after all, what the editor hired you for. (On the other hand, beware of using the

316

seductive power of print for airing private grievances; if a book inspires you to invective or sarcasm for dubious personal reasons, better pass it up. Again, both you and the book deserve better handling.)

Since books are composed of words, ideally an astute, literate reviewer should be able to handle a book on any subject, and indeed some national magazines have successfully assigned books to critics outside the field. Practically speaking, however, as a beginning reviewer, you should get to know as thoroughly as possible the field you choose to work in.

When I started reviewing, I felt competent to write about current fiction because I was, after all, primarily a writer of fiction, besides having read it all my life and having taught literature at Hunter College. Nonetheless, with my first efforts I overprepared — not a bad thing to do, as it turned out. I made sure I was familiar with an author's earlier books so I could see the latest one in the context of a body of work. Naturally this meant more crammed reading and time spent in relation to money earned than was comfortable, but I felt I owed this to the author and my readers. I still do. (Anyone reading this is surely aware that reviewing is not one of life's more lucrative occupations.) Often, especially in brief reviews, hardly more than a sentence or two referring to the earlier works found its way into my final draft, yet I felt that the background knowledge improved my review and gave it a justified tone of authority.

I had trepidations for some time, though, about reviewing nonfiction. What could I claim to know about real facts in the real world? Nevertheless, intrigued by the advance publicity, I asked to review Ellen Moers' *Literary Women* for *The Nation*. Faced with the book's wealth of data, presented by someone who had evidently read every word penned by a woman over the past 200 years, I felt incompetent. Yet, as I read the book, not only did great forgotten chunks of my early studies return to me, but I found whatever else I needed to know on its pages. In my review, besides giving the usual information, I turned my attention partly to the controversy the book had engendered by its considering women authors apart from men, a controversy on which I had very definite and educated opinions.

Encouraged by that venture into nonfiction, I requested of *Ms. Magazine* Ann Cornelisen's *Women of the Shadows,* about the lives of Southern Italian peasant women. Here I worried that my ignorance of agricultural economy, of the difficulties of industrialization, and such, would hamper me. However, I had read other books on the region, and had lived in Italy and traveled through the areas Cornelisen wrote about. I hoped that this firsthand knowledge would stand me in good stead, and I believe it did. But I would hesitate to review a similar book on the lives of peasant women in Turkey or Morocco, places I know nothing about.

In brief, know your subject by study or by firsthand experience, or both. Then if, as occasionally will happen, you are given a book you feel overwhelmed by, stick to what you know and perceive, avoid grandiose generalities, and in the end, trust your instincts. Above all, don't attempt to sound authoritative when there is no basis for authority. I remember how pleased I was, as a beginner, to be offered a book by *The Chicago Tribune Book World,* but how distressed on opening the desired package to find a novel of World War II, filled with details of military strategy, sabotage, fortifications — subjects I knew nothing about and disliked besides. I turned to page one with a sense of duty. In the book itself, I found all I needed to know about strategy, and found in addition, to my pleasant surprise, that like all good novels, *Kramer's War,* by Derek Robinson, was about human beings working out their complex, connected destinies in a situation of great stress. I was able not only to review it but to enjoy it as well. Needless to say, I avoided undue discussion of strategy, fortifications, or deployment of troops.

The above remarks apply once you have the book in hand, but the novice reviewer is probably wondering, How do you get the books assigned? Timing is of the essence. Since newspapers' Sunday sections are prepared weeks ahead and magazines often months ahead, you need to know what titles are coming out well in advance of publication date. *Publishers Weekly,* the invaluable trade magazine, lists forthcoming books, as does *Library Journal.* From their brief and pithy descriptions you can find which books are suitable for you.

Getting the first assignment is difficult, yet a newcomer's prospects are not totally bleak. It's best to try your local papers or weeklies first, even if it means working for no pay temporarily—not advisable as a long-term habit, but worth the initial sacrifice. Send the editor a sample review, your best effort of course, with the names of several forthcoming books you'd like to try, and a few persuasive lines telling why you are especially qualified to review them. Don't be daunted if the first tries fail. The erosion technique—wearing down a solid, recalcitrant object by a light, steady trickle—has been known to work. Certainly competition is stiff, but if editors discover someone with a dash of originality, a capacity for felicitous use of language, a strong sense of organization and a willingness to work doggedly at improving, they will generally succumb. They also, incidentally, will be grateful for a readable, correctly spelled and punctuated manuscript, submitted on time.

Once you have established yourself locally you might try larger markets, sending around tear sheets of previous work. By all means follow up any leads from friends or colleagues. When book review editors send out the word that they're looking for new writers, they usually mean it.

It's extremely important to be aware of the tastes, readership, slants, if any, space limitations, and general tone of the magazine you're writing for. Your chances of impressing *The National Review* with an iconoclastic critique of capitalism are about as great as getting a laudatory review of Richard Nixon's memoirs into *The Village Voice*. In a realistic way, try to suit your review to the publication. If this requires too great a dislocation of your own values, better to try elsewhere. I have found it possible to write for varied periodicals without doing damage to my fundamental opinions about a book. When reviewing *Women of the Shadows* for *Ms.,* I stressed its feminist aspects more than I would have, say, for *The Nation,* where I might have dwelt more on the inequities inherent in the system of land tenure. Both themes were vital and important—the choice was a matter of emphasis, bearing in mind the concerns of prospective readers.

Once you are in the hard-earned position of writing fairly freely for a number of places (that is, once editors have come to trust you), you will find that magazines vary greatly in the way they handle review copy. Very few editors print every word as written. Some, like Emile Capouya, former Literary Editor of *The Nation,* make changes so small, subtle and apt that I, for one, never noticed them at first, only felt vaguely that my review was better than I thought. Others ask for extensive changes, either for style and coherence, or because of space limitations. In any case, it helps to be cooperative with editors, whose experience is usually vast and long. (Unless, of course, their requests involve distorting your opinions for extraneous reasons, which is unacceptable and happens, at least to my knowledge, thankfully seldom.)

Now, suppose you have won the coveted assignment and have the book in hand. How to proceed? The reading is often the hardest part of the job, very different from reading for pleasure. One reads at first with the unsettling sense of needing to remember everything, much like studying for an exam. This compulsion passes, but you do unquestionably owe the book and your audience an attentive reading. Authors frequently complain that their critics seem not to have read the book, or to have read some other book. There is no way of telling whether this is true, but at least new reviewers can avoid the imputation.

I usually read a book twice, once slowly, occasionally marking passages along the way, and the second time quickly, to get a sense of overall shape, flow, and pattern. One soon learns to read with pen in hand—but stopping for real notes fragments the experience of first reading. Note-taking during the second reading is more effective. Both readings are invariably accompanied by familiar conflicts which one learns to take in stride. If I am enjoying the book too much, I worry about losing objectivity, not paying enough attention to how the author achieves his or her effects and simply luxuriating in them. On the other hand, if I dislike the book, I make enormous efforts not to become resentful of my task and thus dislike it more than warranted. I try to look for good points that any one of my innumerable small prejudices may prevent me from noticing. In either case, it is hardly relaxing.

After the two readings I write down my general impressions with illustrations from the book, and organize them under several inclusive headings, which gives me a loose outline. I then proceed with the best intentions of working from this outline, but habitually write the piece straight on, barely glancing at the notes until later, to see that I've covered everything and to locate appropriate examples. It might be suspected that the extra reading, note-taking and outlining are wasted effort. Yet in the end it seems that the intense preparation is somehow needed for the rather swift, "thoughtless" writing process. Also, the outline exists as security in case I run dry halfway through. I don't presume that this method of total immersion, a valiant semblance of scholarly organization, and then an abandoned dash to the finish line can work for anyone else. I do offer it to demonstrate the devious, cumbersome and idiosyncratic ways that reviews get written.

Next come the patient correcting, revising, cutting and moving of parts, drudgery to be sure, but performed with the immense relief of knowing that the thing *exists,* in need only of tinkering. Always, when the review is typed in final form and on its way to the mailbox, I get wild flashes of insight informing me my work is all wrong: I should have kept in what I cut out and cut out what I kept in. These hand-on-the-mailbox insights are an inevitable part of the writing process and should be totally disregarded. (It may help to keep the finished review for a few days to give it a last check before mailing.)

There are, in addition, a few outside impediments to straight thinking that a novice reviewer should be aware of. One is an author's reputation. Depending on the murky depths of a reviewer's secret nature, he or she may be tempted to encourage or to attack new writers (regardless of the merit of the work), or to sustain or stab the reputation of well-known writers (also regardless of merit). To these temptations, the adage "Know thyself" is the best antidote; better still, "Guard against thyself or don't review the book at all." Reviewing books by friends or acquaintances—a common if doubtful practice—requires similar restraint or total abstinence.

Other reviews and publishers' blurbs are powerful obstacles as well. But while the first can be summarily dealt with (never read them till your own review is safely in the mail), advertising, jacket copy, or those ingratiating notes from the publicity staff telling how wonderful the book is, are less easy to avoid. What publicity people say should be regarded as a skillful pass in a complex ball game. The serious danger enters if the uninitiated reviewer's expectations are raised. "Smith's new novel relentlessly plumbs the depths of A, with brilliant insights into B, so that his style is reminiscent of C and D, though paradoxically echoing the uniqueness of E." Smith's book may in fact be a fine one, but a neophyte reviewer diligently in search of A, B, and C is sure to be disappointed, as well as blinded to the book's true worth.

The final questions that keep reviewers tossing in bed at night are, Have I praised a book that everyone will see immediately is idiotic? and Have I panned a masterpiece? The first is more easily dispensed with. It is unlikely that a competent reviewer, after years of reading, will fail to spot awful work. Moreover, it is probably more honorable to err on the side of generosity. But not to recognize genius is to be dull indeed, is it not? I had this experience reviewing a recent novel by a moderately well-known writer. I had read excerpts in a magazine and liked them, but after finishing the whole novel I realized it set enormous goals and failed to achieve them. The book turned out to be the focus of a good advertising campaign; other reviews appeared and were for the most part favorable. I considered retiring. First, though, I went back to the book dispassionately, my review already in print. It was still unsuccessful, and I was glad to have said so.

For one learns, after much time and ink and struggle, that there are no absolute standards of accomplishment, especially today when traditional and experimental modes rightfully flourish side by side. Reviewers' opinions will vary as much as readers'; the difference is that reviewers are expected to have the skill to articulate clearly what they think and why they think it. That is the most, in all conscience, that one can do, and it is no small task. Once it is done, let the reader be left to his own devices.

63

HUMOR IS PUBLISHABLE

By Richard Armour

Two of the hardest forms of writing to publish these days are poetry and fiction. But that doesn't disturb me the slightest, because I don't write either kind. Oh, I wrote some serious, even morbid, poetry when I was in high school. However, I got that out of my system, along with whatever was causing my acne, and never again wrote poetry in the manner of Ezra Pound, T.S. Eliot, or even Edgar A. Guest.

As for fiction, I once wrote a short story. In one of my rare flashes of wisdom, I tore it up. Not at once, of course, but after it came back from sixteen magazines, each time with a printed rejection slip and no encouragement whatsoever.

I admire writers of poetry and fiction. I think they write two of the highest forms of literary art and creativity. So I am sorry if this is a difficult time for publishing their work. I hope there is a change of taste, or whatever is necessary, and that poets and writers of short stories and novels will have their editors knocking at their doors or writing them begging letters: "Please send us something—anything."

But my bent, and with the passing years I am growing more bent than ever, is humor—humor which takes the form of light verse rather than poetry and light nonfiction rather than fiction. The way my mind works, or plays, is indicated by the fact that when I typed the word "difficult" in the paragraph above, it first came out "fiddicult." The word "fiddicult" so entranced me that I found it difficult, or fiddicult, to go on.

If you study the market lists in an inclusive and reliable reference work, such as *The Writer's Handbook,* you will encounter time after time such discouraging comments as "Most articles staff written," "Currently overstocked," "No fiction," "No poetry," "No unsolicited manuscripts considered," and "Query." But you will also find, if you look hard enough, "Humor," "Humorous pieces, 1,000 to 2,000

323

words," "Humorous or human-interest articles," "Satire, sophisticated humor," "Light treatment, lively, enjoyable style," and so on.

Or study the magazines themselves, as I do. Often I find a magazine that uses humor occasionally, in prose or verse, yet makes no mention of it in the brief description in a market list. Many times, over the years, I have come upon a magazine that seemed to me to need humor, but perhaps its editor was not aware that it did. I have tried prose or verse humor on such a magazine and occasionally have broken in, sometimes making the market my own. Thus I had a half page in a medical journal every month for twenty-three years.

So the markets for humor exist. They take more ferreting out than they did when I started to write almost fifty years ago. In those days I was writing for several magazines that no longer exist, such as *Liberty* and *Look,* and others that (I think mistakenly) have given up the humor that once livened their pages.

Now we come to the heart of the matter: writing humor that will sell. I should like to be methodical about this, perhaps even a little pedagogical, and so shall list the points I have in mind. Or rather, the points I *had* in mind, because they are out of my mind, as I myself am often thought to be. (In fact, the most wide-ranging of my books of prose humor, selected from my writings in sixteen magazines, is entitled precisely that: *Out of My Mind.*)

1. It is as hard to make readers laugh as it is to make them cry. In other words, humor of marketable caliber is no easy literary form. Humor in verse (i.e. light verse), for instance, is more than a matter of writing something that rhymes. At its best, it is more rational, if not more intellectual, than much of today's serious poetry, and it is far more concerned with both the correctness and the tricks of technique. Rarely has successful, publishable light verse been written as free verse—without rhyme or meter. Don Marquis is one of the few who managed it. And rarely has it been published when it featured purposely bad meter and outrageous rhymes. Ogden Nash was a genius at parodying poetry and contriving original, unexpected rhymes —rhymes a serious poet would never use. But it would be risky to try to follow in Nash's nimble footsteps.

There is a reason for emphasis on technique in light verse. The serious poet has lofty thoughts and evocative imagery (metaphors, similes, personification, etc.). Lacking these, the light verse writer substitutes the various techniques of meter and rhyme, often trying to surprise.

2. If you wish to write publishable humor in the form of light verse, you must do a little homework, and domework. Read, study, and analyze the works of the best published writers, past and present, of humorous writing. Go back to the work of such as Samuel Hoffenstein, Arthur Guiterman, F.P.A. (Franklin Pierce Adams), Dorothy Parker, Morris Bishop, David McCord, Ogden Nash, Margaret Fishback, and Phyllis McGinley. Phyllis McGinley, by the way, was the only light verse writer to win the Pulitzer Prize, in 1961, though by that time she had become what I would call a writer of light poetry.

3. Prose humor can take the form of either fiction or nonfiction. A short story can be light, even funny. It may even be wild, zany. But it may be merely playful, or have touches that give comic relief to what would otherwise be a serious piece. Humorous or light prose can go beyond the feature or magazine short story to the novel or even to the stage—or screen. There is always the wonderful possibility that a humorous piece can be the basis of a Broadway hit or a film with a major comic star like Woody Allen. You can dream, can't you? I hope you can, because that is one of the things that keeps a writer writing.

4. One further advantage of writing humor in prose is that it can be almost any length, whereas light verse must be kept short (usually four to twelve lines). A good marketable length for prose humor is around 1,200 words, but certain publications use humor pieces that run to about 3,000 words. Thus, a piece of prose humor can be more than a filler. It can be a feature article that will be listed in the table of contents. This gives the writer more of a showcase than a humorous poem and may lead to bigger, if not better, things.

5. But let me come back to earth, or to the more immediately possible, in the marketing of humor. Since, as I have indicated, I am not a writer of fiction, I make use of humor in nonfiction. I do this in two ways: (1) I put a light touch into what might have been a serious article on some such subject as education, the family (and divorce), politics, inflation, aging, travel—just about anything. Or (2) I toy with some personal yet universal bit of trivia, such as plastic plants, paperclips, losing my glasses case, wire coat hangers, or my neighbor's leaves that suddenly became mine.

I have placed more-or-less humorous articles in the first category in *The Christian Science Monitor, The New York Times, Parents, Woman's Day,* the in-flight magazines of several airlines, and so on. I have found even more takers of the second type of short humorous articles, including "The Phoenix Nest" (formerly in the *Saturday Review* but now syndicated by the Associated Press), *Los Angeles* and other regional magazines, and *The Saturday Evening Post.*

6. For me, humor in book form has proved one of the most marketable types of writing. This includes humor in books for children. (Let me say that I think the sense of humor, like the imagination, is livelier in children than in most adults.) A book of humor, if original, timely, and highly polished (though the signs of effort should not show), is almost as publishable as a how-to book. And there is always the possibility of doing a humorous how-to book, which would bring you double rewards.

Despite what many say, humor is not dead. Maybe sick humor is, after getting more and more sickening, and that's all right with me. I try to write healthy humor, perhaps because I have a healthy respect for humor, and when I have written it I try to find a market for it. Usually, but not always, I do. I have to hunt harder than I once did, but I am a determined hunter. Perhaps I need a bird dog, or a word dog.

The world needs humor today and, fortunately, some editors are aware of this. All you have to do to get your humor published is to write publishable humor, and then find the right place for it. It is as simple as that. As a matter of fact, I once wrote, and published, an article on the so-called funny bone. What is funny about the funny bone is that there is nothing funny about it.

64

FREE-LANCING FOR CITY MAGAZINES

By Don Kubit

WHILE free-lancing in itself is a tough enough way to earn a living, making a go of it in economically depressed Detroit nowadays practically qualifies me for a spot, next to the snail darter, on the endangered species list. I just have to believe that if I can survive as a free-lance writer, as I have for years, in a city in which cutbacks and layoffs are daily headlines, I must be doing something right.

I have managed to keep my head above water by writing primarily for *Monthly Detroit,* the area's city magazine, and over the past several years I have had by-lines in the majority of issues—and, more important, got paid. While some may feel that this makes me a regional writer, that geographical chauvinism is precisely why I am able to support myself as a writer.

Detroit is my hometown, so I have both a sense of its history and a participant's feel for what is currently going on around town. Talk to any editor of any city magazine across the country and he'll tell you that that sort of "insider's" knowledge is one of the keys to breaking into print in city magazines.

The growth of city magazines over the past decade has provided local free-lance writers with a rare opportunity. Almost every city magazine *depends* on free lancers to supplement their relatively small in-house writing staff and, consequently, the editors are often more willing to take the time and effort to encourage and develop beginning writers. And, since they are basically competing with Sunday newspaper supplements for local talent, their pay scales tend to be somewhat higher.

From *Boston* to *Los Angeles, Cleveland* to *Corpus Christi,* city magazines share a basic philosophy—to provide the middle-to-upper income, better-educated class of readers, with articles revolving around the "quality of life" in their specific area. Who better to know (and write) about that measure of livability than a person who resides there?

From my own experiences and discussions with a half dozen city magazine editors, I have discovered that the kinds of articles they are looking for fall into designated categories. I have dubbed them the Four Urban P's: PROBLEMS, PERSONALITIES, PLEASURES and PERCEPTIONS. Any one or any combination usually results in a sure-fire "strike."

For the most part, issue-oriented pieces are written by a city magazine's staff writers who have the contacts and facilities to explore crime, drugs, rising politicians, and massive downtown development projects. I would advise free lancers to concentrate more on issues and events within their own communities, e.g., small entrepreneurs; ethnic neighborhoods; the rehabilitation of old houses and movie theaters; the impact of a suburban shopping mall on a town's main street merchants; local political races. There are satellite topics, but every city magazine, regardless of its location or region, has a metropolitan area readership. Residents of one borough or suburb are naturally curious about the goings-on crosstown, because some day they may face similar problems.

Some beginning writers disregard potential article ideas on the grounds that "the local newspapers have already covered that." If it is a major issue, no doubt they have, but city magazine writers have to go beyond the obvious to find an overlooked angle. A few years ago, one of the most over-reported stories in these parts was a battle over a proposed road expansion in the Detroit suburb of Troy. Hardly a heart-wrenching issue, but the local weeklies and the two major dailies in Detroit covered this point-counterpoint situation as if it were a Papal visit. However, in their deadline rush to report all the brickbats, they failed to look at the total picture. With one phone call, I learned that opposition to the planned road-widening started because building the proposed right of way meant cutting down a 50-year-old copper beech.

A second phone call uncovered the fact that a simple driveway separated the offices of the two main antagonists—Minoru Yamasaki, a world-renowned architect fond of quoting Henry David Thoreau, who wanted to turn the road into a pedestrian plaza, *vs.* city manager Frank Gerstenecker, a cost-efficient type who had the facts and figures to show that the road should become an eight-lane highway. My article, "A Tree Grows in Troy," portrayed a classic confrontation of divergent personalities and philosophies.

I suggested that my piece be published in the monthly issue coinciding with the final zoning commission hearing on the road project. Although the hearing received only a one-sentence mention in my article, it was an important news peg that made an otherwise tired, old topic more timely.

Personifying a lifeless cement-and-mortar problem leads us to the second mainstay of city magazine articles—local personalities. People like to read about their neighbors, and almost every city magazine editor would admit that at least part of his function is to serve as a sort of provincial version of *People* magazine. The possibilities for local profiles are nearly endless, with media celebrities at the top of the list—the face behind the voice of a popular disc jockey, the life beyond the anchor of a TV newsman.

Sports personality features are another favorite category, and instead of writing about the highly-publicized All-Star pitcher or All-American tailback, a free lancer would be wise to seek out the little-known center who only snaps for punts and field goals; the lesser-known souvenir concessionaire at baseball games; or the unknown driver of the Zamboni machine, which resurfaces the ice between periods at a hockey game. Don't overlook amateur athletes—young, Olympic-minded gymnasts, a senior citizen softball team, pool hustlers, bowlers, country club caddies, an up-and-coming boxer who works out in a local gym.

Don't forget about people who once lived in your area and went on to fame and fortune elsewhere. Detroit is not exactly considered a breeding ground for celebrities, but its notable list of alumni include Robin "Mork" Williams, Pam "Mindy" Dawber, the Motown sound originator, Berry Gordy, Jr., and his superstar pupil Diana Ross, Gilda Radner, Lily Tomlin, Joyce Carol Oates, and Soupy Sales. The nostalgic reminiscences of ex-residents frequently equal guaranteed sales for city magazine free lancers. There is also what I refer to as the Who-Feeds-the-Ducks? group—a motley collection of potentially interesting profiles, from museum guards to homicide detectives, community volunteers to cabbies, registered nannies to card-carrying witches. I once met a family attorney whose culinary hobby eventually led him to start his own commercial taco factory; the owner of a sports paraphernalia store who was the original proponent of the Super Bowl XVI staged in Pontiac, Michigan. I wrote his story for *Monthly Detroit,* and during Super Bowl week, it gained national attention.

An essential role of every city magazine is to keep its readers informed of what's happening on the social scene. Each month, there is an extensive registry of planned entertainment events for the metropolitan area and an accompanying "restaurant guide."

These tabulations are usually handled by an assigned "listings" staffer, but periodically, this function is expanded into what is called a "service piece"—a ratings game featuring the *best of* this and the *most of* that. These articles generally fall into three categories: 1) food—the juiciest steak, the cheesiest cheesecake, the tangiest chili, etc.; 2) entertainment—the friendliest singles bars, the loudest punk rock havens, the classiest jazz clubs, etc.; and 3) travel—getaways, hideaways and weekend breakaways.

Since all of these classifications are highly subjective, a free-lance writer should not feel that he or she has to be a qualified expert on any given subject in order to write about it. One man's favorite pizza is another man's ersatz Frisbee. If you have an interest and are willing to do the research, your biggest obstacle is defending your choices.

You might even think of a more offbeat approach: ranking roads according to potholes; a list of the most popular books borrowed from local libraries; an inventory of the biggest shoe sizes, submarine sandwiches, salad bars, etc., in your town. The funnier, the more clever and, sometimes, the tackier, the better.

City magazine editors are most receptive to shorter pieces (around 1,000 words) on music, the arts, and local history. If you enjoy and/or know of a struggling painter, a promising sculptor, a talented but overlooked dance company, write about it. Culture sells to a cultured audience.

Whether you live in the city or in the suburbs, it's your town. If you have an interest in something—from politics to potholes—exploit it.

Maybe all you have is an opinion, a personal experience you share with friends and neighbors. Expand it, explore it, write it, and you could well have a marketable article. Every city magazine offers a back-of-the-book final page, a space for an 800- to 1,000-word personal essay presented less for the subject per se than how that view is expressed.

Most city magazines offer free "writer's guidelines." Send for them. They give you a more precise idea of what the publication is looking for and provide an excellent way to make a first contact with an editor.

When you get ready to compose a query letter, be aware of three factors:

1) Never, absolutely never, send carbon copies. If you don't want a form letter response, don't send out a form letter request. Tailor *your* city magazine idea to *your* city magazine editor. It is essential for you to keep abreast of what the magazine has already published. Not only does this allow for possible follow-up pieces, but even a great article idea will be rejected if your subject happens to be on the cover of the issue currently or recently on the newsstands.

2) Be specific. In addition to explaining what your article is about, mention whom you intend to interview, approximate length, the point of view you plan to take, and, as briefly as possible, spell out any credentials you have to qualify you to do the piece. But, don't oversell the article.

3) The writing style of the query letter should be the style you will use in the proposed article. In fact, the first paragraph of your query can be the proposed lead of your piece. City magazines are looking for writers. Introduce yourself with your words. First impressions count.

Finally, here are some of my golden rules for free-lancing for city magazines:

* Be thorough—read and analyze all forms of printed material, from the wedding announcements through the classifieds of daily and weekly newspapers, advertising flyers, newsletters, signs in store windows . . . and become a conscientious producer of story ideas.

* Be curious—if something or someone caught your attention, it's a good bet that your neighbors' interest was also piqued . . . find out what it means.

* Be available—stop by the offices of your city magazine. In addition to looking through their stack of other city magazines for story ideas that would also apply to your town, get to know the staff. And let

them get to know you. There have been many times when I pitched an idea that an editor rejected, but he had a notion of his own, needed a free lancer, and one happened to be sitting right in front of him.

* Be disciplined—clean, accurate copy is a must; meeting deadlines is a given.

* Believe in yourself—the only way to approach free-lancing is not to sell yourself short.

65

POPULAR SCIENCE FOR POPULAR MAGAZINES

By David M. Stewart

BEFORE you read the rest of this article, pick up that stack of magazines sitting on the coffee table, your desk, or the floor in your office. Read the contents and count the articles that could be classified, even if you have to be a little generous, as "science."

Done? My bet is that you found an average of at least one article per magazine, and if you have something like *Mademoiselle, American Way,* or *Science Digest,* you probably found even more—three, eight, or a whole magazineful.

My point should be clear: Science and technology are among the most salable nonfiction topics around. Virtually every magazine's readers have concerns that can be addressed from a scientific perspective, and some are devoted wholly to science and technology. Many newspapers now run a weekly science page or section, and articles on science or technology appear regularly in the news, lifestyle, and Sunday supplement sections.

Editors buy science articles because science attracts readers. There are practical reasons for this: Technology is a dynamic force of change, and we all want to know how it might affect our home, work, and social lives. But readers are just as eager to read about the latest work being done on particle physics, mass extinctions in the Cretaceous era, and the space shuttle's radar photos of the Sahara desert—the practical implications of which are obscure or far in the future. Readers want to know about science mainly because it is fascinating.

What that means for free-lance writers is a vast market that includes some of the best-paying magazines around. And while breaking into that market calls for fresh ideas and clear, logical, and lively writing, you can do it without a degree in physics, biology, or engineering (I majored in philosophy in college). The work is hard, but it's also profitable, useful, and enlightening.

Ideas for popular science articles are legion. Your best sources are:

Newspapers. Quite a few news or feature stories will mention some technological or scientific aspect without pausing to dwell on it. That technology or technique may have broader implications and applications, and that's the seed you need.

Corporate and university public relations offices. Whenever you deal with a company or school, ask to be put on their public relations mailing list, and seek out institutions likely to be doing work you would like to write about.

Scientific journals. Scientific American, Science, and *Nature* are among the more accessible and widely known publications for scientists, and they are full of semi-technical articles from which you can develop ideas. And virtually every scientific discipline supports a number of journals. These sources make your research easier, too, because they generally contain references that can lead you to other sources.

Popular science magazines. Discover, Popular Science, Science 86, and the rest of the varied market of popular science magazines contain ideas in the form of brief items or fillers that could be the basis for feature articles.

Other magazines. It's really hard to avoid finding science articles or ideas, so look everywhere, even in the strangest places, and apply a "sidebar" technique (described below).

Books. You can get ideas just from the titles or covers of the scores of popular science books being published, and many of them are essentially collections of fillers just waiting to be expanded into articles. One I've used in the past is *Omni's Continuum* (Little, Brown and Company) collected from the magazine.

You can glean ideas from your reading by using what I call "sidebar" techniques. A sidebar is a short article within an article, usually set off in a box, on one aspect of a larger subject or closely related to it. In reading through an article, focus on those aspects of a topic that the author doesn't fully explore but which could have been the subjects of sidebars. You can use these to generate articles of your own. An editorial on Olympic cyclers in a cycling magazine mentioned a special scientific training program established by the U.S. Olympic Committee, and that was enough to start my article, "Training the Olympic Elite," for *Southwest Airlines Magazine*. I've even done this with my own articles.

Another approach is to look at the sidebars accompanying a story, or the short fillers you'll find in the fronts or backs of popular science magazines, and decide whether the subjects merit full-length articles. A few fillers and sidebars from different magazines, combined with the publicity surrounding the artificial heart implanted in the late Barney Clark, were the start of my article on bioengineering advances for *USAir*.

Once you've found your idea, you have to convince an editor to give you the assignment. I go through three steps in honing an idea for a query. I start out with a *topic* or *subject* (experimental cars, for example). They I try to *focus* on one aspect of the topic (why experimental cars, which are never turned into production models, are built). Finally, I summarize what the article will say in a *thesis,* a statement which the article will prove ("Experimental cars, despite their apparent impracticality, are useful working laboratories for testing new automotive styling and engineering concepts."). You may want to state your thesis explicitly, but usually you can let your facts demonstrate it by including enough information in your query for an editor to be able to judge whether his or her readers will care about what you are proposing to prove.

Editors of different kinds of magazines are interested in different kinds of topics, and they'll want you to handle your material in a way that will address their readers' interests. There are several general angles for science articles. Consumer articles will tell readers what to look for in a product, and how to determine what they need, then perhaps give an overview of several types or brands. A profile will focus on a person who is doing something scientifically interesting and talk about his methods, struggles, motivations, and achievements. The news article takes a close look at a new technology, problem, or development, often at a university or corporation located in the newspaper's city or state, and informs the reader about it. And what I call "technology salads" unite a number of different technologies that have a general goal and explain their development, purposes, and interrelationships.

You will have to vary the approach and presentation in your query or article according to the particular publication you are aiming for. Generally, the differences between markets are determined by their relative use of technical detail, human interest, and practicality. The strictly science magazines like *Science 86* and *Science Digest* want articles that go deeply into the technicalities of a subject (though not as deeply as a technical journal would). The human element in these is often in the political or social implications, although they give an excellent picture of scientists at work.

In the general publications like the airline magazines, human interest is primary, because as a rule the readers are seeking an entertaining diversion, not an intellectual tussle. I have written two articles on "human powered vehicles," streamlined, superfast bikes and trikes. For *USAir* I talked about what the builders went through to build an HPV and what it was like for a rider to pump his legs at 62 miles per hour; for another publication I wrote an article on things like gear ratios, structural materials, and coefficients of drag.

Readers with no science background will want to know how they can benefit from scientific knowledge. A recent issue of *Mademoiselle*, for example, had articles on dental care, a single woman's uses for a personal computer, and the designs and purposes of a variety of carefully engineered sporting shoes. These articles are light on the technicalities, but you can bet the authors understood the details—and knew how to turn them into practical advice.

These are general observations, and there is no substitute for reading the magazines to which you hope to sell your articles. You'll have to adjust your writing style a bit, too, depending on your market. *Mademoiselle* wants a chatty, friendly style; *American Way* wants it bright and clear; *Popular Mechanics* looks for a dynamic style (I once found the phrase "blow the doors off" about half a dozen times in one issue); *Science 86* prefers the details in a lucid style. If you set the wrong tone in your query or article, you could miss a sale.

A word about assignments: In my experience, most editors will ask you to write at least your first article for them not "on assignment" with a guaranteed payment or kill fee, but "on speculation," with only an agreement to give the finished article serious consideration. However much this may seem to be a cavalier way to treat a writer, the reason editors do it is understandable: They do it to minimize their own risks in working with an unknown writer. After all, most magazines have a group of writers they know they can count on.

If you're a beginning writer, take the opportunity. And deliver an article that the editors will be glad to print. Once an editor buys a piece from you on speculation, you're likely to get firm assignments on anything you write thereafter. If you're an established writer, you may be able to afford to tell an editor that you won't work with that kind of uncertainty. But then, if you're an established writer, you also probably have few fears about a "spec" piece being rejected anyway.

Researching science articles can be an arduous process, and you must gather much more information than you can possibly use. If you have scientific training, and are writing in your field, you already know how to find materials. But if you don't, and if a topic is new to you (as archaeology was to me until recently), you can start with children's books, because they are clearly structured and won't ambush you with a mass of details. They'll give you a map of the terrain you're going to travel through, and as you get to know each field or river you pass through, you'll have some idea of the landscape.

From there you can go to encyclopedias, such as the *Britannica* and the *McGraw-Hill Encyclopedia of Science and Technology;* scholarly works or textbooks on your subject; and magazine and journal articles (cited in several periodical indexes, e.g. the *Applied Science and Technology Index*).

If you're writing about a technology that is sold to consumers, professionals, or industries, the manufacturer's public relations staff can usually provide literature at almost any depth of technicality and arrange interviews; college and government public relations people are also helpful.

You will almost always have to conduct interviews for science articles, because you will eventually run into something that is never explained in laymen's terms, and also because the popular science article, like any other kind of article, needs people to give it vivacity. Even an article that is supposed to be quite technical gains something from showing people who are working at science. I either write to request an interview, including in my letter a synopsis of the kinds of questions I'll want answered, and a stamped return envelope, or I'll call to ask for a later appointment. And I almost always do my interviews by telephone—first, because my interview subjects are usually spread across the country; and second, because unless the article is a profile, in-person interviews waste more time and wander off-course more often.

What is most important is to be clear at all times, and check your writing for ambiguities, inaccuracies, and insufficiently qualified statements. You don't have to get a physics degree to write about photon-induced X-ray emission, but you do have to be an expert at the level your article is written, so that you don't mislead your readers. One of the bonuses about that expertise is that it will increase, and soon it will illuminate virtually everything you learn.

66

OUTLINES THAT SELL BOOKS

By Kenn Oberrecht

UNLESS you're new to the writing business, you probably know that publishers today offer book contracts on the basis of outlines and sample chapters. What might surprise you, however, is the possibility of getting contracts via outlines alone—sans samples. Of the eleven contracts offered me in eight years, seven were based solely on outlines.

The formula I use for writing salable outlines grew mainly out of trial and error and from no small amount of advice from editors, publishers, and others in the book business. If you're where I was a few years ago—on the brink of book publication—perhaps my methods will save you some time and frustration. There are few hard-and-fast rules for outlining, so take what I offer simply as the way one writer outlines and sells his books. The techniques work for me and might put you on the right track.

Page one

Page one is the most important part of my outlines, because this is where I hook or lose editors. It enables them to evaluate my proposal at a glance.

Page one is basically an outline of the outline. After typing my name, address, and phone number in the top left corner, I drop down several spaces and list the main elements of my proposed book. Headings for this list include *Working Title, Alternative Titles, Manuscript Length, Divisions, Completion Time,* and *Illustrations.* Let's examine each.

Titles. As a sales tool, the title is as important as dust-jacket design and paramount to everything else in the book. Spend some time thinking seriously about your title. Jot down the elements of your subject in as few words as possible. Then rearrange these into as many titles as you can think of. List published books in your subject area, both to avoid duplication and to improve on those titles.

Pick your best for a working title, then choose three to twelve others as alternatives, and keep your original list on file.

Manuscript length. If your subject has been written about before, or if you're writing a particular type of book (self-help, how-to, cookbook, biography, etc.), become familiar with related published books, and plan yours to be similar in length to the most successful. It is equally important to be aware of any publisher's current offerings. If a publisher is putting out books of one size, don't jeopardize your chances by offering something considerably longer or shorter.

My first sale was an angling book. Before submitting my outline, I studied other angling books and found that most ranged from 60,000 to 90,000 words. Concurrently, I examined the offerings of several publishers of fishing books and picked my primary target: a house that consistently published books of about 80,000 words. I proposed a book of 75,000 to 85,000 words.

Divisions. Most books are divided into chapters; some are further organized by grouping several related chapters into sections or parts. Your subject will dictate the best arrangement and suitable divisions.

Completion time. Only you can determine how long it will take to write your book, but be careful here, and allow yourself sufficient leeway. If you're an expert on your subject, have files full of supporting material, and can work full time on the project, you might be able to finish your book in a month. Then I would say you could give yourself a three-month deadline, but make it six for safety's sake.

If, on the other hand, you're faced with considerable research and can only work twenty hours a week, you might need six months or more. Add the fudge factor, and agree to deliver in twelve months.

Illustrations. If your book needs illustrations, handle them as you would the text. Find out what the competition is doing, determine what your target publishers want, and make your proposal along those lines. When doing my first book, I found that similar books had from 100 to 150 illustrations, usually black-and-white photographs. In my outline, I proposed 125 photographs.

Text of outline

Subdivisions of this main portion of the outline are grouped under several headings: *Project Description, Style, Length, Markets and Sales Potential, Competing Volumes,* and *Author's Qualifications.*

Project description. This section is next in importance to the page-one summary because, in two or three pages, you distill the essence of the proposed book. The writing must be tight and lively. Be positive and enthusiastic and try to convince the editor that your book will be the best ever written on the subject.

The soundest advice I can give you is to study blurbs on the other books in your subject area. What the blurb writer is trying to do to a potential reader is precisely what you're trying to do to an editor: sell a book.

Style. Each of us has his own style, but most of us work with several styles, adapting them to various subjects and audiences. If you're proposing a textbook, for instance, use an academic style suitable to the field. Psychology books differ in style from history books as much as thrillers differ from romance novels. Further, books on cooking, child rearing, gardening, home improvement, wine, travel, snakes, canoeing, and kazoo playing all differ stylistically, yet they share some similarities.

Keep in mind that popular nonfiction is normally written in an informal, conversational style. It should be grammatically correct, but friendly. Your proposal should clearly demonstrate your ability to write in the style appropriate for the book.

Two paragraphs covered the subject of style in my proposal for a book on the writing craft:

Although *Writing For Real* should prove suitable as a college textbook or supplementary text and will appeal as a popular how-to manual to writers and would-be writers everywhere, it will be neither a stuffy academic tome, nor a formula book written in the too-cute, gee-whiz style favored by some authors these days. Simply, the book will be carefully written and meticulously organized for easy reference.

The subject will be approached seriously and studiously, but not without colorful anecdotes and appropriate humor. Throughout, the purpose will be to inform and motivate the reader, and every effort will be made to entertain him as well.

Length. Mainly, this section deals with the finished book. It's important to envision your book as you will see it on a bookstore shelf. The editor will do so, too.

Take a closer look at some of the books you have already examined in your subject area. Keep in mind that design variations, format, and the use of white space and illustrations can dramatically alter book size. But you should be able to give a reasonable estimate of length and format. Of course, the final decision will be the publisher's.

Markets and sales potential. Although publishers employ people who know more about marketing and sales than the average author does, don't be afraid to address this subject. Your ideas may call the editor's attention to sales possibilities he might otherwise overlook.

Suggest special-interest groups that you think will find your book valuable. Mention similar books that have been marketed successfully by direct mail. If your book seems a natural for one or more book clubs, name them. If you know that a similar book sold 60,000 copies in hardcover, was picked up by two book clubs, serialized in a major periodical, recently sold to a paperback publisher, and you're confident yours will be a better treatment, you can talk specifically, as I did in one of my proposals: "It's not unreasonable to expect hardcover sales to exceed 50,000 copies."

Competing volumes. Make at least one visit to your local library to check the *Subject Guide to Books in Print.* Then, armed with a list of those books most closely related to yours, read, evaluate, and briefly report on as many as possible in your proposal.

Be specific and concise. If you refer to a half-dozen or so books, summarize each in a sentence or two; then demonstrate how yours will excel or improve on them.

If there are no competing volumes, say so. Then explain why your book should be published to fill the obvious void. If you can offer examples of magazine articles on your subject and supporting opinions of well-known experts, all the better.

One of my fishing books was the first in its field. Anticipating criticism of over-specialization, I showed that my subject was as old as fishing itself, that numerous articles had been written about it, and I quoted seven well-known fishing writers. That list of quotations ended up on the back of the dust jacket and was used extensively in promotion and reviews. I'm sure those expert opinions were largely responsible for the contract offer.

Author's qualifications. Here's where you toot your own horn, but with all due modesty. When you're trying to sell a book, your best qualifications are previous books you've had published. But if you're peddling your first book, as all of us once had to, then you'll have to offer other credentials, such as magazine articles you've written, especially those related to your book's subject.

Whether or not you have published anything, be sure to discuss any applicable experience. If you're proposing a book on archery and won the National Field Archery Association Championship three years in a row, that could mean more than previous book sales. Cooking experience might count for more than writing experience in a cookbook proposal.

Everybody is an expert on something, and that expertise can go a long way toward convincing a publisher to offer a book contract.

Contents

Some writers include a table of contents in their outlines; some don't. On the assumption that no editor is going to object to its inclusion, but that some might frown on its omission, I always include one. I also try to outline each chapter in a short paragraph or statement of chapter topics. For example, one chapter of a photography book I currently have in outline form is described this way:

Chapter 20. Communicating With Photographs.
Emphasizes the important communicative aspects of editorial photography and gathers previously discussed principles into a cohesive philosophy. Further convinces the reader of the crucial role photography plays in modern journalism and stresses the ever-present need for effective photographs by magazine and book publishers.

Although my table of contents appears at the end of an outline, this is one of the first sections I start working on. When the project is organized into a workable list of chapters, I know I'm ready to write the outline and send it off to publishers.

Sample chapters

You might need to prepare a sample chapter or two, but that can wait. My feeling is that an editor who has no interest in my idea, or has something similar pending, isn't going to bother reading samples. So why waste money on extra photocopying and postage? And if the idea proves unsalable, preparation of sample chapters will have been a waste of time.

On the other hand, if my proposal sparks interest from the editor, he can always ask for samples. Better yet, he might offer a contract solely on the basis of my outline.

One question I've deliberately left unanswered until now is outline length. I've had good luck with outlines of 10 to 15 double-spaced pages. There's really no set rule for length, other than to make your outline only as long as it must be to cover the proposal and get an editor interested.

If you spend some time on your outline and put your best writing efforts into it, you might soon be doing the most important writing of all: putting your signature on your first book contract.

67

WRITING THE OP-ED ARTICLE

By George W. Earley

Opinions. We all have them, but the difference between yours and mine may well be that I get paid for putting some of mine on paper.

If you live in or near a major city, you've probably seen the market I'm hitting: the newspaper op-ed page.

So-called because its articles appear on the page *op*posite the *edi*torial page, the op-ed page is an ideal market for the beginning writer. But like any other market, it demands that the writer become familiar with editors' needs and requirements for submission.

For the beginning writer, local issues are the best ones to tackle first. Examples of local-interest items can be readily found by reviewing your paper's op-ed page. During one recent two-week period, my local paper, *The Hartford Courant,* carried a mix of serious pieces—abortion, drugs in schools, and state educational reform—and reminiscences—Grandpa vs. the dandelions, Sunday walks in the park, and the Governor's Foot Guard Band. All topics are suited to beginning local writers.

With that as preface, and bearing in mind that the market listing following this article covers specific needs and preferences of a number of papers, let's look at some general requirements.

First, know your market. Make a close study of several dozen local-issue op-ed articles your paper has run. Note the topics covered, the way the articles are structured, and their length. Op-ed pieces generally average about 750 words—a few are shorter and fewer yet are markedly longer. That's tight writing: You'll have to cut and cut and cut again when you first begin doing op-ed pieces. (And when you do get into print, reviewing the published piece against your original manuscript will help you edit your next article.)

Once you feel sufficiently familiar with your target market to be able to write for it, find a topic that's of strong interest to you. The op-ed page is an *opinion* page; if you aren't strongly interested in your topic, it's going to show in your writing and you'll swiftly get a rejection slip.

As your study of them should reveal, op-ed articles generally follow a fairly straightforward three-part format. They open with a statement of opinion, usually on a topical issue, move on to arguments for and against the issue under discussion, and then close with a summing up of the points covered and a restatement of the writer's opinion. You will find variants among different papers; careful study should enable you to tailor this general pattern to your target market.

You don't need formal credentials in your topic . . . but you must have your facts straight! Nothing will kill your reputation as a writer faster than an error-ridden article. Your library can help you get the facts and figures needed to back up an opinion; letters or phone calls to local experts can also elicit useful information and often some good quotes.

With the article done, submission is the next step. Is a query letter needed? Not really. After all, why write a 400-word query letter about a 750-word article? Most papers (see the market listing for exceptions) accept unsolicited manuscripts. However, after you have made two or three sales to your local editor, you might want to ask him if you could discuss new ideas on the phone. I found it useful on several occasions to call my editor and briefly outline an article idea. The go-ahead I received was no guarantee of a sale, but at least I knew that my editor was interested and that no one else had approached him with a similar idea. And cultivating an editor in this way has another advantage. There were times when I sent in an article that was almost salable. Because my editor knew me, I received not a rejection slip, but a letter with comments and suggestions that enabled me to do a salable rewrite. Editors *are* approachable and I have found mine to be very helpful.

After you have developed your skills on local issues for your hometown paper—and especially if you have expertise or special knowledge that would lend itself to pieces submitted outside your local area—you might want to try out-of-town markets. You'll need to research those markets as you did your local ones; your local library, or that of a nearby college, should be able to provide you with a useful sampling of major city newspapers.

Every op-ed submission must be accompanied by a cover letter in which you briefly describe your piece, and indicate any special qualifications you have for writing it. You should also enclose self-addressed, stamped envelopes with all submissions. No SASE, no reply. But keep in mind that many editors will accept photocopied submissions. Just be sure to indicate in your cover letter that the manuscript you're submitting is a Xerox, and that the editor need not return it if he cannot use it. To learn the fate of your article, ask the editor to return a self-addressed postcard on which you've typed the name of your article and the paper to which you sent it. I've been using this submission method for some time now, and find that it works quite well.

One more thing about submissions: Always include your social security number and a daytime telephone number. Both should go on the first page of your manuscript, right below your name and address. Why? Your phone number on your manuscript lets an editor call you to clarify a point or two in an otherwise acceptable manuscript. You could lose a sale if an editor couldn't get in touch with you quickly.

How much will you be paid? Payments range from $25 to $150; the average is about $50, although some papers offer only a flat rate with no increase for subsequent sales. (*The Washington Post* does pay up to $500, but that is for a major [2,500-word] opinion piece.) When a paper lists a payment range of, say, $25 to $75, a first sale will usually bring the lower figure, but you should begin to get more if you continue to sell to that market.

A few other points in closing. Pay attention to those market listings. They're drawn directly from information supplied by the editors of those papers. Don't ignore taboos or seasonal lead times. To do so marks you as less than professional in your approach.

You'll also find that researching an op-ed piece will turn up more data than you can use when you write it. Save everything! Keep a separate file folder for each piece you write, whether it sells or not. Add to those folders any later information you find on your topics. (Also include your submitted manuscript and tear sheets of published pieces.) In time, you may accumulate enough material to do a longer opinion piece for a higher-paying magazine market.

Even rejection can be surmounted. When my op-ed piece on state lotteries was rejected by newspapers in both Connecticut and New York, I resubmitted it—adding a sidebar specific to the Connecticut lottery—to the *Connecticut Weekly* section of the Sunday *New York Times.* They bought it.

Opinions. Everybody has them. I get paid for some of mine, and you can, too!

For market list see page 649.

68

THE PERFECT INTERVIEW

By Joni Winn

I HAVE to know how to ask questions: It's my job. I'm a writer and a talk show host who has been interviewing people for a long time. And I want to tell you how to do it.

Setting up the interview

Make a list of top experts, and I mean *top*. You'll be surprised who will consent to an interview. Remember authors want book publicity, merchants want store publicity, and celebrities want any kind of publicity. Call professors, politicians and organizations whose members have expertise in a particular field.

Begin by explaining what you're doing ("I'm writing on spec for *Redbook* . . ."), what you're after ("I want to convince women that breast self-examination can really save their lives . . ."). Then let your expert ask any questions that will put his mind at ease.

After you agree on an interview time, ask your expert for any funny or exciting anecdotes, dramatic stories, or whatever's appropriate for your article. He may say no, and you should assure him that this is quite all right. But he will continue to ponder, and by the time you meet and ask your first question, he may have recalled several entertaining incidents that will enrich your article.

Many sources are inaccessible except by phone; others prefer a face-to-face meeting. Be willing to accommodate yourself to their preferences. Even when my experts are nearby, I like to use the telephone. Busy experts often appreciate the ease and speed of these interviews, too.

There are exceptions: When I need to describe my source—for a celebrity profile, for example; or when I think I can get better quotes in person (less often than you'd think). When I interviewed Mel Blanc, the voice of Bugs Bunny, Porky Pig, and dozens of other cartoon favorites, it was vital to see him in action. How else would I have known that he actually takes on the *appearance* of each character, every time he does its voice? But such occasions are rare.

The phone saves me time, and because of its anonymity and spontaneity ("How about if I ask you a few questions right now?"), sometimes a source opens up more readily and is less nervous than at a face-to-face appointment.

If your contact agrees to talk for ten minutes, respect that time limitation. You can always say, "I know our time is up, but you're so good in an interview, I wonder if I could ask you two more things." Or, "May I call you back when you have more time?" If the expert feels you will honor his time limits, he just might let you have another crack at it.

Compiling your questions

Many of your questions will come from your outline of the article. If you know enough about the subject to write the piece, you know enough to rough out its general objectives. Quotes from experts will "beef up" your work, adding sparkle and credibility to your writing. Be receptive to change, but let your organized outline lead the way.

Then make a list of pointed questions. Not, "So what's it like to grow asparagus?" or "How does it feel to be married to a Senator?" but questions you have taken time to word in the most provocative way possible. You want your expert to be excited; you want the response to be, "That's an excellent question."

Now put your list through this test:

1. Do my questions address what my readers want to know?

2. Are my questions short enough to be understood easily?

3. What are the three most important points in this article? Should I get quotes on all of them?

4. Am I being careful not to gloss over controversy, just to avoid offending?

5. Have I probed for solutions as well as for problems?

6. Have I covered all the pros and cons?

7. Will the questions produce quotes that illuminate and teach?

8. Have I given the expert an opportunity to offer warnings, tips, suggestions to the reader?

9. What can this mean financially/emotionally/physically/socially/spiritually to my reader?

10. Am I getting the personal side and asking for feelings as well as for facts?

11. Have I asked the interviewee for other sources and referrals: people, books, etc.?

12. Will these questions elicit answers that might be suitable for another publication? If a women's magazine won't buy a piece on sibling rivalry, perhaps it can be rewritten, with unused quotes, for sale to a teen or child-rearing magazine.

13. Have I covered *Who, What, When, Where, Why,* and *How?*

14. Have I covered the past, present, and future?

15. Have I eliminated all the questions that can be answered with a simple "yes" or "no"? When I interviewed actor Jack Palance, who is noted for being difficult in interviews, he initially gave monosyllabic answers. Only after I began rewording my questions to make this impossible, did he give me some good quotes.

16. Did I ask my source how and why he entered this field?

17. Can he rebut other remarks I am likely to hear? For example, in my *Saturday Evening Post* article about high-IQ babies, I asked a supporter of the program to respond to charges of pushing children too fast. I hadn't yet spoken with critics who oppose such ideas, but I knew I would and I knew that this would be one of their arguments. Anticipate the opposing side, so that when you write the article, you can structure the "debate."

18. Did I check for correct name spelling, title, phone number, and address, and the precise name of his specialty or discipline so I won't have to call him back?

In conducting an interview, I like to use a tape recorder and take notes. When I use a tape recorder, I always worry that the tape may somehow get erased or never get recorded in the first place. On the other hand, handwritten notes taken without taped proof are hard to verify if your source accuses you of misquoting him. More important than the writer's peace of mind, however, is the source's. Making your interviewee comfortable is a top priority.

Some frequently interviewed experts say it's disconcerting to watch a reporter scribbling madly as they speak. They prefer the eye contact and relaxed pace a recorder affords. Yet others feel uneasy knowing their every word is preserved on a piece of tape that might someday become "Exhibit A." When a recorder is nearby, they measure their responses so carefully that their quotes sound—and are—totally unnatural. Also, be prepared for the occasional overcautious victim of a previous blistering exposé, who even makes her *own* tape recording of the interview.

Ask your expert if he has any objections to the tape or note method, and be flexible. Then, whether you take notes or use a tape recorder, be as discreet and unobtrusive as possible.

Some people have a bit of the bartender in them and find they can scarcely board a bus or enter an elevator without having five people pour out their life stories to them. But not everyone instills such immediate trust and confidence. Yet the talent of putting others at ease is essential for those rare interviews with reclusive types, who save their gems for one big, blockbusting story.

It takes more than smiling and warmth. It involves honesty, genuine interest, an air of integrity, consideration for your source as a person of value and worth. You must establish a common ground ("We both want the public to know about government spending. . . .") and make it clear that you're in this to educate, not to scandalize or hurt, that you're seeking truth, not exclamation points.

If your source is a conservative member of the megabucks crowd, you may have a hard time getting him to open up if you dress in jeans and look like a holdover from the Sixties. And if your expert is a radical who mistrusts anybody in pinstripes, leave yours in the closet.

Above all, listen. Whenever possible let questions come from the expert's answers. Come back to your list only when you have explored each answer sufficiently. You waste everybody's time if you try to show off your own expertise. Listen not only for content but for style.

And don't be rigid about sticking to your outline. That refugee who you're sure will praise America just may have a surprise or two for you about lack of family ties, pressure to succeed, unfamiliar food, city traffic, and some other negative comments. Or, the mother of twins who you thought would give tips on "how to find twice as much time, etc." might unexpectedly pour out her heart, and you'll end up with a psychological picture of the unusually (close or closed?) relationships between twins, and how they sometimes shut others out of their own private worlds.

As you listen, keep in mind that many of the quotes will have to be paraphrased for the article, simply because you can probably put them better yourself and then just attribute them to your source. Therefore, as you interview, dig especially deep for the punchy phrases and colorful colloquialisms that cannot be improved by paraphrasing.

"How do you mean?", "Really?", "Can you explain?" and "How so?" are good questions to insert after an answer. Often your very best quotes will be in response to your request for amplification.

Phrase questions in a way that flatters your expert. Instead of "Even though you didn't go to the Olympics," say, "I know you're considered one of the world's best skaters. What would you advise a young person . . ." Or "In your many years of experience," not "As someone who has retired from politics. . . ."

When your expert *feels* like an expert, you'll be more likely to get strong, authoritative quotes instead of weak responses, with hedgings, and qualifiers, such as "possibly," "as far as I know," or "but that's only my opinion."

Any zingers or accusations must be worded carefully so as to keep the stream of information flowing. If your source feels he's being exploited or browbeaten, he'll withdraw in a hurry. Sometimes you can best exploit controversy by saying, "Mind if I play the devil's advocate for a moment?"

Get more quotes than you need and use only the best ones. You should use them as seasoning, not the main course.

If you haven't done much interviewing—and even if you have—take a journalism course that forces you to practice. You can also interview friends and ask them to evaluate you afterward. Were they hoping you'd probe deeper just as you darted off to another topic? Did you keep drilling long after you'd pumped all the oil out of the well? Did you make the interview fun? Did you seem confident and relaxed? Did you allow the interviewee to finish his sentences rather than interrupting and leading him along? Did you discover anything you didn't know? If not, chances are your reader won't either.

It's always good to end an interview by asking your source if she has anything else to add. Ask if you may get in touch with her again for further information. Think ahead: Say, "Perhaps you'll allow me to interview you again sometime, for another article."

It is common courtesy to send a thank you note and a copy of the printed article. But do not feel pressured to let your expert proofread the piece *before* it's published. He'll be sure to find what he thinks is a snappier way to put what he told you or a statement he'd rather retract, and before you know it, your article will be cut into worthless ribbons. Even if the changes are minor, you are burdened with doing a useless rewrite.

File your notes and tapes. You may need them for future articles or proof of accuracy. And always write the article as soon after the interview as possible, while quotes and ideas are still fresh.

Now. Time to get started on those questions.

69

ARTICLE OUTLINES BRING SALES

By William E. Miles

"Put it before them briefly so they will read it, clearly so they will appreciate it, picturesquely so they will remember it and, above all, accurately so they will be guided by its light."

Give Joseph Pulitzer a prize for this nearly century-old advice to reporters! Although the publisher of the New York *World* was referring to newspaper stories, his remarks are just as applicable today to magazine article outlines. Brevity, clarity, color, accuracy—that's the gift-wrapping of the package you are inviting an editor to open when you submit an outline of a subject you hope will spark his interest in your article.

An outline should be kept as short as possible, preferably one page single-spaced. Sometimes, of course, the subject demands more detailed explanation—but try not to let it exceed two pages. Within this framework, fill it with enough colorful facts and figures to catch the editor's eye and indicate the authenticity of the material.

Typed on a separate page or pages, the outline should be accompanied by a brief covering letter and sufficient return postage. A sample covering letter might read like this: "Would you be interested in taking a speculative look at a 2,000-word article on the order of the attached outline? My articles have been published in . . ." (naming some of the magazines you have sold to or listing whatever other qualifications you may have). Then, paper-clipped to the covering letter, the outline itself. For example:

PRANKS FOR THE MEMORY

Practical jokes are probably so-called because they are practically never a joke to the victim—who often winds up on something funny as a crutch. Even Mark Twain, an inveterate practical joker much of his life, confessed in his later years that he "held the practical joker in limitless contempt."

The late Bennett Cerf, another humorist who held practical jokers "in low esteem," once waxed particularly indignant over the dirty trick perpetrated on a Chicago bridegroom. After passing out at a bachelor party, he awakened to find his right arm in a cast. His fun-loving friends told him he had broken it in a brandy-inspired brawl—forcing him to spend his entire honeymoon with a perfectly good arm in a painfully tight cast.

Such practical jokers, according to Cerf, are "under no circumstances to be confused with humorists." But American history, dating back to pre-Revolutionary War days, is filled with hundreds of other examples of more harmless exercises in hilarity that don't deserve the harshness of his critical verdict.

One of the earliest of these was conceived by General Israel Putnam, a hero of the French and Indian War, after being challenged to a duel by a British army officer. Putnam selected as his choice of weapons two powder kegs into which he bored holes and inserted slow fuses. When the fuses burned down to an inch of the kegs, the British officer beat a hasty retreat—from barrels filled with onions!

But some practical jokes turn out to be really practical—as in the case of a "green" engineer at the General Electric plant who was assigned by old-timers as a prank the "impossible" job of frosting light bulbs on the inside. Marvin Pipkin not only found a way but, at the same time, devised a method of strengthening the bulbs so they would last much longer—cutting the cost to consumers in half!

An article of mine, based on this outline, appeared in *Elks Magazine*.

If this makes the outline approach to article sales sound easy, it isn't. An outline is only the bare bones of an article and no skeleton key guaranteed to unlock all editorial doors. For every idea that clicks, you may receive a dozen or more rejections. And sometimes the article itself is rejected after the outline has received a speculative O.K. For one reason or another, the article may just not live up to its billing.

But whether it does or not, outlines are not only attention-getters, but time-savers. A complete article can take a month or so to research and write and another month or so languishing in editorial offices awaiting a decison. An outline, on the other hand, requires only cursory research—enough to establish an intriguing lead and some supporting information. Only after the "go-ahead" (if you get it) do you need to start researching the subject in depth.

Editors also answer queries far more rapidly than they return articles—so even a rejection has its bright side. If the query is turned down, you've saved yourself unnecessary work in more ways than one. When outlines are returned, as they usually are, there's no retyping involved (except for another covering letter), if you decide to try elsewhere.

Another important aspect of an outline is that an editor, who likes the general idea, may have some suggestions of his own as to how he'd like it handled. An article I sold to *The Lion* is a good example of this. My original idea was to take a swipe at juries because of the way they were influenced by clever lawyers (and sometimes their own ignorance) into returning strange, far-out verdicts. I had no solutions to the problems in mind when I submitted the following outline to the editor:

THE TROUBLE WITH JURIES

FBI statistics show that 90 out of every 100 murderers are arrested, 50 receive some sort of punishment, and two are sentenced to death. This means that almost half of all accused killers are acquitted after their mandatory trials by jury in cases of first degree murder—presumably the guilty as well as the innocent.

This assumption was borne out by an investigation of the jury system in Pennsylvania which disclosed some juries had reached their verdicts by drawing straws or flipping coins. Other jurors were found to have rushed through their deliberations in order to get to a dance or a lodge meeting on time.

Although Thomas Jefferson described juries as "the best of all safeguards for the person, the property and the reputation of every individual," many legal experts regard them as outmoded relics in this modern age. Trial by jury stems from trial by oath in which the accused, swearing to his innocence, was supported by twelve "oath-helpers," or compurgators, who attested to their belief in his statements. This "jury of peers" was intimately acquainted with the defendant and the circumstances of the alleged crime. But in our day, as Dr. Joseph Catton points out, an attempt is made to select persons who know *nothing* about the offense. "There are those who believe," he adds wryly, "that today's jurors know nothing about anything."

Other criminologists contend that a modern jury is generally made up of persons unfamiliar with the law who often miss the significance of technical rulings by the judge. Even in cases where court rulings are simple and understandable, the jury sometimes ignores them. There is one actual case on record in which members of the jury, disregarding the evidence and the judge's charge, all knelt in prayer—and came up with a verdict!

The editor replied: "I'd be happy to consider your article 'The Trouble with Juries' with one important condition. I'd like to see the piece conclude with some constructive recommendations from authorities on how the jury system could be improved and/or replaced by better systems."

Further research incorporated his suggestions into the article whose whole thrust was changed, including the lead, when it appeared in *The Lion* under the new title, "Of Juries and Judgments."

The lead (aside from the idea) is probably the most important part of an outline, because it's the first thing to attract an editor's eye. One good means of accomplishing this is to tie it to a particular city or state even though the actual subject matter may range far afield. Here's an outline with just such a lead that resulted in a sale to the *Chicago Tribune Sunday* Magazine:

Chicago's long history of accomplishments includes the honor of being the first city to introduce what some engineering experts have called one of the ten most complex and ingenious inventions of the past hundred years. Back in 1893 it put the "zip" in the zipper when a sample of the original slide fastener was placed on display at Chicago's Columbian Exposition for use by the Fair's hootchie-kootchie dancer, Little Egypt, as a rapid skirt-release.

But it was the zipper, not the stripper, that caught the eye of a visitor to the Fair—Colonel Louis Walker of Meadville, Pa.—and he hired the inventor, Whitcomb L. Judson, to improve his original patent on a "locker or unlocker for automatically engaging or disengaging an entire series of clasps by a single continuous movement."

After years of experimentation, the device was finally perfected in 1913 and, four years later, a Brooklyn tailor made the fastener famous by attaching it to money belts which he sold to sailors at the Brooklyn Navy Yard. The Navy itself was soon using the fastener on flying suits. And during the depression, a dress company tried out the novelty as a sales booster—taking the industry by storm. Soon the zipper's long story of "ups and downs" was over. Its slide to success had begun!

Leads come in all shapes and sizes and there are dozens of other ways of writing that all-important first paragraph whose purpose is to sell a particular editor on a particular idea. For instance, the "striking statement" lead:

Lightning, the silent partner of thunder, has frightened more people—and killed fewer—than any other common danger. In fact, your chances of being killed by a lightning bolt are one in a million.

The editor liked this outline lead well enough to keep it intact when my article "Striking Down Lightning Myths" was published in *Wheels Afield*.

Another editorial eye-opener is the "news peg" approach—tying the article to a current happening or upcoming event—or the "anniversary angle" like this outline lead for my article "Meters By The Mile" that appeared in *The Rotarian* more years ago than I care to remember:

Ten years ago last October 1,500 parking meters went on trial in New York City. They were immediately found guilty by protesting motorists who charged that they interfered with their constitutional privileges of life, liberty and the pursuit of free parking space . . .

But why go on? The point is that, varied as they were, all of these leads had one thing in common—an ability to grab the editor's attention and keep him reading. From these examples, you can see that I like to write a lead (and sometimes an ending) that will be used more or less "as is" in the finished article if the outline receives an editorial O.K.

This gives the editor a good idea of what to expect—not only of the subject but of the style in which it will be written. For an outline must persuade the editor that you not only have a good idea, but possess the ability to handle it well.

70

PASSION AND THE MODERN POET

By Dick Allen

I KEEP coming back to passion. It is something all of us have felt, of course, but the severe and sustained passion of the poet is unique. The poet has a passionate need to create lines that seem to stand still but actually tremble and hover a lifetime in the mind: hummingbird lines.

"Batter my heart, three person'd God . . ." (John Donne). . . . "The seal's wide spindrift gaze toward paradise" (Hart Crane). . . . "Downward to darkness, on extended wings" (Wallace Stevens). . . . "You do not do, you do not do" (Sylvia Plath)—these and hundreds of other lines are in my mind daily. It is against them and the poems which sustain them that I measure my own work and the work of my contemporaries.

I do not mean to say that writing poetry is solely a matter of creating memorable lines, "touchstones" as Matthew Arnold called them. Rather, I am saying that the intensity of feeling they contain, their balance and art, is something toward which poets daily strive. The journey of the poet to a place and time when he may have a chance to write great poetry derives in large part from a passion of remembering. That is why the first test of a poet lies in the extent of his love for poetry itself. Virtually every publishing poet I know is a compulsive reader of past and present poetry. There is no quicker way to sort out hobbyist poets from poets who seem to have a chance at doing important work than by asking what they are reading.

The poet who answers that he regularly reads Shakespeare's sonnets, and such poets as Dante, Goethe, Pushkin, Keats, Whitman, Rilke, Akmatova, Montale, and Robert Lowell reveals that he honors and learns from the continuing tradition of poetry. The poet who reads his contemporaries, who subscribes to (or reads in libraries) such magazines as *Poetry, The Hudson Review, The New Yorker, The Atlantic*

Monthly, The American Poetry Review, and many large and small literary periodicals does likewise.

Let's assume that a poet sets out to read, say, the works of Robert Hayden and Adrienne Rich, Richard Howard's translation of Baudelaire's *Les Fleurs du Mal* and Anthony Hecht's *The Hard Hours.* What then?

The dominant mode of twentieth-century poetry is the short personal lyric, usually written in free verse. It is this mode that most college poetry workshops teach and that magazines most frequently publish. Learning to write a passable poem in this mode is not enormously difficult. Technique can be taught to any relatively talented poet. With technique, the poet can write and probably publish the standard contemporary American poem: a lyric that is essentially good, interesting personal journalism, written more or less rhythmically.

I don't mean to disparage such poetry. Just as writing the well-rhymed sonnet was a criterion for measuring a poet's ability in past generations, writing the intense and crafted personal lyric has become the late twentieth-century criterion. As in previous times, poets usually begin with trying to master a way of expression that seems most acceptable to the age in which they live.

The key technical principles for twentieth-century writers, poets included, are the two well-known admonitions of "Show, don't tell" and "Be specific." A great deal of the tension in modern verse derives from the poet's holding back what he or she would otherwise say outright, holding it back so that it will come into the reader's mind as a painting does, as does music, the thought or feeling seeming to have jumped distance and be born from the reader's own sensibility rather than impressed upon it.

"Be specific" forces the beginning poet really to observe the world around him or her and to search for precise words to describe what is seen. A passion for observation is also a passion for knowing and rendering life intensely. In fact, much of contemporary poetry has assumed—consciously or unconsciously on the part of poets—a duty to keep words alive and thus the ideas and feelings they evoke.

With "Show, don't tell" and "Be specific" in mind, the poet unlocks his or her experience. These admonitions intensify the poet's daily doings, meditations, conversations, and memories. What would otherwise be a dull walk on a gray day may turn into one in which the poet

361

notices a small lightning bolt-shaped crack in a neighbor's kitchen windowpane, or how a haphazard arrangement of crocuses and tulips scattered on a suburban lawn makes it look as if the flower clumps were shot there by random cannon bursts. If the neighbor has been going through troubles recently, such imagery may connote it. To think vaguely of a past, lost love but then focus on the pattern of the towel wrapped around her as she stepped from a steamy shower makes that love seem alive in time.

My favorite definition of poetry comes from critic Fred B. Millett's *Reading Poetry:* "Poetry is language measured and supercharged." Supercharged relates to lyric poetry's intensity, which is a matter of many elements. "Language measured" reminds us that anyone serious about writing poetry should train himself in writing in a variety of meters. Knowledge of meter gives the poet maximum freedom; some poems wish to be iambic, or trochaic, or in lines of few or many feet. If a poet can write only free verse, that poet is cut off not only from the past, but from the challenge of writing in many of poetry's greatest traditional forms and modes.

Similarly, the poet who cannot write a decent rhymed poem is not one to be trusted as solidly grounded in the art. If you balk at this, remember that a prevalent kind of rhyming in our century is "slant" or "eye" rhyme. When the poet learns that "window" can be rhymed not only with "snow" but with "threw" and even with "now" or maybe even "blue," enormous possibilities open.

Since a contemporary poem is often valued for its interest—its interesting words, experiences—beginning poets who wish to do other than rake their lives to the coals in the "confessional" manner of Sylvia Plath are sometimes helped by being reminded that the contemporary personal lyric does not have to be an exact rendering of an actual event. "I" poems are not usually literal renderings; the "I" can easily be a persona.

If a poem comes from a train ride to Cleveland but works better when set on a train ride from Montreal, so be it. If "blue chair" works better than the "orange couch" on which a poet actually sat, the fictional aspect of writing allows use of the latter when it will create an emotionally truer and richer poem.

Based on actual experience or not, a great stress of contemporary poetry is on "honesty." The "honest" personal lyric is valued because, reading it, we are reminded that no matter how formula TV shows would convince us differently, each different human life is a remarkably varied and vivid reflection on our own lives. Stereotypes and clichés are clumsy clay representations of the actual wonders and nuances to be seen and felt and heard by those who would truly know that living is more ripples than plains.

When a poet speaks of honesty, what she means is that the best lyrics contain elements that convince the reader that their feeling is not artificial. A poem must not seem to be a hiding place, or counterfeit the "proper" responses to situations with falsifying sentiment. The poet who writes only that she felt bad but resigned when she broke up with her boyfriend, yet does not show how she actually drew his picture in lipstick on her mirror and spat on it is not being honest with her readers. Her consequent poem will almost surely be hollow.

A continual lifetime involvement with reading poetry and with studying technique, as well as an open attitude toward writing poetry can take poets a long way; they cannot, however, give us much poetry that seems to matter ultimately. Good personal journalism and conversation written in free verse lyric poem form, fine descriptive vignettes—if the poet cannot do more she or he will remain at the best marvelously minor.

Everything else being equal, it is the content of the poem that causes it to change lives. In the twentieth century, a misplaced emphasis on "how a poem means" has misled too many poets into writing and teaching as if poetry were primarily a matter of aesthetics. Deep down, the best poets know it isn't, that their passionate intensity comes from a need to communicate deeply felt truths about the world or to tell stories concerning it in words, lines, images, musical throbs that simultaneously seem to hold still and vibrate.

Degrees of passion for subject material and the necessity to deal with ideas as well as feelings divide minor poets from major poets, and craftsmen from geniuses. Content crudely handled in verse has ruined hundreds of thousands of poems; yet without significant content a poet's work will be thin.

It is my conviction that contemporary poetry of the highest order— and who would strive for less?—requires a desperate need to be continually involved with the edges of experience, never to stop trying to write about the great subjects—love, religion, death, who we are, what is our purpose here, how shall we live; to have a living engagement with science and politics, and as many other matters as possible; and then to spend weeks, months, years honing individual works that laugh and shimmer, sob and stare.

71

LIGHT VERSE

By ROBERT WALLACE

A FEW YEARS ago, John Updike, heir to generations of great light verse poets (Dorothy Parker, Franklin P. Adams, Phyllis McGinley, E. B. White, Ogden Nash, Morris Bishop, Richard Armour among them) called light verse "a dying art." He added, "I write no light verse now." (It is hard to remember that Updike's first book was light verse.)

That glum conclusion was no great surprise to those who had watched the shrinking of markets to a mere handful—*The New Yorker* stopped printing light verse in the 1960's—and the dwindling of marketable forms to the clever, topical quatrains:

TAX HANG-UP

For those inclined to play
It fast and loose
Sometimes a tax loophole
Ends up a noose.

Light verse has been in the shadows for twenty years or more. It would be easy to see as its tombstone the fat anthology *The Best of Modern Humor* (Mordecai Richler, ed., Knopf, 1983), which is *entirely prose*. 542 big pages, going back to 1922, and not a shred, not even a single line of Dorothy Parker or Ogden Nash!

But, in Mark Twain's phrase, the report of its death would be "greatly exaggerated."

As long as there is laughter and as long as there is verse, someone will always be bringing the two together. Both fill deep needs. A comic tradition that includes Chaucer, Shakespeare, Pope, and Byron isn't about to vanish. What *has* happened, however, needs understanding before we can see the way ahead clearly.

We are victims, I think, of a distinction made in 1867 by an English light verse poet, Frederick Locker-Lampson. He distinguished between "poetry"—that high, serious art—and what he called, coining the phrase, "light verse." He saw it as "another kind of poetry . . . which, in its more restricted form, has somewhat the same relation to the poetry of lofty imagination and deep feeling, that the Dresden China Shepherds and Shepherdesses of the last century bear to the sculpture of Donatello and Michael Angelo."

Though Locker-Lampson meant the term light verse as praise, this Victorian distinction has turned into a villainous Mr. Hyde, dividing poetry (seriousness) from mere light verse (humor). Joined to the Frankenstein of the twentieth-century's obsession with criticism (which essentially holds that no ordinary reader can really read a poem, novel, or play on his or her own), this distinction has been devastating. Laughter has been read out of the emotions proper for literature. Poetry, struggling under the weight of what can only be called *heavy* verse, has lost touch with the general reader. And light verse, isolated, trivialized, has fallen into the shadows. Ogden Nash doesn't even appear in the 1456 pages of that other could-be tombstone, *The Norton Anthology of Modern Poetry!*

Among the hopeful signs are three anthologies: *The Oxford Book of English Light Verse* (Kingsley Amis, ed., 1978), *The Oxford Book of American Light Verse* (William Harmon, ed., 1979), *The Penguin Book of Light Verse* (Gavin Ewart, ed., 1980). The magazine *Open Places* recently devoted a whole issue—222 pages—to humor, half of it verse. And there is *Light Year,* the annual of light verse and funny poems, which I edit. In its first three issues (totaling 626 pages) are poems by 306 poets, among them beginners as well as many of the finest writers in America: Richard Wilbur, Marge Piercy, X. J. Kennedy, Donald Hall, John Ciardi, May Swenson, Roy Blount Jr., Richard Armour—and John Updike!

And there is this most interesting straw-in-the-wind: as I write, Shel Silverstein's *A Light in the Attic* was on *The New York Times Book Review*'s hardcover best seller list for more than two-and-a-half years. That's a record. If only 10% of the "graduates" of *A Light in the Attic* can be persuaded to go on to other funny poems, there will be a very large, lively, paying audience once again. Perhaps there's gold in them thar hills.

Light verse—maybe we'd better call them *funny poems?*—is coming out of the shadows, and may well be in for a revival.

If I'm even partly right, what can a writer of funny poetry expect? What should he or she do differently, if anything? What will the funny poems of the immediate future be like? Here's some practical advice from the poet-and-editor's crystal ball:

Funny poetry will show a great variety in both subject and form, and will be more sophisticated, more honest, and—often at least—more serious. It will, in short, be more like what it really is: poetry.

1) Freed of the trivializing restrictions, it will find a range of subjects much broader than baldness, going on a diet, jogging, postal rate increases, and such foibles. It will be more topical, less moralizing, and often sillier and just plain merrier. There will be room again for things like Don Marquis's wonderful *archy & mehitabel*. It will, having the space, be peopled with more real and interesting characters. Look for poems like Katharyn Machan Aal's

HAZEL TELLS LAVERNE

last night
im cleanin out my
howard johnsons ladies room
when all of a sudden
up pops this frog
musta come from the sewer
swimmin aroun an tryin ta
climb up the sida the bowl
so i goes ta flushm down
but sohelpmegod he starts talkin
bout a golden ball
an how i can be a princess
me a princess
well my mouth drops
all the way to the floor
an he says
kiss me just kiss me
once on the nose
well i screams
ya little green pervert
an i hitsm with my mop
an has ta flush
the toilet down three times
me
a princess

2) Though epigrammatic quatrains will thrive—like Robert N. Feinstein's

THE OWL

Though I don't wish to seem too fanatical,
I consider the owl ungrammatical.
"To-whit, to-who" he sits and keens;
"To-whit, to-*whom*" is what he means.

—funny poems will often be longer, and both more varied and more daring in form. Look for more free verse, and for poems in complex forms like villanelle and sestina again. Whatever's happening in poetry will be happening in funny poetry. Visual poems, concrete poems, even funny "prose" poems like George Starbuck's

JAPANESE FISH

Have you ever eaten a luchu? It's poisonous like fugu, but it's cheaper and you cook it yourself.

You cut it into little squares as fast as possible but without touching the poison-gland. But first, you get all the thrill you can out of the fact that you're going to do it. You sit around for hours with your closest friends, drinking and telling long nostalgicky stories. You make toasts. You pick up your knives and sing a little song entitled "We who are about to dice a luchu." And then you begin.

3) It will be more sophisticated—often as corny, but probably cleverer. No doubt, sometimes, sexier. It will be less inclined to "nudge" the reader to be sure he gets the point. Titles will be less "cute," more functional, as in Michael Spence's

PROGRAMMING DOWN ON THE FARM

As all those with computers know,
Input-output is called I/O.
But farmers using these machines
See special letters on their screens.
So when they list a chicken fence
To "Egg Insurance and Expense,"
Into what file would it go?
Of course to EIE I/O.

4) It will be more honest and exact, more realistic. Puffy comic exaggeration—"[something or other] makes me tear my hair"—will vanish, as will banal (and untrue) generalities like "A man will stand for anything / Without a fight or fuss, / Except a lady or a lass / Upon a

368

crowded bus." Understatement will turn out to work better, as in Edward Willey's

Marie is bald and doesn't
give a damn. To prove it
she often spits in public
and hates to wear a hat.

I hope she changes
for the better before
she learns to talk.

5) It will often be closer to serious poetry, able to mingle the amusing with the lyrical, as in my

MYTH, COMMERCE, AND COFFEE
ON UNITED FLIGHT #622 FROM
CLEVELAND TO NORFOLK

Clouds, like bird-tracked snow,
spread to dawn-sun five miles below,

while businessmen (& poets) flow
on air streams, to and fro.

Now, of course, we know
Icarus *could* have made a go,

formed Attic Airways Co.,
expanded, advertised, and so

have carried Homer and Sappho
from Athens to Ilo

on reading tours—with, below,
clouds spread out like bird-tracked snow.

Or to mingle the amusing with the genuinely thoughtful—which is to say that it will have simply become poetry again!—as in Howard Nemerov's

POETICS

You know the old story Ann Landers tells
About the housewife in her basement doing the wash?
She's wearing her nightie, and she thinks, "Well hell,
I might's well put this in as well," and then
Being dripped on by a leaky pipe puts on
Her son's football helmet; whereupon
The meter reader happens to walk through

369

And "Lady," he gravely says, "I sure hope your team wins."

A story many times told in many ways,
The set of random accidents redeemed
By one more accident, as though chaos
Were the order that was before creation came.
That is the way things happen in the world:
A joke, a disappointment satisfied,
As we walk through doing our daily round,
Reading the meter, making things add up.

6) And one other, by no means the least consideration: funny poets may expect far more, and better paying, markets than they're used to. That's happening now.

72

THE EXPERIENCE OF THE POEM

BY ANN STANFORD

ONE may think of the ingredients of a good poem as an experience and a fresh perception of that experience. The experience need not be original or new, but the perception should be. Think of Gerard Manley Hopkins' delight in spring, a feeling old as humanity, couched in the freshest of images:

> Nothing is so beautiful as spring—
>> When weeds, in wheels, shoot long and lovely and lush;
>> Thrush's eggs look little low heavens, and thrush
> Through the echoing timber does so rinse and wring
> The ear, it strikes like lightnings to hear him sing;
>> The glassy peartree leaves and blooms, they brush
>> The descending blue; that blue is all in a rush
> With richness; the racing lambs too have fair their fling.

Hopkins' language is vital because his feeling about spring is intense and his own. He has taken the familiar ingredients of a poem about spring and made them into a new vision.

A contemporary example of a poem drawn from everyday experience is May Swenson's "Water Picture,"* which describes the reflection of objects in a pond; it begins:

> In the pond in the park
> all things are doubled:
> Long buildings hang and
> wriggle gently. Chimneys
> are bent legs bouncing
> on clouds below. A flag
> wags like a fishhook
> down there in the sky.

---

* From *To Mix with Time*. Charles Scribner's Sons. Copyright © 1963, by May Swenson.

371

The arched stone bridge
is an eye, with underlid
in the water. In its lens
dip crinkled heads with hats
that don't fall off. Dogs go by,
barking on their backs.
A baby, taken to feed the
ducks, dangles upside-down
a pink balloon for a buoy.

Seen in detail from a new angle, an ordinary experience becomes extraordinary and the substance of poetry. The fresh perception makes the old experience unique.

And the perception is conveyed through language. The words and combinations we choose must be carefully screened to see that they are not the old stereotypes through which we blind ourselves to the world. In his poems, e. e. cummings tore words apart and put the parts back into new combinations so that his language might reveal a new view of the world. Most of us will not follow his way, but we need to be sure we see what we see as it is, not as we think it is. There is a tree before you. What kind of leaves does it have? Are they alternating on the stem? Do they resemble plumes? Are they flat on the air like lily-pads in the water? Hopkins' journal frequently takes account of such phenomena:

Elm leaves:—they shine much in the sun—bright green when near from underneath but higher up they look olive: their shapelessness in the flat is from their being made . . . to be dimpled and dog's eared: their leaf-growth is in this point more rudimentary than that of oak, ash, beech, etc that the leaves lie in long rows and do not subdivide or have central knots but tooth or cog their woody twigs.

Such careful looking, such precision in visual perception, is a first step in writing poetry. If you cannot see what a tree looks like, it will be hard to tell anyone what a feeling feels like. Because in poetry we are dependent on the concrete manifestations of the world to use as symbols of our feelings and our experiences. This is especially true in lyric poetry. But apt suggestive details give credibility to narrative poems and character sketches as well. A good exercise in poetry is to record exactly what you see before you with no large statements about what is there. Simply describe it as if you are seeing it for the first time. An artist practices by carrying a sketch pad and drawing wherever he may be. In the same way, the result of the poet's sketch may not be a poem, but the practice will help develop a technique for handling a more complex subject when it does appear. Here is an example, a description of a shell done as an exercise:

Being which is the size of my palm
almost and fits the upcurled fingers
flat-cupped the thirty-four fingers
end in points set close together
like the prongs of a comb
sea-combing straining the waters
they are printed on your back
brown waves cutting light sand
waves—merging inward
lighter and lighter and closer
whirling
into the self-turned center
of yourself.

Just as there are two kinds of perception—what is seen and what is experienced—there are two kinds of possibilities for exact or innovative language. And there are chances also for trite or easy observation on both levels.

A poem will not always die of a single cliché; indeed, a common observation can even be used for a deliberate artistic purpose. Only someone who has really mastered his craft, however, should dare to use a phrase which borders on the trite. Dylan Thomas sometimes uses old phrases but remakes them by small changes, so that they emerge as live word combinations like "once below a time." But I can think of no poetic situation in which a "rippling stream" or "glassy pond" can add anything but tedium. Worse than the cliché at the literal or visual level, is the cliché at the experiential level, the large abstract concept such as:

Life, like time, moves onward.

The large concept gives the reader a stereotyped experience. Perhaps this is why some very bad poetry appeals to a number of undiscriminating readers: it repeats the stereotype of experience they have in their own minds and gives them nothing new to test it by. A good poem should jolt the reader into a new awareness of his feeling or his sensual apprehension of the world. One of the great mistakes is to make a poem too large and simple.

Poetry is an art which proceeds in a roundabout fashion. Its language is not chosen for directness of communication, for the passing on of facts, like "the plane arrives at five," or "today it is raining," although either of these facts could be a part of a poem. The truth that poetry attempts to communicate is reached by more devious means. Many of the devices thought of as being in the special province of poetry are devices of indirection: the metaphor or symbol, which involves saying one thing and meaning another; paradox, the welding of opposites into a single concept; connotations beyond the direct meaning of a word or phrase, and so on. When we think of the way things are in the world, we find that poetry is not the only area in which the immediate fact is disguised, distorted, or concealed. Poetry does this in order to reach a more complex truth. Other situations involve indirection for other reasons. Purpose determines the directness of statement. Take the guest telling his hostess he enjoyed the party. Did he really? But in saying this he is expressing some other feeling beyond the immediate situation. He may be expressing sympathy or long affection or any number of emotions rather than measuring the quality of his enjoyment of the moment. Take advertising, which often tries to pass along not so much a fact as a feeling about something. Take the art of the magician—the better the more deceiving. For the poet to speak too glibly may be to oversimplify his experience. The poet must constantly ask himself: "Is this the way it really felt? Is this the whole experience? Am I overlooking or suppressing part of it?"

As I write this, a living example has appeared before my eyes. I am looking at the tree just outside the window. If I should give you my visual experience at this moment, I should have to include a lizard that has climbed twenty feet up the trunk and is now looking at me. In my stereotyped picture of trees, birds sometimes come to rest, but not lizards. In my stereotype of the loss of a friend through death, there is sorrow, not anger. But I have felt anger at the death of a friend, and there is a lizard in this tree. The real includes these disparate elements. The poet must think of what he has really experienced. He gives certain real details, certain suggestions. The reader combines these into the experience intended by the poet, the real message of the poem, and so participates in its creation.

The poet uses three types of ingredients in his poem: at the first level is what can be immediately caught by the senses—by sight, by hearing, tasting, feeling, smelling. I call this the literal level: the poet describes what is literally there. This poem of my own is written almost entirely at this level:

THE BLACKBERRY THICKET *

I stand here in the ditch, my feet on a rock in the water,
Head-deep in a coppice of thorns,
Picking wild blackberries,
Watching the juice-dark rivulet run
Over my fingers, marking the lines and the whorls,
Remembering stains—
The blue of mulberry on the tongue
Brown fingers after walnut husking,
And the green smudge of grass—
The earnest part
Of heat and orchards and sweet springing places.
Here I am printed with the earth
Always and always the earth ground into the fingers,
And the arm scratched in thickets of spiders.
Over the marshy water the cicada rustles,
A runner snaps sharp into place.
The dry leaves are a presence,
A companion that follows up under the trees of the orchard
Repeating my footsteps. I stop to listen.
Surely not alone
I stand in this quiet in the shadow
Under a roof of bees.

The sights and sounds caught by immediate sensation are described; the memories are of the same immediate quality. Even the ending of the poem is a literal description, although the reader may find there, if he likes, connotations that go beyond the literal.

Much of modern American poetry is written at this level. If not total poems as here, at least sections of poems. Most readers of modern poetry, many editors, look for this literal quality. Here, as I said earlier, the poet must look carefully and sensitively and report exactly. Notice, next time you read a poem, how much of it contains this literal looking and what details the poet has chosen to give the appearance of reality. Even an imagined experience should have some of this literal quality.

---

* From *The Weathercock*, by Ann Stanford. Copyright © 1955, by Ann Stanford. Reprinted by permission of The Viking Press, Inc.

The next level of poetry is the metaphoric, in which one thing is compared with another. The conventional poetic devices of simile, metaphor, symbol are part of this level. Comparison often mingles with the literal. In Elizabeth Bishop's well-known poem "The Fish," * exact description is aided by comparison:

> I looked into his eyes
> which were far larger than mine
> but shallower, and yellowed,
> the irises backed and packed
> with tarnished tinfoil
> seen through the lenses
> of old scratched isinglass.

The juxtaposing of two things that are not wholly alike but that are alike in some way is one of the ways that poetry creates a new view of the world. Comparisons or analogies can be used thus as part of description, or they can make a total poem. They can be either one-way or two-way comparisons. For example, the fish's eye can be said to resemble isinglass, but isinglass does not remind one of a fish's eye. It is not always necessary or desirable that the comparisons work both ways. Another example, Shakespeare's comparison of true love to a "star to every wandering bark," is effective even though within the poem he is not also comparing a star that guides to love. He is defining love in terms of a star, but not a star in terms of love.

However, often the poet uses a two-way analogy. The doubleness of the analogy is especially effective where the whole poem is in the form of comparison. Here is a poem of mine which satirizes the work of committees.

THE COMMITTEE †
by Ann Stanford

Black and serious, they are dropping down one by one to the top of the walnut tree.
It is spring and the bare branches are right for a conversation.
The sap has not risen yet, but those branches will always be bare
Up there, crooked with ebbed life lost now, like a legal argument.
They shift a bit as they settle into place.

---

* From *Poems: North and South.* Houghton Mifflin Company. Copyright © 1955, by Elizabeth Bishop.
† © 1967 The New Yorker Magazine, Inc.

Once in a while one says something, but the answer is always the same;
The question is, too—it is all *caw* and *caw.*
Do they think they are hidden by the green leaves partway up the branches?
Do they like it up there cocking their heads in the fresh morning?
One by one, they fly off as if to other appointments.
Whatever they did, it must be done all over again.

Here, what is said about the crows can be applied to a committee, but it is also true of crows, at least the ones I have observed in my neighborhood. This, then, is a two-way analogy.

There is another level at which poets sometimes work: the level of statement. Much of Wordsworth's poetry is statement, as:

> This spiritual Love acts not nor can exist
> Without Imagination, which, in truth,
> Is but another name for absolute power
> And clearest insight, amplitude of mind,
> And Reason in her most exalted mood.

This is a hard and dangerous level for most poets. Much poetry, especially amateur poetry, constantly attempts statement without backing it up with the literal or analogic or comparative level. The poem which merely states, except in the hands of a master, falls flat because it does not prove anything to the reader. He is not drawn into the background of the statement. He is merely told. If his own experience backs up the statement, he may like the poem, but he likes it only because of his experience, not because of what the poem has done for him.

Masters of poetry, on the other hand, sometimes make one large statement and spend the rest of the poem illustrating or proving it. Hopkins does this with the statement "Nothing is so beautiful as spring—"; May Swenson does it in a more specific way in "Water Picture." William Carlos Williams in "To Waken an Old Lady" defines old age by describing a flock of birds in winter. His only reference to age at all is the first line, "Old age is." Without the first line to suggest the definition, the poem could be simply a nature description. Emily Dickinson often makes an abstract idea come to life by defining it in visual terms:

> Presentiment is that long shadow on the lawn
> Indicative that suns go down;

377

The notice to the startled grass
That darkness is about to pass.

It would be a rare poem which could exist on one of these levels—
that of literal description, that of metaphor, or that of statement—
alone. Poems usually combine these in varying proportions. There
are dangers to the poetry, besides triteness, at all levels. Flatness,
dullness, and poor selection of details menace literal description.
Metaphor is endangered by irrelevance; a metaphor which does not
contribute in tone or feeling may turn the reader away from the
poem as a whole. Statement is most dangerous, for it must be proved.

A poem which succeeds may also have a fourth level—the transcendental level, where the connotations of the poem extend on beyond the limits of the poem. But the transcendental may hardly be
striven for. We only recognize it when it shimmers in the exceptional
poem.

Meanwhile the poet works at what he can. He looks for the whole
significance of the experience. He renders it—even more, he understands it—through language built around his own view. His new seeing is what will make the experience of the poem worth telling once
more.

73

POETIC DEVICES

By William Packard

There is a good story about Walter Johnson, who had one of the most natural fast balls in the history of baseball. No one knows how "The Big Train" developed such speed on the mound, but there it was. From his first year of pitching in the majors, 1907, for Washington, Walter Johnson hurtled the ball like a flash of lightning across the plate. And as often as not, the opposing batter would be left watching empty air, as the catcher gloved the ball.

Well, the story goes that after a few seasons, almost all the opposing batters knew exactly what to expect from Walter Johnson—his famous fast ball. And even though the pitch was just as difficult to hit as ever, still, it can be a very dangerous thing for any pitcher to become that predictable. And besides, there were also some fears on the Washington bench that if he kept on hurtling only that famous fast ball over the plate, in a few more seasons Walter Johnson might burn his arm out entirely.

So, Walter Johnson set out to learn how to throw a curve ball. Now, one can just imagine the difficulty of doing this: here is a great pitcher in his mid-career in the major leagues, and he is trying to learn an entirely new pitch. One can imagine all the painful self-consciousness of the beginner, as Johnson tried to train his arm into some totally new reflexes—a new way of fingering the ball, a new arc of the elbow as he went into the wind-up, a new release of the wrist, and a completely new follow-through for the body.

But after awhile, the story goes, the curve ball became as natural for Walter Johnson as the famous fast-ball pitch, and as a consequence, Johnson became even more difficult to hit.

When Walter Johnson retired in 1927, he held the record for total strike-outs in a lifetime career (3409), and he held the record for total pitching of shut-out games in a lifetime career (110)—records which have never been equaled in baseball. And Walter Johnson is second only to the mighty Cy Young for total games won in a lifetime career.

Any artist can identify with this story about Walter Johnson. The determination to persist in one's art or craft is a characteristic of a great artist and a great athlete. But one also realizes that this practice of one's craft is almost always painstakingly difficult, and usually entails periods of extreme self-consciousness, as one trains oneself into a pattern of totally new reflexes. It is what Robert Frost called "the pleasure of taking pains."

The odd thing is that this practice and mastery of a craft is sometimes seen as an infringement on one's own natural gifts. Poets will sometimes comment that they do not want to be bothered with all that stuff about metrics and assonance and craft, because it doesn't come "naturally." Of course it doesn't come naturally, if one hasn't worked to make it natural. But once one's craft becomes second nature, it is not an infringement on one's natural gifts—if anything, it is an enlargement of them, and an enhancement and a reinforcement of one's own intuitive talents.

In almost all the other arts, an artist has to learn the techniques of his craft as a matter of course.

The painter takes delight in exploring the possibilities of his palette, and perhaps he may even move through periods which are dominated by different color tones, such as viridian or Prussian blue or ochre. He will also be concerned, as a matter of course, with various textural considerations such as brushing and pigmentation and the surface virtue of his work.

The composer who wants to write orchestra music has to begin by learning how to score in the musical notation system—and he will play with the meaning of whole notes, half notes, quarter notes, eighth notes, and the significance of such tempo designations as *lento, andante, adagio,* and *prestissimo.* He will also want to explore the different possibilities of the instruments of the orchestra, to discover the totality of tone he wants to achieve in his own work.

Even so—I have heard student poets complain that they don't want to be held back by a lot of technical considerations in the craft of poetry.

That raises a very interesting question: Why do poets seem to resist learning the practice and mastery of their own craft? Why do they protest that technique *per se* is an infringement on their own intuitive gifts, and a destructive self-consciousness that inhibits their natural and magical genius?

I think a part of the answer to these questions may lie in our own modern Romantic era of poetry, where poets as diverse as Walt Whitman and Dylan Thomas and Allen Ginsberg seem to achieve their best effects with little or no technical effort. Like Athena, the poem seems to spring full blown out of the forehead of Zeus, and that is a large part of its charm for us. Whitman pretends he is just "talking" to us, in the "Song of Myself." So does Dylan Thomas in "Fern Hill" and "Poem in October." So does Allen Ginsberg in "Howl" and "Kaddish."

But of course when we think about it, we realize it is no such thing. And we realize also, in admiration, that any poet who is so skillful in concealing his art from us may be achieving one of the highest technical feats of all.

What are the technical skills of poetry, that all poets have worked at who wanted to achieve the practice and mastery of their craft?

We could begin by saying that poetry itself is language which is used in a specific way to convey a specific effect. And the specific ways that language can be used are expressed through all of the various poetic devices. In "The ABC of Reading," Ezra Pound summarized these devices and divided them into three categories—phonopoeia (sight), melopoeia (sound), and logopoeia (voice).

SIGHT

The image is the heart and soul of poetry. In our own psychic lives, we dream in images, although there may be words superimposed onto these images. In our social communication, we indicate complete understanding of something when we say, "I get the picture"— indicating that imagistic understanding is the most basic and primal of all communications. In some languages, like Chinese and Japanese, words began as pictures, or ideograms, which embodied the image representation of what the word was indicating.

It is not accidental that our earliest record of human civilization is in the form of pure pictures—images of bison in the paleolithic caves at Altamira in Northern Spain, from the Magdalenian culture, some 16,000 years B.C. And there are other records of stone statues as pure

381

images of horses and deer and mammoths, in Czechoslovakia, from as far back as 30,000 years B.C.

Aristotle wrote in the "Poetics" that metaphor—the conjunction of one image with another image—is the soul of poetry, and is the surest sign of genius. He also said it was the one thing that could not be taught, since the genius for metaphor was unaccountable, being the ability to see similarities in dissimilar things.

Following are the principal poetic devices which use image, or the picture aspect of poetry:

image—a simple picture, a mental representation. "That which presents an intellectual and emotional complex in an instant of time." (Pound)

metaphor—a direct comparison. "A mighty fortress is our God." An equation, or an equivalence: A = B. "It is the east and Juliet is the sun."

simile—an indirect comparison, using "like" or "as." "Why, man, he doth bestride the narrow world/Like a Colossus..." "My love's like a red, red rose."

figure—an image and an idea. "Ship of state." "A sea of troubles." "This bud of love."

conceit—an extended figure, as in some metaphysical poetry of John Donne, or in the following lines of Shakespeare's Juliet:

> Sweet, good-night!
> This bud of love, by summer's ripening breath,
> May prove a beauteous flower when next we meet...

SOUND

Rhythm has its source and origin in our own bloodstream pulse. At a normal pace, the heart beats at a casual iambic beat. But when it is excited, it may trip and skip rhythm through extended anapests or hard dactyls or firm trochees. It may even pound with a relentless spondee beat.

In dance, rhythm is accented by a drumbeat, in parades, by the cadence of marching feet, and in the night air, by churchbell tolling.

These simple rhythms may be taken as figures of the other rhythms of the universe—the tidal ebb and flow, the rising and setting of the sun, the female menstrual cycles, the four seasons of the year.

Rhythm is notated as metrics, but may also be seen in such poetic devices as rhyme and assonance and alliteration. Following are the poetic devices for sound:

assonance—rhyme of vowel sounds. "O that this too too solid flesh would melt..."

alliteration—repetition of consonants. "We might have met them dareful, beard to beard, And beat them backward home."

rhyme—the sense of resonance that comes when a word echoes the sound of another word—in end rhyme, internal rhyme, perfect rhyme, slant or imperfect rhyme, masculine rhyme, or feminine rhyme.

metrics—the simplest notation system for scansion of rhythm. The most commonly used metrics in English are:

iamb $(\smile \prime)$
trochee $(\prime \smile)$
anapest $(\smile \smile \prime)$
dactyl $(\prime \smile \smile)$
spondee $(\prime \prime)$

VOICE

Voice is the sum total of cognitive content of the words in a poem. Voice can also be seen as the signature of the poet on his poem—his own unmistakable way of saying something. "Only Yeats could have said it that way," one feels, in reading a line like:

That is no country for old men...

Similarly, Frost was able to endow his poems with a "voice" in lines like:

Something there is that doesn't love a wall...

Following are the poetic devices for voice:

denotation—literal, dictionary meaning of a word.

connotation—indirect or associative meaning of a word. "Mother" means one thing denotatively, but may have a host of other connotative associations.

personification—humanizing an object.

diction—word choice, the peculiar combination of words used in any given poem.

syntax—the peculiar arrangement of words in their sentence structures.

rhetoric—"Any adornment or inflation of speech which is not done for a particular effect but for a general impressiveness..." (Eliot)

persona—a mask, an assumed voice, a speaker pretending to be someone other than who he really is.

So far these are only words on a page, like diagrams in a baseball book showing you how to throw a curve ball. The only way there can be any real learning of any of these devices is to do endless exercises in notebooks, trying to master the craft of assonance, of diction shifts, of persona effects, of successful conceits, of metrical variations.

Any practice of these craft devices may lead one into a period of extreme self-consciousness, as one explores totally new reflexes of language. But one can trust that with enough practice they can become "second nature," and an enhancement and reinforcement of one's own intuitive talents as a poet.

74

EVERYONE WANTS TO BE PUBLISHED, BUT...

By John Ciardi

AT A RECENT writers' conference I sat in on a last-day session billed as "Getting Published." Getting published was, clearly, everyone's enthusiasm. The hope of getting published will certainly do as one reason for writing. It need not be the only, nor even the best, reason for writing. Yet that hope is always there.

Emily Dickinson found reasons for writing that were at least remote from publication. Yet even she had it in mind. She seems to have known that what she wrote was ahead of its time, but she also seemed to know that its time would come. If Thomas H. Johnson's biography of her is a sound guide, and I believe it is, she spent her last ten years writing her "letters to the future." The letters, to be sure, were addressed to specific friends; yet they were equally addressed *through* her friends to her future readers. As Hindemith spent ten years composing his quartets and then ten more creating the terms by which they were to be assessed critically, so Emily spent ten years writing her poems (1776 of them, if I recall the right number), and then ten more years stating the terms for their reception.

Even she, then, had an audience (which is to say, publication) in mind. Nor do I imply that the desire to publish is an ignoble motive. Every writer wants to see himself in print. No writer, to my knowledge, has ever been offended when his published offerings were well received. The desire to publish becomes ignoble only when it moves a writer to hack and hurry the work in order to get it into print.

Poetry, of course, is relatively free of commercial motive. Every generation has its Edgar Guest. Ours, I suppose, is Rod McKuen. These are writers whose remouthing of sentiments catches some tawdry emotional impulse in commercial quantities. Yet such writers—or so I have long suspected—must come to believe seriously in the inanities they write. I doubt that they have sold out to the dollar sign: more tragically, they have sold out to themselves.

Such writers aside, it is hard to imagine that anyone would think to bribe a poet to write a bad poem. It would follow then (all temptation to cheat being out of the equation) that the only reason for writing a poem is to write it as well as one possibly can. Having so written it, one would naturally like to see it published.

I was, accordingly, in sympathy with the conference members—but I was also torn. For I had just spent days reading a stack of the manuscripts these people had submitted, and I had found nothing that seemed worthy of publication. I sat by, thinking that session on getting published was an exercise in swimming in a mirage. I even suspected a few of those present of drowning in their mirages.

Then one of the hard-case pros on the conference staff delivered a statistic. "You want to get published?" he said. "Fine. Look at the magazines. What are they publishing? The answer is, roughly, 98 percent nonfiction and not quite half of one percent poetry. Yet of the manuscripts submitted at this conference, seventy-six are poetry and only two are nonfiction." He paused. "Now you tell me," he said, "where are you going to get published?"

The hard case, as it happened, was a successful nonfiction writer for the large-circulation magazines; he had dismissed from consideration the literary quarterlies that do publish poetry, sometimes without payment, but sometimes with an "honorarium." To the quarterlies, I would certainly add our two excellent poetry tabloids, *The American Poetry Review* and *Poetry Now.*

For poetry does get published, though not on terms that would be attractive to the big-circulation pros. Poets *qua* poets do not run into serious income tax problems. So be it. If a little is all one asks, then a little is enough. I have never known of anyone who turned to poetry in the expectation of becoming rich by it. Were I to impersonate the hard-case pro at that conference, I could argue that a writer writes as an alcoholic drinks—which is to say, compulsively, and for its own sake. An alcoholic expects no special recognition for being helpless in his compulsion: Why should a poet expect money and recognition for his compulsion?

The fact is that the good poets do generally find their rewards and recognitions. Ego being what it is (and the poet's ego more so), any given poet may think his true merit has been slighted. For myself, whatever I have managed to make of my writing (and it has been a love affair, not a sales campaign), I have always felt that my own satisfaction (or at least the flickering hope of it) was a total payment. Whatever else came has always struck me as a marvelous bonus. And there have been bonuses—grants, prizes, even a small, slow rain of checks. How could I fail to rejoice in that overflow of good? I wish it to every writer, and wish him my sense of joy in it.

But there is more to it. The hard case's manuscript count stayed with me. Can seventy-six poets and two nonfiction writers be called a writers' conference? He hadn't mentioned fiction, and I never learned how many fiction manuscripts had been turned in. But why, I asked myself, would seventy-six turn to poetry and only two to nonfiction? All writing is writing; all of it is part of one motion. I have enjoyed trying different sorts of writing. This present piece, for example, is nonfiction. It is part of the same exploration that poems take me on.

I asked myself the question, but I know I already had the answer —at least part of it—from the poems I had read and criticized. The poems had been bad, and I had fumbled, as one must, at trying to say why I thought they were bad. I wished on that last day that the conference were just starting and that I had ahead of me another chance to identify the badness of the poems. But perish that thought: I was emotionally exhausted.

Yet on that last day the reason so few of the conference members had turned to nonfiction seemed clear to me. Even to attempt nonfiction a writer must take the trouble of acquiring some body of information. The poems I had read lacked anything that could be called a body of information. The writers seemed to have assumed that their own excited ignorance was a sufficient qualification for the writing of poetry.

I wanted to go back and say to my conferees, "Your poems care nothing about the fact!" Isn't that another way of saying they were conceived in ignorance? Not one of the poets I read had even tried to connect fact A to fact B in a way to make an emotional experience of the connection. The writing lacked *thingness* and a lover's knowledge of thing.

Consider these lines by Stanley Kunitz (the italics are mine):

> Winter that *coils* in the thickets now,
> Will *glide* from the fields, the *swinging* rain
> Be *knotted* with flowers. On every bough
> A bird will *meditate* again.

387

The diction, the rhyming, the rhythmic flow and sustainment are effortless, but how knowledgeably things fall into place! Winter *coils* in the thickets because that snow that lies in shade is the last to melt, thinning down to scrolls of white by the last thaw. Winter will then *glide* from the fields—and what better (continuous, smooth) motion for the run-off of the last melt? The *swinging* rain (what word could better evoke our sense of April showers?) will then be *knotted* (as if) with flowers while birds (as if) *meditate* on every bough. The rain, of course, will not literally be knotted with flowers, nor will birds, literally, meditate. Yet what seems to be a scientific inaccuracy is of the central power of metaphor. Metaphor may, in fact, be conceived as an exactly felt error.

Metaphor is supposed to state the unknown in terms of the known. It is supposed to say X equals Y. Yet when we say "John is a lion," we do not think of John with a mane, with four clawed paws, nor with a pompon tipped tail. We extract from "lion" the emotional equivalent we need and let the rest go. The real metaphoric formula is X does-and-does-not-equal Y. Kunitz understands this formula. His knowledge of it is part of his qualification as a master poet.

There is more. More than can be parsed here. But note how the italicized words *hearken* to one another, each later term being summoned (by some knowledge and precision in the poet) by what went before. The italicized words form what I will dare to call a chord sequence by a composer who has mastered musical theory.

The passage, that is to say, is empowered by a body of knowledge of which I could find no trace in the poets I had been reading at the conference. My poets had been on some sort of trip. Their one message was "I feel! I feel!" Starting with that self-assertive impulse (and *thing* be damned), they then let every free association into the poem. They were too ignorant even to attempt a principle of selection.

I do not imply that I know what any given poem's principle of selection ought to be. To find the principle that serves best and to apply it in a way to enchant the reader is the art and knowledge of the poet. Everything in a good poem must be *chosen* into it. Even the accidents. How else could it be when one stroke of the pen will slash a thing out forever? All that has not been slashed out, it follows, is chosen in.

Ignorance, as nearly as I could say it (too late), was what had really stifled the poems I had read. The writers had not cared enough to learn their own art and use their eyes.

They will, I suppose, get published. Some of them somewhere. But have they earned the right to publication? I ask the question not to answer it. It is every writer's question to ask for himself.

75

WRITING POETRY FOR CHILDREN

By Myra Cohn Livingston

I NEVER intended to write poetry for children. It was a complete accident, and even today I marvel that it happened at all. I was eighteen, in college, and writing what I considered far more important—poetry about love! My instructor at Sarah Lawrence College, Katherine Liddell, had given us an assignment; we were to use alliteration and onomatopoeia. I turned in some verses. "These," she said to me in her converted closet-conference room, reeking with the odor of Sano cigarettes, "would be wonderful for children. Send them to *Story Parade*" (a magazine for boys and girls published by Simon & Schuster). I grudgingly followed her instructions—the accompanying letter, the self-addressed stamped envelope. Several weeks later the envelope came back. I threw it onto a pile of papers and three weeks later became so angry with Miss Liddell's folly, that I ripped it open to confront her with her error. I caught my breath. The editor had carefully clipped three of the poems, and there was a letter accepting these for publication.

It took me eleven years for my first book, *Whispers and Other Poems,* written when I was a freshman, to be accepted for publication by the same editor, Margaret K. McElderry, who had seen the manuscript when I was in college and encouraged me to continue writing. I know now that during the war years few new books were published, and certainly poetry for children was far down on the list of desired manuscripts. In those days, I read *The Writer* religiously, hoping to find someone who would want my work, and collected a sheaf of rejection slips.

But I did not write and never have consciously written *for* children. I cannot understand why the world appeared to me from the start as through the eyes of a child—of my own childhood—or why, even today, most of the poetry I write comes out that way. The only clue I have is that, even as an anthologist, I am drawn to (or write) those poems that speak to the subjects, emotions, and thoughts of children in a diction they understand.

My own poems have often been called "deceptively simple"; the first review of *Whispers* scathingly accused me of writing about "simple, everyday things," as though this were some sort of evil. Perhaps this is because many adults forget that to the child, these very things are what pique his curiosity, engage his attention. As the poet-in-residence for our school district, in my visits to schools and libraries throughout this country, and in teaching courses for teachers at U.C.L.A. Extension, I note that today's child is very different, in many respects, from the child I was, or that my children are, but that many things remain eternal. Children may know more facts, be more worldly wise, but the curiosity, wonder and fresh way of looking, the joys and pains and doubts, seem just as they always were.

I would like to suggest that anyone who wishes to write poetry that children might enjoy face up to a few basics about this vocation. The climate today is far more receptive to poetry than it was a number of years ago when the English—Walter de la Mare, Robert Louis Stevenson, and A. A. Milne—dominated the field. America has given us Elizabeth Madox Roberts, David McCord and Harry Behn, to mention but a few—and there are many exciting middle-aged and young poets publishing today whose work is excellent. We no longer have to take second place to the English, but we do have to recognize that poetry is still somewhat of a stepchild in juvenile literature. Children, themselves, are more apt to read a story in a picture book than to read poetry, for most adults and teachers feel uncomfortable about presenting it. Even Mother Goose is not as well known as once she was. And poetry demands an involvement of the emotions, whether it be laughter or wonder or a more serious way of viewing the world.

The crisis we seem to face now is the mistaken notion that *anyone* can write a poem. The Poets-in-the-Schools program, in many areas, has too often, in my opinion, fostered undisciplined writing, that which John Ciardi has called "a spillage of raw emotion." Any word or series of words written down are called "poems." This, as I see it, is a great disservice to the children who are falsely praised, but it also applies to older aspiring poets. Many of the high school and college students have had no real discipline. Metrical feet, scansion, forms are unknown. Of course, we do not want didactic, sing-song verse, the moralizing of a Henley's "Invictus" or the elusive fairies of Rose Fyleman. What we do need is true poetry that takes into account the interests and yearnings of the young and leads them toward a process of humanization.

In offering suggestions to the person who wishes to write such poetry, I would ask that he ask himself if anything of the child remains in him—a way of looking, tasting, smelling, touching, thinking; if he is in touch with the contemporary child and his way of viewing the world, if he is truly comfortable with children. I would also suggest that he make the commitment to learn the basics of writing in disciplined forms and meters. One cannot, for example, attempt a limerick without knowing how to use the iambus and anapest correctly, nor even free verse without knowing why it *is* free verse.

Another, and perhaps more elusive point, is that the writer understand and believe that poetry for children is not second-best; there is a tendency on the part of many to feel that a so-called children's poet is one who has failed in writing adult poetry, or that it is "easy" to do. The poet who writes for children exclusively is a sort of second-class citizen.

Although I have spent almost twenty years sharing with young people poetry ranging from Mother Goose to T.S. Eliot, it is difficult to give any definite answer as to what sort of poetry children like best. We know through experience that levity is always high on the list, and humor is important, for it counters the view of poems as soul-building messages in high-flown diction. But many a child prefers the more serious. The more a young person is exposed to poetry, the more refined is his taste in this, as in all arts. I would hope that any writer aspiring to publish poetry would not write for what he thinks is the juvenile market, but rather concentrate on his own strengths. The word-play of David McCord is something that comes naturally to his art; curiosity and a love for nature are intrinsic to Harry Behn's work; and Elizabeth Madox Roberts wrote about experiences of her own as a child.

My own poetry has gone through a series of changes. Trained in the traditional rhyme/meter school, I have at times broken away to free verse, knowing that the force of what I wished to say had to dictate the form. Yet I do not feel I could have made this break without a sure knowledge of the disciplines, taught to me by Robert Fitzgerald and Horace Gregory. I know that there are many who would take issue with me, who feel that anything one wishes to put down, if arranged in a certain order, is a poem.

This change may best be shown by contrasting my first published poem, "Whispers," to later work:

> Whispers
> tickle through your ear
> telling things you like to hear.
>
> Whispers
> are as soft as skin
> letting little words curl in.
>
> Whispers
> come so they can blow
> secrets others never know.

Most of my verse in *Whispers, Wide Awake, Old Mrs. Twindlytart* and *The Moon and a Star* was written in traditional forms. But in *A Crazy Flight* (published in 1969), what I wanted to say suddenly refused to be confined by rhyme. The need to use repetition and a freer form of expression asserted itself in a poem that also picked up some current speech patterns of the children I was then teaching:

THE SUN IS STUCK

> The sun is stuck.
> I mean, it won't move.
> I mean, it's hot, man, and we need a red-hot
>   poker to pry it loose,
> Give it a good shove and roll it across the sky
> And make it go down
> So we can be cool,
> Man.

Yet, *The Malibu,* my poem inspired by the moon landing and America's concerns with litter, combined both the rhyming couplet and some elements of free verse:

ONLY A LITTLE LITTER

Hey moonface,
man-in-the-moonface,

do you like the way
we left your place?

can you stand the view
of footprints on you?

is it fun to stare
at the flags up there?

did you notice ours
with the stripes and stars?

does it warm you to know
we love you so?

moonface,
man-in-the-moonface,

thanks a heap for the rocks.

In *The Way Things Are,* the meter follows a child's pattern with a different rhyme pattern, in "Growing: For Louis."

It's tough being short.

Of course your father tells you not to worry,
But everyone else is giant, and you're just the
way you were.
And this stupid guy says, "Hey shorty, where'd
you get the long pants?"
Or some smart beanpole asks how it feels to
be so close to the ants?
And the school nurse says to tell her again how
tall you are when you've already told her.
Oh, my mother says there's really no hurry
And I'll grow soon enough.

But it's tough being short.

(I wonder if Napoleon got the same old stuff?)

But the rhymed couplet creeps up again and again in *4-Way Stop* (published in 1976):

OCEAN AT NIGHT

Mother Wave sings soft to sleep
the fish and seaweed of the deep

black ocean, and with quiet hands
pats to peace her tired sands,

her kelp and driftwood; fills her shoals
with gleaming tides, and gently pulls

across her bed the pale moonlight.
And this is night. And this is night.

Throughout these later books are outcroppings of free verse with which I am still experimenting, but there is an inherent pull that constantly draws me back to the containment of fixed forms. I have finally begun to tackle the haiku and cinquain, most demanding in their use of words:

Even in summer
bees have to work in their orange
and black striped sweaters.

Like any other poet, I feel that the most important factor in my poetry writing is not that I set out to write in any given form, but that I must find the right form for the subject matter. For this is when —and only when—the poem "comes right" for me.

What is right for me is not so for everybody. There are no surefire methods, although I do believe that one must know the basics and rules before breaking them. Even children need these rules, for without them, they flounder and grow dissatisfied with what they are doing. What we all have in common is that we are still learning, and, I hope, growing and changing.

395

76

POETRY'S SLANT VISION

BY JOSEPHINE JACOBSEN

POETRY IS the most honored and least read form of literature. Many intelligent and highly literate readers haven't read a poem since leaving college. The most common complaint is, "I'm just not up to poetry. I honestly don't feel that I understand it." Usually added: "I wish I did."

The same person will attribute this impenetrability to the difficulties of modern poetry, saying or implying that if only poets wrote like Tennyson or Wordsworth, the complainer would be an avid reader. But both the speaker and the spoken-to know that this is doubtful, to put it kindly.

Why then does poetry hold, as it does, a place of such respect in the minds of its non-readers? I think it is because there is a deep feeling, conscious or not, that if it can be reached, there is in poetry some sort of truth, of illumination, of pleasure, some quintessentially *different* quality that exists nowhere else. And those who know poetry, as readers or as writers, know, too, that this is nothing less than the truth. William Carlos Williams said it once and for all, bluntly: "You have no other language for it than the poem."

Among the greatest rewards a poet can have is one of those letters that arrive from an unknown reader, saying that some particular poem has penetrated to an area nothing else has reached—has released an emotion or a comprehension which the reader has never been able to express, to put into language—that magic which enables us to understand what we mean.

How it does this, like anything to do with true art, is partly a mystery; but its comprehensible part is made up of a number of strengths. One of these strengths is its ability to overcome an initial hazard: its own medium. While the painter, the sculptor, the musician, work in a medium that is not pinned down by any dictionary, or assumed to be within reach of anyone over the age of two, the poet has to work in one that is everyone's property; the medium in which advertisements are composed, news is relayed, orders are given, the thousand details of daily life are expressed.

Form and vocabulary are the poet's basic tools. The qualities he wants in his work—strength, concision, penetration, memorability—all must come through these. There is the classic argument, which never will be resolved, between established and free forms, between those who feel that both rhyme and rhythm are more dangers than aids, and those who see them as part of the very marrow of the poem. It seems to me a bootless, though occasionally pleasurable, contention. The approach of the individual poet is deeply built into his poetic genes. Never can he successfully write against his own grain, to please reader, editor, or even himself. There is a quality that makes all poetry a whole, but it will never be a right-or-wrong choice of concept. The poet will find in his own work changes (or else he should stop writing), but they will be organic, not imposed. The fact that my own work has moved from an originally lyric, usually rhymed, somewhat head-long form, subsequently to one looser, more superficially informal and explorative; and then, at the moment, to one highly compressed, in which the aim is an explosion tightly contained, certainly doesn't point this development out as the necessarily desirable path.

As in politics, or for that matter in anything else, the extremes rarely listen to one another. Those who cling to rhyme and scansion, to inherited forms, often won't admit that there are always perils, and have their own danger of dullness and monotony, and the lack of living invention; and those who totally equate originality with the bizarre, rather than the discovered connection, are determined not to admit the profound need for rhythm, for some form of varied repetition, however subtle, which is an essence of poetry. The enduring response to nursery rhymes, to street games, simply cannot be denied. Can anyone argue that "I, said the fly/With my little eye/I saw him die . . ." or "One, two, button my shoe/Three, four, shut the door" survive because of their intellectual content? But then, before one can turn around, this is being used for an argument that poetry can thump along like a street band.

Beginning poets—and for that matter, all others—need constantly to be aware of reverse options, and possibilities, and above all to beware of that modishness that is the enemy of poetry—the ear cocked constantly to the critical or editorial reaction, instead of being ruled by the response to the individual poem's necessity. Each poem *has* its own necessity. Every poet has experienced the false start, the realization that somehow the poem is being forced into a form—or even more dangerously—a tone, that is not its own.

But before all the decisions on form, comes the matter of language—this particular poem's language. Nothing is more dangerous to a poem than the idea that poems are composed in a special language, that "poetic words" are of its essence. Such words are far more useful to prose, which controls and incorporates them, though they are dangerous enough there. It is the way words are used and the relationships between them that turns them into poetry. It is the connections they make, the sounds by which they respond to each other, the surprises of their possibilities, that make for the quality of poetry. That surprise, which is one of the essential ingredients of poetry, comes in part from the sudden transformation of a word—a revelation of its meaning, what it can say, here, now. There is an oblique quality in poetry that has nothing to do with obscurity or preciousness, with anything that lacks the particular truth. To be chary of poets' dicta, I would quote only one other—Emily Dickinson's "Tell all the truth/but tell it slant." The elaborate, the self-conscious, is hostile to poetry. Everyone who has dealt with masses of the poetry of beginners knows that its most common fault is a lack of original imagination clothed in purportedly "poetic" language.

"Poetry is. . . ," "Beauty is . . ." are sentences never to be completed. "One of the things poetry is . . ." is, on the other hand, an endlessly fascinating and often valuable attempt.

An experienced poet is rarely in need of advice other than that he must give himself. A beginning poet, however talented, is a different matter. We constantly use the expression "beginner," but it is a very tricky one. There is the beginner in the common sense of the term, one who has little experience in wrestling with his art. But the question of "beginning" is vital to all poets. One of the innumerable pitfalls in the writing of poetry is self-repetition; the danger that, having discovered that there is a kind of poem one can accomplish successfully, one will linger in that tried territory, putting a bit of extra polish, of extra ingenuity, on a poem which breaks no new ground, shows no sign of

398

the discoveries that life forces upon us. Such work, however expert, has about it something sad, and limited. The worst part of this is that the poet, conscious that his poems of this year, in their vision, are identical to those of earlier years, often is driven to substitute linguistic shock and wrenched syntax for poetic growth. One needs to repeat that growth with its altered vision, is organic, not imposed. Of course this is frightening, but whoever said that the writing of poetry was an unintimidating occupation?

On one of the early space-flights, the astronauts took along, among other forms of life, a spider, to see how the problem of weightlessness would affect *her* occupation. The spider, at first baffled, after repeated attempts finally managed a new method of constructing its troublesome web—and to a poet that was one of the exciting results of the flight. I wrote a poem about that, and it ended, "You frighten me very much. Am I to understand then/that there is no end, absolutely no end, to beginning?" Every poem is a web constructed by that spider.

The necessity to discard or modify concepts and methods is often a painful one, and the immediate results often discouraging. But like the spider web, one of the things a poem does is to demand a different, a hitherto unperceived connection. The theme, the subject matter, will have been used a thousand times; but the poem will make a surprising but valid connection, will see things by its own instinct. In the reader, it will require a leap of recognition; but the honest truth must be there to be recognized. Nothing sows distrust and distaste more quickly than the reader's realization that what seemed originally a new and marvelous flower, turns out to be, on closer inspection, rootless and artificial—whether made of cheap paper or silk. That distrust expands from the poem to the poet. No cliché can be more flattening.

Another of poetry's primary demands is that of particularity. No quality is more vital. Generalization is poison to the poem. And it is generalities that especially beset the beginner. In the excitement and optimism of that moment in which the possibility of that poem occurs, there is an attempt to conquer a giant theme. The poem will be ambitious, but vague. It will talk about "beauty" "love" "evil" without one flash of intimate, particular revelation. I remember struggling to read with an open mind a submitted poem of which the title was "Life." I really knew that the problem was probably a beginner's necessity to explain somehow that the impulse driving him to write the poem had significance and universality. The poem can bring us to the universals of "beauty" "evil" "death" "love" only through the most focused concentration on the particular.

Keats writes of joy. But joy is a figure, *whose hand is ever at his lips/ bidding adieu.*

The poor poet is caught between the demands of the particular, and the necessity that the particular should relate to some aspect of the universal.

The second most common cause for disaster for the tyro poet is the unconscious belief that because something has happened to him for the first time, it is of interest to the reader. His excitement, his revelation, is a preparation, not a product. A disaster, a joy, a perception, will go into the human experience, which is the raw material for poetry; but, untransformed, *unprocessed,* so to speak, it can tell us nothing that moves us. *There is no other language for it but the poem.* Poetry has no purpose; but its happiest side-effect is the unknown reader who writes, "That is what I have known and never been able to express . . ."; "that has given me, in language, the relief of recognition"; "that has allowed me to communicate with myself."

Poems such as William Carlos Williams's "Asphodel That Greeny Flower," or Auden's "Lay Your Sleeping Head, My Love," or Yeats's "Sailing to Byzantium," rise to their accomplishment by the indispensable qualities of strong emotion under technical discipline, used so that the reader instantly feels that there is "no other language for it but the poem." And of course at the core, there is always that X, never totally subject to analysis, but always unarguable.

Obviously, the language of poetry alters with time—it develops, incorporates, discards—especially discards. While certain words and phrases remain alive and untarnished in their own context—those of the Elizabethan lyrics, for example—they would seem artificial and even ridiculous in the context of contemporary life, the only material from which we can make our own poetry. Constantly, new influences, especially those of our inescapable daily history, enter our work, bringing with them their own vocabularies. But any word that leaps out at the reader, claiming attention beyond its service to the poem, will be fully as destructive as the prostrate cliché. Poor poet, walking his narrow line between opposed dangers: the danger of producing guess-what-happened-to-me-last-night verse, on the one hand, or the artificiality of something disconnected from his own emotional experience, on the other; between a flat lack of originality, and a wrenched and effortful invention; between a plodding rhythm and assured rhyme, and a secret invasion by prose; between the fatal generalization, and true poem's universality.

And the strange thing is that, in the process of writing the poem, it is dangerous for the poet to be conscious of any of these perils. Thinking about what the poem must *not* be, is fatal. That is criticism; that comes later. Like the centipede, which questioned as to its method of locomotion, never moved again, the poet, considering the *how* of what he is doing as he does it, is lost. Better a hundred blunders, a hundred discarded poems. Like the athlete, the poet cannot stop in mid-career, to analyze the poetic motion. All that has been learned, been experienced, will go into his poem. But, reading it over at once, then again days later, the poet has vanished, and a cold and demanding eye is fixed on each word of each line.

It is possible to argue that good poetry is becoming more difficult to write. We have lost many common assumptions; changes hurtle forward at a previously inconceivable speed, giant problems of total destruction, of transformations of life, surround us. But it is also possible—and I think true—to say that never has poetry been such a necessity, never have we needed that momentary order and peace brought by the poem, as we do right now. Auden said that poetry changes nothing; the event will go forward just as though the poem did not exist. But it does change something—us. Through the slant vision of poetry we learn new truth, and for that truth we have indeed no other language.

77

TEN GOLDEN RULES FOR PLAYWRIGHTS

By Marsha Norman

Budding playwrights often write to ask me advice on getting started—and succeeding—in writing plays. The following are a few basics that I hope aspiring playwrights will find helpful.—M.N.

1. Read at least four hours every day, and don't let anybody ask you what you're doing just sitting there reading.

2. Don't write about your present life. You don't have a clue what it's about yet. Write about your past. Write about something that terrified you, something you *still* think is unfair, something that you have not been able to forget in all the time that's passed since it happened.

3. Don't write in order to tell the audience how smart you are. The audience is not the least bit interested in the playwright. The audience only wants to know about the characters. If the audience begins to suspect that the thing onstage was actually written by some other person, they're going to quit listening. So keep yourself out of it!

4. If you have characters you cannot write fairly, cut them out. Grudges have no place in the theatre. Nobody cares about your grudges but you, and you are not enough to fill a house.

5. There must be one central character. One. Everybody write that down. Just one. And he or she must want something. And by the end of the play, he or she must either get it or not. Period. No exceptions.

6. You must tell the audience right away what is at stake in the evening, i.e. how they know when they can go home. They are, in a sense, the jury. You present the evidence, and then they say whether it seems true to them. If it does, it will run, because they will tell all their friends to come see this true thing, God bless them. If it does not seem true to them, try to find out why and don't do it any more.

7. If, while you are writing, thoughts of critics, audience members or family members occur to you, stop writing and go read until you have successfully forgotten them.

8. Don't talk about your play while you are writing it. Good plays are always the product of a single vision, a single point of view. Your friends will be helpful later, after the play's direction is established. A play is one thing you can get too much help with. If you must break this rule, try not to say what you have learned by talking. Or just let other people talk and you listen. Don't talk the play away.

9. Keep pads of paper near all your chairs. You will be in your chairs a good bit (see Rule 1), and you will have thoughts for your play. Write them down. But don't get up from reading to do it. Go right back to the reading once the thoughts are on the paper.

10. Never go to your typewriter until you know what the first sentence is that day. It is definitely unhealthy to sit in front of a silent typewriter for any length of time. If, after you have typed the first sentence, you can't think of a second one, go read. There is only one good reason to write a play, and that is that there is no other way to take care of it, whatever it is. There are too many made-up plays being written these days. So if it doesn't spill out faster than you can write it, don't write it at all. Or write about something that does spill out. Spilling out is what the theatre is about. Writing is for novels.

78

GUIDELINES FOR
THE BEGINNING PLAYWRIGHT

By Louis E. Catron

YEARS OF teaching playwriting probably have been more educational for me than for my students. Several hundred young playwrights have taken one or more of my classes since I first started teaching at the College of William and Mary in 1966, and they have taught me that writing a play can be simplified—maybe not made "easy," but certainly "easier"—if certain boundaries are imposed.

We began experimenting with guidelines because so many playwrights were expending too much creative energy chasing nonproductive fireflies. We found that these limitations help playwrights over difficult hurdles. More, they are highly important for the overall learning process.

To be sure, for some writers the very idea of imposed limits appears to be a contradiction in significant terms. How, they ask, can I do creative writing if you fence me in?

Their objections have merit. Limitations often inhibit the creative mind, and many creative people expend a great deal of effort seeking clever ways of circumventing the rules. Certainly I've had students react to the guidelines with the fervor of a bull to a red flag and we've had to arm wrestle about the rules.

Nonetheless, imposition of limitations is a way of life in all creative arts. Theatre is no exception. As a play director, for example, I have found that one key portion of my job is establishing parameters of character for actors, holding these walls tightly in place during rehearsals, and encouraging the performers to create depth within those limitations.

We're talking about the contrast between the casual and sloppy meandering of a Mississippi River versus a tightly confined Colorado. The former changes directions so often that it confuses even experienced riverboat captains, but the latter is held so tightly in direction that it cuts the Grand Canyon. Discipline is essential for the creation of beauty.

The beginning playwright is encouraged to accept the following guidelines to write his or her first play. Later plays can be more free. Indeed, deliberately breaking selected guidelines later will help you better understand the nature of dramatic writing. For now, however, let these guidelines help you in your initial steps toward learning the art and craft of playwriting.

1. *Start with a one-act play.* A full-length play isn't merely three times longer and therefore only three times more difficult. And that a one-act is simpler doesn't mean it is insignificant. The one-act play can be exciting and vibrantly alive, as has been shown by plays such as *No Exit* (Sartre), *Zoo Story* (Albee), *The Maids* (Genet), *the Dumb Waiter* (Pinter) and *The Madness of Lady Bright* (Wilson).

Starting with the one-act lets the writer begin with a canvas that is easily seen at a glance, instead of a mural that covers such a huge space perception doesn't grasp it all.

The one-act typically has only a few characters, is an examination of a single dramatic incident, and runs about half an hour in length. It usually stays within one time frame and one place. Because there are fewer complexities, you'll be able to focus more upon the actual writing, and you'll have less concern about a number of stage problems which come with full-length plays.

2. *Write about something you care about.* Writing manuals usually tell the beginner to write "about what you know best." I think that can lead a beginner to think in terms of daily, mundane events. Better, I believe, is for the beginner to *care;* if the playwright is involved with the subject, that interest will pull an audience along.

3. *Conflict is essential to drama.* Quibble me no quibbles about plays which may not have conflict. For *your* first play, there should be conflict. Drama is the art of the showdown. Force must be opposed by force, person (or group) by person (or group), desire by desire.

If there's no conflict, the dramatic qualities are lost. The result may still hold the stage, but the odds against it are increased. More important, even if the one-act has no conflict and yet holds the stage, the playwright hasn't learned that all-significant lesson about showing conflict. You'll want to know that when you write more.

405

4. *Let there be emotion.* People *care,* in your first play, I hope; people feel strongly, whether it is love or hate, happiness or despair. If you are able to get them emotional, your characters more than likely are going to be active and going somewhere. The audience will care more about emotional people than those dull-eyed, unfeeling dramatic deadbeats.

5. *Stay within the "realistic" mode.* Realism deals with contemporary people, the sort who might live next door, in their contemporary activities, and with selective use of ordinary speech. It avoids the aside and the soliloquy. It is quite comfortable inside the traditional box set. Realism is selective, and sometimes critical, in its presentation of objective facts.

Realism is the familiar mode you've seen most often: it dominates television, and only a handful of movies break away from realism. No doubt you've also seen it on stage more than any other mode. Because you know it best, your first play will be easier to write if you stay in realism. Expressionism, absurdism, symbolism, epic: avoid these for your first experience with playwriting.

(Examples of realism would be full-length plays like *Ghosts* or *A Doll's House,* both by Ibsen, or one-acts like *Ile* and other sea plays by O'Neill. More recent plays tend to be eclectic—primarily but not totally realistic, like the full-length *Death of a Salesman,* by Arthur Miller, or the one-act *Gnadiges Fraulein* by Tennessee Williams.)

6. *Limit the number of characters.* Too many characters and you may lose some: they'll be on stage but saying and doing nothing, so you'll send them off to make dinner or fix the car while you focus on the remaining characters you like better. Consider eliminating those who are dead.

Strenuously avoid "utilitarian" characters—those people who make minor announcements (in older drawing-room plays they say little more than, "Dinner is served"), or deliver packages or messages (Western Union's delivery boy, remember, is as much a relic as the butler). Such characters tend to be flat and no fun for playwright, performer or audience.

Some utilitarians are confidants, on stage to serve as ears so the protagonist will be able to speak inner thoughts without resorting to the soliloquy. The confidant in this sort of case turns out to be about as vital as a wooden listening post.

Confidants, by the way, are easily recognized: their faces are covered with a huge question mark. They seem to be asking questions eternally, without any apparent interest in question or answer. The playwright uses the confidant to get to the answer. If such a person is necessary, let the character be more than a pair of ears.

Just how many characters should be in the play?

Three is a good number for the first play. The triangle is always helpful; three characters allow development of good action and conflict and variety. More, and there's the risk of excess baggage; less, and the characters may quickly become thin and tired.

7. *Keep them all on stage as long as you can.* All too often I've seen plays developing potentially exciting situations, only to be deflated by the exit of a prime character. The audience will feel let down—promised excitement evaporated through the swinging door.

A flurry of activity with entrances and exits is deceptive. There may be a feeling of action but in truth there's only movement of people at the door. The more such business, often the less the drama: in class we begin to comment jokingly about wanting a percentage of the turnstile concession.

The beginning writer needs to learn to keep all characters alive and actively contributing to the play's action. So, then, you need to try to keep them all on stage as long as you possibly can. If you have a character who keeps running out, perhaps he ought to be eliminated.

You needn't invent a supernatural force to keep them in the same room, by the way, although I've seen my student writers come up with fascinating hostage or kidnap situations and locked doors in order to justify keeping everyone present. All of that is clever, but all you need is action that involves all the characters.

8. *No breaks: no scene shifts, no time lapses.* Just as some playwrights have people leaving when stage action is growing, so also are there authors who cut from the forthcoming explosion with a pause to shift scenery or to indicate a passage of time. There is a break in the action and that always is disappointing. Such lapses are all too often barriers to the play's communication with the audience.

If you have in mind a play that takes place first in an apartment, then in a grocery store, then in a subway, you have let the motion pictures overly influence your theatrical concept. It just won't wash, not in a one-act stage play; with so many sets and breaks producers will shy away from your script. (Yes, yes, you can cite this or that exception, but we're talking about a beginner's first play, not a script by someone with an established reputation.)

Reduce the locales to the *one* place where the essential action occurs, and forget the travelogue. So also with the jumps in time: find the *single* prime moment for these events to take place.

Later you can jump freely in time and space, as Miller does so magnificently in *After the Fall*. Your first play, however, needs your concentrated attention on action, not on inventive devices for jumping around through time and space.

9. *Aim for a thirty-minute play.* One-act plays are delightfully free of the restrictions placed upon full lengths, and can run from only a few minutes to well over an hour. The freedom is heady stuff for a beginning writer.

Aim for around half an hour. Less than that and you probably only sketched the characters and action; much longer, and you might exhaust your initial energies (and your audience!). Your goal, of course, is to be sure you achieve adequate amplification; too many beginners start with a play only eight or ten minutes long, and it seems full of holes. Your *concept* should be one that demands around half an hour to be shown.

10. *Start the plot as soon as you can.* Let the exposition, foreshadowing, mood and character follow the beginning of the plot (the point of attack). Get into the action quickly, and let the other elements follow.

11. *Remember the advantage of the protagonist-antagonist structure.* Our era of the anti-hero apparently has removed the protagonist from the stage. Too bad. The protagonist is a very handy character indeed, and the protagonist-antagonist structure automatically brings conflict which, you recall, is essential for drama.

The protagonist is the "good guy," the one with whom we sympathize and/or empathize, the central character of the play. A better definition: *The one whose conscious will is driving to get a goal.* The antagonist stands firmly in the way. Both should be equal forces at the beginning of the play: if one is obviously stronger, the conflict is over quickly and so should the play be.

(If you do not fully understand the personality of a true protagonist, look at Cyrano in Hooker's translation of Edmond Rostand's *Cyrano de Bergerac*. Cyrano is so strongly a conscious will moving actively that it takes several antagonists to balance him.)

12. *Keep speeches short.* Long speeches often grow boring. Sometimes they are didactic; the playwright delivering The Play's Message. Always they drag the tempo. But the worst sin of a long speech is that it means the playwright is thinking just of that one character and all the others are lying about dead.

Short speeches—quick exchanges between characters—on the other hand keep all of them alive and make the play appear to be more crisp and more vital. The play will increase in pace and you'll automatically feel a need to increase the complications.

How long is "short"? Let the dialogue carry but one idea per speech. Or, to give you another answer, let your ear "listen" to the other characters while one is talking, and see who wants to interrupt. A third answer: try to keep the speeches under, say, some twenty words.

One grants the effectiveness of the "Jerry and the Dog" speech in Albee's *Zoo Story*. It makes a nice exception to this guideline. But there are very few such examples, and there are many more examples of plays where the dialogue is rich and effective because the playwright disciplined the talky characters.

13. *Complications are the plot's heartbeat.* John wants Mary. Mary says fine. Her family likes the idea. Her dog likes John. His parrot likes Mary and the dog. So John and Mary get married. They have their 2.8 kids, two cars, a dishwasher, and they remember anniversaries. Happiness.

Interesting? Not very. Dramatic? Hardly.

John wants Mary. Mary is reluctant, wondering if John simply is in love with love. John is angry at the charge. Mary apologizes. John shows full romanticism. Mary worries again. Mary's grandmother advises Mary to take John to see what love really is by visiting Mary's older sis who everyone knows is happy in marriage. Mary and John visit. Sis and her husband Mike are having a violent fight; mental cruelty; damning ac-

409

cusations. Sis gets John to help her and he unwillingly does; Mike pulls John to his side; Mary yells at John for causing trouble.

That's the first ten minutes.

I think you'll grant it has more potential than the first sketch. *Complications* keep it vital, moving, alive. *A play depends upon conflict for its dramatic effect, and complications are the active subdivision of the basic conflict.*

So, then: the traditional baker's dozen—thirteen guidelines which will help you with your first play. They will help you avoid pitfalls which have lamed so many playwrights, and they will give you a basic learning experience which will help you with future plays.

79

BEFORE YOU WRITE YOUR PLAY

By Lavonne Mueller

Garcia Lorca once said that a drama was "weeping and laughing." But that "weeping and laughing" is not gratuitous. It involves careful planning. You must be prepared to plot all emotions on a definite journey—a journey that follows a very clear course toward a destination.

Simply put, you might say a play is an action that goes in a step-by-step pattern from a beginning, through a series of conflicts or problems to a final untangling of those problems. And whatever problem you present when the curtain rises must be answered when the curtain falls.

A good way to ensure a clear step-by-step process in developing your play is to make an eight-point outline before you begin. These eight points are what I always define before I begin writing a play:

1. The Germ

It was Henry James who called the first idea for a creative work—the *germ*. James received the "germ" for a novel from a casual remark at a dinner table.

A "germ" can come to you at any time or place. It is merely a word, phrase, sound, or sight that makes you pause and consider it for some artistic framework.

The "germ" for my play *Warriors from a Long Childhood* was a story I heard when I was a child growing up on an Army post. This tale dealt with four American GI's who were prisoners of war during the Korean conflict. When the war was over, the men were afraid to leave one another—in fact, the military police had to literally carry each soldier home. I wondered what kind of bonding made those men become so attached to each other. I decided they had probably created a family unit—one assuming the role of the father, one the mother, one a brother, and the more dependent sick man being the infant.

In my most recent play, *Little Victories*, the "germ" came from a casual remark I made to women at a playwriting conference. I told the group that women should write about war; after all, one of the greatest generals the world has known was a woman. I was amazed that nobody in the room knew who this woman general was. That's when I decided I wanted to write about Joan of Arc—not as a saint but as a soldier. And in *Little Victories*, I placed Joan on a battlefield, dealing with archers and captains.

A patch of dog-tooth violets I once saw in a field of weeds was still another "germ." These violets had a poetic loneliness that reminded me of *displacement*. I suddenly thought of someone who had always worked outside—a farm woman perhaps—who out of necessity found she had to work in a factory. What kind of emotions and problems would this entail? I let the "germ" grow until it became my play, *Killings on the Last Line*.

The important thing is to let yourself be open to "germs." Anything that alerts your interest is a possibility for an emerging play.

For the first point on your outline, jot down the origin of your germ. This is important to note because the "germ" is often the true core of what you hope to capture in your drama.

2. Preparation

There is not much action in the beginning of your play. Your purpose is to introduce your audience to the characters.

In my play *Killings on the Last Line*, there are eight women who come immediately on stage as the curtain goes up. In the first draft, I brought all eight women on at the same time. I found that this was confusing: It was hard to sort out the different personalities at once. So in the final draft, I brought the characters out in three groups—a woman and her daughter first; then after several short speeches, three more women. And when the five characters were integrated after several pages of dialogue, I introduced the remaining three.

In the beginning pages of *Killings on the Last Line*, I provide some important details for the audience. Eight women work together in a chemical factory. It's a half day, and the women are happy because of this: Most of them dread the tedium of their work; they also fear chemical contamination. One woman has to hide her baby in the washroom of the factory because she can't afford a sitter.

Under preparation, list the number of characters and how they will be introduced. Make a note of some initial details about their lives.

3. Dramatic question

This is a very important part of your drama. One character (or more) now knows the exact nature of his or her problems and should voice it to another character or characters so that the audience is specifically aware of this concern. The *question* may be given in a single speech, line, or action. The answer to this question will end the play.

In *Killings on the Last Line,* a woman worker tells the other workers that a baby hidden in the washroom could endanger all their jobs. If the baby is discovered by the factory officials, it could mean a mass firing on their assembly line.

Question: What do we do about the baby? This "question" is the tension throughout the play.

Under dramatic question, write the question that you want to be the central tension of your play.

4. Rising action

Out of that *dramatic question* about a problem comes a whole series of complications. Characters will try to solve their problems and thus create suspense for the audience. The audience will wonder: How can the problem be solved? How will the play end?

In *Killings on the Last Line,* the mother of the hidden baby tells the other women:

ELLIS

I give him phenobarbitol to sleep.
It's a good little thing. Out like a light all the time.

Later, when the mother has to leave her machine for a few seconds to check on the baby, she is warned by the others that the machine records every second of work-time that is lost. And when one of the supervisors comes through for the morning check, tension builds as he comes close to discovering the hidden child.

In *Little Victories,* Joan of Arc is told that many of her captains are refusing to follow her. Archers are running off to the hills—deserting. One officer wants to kill her.

413

For rising action, list three or four complications involving your characters.

5. Turning point

You are now at the peak of your play—the most tense moment. This is what you've been building up to through your *rising action*. Tension may continue to increase after the *turning point*, but it will not be as dramatic. The characters are at the point where they must do something important or make a decision. The audience at this time should be on the edge of their seats.

In *Killings on the Last Line*, a minor supervisor walks into the washroom for a maintenance check. She senses something is hidden. The mother becomes frantic. The other workers are agitated.

MAVIS (supervisor)

I don't know what is hid in here . . . dog . . . cat . . . I don't wanna know. But you git it gone tomorrow.

ELLIS

Mavis, you put your own little Royce to yer car in the parkin lot . . . when he had hisself a cold 'n couldn't go ta school.

MAVIS

That was a long time ago.

ELLIS

Before you was supervisor.

MAVIS

Git it gone. Tomorrow. Ok? Now I ain't seen me nothing, ok? You git yourself back to work.

When the supervisor leaves, the mother frantically tells the women she will find another hiding place for the baby. But one woman, Hidelman, says the baby can't stay—for the good of everybody's job. A fight soon follows, and the assembly line is in even more danger.

In *Warriors from a Long Childhood*, the prisoners live together in a makeshift hut after the guards have gone and the war is over. They have deteriorated mentally and physically. When one of the men resorts to begging from a child in a nearby village, Chris, the father figure in the group, is horrified and realizes they must all go home.

CHRIS

Look at us. We're bums . . . bums!
(HE TURNS AWAY FROM THE MEN, AFTER A PAUSE.)
There's a special Army train going through here tonight. For Seoul. We're getting on.

TONY

Whattaya mean . . . we're getting on?

CHRIS

Leaving!

TONY

Breaking up?

Tony's action of begging constitutes a turning point and forces Chris to realize how far the group has deteriorated.

Under turning point, you will want to note what might be a "tense high point" for your play. What action can you invent to force your characters to change their course of action? List two possible confrontations.

6. Falling action

Everything begins to "come down" from the *turning point*. Information falls together for the dramatic answer. Characters are collecting their information in order to arrive at a solution.

In *Killings on the Last Line,* the workers' union issues a bulletin that says some towels and uniforms in the factory are possibly contaminated. Ellis, the mother, has wrapped her child in these contaminated materials. This information now causes the women to band together—they all feel vulnerable. Hidelman, previously the most antagonistic toward the mother, now says:

HIDELMAN

Ellis, you go home tonight and burn all them old uniforms and towels you took. Hear me! You git them off that kid . . . and don't feed him no more creamers from the cafeteria.
(PAUSE)

415

Ellis . . . if you don't, I'm coming over there and burn 'em myself.

The women realize they must talk to the factory officials. The "spills" are at a dangerous level.

HIDELMAN

Look at my fingernails!

ELMHURST (factory supervisor)

They're dirty.

HIDELMAN

Look a-gin. That ain't dirt. (PAUSE) Skin under there's dark blue. From exposure to aldrin spills.

ELMHURST

You show me one monitor that has registered spills. (PAUSE) Didn't I get your people safety showers?

HIDELMAN

It's not enough. That stuff goes through unbroken skin.

The urgency of contaminated towels and uniforms—as well as the chemicals under their fingernails—forces the workers to act on the problem.

Under falling action, list some vital information that will cause your characters to arrive at a solution.

7. The dramatic question answered

If you want to be technical, this part of the play is called a *denouement*. This is the untying. In other words, all the tangles of the play have been unraveled. The dramatic question is answered, and the characters arrive at some sort of solution.

In *Killings on the Last Line,* the women demand that the mother bring the baby out of its hiding place and into the open. It is their way of demonstrating that they are not going to hide their fears anymore. They are now a force for management to confront.

Answer: Bring the baby out of its hiding place. Make the leadership in the factory deal with the workers' problems.

416

Answer your "dramatic question" in one or two sentences. What can the character or characters do to solve their problems?

8. Wrap-up

Now you are letting the audience see your characters adjust to the solution of their problems. This is the time you give your people a graceful farewell and prepare your audience for the final curtain.

In *Killings on the Last Line,* the women slowly leave the factory. As they do, the mother says:

ELLIS

My baby . . . he's gonna be all right, ain't he?

QUASHIE

Yes, darlin. Now you just think about everything outside on the ground pushing up—flowers and grass—gettin' themselves born hard and hurtin, like all life.

I end the play showing that the women will struggle; that is the life force. That is the eternal hope of human beings.

In the wrap-up, list several ways you can smoothly let your characters leave the stage. A good last line is very effective.

When you have outlined these eight points, you are ready to write your play. The spine is securely formed. You now have the luxury of concentrating on the "weeping and laughing."

For market list see page 710.

80

HOW TO SELL YOUR TELEVISION SCRIPT

By Richard A. Blum

MARKETING a television script requires strategy, determination, and a realistic understanding of the industry. The marketplace is extremely competitive, and even the best projects written by established professionals might end up on the shelf. Still, an *excellent* original script—submitted to the right person at the right time—might suddenly break through all barriers. The key word is *excellent*. It makes no sense to submit a script unless you feel that it is in the most polished form (even then it will be subject to rewrites), and that it represents the highest calibre of your creative potential. One might think producers are inclined to see the masterpiece lurking behind a rough draft script. More likely, they'll focus on the weaknesses, compare it to top submissions, and generalize about the writer's talents. So, if you feel uncertain about the professional quality of a work, hold off submitting it. Your next work might show you off to better advantage.

Since unsolicited scripts tend to be lost or "misplaced" by production companies, it's a good idea to have a sufficient number of copies. The *minimum* number you will need is three—one for your files, one for submission, and one for inevitable rewrites. More realistically, you'll probably want additional copies for two or three producers, an agent or two, and your own reserve file for unanticipated submissions. Incidentally, fancy covers and title designs are totally unnecessary. Three inexpensive brads can be punched through the left hand margins of the manuscript. Scripts are usually printed or photocopied to avoid the smudged look of carbons.

The Writers Guild

The Writers Guild of America protects writers' rights, and establishes minimum acceptable arrangements for fees, royalties, credits, and so on. You are eligible to join the Guild as soon as you sell your first project to a signatory company (one who has signed an agreement with the Guild). A copy of your contract is automatically filed and you will then be invited to join the membership. Before you sell the new project, you *have* to be a member of the Guild; otherwise, no signatory company can hire you.

The one-time membership fee for Writers Guild of America, West (Los Angeles) is $1,500, plus 1% of yearly earnings as a writer (or $25 quarterly, if you earn less than $1,000 as a writer). The membership fee for Writers Guild of America, East (New York) is $750. Dues are $50 per year, plus 1½% of annual earnings as a writer.

Any writer can register a story, treatment, series format, or script with the Writers Guild of America. The service was set up to help writers establish the completion dates of their work. It doesn't confer statutory rights, but it does supply evidence of authorship which is effective for ten years (and is renewable after that). If you want to register a project, send one copy with the appropriate fee ($15 for nonmembers; $5 for members) to: Writers Guild of America West, Registration Service, 8955 Beverly Blvd., Los Angeles, CA 90048, or Writers Guild of America East, Inc., 555 West 57th Street, New York, NY 10036.

You can also register dramatic or literary material with the U.S. Copyright Office—but most television writers rely on the Writers Guild. The Copyright Office is mainly used for book manuscripts, plays, music or lyrics, which the Writers Guild will not register. For appropriate copyright forms (covering dramatic compositions), write to: Register of Copyrights, Library of Congress, Washington, D.C. 20540.

The release form or waiver

If you have an agent, there is no need to bother with release forms. But if you're going to submit a project without an agent, you'll have to send to the producer or the production company for a release form—or waiver—in advance. (Addresses of selected production companies are listed at the end of this chapter.) Most production companies will return your manuscript without it. The waiver states that you won't sue the production company and that the company has no obligations to you. That may seem unduly harsh, but consider the fact that millions of dollars are spent on fighting plagiarism suits, and that hundreds of ideas are being developed simultaneously and coincidentally by writers, studios, and networks.

The waiver is a form of self-protection for the producer who wants to avoid unwarranted legal action. But it also establishes a clear line of communication between the writer and producer. So rest assured, if legal action is warranted, it can be taken.

The cover letter

When you prepare to send out your project, draft a cover letter that is addressed to a *person* at the studio, network, or production company. If you don't know who is in charge of program development, look it up in the trade papers, or telephone the studio receptionist. If she says, "Mr. So-and-So handles new projects," ask her to *spell* "Mr. So-and-So." That courtesy minimizes the chance of embarrassment, and maximizes the chance that the project will wind up at the right office.

The letter you write should sound professional. There's no need to offer apologies for being an unsold writer, or to suggest that the next draft will be ten times better than this one. If a cover letter starts off with apologies, what incentive is there to read the project?

Here's the tone a cover letter might have:

Dear_____

I've just completed a mini-series called FORTUNES, based on the book by Frank Tavares. I've negotiated all TV and film rights to the property, which is a dramatic adventure series about a family caught in the California Gold Rush. I think you'll find the project suitable for the mini-series genre. It's highly visual in production values and offers unusual opportunities for casting.

I look forward to your reaction. Thank you for your cooperation.

Sincerely,

The letter doesn't say I'm an unsold writer in the midwest or that Frank Tavares is my friend and let me have the rights for a handshake. Nor does it take the opposite route, aggressively asserting that it is the best project the studio will ever read. There's no need for such pretentions. The cover letter sets the stage in a simple and dignified manner. The project will have to speak for itself.

Submitting a script

Independent producers represent the widest span of marketing potential for the free-lance writer. If one producer turns down an idea,

420

there are many others who might still find it fresh and interesting. However, the smaller independent producer is not likely to have the financial resources to compete with the development monies available at the network or studio.

Production companies do have that bargaining power. The distinction between smaller independents and larger production companies is their relative financial stability and current competitive strength on the airwaves. Production companies form and dissolve according to the seasonal marketing trends and network purchases. The more successful production companies have become mini-studios in their own right, with a great number of programs on the air and in development. Some of the more recognizable entities are M. T. M. Enterprises (Mary Tyler Moore), Embassy TV (Norman Lear), and Lorimar Productions (Lee Rich).

The major motion picture studios are in keen competition with production companies. Only six major film studios have aggressive and viable television divisions: Columbia Pictures—TV; Paramount Pictures—TV; Metro-Goldwyn-Mayer (M.G.M.)—TV; 20th Century-Fox—TV; Universal—TV; and Warner Brothers—TV. (Addresses at the end of this chapter.) They represent highly fertile ground for program development; strong deals can be negotiated by agents for the right project.

At the top of the submission ladder is the network oligarchy: ABC, CBS, NBC. Once a project is submitted at this level, there's no turning back. If a project is "passed" (*i.e.,* turned down), it's too late to straddle down the ladder to independent producers. *Their* goal is to bring it back up to the networks (who in turn must sell to the sponsors).

The closer the project comes to the network, the more limited the number of buyers. As the submission moves up the ladder, it faces stiffer competition and fewer alternatives. So you see that the marketplace is highly competitive, although not totally impenetrable. Your submission strategy will depend on knowing the marketplace trends and organizing a campaign to reach the most appropriate people and places.

There's no better way to stay on top of marketing and personnel changes than reading the trade papers—*Daily Variety* (1400 N. Cahuenga Blvd., Hollywood, CA 90028) and the *Hollywood Reporter* (6715 Sunset Blvd., Hollywood CA 90028). The trades reflect the daily pulse of the entertainment industry on the West Coast. Moreover, each paper offers a weekly compilation of production activities ("TV Production Chart," "Films in Production," etc.), which lists companies, addresses, phone numbers, and producers for shows in work. A careful scrutiny of those lists will provide helpful clues to the interests and current activities of independent producers, production companies, and studios.

A similar resource is the "Television Market List," published regularly in the *Writers Guild of America Newsletter* (8955 Beverly Blvd., Los Angeles, CA 90048). It lists all current shows in production or preproduction, and identifies the story consultant or submission contact for each show. The WGA's market list states whether or not a show is "open" for submissions, and whom to contact for assignments. A careful reading of these and other publications, such as *Ross Reports Television* (40–29 27th St., Long Island City, NY 11101), a monthly magazine that lists new television programs and their producers, can help bring you closer to making knowledgeable and practical decisions about marketing your own projects and scripts.

In the network marketplace, you have a choice of submitting a script to a great number of places at the same time or sending it selectively to a few individuals. The specific strategy depends on the needs of the marketplace at the time. You should determine which producers and production companies are particularly interested in the type of project you have developed.

Options, contacts, and pay scales

If a producer is interested in a project he or she will propose a *deal, i.e.,* the basic terms for a contract. If you have no agent, now is the time to get one. *Any* agent will gladly close the deal for the standard 10% commission. An attorney would be equally effective, or if you have an appropriate background, you might want to close the deal yourself. The need for counsel depends on the complexity of the proposed deal, and the counter-proposals you wish to present.

On the basis of your discussions, a *Deal Memo* is drawn up which outlines the basic points of agreement—who owns what, for how long, for how much, with what credits, royalties, rights, and so on. The deal memo is binding, although certain points may be modified if both parties initial it. The *Contract* is based on the terms of the deal memo and is the formal legal document. If you're dealing with a producer who is a signatory to the Writers Guild (most established producers are), the contract will adhere to the terms of the Minimum Basic Agreement (M.B.A.) negotiated by the Writers Guild of America.

A producer can either option your work, purchase it outright, or assign you to write new material. If the property is *optioned,* the producer pays for the right to shop it around (which means the project can be submitted by the producer to a third party, e.g., the network). During the option period, you can't submit the project to anyone else. Typically, option money is relatively small; perhaps $1,500 or $2,500 for a six-month period. But the writer will be paid an additional sum of money if the producer elicits interest and moves the project forward. If the producer fails to exercise the option (*i.e.,* if the option expires), the rights revert back to the writer.

A *Step Deal* is the most common form of agreement between producers and free-lance writers. It sets forth fees and commitments for story and teleplay in several phases. The first step is at the *story* stage. When the writer turns in a treatment, the producer pays for it—at least 30% of the total agreed upon compensation—but the producer does not have to assign that writer to do the script. If the writer *is* retained, the producer exercises the *first draft* option. When that draft of the script is turned in, the writer receives a minimum of 40% of the total agreed upon compensation. Now the producer has the final option—putting the writer to work on the *final draft.* Once that script is received, the writer is entitled to the balance of payment. The *Step Deal* is a form of protection for the producer who can respond to the quality of content, the inviolability of delivery dates, and the acceptability of the project to the networks. It also guarantees the writer that his or her work will be paid for, whether there is a cut-off or a go-ahead on the project.

How to get an agent

A good agent is one with a respectable track record, a prestigious list of clients, and a reputation for fairness in the industry. There is no magical list of good agents, although the Writers Guild does publish a lists of agents who are franchised by the Guild. (Send $1.00 to Writers Guild West, *Attn: Agency List,* 8955 Beverly Blvd., Los Angeles, CA 90048.) Names and addresses of literary and dramatic agents appear in *Literary Market Place* (Bowker), available in most libraries. A list of agents can also be obtained by sending a stamped, self-addressed envelope to Society of Authors' Representatives, P.O. Box 650, Old Chelsea Sta., New York, NY 10113.

If you have no agent representing you, it's difficult to get projects considered by major producers. One of the best ways is to submit your work to an agent who already represents a friend, a professor, a long-lost uncle in the industry. If you are recommended by someone known to the agency, it makes you less of an unknown commodity. If you have no contact, make a list of possible agents for your project, and prioritize them in your submission status file. You might send the project to one top agency for consideration, or to a select number of agencies at the same time.

A brief cover letter might introduce you as a free lancer looking for representation on a specific project. If you don't get a response within six to eight weeks, you can follow up with a phone call or letter, and submit the project to the next agent on your list. Don't be discouraged if you get no response at first; just keep the project active in the field. If the script or presentation is good enough, you might eventually wind up with some positive and encouraging response from the agency.

If an agent is interested in your work, he or she will ask to represent it in the marketplace. If the work sells, the agent is entitled to 10% commission for closing the deal. If the work elicits interest but no sale, you have at least widened your contacts considerably for the next project.

The larger agencies offer an umbrella of power and prestige, but that elusive status is seriously undermined by the sheer size of the agency itself. Many clients inevitably feel lost in an overcrowded stable, and newcomers can hardly break into that race. In contrast, a smaller literary agency provides more personalized service, and is more open to the work of new talent. If you're going to seek representation, the smaller agency is the likely place to go. But don't be fooled by the label "small." Many of these agencies are exceptionally strong and have deliberately limited their client roster to the cream of the crop. In fact, many smaller agents have defected from executive positions at the major agencies. So you'll have to convince them you're the greatest writer since Shakespeare came on the scene—and that your works are even more salable.

How do you prove that you have the talent to be a star talent? It's all in the writing. If your projects look professional, creative, and stylistically effective, you're on the right track. Indeed, you can call yourself a writer. If the artistic content is also marketable and you back it up with determination and know-how, you might just become a *selling* writer.

And that is the "bottom line" for success in the television industry.

Networks, Studios and Production Companies

(Note: New submissions should be addressed to the Head of Program Development.)

NETWORKS

ABC-TV
4151 Prospect Ave.
Los Angeles, CA 90027
or, 1330 Ave. of the Americas
New York, NY 10019

CBS-TV
7800 Beverly Blvd.
Los Angeles, CA 90036
or, 51 West 52nd St.
New York, NY 10019

NBC-TV
3000 W. Alameda
Burbank, CA 91523
or, 30 Rockefeller Plaza
New York, NY 10020

MAJOR STUDIOS

Columbia Pictures-TV
3000 Colgems Sq.
Burbank, CA 91505

MGM-TV
10202 W. Washington Blvd.
Culver City, CA 90230

Paramount Pictures-TV
5555 Melrose Ave.
Los Angeles, CA 90038

20th Century Fox-TV
10201 W. Pico Blvd.
Los Angeles, CA 90064

Universal Studios-TV
100 Universal City Plaza
Universal City, CA 91608

Warner Bros.-TV
4000 Warner Blvd.
Burbank, CA 91505

SELECTED INDEPENDENT PRODUCTION COMPANIES

Embassy Television Corp.
100 Universal City Pl.
Universal City, CA 91608

Lorimar Productions
3970 Overland Ave.
Culver City, CA 90230

M.T.M. Enterprises
4024 Radford Ave.
Studio City, CA 91604

Aaron Spelling Productions
1041 N. Formosa
Los Angeles, CA 90046

81

CREATING TELEVISION STORIES AND CHARACTERS

By Stewart Bronfeld

CREATING stories and the characters in them is what script writing is really all about. The rest — the technology, the business, the timing and the luck—are also found in a thousand other activities of life. But when, in the matrix of a blank page, a story starts to emerge which never before existed, and characters are born and develop who never lived before that moment, something very special is happening. It is part craft, part art and (there's no other word) part magic.

The magic of the creative process remains basically mysterious, like any other kind of birth. The art is a product of the artist's personality and thus differs with each person. But the craft is based on experience, common sense and professional techniques and *can* be learned and practiced.

Principles and rules and fashions of playcraft change but one bedrock truth remains constant: *the basis of effective drama is conflict.* Learn this and you learn a lot. Sophocles knew it. Shakespeare knew it. And the writer of the script for that popular TV series you saw last Tuesday knew it. The conflict of man against man, man against woman, man against nature, man against himself—the clang of two opposing forces coming against each other makes for drama. The conflict may be Big and Important—the numberless masses tearing down the mighty regime of the Czar in *Dr. Zhivago.* Or it may be small and wistful—a fat, homely butcher and a plain neighborhood girl making a clumsy grab at a chance for love in *Marty.*

Consider one of the most successful motion pictures of all time, *Gone With the Wind.* Along with her skill for recreating a colorful time and place and sheer storytelling art, Margaret Mitchell built her story with such effective dramatic conflicts that both the book and the movie are still very much alive (and making money) today. While the Civil

426

War itself was not directly one of the conflicts (for conflict implies two opposing forces and the North almost never appears in her work), it served as a suitable backdrop for the interplays of strong dramatic conflicts with which the author fashioned her story and characters:

The Old South versus the emerging reality of a new and different world.

Rhett Butler, who could have any woman he wanted—*except* the one he wanted most.

Scarlett O'Hara, beautiful enough to attract any man *she* wanted—except the one she wanted most.

Ashley Wilkes, torn between wanting Scarlett and needing Melanie.

These characters, with their frustrations and longings, could have become no more than soap opera figures—just as *Macbeth* could have become no more than a murder melodrama. The difference, in both cases, was that the authors had the gift of imparting life to their characters and meaning to their conflicts. Thus audiences *cared;* they still do.

Examine any good story and you will discover the conflict that motivates the main character(s) and moves the plot along. One of Somerset Maugham's most enduring stories is *Of Human Bondage,* whose very title highlights the conflict of the young surgeon fighting against his imprisoning love for a worthless girl. But just as enduring, if not as deep, are Laura Lee Hope's children's books about the Bobbsey Twins, each of which gets the kids into some conflict which, happily, is resolved in the final pages.

Sometimes if you look carefully you find the same basic conflict in widely different stories. In *Tom Sawyer,* it is wanting to be good to a loved one (Aunt Polly) versus the pull of adventure with wilder companions. The same conflict (in a dog instead of a boy) is the basis for the drama in *The Call of the Wild.* And, in essence, nearly the same conflict is at the heart of the story of the opera *Carmen.*

The knowledge that conflict makes for drama is a nuts-and-bolts tool which writers can use—especially when they sit at their writing desk caught up in a conflict of their own, namely, "I've got a rough idea of a plot but I don't know what to do with it." First, *think of the plot in terms of the conflict or conflicts involved.* If you cannot identify any, you probably do not have the basis for a very strong story idea. This in itself is an accomplishment, for it can save hours of work, reams of paper and pangs of disappointment later.

427

What contributes drama to the plot is not the conflict itself, but rather what the character does and how he or she does it in response to that conflict. People are naturally more interested in people than they are in circumstances. What engages their attention is not so much the adventure as the adventurer, not the danger so much as how the people react to what is menacing them, not the surprise ending, but how the characters in the story are affected by, and respond to, the surprise.

This simple but fundamental fact that people are primarily interested in people is the basis for another important tool of scriptcraft: *characterization,* the development in a character of specific personality traits. Examine most successful movies and television series and you will find they often have one thing in common: a well-drawn central character (or characters) whose personality traits are clearly defined. These traits may be good ones or bad ones, but they are distinctive. Early in a movie, over the weeks in a TV series, these characteristics become familiar to the viewer. They add a dimension of depth and reality to the character. Another (and perhaps paramount) reason for the enduring success of *Gone With the Wind* is the author's skillful use of characterization; Rhett Butler and Scarlett O'Hara were so vividly conceived and depicted that millions of readers and viewers have found it impossible to believe they are not real people.

On television, the mortality rate of new programs is appalling. Not many new shows survive a season's journey through the ratings mine field. Half-hour comedies are especially popular with viewers, and so smoke pours out the stacks of the Hollywood fun factories day and night as they churn out an endless assembly line of new shows, in which "wacky" characters do "wacky" things—and get "wacky" ratings and disappear. Sometimes, before they expire, they are desperately switched from one time slot to another, scrambling around the network's program schedule like escaped hamsters.

Why do so few of them take root and prosper? The answer, I think, is that they are sitcoms, or situation comedies—which means their emphasis is on ever-zanier "situations," with the people in them seldom developed beyond the cartoon character stage. But there *are* half-hour comedies that become popular successes with longtime runs and high ratings. While they also may be called sitcoms in the trade, these shows might be more accurately called "charcoms," for their humor comes not from artificially contrived "situations," but from artfully created characterization.

Among them was one of the most successful television series of all time, *The Mary Tyler Moore Show,* which ended only because the star grew tired of the weekly grind. The program immediately became a top success on the rerun circuit and established something of a record for the price paid for syndication rights. The secret of the show's success was clearly the effective characterization established by the original creators and skillfully followed by all the subsequent script writers. The funny situations almost always resulted from, or were related to, the regular cast's character traits, which were familiar to every viewer. Proof of the power of good characterization is the fact that no less than three of the show's characters were spun off into successful series of their own: Rhoda, Phyllis and Lou Grant.

What makes this kind of "charcom" so successful is also what makes many dramatic series attain great popularity while their competition regularly arrives and departs. This includes action-adventure shows. *Kojak,* for example, was a tremendous hit, and still is, in its syndication afterlife. But *Kojak* was never really about cops-and-robbers and drug busts; it was primarily about Lieutenant Theo Kojak.

Therefore, whether you are writing a script for a television series, a single original teleplay or a movie, a prime factor to consider is the importance of character creation. Even when you feel your plot is the paramount consideration in a particular script, your characters should never be mere puppets manipulated to suit it. It does not always take a full-scale portrait to make a character come alive; sometimes a few well drawn strokes can do it.

The best and strongest plots, however, are those that evolve naturally, even inevitably, out of the characterization. These stories have more impact, because they are more believable. There is good reason for this. In the lives of most of us, very few important things happen for totally external reasons; what happens to us is often the result of what we do—and what we do is often the result of what we are. That is true of you and me and your potential viewers. If it is also true of your characters in what you make happen to them, they will be perceived not as concoctions, but as living characters with a dimension of depth and reality. Thus your story will not merely gain the attention of the audience; it will make some impact upon them. There's a difference; it means they will *care* about what they are watching. And, as producers, directors and story editors well know, when an audience feels an involvement, it shows in the ratings and at the box office.

Let us see an example of plot developing out of characterization. Jane is a timid young woman, terrified of asserting herself, due in large part to her overbearing mother. She is constantly driven to gain her mother's approval, seldom succeeding. A situation arises at work wherein problems are causing the company's management to consider going out of business. Jane, who has a keen and analytic mind, has diagnosed the problems and feels she has a solution that may save the company. The frantic meetings of the managers behind closed doors are getting louder each day.

Conflict: Jane's desire to offer her solution, thus possibly becoming a heroine, getting her reward and making her mother proud of her—versus her inability to push herself into the councils of upper management and possibly be rebuffed and humiliated. It's not *Hamlet,* but it is the basis for an interesting human drama with which the audience can identify.

The point is that the characterization I created for Jane does not function merely as a kind of outer garment she wears as she makes her way through the plot; the plot evolves directly out of her characterization. If I changed the kind of person Jane is, my plot would no longer work. The two—characterization and plot—are welded together.

Some writers may have an intuitive ability to create a fully defined character as they go along; however, it cannot hurt (and will always help) to write a detailed sketch or profile of any major character first. Creatively, the more you "know" about a character the more you contribute to his or her reality in the script. Practically, facets of the character's personality will often strongly suggest plot ideas. (When one of my characters is especially well defined, I occasionally become aware that he or she is really writing the scene, while I follow along at the typewriter, interested and even curious to find out what will happen next.)

However, writers do vary in both their skill and their inclination for characterization. For some writers, formulating a plot is paramount, and the people caught up in the action are merely vehicles to advance the story line. Obviously, if a plot is compelling enough, viewers will be interested in what is happening even though they are not particularly interested in those to whom it happens. Many movies and television series attest to this. While I believe a more memorable story will evolve out of characterization, I would much rather see a script with an intriguing plot moving at a well-orchestrated pace even though with cardboard characters, than one with vividly sketched characters whose personalities are fascinating, but *nothing really happens.*

There is a test the script writer should apply to his or her work as it proceeds to be sure that there is a consistent plausibility to the characters and the plot. The test is *motivation.* Motivation makes the difference between actions seeming real or staged. People are not robots; they generally do what they do for a reason. Sensible people act from sensible reasons and fools act from foolish reasons. The writer looks at each action of the main characters and asks, "Would this particular person do this, in this particular circumstance?"

The movies of the thirties and forties, mostly ground out by writers on a weekly salary, were often written as fast as they were typed, and frequently had no time to bother with motivation. Now they live on mainly at 2:30 A.M. on television and there is a reliable way to identify them in the TV listings: the word *decides.* "An heiress decides to run off with her gardener . . ." "A millionaire decides to take a slum kid into his household . . ." Whenever you see the word *decides* in a movie listing, you know that the only motivation involved is that it was Thursday and the script was due in the producer's office by Friday. When you look over your script after a cooling-off period, try to be objective enough to note whether your character "decides" to do something just because, solely for plot purposes, you want him to. If he does, if proper motivation is lacking, it is a sign that the scene (or possibly a larger segment of the script) requires rethinking and rewriting.

There is another element in any kind of story, one not so susceptible to definite guidelines. I refer to *theme.* Writers generally are writers because they have an inclination (or perhaps an impulsion) to communicate. But the reason any individual writes any particular story must vary, not only with each writer but with each story he or she writes. We all have different interests, different outlooks on life and different matters we consider important; if these motivate us when we sit down to do our communicating—our writing—our work will reflect a theme.

431

In a story, plot is what happens. Theme is the larger framework of meaning in which it happens. Larger stories have larger themes, and lesser stories have lesser themes. In the powerfully written and expansively produced *The Godfather,* the theme was that evil is self-consuming. In a program I saw last night in a half-hour comedy series, the theme was the importance of good friends later in life.

Do not confuse a theme with a "message." The writer should not be trying to make a commentary on his or her theme, only to *air* it. Reflection on the meaning should rest with the viewer.

Do all writers have themes for their stories? The answer is, not all the time (and not always consciously). But a theme is an asset to any literary work. First, it elevates the story because there is some central meaning to it all. Then, it assures a better, more unified construction to the script, for it provides a general reference point to guide the direction of the plot and the development of the characters.

Herman Melville wrote, "To produce a mighty book, you must choose a mighty theme." You will find, however, that when it happens, it is more as though the mighty theme chose *you.*

82

BEFORE THE FINAL CURTAIN

By Jean Raymond Maljean

AFTER TYPING FINAL CURTAIN on that play manuscript, you may have had an inkling that the word FINAL was premature.

What actually has come to an end is your solitary command over this property. Now you'll wrangle with the director, alternately winning and losing battles over sweeping changes in the original script. Actors and actresses will press you, via the director, to alter their lines, business, and characterization.

The conflict will not be confined to your plot. Amidst all these creative minds, you have a hassle on your hands. A good thing, too. It may be your baby, but it takes teamwork to deliver it into the world. Through tedious rehearsals you'll cut, change, and add scenes all the way until opening night. Assuming your play was optioned by a successful producer or organization, you'll be sitting in the theater as hundreds of ticket holders arrive, each a survivor of bumper-to-bumper driving through heavy traffic, having suffered an exorbitant price for dinner, baby sitter, and parking. What kind of evening's entertainment have you prepared to reward their faith in the work of a new playwright?

Do you know what they want?

Do they know?

Audiences are not certain about that. The critics who will also be on hand can articulate what reaction the audience feels in the reviews the next day—not that all critics are infallible, but they do make a study of theatrical successes and failures.

Over the years I have compiled the following checklist, after observing what critics like and dislike about the plays they have reviewed. You should test your script against each item before the critics have a chance to do so.

And until you do, hold that FINAL CURTAIN.

• Who is your protagonist? The story may follow the lives of many but, to prevent diffusion, the audience must identify with one central character.

• Does the audience know a great deal about this person? Do they care what happens to him or her? If not, what's all the fuss about?

• Is your central character's conflict against another person? The environment? Him- or herself? A play without conflict is not a play, and the conflict will be between you and your audience.

• Endow the antagonist with redeeming virtues. No bad guys, please. Allow the player to feel justified in portraying the role with conviction. One playwright's antagonist could be another playwright's protagonist.

• Does your protagonist change as a result of the struggle? Or does he "just come to think of things in a new light" and decide to change his mind? Or hers? People don't just "change their minds" in plays, any more than they do in real life. People change when conflict turns them inside out and wrenches them away from their former pattern of living. If this is one of your writing faults, change your mind.

• Have you written a play or a manuscript? Is it something you can visualize, moving, changing shape—or is it simply a printed page to be read? I've composed a limerick to illustrate:

A playwright who used language purely
Placed semicolons and commas securely.
He wrote for the page
But not for the stage
So his audience left prematurely.

• What does your protagonist want? If he doesn't want something with all of his heart and soul and mind and body and every fiber of his being, he is an excessively boring person.

• Is your story about people or about plot? Start with people. They'll find lots of plots and help you work them out. Try to avoid average people. Average people are boring to audiences, even to average audiences. You may press your ear against the wall to eavesdrop on "average" neighbors who are fighting, but you won't plunk down $20 for a theater ticket to watch it. Try to create salty, contradictory, lovable, hateable, strong-willed individuals.

• Emotions. Have you made the audience cry, laugh, fume with rage, shiver with fright, tingle with nostalgia, etc.? Put your audience through the wringer. It's what they want.

• Is there enough action onstage to keep the audience's attention riveted on the development? Nothing wastes an evening in the theater like two lovers talking to each other endlessly without action. Too many plays are just chit-chat.

• Does the plot build? Is there rising action throughout?

• Is it real action or just "business"? You're not going to get away with a static play by having your actors hammering and sawing and jumping around, entering and exiting frequently, or making them move furniture all over the stage.

• And don't use the ploy of moving the plot forward by phone conversations. These are deadly! Audiences tire of this device and are also irritated by a play that is broken into many small scenes. Sometimes this works, but usually it keeps the audience from losing themselves in the story.

• If it's suspense you're after, you must build ever-increasing fear by fueling the plot with more and more new dangers, even if nothing horrible happens until the end. Recently, I read a play that will certainly be panned if it is ever produced. A killer is loose. Two men with shotguns wait for him to appear. They wait and wait and wait—and so does the audience. Waiting is not suspense. Waiting is waiting, and that is sleep inducing.

• If any action happens offstage, can it be brought onstage? The audience doesn't want to hear about it, they want to see! A distinction between action and movement must be made here. When a director reads your play, he retains important happenings but crosses out all stage directions such as, "crosses to stage right, sits on chair," etc. Don't usurp the director's blocking privileges.

• Is your exposition exciting? Some believe that it's not possible to make exposition entertaining, but it can be done with a few more months' work. In the old days, plays opened with two servants swinging feather dusters as they spoke to each other about what had taken place before the play started. Unfortunately, there are still some remnants of feather-dusting in plays by neophytes. A good hint: Chop off the first 6 pages of your script and watch the exposition improve. Free of verbal fat, the action will get off to a fast start. You may easily restore any essential lines that have thus been displaced. Another hint: Finish the play, then go back and rewrite the exposition when you've come to understand what you're trying to do.

• Have you finished all of your exposition by the end of Act I? By Act II, you should have nothing but rising action headed straight for the denouement.

• Do you know how to divide the two acts? An audience has more patience in the beginning, so make Act I long and Act II short. But, whatever you do, be sure to end Act I with a cliff-hanger so that everyone will show up again after intermission.

• Don't preach or explain too much. Don't insult the intelligence of your audience.

• Are your characters entirely different from one another? If any two are similar, fire one of them. Orchestration is the key. You must also remember that the producer who reads your play must pay a salary for each player that you "hire" by writing him or her into your script.

• Is the vocabulary and speech pattern of each character distinctive? Eavesdrop on authentic conversations. Take notes on how people talk to one another.

• Will the audience learn about your characters by what they do, through their actions and reactions? (No one should have to explain himself.) Show, do not tell!

• Did you create personas so exciting and powerful that an actor or actress would want to use a scene from your play as an audition piece? Consider the player. He or she is sick to death of picking up parts that mouth some pet philosophy of the playwright. He wants to portray someone who is good and bad, who has human frailties and virtues. Try to take a part in a play reading as a performer, and you'll soon realize how disappointing it can be to take the part of a wooden dummy. Think like an actor or actress when you write. Cast yourself in some of your own roles and walk around reading aloud. Plays are for acting.

• Did you keep your lines short, or do you have actors spouting two or three sentences in each line? Except for some unusual plays, most lines should resemble ping-pong volleys with occasional paragraphs of greater length to vary the rhythm.

• Did you make the mistake of repeating something to be certain the audience will remember? Cut repeats: even stupid people keep track of an exciting story.

• Does each line move the play forward? If not, cut the line and save it for another play, so it won't be a total loss.

• Have you cut your play down to the bone? No, you haven't. Go right back and cut out all those lukewarm lines. Then when it's lean, make another major cutting. Slash away. You do it in your garden; why not with something as important as a play? After you make the cuts, see how it flows. An otherwise perfect script could be totally ruined by excessive length—125 pages could deal the death blow.

• Have you prepared the way for major action by planting seeds? Don't just drop something on the audience. They want to guess ahead. Let them be part of the experience. If your protagonist drives a sword through someone in Act II, that instrument should have been introduced in Act I in some minor way. Also, the entrance of each character should be prepared for.

• Does your play break new ground? If it covers an idea that is not new, is it presented in a new or unique way? Also, re-examine your script to make sure you haven't rewritten one of the great classics all over again. Once was enough. (This is the most common fault. Check it out again.)

• Can you summarize the premise of your play in one sentence? If not, the play may be attempting to say more than is possible within the framework. That will cause diffusion and confusion. The premise of a play is usually a statement like "Pride goeth before a fall," "Love is blind," or "Greed can bring about destruction." Keeping it in mind will assure unity throughout. Anything that does not lead to your premise should be pruned away from the script.

437

• Did you use lots of four-letter obscenities because it's chic? They don't shock anymore. When the fad disappears, and it will, your play will be dated. And never use current jargon, if you want your play to enjoy a long life.

I originally compiled this list to remind myself of the faults most often cited by critics, but I keep forgetting them. In fact, I wrote the first draft of this article on the backs of pages of my plays that were rejected for such infractions.

83

THOUGHTS IN THE RABBIT HOLE

By Anne Lindbergh

WHEN my niece was a little girl there were two Willys in her life: One was a friend of her father's, the other a dog. She answered the phone one day when her parents were out, and the voice at the other end instructed her to tell her father that Willy had called. "Willy the man or Willy the dog?" she asked.

The caller was Willy the man, but he could just as well have been Willy the dog, in which case my niece would have given the message unconcernedly except, perhaps, for remarking that it was the first time the dog had called on the phone.

I remember crossing a bridge over the railway tracks of the "Gare de Lyons" in Paris with my son, who lived in that city until he was nine. "What's down there?" he asked. "It's the 'Gare de Lyons'," I told him, "the Lyons station." He examined it carefully before saying, "I think you're wrong. It's a train station."

Small children come up with "cute" sayings all the time. We repeat them to our friends and laugh. They *are* funny, but what makes them funny is the key to a successful children's fantasy: a child's willingness to consider and eventually accept what most adults would reject as a preposterous situation.

I began to use fantasy more and more in writing my books for children as I became better acquainted with children. As a child, I loved reading *Alice in Wonderland, Mary Poppins,* E. Nesbit's trilogy *(The Five Children and It, The Phoenix and the Carpet,* and *The Story of the Amulet),* and later, C. S. Lewis's *The Lion, the Witch, and the Wardrobe,* followed by the further chronicles of Narnia. I read and reread them but didn't stop to ask myself why, or what they had in common. Now, raising my own children, listening to them and their friends, and hearing what children have to say about the books I write, I am beginning to find out.

Children have different tastes in their reading, of course, just as adults do. But the children who read the sort of books I used to read like them because they appeal to their credulity and their imagination at the same time. The characters and settings in the stories are familiar: The characters could be the readers themselves, and the stories could take place in their own homes. But the situation that is "impossible" in real life actually occurs in these books. The dog speaks on the telephone, lions are in the station, and the child in the story is only mildly surprised.

When Mary Poppins arrives at number seventeen Cherry-Tree Lane, lifted and blown by the east wind toward a very ordinary family, Michael Banks simply comments, "How funny! I've never seen that happen before!"

My favorite example of a child's accepting the preposterous is Alice. She is sitting outdoors with her sister on a hot day, feeling very sleepy and a little bored. A white rabbit runs by, talking to itself—in English. If Alice had been ten years older, she would have questioned her sanity, looked for the hidden mechanism, or for the ventriloquist. Instead, she decides to follow the rabbit because "it flashed across her mind that she had never before seen a rabbit with either a waistcoat pocket or a watch to take out of it." So down the rabbit hole she goes (a rash action, and one that worried me as a child), but does she leave reality behind when she slides into the dark tunnel? On the contrary, she takes time to inspect a jar of marmalade, consider altitude, longitude, and the distance to the center of the earth, and wonder if her cat, Dinah, will be fed at teatime. The only difference between Alice and today's reader on an ordinary trip is that the reader would be on a plane to California, while Alice was on her way to Wonderland.

The adventures in Wonderland were enthralling, but detached from my own world, and they seemed to function on a whole new set of rules. Who needed new rules? I was quite happy reading how a child differed from me only in that she had hit on a good thing, could bend or break the *existing* rules.

It would be dull if the child who has had the luck to find the rabbit hole, the mirror, or the magic picture, walked through to find a world no different from the one he or she had left behind. A few talking beasts liven things up, but the most endearing aspects of fantasy are usually those that relate to a child's everyday life. The child reader may not remember that Alice ran a caucus race with a mouse, two crabs, a duck, and a dodo, but rarely forgets the contents of Alice's pocket—a box of comfits (just enough to go around as prizes) and a thimble.

From talking to my readers, I have found that the details they relish are found in inventories, rather than in meticulous descriptions. Readers of my first book, *Osprey Island,* like the lists of supplies that Charles, Amy, and Lizzie took through the magic painting to camp on Osprey Island, or the contents of the trash cans in which August rummaged when he followed the rag-bag lady. A fourteen-year-old boy who lived next door, after reading the final version, commented, "It's still an O.K. book, but why did you leave out all those good parts about the food they ate?" He enjoyed reading how it felt and looked to be absorbed into a painting on the wall, and how time played tricks on children who played with magic, but he also wanted to know what Charles, Amy and Lizzie spread on their sandwiches.

Readers cling to familiar details in fantasy because these provide constant reminders that the readers are participating, that if they had the luck to find the magic painting, they would know what to wear, to put into their pockets, and pack for lunch. I think this is the basic difference between the fantasies I liked to read and later write, and the fairy tales that were read to me as a very young child. Seven-league boots and a cloak of invisibility are all very well in the land of giants and dragons, but if you have painted a "window" of a mountain lake on your bedroom wall and step through with the intention of camping there, what you really need are sensible shoes and a warm jacket.

I don't mean to imply that older children become less imaginative. On the contrary, they simply stop being apprentice imaginers who need the entire fantasy worked out for them, and go into practice. Given an invitation to step into the painting, they like to make out their own lists and pack their own knapsacks. For this reason, in the fantasies I write, I use magic primarily as a means, rather than an end. The painting of Osprey Island is a way of carrying my characters, all of whom could be my readers, into a new environment, where they will have to fend for themselves and use their own ingenuity, *without coaching from adults.* The children in *Osprey Island* could easily have been taken by boat to the island in Maine, equipped with tents, sleeping bags, and a collapsible cooking stove, but their parents would have done all the thinking. It wouldn't have been nearly as much fun, either for those children or for the readers.

"Fun" is a key word. Although I would like my readers to work out the practical problems of magic and time travel along with my characters, I believe that fantasy in children's books is primarily entertainment. It shouldn't be mindless entertainment (the reader is quickly bored when it is), but it should be fun.

Many children like to take off into a realm of fantasy and stay there, leaving their everyday lives behind until the end of the story, a little the way adults like to "get away from it all" on a vacation. But my favorite sort of vacation is one in which you stay at home and make short forays to museums and restaurants as if you were a tourist in your own life. That is the way I use fantasy in my books.

My characters travel back and forth—city, country, past, future—but they always keep in touch with home. A friend suggested to me that the children who prefer this treatment of fantasy are the ones who like to keep one foot in the door, and need the reassurance of an easily accessible home base. That may be true, but they are also the children who delight in the idea of flirting with magic and want as many opportunities as possible to do so in a story.

After stealing Mary Poppins's compass on "Bad Tuesday" and summoning North, South, East and West in one fell swoop, Michael Banks ends up in bed with a cup of warm milk. Reassuring, yes, but why not? As a child I wouldn't have bothered to reread the chapter if Michael had gone to the North Pole and stayed there.

In *The Story of the Amulet,* the final book of E. Nesbit's trilogy, the children travel in time as well as in space. First published nearly eighty years ago, this book added a new dimension to the genre: Not only could children go to the four corners of the earth and come safely home without having lost more than a few minutes of their time (there seems to be an unwritten rule in magical excursions that no matter how long you are gone, the hands of the clock have hardly moved when you get back home), but they could now travel into the past and even change it. For both the author and the reader, this was like being given a new toy. In their search for the missing half of the amulet, the children travel to 6,000 B.C., and Robert terrifies an entire Egyptian village with a cap pistol. After a lengthy and nearly disastrous visit, he and his brother and sister tumble back into their own time, where "Old Nurse met them with amazement. 'Well, if I ever did!', she said. 'What's gone wrong? You've soon tired of your picnic.'"

442

This last escapade (I keep wondering if it was inspired by Mark Twain's *A Connecticut Yankee in King Arthur's Court,* published seventeen years earlier, in which the appearance of gunpowder at Camelot creates much the same effect) represents a totally new and delightful way of flirting with magic, one which had since been used again and again by authors of children's fantasies. In *A Swiftly Tilting Planet,* Madeleine L'Engle sends Charles Wallace to "before this planet's Might-Have-Been" and has him work his way up to present time, rearranging events in order to prevent a nuclear disaster. In *The Shadow on the Dial,* the book I am working on now, a brother and sister go back to the beginning of the century and make a few changes to help their great-uncle find his Heart's Desire.

I remember being wildly excited as a child by the possibility of going back to rearrange the past. Ideas rushed into my mind, ranging from preventing Lincoln's assassination to marrying my maternal great-grandfather to someone nicer.

Then there's the future. I have noted that in "my kind" of fantasy, there is relatively little travel into the future. In fact, when there is too much of it, a book crosses the line to science fiction. Here and there in my books, a child has a glimpse of himself as an older child and adult (and usually doesn't like what he sees), but in general he sticks to the past and present. On the other hand, authors have had a wonderful time bringing characters out of the past into *their* future, which is usually the present for the children in the book. In *The Story of the Amulet,* Nesbit brings the Queen of Babylon to early twentieth-century London, where she tries to reclaim her jewelry from a display at the British Museum, and causes quite a disturbance. The author puts the child protagonist in a situation that is terrifying, irresistible, and screamingly funny.

Thinking about these books makes me want to go on a two-week binge and read each one of them over again, along with my other old favorites. Reading any well-loved book—fiction or nonfiction, adult or juvenile—is a little like falling down the rabbit hole or stepping through the arch of the amulet. You travel anywhere, to any time, and come back home for tea. But the story in which a child encounters magic not in outer space or fairyland but on his own street, in his own house, has an appeal that I have never found in other books.

Reading fantasy can be entertainment, escape, or even a form of tranquilizer, but its best side keeps the child alert and constantly on the watch. Few children expect to find a spaceship on the corner to speed them off toward the moons of Jupiter. But there is always a very slight possibility that one day they will open a door and find themselves in another country, or touch the seascape hanging on the wall to discover that the waves are wet and taste of salt.

84

WRITING NONFICTION BOOKS FOR YOUNG READERS

BY JAMES CROSS GIBLIN

WHERE do you get the ideas for your nonfiction books?" is often the first thing I'm asked when I speak to writers. My usual reply is, "From anywhere and everywhere."

I've found a good place to start in the search for ideas is with your own interests and enthusiasms. It also helps if you can make use of personal experience. For example, the idea for my *The Skyscraper Book* (Crowell) really had its beginnings when I was a child, and loved to be taken up to the observation deck of the Terminal Tower, the tallest building in my home city of Cleveland.

Years later, after I moved to New York, I rented an apartment that was just a few blocks away from the Flatiron Building, one of the city's earliest and most striking skyscrapers. No matter how many times I passed the building, I always saw something new when I looked up at the carved decorations on its surface.

Although I had edited many books for children, I'd never thought of writing for a young audience until I was invited to contribute a 500-word essay to *The New York Kid's Book*. I chose the Flatiron Building as my topic because I wanted to find out more about it myself.

That piece led to an expanded magazine article (for *Cricket*) called "Buildings That Scrape the Sky," and then to *The Skyscraper Book*. In the latter I was finally able to tell the story behind Cleveland's Terminal Tower, the skyscraper that had fascinated me forty years earlier.

Besides looking first to your own interests and knowledge, you should also be open to ideas that may come your way by luck or chance. The idea of *Chimney Sweeps* (Crowell) literally came to me out of the blue when I was flying to Oklahoma City on business.

The plane stopped in Chicago and a tall, rangy young man carrying

445

what I thought was a musical instrument case took the seat next to me. We started to talk, and I discovered that the man—whose name was Christopher Curtis—was a chimney sweep, and his case contained samples of the brushes he manufactured at his own small factory in Vermont. He was on his way to Oklahoma City to conduct a seminar for local sweeps on how to clean chimneys more efficiently.

Chris went on to tell me a little about the history of chimney sweeping and its revival as a profession in the last decade, because of the energy crisis. In turn, I told him I was a writer of children's books, and that he'd fired my interest in chimney sweeps as a possible subject.

We exchanged business cards, and a month or so later I wrote to tell him that I'd followed up on the idea and had started researching the book on chimney sweeps. I asked him if he'd be willing to read the manuscript for accuracy. He agreed to do so and volunteered to supply photographs of present-day sweeps that could be used (and were) as illustrations in the book.

According to an old English superstition, it's lucky to meet a chimney sweep. Well, meeting Christopher Curtis was certainly lucky for me!

Evaluating an idea

Once you have an idea for a book, the next step is to decide whether or not it's worth pursuing. The first thing I do is check R. R. Bowker's annual *Subject Guide to Children's Books in Print,* available in the reference department of most libraries, to see what else has been written on the subject. With *Chimney Sweeps,* there was nothing at all. In the case of *The Skyscraper Book,* I discovered that there were several books about *how* skyscrapers are constructed, but none with a focus on *why* and *by whom* they're constructed, which was the angle of the book I wanted to write. There may be many books on a given subject, but if you find a fresh or different slant, there'll probably be room in the market for yours, too.

Another thing to weigh when evaluating an idea is the matter of levels: A subject worth treating in a book usually has more than one. For instance, when I began researching *Chimney Sweeps,* I soon realized that besides the obvious human and social history, the subject also touched on economic and technological history. Weaving those different levels together made the book more interesting to write—and I believe it makes it more interesting for readers also.

446

A third important factor to consider is what age group to write the book for. That decision has to be based on two things: the nature of the subject and a knowledge of the market for children's books. I aimed *Chimney Sweeps* at an older audience, because I felt that the subject required more of a sense of history than younger readers would have. At the same time, I kept the text as simple and compact as possible, because I knew that there's a much greater demand today for children's nonfiction geared to the upper elementary grades than there is for Young Adult nonfiction.

After you've checked out your idea and decided what slant to take with it, and what age group to write for, it's time to begin the research. An entire article could be devoted to research methods alone. The one thing I feel it's safe to say after writing seven books is that each project requires its own approach, and you have to discover it as you go along.

When I was researching *The Scarecrow Book* (Crown, 1980), I came up against one stone wall after another. It seemed no one had ever bothered to write anything about scarecrows. Research became a matter of following up on the skimpiest of clues. For example, a brief mention in a magazine article that the Japanese had a scarecrow god led me to the Orientalia Division of the Library of Congress, where a staff member kindly translated a passage from a Japanese encyclopedia describing the god and its relation to Japanese scarecrows.

The Skyscraper Book presented the opposite problem. There was so much background material available on skyscrapers that I could easily have spent ten years researching the subject and never come to the end. Choices had to be made early on. I settled on the eight or ten New York skyscrapers I wanted to discuss and sought detailed information only on those. I did the same thing with skyscrapers in Chicago and other cities around the country.

Chimney Sweeps opened up the exciting area of primary source material. On a visit to the Economics Division of the New York Public Library, I discovered the yellowing transcripts of early 19th-century British investigations into the deplorable living and working conditions of child sweeps.

Fireworks, Picnics, and Flags: The Story of The Fourth of July Symbols (Clarion) introduced me to the pleasures of on-site research. I had spent two days at beautiful Independence National Historical Park in Philadelphia. I toured Independence Hall, visited the rented rooms nearby where Thomas Jefferson drafted the Declaration of Independence, and watched a group of third-grade youngsters touch the Liberty Bell in its pavilion. I won't soon forget the looks of awe on their faces.

Whenever I go out on a research expedition, I always take along a supply of 4 × 6-inch cards. At the top of each one, I write the subject for handy reference when I file the cards alphabetically in a metal box. I also write the title, author, publisher, and date of the book I'm reading so that I'll have all that information on hand when I compile the bibliography for my book. Then I go on to jot down the facts I think I might be able to use.

I try to check each fact against at least two other sources before including it in the text. Such double-checking can turn up myths that have long passed as truths. For instance, while researching *Fireworks, Picnics, and Flags,* I read two books that said an old bell-ringer sat in the tower of Independence Hall almost all day on July 4, 1776. He was waiting for word that independence had been declared so that he could ring the Liberty Bell.

At last, in late afternoon, a small boy ran up the steps of the tower and shouted, "Ring, Grandfather! Ring for Liberty!" The old man did so at once, letting all of Philadelphia know that America was no longer a British colony. It makes a fine story—but according to the third source I checked, it simply isn't true.

By no means will all of the facts I find appear in the finished book. Only a small part of any author's research shows up in the final manuscript. But I think a reader can feel the presence of the rest beneath the surface, lending substance and authority to the writing.

Picture research

With most of my books, I've gathered the illustrations as well as written the text, and this has led me into the fascinating area of picture research. On *The Scarecrow Book,* for example, I discovered the resources of the Prints and Photographs Division of the Library of Congress, where I located several stunning photographs of Southern scarecrows taken during the 1930s. Later, in a back issue of *Time* magazine, I came across a story about Senji Kataoka, a public relations officer with the Ministry of Agriculture in Tokyo, whose hobby was taking pictures of scarecrows. Over the years, the article said, Mr.

Kataoka had photographed more than 2000 examples in the countryside around Tokyo.

I decided to follow up on this lead, remote as it might prove to be. From the Japanese consulate in New York I obtained the address of the Ministry of Agriculture in Tokyo, and wrote Mr. Kataoka there. Six weeks later his answer arrived in neatly printed English, along with eight beautiful color snapshots of scarecrows. I wrote back saying I needed black-and-white photos for the book and Mr. Kataoka immediately mailed me a dozen, four of which were used in the chapter on Japanese scarecrows. Another appeared on the jacket. When I asked Mr. Kataoka how much he wanted for his photos, he said just a copy of the book.

Experiences such as these have taught me several important things about doing picture research. The first is: Never start with commercial photographic agencies. They charge high reproduction fees which are likely to put you in the red if your contract states that you are responsible for paying such costs.

Instead, try non-profit sources like U.S. government agencies, which provide photographs for just the cost of the prints; art and natural history museums, which charge modest fees; and national tourist offices, which will usually give you photographs free of charge, asking only that you credit them as the source.

Other good sources of free photos are the manufacturers of various products. Their public relations departments will be happy to send you high quality photographs of everything from tractors to inflatable vinyl scarecrows in return for an acknowledgment in your book.

Selling

Writers often ask me if they should complete all the research for a nonfiction book before trying to sell the idea to a publisher. That's usually not necessary. However, if you're a beginner you should do enough research to make sure there's sufficient material for a book. Then you'll need to write a full outline and draft one or two sample chapters. After that, you can send query letters to publishers and ask if they'd like to look at your material.

If a publisher is interested, you should be prepared to rewrite your sample chapters several times before being offered a contract. That happened to me with my first book, *The Scarecrow Book,* and looking back now I'm glad it did. For it helped me and my collaborator, Dale Ferguson, to sharpen the focus of that book.

Of course it's different after you become an established author. Then both you and your editors know what you can do, and generally a two- or three-page proposal describing your new book idea will be enough for the publisher to make a decision.

Once you have your contract for the book in hand, you can proceed with the writing of the manuscript. Some authors use electric typewriters, others have turned to word processors. I write longhand in a spiral notebook and mark in the margins the date each passage was drafted. That encourages me as I inch through the notebook, working mainly on Saturdays and Sundays and during vacations from my full-time editorial job.

Achieving a consistent personal voice in a nonfiction book takes me at least three drafts. In the first, I get down the basic material of the paragraph or section. In the second, I make certain the organization is logical and interesting, and I then begin to smooth out those spots where the style of the original research source may be too clearly in evidence. In the third draft, I polish the section until the tone and voice are entirely mine.

After I deliver to the editor the completed manuscript and the illustrations I've gathered, I may heave a sigh of relief. But chances are my work won't be over. The editor may feel that extensive revisions are necessary; sections of the manuscript may have to be reorganized, others rewritten. Perhaps the editor will want me to compile a bibliography, or a glossary of unfamiliar words used in the text.

At last everything is in place, and a year or so later—during which time the manuscript has been copyedited, designed, and set in type—the finished book arrives in the mail. That's an exciting moment, followed by a few anxious weeks as you wait for the first reviews to appear. The verdict of the critics isn't the final one, though. There's yet another stage in the life of any children's book: the reaction of young readers.

Perhaps a boy will come up to me after a library talk and tell me that he was inspired to find out more about the skyscrapers in his city after reading *The Skyscraper Book.* Or a girl will write to say that the chapter on a day in the life of a climbing boy in *Chimney Sweeps* made her cry. It's only then that I know I'm on the way toward achieving my goal—to write lively, accurate, and entertaining books for young people.

85

WRITING FOR YOUNG ADULTS

By Norma Fox Mazer

WRITING for young adults today is particularly satisfying. These young people are going through the most intensely felt time of their lives. They are a devoted audience and, once caught by one of your books, they will read all of them and wait impatiently for the next one to appear. To write for this audience, it's not necessary to know their slang or the latest fad. It is important to understand their fears, dreams and hopes, but it is vital to know your *own* point of view: what you, the writer, think, feel, fear, understand and believe. You cannot write a deeply felt, satisfying book without a point of view on your material.

The storyteller brings order to events that in life might be random, purposeless, even meaningless. It's this sense of orderliness and meaning that makes the novel so satisfying. But to create that order, the writer should be aware of certain rhythms and patterns. To begin with, a story needs those simple classic elements: a beginning, a middle, and an ending. Most books have a beginning and an ending of sorts, but a great many fall down in the middle. If the writer flounders, the reader gets the sense of the writer's despair: I've come this far—what do I do now?

There are two things I think will help the new writer. One is to work with a unity of opposites as the foundation for your story—two characters locked together but intent on opposite goals. In my novel *Taking Terri Mueller,* Phil and Terri are father and daughter; that is their essential unity. They are further united by the deep love between them, and this, in turn, is reinforced by their life style, which isolates them from other people. This is the background of the struggle that ensues between them. Terri is determined to know the truth about her past. Phil is equally determined that she should not. There they are, united, unable and unwilling to get away from each other, and wanting completely different things.

When you first come up with an idea for a novel, test it by asking yourself a few questions: What is the basic unity? (It does not have to be two people. The unity of a character and an animal, or a character and nature, such as a landslide or a hurricane, is just as valid.) What is the opposition? Can I put the idea of the story into a paragraph that will suggest the unity of opposites? *Taking Terri Mueller* began with a single sentence. "A girl has been kidnapped by her own father."

When a writer works with a powerful unity of opposites, there are scenes that almost demand to be written. Long before I knew how I would develop the story to the point at which a confrontation about Phil's lying takes place between Terri and Phil, I knew that scene had to be written. All I had to do was work my way through the story toward that point. This key scene comes about midway through the novel, when the reader has been fully engaged with Terri's struggles and her father's painful desire to keep her ignorant of the truth.

The second thing I find helpful in writing a novel is to think in threes. Three is a magic number. Human beings respond to threes. A story must rise and fall three times to satisfy the reader. When I'm planning, I often divide the book into three sections. Then each section can also be divided twice into three parts. And in most chapters, there is a threefold rise and fall. Let me give one illustration from the key chapter in *Taking Terri Mueller:*

Terri and her father Phil have a close, affectionate and trusting relationship. Her only other relative is her Aunt Vivian. Now it's time for Aunt Vivian's once-a-year visit, a wonderful event to which Terri looks forward all year.

She wants to make the most of the visit, yet it's marred almost from the beginning. Three things happen. First, Vivian dislikes Nancy, Phil's new girlfriend, creating a strained atmosphere. Secondly, Terri sees a wallet snapshot of her aunt, who is said to have no other family, with two young boys. And finally, Terri overhears a conversation between her father and her aunt that strongly suggests there are secrets between them.

There are other ways to use the rhythm of three. For instance, a working rule of thumb for fixing a character in the reader's mind is to repeat something about that character three times. Although it needn't be a physical characteristic, the obvious and old example is the mole on the nose. Use a bit of subtlety in repeating the detail—certainly don't say it the same way each time—but within the first five or six chapters, working in the "mole" helps the reader visualize the character, especially if the detail can be used to shed light on the character's personality or state of mind.

In a description of Terri, I work on her appearance, but also on her state of mind.

> She was a tall girl with long hair that she sometimes wore in a single braid down her back. . . . She was quiet and watchful and didn't talk a lot, although she liked to talk, especially to her father, with whom she felt she could talk about anything.

The end of that description reveals something much more important than that Terri has long hair: her trust in her father. That he betrayed this trust is one of the central themes of the book. In the next chapter, Nancy thinks Terri is older than she is. Terri says, "You only thought so . . . because I'm tall." Thus, through dialogue, I repeat one of the points of Terri's description. And through narration we also learn that Terri is almost always the tallest girl in her class. But what's important here is not Terri's height, but her emotional maturity. And this is reinforced when Nancy says that it isn't Terri's being tall—but her poise—that made her think Terri was older.

In creating characters, remember that key word—create. You are not making a real human being, but an illusion of a human being. It would be impossible, confusing, and boring to put down on paper all the elements that go into any one actual person. Your job as a writer is to make your readers believe. Therefore, on the one hand your character needs a certain consistency, and on the other hand those very contradictions that are part of being human.

It's good to give your readers a sense of how your characters look, but what's basic are words and actions. What the characters say. What the characters do. I, the author, tell you, the reader, that Terri is a warmhearted girl, but if what you see her do is trip up a little old lady, then you know I'm lying to you. When I'm struggling with a character, I remind myself of the basic dictum: show, don't tell. I wanted to show Terri's longing for a family. Rather than say it, I showed Terri looking at a friend's family snapshots. Terri's interest and eagerness bring home to the reader her underlying sense of isolation and loneliness.

I've been speaking here of the young adult novel, and yet most of the

453

things I'm saying should apply to any novel. Still, the young adult novel stands in a class by itself. Briefly, I'd like to mention what, in general, distinguishes the young adult novel from any other novel.

The first and most obvious point is the age of the protagonist. Nearly always, the main character is going to be a person the same age or slightly older than the people in your audience. In the young adult novel, there tends to be a very close identification between the reader and the protagonist. A reader wrote me recently, "I hope you know your book describes my life." Literally, it couldn't have, since story, setting, and characters were all products of my imagination. Yet this reader believed in the reality of the world I created. To achieve this sense of verisimilitude, when you write you cannot stand above or to one side of the character, you cannot comment as an older, "wiser" adult, but you must see and report the world through your protagonist's eyes. This limitation, more than anything else, makes the difference between a novel written for this audience and one written for an adult audience.

Although it's important to recognize who your audience is, it's simply death to allow a patronizing attitude to creep into your writing. Your readers deserve your best. The one time I focus on the fact that I'm writing for teenagers is in the early stages when I'm searching for the right idea. Clearly, some book ideas are better than others.

I consider this early stage of writing the novel, which is really an almost non-writing stage, the most important. Concept is all. A silly or unimportant concept can mean months of wasted work.

Questions: Is the idea about young people? Is there an opportunity for the characters to work out their own problems and destinies? Is there a chance for consideration of some serious subjects? Is there also a place for the playful scene or character? I like to achieve a balance. Even in *Taking Terri Mueller*, which is about the terribly serious problem of childnapping, there are a few funny scenes with her father, a scattering of amusing dialogues with her girlfriend.

There are rewards in writing for young adults. There is hardly a subject or an idea that can't be tackled. I have written short stories, serious realistic novels, a time fantasy and, in *Taking Terri Mueller*, a mystery.

Perhaps the first real lesson I learned about writing was that not only did I have something to say, but, whether I recognized it or not, it was there, inside me, waiting to be said. I'm convinced this is true for everyone. Each of us has a unique point of view on the world; the struggle is to get in touch with that uniqueness and bring it into our writing.

My method is to write a first draft in which I spill out everything. The inner censor is banished. I do not allow myself to ponder over the "right" word, to search for the felicitous phrase or struggle for the beautifully constructed sentence. For me, a first draft means putting the truth of a story before all else. It means digging down for all those unique, but what-if-no-one-else-agrees-with-me thoughts, bringing them into the light and onto paper.

Then there is your audience. Is there another group of readers who are quite so enthusiastic, who are ready to laugh and cry over your book, who will cheer you on and write to you in droves? What can compare with the thrill of receiving a letter like the one that came in my mail from a girl in Pennsylvania: "Once I began to read about Terri, I could not get my eyes away from the book."

Each time I approach the writing of a new young adult novel I wonder, "Can I do it again? Will I do this story justice? Will I write a book readers will enjoy? What does this story mean? And aren't there enough books in the world already?"

No, not as long as there are readers and writers. Not as long as there are people like me, like you, like all of us who, like the writer Katha Pollitt, believe that we "go to fiction for the revelation of character, the rich presentation of lived life and the daily clutter of things."

86

MESSAGES BELONG IN TELEGRAMS

By Connie C. Epstein

Sam Goldwyn, driving force of Metro-Goldwyn-Mayer, once said, "If you want to send a message, send a telegram." Although he is not usually thought of as a source of good advice for children's authors, his remark is one the aspiring writer for the young would do well to take to heart. Message writing is usually bad writing, and children's books appear to be especially vulnerable to it. In fact, it may be the reason children's writing is often considered a lesser art.

Katherine Paterson, a Newbery Medal winner, expressed her feelings about message writing very cogently: When an interviewer asked her, "What are you trying to do when you write for children?," he was clearly disappointed when she answered that she was simply trying to write as good a story as she possibly could. She concluded, "He seemed to share the view of many intelligent, well-educated, well-meaning people that while adult literature may aim to be art, the object of children's books is to whip the little rascals into shape."

What is message writing? After all, every writer has a point of view, and without it a book is boringly bland. My definition is that the message writer believes in one or more universal truths that hold for everyone, whatever the circumstances. The artistic writer, on the other hand, is interested in people as individuals, the way each behaves and why. She or he describes them as clearly as possible and then trusts the reader to draw the appropriate conclusions from the actions of the characters.

All kinds of messages have shown up in children's books ever since children's writing was first considered a form of its own. At first, proper manner, good habits, and virtuous behavior were a prime concern. Today's writers continue to worry about virtuous behavior, but the problems have changed. Instead of thumb-sucking, stories deal

456

now with the terrors of drug addiction. Or writers may feel they should instill proper attitudes toward social problems such as racism, sexism, and ageism.

Some of the early children's cautionary tales seem startling, to say the least, in this day and age. There is the famous *Struwwelpeter (Slovenly Peter)* by Heinrich Hoffman, published in Germany in 1845. It was considered a great advance in the development of children's books, for it used the technique of comic exaggeration, a largely missing ingredient until then. Still, to cure Little Suck-a-Thumb of his bad habit, the tailor cuts off his thumb with his shears. The illustration shows the blood dripping down, and the caption reads, "That made little Conrad yell."

I learned good table manners from a book that had dropped the violence but retained both the preaching and the humor. Certainly it pulled no punches when it advised on right and wrong. This Manual of Manners for Polite Infants was titled *Goops and How to Be Them* by Frank Gelett Burgess, first published in 1900, a collection of verses about a strange subculture of bald, round-headed beings. The opening poem read:

> The Goops they lick their fingers,
> And the Goops they lick their knives;
> They spill their broth on the tablecloth—
> Oh, they lead disgusting lives!
> The Goops they talk while eating,
> And loud and fast they chew;
> And that is why I'm glad that I
> Am not a Goop—are you?

We recited these lines in a chorus whenever any one of the three children in our family made a slip at the dinner table and, strangely, thought they were funny rather than irritating. Perhaps the silliness was a relief in contrast to the parental lecture. Anyway, the priggishness didn't offend us and apparently doesn't offend children today, for I find to my surprise that the book is still in print.

Humor, in fact, has saved many a morality tale. One that I was most closely connected with was *The Chocolate Touch* by Patrick Skene Catling, a modern variation on the legend of King Midas (Morrow). In it, everything the hero touches turns to chocolate, and it preaches the evils of greed unabashedly, but a number of the effects are really very funny. In retrospect, I think it was more popular with children than with critics, so much so that Morrow brought out a new reillustrated edition with considerable success.

Judging from the manuscripts submitted to children's book editors, I would say that the temptation to pass along a constructive message to children continues unabated. Everyone who cares about young people these days worries about the problems of addiction to alcohol and drugs. This topic turns up constantly. Sometimes the concern takes such precedence over characterization that we get dialogue like the following:

> "If Sandy hadn't messed with drugs, she'd still be alive. . . ."
> "Well, it won't ever happen to me," Tommy answered.
> "I'm sure Sandy thought it would never happen to her."
> "I guess you're right. After all, a lot of famous people have overdosed—Janis Joplin, Jimmy Hendrix."

I can't believe that any two teen-agers ever talked to each other this way, and I doubt that any other reader would be convinced, either. Unfortunately, drug addiction is not solved so simply, and this whole story loses credibility because the writer has clearly put the message before characters and plot, a reverse of writing priorities.

Because this writer has taken his message so seriously, the reader cannot take him seriously—certainly not as an author. Adult writing-in-progress rarely suffers from the disease of wishful thinking in quite so virulent a form, with the possible exception of religious work, in which the message is truly the medium. To master their craft, children's fiction writers must constantly guard against wishful thinking and not play their characters false, or they always will be considered lesser artists.

Some people are surprised that a topic as unpleasant as drug addiction appears in juvenile writing at all, but the extent of this modern plague has pretty well settled the question. Regrettably, it is part of the scene for teen-agers in most large urban areas. More to the point is the artistry with which the subject is handled. When believable characters and plot are created, the problem falls into perspective.

The danger is the "single-issue novel," narrated in first person so that it is limited to the scope of one, sometimes immature, sensibility. All too often, the characters in such a story are defined entirely in terms of their attitude toward the problem—in this case addiction. It is their only topic of conversation and the sole motive for their actions. If characters and plot are given proper priority, however, then the problem is only one part of the whole, and the story is probably not considered a problem novel at all.

The present-day problem novel seems to me simply the latest form of message writing. Even now when we smile about the Goops of the past, children's fiction is still afflicted with obvious messages.

Manuscripts written for little children usually do not get entangled with complicated social problems, but they sometimes try even more earnestly to instruct in good behavior. In one manuscript I saw last year entitled *The Little Ice Cream Truck Who Hated Snowballs,* a personalized truck explained to a group of children the dangers of throwing things at moving vehicles. Perhaps this concept would work visually as an animated television commercial for Good Humor sticks, but between covers it seems a thinly disguised tract.

Another recent example carried the title *Aunti-Pollution and the Bubble-Gum Mess.* Aunti-Pollution was a turtle who stepped on a wad of gum and needed the help of all her animal friends to make her clean again. Pollution is of crucial importance today, but presenting it in terms of do's and don'ts for the young runs the risk of turning them off with a lecture or, at the least, of making them always uncertain exactly how the word *anti* is spelled.

When messages dominate a story, all the characters are likely to be stick figures, but one type suffers especially: the villain. Adventure tales desperately need a good, credible villain to make them work properly, yet all too often the writer wants to shield child readers from evil and cannot bring himself to describe wrong-doing with conviction or, for that matter, with understanding. In fact, the villain in this kind of story may be more important to its success than the hero, and you should be sure to develop him or her with just as much or even more care.

Of course, citing examples of what not to do is much easier than offering advice on good technique. Recently the children's writer Beverly Cleary had the following to say about messages:

There are those who feel that a children's book must *teach* a child. I am not one of them. Children prefer to learn what is implicit in a story, to discover what they need to know. As a child I was tired of being taught when there was so much room for improvement in adults.

459

These remarks were made in acceptance of an award for her story, *Ramona and Her Mother,* in which Mrs. Cleary did reluctantly allow there was a message. She didn't know it was there until she had finished the book (which is a good thing to remember: let the characters grow naturally and the moral will emerge of itself), and then the message turned out to be for adults, not for children at all. Ramona learns at last that though she has done exasperating things like squeezing out an entire tube of toothpaste, her mother does love her. So Mrs. Cleary concluded, "If there are any adults in the audience who feel that a book for children *must* have a moral, here it is: Children need to be told in words that their parents love them."

In other words, the child's point of view should be paramount. Try to imagine how the *child* in your dramatic situation would feel, and relate adult reactions to this feeling. If you are truly seeing the world through the eyes of children, you can hardly send them a message about it at the same time. Perhaps the biggest challenge for the children's writer is the leap in point of view that must always take place. From memory, instinct, and observation, the writer is always re-creating another, slightly different sensibility. The adult writer is frequently able to take the far easier course of writing from his or her personal reactions and perspective.

Children's writing is said to have come of age in the United States since World War II, for in that period it came to be recognized as a distinct area of publishing with formal standards of its own. Those who care agree that children deserve the finest writing and resent the notion that it is in any way a lesser art. But until we remember to use Western Union, not children's books, for our messages, I suspect they won't be completely accepted in the mainstream. Sam Goldwyn was a smart man, and we should listen to him.

87

SCIENCE FICTION FOR YOUNG READERS

By Douglas Hill

THE DISTINGUISHED American poet, novelist and science fiction writer Thomas M. Disch once rather sourly remarked that "all science fiction is children's fiction." His tongue may have been in his cheek, but he was reflecting a fairly general view that there is still something slightly disreputable about SF (which is the proper abbreviation, not "scifi"). Hence, there must be something slightly peculiar, if not immature, about those who persist in reading it into adulthood.

Nonetheless, a great many of us do persist, maintaining and usually enlarging that addiction that we first acquired when we were around 12 or 13. For that matter, the vast majority of SF *writers*, including me, started out as young fans, or addicts.

When I began writing SF for young readers—after some ten years and nearly 20 books of adult nonfiction—I felt it had to be a simple enough process. I could clearly remember what I liked reading when I was 12 or 13, so I set out to write along those lines.

And though it did not by any means turn out to be quite as simple as that, the basic premise was accurate: Children who develop an interest in SF do not leap directly from Marvel Comics to the luminous riches of novels by Ursula K. Le Guin. They progress through SF by stages—and the early stages are, without a doubt, children's fiction.

When I began writing science fiction books for children (my first, *Galactic Warlord,* was published in 1979 in England), I went straight into space adventure. There are plenty of other options within the incredible breadth of SF—the future on Earth, time travel, alternative universes, alternative pasts or futures, contacts with extraterrestrials (cuddly or otherwise). But as a kid I had liked reading about adventures on other worlds; I'd had an idea for an interplanetary hero with a particular problem and purpose; and I was encouraged by the fact that television and films were creating a huge audience for space adventure, even in 1977 B.S.W. (Before *Star Wars*).

So out into the galaxy I went, with my hero, the Last Legionary, and a cast of rather more than thousands. And I found—because this was my first crack at any kind of longer fiction, let alone children's fiction— that I had to learn a great many ground rules, mostly the hard way. Some of them may seem fairly obvious to experienced professionals, but they may help to clarify the thinking and planning of anyone contemplating a similar lift-off into SF.

The ground rules fall into two categories, with a certain amount of overlap. I had to learn about writing *adventure* fiction, for children today; and I had to learn about writing more or less specialized *genre* fiction.

The adventure element seemed paramount at first, mainly because I have never written anything like it. I had stumbled, probably by instinct, onto the first main prerequisite, a clearly defined and fairly fundamental "good *vs.* evil" plot—otherwise defined as a good guy against a number of bad guys. No matter how many subplots or temporary diversions you want to weave in, that central plot must always be clearly defined and visible, a broad, straight and well signposted freeway with a discernible goal in view.

So, too, the characters must be clearly defined and distinguishable— but that is made easier in SF, where aliens and mutants with weird names and weirder shapes can easily be distinguished from a very human hero. In the same way, space adventure readily provides the unusual or exotic settings on other worlds that can lend tone and atmosphere, heighten the sense of excitement or menace, and add integrated little plot twists.

Of course, adventure fiction requires you to place the emphasis on drama and suspense and action, rather than on subtle interplay of character or delicate tapestries of descriptive prose. These days, if you interrupt the progress of the story with too many pages of descriptive writing, a young reader is likely to toss the book aside and watch TV. So you keep description to a minimum, sometimes just a few spare sentences to prime a young reader's imagination, and let him take it from there.

Pace is the key word: You start off with a "hook," an attention-getting bit of action or excitement, and then you keep it moving—even accelerating as you approach the climax.

Naturally, there will be lulls, brief transitional passages when the characters talk among themselves, or travel from one place to another, or in other ways slow down for a short while and perhaps let the reader's pulse rate settle. But even in these lulls, there are valuable chances to underline the "what will happen next?" suspense—as well as useful possibilities for character development, comic relief, scenery changing, signposting time shifts and plot twists, and so on.

At such times the usefulness of giving the hero a companion, a sidekick, is especially clear. Hero and friend can converse, and so can not only expand the characterization and make a tension-easing joke or two, but can also clarify the narrative—reminding the reader where the story is, where it's likely to go next, and where it must go ultimately (that "discernible goal" of the overall plot). It's for this reason, among others, that the Lone Ranger has Tonto, Batman has Robin, and my hero has a sardonic winged alien chum named Glr.

I could go on and on about what I've learned in the course of writing adventure fiction, but the best writers make their own rules, and break them, and get away with it. "Rules" is probably the wrong word, with its overtones of restraint and contrivance—which can be fatal to a high-tension, fast-moving adventure story if it means forcing the narrative into directions where it doesn't want, naturally, organically, to go.

For instance—I always make fairly substantial synopses of my books at the start, partly for my own use and partly because the publishers need them as a basis for commissioning the work. But more often than not the book will break away from the synopsis at many integral points, because as the characters take on a life of their own within the plot framework, they also begin to assume some control—showing the writer better ways to move smoothly through the transitions, to develop the story and tie up the loose ends in a natural and unlabored way.

Still, that initial synopsis or outline is crucial, if you want to prevent too much meandering away from the main plot line and allocate the action to various chapters in the proper proportion. My books for children tend to be about 35,000 words long, and the chapters are also necessarily short—averaging about 2,000 words each, tailored to the attention span of a youngster of the 1980s. Also, many of the chapters end with something akin to a cliffhanger, something that slightly raises the voltage of suspense and makes the reader want to hurry on. And I'm simply not adept enough to parcel out the drama and action in the right chapter proportions as I go along, while at the same time trying to handle all the other elements.

I need a synopsis, or plan, to keep me on line—as, I think, most writers do. I also need to put a book through several revised versions, usually five or six. But a plan is not sacred: you control it, not the other way around, and you can alter or abandon it whenever a better idea or pattern comes into your mind.

As for the writing of *genre* fiction, in my case science fiction, I can again offer general hints from my experience, without insisting that they are hard-and-fast rules or restraints.

The fact that much science fiction takes place in the future and/or on alien planets can seem to mean that in dreaming up a story, nothing is *impossible*. The future offers a nearly infinite scope for change and development of the human condition; and alien worlds offer a literally infinite universe of possibilities. So it would seem that you can really let your imagination off the leash, in SF. But in fact that freedom only goes so far.

The watchword here is credibility. If you want to invent an alien race, or to depict humanity as developing in some wildly unusual genetic way, you have to keep it *believable*—within its own imaginative context. As a very simple example, suppose you want your future human beings to be winged. You can't just attach angelic pinions to people as they are now, and get on with your story. Human beings would have to have changed and evolved in other ways—with alterations to bone structure and musculature, with social and cultural changes (flying people wouldn't live in one-story bungalows), and so on.

The SF imagination can be brought back to earth, so to speak, with this need to achieve credibility. You also need to avoid too much complexity, because again you don't want to halt the progress of the story for pages and pages of description and explanation. And you don't want to introduce your strange aliens or mutations, or fantastic technological devices, merely for their *own* sake, just to be clever or to add extra exotic texture. They should play a functional role in the plot (unless they are only glimpsed in passing, very briefly, as part of the otherworldly background).

Also, you needn't be over-conscious of the generic term "science fiction," which is something of a misnomer. Young readers don't want essays on the future of astrophysics or biochemistry with a light sugar coating of dramatic action. They want a good absorbing story, though SF often does, broadly, confront important issues having to do with man's uneasy relationship with science and the general "future shock" of a high-tech society. But not even adult readers of SF, on the whole, like to be overwhelmed by science or handed a thinly disguised sociological treatise. Science fiction is just a special form of imaginative fiction, and the emphasis is on the fiction.

But at the same time you can introduce a few touches of science and technology as part of the exotic (but credible) background. Children will happily accept brief allusions to advanced forms of spacecraft, or futuristic machines, and you merely need to include a phrase or two of explanation where the meaning isn't already clear from context. And then it can help if the writer has at least a smattering of up-to-date scientific awareness, if only to avoid "howlers"—like populating the bleak barrenness of Mars or Venus with civilized, intelligent beings, or indeed any kind of life at all. Never forget that scientific and technological "progress" is high-speed, and accelerating. When I began reading SF as a young reader, space shuttles and holograms and micro-chips were still science fiction.

Even more important may be the need to have an adequate awareness of the genre in all its forms. Many young readers may prefer to dip into SF only now and then, but many more are hard-core fans, or addicts. And, as I said earlier, nearly every SF *writer* I know of began in the same way, as a juvenile fan. SF is a genre that breeds addicts—a merry, ingroup world of fan magazines and conventions and specialized, cultish expertise. It's not easy to wander in from the outside and write an SF story that is believable and effective and that doesn't unknowingly make use of some already overused device or terminology. You need to be aware of the competition—not just other SF books, not just films and TV, but also the comics, the video games, the fantasy board games, the toys . . .

It can be daunting, but children today are immersed in it, and so you must be, too, or else you're likely to start a story about a little green alien marooned on Earth—or about a space-traveling hero named Luke Skywalker. I came close enough to a version of the latter, in 1977, when I was planning to name my hero "Kyle Wandor." But then there was a British TV series called *1990* with a hero named Kyle; and an

American fantasy writer produced a series featuring a hero named Wandor. So my Last Legionary is now known as "Keill Randor," and he seems quite happy about it.

There are, of course, advantages for the writer in the present bombardment by SF. Addicts of SF generally tend to be collectors, which means that they like to own all the work of a writer they like. It also means that they are quite happy with the series format—trilogies, quartets and so on—though of course each book should be as self-contained as possible, like the episodes of a TV series (as opposed to a serial).

A principal advantage in the current abundance of TV and film SF lies in the impetus it gives young people to read books. That may seem a contradiction, but consider—SF is imaginative fiction, and the imagination flourishes best when it has room to operate. TV and films provide *everything,* in full color, leaving hardly any room for imaginative children to dream about what the strange planet and its eerie alien beings might look like, because the visuals give them so much detail. But an SF book, sketching its descriptions with a few swift and telling strokes, leaves enormous scope for the readers to go on dreaming, to add the fine detail and extra exotic flourishes.

If reading adventure space fiction can lead some children into reading other kinds of SF (and more books generally), the writer can feel gratified. Children may well see not only that the SF they enjoy at the movies or on TV has its counterparts in book form, but that the written word can offer more exciting, positive, lasting pleasures.

88

WRITING BOOKS FOR YOUNG PEOPLE

By Avi

IT's always difficult for me to set down a coherent plan that will describe how I write my books for young people. Like many writers, I work very hard not to set rules for myself. In fact, I have but one rule in which I have complete faith. Considering it's the only foolproof one I've got, I'd best save it for the end.

When asked *how,* therefore, I fall back to describing my process. It works—sometimes—for me, and that's the best I can do.

The question that's addressed to me more than any other (adults as well as kids, by the way) is: "Where do you get your ideas?" The answer is, everywhere. Ideas do not come whole cloth. They are amalgams of random thoughts, observations, moods, squeezed into shape by the way I look upon the world.

For example, my book *Sometimes I Think I Hear My Name* (Pantheon) is based on a) the particular living circumstances of a kid I knew; b) a remark about locale by a writer friend; c) a passing reference by my wife to the way some kids were living; d) the off-chance remark of another friend about a parent, and e) a quote from Ross MacDonald, "Most fiction is shaped by geography and permeated by autobiography, even when it is trying not to be."

Clearly, all these elements did not come together in one explosion. They rattled about in my head until they were linked. How so? This, I suspect, is the crucial part. My primary perception of the world is that of story. Because I have always read a great deal (still do), I have taught myself to think about people, circumstances, events, not in terms of singular occurrences, but in the context of evolving narratives that contain beginnings, endings, tensions, and locales. This means I am never without ideas. I've got six books in my head right now.

I think that each person has a way of looking at the world. I'll bet your dentist, upon meeting someone, notices teeth. The clothing designer will measure your cut, taste, and budget. Your car mechanic notices less about you than the year, condition and probable disasters of your auto. In just the same fashion, you can learn to look at the world from a novelist's point of view. It does require you to read a great deal and to think novelistically. Even that can be further defined; it's the 19th-century novel that holds me.

Out of a rather casual, on-going observation of things in a narrative fashion, I move on to constructing my novels. The key question for me has always been, not, how do I find ideas, but rather, how do I choose the ones I wish to work on? Not all ideas make good books for me.

I do it by building a brief outline that consists, in the main, of a series of *events,* usually no more than twenty. Since my perception of plot has to do with interlocking events that have a culmination, in time these events become chapter concepts. Here is an outline for a book I once started, but never finished. It's quite typical.

1. How it happened. Then.
2. Later. Nicholas meets Henry. Decision.
3. In school. Roger. Laying out plan.
4. In class. Dick. Punishment. Revenge.
5. Establish boy(s). Being punished.
6. Result.
7. The first coming of the ghost.
8. Boys see G. What to do.
9. With parents. Expose it! Win reward!
10. Return to school. First clues. Suspect.
11. Second suspect. Mountain digging.
12. Other boys.
13. Third suspect. Parents again.
14. Ghost again. Demands. Boxes. Slips. Clues. Fire.
15. Attempt to expose R. Triumph for R.
16. Two crises.
17. Evidence reviewed.
18. The empty box. More clues.
19. Great crisis.
20. Ghost revealed. Climax.

The outline is, as you can see, crude, and much of it sits in my head, rather than on paper. In that sense, the outline helps me recall my thoughts.

Usually, for a while, I don't go beyond the construction of an outline.

I sit back and think and think, and having done that, think a while more. Occasionally I've jumped in quickly upon the page with a new idea, but more often than not, I'll think it over for a period of months, maybe a couple of years. I will fuss with that event-outline a good bit, adding, subtracting, but always keeping it brief, to the point, and focused on *events*. I make no notes about persons, places, characters. I think about it. Above all, I try hard not to think what I *mean*.

I should say that I don't talk about works-in-progress, for two reasons. The first is that my great desire to communicate is best plugged into my typewriter. If I *tell* my tale, I find myself with much less desire to *write* it. More important, I'm afraid of committing myself to explaining my story before it exists. I don't want to fence myself in.

As for getting around to writing, that start is focused on the first chapter, the first page. I do believe that with the children's book, that first page, that first paragraph, is crucial. The kids don't give you much time to set your hook, and if you provide too much information they simply can't absorb it all. I strive for a quick sense of conflicting forces, an unanswered question, a loss of balance. I labor a great deal over these opening words and pages, not just for their readability but because they set the tone, the mood, the pace, even—and this is *very* crucial to me—the rhythm.

Given the opening gambit (which I think is exactly the right word here), I set to work from page one, right on through, with one eye on that "event" outline. But the fact is I'm never really sure where I am going. For example, when I wrote *The History of Helpless Harry* (Pantheon), I was intent on composing a grim, relentless tragedy about a kid whose fearfulness made him positively evil. There was not the slightest notion of anything funny. After a crucial suggestion by my astute agent—many, many rewrites and three years later—one reviewer wrote: "This is an invitation to farce, and farcical indeed is the web of misconstructions that follow." Wrote another critic of my would-be demonic youth: "This tale offers . . . a hero who makes the reader stand up and cheer."

So much for my relentless tragedy.

This kind of thing happens to me often because I allow myself to react to the books as I write them. I write, I have a suspicion, to discover what will happen. It's a journey. I read my books as I write them, responding to that reading, making countless adjustments, major and minor, as my *developing* perception of what I am writing evolves. Not infrequently I'll work on a book for months before I describe a character's physical being. It takes that long to see.

Just the other day, typing a manuscript for perhaps the tenth time, I was pounding toward the climax when I suddenly realized that my main character would not be saying what *I* had him saying. What he wanted to say was . . . and so he did, in the eleventh rewrite.

Here, for example, is the evolution of the last lines from the first chapter of my *A Place Called Ugly*. This sequence of versions runs from first draft to the printed text.

A tremor of panic forced Owen to swallow hard: he had done it. He was alone.

Owen was alone. A tremor of panic made him swallow hard.

Alone, a tremor of panic made Owen swallow hard.

And all of a sudden I had this feeling of panic. I mean, I had done it. I was alone.

Suddenly, I had this feeling of panic. I mean, I had done it. I was alone.

And what did I feel? Panic. I was really alone.

In seconds there was nothing but silence. They had gone.

Taking hold, they sped away. They were gone.

They were gone, and I was alone.

Mind, in a couple of drafts these lines do not appear at all as I experimented with totally different plot evolutions. And, in other drafts, these lines remained intact (for a time), while still other sections were being redone. I know I must have rewritten one part of the book, a few pages which contain, I think, the heart of the story, at least forty times. Most of those versions, I'm happy to say, were thrown out.

In this sense I describe myself as a very slow writer who works quickly. Fifteen rewrites for me is not uncommon, and the difference between first and last version is day and night. My first drafts are simply awful. I wouldn't show them to my cat. What *emerges* can be, and often is, O.K. But good Lord, there are times I feel as if I'm not writing, not for fun anyway, until I'm into the manuscript for six months.

It is here that my conceptual view of the novel's form becomes so critical. I reread what I rewrite endlessly. I respond to my work as

470

listener, seeking that right voice, tone, flow. I read my books out loud so I can hear them. Amazing what you hear. Read to a class of young people, and that relentless, restless shifting of feet is every bit as eloquent, as critical as a major media review. Considering its place in the process, it's usually more helpful.

How long does this entire evolution take? It varies. Generally speaking, I find that my best books are written in two phases. First, a fast, intense period of writing in which an entire crude first draft is made complete. This is followed by a long, slow period, during which time I untangle or realize that draft's potential. On the one hand, there is the emotional uniformity of that mad dash toward the finish; on the other, the often difficult, sometimes tedious, technical process during which I labor to make the emotional base readable. And, believe me, it's an everyday effort.

The crux of all this is a kind of hard honesty. If the work doesn't feel right, I *must* respond accordingly. Sometimes, I suppose, I try to fool myself, but I know. If you are not going to be absolutely honest with yourself, forget it. It will never go. And I'm not just thinking of plot and character, but of words, rhythm, that slender, silken, but always *spoken* thread that beads your vision into an ornament of articulation.

Betty Miles, one of our best writers for young people, once described to me that time after the book is essentially done, when one is free (and relaxed) to make those countless changes, those tiny touches that transform adequacy into an adventure. How true she spoke. At last one feels that one is truly plying the writer's craft.

Fortunately, I've been blessed with a few friends who provide me with readings to which I can respond; a close, working relationship with a top agent; and fine editors. Rarely do these people announce something I've completely overlooked—though that has happened. What I get mostly from them—in the basic stages of development—are echoes of my own thoughts and doubts, which bring me back to the typewriter. Later on, as the manuscript is given final shape, the creative interchange between me and the editor becomes crucial. You can't bring the ship to port without the pilot. I always listen. I never argue. Then, rewrite once more.

This kind of honesty is particularly vital in the children's book field. Young people have an essentially empirical understanding of the world. Their cognitive development is founded not on abstract ideas, but on

471

their concrete experiences, experiences centered on self. It is that characteristic that makes kids naïve, blunt, crude, insulting, cruel, refreshing, candid . . . depending on your perspective. The point is that they bring this critical apparatus to the books we write for them. They are much more demanding than the average adult reader. A hard audience to please: Give them a world they can understand and they will read you. Give them a world that expands, or better, defines, their often unspoken, often hidden perceptions and extraordinary sensibilities, and they will embrace you.

What I have described above is much the way my books come to be. When it comes to rules, I just don't believe in them. Except one: Write on heavy paper. When you are through for the day (every day), it'll give you the feel that you've accomplished something.

89

CLUES TO THE JUVENILE MYSTERY

BY JOAN LOWERY NIXON

WHEN I see the words 'mystery,' 'secret,' or 'ghost' in the title of a book for children," a librarian once told me, "I automatically order five copies, because I know the books will be read so eagerly they will soon be in shreds."

And when I announced to my family that I thought I'd switch from writing for adults to writing for children, one of my young daughters immediately said, "If you're going to write for children, you have to write a book, and it has to be a mystery!"

What are the magic ingredients of a mystery novel for the eight-to-twelve age group that draw young readers to it? What does a writer need to include in his story so that his readers won't be able to put the book down until they have come to the last page?

In a mystery story the idea is often the starting point. Sometimes this idea can come from a magazine article or news item. I once read an article about artifacts being smuggled out of Mexico that led to research on the subject and eventually to a juvenile mystery novel.

Sometimes the idea can come from experience. When we moved to Corpus Christi, Texas, we found ourselves in the middle of a hurricane. The eye of the storm missed our city, but the force of the rain, wind, and waves caused tremendous damage. The area had been evacuated, but I wondered what someone would have done who couldn't leave—who, for some reason, had been left behind in the confusion. The beach houses could not withstand the force of the storm, or stay intact, but what if high on the hill there stood a stone "castle," strong enough to survive the storm and to shelter its occupants? And what if this castle were known to have as its only occupant a ghost? Out of these questions came my book *The Mystery of Hurricane Castle*.

A study of the New Orleans French Quarter, with its legends of pirate treasure and its modern day fortune-tellers, grew into a mystery novel; and the idea of someone trapped on a cruise ship, or unwilling to leave when the "all ashore" is sounded for guests, because he thinks he has just overheard the plans for a murder, developed into *The Mystery of the Secret Stowaway.*

A mystery novel should give the reader an interesting background that will expand the child's horizons. Phyllis A. Whitney, in her excellent mystery novels for children, has taken her readers to many exciting and unusual foreign settings. But even the author who cannot travel can make a small town on the coast of Maine, or a truck stop in the middle of the Arizona desert, colorful and interesting to the child for whom this too is a new experience.

Deciding upon the main character is the next step in developing the mystery novel. It is his story. He (or she) will have to solve the mystery, and he will go about it in his own individual way.

It is important to make the main characters well-rounded, interesting and actively alive. The children who read the novel will want to identify closely with them and eagerly follow their adventures to the last page. They should have a minor fault or two—something with which children feel familiar. Maybe the boy's in trouble because he can't seem to remember to keep his room tidy, or perhaps the girl's impatient and plunges into things without thinking.

The main character preferably should be twelve or thirteen years old—at the top of this age group. Eight-year-olds will read about older children, but older children do not want to identify with younger children. Plots featuring boys and stories with girls as main characters are equally popular.

Once an editor told me, "Most of the mysteries I get take place during the summer vacation. I'd like to see one in which the main character was going to school." So in *The Mysterious Red Tape Gang,* I placed my main character right in the middle of the school year. His problem with turning in homework on time gave him a character flaw and added some humor to the story.

A little light humor can be a good ingredient in a mystery novel. I learned this lesson when I was writing my first mystery. I read chapters to my children, and my fifth-grade daughter would sometimes say, "It's scary for too long. Put in something funny." What she was telling me, in essence, was to break the mood of suspense occasionally. The author can't, and shouldn't, sustain tension in the story from beginning to end. It should have peaks of suspense and valleys—breathing space, one might say, and natural humor is a good ingredient to use for this purpose.

In order to make the main character more of a "real person," I think it's good to give him a personal problem to handle along with the mystery to solve. For example, in one story I let my character's fear of a neighborhood bully turn to compassion and a tentative attempt at friendship as he began to realize what made this boy behave like a bully. In another, I matched two girls as friends—one who thinks her younger brothers and sisters are a burden, and the other an only child who lives in an adult world. Each girl learns from the other, and each learns to appreciate her own family life.

The story must be told from the main character's viewpoint only, although if there are two characters traveling this mysterious road together—friends, brothers, or sisters—the viewpoint can include them both. You are telling the story through your main character's eyes, and it's important not to have anything happen of which he or she isn't aware. She may see an obvious clue and overlook it, thinking it's not important; or he may sidetrack his efforts, and thereby come closer to danger, thinking something is important that is not; but in either case, it is that main character's story alone and the author of the juvenile mystery must keep this in mind.

As to clues, children love the puzzle in a mystery. They love to find obvious clues which the main character seems to miss. They love to search for clues which the main character has discovered, but the readers haven't figured out. Both types of clues are needed in a mystery, but the hidden clues shouldn't be too well hidden. After the solution of the mystery is reached, at the end of the story, the reader should think, "Of course! I remember that! I should have known it all along!"

Sub-mysteries, which are complications, unexpected scary situations, or new questions raised, should be used throughout the story. They all tie into the main mystery, although some of them can be solved along the way. Each chapter, through action and suspense, moves the mystery closer to its solution, and each chapter should end with something tense or a little frightening—a cliff-hanger ending—so that the reader cannot stop at the end of the chapter, but must read on to see what happens. An example is this chapter ending for *The Mysterious Red Tape Gang:*

> Linda Jean grabbed my arm and squeezed so tightly that ti.e pressure of her fingers was painful. "Mike," she whispered, "those men might hurt my father!"
> The same thought had occurred to me. I wanted to answer her; but my mouth was dry, and I tried to swallow.
> Mr. Hartwell's face looked awful. He was like a trapped animal.
> "Mike!" Linda Jean whispered. "You've got to do something!"

Children read for pleasure, not for all the reasons for which adults read—because the book is a best seller, or because one received it as a Christmas present. If a child doesn't like a book, after the first page or two, he puts it down and looks for something else to read.

Therefore, the story should immediately introduce the main character, lead into the mystery as soon as possible, and grab the reader. In the opening paragraphs of *The Mysterious Red Tape Gang,* I set the scene, established the mood of the story, introduced my main character, told something about the other characters who would be important, and gave the first hint of mystery to come:

> My father gets excited when he reads the newspaper at the breakfast table. Sometimes a story makes him mad, and he reads it out loud to my mother. And all the time he reads, he keeps pounding his fist on the table.
> Once, when his fist was thumping up and down, my little brother, Terry, carefully slid the butter dish over next to my father just to see what would happen. Terry had to clean up the mess, but he said it was worth it.
> Sometimes my father reads a story to me, because he says a twelve-year-old boy ought to be aware of what could happen if he fell in with bad companions.
> At first I tried to tell him that Jimmy and Tommy Scardino and Leroy Parker weren't bad companions, but I found out it was just better to keep quiet and listen.
> "Michael," he said one morning, "listen to this! The crime rate in Los Angeles is rising again! People are being mugged, cars being stolen. A lot of it is being done by kids! Watch out, Michael!"
> I nodded. What I had planned to do after school was work on the clubhouse we were building behind our garage, along with Tommy and Jimmy and Leroy. None of us wanted to steal cars. In the first place, it's a crime, and in the second place, we can't drive.

The mystery novel should have plenty of action. The old-fashioned mental detection type of story, with lots of conversation and little action, is out of date even with adult readers. With children it's doubly important to include a great deal of action and excitement in mystery stories.

However, dialogue is important, too. Dialogue not only breaks up a page and makes the story look more inviting in print, but it draws the reader into the story in a way narrative description cannot do. A careful mix of dialogue with lots of action usually results in a fast-paced, suspenseful story.

The ending of a mystery novel is important to the writer, because it's one of the first things he must think about in planning his book. After he has mentally worked out the idea of the mystery, who his main character will be, and how the story will begin, he should decide how it will end. Once this is established, the middle will fit into place, with the clues planted and the direction of the action set. I find it helpful to make an outline, chapter by chapter, so vital clues and important bits of planted information won't be omitted.

A good mystery should always be logical, and the ending should be satisfying. It should never depend on coincidence. The main character must solve the mystery. If it's necessary to bring in adults to help out—such as the police or someone who could give advice—it must be the decision of the main character to do so.

The ending of a mystery novel should satisfy the reader, because it should present an exciting climax. The solution of the mystery should contain all the answers, so a drawn-out explanation of who-did-what-and-why isn't needed. Throughout the story the reader must be given reference points he can remember—well-planted clues. Just a page or two should be used to end the story and tie up all the loose ends concerning the main character's relationship with others in the book.

Stories for the reader of eight to twelve shouldn't be gory or horrifying: characters can be captured or threatened, but description should be kept within the bounds of good sense. The occult can be used in stories for this age, and can be left unexplained, if the author wishes, as the witchcraft in Scott Corbett's *Here Lies the Body*. At the author's whim, ghosts can be explained, or left forever to haunt future generations.

As for the title: Writers should remember the key words for which librarians look and make their titles mysterious or frightening. Some child who wants the pleasure of following a character through a scary adventure will reach for that book.

Mysteries for the readers of grades one to three, who are learning to read, have become increasingly popular with editors. These are "light" mystery novels—not as involved, and not as frightening as mystery novels for older brothers and sisters. The mystery tends to be more of a puzzle to solve than a threatening situation to investigate.

These stories are designed for 42 or 43 pages in a 48-page book. On each page, there are from one to eight lines, with six to eight words to a line. The vocabulary is not controlled, but is kept within the boundaries of common sense as to words a very young reader could read and understand.

As in the mystery for the eight-to-twelve-year-olds, the story opens with action and interest, and immediately introduces the main character. Within the limited number of words, the characters and the stories cannot be written with as much depth; but along with the mystery, the main character's relationship with others can still be shown. The plot should include a surprise kept from the reader, which sustains the suspense.

In *The Secret Box Mystery,* no one can guess what Michael John has brought to school in a box for his science project, even when it gets loose in the room. In *The Mysterious Prowler,* someone leaves a nose print on Jonathan's window, bicycle tracks across his muddy yard, and calls on the phone but won't speak; and Jonathan sets out to discover who the prowler is.

As in the eight-to-twelve novel, the solution of the mystery in books for beginning readers is in the hands of the main character, although he or she is allowed to have a little more help from friends.

90

STORYTELLING: THE OLDEST AND NEWEST ART

BY JANE YOLEN

SOME time ago I received one of those wonderful letters from a young reader, the kind that are always signed mysteriously "Your fiend." This one had an opening that was an eye-opener. It read:

Dear Miss Yolen:
   I was going to write to Enid Blyton or Mark Twain, but I hear they are dead so I am writing to you...

Of course I answered immediately—just in case. After all, I did not want that poor child to think that all the storytellers were dead. Because that was what the three of us—Enid Blyton, Mark Twain, and Miss Yolen—had in common. Not style. Not sense. Not subject. Not "message or moral." The link was clear in the child's mind just as it was in mine. Blyton, Twain, and Yolen. We were all storytellers.

Nowadays most of the storytellers *are* dead. Instead, we are overloaded with moralists and preachers disguised as tale tellers. Our medium has become a message.

So I want to talk to you today about the art of and the heart of storytelling; about tales that begin, go somewhere, and then end in a satisfying manner. Those are the tales that contain their own inner truth that no amount of moralizing can copy. The Chinese, the *New York Times* reported in 1968, were recruiting "an army of proletarian storytellers" who were ordered to fan out into the countryside and "disseminate the thoughts of Chairman Mao." They told the kind of stories that end: "As a result, the evil wind of planting-more-watermelons-for-profit was checked." These tales waste no time in getting their message across. But they are sorry excuses for stories. As Isaac Bashevis Singer has said: "In art, truth that is boring is not true."

Storytelling may be the oldest art. The mother to her child the hunter to his peers, the survivor to his rescuers, the priestess to her

479

followers, the seer to his petitioners. They did not just report, *they told a tale.* And the better the tale was told, the more it was believed. And the more it was believed, the truer it became. It spoke to the listener because it spoke not just to the ears but to the heart as well.

These same stories speak to us still. And without the story, would the tale's wisdom survive?

The invention of print changed the storyteller's art, gave it visual form. Since we humans are slow learners, it took a while to learn that the eye and ear are different listeners. It took a while to learn the limits and the limitlessness of two kinds of tellers—the author and the illustrator—in tandem. And it has taken us five centuries, dating from Gutenberg, to throw away the tale at last.

Children, the last audience for the storytellers who once entertained all ages, are finding it hard to read the new stories. Their literature today is full of realism without reality, diatribes without delight, information without incantation, and warning without wisdom or wit. And so the children—and the adults they grow into—are no longer reading at all. The disturbing figure I heard only last month is that 48% of the American people read no book at all in the past five years.

And so I dare. I dare to tell tales in the manner of the old storytellers. I do not simply retell the old tales. I make up my own. I converse with mermaids and monsters and men who can fly, and I teach children to do the same. It is the only kind of teaching I allow in my tales.

What of these stories? There is a form. First, a story has a beginning, an opening, an incipit. Sometimes I will use the old magical words "Once upon a time." Sometimes I vary it to please my own ear:

Once many years ago in a country far to the East....

There was once a plain but goodhearted girl....

In ancient Greece, where the spirits of beautiful women were said to dwell in trees....

Once on the far side of yesterday....

In the time before time, the Rainbow Rider lives....

Once upon a maritime, when the world was filled with wishes the way the sea is filled with fishes....

But always a story begins at the beginning. That is surely a simple thing to remember. Yet my husband begins reading any book he picks up in the middle and, if he likes it, he will continue on. He says it does not matter where he begins, with modern books—and he is right. If stories and books no longer start at the beginning, why should the reader? And if, as Joyce Cary says, "... reading is a creative art subject to the same rules, the same limitations, as the imaginative process...," then a story that begins in the middle and meanders around and ends still in the middle encourages that kind of reading.

Now I am not saying that a story has to move sequentially in time to have a beginning. One does not have to start with the birth of the hero or heroine to start the story at the beginning. Still, there must be a reason, a discernible reason, for starting a tale somewhere and not just the teller's whim. The person who invented the words "poetic license" should have his revoked.

What of the story's middle? First it should not be filled with middle-age spread. But also, it should not be so tight as to disappear. Do you remember the nursery rhyme:

> I'll tell you a story
> About Jack O'Nory,
> And now my tale's begun.
> I'll tell you another
> Of Jack and his brother,
> And now my tale is done.

Where is the middle of that story? It should be the place in the tale that elicits one question from the reader—*what then*? The middle is the place that leads the reader inevitably on to the end.

Is that not a simple task? I run a number of writers' groups and conferences, and all persuasions of writers have passed through. There are the naive novices who think that children's books must be easier to write because they are shorter and the audience less discriminating. There are the passable writers, almost-pros who have had a story or two published in religious magazines and are ready to tackle a talking animal tale or—worse—a talking prune story where inanimate objects converse on a variety of uninteresting subjects. And there are the truly professional writers whose combined publications make a reasonable backlist for any publishing company. And they all have trouble with the middles of stories.

The problem is one of caring. Too few writers today care enough about storytelling. If they should happen in the throes of "inspiration" to come upon a beginning and an ending, then they simply link the two together, a tenuous lifeline holding two climbers onto a mountain.

Of course the middle *is* the mountain. It is the most important part of the book, the tale, the story. It is where everything important occurs. Perhaps that is why so few people do it well.

What of the end? Ecclesiastes says: "Better is the end of a thing than the beginning thereof." An overstatement perhaps. But if the end is not *just* right, and is not filled with both inevitability and surprise, then it is a bad ending.

Adults are quite willing to forgive bad endings. I saw only recently a review of an adult book that said, in essence, the ending is silly, unconvincing, and weak, but the book is definitely worth reading. Children will not forgive a weak ending. They demand a rounding off, and they are very vocal in this demand. I remember reading a story of mine in manuscript to my daughter, then age seven. It was a tale about three animals—a sow, a mare, and a cow—who, tired of men and their fences, decided to live together. When I finished reading, with great feeling and taking the dialogue in special voices, I looked up at my audience of one. She looked back with her big brown eyes.

"Is that all?" she asked.

"Well, that's all in this story," I said, quickly adding "Would you like another?"

She tried again. "Is that all that happens?"

"Well, they just...I mean they...yes, that's all."

She drew in a deep breath. "That *can't* be all," she said.

"Why?" I asked, defeated.

"Because if that's all, it's not a story."

And she was right. I have not yet worked out a good ending for that story, though I am still trying. G.K. Chesterton noted this about fairy tale endings, which are sometimes bloodier than an *adult* can handle. He wrote: "Children know themselves innocent and demand justice. We fear ourselves guilty and ask for mercy."

But lots of stories can still have a beginning, a middle, and an end and not be right. If they are missing that "inner truth," they are nothing. A tale, even a small children's tale filled with delight, is still saying something. The best stories are, in Isak Dinesen's words, "a statement of our existence." Without meaning, without metaphor, without reaching out to touch the human emotion, a story is a pitiable thing; a few rags upon a stick masquerading as life.

I believe this last with all my heart. For storytelling is not only our oldest art, it is our oldest form of religion as well; our oldest way of casting out demons and summoning angels. Storytelling is our oldest form of remembering; remembering the promises we have made to one another and to our various gods, and the promises given in return; of recording our human-felt emotions and desires and taboos.

The story is, quite simply, an essential part of our humanness.

91

WRITING THE PICTURE BOOK STORY

By Mary Calhoun

You want to write for children. Picture books. You tell stories to your children or the neighbor's children, and they just love your stories. *And this is good.* If you're telling stories, you already have the first qualification for writing picture books: You are a storyteller. The person who can spin a yarn is the golden one who will fascinate the four-to-eight-year-olds.

Then why aren't the publishers snapping up your stories and publishing them in beautiful four-color editions? Just what I wanted to know when I first started writing down the stories I'd told my boys. Rejection notes from editors commented:

"Too slight."

"Not original."

"We've used this theme several times."

"Too old for the age group."

I can't tell you all the reasons editors reject picture book scripts—such as "might encourage kids to make mess in the kitchen," "might encourage kids to try this and kill themselves." You'll just have to experience some of the rejections yourself. However, these are the general heart of why picture books are rejected:

"Not enough body and plot."

"Idea not big enough."

"Not ready to be a book."

"Things happen to the hero rather than he making things happen."

"Action too passive."

"Basic situation not convincing."

And over and over, "Too slight."

Sound familiar? Use the rejection list to check your stories—my compliments. The thing is, there's a lot more to writing for children than reeling off a story.

Now about picture **books**.

First, definitions: A picture book is one with pictures and a story to be read to or by a child between the ages of three and eight. (Publishers usually say four-eight, but many a "mature" three-year-old can enjoy having a picture book read aloud to him.)

Of course, there are other picture books for young children. For the two- and three-year-old there are the counting books, the ABC books, the "see-the-cat" books. There are picture books with a very slim text line, books conceived by the artists mainly for the sake of the art work. (No, you don't have to supply the artist for your story; the editor will do that.) There are the "idea" books: non-fiction—exploring "what is night?", "what is time?"—and such books as *A Hole Is to Dig* and *Mud Pies and Other Recipes,* charming ramblings on an idea, but not stories.

Here let's concern ourselves with the traditional picture book, one with a story from which the artist gains his inspiration for the pictures.

What goes into a picture book story?

As I see it, the elements are four: idea, story movement, style and awareness of audience.

First of all, the *idea*. Without a good idea, the writer is dead. Most often, I'd guess, a picture book script is rejected because the idea isn't good enough. What's a good idea? Make your own definition; I suppose each writer and editor does. I'd say, though, that basically the hero is vivid, the basic situation and the things that happen in the story are fascinating to a child. And generally there is a theme, some truth you believe, such as "you can master fear." Not a moral tacked onto the story, but the essence of the story, the hero and events acting out the theme.

How do you come by good ideas? Perhaps in the long run only heaven can help you, but it seems to me that primary is rapport with children—and a strong memory of your own childhood feelings and reactions.

"Tell me a story" many times a day keeps the old idea-mill grinding. Many of my picture book and magazine stories grew directly from contact with my children.

One day I hugged Greg, saying, "You're an old sweet patootie doll." "What's a patootie doll?" asked Greg, so I launched on a spur-of-the-moment tale. The theme was (I discovered after I'd written down the story) "know who you are and be glad for it." *The Sweet Patootie Doll* was first published in *Humpty Dumpty's Magazine* and later became my first published picture book.

A magazine story, "Cat's Whiskers", came into being because Greg was always climbing into things and getting stuck—in buckets, under the porch, even in the washing machine. I coupled this with the idea that cats use their whiskers to measure whether they can get through openings; in the story the boy sticks broomstraws on his face for whiskers, and the story goes on.

However, here was a story idea too slight for a picture book. Not enough happened, really, and there was no real theme in the sense of a universal truth.

This brings us to a point valuable to beginning writers: If your story is rejected by book editors, try it on the children's magazines. The magazines have high standards, too, of course, but they can be your training ground and means of being published while you learn. It was my lucky day when a book editor said, "Not ready to be a book. Have you thought of sending it to a magazine?" My story, "Lone Elizabeth," went through many rewritings, but finally was published in *Humpty Dumpty's Magazine*. "Bumbershoot Wind" was termed "too slight" by a book editor but appeared in *Child Life*.

Actually, all of the elements of a story are tied into the idea, but let's go on to consider them in detail.

Story movement. I choose to call it this, rather than plot, for this suggests just what a story for children must do: move. Children like a story that trots right along, with no prolonged station-stops for cute conversation or description. Keep asking yourself (as the child does), "What happened next?"

In picture books there needs to be enough change of action or scenery to afford the artist a chance to make different pictures. Some stories are very good for telling aloud, but when you look at them on paper, you see that the scene hasn't changed much.

A book editor pointed this out for me on my "Sammy and the Something Machine." In this fantasy, Sammy makes a machine out of which come in turn mice, monkeys, mudpies, pirates and hot dogs. (It grew from my Mike's chant at play, "I'm making, I'm making!") This story went down on paper perfectly well in *Humpty*

Dumpty's Magazine, where there are fewer illustrations than in a picture book. But the scene doesn't change; there's that machine, over and over, turning out different things.

When your story is moving along vigorously, the scene changes will follow naturally—*if* the idea is storybook material. If the story moves but there's not much possibility for picture change (better let the book editors decide this), it may still be a fine story for some magazine.

Style. Of course, your style will be your own, and only you can develop it through writing and trying out and thinking about it and forgetting about it as you plunge ahead in the heat of telling a story.

The story content to some extent will indicate the style, that is, choice of words, length and rhythm of sentences. The story may hop joyously, laugh along, move dreamily, or march matter-of-factly. For study, you might read aloud folk tales and attune your ears to varieties in cadence: the robust, boisterous swing of a western folk tale; the rolling, measured mysticism of an Indian folk tale; the straightforward modern "shaggy dog" story; the drawling wry humor of the southern Negro folk tale.

If you already are telling stories to children, you're on your way to developing your style. However, "telling" on paper is slightly different from telling aloud, where the *effect* is achieved by a few judiciously chosen words and the swing of sentences.

I've had some success with one approach to the written story, and I've seen examples of it in other picture books. I call it "vividry." To me it's more vivid and succinct to say that than "vivid effect," and this explains what "vividry" is: words chosen with economy for their punch. For example, in a certain book I choose to say "little mummy mice." "Mummified mice" might be more proper, but to me it sounds textbookish. "Mummy mice" rolls off the tongue and seems a more direct idea-tickler for the child.

In college journalism courses, our bible was Rudolf Flesch's *The Art of Plain Talk*. From it we learned the value, in newspaper writing, of using sentences of short or varied length; strong verbs; short, strong nouns and many personal pronouns. Flesch might have been writing a style book for children's picture books.

We all know the delight in finding "the exact word" for a spot in a story. Never is this more effective than in children's books. Magazines for children generally have word-length requirements. Try putting a full-bodied story into 800 to 1,000 words. Every word counts. Writing for the magazines can be excellent training in choosing words and cutting out the lifeless ones.

I'm not saying, however, that big words have no place in a picture book script. Writing "controlled vocabulary" books for the young is a specialized art, and those books are used mostly by teachers and parents to stimulate a child's desire to read. Several book publishers now put out series of "easy-to-read" books. If you are interested in this field, read some of the books and query the editors on requirements. In the general picture book, though, I think children like to come upon an occasional delightfully new and big word. Haven't you seen a four-year-old trotting around, happily rolling out "unconditionally" or some other mouthful he's just heard? It's the *idea* of the story that the writer suits to the age group, not every given word in the story.

And this brings us to *awareness of audience*. I've mentioned rapport with children. If you're around them you know what they're thinking and wishing, what their problems are. And you'll know if a story idea is too old for the three-to-eight-year-olds or just plain wouldn't interest them.

With a small child underfoot or in tow, you see the details of the world that fascinate him: how a spot of sunlight moves on the floor; a cat's relationship with his tail (I used this one in "Tabbycat's Telltale Tail"); or the child's own shadow. (I haven't been able to make a good story of this; maybe you can.)

A child will watch a hummingbird moth at work in a petunia bed and report wisely, "He only goes to the red ones. White petunia must not taste good."

All of this, *plus awareness of the child's emotions, plus turning your mind back to remember how it was with you as a child,* tells you what to put into a picture book.

And then there's the other way to be aware of your audience: reading, reading all the good books and stories written for that age. Then you begin to see what has pleased children. You get the feel of what is suitable for that age group. You also see what has already been done, so that your own ideas can be fresh, not trite. You read "The Three Pigs," and the books about the Melops and you say to

488

yourself, "Very well, but a story about a pig has never been told just in *this* way," and you start off on your own particular pig story. As you read (perhaps to a child to catch his reactions, too), you may begin to draw your conclusions of what is good in children's literature, what is slightly sickening, how the stories are put together, what has worked.

It has interested me, for instance, to notice how many of the traditional stories are built on what I call a "core of three." Three brothers, three mistakes, three attempts at a solution. "The Three Pigs" makes me wonder if the composer weren't slyly trying to see just how many times he could use three. Three pigs, three encounters with men carrying building materials, three houses visited by the wolf, "chinny-chin-chin," etc. In so many of the stories, the use of three attempts to solve the problem is effective in building intensity to the climax.

So there you have it: idea, story movement, style and awareness of audience. Study them, use them in your rewrites, let them sink into your subconscious.

And then don't worry about techniques as you tell the story. For the first, last and most important thing is: you must *like* the story! You're having a ball telling it. Right at this moment, it's the most wonderful story ever told to man or child.

That, finally, is what gives the story sparkle and makes editors say, "This will make a wonderful picture book!"

92

WRITING BIOGRAPHIES
FOR YOUNG PEOPLE

BY ROXANE CHADWICK

EIGHT-YEAR-OLDS are naturally curious. They touch a cactus to see if the spines really hurt. They manipulate household gadgets, often breaking them, to see how they work. Their curiosity extends to all areas of life. One of their unanswered questions is what is life all about. This question leads them to read biographies. Biographies written especially for children give them some answers by showing them one person's life and hinting at its meaning.

Biographies for young people are as diverse as the lives of the people they are about. They cover a wide range of personalities and their accomplishments—scientists, rock stars, sports heroes, writers, political and historical figures, educators, statesmen, explorers, theatrical performers, dancers, artists. They run in length from 3,000 to 7,000 words for eight-year-olds; 20,000 to 25,000 words for "partial biographies" for nine-to-twelve-year-old readers; and 50,000 words for biographies covering the entire life of a person, aimed at the teen-age reader.

Biographies show children the possibilities open to them in the course of their own lives. They may decide to follow the professions, try to emulate career paths, patterns of behavior, reactions and responses to crises and setbacks. Through the biographies, the readers can come to know people they could never meet.

The most important step in writing a successful biography is choosing a subject from the millions of interesting men and women who have peopled this earth. In making this choice, writers have to please children, editors, and themselves. Most editors, librarians, and parents who buy biographies look for books about individuals who have made positive contributions to society. An editor also looks for biographies that will in general fit the company's list and will fill gaps in particular age groups and subjects.

An important consideration for the writer in selecting the subject for a biography is the number of biographies already in print about that person. Several years ago, writers discovered that biographies about women and minorities had been neglected. Consequently, many first-time biographies about accomplished women and others previously overlooked or ignored were published, and there are still many important people whose biographies are not yet written. By checking *Children's Books in Print* (found in public library reference rooms), writers can discover what books on an individual, if any, are available.

Before writers begin extensive research for a juvenile biography, they should query editors about their proposed books because many publishers have biography series limited to specific areas. Dillon Press has a series of collective biographies called "Contributions of Women," which covers women in such fields as dance, education, and science; EMC has a "Headliners" series on entertainers and politicians, aimed to attract reluctant readers; Oxford University Press publishes a series on artists. Several other publishers have series of children's biographies of Americans: Garrard's calls their "Americans All," and Creative Education's series is "Gallery of Great Americans." Consult publishers' catalogues (usually obtainable on request from the publishers) to see what series a particular house specializes in. Then write a query to find out if a proposed biography will be of interest to that publisher.

The most important criterion for a writer to use in choosing a subject for a biography is his or her personal interest in the individual. If the writer's interest is not strong or wanes during the course of the writing, the book will suffer and though it may get published, the young people reading it will detect this lack of enthusiasm.

When I took my first solo, cross-country flight, I developed an appreciation and respect for fliers. I had prepared scrupulously for the flight, mapping the route and calculating the course. Fifteen minutes into the flight, I crossed a lake, but according to the map there were no lakes on that route! I was lost; I panicked.

When I had landed safely, I began to wonder what made pioneer fliers risk their lives. With primitive radio systems and navigational equipment, they braved dangers known and unknown on flights around the world and across oceans. They often were lost, but they persisted in planning increasingly dangerous flights. Thus, when an editor asked me about writing a biography, the first name to spring to my mind was

Amelia Earhart. Her life was exciting enough to hold any child's attention. She had contributed to the advancement of aviation and women's rights. My interest in her was strong. The only drawback was that several books about her had already been published.

I borrowed all the children's biographies of Amelia Earhart through interlibrary loan, and read each one carefully. The life stories about her assumed that girls had no interest in technical information. Actually, today's children, boys *and* girls, are fascinated by how things work. I felt that the technical aspects of flying, as well as Amelia Earhart's significant role in the development of aviation, had been overlooked, and when I queried publishers about the Amelia Earhart biography I wanted to write, I included an annotated list of published juvenile biographies about her. I also explained what my book proposed to cover and why.

Authenticity and accuracy are absolutely essential in writing biographies, no matter what combination of research sources and methods you use. *Biography Index, The Readers' Guide to Periodical Literature,* and *Books in Print,* as well as *Children's Books in Print* (mentioned earlier) are good starting points for research. They point the way to numerous other valuable sources. Studying maps, getting in touch with businesses or industries related to the work of the subject, reading newspapers on microfilm (either in libraries or in the libraries of the newspapers themselves, with permission), writing letters to historical societies, government agencies (state and federal), and museums are some of the techniques biographers can use. Visiting the subject's hometown and interviewing people who knew the person or had some connection to the subject through friends or family can yield anecdotes and other material that will add zest to a biography. If you are writing about a living person, he or she may be willing to grant an interview, but you should be sure to write ahead to see whether your trip will be worthwhile and productive.

It is essential to take careful, detailed notes and keep track of all your sources. Although children's biographies are not usually footnoted when published, making notes as you go along in the various drafts will save you time in rechecking facts later on. In the final copy, simply omit these notes and file them in case any questions arise.

Still another important research tool is a chronological list of significant events in the subject's life, which may be correlated with important political and social events in the world, if relevant. Such a chronological record is necessary for a person like Amelia Earhart, who moved from place to place constantly.

In addition to the chronological events in the subject's life, biographers need to research the person's background, family, education and professional experiences. A general history of the period in which the subject lived will reveal events that may have influenced the individual's life. Histories about a particular field can show the person's contribution to its development, as for example, the history of aviation shows Amelia Earhart's pioneering efforts in flying.

Research is only the beginning. A collection of facts does not make a biography. From facts, a biographer must shape a story that tells how one person lived. A biography is a story of a person, with a theme, a plot, and vivid characters.

The theme of a biography can give a reader a clue to what the subject's life was all about and reflect the dominant thread that pervaded that life, thus shaping the cumulation of facts and anecdotes into a work of art. In the case of my book about Amelia Earhart, I found that confronting a challenge was an underlying factor in her life; she challenged not only herself, but also others—the children she worked with and the college women she counseled. I used her zest for challenge as a theme.

Like any story for children, a biography needs a plot as well as a theme. The events in the subject's life are the outline, the framework of the plot, but plotting is not simple. Because children's biographies must be short, it is impossible to tell everything that happened in a person's life, and a biographer must therefore choose the events that best illuminate that person and express the theme most effectively.

One successful way to approach the problem, given the word limitations, is to write a "partial biography." Writers often cover a person's life from teen-age until he or she achieves success, but any significant, productive period in the subject's life can make a good book.

Another approach especially successful in biographies for young readers is the "biographical episode," which describes one important event in the subject's life. *Lincoln's Animal Friends* by Ruth Painter Randall is an example of such episodes, stories of Lincoln's encounters with animals. Still another type of biography was published by Value Communications and called "Value Tales." Written in easy-to-read format for young readers, each of these books focused on one personal value—friendship, fairness, humor, etc.—as demonstrated by the life of a particular individual.

While in adult biographies writers need to tell the "whole truth," in children's biographies it is possible to omit certain episodes or periods that may not be suitable to their age (scandals, personal problems that do not relate to the subject's achievements) and would be outside of their experience or understanding. This does not mean, however, that a biographer is allowed to manipulate facts or change the essential character of the subject. These biographies for children must be true to the events and person's life and work to the extent these are included in the book.

Biographies for young people do not deal exclusively with the sunny side of life. Eleanor Coerr wrote a touching profile of a girl with leukemia caused by the bombing of Hiroshima. *Sadako and the Thousand Paper Cranes,* the story about the last year of this Japanese girl's life, is full of bitter truths.

In fictionalized biography and biographical fiction, plots can be made exciting by adding undocumented dialogue and details for flavor. The challenge for the writer of authentic biography is to make the plot of the story accurate and exciting.

The need to be factual poses difficulties not only in plotting, but also in delineating main characters vividly. Words and thoughts reported in the book must be words that the hero has recorded or is known to have spoken or could logically have said. Biographers skirt this rule sometimes by using "perhaps he meant" or "perhaps she thought," a device that should be used sparingly.

In the past, stereotyped characters were allowed in children's biographies in the hope that children would copy the characters' virtues. Stories of the ever-truthful Washington or always-thrifty Benjamin Franklin abounded. Children today find virtuous characters who never tell a lie or play a prank unbelievable. Ironically, these caricatures may give children a message opposite to what well-meaning writers intended. Instead of saying, "By being truthful and thrifty, you too can become famous," they imply, "Because of your imperfections, you could never be this good."

Today, biographers attempt to portray the whole man or woman through vivid details and amusing anecdotes. In *Joseph Haydn, The*

Merry Little Peasant, Opal Wheeler and Sybil Deucher show Haydn cutting off the pigtail of a fellow singer. In Ingri and Edgar d'Aulaire's *Abraham Lincoln,* Lincoln plays a prank on his stepmother. He holds a child upside down to make footprints on the ceiling. These are characters children can relate to—imperfect people who have even been naughty, but who did wonderful things despite their human frailties.

Even after the theme, plot, and character of your subject have been woven into a book, your work is not yet finished. A bibliography, statistics, appendixes, maps, or additional background information that may be relevant (this applies primarily to biographies for teen-agers) must be completed and checked, and the manuscript must be polished before you submit it to a publisher. Although such material is not always used in the published book, it often can add scope and authenticity to a biography, as in the case of a map of Amelia Earhart's around-the-world flight path. Any records that the subject set may also be of interest to readers and lead them to further reading in the field. And the bibliography about the period or subject is often omitted, but is an important part of a biography.

While you are completing your work on these appendixes, your manuscript can "cool" and when you go back to it, you can read it with more detachment and objectivity. Check it for clarity, liveliness of style, spelling, and grammar, and be sure to explain any terms that may not be generally familiar to young readers.

The finished biography won't provide youngsters with a blueprint for life, but it will give them some clues. Children can see how one person lived, and even how he or she died is often significant. Readers can discover what factors influenced this person's life, and as they learn about the lives of others, they can begin to understand and plan their own lives.

93

WRITING FOR YOUNG CHILDREN

By Charlotte Zolotow

CHILDREN's book writing includes fiction for children from picture books on up to the young adults, non-fiction—biography, autobiography and factual books—and of course poetry. In short, it includes every category of adult writing that exists, and everything that is true of distinctive writing for adults is also true of fine literature for children.

But there is in writing for children an additional skill required. It is easier to address our peers than those who are different from ourselves. And children are different from adults because they live on a more intense level. Whatever is true of adults is true of children, only more so. They laugh, they cry, they love, they hate, they give, they take as adults do—only more so. And this is what makes writing for children different from writing for adults.

One must first of all, over and above everything, take children seriously and take writing children's books seriously. Over and over I have met people who feel that writing for children is a first step to doing "something really good." A fairly successful, but undistinguished author of many children's books said to me one night, "Some day I'm going to do something really good. I'm going to write a novel or a play."

What this gentleman's abilities as an adult writer will be, I don't know. His children's books, however, lack something. There is nothing in them that would make a child put one down and say, "What else has this person written?" (A question children have asked many times after first reading a book by Ruth Krauss, Maurice Sendak, Else H. Minarik, Laura Ingalls Wilder, Margaret Wise Brown, E. B. White, Marie Hall Ets, E. Nesbit, P. L. Travers, Beatrix Potter— the great writers of children's literature.)

This remark of his made me understand why. *He doesn't respect what he is doing.* If he ever gets to his serious play or novel, it won't be that he came via children's books, but that he finally did take seriously what he was doing. I don't think writers of this sort should be writing for children at all. Children's books are an art in themselves and must be taken seriously. Anyone who regards them simply as a step along the way to "real" writing is in the wrong field.

I should make clear here that when I use the word *seriously* I don't mean *pompously*. I don't mean that every word is holy or that it should be heavy-handed. Some of the most delightful humor in books today is in the books for children. Some of the wildest kind of nonsense is there, too. But the writers are saying something seriously in their humor and in their nonsense—something that is real to them and meaningful to them—and they are saying it the best way they can without writing down to an audience whose keenness and perception they must completely respect.

There is a popular misconception about children's books that exists even among literate people. And it exists most particularly in the area of the picture book. A television writer once told me, "I never read my children what's in a picture book. I make up my own story to go with the pictures." He was quite pleased with himself—had no idea of the absurdity his smug assumption "that anyone can write a children's book" contained. He didn't realize that though his stories might amuse his own kids, delighted with the sound of his voice, the expression of his face, and the feeling of well-being his spending time with them gave them, a *published* story must be a finished, well-rounded work of art. In cold print, a story has to be good. The wandering, sketchy bedtime stories we tell our children have to be formed and shaped and sharpened before they can be printed, illustrated, bound in a book to be read over and over again to thousands of children who are strangers to the author's face and voice.

Some of my own books have indeed come out of stories I originally told my children, but years later, and after much thought, much reforming, reshaping, pruning, and in a voice or style that was a writer's, not a mother's. There is an immense difference.

In some picture books there are just a few words on a page. Certain immortal lyrics are four lines long. A sonnet has only fourteen lines. But the brevity doesn't mean they are "easy" to write. There is a special gift to making something good with a few words. The ability to conjure up a great deal just from the sound of a word and its relation to the other words in the sentence, the gift of evocation and denotation, is not only special to the poet but to children themselves. To say that he has had a good time at school that morning, a child may simply tell you, "The teacher wore a purple skirt." The recipient of this confidence would have to be close enough to the particular child to know that purple is her favorite color; that summing up a whole morning's events by that color is equivalent to having an adult say, "excellent wine"; that, in fact, in this child's vocabulary "purple" is a value judgment and the sign of a happy morning. And since children themselves so often use this oblique, connotative language, the writer who is fortunate enough to have retained his own childlike vision can speak to them in this special poetic shorthand that evokes worlds in a word.

A picture book writer must have this gift of using words carefully, of identifying with, understanding, projecting himself into the child's world. He must know and feel what they know and feel with some of the freshness of their senses, not his experienced adult ones. He must know what children care about a given situation. This is usually quite different from what an adult in a similar situation is thinking, wanting, seeing, tasting, feeling; and sympathy and empathy (and memory) are necessary, not condescension, not smugness, not superiority, not serious observation from an adult point of view.

And while the brevity of a picture book makes the author's use of words particularly selective, the rest of what I've said applies not only to picture books but to books going up in age group to the young adults. It is a question of experiencing at that particular level how the small or "middle-aged" child feels.

The best children's book writers are those who look at the world around them with a childlike vision—not childish, which is an adult acting like a child—but with that innocent, open vision of the world that belongs to the various stages of growing up, a clearer, more immediate, more specific, more honest, less judging vision than the adult one.

Children come fresher, with less cant, less hypocrisy, less guilt, to the world around them than even the most honest adults are apt to. Children smell good and bad things without inhibition. They taste, they hear, they see, they feel with all their senses and not so much interfering intellect as the adult, who will label things by applied standards, preconceived standards of good or bad—a good smell or a bad smell, a good taste or a bad taste. Children are realists of the first order. They have fewer preconceived ideas than adults. To them, flowers may smell bad. Manure may smell good. They have no fixed judgments yet. Most things are still happening to them for the first time. The first time water comes from a faucet, heat from a radiator, snow falls, the *real* itself is *magic*.

Because of this, children are open to belief in fantasy—fairies can exist if snow can fall, magic can happen if there are cold and heat, moon and stars and sun. Nothing is routine yet. They live more immediate lives than adults, not so much of yesterday or tomorrow. They are open to the moment completely. They respond to every detail around them completely. (That is why they are so often tiring to be with.)

I remember once the poet, Edwin Honig, came to visit us. He had never met our daughter Ellen, who was then four. They liked each other immediately. And when she offered to show him the house, he left his drink on the front porch and went off into the house with her. When I came in a few minutes later, he was holding her in his arms, and she was pointing into the living room.

"That is the fireplace where we have fires in winter.

That is the rubber plant where one leaf died.

That is the radio where we had the tube fixed.

That is the best chair but our dog sits in it." She might have invited him to see if he could smell the dog in the chair if I hadn't come in.

"You know," Honig said to me, "she's living everything here for me."

A poet could understand this. And in this sense that is what everyone who writes for children must be.

Always remember that the field of children's books is exciting and specialized. It is full of pitfalls that adult writing is free from, not the least of which is that a child's point of view is so different from that of an adult—more different at three than at six, and more so at six than at nine. And even when the child and adult reaction is identical—at any age level—in being hurt, in wanting, in hating, in loving, it is more intense. Adults are like a body of water that has been

499

dammed up, or channeled. Children haven't these constrictions yet on their emotions. They abandon themselves to emotion, and therefore everything from a cake crumb to an oak tree means more to them.

If you are to write for children, you must be absolutely honest with yourself and with them. Willa Cather once advised a young writer never to hold back on any idea or phrase when it fitted something he was writing, in the hope of using it later in something better. Never hold back on what fits the book you are writing for children either. Remember how you felt about things when you were a child; remember, remember that adults might laugh and say, "tomorrow he'll forget," but right then, at the moment, the child feels and believes in his pain or his joy with his whole being.

A famous children's book editor once said, "Young people can and will accept the very best truly creative people will give them." And in a *New Yorker* article about Maurice Sendak, one of the finest children's book artists and writers today, it was stated, "Too many of us . . . keep forgetting that children are new and we are not. But somehow Maurice has retained a direct line to his own childhood."

This is what anyone who wants to write for children must do.

94

BREAKING INTO THE BIG MARKETS

By Sondra Forsyth Enos
Executive Editor, *Ladies' Home Journal*

WHEN James B. Conant was president of Harvard University, he kept among other objects on his desk a statuette of a turtle, on whose base was the inscription: "Consider the turtle. He makes progress only when he sticks his neck out." There could perhaps be no more fitting admonition to free-lance writers than that one. I have a great deal to share with you about the business of selling what you write, but what I would like most of all is to inspire you, to instill in you the conviction that you can and will succeed—in short, to give you the courage to stick your neck out.

To start with, let me debunk the long-standing myth that unsolicited queries from unknown, unagented writers are never read with much attention or consideration. That's simply not true. I have been on the staff of three major national magazines, and I've discussed this subject with editors at many other magazines. The consensus is that while we all receive reams of so-called slush submissions—as many as five hundred pieces of mail a week at *Ladies' Home Journal,* for example—someone on each staff opens and reads every single submission. You see, we all *want* to discover new talent "over the transom," or to include in our stables established writers who have not yet worked for us. Believe me, it is a thrill to find in the morning's mail a sparkling query by a clearly gifted writer, who has come up with an idea that is just right. When that happens, I lose no time contacting the writer, even if he or she has no publishing credits at all. I would have to give a rank beginner a go-ahead on spec—speculation—of course, not a firm assignment, but that's an opportunity no one should turn down. Editors don't ask to see pieces on spec unless they are serious about wanting them to work out.

501

But that's enough of a pep talk for the moment. Let's get on to the nuts and bolts of breaking into the big markets.

Rule Number One: *Read your target markets.* If you want to sell me an article, go to the library and read every issue of *Ladies' Home Journal* for the last year or two. Try to absorb the tone and style, and decide who the average reader must be. Learn to think the way we, the editors, think. I am often asked what sort of manuscripts we buy, and this amazes me, because what we buy is out there on the newsstands every month for anyone to see.

Rule Number Two: *Offer ideas that are as fresh and unique as possible.* Editors read and research a lot, trying to come up with ideas and stay a jump ahead of the readers. We clip items, spot trends, and meet to share what we have gleaned. The result is that if there is, say, a rise in the rate of Caesarean deliveries, we're going to know about it right away, and if we decide we want a piece on the topic, we'll surely call one of our regular writers and assign the piece that afternoon, before your query on the subject, however compellingly written, can even reach us.

What's a writer to do, then? My suggestion is that you forget national topics for the moment, and look instead in your own backyard. For instance, suppose your hometown newspaper carries the story of a brave family coping with a gravely ill child, who has a rare and perhaps incurable disease, and let's say the family has inadequate medical insurance, so theirs is a double tragedy. Now there is a story of human courage which I would never know about unless you brought it to my attention. And if you had done your homework, reading *LHJ* from cover to cover, you'd know that we run at least one such "ordeal story" in almost every issue. You would also have noticed that we frequently run fact-filled boxes along with such articles, detailing where people in similar straits can get help or find support groups or financial assistance. Knowing all that, you would then send me a query, preferably noting that the people involved had agreed to give you an interview. If your query were exemplary, I'd surely bite. In fact, I did, when Beverly Jacobson of Scarsdale, New York, sent me a query on this very case. The result was a much-loved article, "The $300.00 Medical Bill," which ran in our August 1982 issue.

Rule Number Three: *When you stick your neck out, make the best impression possible.* Of course, I wouldn't have responded positively to Beverly Jacobson's query if it hadn't been so thoroughly professional, with a warm, attention-grabbing lead that could actually have been the lead for her story, and then a crisp summation of the facts in the case. She kept her query to under two pages, and she let me know that she had already approached the people involved and that they were willing to be interviewed and photographed, and that they would agree, for an honorarium, to give the story as a magazine exclusive to *Ladies' Home Journal.* Beyond that, successful writers know that neatness counts. You don't need a fancy letterhead or a word processor, but do spring for a fresh typewriter ribbon, and remember to include your full name, address, and telephone number.

Rule Number Four: *Don't send a completed manuscript.* There are a few exceptions to this rule—for example, short humor pieces, essays, fillers and anecdotes—but in most cases editors prefer to read brief queries. Even if you have written the entire piece, please follow this rule.

Rule Number Five: *Don't phone a query.* If you are a writer whose work I know, you may break this rule. Otherwise, you need to show me how you write by sending a written query.

Rule Number Six: *Send a resume and clips, if you have them.* Naturally, if you have no previous publishing credits, you'll have to take your chances and hope your query is a stand-out. It will not automatically be passed on to a top editor, as it would be if you had clips, but if it's good, I can guarantee you that the slush readers *will* pass it on.

Rule Number Seven: *Don't worry about getting an agent.* I know that the phrase "literary agent" has a certain glamour to it, conjuring up visions of lunching at the Four Seasons or La Cote Basque. But it is really not necessary to be represented by an agent when you are submitting nonfiction to magazines. If you also write books, you and your agent can decide whether or not he or she will also handle your magazine work.

Rule Number Eight: *Meet your deadlines.* This is most important if an editor is planning to use your piece for a specific issue. On the other hand, don't be disappointed if you do get your story in on time, and then it's bumped from the issue and put on hold for a future issue. Scheduling each issue of a magazine is a delicate task, and we always have a sound reason for whatever changes are made.

Rule Number Nine: *Send full names and addresses of all your sources.* This is true for your experts and your case history people as well, so that we can fact-check quickly. Also send a bibliography for secondary sources, and keep all of your notes and tapes on file in case we need to go back to them.

Rule Number Ten: *Expect to be edited.* The best writers always seem to be the ones who are the most eager to cooperate in the editing process, recognizing that it is a joint venture designed to polish and clarify their work. So be available by phone throughout the editing process, and read your copy of the edited manuscript the minute it reaches you, so that you can call with any changes.

There you have them: my ten rules for getting out of the slush and into print. But just to make sure you really go for it, let me close with my all-time favorite break-in-over-the-transom story. Some years ago there was a young Michigan woman who wanted to be a published writer. She wrote all the time, and she read *The Writer* religiously every month, but she never put anything in the mail because she was afraid to stick her neck out. She was afraid of getting rejection slips, of being out of her league. Then one summer, she was on the island of Crete with her new husband. They had dinner at an intimate little taverna on the Mediterranean in a tiny town on the south coast, called Ierapetra. It wasn't a tourist town, and they were the only Americans at table that evening. The food was delicious and the atmosphere enchanting. "You ought to write an armchair travel piece about this place for *Gourmet,*" her husband suggested. She was touched by his faith in her writing, and so the next day she borrowed the only English language typewriter in town, from the schoolmaster, and she wrote a query and sent it off to *Gourmet.* A few weeks later, she got a go-ahead on spec. Breathlessly, she wrote the story, sent it off, and waited. She was rewarded in a month with a lovely acceptance letter and a $300 check. She had broken in over the transom!

I was that young woman. I'm glad I stuck my neck out. You will be, too.

95

SELLING TO MEN'S MAGAZINES

BY JACK BRADFORD OLESKER

I GET angry when I read articles that suggest the short story is dying, that markets for it are vanishing. I suppose a great many markets for short fiction have dried up since the days of the pulps. But I get angry because as a men's magazine editor, I opened my mail every day hoping to find a short story I could buy. When I did find one, I would be willing to work closely with the author on revisions, pay him a healthy sum for his story, and give him exposure in a national magazine. Like many of my colleagues, I was always looking for short fiction. Magazines like *Playboy, Penthouse, Cavalier, Gallery* and *Genesis* all use short stories.

The volume of submissions I received is mind-boggling. But of the thousands and thousands of submissions received in the editorial offices of men's magazines, only a few deliver what editors are looking for. Precisely what editors are looking for and, more important, what they are *not* looking for, is what this article is about.

Why manuscripts are rejected

Writers of short fiction spend an inordinate amount of time worrying about the *category* of fiction a magazine will buy. This is a mistake. A particular magazine may feel it doesn't want to see detective or suspense fiction. It may have a reputation for publishing mainstream or slice-of-life stories. But let a well-crafted short story about a private eye come in, and they'll buy it in a minute.

Don't worry so much about the *kind* of fiction you want to write. Worry more about the *form*. This is the key to breaking into the men's field. Disregard the categories, look at the structure. Learn the structure.

The most common reason men's magazine editors have for rejecting short stories is that the vast number of submissions are not short stories at all. They are fourteen pages of sexual incident after sexual incident strung together. And sexual incidents do not a short story make.

I think this error on the writers' part comes from a basic confusion between the photographic and the editorial sections of men's magazines. While it's true that many magazines want short stories that are titillating and erotic, it's also true that fiction must accomplish something more. Fiction must involve the reader in a story. This is the big plus short stories have over photo features. They involve the mind as well as the libido.

The other side of the coin is that fiction in men's magazines must compete with the pictorial sections for the reader's attention. Your stories must grab the reader quickly. The opening must nail the reader, forcing him to read the next paragraph and the next and the next, until he is so involved with the characters and plot that he forgets about thumbing to the centerfold.

One of the main criteria I used when reading submissions was that I had to be hooked by the end of the first page. If I wasn't, I would usually slip the story back in the SASE and go on to the next.

The opening need not be an erotic scene—though certainly it can be. But it also can be . . .

It was kind of a celebration. I'd just finished eleven weeks of work on a film for Columbia. Every muscle in my body ached. The public has this strange idea that stuntmen don't get hurt when they do stunts in the movies. Don't believe it. Try falling off a three-story building some time—even if there are airbags or mattresses stacked and waiting—and see how you feel. The strain on your body is tremendous. And staging a fight isn't a piece of cake either. Sylvester Stallone found out you can't pull every punch when they were filming *Rocky*.

That's the opening from a short story entitled "Fall Guy" (before the television series of the same name hit the air, by the way) that I published in *Hustler* a number of years ago. The opening involves the reader, because stuntmen are interesting people in a dangerous business, and you want to know more about this fellow and what's going to happen to him. You want to keep reading.

507

The battle over the importance of plot vs. character in fiction has raged for centuries. Character development is important in men's fiction. But plot is at least as important—maybe even more important.

Men's fiction is generally fast-paced and hard-hitting. There has to be conflict. Something should *happen* to the main characters. I know that sounds simplistic, but I say it because so many submissions are lacking in dramatic action. Climbing from one bed to the next is not dramatic action. People being shot at, kidnapped, climbing a mountain, escaping from an oppressive government, or going on a hunting trip—that's action.

You, the writer, must weave action into a compelling plot. Let's look at a hunting trip. I recently bought a short story for *Genesis* entitled "The Huntress." It opened with a woman picking up her boyfriend at 3:30 in the morning to go hunting. I liked the idea of an outdoors story, and the woods offered an interesting setting.

As it turned out, Diana was quite a hunter—the mythical Goddess of the Hunt—and the male character got considerably more than he had bargained for. I bought the story because the mythological element of a goddess-come-to-life—an evil goddess in this case—gave my readers that something extra every editor is searching for.

The "hunt" in this story was for human quarry. There were little hints all along the way that there was something dreadfully different about this particular hunting story, and I found myself pulled further and further into it.

All the vital elements of plot were there: a strong setting, interesting characters, and conflict when at the end, the man rebels against his bloodthirsty companion. Unfortunately for the protagonist, he rebelled too late.

Ah, yes. We're not talking about *Reader's Digest,* here. Most men's magazines—though not all—require erotic passages in the fiction they buy. Writing convincing sex scenes is difficult. Study is important. Read short stories published in men's magazines and *study* the sexual passages.

One of the major shortcomings I noticed in sex scenes of submissions I received was that they emphasized acrobatics. This may be a result of the deluge of sex manuals on the market.

What writers fail to realize when writing erotic passages is that readers aren't looking for instruction. They are looking for arousal.

Emphasis should be on the sensory experience, on the riveting emotions, on the pulsing passion. That this is difficult is undeniable, perhaps because most of us are Puritans at heart. But it can be mastered—at least in *writing!*

Another difficulty in writing erotic passages is a tendency to overwrite. Purple prose, flowery language, excruciatingly adjectival descriptions, should be avoided. To guard against this, read these passages back aloud. If you groan—as I often do—then you've overwritten the section.

As with the best love-making, the best erotic writing is natural.

A helpful hint: We're living in the eighties. Women no longer play a totally submissive role in sexuality or in plots. They are sexual *partners*—if not always full partners—in men's fiction. They do not exist solely for the satisfaction of men. Multiple points of view showing the female characters' sexual enjoyment are encouraged, and help enhance the eroticism of the stories.

There are some topics most men's magazines will not deal with in fiction. This is partly because of obscenity laws in the United States and foreign countries. I also like to think it's partly due to the sensibilities and morals of men's magazine publishers.

Stories dealing with incest, rape, extreme brutality, torture, bestiality and sex between or with minors get the reject slip.

O.K. I've told you not to be concerned about the category of fiction you're writing—be it detective, suspense, etc. But the truth is that certain categories lend themselves to men's fiction.

Detective fiction has long been a staple. The private eye with a gorgeous client in trouble is almost a cliché. Still, it works. But men's magazine editors would like to see more submissions of other categories.

Adventure and suspense are almost always welcome. Whether it is the story of man fighting against nature, against himself or another man, suspense can supply the kind of fast-moving plots editors like. The best plots grab the reader by the scruff of the neck and drag him through a story until he is breathless with excitement.

Certain magazines—*Playboy* and *Penthouse* come to mind—prefer slice-of-life fiction. *Esquire* has long been known for that kind of story.

Occult and supernatural tales are popular with some editors. Stories that deal with horror and creeping evil provide gripping entertainment.

Nowhere is it more important to know the markets than in men's fiction. Read the many men's publications and see what they are publishing.

It's unlikely I would buy a story for *Genesis* that *Playboy* would purchase. Some magazines favor plotted stories that are highly erotic throughout. Others want fiction with only one or two erotic episodes. Still others buy fiction that have no sexual scenes.

You must target your story for the right market. Just sending off a story blind is the same as buying a suit off the rack without trying it on, and hoping it'll fit.

Editors can and will help you tremendously. The secret is, you've got to ask them. Most editors really like writers, and they want to help them. Honest.

Write to an editor and tell him you'd appreciate some "inside tips" on what he's looking for in short stories. A short, carefully constructed query asking the editor if he is looking for something specific might just catch him when he's between manuscripts and has time to send you more than just a mimeographed editorial tip sheet.

Even if he can't send you a detailed letter, he'll remember your name later, because you've made yourself an individual rather than just one of hundreds of writers who submit a manuscript cold.

I'd feel foolish mentioning these offenses, except for the large number of writers who make them. Story lengths set by magazines are not arbitrary. Space limitations dictate how long a story can be. In my fiction guidelines, I told writers we wanted stories between twelve and sixteen pages. Once, I sent these guidelines to a writer who promptly sent me back a story twenty-six pages long! It got the reject slip. Edit and cut your stories before you send them, so they fit the editorial requirements.

Always, *Always,* ALWAYS enclose an SASE. Failing to do so brands you as either a novice, a tightwad or both. Submissions that don't have SASEs usually don't get returned.

Hard-to-read manuscripts do not endear you to an editor. Nor does erasable bond, which is about as easy to read as Saran Wrap. And faded typing from worn-out ribbons also slows down our reading—and, hence, the flow of the story. Most editors don't mind photocopies as long as they're clear and on good paper.

510

Few areas in publishing offer the opportunities for writers that are found in the men's magazine field, which consumes great quantities of fiction every month, and pays well. The chances for a new writer to break into men's magazines are better than in almost any other type of magazine.

Men's magazines are a veritable gold mine, waiting to be worked. But, as with gold prospecting, it requires preparation, study, diligence, and hard work. If you're willing to put out the effort, you just might strike the mother lode.

96

WHAT WRITERS SHOULD KNOW
ABOUT LITTLE MAGAZINES

BY BRUCE MCALLISTER

WHY should any writer care about "little magazines"—about a market that isn't really a market, about magazines that usually pay only in copies and always seem to have such odd names?

Because, many insist, it is in the three thousand little magazines published in this country today—from *Alcheringa* to *Epos* to *The Paris Review* to *Zahir*—that literary poetry and serious fiction remain alive. It is here that both established writers and beginners can experiment with new forms and visions, or refine their traditional crafts. It is here that budding "literary" writers can see their work in print sooner rather than later, and at the same time receive a helping editorial hand during the long years of craft apprenticeship.

Editors of little magazines are in a special position. They can take up the slack from the "big magazines," where only a fraction of the best poetry and fiction written each year can see print. They can also do what few readers and editors for *The New Yorker, Redbook, Esquire* and *The Nation* can: comment personally on your poem or short story even if it isn't yet ready for publication. "Litmag" editors, it turns out, frequently offer helpful insights, suggestions for revision, or, at the very least, a line of encouragement.

But to receive this personal attention you must act like a "little magazine pro," not "amateur." Like any overworked New York editor, the editor of a "little magazine" reads dozens of submissions each week and has learned to differentiate between "pros" and "amateurs." How you present yourself determines not only how your "little magazine" editor will read your work, but also how much time he or she will take responding to it.

My own experience as editor of a literary magazine convinces me that too many apprentice writers make no effort to learn the protocol and etiquette of The Little Magazine World. Some of the following *do's* and *don'ts* are carry-overs from the world of general magazines; some are peculiarities of the little magazine world itself. But all reflect the experience—sometimes painful, sometimes joyous—of fellow editors and the thousands of writers who have sent their poetry and fiction to little magazines over the years.

Submission mechanics

1. *Keep it clean, keep it simple:* Don't use paper clips, staples, scented stationery, colored stationery, flamboyant letterhead stationery, easy-erase paper, onion-skin paper, notecards, notebook paper, pencil, typing ribbons other than black, scented ink, script typewriters. *Do* use 16- or 20-pound white bond for both your submission and your cover letter, and elite or pica face. Don't XXX over words, and beware of piling up that infamous "white ink." Instead, make corrections with those little slips or strips of correcting paper. (Better yet, retype!)

2. *Be sensible:* Don't fold your pages separately, or into fourths. Don't mail three poems flat in a large manila envelope. (Unless you're submitting a full-length short story—ten pages or more—the white business-size envelope is the standard manuscript vehicle.) Type one poem or mini-fiction per page.

3. *Keep your typewriter under control:* Don't type "Copyright 1986" or "First North American Serial Rights" on your submission. Don't note the number of lines in a poem, and unless it's a full-length short story, don't note the wordage on your fiction. Don't type your poems all in caps or use "—30—" to signal the end of a poem or short story. Unless you're an experimental poet working in "visual" or "concrete" forms, don't play around with typographics (+, #, *, !!!, ???), which distract from the words. All you need is your name and address in the upper left-hand corner of each poem or short story, centered below that the title of the piece (all in caps or underlined), and below that the work itself (if poetry, either single- or double-spaced; if fiction, always double).

4. *Be a little magazine professional:* Only amateurs flood an editor with fifteen or twenty poems at a time. Choose your three or four strongest poems. If they're good enough, your editor will ask to see more, and finally you may hear, "Yes, I'd like to use *this one*." Nor

should you send a single poem to an editor; that's what "weekend poets" do. Never pad out a group of three strong poems with two weaker ones simply to get five. If you're a writer of prose poems or experimental mini-fictions, the same rule applies; send them in batches of 2–5 for a total of 5–10 pages.

Always enclose a stamped self-addressed envelope (a white business-size envelope folded into thirds is standard). Telling an editor you don't need your poems back leaves the impression that you don't care very much about your work or that you have multiple submissions circulating. Besides, a pro *never* does this. Don't send photocopies if you can avoid it, and unless you're a Pulitzer Prize winner, never have your literary agent submit poems for you.

Don't send long, chatty cover letters unless you already know the editor—and even then remember, editors are busy people. Many pros use no cover letters at all, but since most "litmag" editors wouldn't be in the business if they didn't enjoy people contact, a brief cover letter is preferable to none: "Dear——: Any consideration of the enclosed would be greatly appreciated. Sincerely . . ." If you've already published in other little magazines, your editor probably wouldn't mind hearing—but tread gently: "I've had _____ in _____, _____ and _____, among others." Don't cite credits that aren't relevant (nonfiction books, genre fiction, ad copy, or greeting card verse) and don't list all thirty magazines you've appeared in. Choose the most prestigious three, list them, and finish with "among others." Never tell an editor, "Just respond on the enclosed card. I don't need the poems back." Never tell her to call you; never tell her you'll call her; never tell her you'd very much like to get back constructive comments "because that's the only way I'll grow." Only amateurs say these things.

What you'll receive back from your editor depends on the kind of little magazine you've submitted to and the personality of the editor. If you submit to little magazines long enough, you'll see *everything:* mimeographed rejection slips, outrageous letterhead stationery, hard-sell ads seconding as rejection slips, odd form letters (like "*Mom* says _____Yes _____ No" with the appropriate blank checked), notecards with a scrawled "No, thanks," and of course, ordinary printed rejection slips.

But what you will also begin to see are *personal comments*. Suggestions for revision. Encouragement. Invitations to send more. "Not these, but we'd like to see others.' " " 'Honeymoon' is the strongest poem of the lot." "If you can tighten up this story we'd like to see it again. P.S. Cutting the first three pages might help—just a suggestion."

When an editor sends you an encouraging note, no matter how abbreviated, by all means try him with more material—and soon. But make it your best. You'd be surprised how many writers, even pros, never follow up on editorial encouragement. The cover letter to your follow-up should remind the editor that he was encouraging: "Thanks very much for the encouraging note on the last short story. Any consideration of the enclosed would be greatly appreciated too." If it's appropriate, you might add, "Your remarks on the second stanza seem right and are appreciated." If an editor has told you, "I like the third poem, but there is something wrong with the second stanza," he won't mind if you revise the poem and resubmit. Your cover letter on the re-submit might well read: "Thanks very much for the comments on the last batch of poems. Your specific suggestions on _____ were appreciated; and I'm enclosing a rewrite of that poem as well."

If an editor is taking forever with your submission, ask yourself how long it's *really* been. (You *should* be keeping records.) In the little magazine world you'll find editors who take six months to answer, and a surprising number of editors aren't around in the summer (many are college professors). But if after four months you still haven't heard a word, you have a right to send a gentle prod: "Last May I sent you a group of poems. Did it reach you? If so, fine. If not, please let me know on the enclosed card and I'll try again." I agree, four months is a long time, but we're talking about another world—one where magazines are usually labors of love, money-sinks for the editors' avocations, and they deserve a little patience.

If you wish to free up those poems or that short story (you have reason to believe the magazine in question has gone the way of dinosaurs), you might add: "If I haven't heard from you in three weeks, I'll assume you can't use my _____ and will go ahead and submit them elsewhere. Thank you. Sincerely, ..." A deadline protects you from a "simultaneous submission" bind; if you've given an editor one, you're free to submit your work elsewhere once the deadline has passed.

Sending your work blindly to magazines, any pro will tell you, is a waste of postage. But how can you possibly get to know three thousand little magazines? You can't and you don't have to. Just be sure that when you *do* send your work out it's to a "sympathetic" magazine. "Homework" is the key.

There are a number of ways to do your homework, and the wise writer does them all simultaneously. Purchase or consult at the public library a copy of *The International Directory of Little Magazines and Small Presses* (Dustbooks, P.O. Box 100, Paradise, CA 95969), and look up those magazines that list as their representative contributors poets and fiction writers you happen to like, or writers who are working the same veins and in the same forms you are. (If you find that none of the writers listed are familiar to you, you may assume that you just aren't keeping up with *contemporary* fiction and poetry. And you must. Writers who want to grow never stop reading, and they know that they must read "contemporary" as well as "modern" and "classical" writings. As any pro will tell you, you can't write what you don't read.).

When you've found a dozen magazines "sympathetic" to your kind of poetry or prose, send for sample copies. This will cost you something, but the investment is worth it. Bookstores and newsstands in major metropolitan areas or college towns often carry the more important literary quarterlies as well as the smaller, regional ones, as do many public and university libraries. Locate copies of as many different "litmags" as you can and read them, keeping in mind that your goal is a panoramic view of the little magazine world. Without this view you'll have no sense of how or where your own work may fit the scheme of things, and without that sense, you'll never find the magazines and editors right for you.

The International Directory of Little Magazines and Small Presses offers information on editors' response times, payment, circulation figures and "manuscript needs"—all invaluable if you're out to avoid *faux pas* with your editors. Other publications like *The Writer, CODA: Poets and Writers Newsletter* (201 W. 54th St., New York, NY 10019), and *Literary Markets* (4340 Coldfall Rd., Richmond, BC, Canada VFC 1P8) also carry lists of little magazines seeking manuscripts (get up-to-date information wherever you can, however you can). Little magazines are notorious for coming and going without telling anyone, or simply changing their editorial tastes.

If you've created the very best verse or fiction you are capable of, as should always be the case, there is an editor of a little magazine out there who will thank you for it, and from such humble beginnings will grow one of those editor-writer relationships that writers dream of.

516

97

PANNING FOR GOLD IN THE SLUSH

BY DAVID GROFF

THEY come in by the dozens every day, in the mailrooms of publishing houses across the country: query letters, sample recipes, chapters of novels, ten-point plans for instant wealth, exercise programs, outlines of romances, three-volume family sagas, even an occasional illustrative kiwi. Writers from Nome, Huntsville, Pontiac, San Diego, Rockford and countless small towns have sealed an envelope, addressed it to "the Editor" and taken it to the post office, hoping against hope that in a few weeks an editor will write or call to make an offer for their work.

I'm the one at the other end; I open the mail. As an editorial assistant at a New York publishing house, one of my jobs is to read through those unsolicited submissions, which we rather cruelly call "slush." At the beginning of last week, I had about five feet of mail stacked on the shelves beside my desk. During these afternoons of tearing open envelopes and cutting the string on packages, I read hundreds of letters and scanned innumerable chapters and proposals. I returned all but three submissions. And I felt depressed; no one likes to reject the efforts of other people.

Reading slush is like being the director of an open audition: Even though I may not be sure what role I am casting for, I hope that someone is going to sing so lustily, or dance with such vigor, that I'll find myself making a brand-new part in the show for the next Judy Garland. There's a feeling of exhilaration as I first sit down to read—to have spread before me so many exercise books, novels and systems for spiritual happiness: so much promise in one tall pile. But after a very short time, anticipation gives way to panic (Will I ever finish?), then to anger (Why don't these folks read books instead of writing them?), and finally to guilt and depression (I can never do justice to the efforts of these people; I'm failing thousands!).

I can't feel joy at the day's fourth submission of cartoons about jogging, even if two of the drawings are funny. I can't give my complete attention to still another inky novel about a girl from Texas who wants to be an opera singer. Didn't this person check to find out our company doesn't publish poetry? Couldn't that novelist afford a new typewriter ribbon?

Nevertheless, I shouldn't leave the impression that even the majority of unsolicited mail is badly thought out or illiterate. Much of it is fairly well done, and there is probably going to be at least one stunning passage in that novel about the Texas opera singer. Most writers, after all, are readers—and most writers write versions of what they have read. Someone, for instance, will have studied Isaac Asimov and will submit a long saga in which overintelligent robots are pitted against human beings. Someone else, having taken *The One Minute Manager* to heart, will use his experience as an executive to write another book on office management techniques. Another writer will substitute dead rats for Simon Bond's dead cats. And I've received at least a dozen outlines for books based on *The Preppie Handbook:* "The Maven Handbook," "The Tacky Handbook," "The Football Widow's Handbook." Right now I'm getting a lot of novels about Vietnam, and I think I'm detecting another trend as well: books that open the day after the ABC television movie "The Day After." But what an editor is really looking for is a novel or a nonfiction proposal so fresh, so unexplainably promising, that he or she is willing to invest the company's money and a year's worth of effort publishing that book.

Of course, there is nothing new under the sun, and originality is a matter of style as much as it is a matter of content. But I can think of several novels and proposals I've seen that did feel extraordinarily fresh and worthwhile. Next January my company will be publishing a book of short stories by a young, unknown writer who is on intimate terms with the Caribbean and the mysteries of its society and politics; his stories explore a whole new region that American readers will find fascinating. Also, I have found myself eager to read a nonfiction book proposal dealing with the situation of gay men and women in the McCarthy era, and another dealing with Vietnamese immigrants coping with life in America. Generally, writers do their most effective work when they use whatever particular expertise they have. Whether they are recreating suburban California in fiction, investigating the quasi-legal activities of

518

art dealers, outlining an exercise program for infants or writing a guidebook for owning a boyfriend, they'll find their knowledge carrying them a long way, provided they write with style, particularity, and verve.

Publishing is a risky business. About seventy-five percent of all trade books don't even earn the advance paid the author. But it's not a monolithic industry; its ways of operation may be unpredictable and unsystematic, but book publishing is not a den of caprice and favoritism. You don't have to lunch at the Four Seasons to have your manuscript see print. Editors are always searching out new books by new and unknown authors. When all is said and done, there is only one general requirement for publication: You have to be good. You have to be good enough to make other people care.

What does it mean to be good? How does a writer make a reader care? More specifically, how can you grab the attention of editors reading hundreds of pages a week? While no one can offer a sure-fire formula, here are some major and minor ways writers who want to be authors can make their manuscripts stand out. Some of these are simply suggestions about the mechanics of submitting a manuscript; others address some of the bigger issues and will, I hope, give an overall idea of what most publishers are receptive to.

—Know your publishing house. If you are writing a category romance, don't bother sending it to Knopf; Knopf doesn't publish any category romance. Over the years many publishers have specialized—in textbooks, literature, poetry, psychology, the occult, business. Send away for the publishers' catalogues, so you will have a sense of what sorts of books different hardcover and paperback houses emphasize; you'll save a lot of time, energy and stamps by sending your work only to those houses truly interested in the genre you're writing in. Consider, too, whether your book would be best served by publication in hardcover or mass-market paperback. I've read dozens of novels, especially romances and thrillers, that would be superb paperbacks but do not demand the sort of backing—reviews, and large advertising and promotion budgets—that hardcover houses provide.

—Know your editor. Get access to a current copy of *Literary Market Place* (since editors move around more than movie stars, an old *LMP* is about as useful as the Domesday Book). Pick out an editor—any editor, but preferably one who is listed (as many are) with a specialization in your field of interest. You're much more likely to get a good response when you write to a real-live editor by name, even if he or she has no idea who you are. This won't necessarily rescue you from a form rejection slip, but at least you'll reach the desk of someone influential.

—Don't send only a query letter. It's almost impossible to conclude anything from a single page, so include an outline, a sample chapter, and a proposal for your nonfiction manuscript, or several chapters of your novel. Within reason, the more material you send, the better. Unpublished writers very seldom get contracts for works yet to be written. The submission may cost more to mail, but it's to your advantage to have lots of good words already down on the page.

—Do send a cover letter with your submission. Try to sound like a specific human being and not just a name in the telephone directory. Contrary to public belief, editors do like human beings.

—Do not send cash. Do not send stamps. Send a self-addressed envelope with the stamps in place, if you want to see your manuscript again. Manuscripts with stamped return envelopes somehow don't get mislaid as frequently as those accompanied only by stamps or a dollar bill, or nothing at all. It's best to make it clear if you want your manuscript returned or if you simply want a reply. If you haven't received a response within six weeks or two months, feel free to send a query (also with SASE)—but be prepared: Publishers seldom have the time and manpower to log in every submission, and the volume of mail received means that things do get lost. Be sure to keep a copy of everything you send a publisher.

—Neatness counts. If your manuscript is messy, retype it. If it comes back messy from the publisher, photocopy it again before you send it to someone else. Nothing can make a reader at a publishing house leap to the wrong conclusion faster than a submission that obviously has popped through many pairs of hands.

—Test your work beforehand on savvy people who do not have a vested interest in keeping you happy. Ask yourself why someone else should read your manuscript instead of watching "Fantasy Island." But if your work is rejected, remember that some of those stories of eventually successful books having been rejected countless times are true. Tastes vary, and lightning strikes.

But showing your work to someone whose opinion you respect is a great way to see it freshly. Even the idea that another person is looking over the fruit of your efforts may provide you with a whole new angle on what you are doing. You find yourself asking the questions your readers might be asking: Why would this work appeal to those specific readers? Can they see what you are seeing as clearly as you see it, or did they need to be present at the creation?

—Writers aren't at their best working in a garret. Even Proust would have benefited if he'd left his cork-lined room to wander the streets of Paris. A writer should mingle as much as possible with other writers, both published and unpublished, for creative inspiration as well as to become savvy about the business of publication. There are dozens of ways to do this, from going to writers conferences to conversations over drinks. It's my belief that most serious writers should invest the time it takes to become a member of the writing community. Not only does your knowledge of the world of writers increase your chances of publication, but it's reassuring, enlightening, and fun.

—Start small. Maybe you aren't ready to publish a book yet. Maybe your novel should be introduced to the world as a series of short stories published in magazines. Maybe your nonfiction book idea could be one or more (lucrative) magazine articles. With a critical eye, and with the help of the market section of *The Writer* Magazine or *The Writer's Handbook,* investigate various periodicals. Editors at book companies are always on the lookout for magazine articles and stories that may be developed into books. A writer can save a lot of perspiration when his previously published work brings him to the attention of an editor or an agent.

—It's not easy to gain the support of a literary agent, but if an agent expresses interest in you, it can definitely increase the chances of publication for your book. Of course, having an agent is no guarantee of publication, and many writers do quite well on their own. But look before you leap; make sure you know exactly what an agent will do for you, and what that agent's track record is.

—Once you receive a favorable response from an editor, take heart; you are not just being humored. If you have been told you write well but that for some specific reason your manuscript wasn't right for publication, send a thank you note. If you have something else you think might suit that editor, send it soon, or write to explain when you'll have more material.

If an editor begins to talk seriously about revisions in the form or substance of your work, listen carefully (but of course feel free to disagree). Don't expect money to be discussed right away, although sometimes that happens. Your submission will still have to receive the approval of the entire editorial board of the publishing house, and often will be discussed with marketing honchos as well; any of these people could shoot down your novel or book idea, even if your editor is solidly behind it. If and when the publisher offers you a contract, make sure you have legal advice, or the advice of a literary agent.

Of course, no number of helpful hints can replace the fundamentals any writer needs: talent, persistence, a sure grasp of the English language, luck, a taste for perfection, and (in some ways the most important) a sense of responsibility toward the rest of the world.

Good writing—the kind that makes me pay attention as I sit at my desk at the end of a long day—is not simply an expression of a writer's temperament, financial motivations, neuroses or beliefs. A truly good writer wants to communicate, *not* to express: He or she has information about the world to get across to me in the most vivid, effective and detailed manner possible. A good writer does everything possible to deliver that world—and to make me care.

I try to care back. There are few thrills greater than helping those three-hundred typewritten pages become a bound book people will want to read. There are certainly easier ways of making money than writing (or editing), but book publishing is one of the few commercial activities around that tries with some consistency to maintain the vigor of the language and the value of human communication. I love to walk into a bookstore and see someone engrossed in a book I worked for—and I can understand the even stronger response a newly published writer feels toward that scene. After all, communication is—at its very best—an act of love.

98

THE EDITOR'S SIDE

By Olga Litowinsky

I HAVE written books as well as edited them, and know full well the many frustrations a writer can experience. I remember waiting six months for a check due on acceptance of a manuscript on which I had labored over a year. My books were also not promoted enough, went out of print too soon and did not make me rich and famous (ah, there's the rub!). Obviously, this was the publisher's fault. We all know that.

On the other hand, I am forever grateful to the editor of my first novel, who returned the manuscript looking as if a chicken had wandered delicately over every page. I resented every change she tactfully suggested, but after some thought, duly made all but one. I resisted that one only because I had to take a stand *somewhere*. My next editors were charming. Even though one of them insisted a passage was unintelligible to her no matter how many times I told her it was perfectly clear, we are still friends (I did make the change). The other editor was sorry there weren't more ads for the book, and I remain embarrassed at the outrage I directed toward him, even though it wasn't his fault.

Now let's discuss some points from the editor's side of the desk:

1. *Time*. Since every writer considers him/herself the *only* writer an editor has, of course the editor should take the new manuscript home and spend the evening (or weekend) reading it. We get paid about the same as schoolteachers. While we know teachers are underpaid, they at least get lots of time off. Editors get standard corporate vacations, go to conventions on weekends, and are expected to keep up with the flow of manuscripts. Reading manuscripts is *work* when read during one's *leisure* time.

2. *Form rejection slips*. How nice if we could write a thoughtful note to each of the authors of the 5000 manuscripts we receive. The form

523

rejection slip has turned out to be the kindest and quickest way to say no thank you. When an editor does offer a gentle criticism to a promising writer of a mediocre work ("You might consider developing the characters a wee bit more"), we are usually branded as insensitive louts. It's a no-win situation.

3. *The flow of words.* Is an editor to allow murky or ungrammatical passages to go out to the world? Reviews are of the writer's work, not of the editor's; rarely have I seen a book criticized for being poorly edited, often for being poorly written. Am I wrong to think one of my functions as an editor is to aid the writer in presenting the best face possible to the world? I admit that when I was younger, I did overedit as a means of satisfying my ego, of making the book "mine" in a way it did not have a right to be. I still remember Ben Bova's question to me: "Is this book mine or yours? Perhaps you should try writing one of your own." It was a valuable lesson in keeping my mitts off when it *wasn't* necessary. Since then I learned to trust my writers more.

Editors are not perfect (surprise!). Yet there is no one else an author can trust to be impartial and honest about his or her writing. Husbands, wives and friends are either "too busy" or too adoring; other writers are often jealous; reviewers may have private axes to grind. Editors sit between the virgin manuscript and the public. We are the first real reader the book is exposed to, and like a kindly parent, we are the first to say "your slip is showing." Writers—even the very best—are not perfect either; they can have blind spots. I was mortified recently when an editor returned an article I had done, asking me to "please change all the passive voices to active." How many times have I asked my writers to do the same?

4. *Editing on a word processor.* Like most editors I know, I've never done it and don't want to have to squint at a screen all day long. I'm not sure I trust the dang things yet. When it becomes inevitable, I guess I'll do it, but for now I like my Blackwing pencils.

Because I am a writer as well as an editor, I've become more sensitive to my writers' concerns. But being a writer doesn't change for me some of the fundamental defects in the editorial and publishing process. Too much work, not enough staff, not enough money. We will all say we do what we do because we love it, although recently quite a few potential editors have gone off to become lawyers, doctors and M.B.A.s because they don't believe in taking vows of poverty.

But what bothers me most is that it's a rare writer who ever says thank you to the person who's worked hard (and anonymously) to make the writer look good. Turnabout, they say, is fair enough. The next time a writer is between books, why doesn't he or she spend a few months at the publisher's office to get a better idea of what it's like on this side of the desk? Perhaps if writers and editors were more sympathetic to each other's problems, we could dispense with petty resentments and back-biting and get on with the work.

99

THE 10% SOLUTION

By Anita Diamant

EACH time that I have had the privilege of talking to a group of writers, the consensus seems to be that it is harder today to find a good agent than a publisher. True? Well, legitimate agents work on a 10% commission basis, and of the manuscripts submitted to an agent by new writers only a very small percentage will prove to have sales potential. The agent will have spent time and energy in appraising these materials with no certainty of any income. After all, 10% of nothing doesn't really help to pay the rent!

But does this mean that in the field of book publishing, a new writer, or even a once-published writer, must attempt to sell a work himself? Not necessarily. There is no question about the fact that an agent can be enormously helpful to both an experienced and a new writer, depending upon the kinds of personalities involved and the type of relationship that can be established. While an agent is primarily the writer's business representative, it would be most unusual if a personal relationship between them did not come into being. I like to feel that my writers are not only my clients but also my friends, based upon our mutual interest and respect for each other.

It is important, however, for the writer to understand the function of a literary agent — what to expect from the agent and what a literary agent either can or cannot be asked to do. I feel that I can help my clients, not just by selling what they write, but also by advising them about the potential markets for the work they are planning and assisting them in smoothing out problems of plot and treatment in their manuscripts. Writers may expect agents to be so experienced that the advice they give their clients would be invaluable. But it is unrealistic for a writer to expect the agent to act as a publicity director, to handle bookstore sales, to act as a banker, or to offer psychiatric advice.

How can a writer obtain the services of a suitable agent? Although our agency is not eager to take on any number of unpublished writers, we do read and answer every letter of inquiry sent to us. It is extremely helpful for a prospective client to tell us something about his or her work, background, and why he or she feels he has a salable work in progress. We are frequently tempted to ask for sample chapters and an outline of the proposed book, and in many instances, we have found salable manuscripts in this way. The cliché, "Write, don't telephone," applies here, because our office time is taken up largely with numerous telephone calls from our clients, publishers, and editors, and we simply cannot take additional time to answer telephone queries from new writers.

When my assistant was asked what literary agents really do, he answered simply, "They talk on the telephone and go out to lunch." And while this may seem simplistic, frankly this kind of activity takes up much of our time. Lunches are important, for this is when agents meet editors and publishers to discuss projects. It is so much easier to sell a book on a personal, eyeball-to-eyeball basis, and any good agent can, through the dramatic presentation of an idea, create enormous interest on the part of an editor. (Of course, there are times when a writer does not fulfill that excitement in the presentation of the material!)

You are probably aware of the fact that legitimate literary agents do not advertise for writers, any more than legitimate publishers advertise for book properties. Then how does one go about finding an agent? The best way, of course, is through recommendation. If a writer has a friend who has had a book published, he can ask this person for the name of his agent. He then may write a letter to the agent, mentioning the recommen-

Agents are listed in *Literary Market Place,* published by R. R. Bowker Company, and the Society of Authors' Representatives (P.O. Box 650, Old Chelsea Sta., New York, NY 10113) also publishes a list of members, which will be sent if a stamped, self-addressed envelope is enclosed. In addition, a newer group of agents, the Independent Literary Agents Association (21 W. 26th St., New York, NY 10010) will send a list of members to those enclosing a stamped return envelope. Any agent listed in these three sources would be knowledgeable and reputable and would have a grasp of the markets and the requirements of various publishers today.

There are times when a new writer may be able to start on his own, and in the case of specialized books, such as books on crafts, juveniles and certainly academic subjects, a writer may find it relatively easy to make a direct contact and sell a manuscript. Many publishing houses, however, will not read manuscripts that come "over the transom," and consequently, if at all possible, a writer should attempt to find an agent. Also, there are some editors who find it difficult to deal directly with a writer and prefer to talk to an agent about business matters. (We have even had to shift a successful author from one large publishing house to another because of an unfortunate relationship between the writer and the editors at the first house.) The agent should always negotiate for the client and should run interference between editor and writer, when necessary.

When a writer complains — and not always unreasonably — about the lack of promotion and publicity for his book and the fact that it cannot be found in major bookstores, the agent takes up the complaint with the publisher. Acting as the intermediary, the agent, who is most apt to know when the complaint is justified, either telephones or makes a personal call on the publisher to straighten out the problem.

The agent frequently assumes the role of arbiter between two writers working together, since many collaborations, I find, begin happily and end disastrously.

An agent is most important to a writer in reading and working out the details of a book publisher's contract. While there are standard clauses that can rarely be changed in any publishing contract, still, the agent is more likely than the writer to know the customs and mores of the business and will be able to determine just what is negotiable and what will have to remain intact. At a writers' conference at which I was a speaker, I found that many writers were curious about the comparable benefits of using a lawyer against those of using a literary agent. There are many attorneys who specialize in literary properties and who can be extremely helpful in advising their clients about specific clauses in a contract. But the average lawyer has had little experience in this highly specialized form of legal document and may "make waves" that may not be beneficial to the writer's interests. On one occasion I sold a book manuscript to a major publisher for a new client who in turn had her lawyer read the contract. He made changes in minor clauses that worked against the author's interests!

In negotiating contracts, agents make every effort to retain subsidiary rights, such as first serial excerpt, foreign rights, television, motion picture, and so on, for these in many cases bring the authors larger sums than the initial book publication. But agents are aware that in the case of new writers, publishers will not yield on the usual 50-50 split in the proceeds from the sale of paperback or book-club rights. Also, many of the clauses that refer to the author's liability are difficult to alter, and here again, agents know just how far they can go in requesting changes in the contract.

Apart from benefiting from the agent's know-how in negotiating contracts, a writer also benefits from the agent's knowledge of the kind of publisher to whom a particular work should be submitted, and the form in which the material is most likely to be sold. For example, when I read a novel manuscript, I must determine at once whether it would be best to submit it for hardcover publication, or whether it should go directly to a paperback publisher. There is, of course, a difference: Though many books on the hardcover best-seller list are similar in style to paperbacks, a book must be fast-moving and filled with incident to appeal to the paperback audience. Also, I have to make the same kind of decision in deciding where to submit a nonfiction book idea for what we term the "oversize paperback," instead of a standard rack-size. The oversize paperback is a new and very profitable market today, and it has opened up many possibilities for nonfiction writers.

The work of literary agents has become so specialized that they have to decide not only which publisher would be best for a manuscript, but also which editor would offer a relationship that might be most *simpatico* for the author. If possible, I like to have my client and the editor meet at the very outset, so that they can work together without having any misunderstandings later on. This, of course, works most effectively when the contract for a book is signed before the book is completed.

At times, the agent is also faced with the important decision of whether to auction a manuscript or just to offer it on a multiple-submission basis. It should be stressed that auctions and multiple submissions are techniques that can be used *only* by agents, not by writers themselves. These are techniques by which we try to get a quick response from a publisher. In the case of a multiple submission, we send out several copies of the proposal or manuscript simultaneously to various publishers. But the whole purpose of this lies in telling each publishing house that a multiple submission is being made: Each house understands that it is in competition for the property offered. The same procedure is followed with an auction, but in this case the agent informs the publishers that there is a "floor" — a minimum advance that the author will find acceptable. Each house is then given a brief period to make an offer over the "floor." Although such auctions have received wide publicity recently, these are highly competitive techniques and should be used only very rarely — and then only by professionals.

This is another instance in which an agent's experience in professional matters is useful in making decisions for the benefit of the author. And that is why it is so important for a writer in selecting an agent to feel that he or she can place complete trust in the judgment of such a representative. Agents can make mistakes, of course, but they are likely to make fewer if they are dealing from knowledge and experience.

An agent receives a 10% commission on all domestic sales of manuscripts, including all rights, such as sales to magazines, television, syndicates, films, cassettes, and so on. However, in the case of British sales, we charge 15%, and on other foreign sales, a 20% commission. The increased commissions are charged because we all have representatives abroad who in turn have to be compensated for their work.

Is it worth 10% of a writer's income to have an agent? I am prejudiced, of course, but I sincerely think so. After all, an agent's function does not cease when a writer becomes established, witness the fact that such top authors as Irving Wallace, Arthur Hailey, Harold Robbins, and Erica Jong are all represented by agents. And I feel certain that all these successful writers would agree that they are more than reimbursed by the "10% solution."

100

WHAT EVERY WRITER NEEDS TO KNOW ABOUT LITERARY AGENTS

By Ellen Levine

Q. *At what stage in their careers should writers look for an agent— or will a good agent find them?*

A. Most agents prefer to begin a working relationship with a writer when there is a book-length work to market, rather than articles or short stories. Some agents prefer writers who already have publication credits, perhaps magazine publication of shorter work. However, a writer who has never published before, but who is offering a book which deals with a unique or popular topic may also have an excellent chance of securing an agent. Quite a number of agents are actively looking for new writers, and they comb the little magazines for talented writers of fiction. They also read general interest and specialty magazines for articles on interesting subjects, since they might contain the seeds for books. Some agents visit writers conferences and workshops with the express purpose of discovering talented authors who might be interested in representation.

Q. *How does a writer go about looking for a legitimate agent?*

A. Writers can obtain lists of agent members from two professional organizations—The Society of Authors' Representatives (SAR) or The Independent Literary Agents Association (ILAA)— by writing to these organizations at (for SAR) P.O. Box 650, Old Chelsea Station, New York, NY 10113 and (for ILAA) 21 W. 26th St., New York, NY 10010. Writers can also obtain a more complete list of agents by checking the "Agents" section of *Literary Market Place* (LMP), available from R. R. Bowker, 205 E. 42nd St., New York, NY 10017, or as a reference work at the local library. Finally, the Authors Guild at 234 W. 44th St., New York, NY 10036 will supply a list of agents.

Q. *How important is it for an agent to be a member of SAR or ILAA?*

A. It is not essential for a good agent to belong to either organization, but membership is very helpful and adds credibility and professionalism to the agency. These organizations schedule meetings to discuss issues and problems common to the industry and their members work together to solve them. Expertise is often shared; panels and seminars are regularly scheduled, often including key publishing personnel. There are also certain codes of professional ethics, which members of each group subscribe to. This, of course, is to the writer's advantage.

Q. *Do literary agents specialize in particular types of material— novels, plays, nonfiction books, short stories, television scripts? Are there some categories that agents could not profitably handle that could better be marketed by the authors?*

A. Most of the agents' listings in LMP specify which kind of material the agency handles. A few agencies do have certain areas of specialization such as screenplays, or children's books, as well as more general fiction and nonfiction.

Q. *Should a writer query an agent (or several agents) before sending him or her his manuscript(s)?*

A. It is acceptable for a writer to query more than one agent before sending material, but it should be made clear to the agent that the writer is contacting several agents at one time. It is even more important for the writer to clarify whether he plans to make multiple submissions of a manuscript. Most agents prefer to consider material on an exclusive basis for a reasonable period of time, approximately four to eight weeks.

Q. *What do agents look for before accepting a writer as a client?*

A. An agent usually takes on a new client based on his or her enthusiasm for that writer's work and a belief that it will ultimately be marketable.

Q. *Once an agent has agreed to take a writer on as a client, what further involvement can the agent expect and legitimately ask of the writer?*

532

A. It may take longer to place the work of a new author, and the client should be patient in the process. If the writer has made contact with a specific editor or knows that there is interest in the work from a specific publisher, he or she should inform the agent. The writer should feel free to continue contacts with book editors with whom he or she has worked, and to discuss ideas with magazine editors.

Q. *Do most agents today ask for proposals, outlines, synopses, etc., of a book-length work before taking on the job of reading and trying to market the whole book? Do agents ever prepare this type of material, or is that solely the author's function?*

A. This varies among agents. A popular procedure for consideration of material from a prospective client is the request of an outline or proposal and the first 50 or 100 pages. If the book is complete, some agents might request the completed manuscript. It is common practice to submit a nonfiction work on the basis of one or more chapters and a synopsis or outline. The extent of the sample material needed is often based on the writer's previous credentials. It is generally the author's job to prepare the outline and the agent's to prepare the submission letter or the "pitch."

Q. *When, if ever, are multiple queries or submissions allowable, acceptable, desirable? By agent or by author?*

A. If an author is working without an agent, multiple submissions to publishers are acceptable only if the author informs the publisher that the book is being submitted on that basis. However, this can sometimes backfire since those publishers who will read unsolicited manuscripts may not care to waste the staff's reading time on a manuscript that is on simultaneous submission to five other publishers. Multiple queries with one-at-a-time submissions upon receipt of a favorable reply are probably more effective for a relatively new author. However, if a writer has a nonfiction project that is obviously very desirable or timely (an inside story, a current political issue), it is of course expedient to proceed with a multiple submission. This should be done carefully, informing all the participants of the deadline, ground rules, and so on. Agents must judge each project individually and decide on the appropriate procedure. If more than one publisher has expressed an interest in a specific writer or project, a multiple submission is not only appropriate, it is fair and in the author's best interest if there are competitive offers. If a book is very commercial, an auction may well be the result of a multiple submission. If other factors, such as a guaranteed print order or publicity plans are important, a multiple submission without the necessity of taking the highest bid may bring the best results. If an agent routinely makes multiple submissions of all properties, credibility may be lost. If this practice is reserved for the projects which warrant it, the procedure is more effective. It is usually not appropriate to send out multiple copies of a promising first novel. It may be for the inside story of last week's Congressional investigation.

Q. *What business arrangements should a writer make with an agent? Are contracts common to cover the relationship between author and agent? How binding should this be and for what period of time?*

A. Author-agent business arrangements vary among agencies. Some agents will discuss commission, expenses, and methods of operation with their authors, and this informal verbal agreement is acceptable to both parties. Others will write letters confirming these arrangements. Several agencies require contracts defining every detail of the business arrangements, and others require formal, but less extensive contracts. Written agreements often contain a notification of termination clause by either party with a period varying from 30 days to a full year. A few of the agency agreements require that the agency continue to control the subsidiary rights to a book even after the author and agent have parted. Most agents include what is known as an "agency clause" in each book contract the author signs, which provides for the agency to receive payments for the author due on that book for the complete life of the contract, whether or not the author or agent has severed the general agency agreement. In a few cases this clause will contain the provision mentioned above (compulsory representation of the author's retained subsidiary rights). It is important for a writer to discuss these and all aspects of the agency's representation at the beginning of the relationship. In addition to understanding clearly commission rates and expenses he or she will be required to pay, a writer might want to discuss such matters as expectations for consultation on marketing, choice of publishers, the number of submissions to be made, frequency of contact with agent, and so on. *Poets and Writers, Inc.* at 201 West

54th Street, New York, NY 10019 has published a helpful handbook entitled *Literary Agents: A Writer's Guide* ($5.95), which addresses these issues. Commissions vary among agents. The range is often between 10% and 20%. Some agencies may vary the commission for different rights, charging 10% or 15% for domestic sales and 15% or 20% for foreign sales. Certain agencies have different rates for different authors, depending upon the length of time the author has been with the agency, the size of the publishing advance, or the amount of editorial and preparatory work the agent must do before marketing the book. Some agents work more extensively in an editorial capacity than others and may make detailed suggestions and ask for revisions before marketing a work.

Q. *Can a writer express a preference to the agent concerning the particular publishing house or kind of house he would prefer for his book?*
A. Writers should share with their agents any preferences or ideas they may have about their work, including which publishers would be most appealing, and in which format they envision their books. However, writers should not be dismayed if their agents feel in some cases that a particular preference may be unrealistic or inappropriate.

Q. *How much of the business side of publishing does the writer need to deal with, once he is in the hands of a competent agent?*
A. An agent acts as a writer's business representative for his publishing affairs. Most agents do not act as a writer's overall financial manager, and if an author begins to earn a substantial income, he or she may be well-advised to consult with a C.P.A. and/or tax attorney. The prudent writer, while entrusting his business affairs to his or her agent, will want to stay informed about these matters.

Q. *How much "reporting" can a writer legitimately expect from the agent who has agreed to handle his work?*
A. This would depend on the agent's individual style and the writer's need and preference. Many agents keep clients informed about the progress of submissions by sending copies of rejection letters; others do not, and will give the writer a summary periodically. A writer

should be kept informed of all important events and conversations with editors and co-agents about his or her work; for instance, a favorable *Publishers Weekly* review that has come in, a substantial delay in publication, a paperback auction date that has been set. On the other hand, writers should not expect daily contact with an agent as an established routine.

Q. *What involvement, if any, should a writer have in the contract that the agent makes with a publisher? Does he have the right, responsibility to question the terms, change them, insist on higher royalty rates, advertising, etc., or is this left entirely to the agent, along with the sale of substantial rights?*

A. It is the agent's responsibility to consult with the author before accepting any of the basic terms of an offer such as the advance, royalties, subsidiary rights, and territories granted. If the author has any particular reasonable requests which he or she would like to include in the contract, such as approval or consultation on the jacket design, it is the author's responsibility to let the agent know before the start of negotiations. The choice of an agent should imply the author's trust and confidence in the agent's expertise in negotiating the contract and securing the best possible financial and legal terms for the author. Authors should read contracts carefully and ask questions about any provisions, if necessary. However, it is not reasonable for an author to ask for changes in every clause or expect provisions that are extremely difficult to obtain, particularly for authors who have not had best sellers. For instance, advertising guarantees in contracts are not common for new authors. If the author has chosen a skillful agent, he or she should have confidence in the agent's explanation of what is or is not feasible in a contract with a particular publisher.

Q. *If an agent feels that he cannot place a manuscript and the author feels that it is marketable, or, at least, worthy of publication, can the author try to sell it on his own?*

A. If this happens on occasion and the agent has no objection, the author should feel free to try after discussing what he or she plans to do. The agent will want to be informed so that no prior obligation, such as an option requirement, is breached. If the author's agent repeatedly

536

feels that the author's manuscripts cannot be placed, perhaps it is time for the author and agent to re-examine their relationship and discuss a change.

Q. *What services, other than the marketing of the manuscripts, negotiating the terms of their publishing contracts and related business arrangements may authors reasonably expect from their agents?*

A. In addition to marketing manuscripts, agents often help authors in formulating book ideas, passing along book ideas from editors when appropriate, and making introductions to appropriate editors if the author is between projects and free of contract obligations. Agents also follow up on various details of the publication process, such as production schedules, publicity, promotion, suggestions of other writers who might offer a quote for the jacket. The agent should also disseminate reviews, quotes, and information on subsidiary rights sales such as reprint and book club sales. Agents also examine royalty statements and, when necessary, obtain corrected statements.

Authors should not expect an agent to act as a secretary, travel agent, or bank. On the other hand, it is inevitable that a more personal bond may often form in the author/agent relationship, and in certain cases, agents do become involved to varying extents in friendships with their clients. In fact, hand-holding, "mothering" and counseling are not unfamiliar to many agents in dealing with certain authors. This is really a function of the agent's personality and often a conscious decision about how personally involved with his or her clients that particular agent wishes to be. A client should not expect that agent to solve his or her personal problems routinely.

Q. *How would you sum up the major role the agent plays in selling an author's work?*

A. If a manuscript is marketable, a good agent can short-circuit the random process of submissions by knowledge of the market, publishers, and the tastes and personalities of specific editors. However, an agent cannot place unsalable work. An agent can also be effective in the choice of marketing strategy for a particular work—should the book be sold as a trade paperback? Is a "hard-soft" deal best for the project? Would the author best be served by an auction, or would select individual submissions with editorial meetings be best?

537

PART IV

WHERE TO SELL

This year's edition of THE WRITER'S HANDBOOK includes completely revised and updated market lists, and writers at all levels of experience should be encouraged by the number and variety of opportunities. Editors, publishers, and producers continue to rely on free lancers for a wide range of material—from fiction and articles to play scripts, opinion essays, and how-to books—and are very receptive to talented newcomers.

One of the best magazine markets for beginning free lancers remains the field of specialized publications, including city and regional magazines, travel and inflight publications, and those covering such fields as health, science, consumer issues, animals, sports, and art. Writers with experience in and enthusiasm for a particular field—whether it's hang gliding, gardening, ceramics, beer brewing, home remodeling or doll collecting—will find their knowledge particularly helpful, since editors are always seeking authoritative articles. No matter what the field, there is usually at least one publication devoted to it, making this market in general an attractive one for writers with a specialty.

One of the fastest-growing nonfiction fields open to free-lance writers is the market for technical, health, and computer writing, with articles on those topics used in almost every publication on the newsstands today—from the major women's magazines to the more specialized science publications. Editors here are looking for writers who have an ability to translate technical material into lively readable prose—often the most important factor in determining a sale.

While beginners may find some of the more established markets difficult to break into, there are thousands of lesser-known publications, where editors are willing to consider the work of first-time free lancers. Some of the best opportunities are closest to home, as editors of city and regional publications like to work with local writers. Many newspapers accept op-ed pieces from free lancers as well, and though subject matter varies greatly, writers should concentrate on topics not covered by syndicated columnists (economics, foreign affairs, etc.): pieces with a regional slant are particularly welcome here.

It is especially important for free lancers to keep in mind how many opportunities exist for nonfiction, since the paying markets for fiction are somewhat limited. Many of the general-interest and women's magazines do publish fiction, but use mostly the work of established writers. We highly recommend that new free lancers look into the small, literary, and college publications which always welcome the work of talented writers. They usually pay in copies only, but publication in literary journals can lead to recognition by editors of larger-circulation magazines, who often look there for new talent.

The market for poetry in general-interest magazines also continues to be tight, and the advice for poets, as for fiction writers, is to try to get established and build up a list of publishing credits by submitting material to literary journals. Poets should also keep in mind that local newspapers often use verse—especially on holidays and special occasions—and local magazines too, may be partial to the work of poets living in the area.

In the field of drama, community, regional and civic theaters and college dramatic groups offer the best chance for the new playwright to see his work "come alive" on the stage. Indeed, aspiring playwrights who can get their work produced by any of these theaters have taken an important step toward breaking into the competitive dramatic field— many of today's well known playwrights received their first recognition in the regional theaters. In addition to producing plays and giving dramatic readings of new works, many theaters also sponsor annual competitions or new play festivals.

Though a representative list of television shows is included in this section of the HANDBOOK, writers should be aware of the fact that this market is inaccessible without an agent, and most writers break into it only after careful study of the medium, and a long apprenticeship.

The book publishing field has become increasingly competitive, especially for writers seeking their first sale. There is, however, good reason for beginners to be optimistic, since publishers are accepting the work of talented newcomers—as witnessed by the dramatic increase in the number of first novels published over the past few years. Nonfiction books by writers with knowledge in a particular field—careers, psychology, finance, cooking, or woodworking, for instance—are also popular, and writers who combine talent with persistence and determination may very well see their books in print.

All information in these lists concerning the needs and requirements of magazines, book publishing companies, and theaters comes directly from the editors, publishers, and directors, but writers should realize that editors move and addresses change, as do requirements. No published listing can give as clear a picture of editorial needs and tastes as a careful study of several issues of a magazine, and writers should go to their local library to look at back issues of any publication to which they'd like to submit material, or write directly to the editor for a sample copy (often free or available at small cost).

ARTICLE MARKETS

The magazines in the following list are in the market for free-lance articles of many types. Unless otherwise stated in these listings, a writer should submit a query first, including a brief description of the proposed article and any relevant qualifications or credits. A few editors want to see samples of published work, if available. Manuscripts must be typed double-space on good white bond paper (8½ × 11), with name, address, and telephone number at the top left- or right-hand corner of the page. Do not use erasable or onion skin paper, and always keep a copy of the manuscript, in case it is lost in the mail. Submit photos or slides only if the editor has specifically requested them. A self-addressed envelope with sufficient postage to cover the return of the manuscript or an answer to query should accompany all submissions. Response time may vary from two to eight weeks, depending on the size of the magazine and the volume of mail it receives. If an editor doesn't reply within what seems to be a reasonable amount of time, it's perfectly acceptable to send a polite inquiry. Many publications have writer's guidelines, outlining their editorial requirements and submission procedures; these can be obtained by sending a self-addressed, stamped envelope (SASE) to the editor.

GENERAL-INTEREST PUBLICATIONS

ACROSS THE BOARD—845 Third Ave., New York, NY 10022. Hal Goodman, Man. Ed. Articles, to 5,000 words, on a variety of topics of interest to business executives; straight business angle not required. Pays $100 to $750, on publication. Query.

ALLIED PUBLICATIONS—P.O. Drawer 189, Palm Beach, FL 33480. Mark Adams, Ed. Short articles, to 800 words, of a general and noncontroversial nature on home, family, children, teenagers, travel, hobbies, pets, decorating, fashion, beauty, sports, health, longevity. Pays 5¢ a word, up to $25, on publication. Publications include *Modern Secretary, Exhibit, Woman Beautiful, The Hairstylist, Magazine of Flowers, Modern Living and Reader's Nutshell, Management Digest, Trip & Tour,* and *Modern Tech.* Editorial guidelines available.

AMERICAS—OAS, Administration Bldg., 19th and Constitution Ave., Washington, DC 20006. A. R. Williams, Man. Ed. Features, to 2,500 words, on life in Latin America and the Carribean. Wide focus: anthropology, the arts, travel, science and development, etc. No political material. Query. Pays from $200, on publication.

AMTRAK EXPRESS—140 E. Main St., Suite 11, Huntington, NY 11743. Christopher Podgus, Ed. General-interest articles on business, health, books, sports, personal finance, life style, entertainment, travel (within Amtrak territory), technology, and science, for Amtrak travelers. Submit seasonal material three to six months in advance. Pays on publication, $300 to $700 for 1,800- to 3,000-word manuscripts; $250 to $600 for department pieces of 1,500 to 2,500 words. Query with published clippings.

BETTER HOMES AND GARDENS— 1716 Locust St., Des Moines IA

50336. David Jordan, Ed. Articles, to 2,000 words, on home and family entertainment, building, decorating, food, money management, health, travel, pets, and cars. Pays top rates, on acceptance. Query.

BON APPETIT—5900 Wilshire Blvd., Los Angeles, Ca 90036. Barbara Varnum, Articles Ed. Articles on fine cooking, cooking classes, and kitchens. Query, with samples of published work. Pays varying rates, on acceptance.

CAPPER'S WEEKLY—616 Jefferson St., Topeka, KS 66607. Dorothy Harvey, Ed. Articles, 300 to 500 words: human-interest, personal experience for women's section, historical. Pays varying rates, on publication.

CATHOLIC DIGEST—P.O. Box 64090, St. Paul, MN 55164. Address Articles Ed. Articles, 2,000 to 2,500 words, on Catholic and general subjects. Pays from $200 for original articles, $100 for reprints, on acceptance.

CHATELAINE—Maclean Hunter Bldg., 777 Bay St., Toronto, Ont., Canada M5W 1A7. Mildred Istona, Ed. Articles, 3,000 words, for Canadian women, on current issues, personalities, medicine, psychology, etc. Pays $750 for personal-experience pieces, from $1,000 for articles, on acceptance.

THE CHRISTIAN SCIENCE MONITOR—One Norway St., Boston, MA 02115. Robert C. Nelson, Feature Ed. Articles on travel, education, food and lifestyle; interviews; literary essays, to 800 words, for Home Forum; guest columns, to 800 words, for editorial page. Pays varying rates on acceptance.

CLASS—27 Union Sq. W., New York, NY 10003. René John-Sandy, Ed. Articles, to 2,500 words, of interest to the Third World population living in the U.S., and inhabitants of the Caribbean Islands. Pays 5¢ to 20¢ a word, after acceptance. Query.

COSMOPOLITAN—224 W. 57th St., New York, NY 10019. Helen Gurley Brown, Ed. Guy Flatley, Man. Ed. Articles, to 4,000 words, and features, to 2,500 words on issues affecting young career women. Pays $1,500 to $2,000 for full-length articles, less for features, on acceptance. Query.

COUNTRY JOURNAL—Box 870, Manchester Center, VT 05255. Tyler Resch, Ed. Articles, 2,500 to 3,000 words, for country and small-town residents: practical, informative pieces on contemporary rural life. Pays about $500, on acceptance. Query.

COUNTRY PEOPLE—5400 S. 60th, Greendale, WI 53129, Dan Johnson, Assoc. Ed. Articles, 500 to 1,000 words, for a rural audience. Taboos: tobacco, liquor, and sex. Pays $125 to $150, on publication. Query.

DALLAS LIFE—*The Dallas Morning News,* Communications Center, Dallas, TX 75265. Melissa East, Ed. Well-researched articles and profiles, 1,000 to 3,000 words, with photos, on contemporary issues, personalities,or subjects of strictly Dallas-related interest; short humor features, also Dallas-related, 500 to 750 words. Pays 10¢ and up a word, on acceptance. Query.

DAWN—628 N. Eutaw, Baltimore, MD 21201. Bob Matthews, Exec. Ed. Illustrated feature articles, 1,500 words, on subjects of interest to black families. Pays $100, on publication. Query.

DIVERSION MAGAZINE—60 E. 42nd St., Suite 2424, New York NY 10165. Stephen N. Birnbaum, Ed. Dir. Articles,1,200 to 3,000 words, on travel, sports, hobbies, entertainment, food, etc. for physicians. Photos. Pays from $350, on publication. Query.

DYNAMIC YEARS—215 Long Beach Blvd., Long Beach, CA 90801.

Lorena F. Farrell, Exec. Ed. General-interest features, 1,000 to 3,000 words, and column items, 350 words, with emphasis on fitness and diet, retirement planning, personal finance and investment, health, lifestyles and celebrities, sports, relationships, travel, professional life and advancement, the world of work, second and third careers, etc., all geared to the 45 to 60 age group. Photos. Pays $150 to $350 for column pieces, $500 to $2,000 for features, extra for photos, on acceptance. Query.

EARTHTONE—Publication Development, Box 23383, Portland, OR 97223. Pat Jossy, Ed. Feature articles, 1,500 to 2,000 words, on gardening, energy, health, nutrition, home projects, food, recreation, etc. Profiles, interviews. Pays $50 to $300, on publication.

EBONY—820 S. Michigan Ave., Chicago, IL 60605. Herbert Nipson, Exec. Ed. Articles, with photos, on blacks: achievements, civil rights, etc. Pays from $150, on publication. Query.

EQUINOX—7 Queen Victoria Rd., Camden East, Ont., Canada KOK 1JO. Frank Edwards, Exec. Ed. Articles, 4,000 to 8,000 words, on popular geography, biology, astronomy, sciences, the arts, industry, and adventure. Department pieces, 500 to 750 words, for "Nexus" (science and medicine) and "Habitat" (man-made and natural environment). Pays $1,000 to $2,000 for features, $250 to $350 for short pieces, on acceptance.

ESQUIRE—2 Park Ave., New York, NY 10016. Gene Stone, Sr. Ed. Articles, 250 to 7,000 words, for intelligent adult audience. Pays $250 to $1,500, on acceptance. Query.

FAMILY CIRCLE—488 Madison Ave., New York, NY 10022. Susan Ungaro, Articles Ed. Articles, to 2,500 words, on child care, consumer affairs, changing lifestyles, health and fitness, jobs, money management, food, travel, gardening; true-life dramas. Query required. Pays on acceptance.

FORD TIMES—Rm. 765, P.O. Box 1899, Dearborn, MI 48121–1899. Arnold S. Hirsch, Ed. Articles, to 1,500 words, on contemporary American life and trends, travel, outdoor activities. Profiles of personalities, well-known and not. Pays to $750, on acceptance. Query.

FRIENDLY EXCHANGE—Locust at 17th, Des Moines, IA 50336. Adele Malott, Ed. Articles, 1,000 to 2,500 words, for traditional, home-owning families, on domestic travel, gardening, home decorating, personal finance, sports and the outdoors, consumer interests, etc. with Western U.S. tie-in. Pays $600 to $800 for features. Departments are generated exclusively by reader mail. Pays on acceptance. Query.

FRIENDS—30400 Van Dyke, Warren, MI 48093. Tom Morrisey, Ed. Active lifestyle articles and upbeat subjects for owners of Chevrolet cars and trucks. Must have Chevy tie-in. Photos (4 color trans.). Pays from $400, on acceptance.

GENTLEMEN'S QUARTERLY (GQ)—350 Madison Ave., New York, NY 10017. Eliot Kaplan, Managing Ed. Articles, 1,500 to 4,000 words, on politics, personalities, life styles, trends, grooming, sports, travel, business, etc. Columns: "Male Animal" (essays by men on life); "All About Adam" (nonfiction by women about men); "Games" (sports); "Health" and "Humor." Other columns cover fitness, nutrition, investments, travel, music, wine and food. Pays $750 to $2,000 for columns of 1,000 to 2,500 words. Pays $750 to $3,000, on acceptance, for full-length articles. Query with published clips.

GLAMOUR—350 Madison Ave., New York, NY 10017. Ruth Whitney, Ed.-

544

in-Chief; Janet Chan, Art. Ed. Articles on careers, health, psychology, interpersonal relationships, etc.; editorial approach is "how-to" for women, 18 to 35. Fashion and beauty material staff-written. Pays from $1,000 for 1,500 to 2,000-word articles, from $1,500 for longer pieces, on acceptance.

GLOBE—2112 S. Congress Ave., West Palm Beach, FL 33413. John Cooke, News Editor. Factual articles, 500 to 1,000 words, with photos: exposés, celebrity interviews, consumer and human-interest pieces. Pays from $50 to $1,500.

GOOD HOUSEKEEPING—959 Eighth Ave., New York, NY 10019. Joan Thursh, Articles Ed. Personal-experience articles on an inspirational or trend-setting events; personal medical pieces on unusual illness, treatment, and result. Short, essay-type reminiscences on some aspect of family life or relationships. Well-researched medical and health articles by writers with credentials in the field. Full-length articles run to 2,500 words; 750 to 1,000 words for short essay-type pieces. Query first with two writing samples. Pays $500 to $750 for short articles, $1,000 to $1,500 for full-length pieces, on acceptance. Buys all rights. Guidelines available.

GOOD READING MAGAZINE—Litchfield, IL 62056. Articles, 500 to 1,000 words, with B/W photos, on current, factual subjects of general interest; business, personal experiences which reveal success in human relationships. Pays $10 to $100.

GRIT—208 W. Third St., Williamsport, PA 17701. Joanne Decker, Assignment Ed. Articles, to 500 words, on religion, communities, jobs, recreation, families and coping. Pays 12¢ a word, extra for photos, on acceptance.

HARPER'S MAGAZINE—2 Park Ave., New York, NY 10016. No unsolicited articles or queries. Considers manuscripts submitted through an agent only.

HISTORIC PRESERVATION—1785 Massachusetts Ave., N.W., Washington DC 20036. Thomas J. Colin, Ed. Articles from published writers, 1,500 to 4,000 words, on historic preservation, maritime preservation and people involved in preservation. High-quality photos. Pays $300 to $850, extra for photos, on acceptance. Query required.

HORTICULTURE—755 Boylston St., Boston, MA 02116. Steven Krauss, Man. Ed. Authoritative, well-written articles, 1,500 to 3,000 words, on all aspects of gardening and horticulture. Pays competitive rates. Query.

HOUSE & GARDEN—350 Madison Ave., New York, NY 10017. Louis O. Gropp, Ed.-in-Chief. Shelley Wanger, Articles Ed. Articles on decorating, architecture, gardens, the arts. Query. Rarely buys unsolicited manuscripts.

HOUSE BEAUTIFUL—1700 Broadway, New York, NY 10019. Carol Cooper Garey, Dir. Copy/Features. Service articles related to the home. Pieces on beauty, travel and gardening mostly staff-written. Pays varying rates, on acceptance. Send for writer's guidelines. Query with detailed outline and SASE.

INQUIRER MAGAZINE—*Philadelphia Inquirer,* Broad and Callowhill Sts., Philadelphia, PA 19101. David Boldt, Ed. Local-interest features, 500 to 7,000 words. Profiles of national figures in politics, entertainment, etc. Pays varying rates, on publication. Query.

INTERNATIONAL LIVING—824 E. Baltimore St., Baltimore, MD 21202. Elizabeth Philip, Ed. Newsletter. Short pieces and features, 200 to 1,000 words, with useful information on living abroad, investing overseas, and unusual travel bargains. Pays to $200, on acceptance.

LADIES' HOME JOURNAL—3 Park Ave., New York, NY 10016. Articles on contemporary subjects of interest to women. Personal experience and regional pieces. Queries only (with SASE) to Exec. Eds. Jan Goodwin or Sondra Forsyth Enos. Not responsible for unsolicited manuscripts.

LIFE—Time-Life Bldg., Rockefeller Center, New York, NY 10020. Richard A. Burgheim, Asst. Man. Ed. General-interest articles, 3,000 to 5,000 words. Pays varying rates, on acceptance. Query. Rarely buys free-lance material.

McCALL'S—230 Park Ave., New York, NY 10169. Robert Stein, Ed. Judy Stone, Art. Ed. Interesting, unusual and topical first person essays, narratives, reports on health, home management, social trends relating to women of all ages, 1,000 to 3,000 words. Humor. Human-interest stories. Job column. Pieces for VIP-ZIP and regional sections: consumer, travel, crafts. Essays, 1,000 words, for "Back Talk," a forum for airing fresh and often controversial views on all subjects. Pays top rates, on acceptance.

MADEMOISELLE—350 Madison Ave., New York, NY 10017. Kate White, Exec. Ed. Articles, 1,200 to 2,500 words, on subjects of interest to literate young women. Pays from $350, on acceptance. Query.

MARRIAGE & FAMILY LIVING—St. Meinrad, IN 47577. Kass Dotterweich, Man. Ed. Articles, to 2,000 words, on husband-wife and parent-child relationships. Pays 7¢ a word, on acceptance. Query.

MD MAGAZINE—30 E. 60th St., New York, NY 10022. A. J. Vogl, Ed. Articles, 750 to 2,500 words, for doctors, on the arts, history, other aspects of culture. Fresh angle required. Pays from $200 to $700, on acceptance. Query.

METROPOLITAN HOME—750 Third Ave., New York, NY 10017. Service and informational articles for metropolitan dwellers in apartments, houses, co-ops, lofts, and condominiums, on real estate, equity, wine and spirits, collecting, etc. Pays varying rates. Query.

MODERN MATURITY—215 Long Beach Blvd., Long Beach, CA 90801. Ian Ledgerwood, Ed. Service articles on living, food, health, employment, travel, and leisure activities, for persons over 50 years. Nostalgia, inspirational articles, personality pieces, Americana, to 2,000 words. Photos. Pays $150 to $2,500, extra for photos, on acceptance.

THE MOTHER EARTH NEWS—105 Stoney Mt. Rd., Hendersonville, NC 28791. Roselyn Edwards, Submissions Ed. Articles, with photos, on alternative life styles, for rural and urban readers: home improvements, how-to's, indoor and outdoor gardening, family pastimes, etc. Also, self-help, health, food-related, ecology, energy and cosumerism pieces. Profiles. Pays varying rates, on acceptance. Send for writers' guidelines.

MS.—119 W. 40th St., New York, NY 10018. Address Manuscript Ed. Articles relating to women's roles and changing lifestyles; general interest, how-to, self-help, profiles. Pays varying rates, on acceptance. Query.

NATIONAL ENQUIRER—Lantana, FL 33464. Articles, of any length, for mass audience: topical news, the occult, how-to, scientific discoveries, human drama, adventure, personalities. Photos. Pays from $325. Query; no unsolicited manuscripts accepted.

NATIONAL GEOGRAPHIC—17th and M Sts. N.W., Washington, DC

20036. First-person articles, 6,000 words maximum, on travel, exploration, mountaineering, seafaring, archaeological discoveries, natural history, industries, commodities, science, occupations, living patterns. Photos. Pays to $8,000, extra for photos, on acceptance. 500-word query required; address Sr. Asst. Ed. No unsolicited manuscripts.

NATURAL HISTORY—American Museum of Natural History, Central Park West at 79th St., New York, NY 10024. Alan Ternes, Ed.-in-Chief. Informative articles to 3,500 words, by experts, on anthropology and natural sciences. Pays $750, on acceptance. Query.

NEW AGE—342 Western Ave., Brighton, MA 02135. Articles, for readers interested in self-development and awareness, on natural foods, holistic health, education, disarmament, etc. Pays from 10¢ a word, on publication. Query.

NEW REALITIES—680 Beach St., San Francisco, CA 94109. James Bolen, Ed. Articles on holistic health, personal growth, parapsychology, alternative lifestyles, new spirituality. Pays to $150, on publication. Query.

NEW WOMAN—215 Lexington Ave., New York, NY 10016. Pat Miller, Ed. "Read the magazine in order to become familiar with our needs before querying." Articles on new lifestyles. Features on financial and legal advice, building a business, marriage, relationships, surviving divorce, innovative diets. Pays varying rates, on publication. Query.

NEW YORK—755 Second Ave., New York, NY 10017. Edward Kosner, Ed. Laurie Jones, Man. Ed. Feature articles of interest to New Yorkers. Pays from $350 to $3,500, on acceptance. Query required; not responsible for unsolicited material.

THE NEW YORK TIMES MAGAZINE—229 W. 43rd St., New York, NY 10036. Address Articles Ed. Timely articles, approximately 4,000 words, on new items, forthcoming events, trends, culture, entertainment, etc. Pays $350 to $500 for short pieces, $1,000 to $2,500 for major articles, on acceptance. Query.

THE NEW YORKER—25 W. 43rd St., New York, NY 10036. Address The Editors. Factual and biographical articles, for "Profiles," "Reporter at Large," "That Was New York," "Annals of Crime," "Onward and Upward with the Arts," etc. Pays good rates, on acceptance. Query.

OMNI—1965 Broadway, New York, NY 10023–5965. Gurney Williams, III, Ex. Ed. Articles, 2,500 to 3,000 words, on scientific aspects of the future: space colonies, cloning, machine intelligence, ESP, origin of life, future arts, lifestyles, etc. Pays $750 to $2,500, less for short features, on acceptance. Query.

PARADE—750 Third Ave., New York, NY 10017. Fran Carpentier, Articles Ed. National Sunday newspaper supplement. Factual and authoritative articles, 1,000 to 1,500 words, on subjects of national interest: health, education, consumer and environmental issues, science, the family, sports, etc. Profiles of well-known personalities and service pieces. No fiction, poetry, games or puzzles. Photos with captions. Pays from $1,000. Query. Self-addressed, stamped envelope required.

PENTHOUSE—1965 Broadway, New York, NY 10023–5965. Claudia Valentino, Man. Ed. Peter Bloch, Exec. Ed. General-interest or controversial articles, to 5,000 words. Pays from 20¢ a word, on acceptance.

PEOPLE IN ACTION—1720 Washington Blvd., Ogden, UT 84404. Caroll McKanna Halley, Ed. Upbeat personality profiles about people overcoming, enjoying, helping others, 600 to 1,200 words; Pays 15¢ a word, $35 for color photos, on acceptance. Query or send manuscript with photos (no black & white). Celebrity Chef feature, 400 to 600 words, must include recipe; need not be celebrity. One-year lead time.

PEOPLE WEEKLY—Time, Life, Inc., Rockefeller Center, New York, NY 10020. Hal Wingo, Ass't. Man. Ed. Considers article proposals only, 3 to 4 paragraphs, on timely, entertaining, and topical personalities. Pays good rates, on acceptance. Most material staff written.

PLAYBOY—919 N. Michigan Ave., Chicago, Il 60611. James Morgan, Articles Ed. Sophisticated articles, 4,000 to 6,000 words, of interest to urban men. Humor; satire. Pays to $3,000, on acceptance. Query.

PLAYGIRL—3420 Ocean Park Blvd., Suite 3000, Santa Monica, CA 90405. Ruth Drizen, Sr. Ed. Feature articles, 2,500 to 3,000 words, for contemporary women, age 20 to 35. Celebrity interviews, 3,000 to 4,000 words. Pays negotiable rates. Query with published clips.

PRIME TIMES—Suite 120, 2802 International Ln., Madison, WI 53704. Joan Donovan, Assoc. Man. Ed. Articles, 500 to 2,500 words, for over-50 or retired credit union people. Departments, 850 to 1,000 words. Pays $125 to $750, on publication, for first and second rights. Query.

PSYCHOLOGY TODAY—1200 17th St. N.W., Washington, D.C. 20036. Address Manuscripts Ed. Most articles assigned to researchers in the social sciences. Query.

READER'S DIGEST—Pleasantville, NY 10570. Kenneth O. Gilmore, Ed.-in-Chief. Unsolicited manuscripts will not be read or returned. General-interest articles already in print and well-developed story proposals will be considered (include SASE). Send reprint or query to any editor on the masthead.

REDBOOK—224 W. 57th St., New York, NY 10019. Annette Capone, Ed.-in-Chief. Karen Larson, Articles Ed. Articles, 1,000 to 3,500 words, on subjects related to relationships, sex, current issues, marriage, the family, and parenting. Pays from $750, on acceptance. Query.

ROLLING STONE—745 Fifth Ave., New York, NY 10151. Magazine of modern American culture, politics, and art. No fiction. Query; "rarely accepts free-lance material."

THE SATURDAY EVENING POST—1100 Waterway Blvd., Indianapolis, IN 46202. Ted Kreiter, Exec. Ed. Articles, 2,500 to 3,000 words, on education, medicine, the arts, science, politics. Articles on sports, home repairs (with photos). Photo essays. Pays varying rates, on publication. Query with outline.

SATURDAY REVIEW—214 Mass. Ave., N.E., Suite 460, Washington, DC 20002. Frank Gannon, Ed. Interviews; profiles; and reviews of events and books, 800 to 2,500 words. Pays varying rates, on publication.

SAVVY—3 Park Ave., New York, NY 10016. Wendy Reid Crisp, Ed. Service articles and business features for women executives. Writers must be familiar with the magazine before submitting material. Pays $300 to $1,500, on acceptance. Query.

SELF—350 Madison Ave., New York, NY 10017. Phyllis Starr Wilson, Ed. Articles for women of all ages, with strong how-to slant, on self-development. Pays from $750, on acceptance. Query.

SHOW-BOOK WEEK—*Chicago Sun-Times,* 401 N. Wabash Ave., Chicago, IL 60611. Henry Kisor, Book Week Ed. Articles, profiles and interviews, to

1,000 words, relating to fine arts or lively arts. Pays $50 to $125, on publication. Query.

SIGNATURE—641 Lexington Ave., New York, NY 10022. Barbara Coats, Articles Ed. Magazine of the Diners Club and Citicorp. Articles, 1,300 to 2,000 words, on travel, sports, entertainment, wine, spirits and gastronomy for well-traveled, upper-class readers. Pays from $700, on acceptance. Query.

SMITHSONIAN—900 Jefferson Dr., Washington, DC 20560. Marlane A. Liddell, Articles Ed. Articles on history, art, natural history, physical science, etc. Query with SASE.

THE STAR—660 White Plains Rd., Tarrytown, NY 10591. Dick Kaplan, Managing Ed. Topical articles, 50 to 800 words, on human-interest subjects, show business, lifestyles, the sciences, etc., for family audience. Pays varying rates.

SUCCESS—342 Madison Ave., New York, NY 10175. Scott DeGarmo, Ed.-in-Chief. Profiles of successful individuals, executives; entrepreneurs; psychology, behavior, and motivation articles, 500 to 3,500 words. Columns on personal finance and health. Pays $250, on acceptance. Query.

SUNDAY—*The Chicago Tribune,* 435 N. Michigan, Chicago, IL 60611. Mary Knoblauch, Ed. General-interest articles, to 5,000 words. Pays on publication. Query.

TOWN & COUNTRY—1700 Broadway, New York, NY 10019. Address Features Dept. Considers one page proposals for articles. Rarely buys unsolicited manuscripts.

TRAVEL & LEISURE—1120 Ave. of the Americas, New York, NY 10036. Pamela Fiori, Ed.-in-Chief. Articles, 800 to 2,500 words on destinations and leisuretime activities. Regional pieces for regional editions. Pays $600 to $2,000, on acceptance. Query; articles on assignment.

TROPIC—*The Miami Herald,* One Herald Plaza, Miami, FL 33101. Gene Weingarten, Ed. Essays and articles on current trends and issues, light or heavy, 1,000 to 4,000 words, for sophisticated audience. Pays $400 to $1,000, on publication. Query with SASE.

TV GUIDE—Radnor, PA 19088. Andrew Mills, Ass't Man. Ed. Short, light, brightly-written pieces about humorous or offbeat angles of television. Pays on acceptance. Query.

US—215 Lexington Ave., New York, NY 10016. Richard Sanders, Exec. Ed. Non-entertainment features, human-interest stories, 1,200 to 1,500 words, with emphasis on dramatic, controversial or trendy. Pays $500, on publication. Query, with published clips.

USA WEEKEND—1515 Broadway, New York, NY 10036. Tom Plate, Ed., John Tarkov, Exec. Ed., Tim Mulligan, Man. Ed. Short, lively articles on prominent individuals, health, medicine, money management and family advice. Pays from $200, on acceptance. Query.

VANITY FAIR—350 Madison Ave., New York, NY 10017. Tina Brown, Ed. Articles, 500 to 2,000 words. Pays on acceptance. Query.

VOGUE—350 Madison Ave., New York, NY 10017. Amy Gross, Features Ed. Articles, to 1,500 words, on women, entertainment and the arts, travel, medicine and health. General features. Rarely buys unsolicited manuscripts. Pays good rates, on acceptance.

549

VOLKSWAGEN'S WORLD—Volkswagen of America, Troy, MI 48099. Ed Rabinowitz, Ed. Articles, 600 to 1,000 words, for Volkswagen owners: profiles of well-known personalities; inspirational or human-interest pieces; travel; humor. Photos. Pays $150, per printed page, on acceptance. Query. Guidelines on request.

WASHINGTON POST MAGAZINE—*The Washington Post,* 1150 15th St., NW, Washington, DC 20071. Stephen L. Petranek, Man. Ed. Personal-experience essays, profiles and general-interest pieces, to 4,000 words, on business, arts and culture, politics, science, sports, education, children, relationships, behavior, etc. Pays from $100, after acceptance.

WEEKLY WORLD NEWS—600 S. East Coast Ave., Lantana, FL 33462. Joe West, Ed. Human-interest news pieces, about 500 to 1,000 words, involving human adventure, unusual situations, and off-beat stories from foreign countries. Pays $125 to $500, on publication.

WESTWAYS—Box 2890, Terminal Annex, Los Angeles, CA 90051. Mary Ann Fisher, Ed. Articles, 1,000 to 1,500 words, and photo essays, on western U.S., Canada, and Mexico: history, contemporary living, travel, personalities, etc. Photos. Pays from 20¢ a word, extra for photos, 30 days before publication. Query.

WISCONSIN—*The Milwaukee Journal Magazine,* P.O. Box 661, Milwaukee, WI 53201. Beth Slocum, Ed. Trend stories, essays, humor, personal-experience pieces, profiles, 500 to 2,000 words. Pays $75 to $500, after publication.

WOMAN'S DAY—1515 Broadway, New York, NY 10036. Rebecca Greer, Articles Ed. Articles, 500 to 3,500 words, on subjects of interest to women: marriage, education, family health, child rearing, money management, interpersonal relationships, changing lifestyles, etc. Dramatic first-person narratives about women who have experienced medical miracles or other triumphs. "Reflections": short, provocative personal essays, 1,000 to 1,500 words, humorous or serious, dealing with concerns of interest and relevance to women. Pays $2,000 for essays, tops rates for articles, on acceptance.

WOMAN'S WORLD—177 N. Dean St., Englewood, NJ 07631. Janel Bladow, Sen. Ed. Articles, 800 to 2,500 words, of interest to middle-income women between the ages of 18 and 60, on love, romance, careers, medicine, health, psychology, sex, travel, dramatic stories of adventure or crisis. Pays $300 to $1,000, on acceptance. Query.

WORKING WOMAN—342 Madison Ave., New York, NY 10173. Anne Mollegen Smith, Ed. Articles, 1,000 to 2,500 words, on business and personal aspects of working women's lives. Pays from $400, on acceptance.

YANKEE—Dublin, NH 03444. Judson D. Hale, Ed. Articles, to 3,000 words, with New England angle. Photos. Pays $100 to $700 (average $450 to $550), on acceptance.

CURRENT EVENTS, POLITICS

AFRICA REPORT—833 U.N. Pl., New York, NY 10017. Margaret A. Novicki, Ed. Well-researched articles by specialists, 1,000 to 4,000 words, with photos, on current African affairs. Pays $150 to $250, on publication.

THE AMERICAN LEGION MAGAZINE—Box 1055, Indianapolis, IN 46206. Daniel S. Wheeler, Ed.-in-Chief. Articles, 750 to 2,000 words, on current world affairs, public policy, and subjects of contemporary interest. No fiction or exposés. Pays $100 to $1,000, on acceptance. Query.

AMERICAN POLITICS—810 18th St., NW, Suite 802, Washington, DC 20006. Andrew C. L. Jones, Ed. Timely articles on issues, trends, and figures in American politics; profiles; local pieces of national interest, 3,000 to 3,500 words. Payment varies, on publication. Query.

THE AMERICAN SCHOLAR—1811 Q St., N.W., Washington, DC 20009. Joseph Epstein, Ed. Non-technical articles and essays, 3,500 to 4,000 words, on current affairs, the American cultural scene, politics, arts, religion and science. Pays $350, on acceptance.

THE ATLANTIC—8 Arlington St., Boston, MA 02116. William Whitworth, Ed. In-depth articles on public issues, politics, social sciences, education, business, literature, and the arts, with emphasis on information rather than opinion. Ideal length: 3,000 to 6,000 words, though short pieces (1,000 to 2,000 words) are also welcome. Pays $1,000 to $7,000, on acceptance.

COMMENTARY—165 E. 56th St., New York, NY 10022. Norman Podhoretz, Ed. Articles, 5,000 to 7,000 words, on contemporary issues, Jewish affairs, social sciences, community life, religious thought, cultural activities. Pays about 20¢ a word, on publication.

COMMONWEAL—232 Madison Ave., New York, NY 10016. Peter Steinfels, Ed. Catholic. Articles, to 3,000 words, on political, social, religious and literary subjects. Pays 3¢ a word, on acceptance.

THE CRISIS—NAACP, 186 Remsen St., Brooklyn, NY 11201. Fred Beauford, Ed. Articles, to 1,500 words, on civil rights, problems and achievements of blacks and other minorities. Pays in copies.

ENVIRONMENT—4000 Albemarle St., N.W., Washington, DC 20016. Jane Scully, Man. Ed. Articles, 2,500 to 6,500 words, on environmental, scientific and technological policy and decision-making issues. Pays $75 to $300, on publication. Query.

FOREIGN POLICY JOURNAL—11 Dupont Circle, N.W., Suite 900, Washington, DC 20036. Charles William Maynes, Ed. Articles, 3,000 to 5,000 words, on international affairs. Honorarium, on publication. Query.

FOREIGN SERVICE JOURNAL—2101 E St. N.W., Washington, DC 20037. Stephen R. Dujack, Ed. Articles on American diplomacy, foreign affairs and subjects of interest to Americans representing the U.S. abroad. Pays 2¢ to 10¢ a word, on publication. Query.

THE FREEMAN—Foundation for Economic Education, Irvington-on-Hudson, NY 10533. Paul L. Poirot, Ed. Articles, to 3,000 words, on economic, political and moral implications of private property, voluntary exchange, and individual choice. Pays 5¢ a word, on publication.

INQUIRER MAGAZINE—*Philadelphia Inquirer,*Broad and Callowhill Sts., Philadelphia, PA 19101. David Boldt, Ed. Local-interest features, 500 to 7,000 words. Profiles of nationa figures in politics, entertainment, etc. Pays varying rates, on publication. Query.

INQUIRY—1320 G. St. S.E., Washington, DC 20003. Doug Bandow, Ed. Libertarian monthly. Articles to 5,000 words, on civil liberties, economics, foreign policy and current political developments. Columns, 1,000 to 2,500 words, on law, politics, education, economics, and media. Pays 10¢ a word, on publication. Free sample copy. Query first.

INTELLECTUAL ACTIVIST—131 Fifth Ave., New York, NY 10003. Articles, 2,000 to 4,000 words, analyzing current political issues, especially articles on economic and social issues that affect individual rights—from energy and national health insurance to defense and antitrust law. Query. Editorial guidelines available. Pays $200 to $500, on publication.

MIDSTREAM: A MONTHLY JEWISH REVIEW—515 Park Ave., New York, NY 10022. Joel Carmichael, Ed. Articles; reviews. Pays 5¢ a word, on publication.

MOMENT—462 Boylston St., Boston, MA 02116. Nechama Katz, Man. Ed. Sophisticated articles, 2,000 to 4,000 words, on Jewish political, social, literary and religious issues. Pays from $100, on publication. Query.

MOTHER JONES—1663 Mission St., San Francisco, CA 94103. Deirdre English, Ed. Investigative articles, political essays, cultural analyses. Pays $750 to $1,000, after acceptance. Query.

THE NATION—72 Fifth Ave., New York, NY 10011. Victor Navasky, Ed. Articles, 2,000 to 2,500 words, on current issues. Pays about 2¢ a word up to $150 on publication. Query.

THE NEW YORK TIMES MAGAZINE—229 W. 43rd St., New York, NY 10036. Address Articles Ed. Timely articles, approximately 4,000 words, on new items, forthcoming events, trends, culture, entertainment, etc. Pays $350 to $500 for short pieces, $1,000 to $2,500 for major articles, on acceptance. Query.

THE NEW YORKER—25 W. 43rd St., New York, NY 10036. Address The Editors. Factual and biographical articles, for "Profiles." "Reporter at Large," "That Was New York," "Annals of Crime," "Onward and Upward with the Arts," etc. Pays good rates, on acceptance. Query.

NUCLEAR TIMES—298 Fifth Ave., New York, NY 10001. Renata Rizzo, Man. Ed. Terse, timely news articles, to 1,500 words, on the nuclear disarmament movement, the arms race, nuclear weapons and nuclear war. Pays 12¢ a word, on publication.

PRESENT TENSE—165 E. 56th St., New York, NY 10022. Murray Polner, Ed. Serious reportage and personal journalism 2,000 to 3,000 words, with photos, on developments concerning Jews worldwide; profiles of Jewish life. Pays $100 to $250, on acceptance. Query.

THE PROGRESSIVE—409 E. Main St., Madison, WI 53703. Erwin Knoll, Ed. Articles, 1,000 to 3,500 words, on political, social problems. Light features. Pays $75 to $300, on publication.

PUBLIC CITIZEN MAGAZINE—P.O. Box 19404, Washington, DC 20036. Bimonthly. Elliot Negin, Ed. Investigative reports and articles of timely political interst, 500 words to feature length, for members of Public Citizen: consumer rights, health and safety, environmental protection, safe energy, tax reform and government and corporate accountability. Photos, illustrations. Pays to $750.

ROLL CALL: THE NEWSPAPER OF CAPITOL HILL—201 Mass. Ave. N.E., Washington, DC 20002. Sidney Yudain, Ed. Factual, breezy articles with political or Congressional angle: Congressional historical and human-interest subjects, political lore, etc. Political satire and humor. Pays modest rates, on publication.

THE SPOTLIGHT—300 Independence Ave., S.E., Washington, DC 20003. Vincent J. Ryan, Man. Ed. Articles covering national and world political affairs of type not appearing in the Establishment press. Pays on publication. Query required.

TROPIC—*The Miami Herald,* One Herald Plaza, Miami, FL 33101. Gene Weingarten, Ed. Essays and articles on current trends and issues, light or heavy, 1,000 to 4,000 words, for sophisticated audience. Pays $400 to $1,000, on publication. Query with SASE.

VFW MAGAZINE—Broadway at 34th, Kansas City, MO 64111. Magazine for Veterans of Foreign Wars and their families. James K. Anderson, Ed. Articles, 1,000 words, on current issues, solutions to everyday problems, personalities, sports, etc. How-to and historical pieces. Photos. Pays 5¢ to 10¢ a word, extra for photos, on acceptance.

VILLAGE VOICE—842 Broadway, New York, NY 10003. David Schneiderman, Ed.-in-Chief and Pub. Articles, 500 to 2,000 words, on current or controversial topics. Pays $75 to $350, on acceptance. Query.

WASHINGTON DOSSIER—3301 New Mexico Ave., NW, Washington, DC 20016. Kitty Chism, Ed. Features with a Washington, D.C. slant. Sophisticated investigative pieces, personality profiles, service articles, etc., 1,000 to 2,500 words. Pays 10¢ to 20¢ a word, on acceptance. Query.

THE WASHINGTON MONTHLY—1711 Connecticut Ave., N.W., Washington, DC 20009. Charles Peters, Ed. Investigative articles, 1,500 to 5,000 words, on politics, government and the political culture. Pays 10¢ a word, on publication. Query.

WASHINGTON POST MAGAZINE—*The Washington Post,* 1150 15th St., NW, Washington, DC 20071. Stephen L. Petranek, Man. Ed. Personal-experience essays, profiles and general-interest pieces, to 4,000 words, on business, arts and culture, politics, science, sports, education, children, relationships, behavior, etc. Pays from $100, after acceptance.

REGIONAL AND CITY PUBLICATIONS

ADIRONDACK LIFE—420 E. Genesse St., Syracuse, NY 13202. William K. Verner, Ed. Features, about 3,000 words, are geared to an upstate New York audience, and focus on outdoor activities (hiking, canoeing, camping, etc.), arts, crafts, wilderness preservation, and history. Photos are a plus. Pays $175 to $300, on publication.

ALASKA—Box 4-EEE, Anchorage, AK 99509. Tom Gresham, Ed. Articles, 1,500 words, on life in Alaska and northwestern Canada. Pays on acceptance. Write for guidelines.

ALASKA OUTDOORS—Box 82222, Fairbanks, AK 99708. Christopher Batin, Ed. Articles, 1,400 to 1,800 words, on outdoor recreational activities in Alaska. How-to's, fillers, humor, and investigative pieces on Alaska's natural resources. Pays $100 to $200, extra for photos, on acceptance. Query required.

ALOHA, THE MAGAZINE OF HAWAII—P.O. Box 3260, Honolulu, HI 96801. Rita Ariyoshi, Ed. Articles, 1,500 to 4,000 words, on subjects of regional interest. Poetry and fiction that "illuminates the Hawaiian experience." Photos. Pays 10¢ a word, on publication. Query first.

AMERICAN WEST—3033 N. Campbell Ave., Tucson, AZ 85719. Mae Reid-Bills, Managing Ed. Bimonthly. Articles that "celebrate the West, past and present. Pays $200 to $800, on acceptance for features (2,500 to 3,000 words) and department pieces (900 to 1,000 words). Query first.

ANTIQUING HOUSTON—Box 40734, Houston, TX 77240. Susan C. Taber, Ed. Articles on antiques and collectibles, 300 to 1,000 words. Poetry, 4 to 20 lines, and fillers, 4 to 15 lines, on antiques and collectibles. Pays $5 to $50, on acceptance.

ARIZONA—The *Arizona Republic,* Box 1950, Phoenix, AZ 85001. Paul Schatt, Ed. Articles, 500 to 2,500 words, on people and issues of interest to Arizona readers. Humor, cartoons. Photos. Pays $40 to $400, before publication.

ARIZONA FOOTBALL—P.O. Box 2258, Prescott, AZ 86301. Fred Stewart and Ray Trevino, Eds. Articles, 250 to 500 words, on Arizona football. Pays $25, extra for photos, on acceptance.

ARIZONA HIGHWAYS—2039 W. Lewis Ave., Phoenix, AZ 85009. Richard G. Stahl, Managing Ed. Articles on travel in Arizona and environs (including Mexico); pieces on history, adventure, personalities, nature, arts and crafts, humor, lifestyles, nostalgia, archaeology, and Western nonfiction romance—all with an Arizona slant. Pays 25¢ to 30¢ a word, on acceptance. Average length of articles is 2,000 words. Query first.

ARKANSAS TIMES—Box 34010, Little Rock, AR 72203. Bob Lancaster, Ed. Articles, to 6,000 words, on Arkansas history, Arkansas people, travel, politics. All articles *must* have strong AR orientation. Fiction, to 6,000 words. Pays $100 to $300, on acceptance.

ATLANTA—6285 Barfield Rd., Atlanta, GA 30328. Neil Shister, Ed. Articles, 2,500 words, on Atlanta subjects or personalities. Pays $600 to $1,000, on publication. Query.

ATLANTA BUSINESS CHRONICLE—1800 Water Place, Suite 100, Atlanta, GA 30341. Business articles on Atlanta companies, 1,500 to 3,000 words. Queries required. Payment is negotiable, on publication.

THE ATLANTIC ADVOCATE—P.O. Box 3370, Gleaner Bldg., Prospect St., Fredericton, N.B., Canada E3B 5A2. Harold P. Wood, Ed. Well-researched articles on Atlantic Canada and general-interest subjects; fiction, to 1,500 words. Pays to 8¢ a word, on publication.

ATLANTIC CITY MAGAZINE—1637 Atlantic Ave., Atlantic City, NJ 08401. Bill Tonelli, Ed. Lively articles, 500 to 5,000 words, on Atlantic City and

Southern New Jersey: casinos, business, personalities, environment, local color, crime, for locals and tourists. Pays $100 to $600, on publication. Query.

AUGUSTA SPECTATOR—P.O. Box 3168, Augusta, GA 30904. Faith Bertsche, Pub. Fiction to 2,000 words. Poetry; submit to Jan Cwalina, 19 Troon Way, Aiken, SC 29801. Articles on the arts, local history, travel, to 2,000 words. Pays to $25 for stories and articles, in copies for poetry, on publication. Query first.

AUSTIN—Box 1967, Austin, TX 78767. Hal Susskind, Ed. Articles, 800 to 1,500 words, on Austin. Photos; cartoons. Pays varying rates, on publication. Query.

AVENUE—145 E. 57th St., New York, NY 10022. Michael Shnayerson, Ed. Articles, 2,000 to 2,500 words, for Upper East Side New Yorkers, and residents of affluent suburbs around the country. Profiles of Upper East Siders in business and the arts, food, fashion. Fiction. Pays $400 to $500, on publication. Query.

AVENUE M—100 E. Walton, #36A, Chicago, IL 60611. Art Desmond, Ed. Articles, 500 to 1,000 words, on lifestyles, finance, and travel, for residents of Near North area of Chicago. Profiles. Pays $25 to $50, on publication. Query preferred.

BALTIMORE MAGAZINE—26 S. Calvert St., Baltimore, MD 21202. Alan Sea, Managing Ed. Articles focusing exclusively on the people, places and events in the Baltimore metropolitan area. Articles, 500 to 3,000 words, giving consumer advice, investigative pieces, profiles, humor and personal-experience pieces. Pay varies, on publication. Queries are required.

BOSTON GLOBE MAGAZINE—*The Boston Globe,* Boston, MA 02107. Ande Zelman, Ed. Weekly Sunday magazine. General-interest articles, humor, interviews (not Q & A) and profiles; articles on history, nostalgia, arts, science, and medicine. Regional tie-in is not required, but a "news peg" is important. Pays $500 to $1,000, on publication, for articles of 2,500 to 5,000 words. Queries required; enclose published clips and SASE.

BOSTON MAGAZINE—300 Mass Ave., Boston, MA 02115. Informative, entertaining features, 1,000 to 4,000 words, on Boston area personalities, institutions and phenomena. Pays $250 to $1,200, on publication. Query David Rosenbaum, Articles Ed., or Kate Broughton, Service Features Ed.

BUFFALO—See *Living Publications.*

BUFFALO SPREE MAGAZINE—Box 38, Buffalo, NY 14226. Jo V. Shotell, Ed. Quarterly. Articles with a regional slant, to 1,500 words. Payment is $75 to $100, on publication.

CALIFORNIA—11601 Wilshire Blvd., Los Angeles, CA 90025. Katherine Pandora, Assoc. Ed. Articles with a California focus on politics, business, environmental issues, ethnic diversity, and sports. Service pieces, profiles, and well-researched investigative articles. Query. Pays $750 to $2,500 for features, $200 to $750 for shorter articles and columns.

CAPE COD GUIDE—Long Pond Rd., Plymouth, MA 02360. Walter Brooks, Pub. Features, two typed pages, that "advance the temporary pleasure of our vacation readers." Pays $25 to $40, on publication. Include artwork or photos.

CAPE COD LIFE—P.O. Box 222, Osterville, MA 02655. Brian F. Shortsleeve, Publisher. Bimonthly. Articles on current events, business, history, art, gardening in Cape Cod, Martha's Vineyard, and Nantucket region. Pays $3 per column inch, on publication, for articles of 2,000 words. Photos are a plus. Poetry is used every other issue. Queries are required.

CAPITAL DISTRICT—See *Living Publications.*

CAPITOL, THE COLUMBUS DISPATCH SUNDAY MAGAZINE—Columbus, OH 43216. Articles, to 5,000 words, preferably related to Ohio. Photos. Pays negotiable rates, extra for photos, after publication.

CENTRAL FLORIDA MAGAZINE—P.O. Box 7727, Orlando, FL 32854. Rowland Stiteler, Ed. Articles on business, sports, cars, and travel; profiles. Pays 5¢ to 10¢ a word, on publication. Query first.

CHARLOTTE MAGAZINE—P.O. Box 221269, Charlotte, NC 28222. Frederick J. Keitel III, Publisher. Articles on subjects of interest to young, affluent professionals in the Charlotte area—arts, home, fashion, events, lifestyle, sports and personalities. Article lengths: 500 to 750 words, 1,200 words, or 1,600 words, Query. Payment is negotiable or 10¢ a word, on publication. All material (with the exception of short humorous pieces) must have a regional slant.

THE CHARLOTTE OBSERVER AND THE CHARLOTTE NEWS—Box 32188, Charlotte, NC 28232. Cynthia Struby, Features Ed. Newspaper features, travel articles, 500 to 1,000 words, for audience in NC and SC, Pays $25 to $75, on publication.

CHESAPEAKE BAY MAGAZINE—1819 Bay Ridge Rd., Annapolis, MD 21403. Betty D. Rigoli, Ed. Articles, 8 to 10 typed pages, related to the Chesapeake Bay area. Articles on boating, fishing, nature, and history; profiles. Pays $50 to $85, on publication. Photos.

CHICAGO—303 E. Wacker Dr., Chicago, IL 60601. Don Gold, Edit. Dir. Articles and fiction, 1,000 to 5,000 words, related to Chicago. Pays varying rates, on acceptance. Query.

CHICAGO HISTORY—Clark St. at North Ave., Chicago, IL 60614. Timothy C. Jacobson, Ed. Articles, to 4,500 words, on urban political, social and cultural history. Pays to $250, on publication. Query.

CHICAGO TRIBUNE MAGAZINE—See *Sunday.*

CINCINNATI ENTERTAINER—18 E. 4th St., Suite 601, Cincinnati, OH 45202. Susan Conner, Ed. Interviews, profiles, articles, on entertainment; columns, 750 words. Fiction, 750 words. Pays $15 per printed page, and copies.

CINCINNATI MAGAZINE—35 E. Seventh, Suite 300, Cincinnati, OH 45202. Laura Pulfer, Ed./Pub. Articles, 1,000 to 3,000 words, on Cincinnati people and issues. Pays $75 to $100 for 1,000 words, on acceptance. Query with writing sample.

COASTAL JOURNAL—Box 84, Lanesville Sta., Gloucester, MA 01930. Joseph Kaknes, Ed. Articles, 2,000 words, on the New England coast, past, present and future trends, current events, personalities and nautical history. Fiction, same length. Fillers. Photos. Pays $100 to $150, on publication.

COLORADO BUSINESS—1621 18th St., P.O. Box 5400-TA, Denver, CO 80217. Jim Craig, Ed. Articles, to 1,500 words, on banking, real estate, transportation, manufacturing, etc., in Colorado. Pays 10¢ a word, on publication. Query.

COLORADO HOMES & LIFESTYLES—Suite 154, 2550 31st St., Denver, CO 80216. Joseph Kim Bella, Exec. Ed. Articles on topics related to Colorado: travel, fashion, design and decorating, gardening, luxury real estate, art, life styles, people, food and entertaining. Pays to 20¢ a word, on publication. Query.

COLORADO SPORTS MONTHLY—P.O. Box 3519, Evergreen, CO 80439. Robert J. Erdmann, Ed. Articles, 1,500 to 2,000 words, on individual participant sports in Colorado. Pays varying rates on publication. Query.

COLUMBUS HOMES & LIFESTYLES—P.O. Box 21208. Columbus, OH 43221. Features, for upscale readers, 35+ years, on history, nostalgia, interviews and profiles, photo features, with a central Ohio slant. General-interest articles on interiors, gardens and landscaping, and collectibles. Pays $50 to $200, or 6¢ a word, on publication. Query with clips.

COMMONWEALTH, THE MAGAZINE OF VIRGINIA—121 College Pl., Norfolk, VA 23510. Deborah Marquardt, Ed. Sophisticated articles, 1,500 to 3,000 words, with Virginia focus. Short pieces on current events and trends. Pays 10¢ a word. Query.

CONNECTICUT—636 Kings Hwy., Fairfield, CT 06430. Albert E. Labouchere, Ed.-in-Chief. Articles, 1,500 to 2,500 words, on Connecticut topics and issues, people and style, etc. Pays $200 to $700, on publication.

CONNECTICUT TRAVELER—2276 Whitney St., Hamden, CT 06518. Elke P. Martin, Man. Dir. Articles, 500 to 1,200 words, on travel and tourist attractions in New England. Photos. Pays $50 to $175, on publication. Query.

CORPORATE MONTHLY—105 Chestnut St., Philadelphia, PA 19106. Bruce Anthony, Pub. and Ed. Articles of interest to the regional business community, 1,500 to 2,000 words. Pays varying rates on publication. Query required.

COUNTRY MAGAZINE—P.O. Box 246, Alexandria, VA 22313. Philip Hayward, Ed. Articles, 2,000 words, related to life in the Mid-Atlantic region: travel, outdoor sports, gardening, antiques, history, architecture, environment, etc. Fiction. Short poetry. Photos. Pays $3.50 per column inch, extra for photos, on publication. Query preferred. Include SASE.

CRAIN'S DETROIT BUSINESS—1400 Woodbridge, Detroit, MI 48207. Peter Brown, Ed. Business articles, 500 to 1,500 words, about Detroit, for Detroit business readers. Pays $75 to $150, on acceptance. Query required.

D—3988 N. Central Expressway, Dallas, TX 75204. Lee Cullum, Ed. In-depth investigative pieces on current trends and problems, personality profiles, and general-interest articles on the arts, travel, fashion, and business, for upper-class residents of Dallas. Pays $350 to $500 for departments, $800 to $1,200 for features. Query.

DALLAS—1507 Pacific Ave., Dallas, TX 75201. Ann Schiffler, Ed. Articles on local businesses—airlines, sports franchises, hospitals, etc. General-interest features on business trends. Feature articles run from 2,500 words; 1,500 words for department pieces. Pays $100 to $600, on acceptance. Queries required.

DALLAS CITY (formerly *Westward*)—1101 Pacific Ave., Dallas, TX 75202. Sunday magazine of the *Dallas Times Herald*. Ron L. Ruggless, Managing Ed. Articles, 2,500 words, on contemporary, urbane topics of interest to people living in the Dallas/Fort Worth area. Departments include food, fashion, homes, and self help. Short essays, 500 to 750 words, on current topics. Pays $100 to $750, on acceptance. Query.

DALLAS LIFE—*The Dallas Morning News,* Communications Center, Dallas, TX 75265. Melissa East, Ed. Well-researched articles and profiles, 750 to 2,000 words, on contemporary issues, personalities, or subjects of strictly-Dallas related interest. Short Dallas-oriented humor features, 750 to 1,000 words. Pays from 25¢ a word, on acceptance. Query required.

DELAWARE TODAY—P.O. Box 4440, Wilmington, DE 19807. Peter Mucha, Ed. Service articles, profiles, news features, on topics of local interest. Best bets for out-of-state writers are articles on finance, high-tech consumer items or cars. No fiction, humor, poetry. Pays $75 to $125 for department pieces, $125 to $300 for features, on publication. Query required; enclose writing sample.

DENVER LIVING—See *Living Magazines.*

DETROIT MAGAZINE—*Detroit Free Press,* 321 W. Lafayette Blvd., Detroit, MI 48231. Articles, to 3,000 words, with a Detroit-area or Michigan focus, on issues, lifestyles, business. Personality profiles; service pieces; humor. Pays $100 to $500.

DOWN EAST—Camden, ME 04843. Davis Thomas, Ed. Articles, 1,500 to 2,500 words, on all aspects of life in Maine. Photos. Pays to 10¢ a word, extra for photos, on acceptance. Query.

ENQUIRER MAGAZINE—*The Cincinnati Enquirer,* 617 Vine St., Cincinnati, OH 45201. Betsa Marsh, Ed. Articles, 1,000 to 2,700 words: profiles, in-depth pieces on business, sports, psychology, science, religion, life styles and entertainment. Pays $85 to $350, on publication. Query.

ERIE & CHAUTAUQUA MAGAZINE—Charles H. Strong Bldg., 1250 Tower La., Erie, PA 16505. Mary J. Brownlie, Ed. Feature articles, to 2,500 words, on issues of interest to upscale readers in the Erie, Warren and Crawford counties (PA), and Chautauqua (NY) county. Investigative pieces. Personality profiles, to 1,500 words. Pays $35 per published page, on publication. Query preferred, with writing samples. Buys all rights. Guidelines available.

FLORIDA GULF COAST LIVING—1311 N. Westshore Blvd., Suite 109, Tampa, FL 33607. Milana Petty, Ed. Articles, 750 to 1,200 words, for the active home buyer on the Gulf Coast: home-related articles, moving tips, financing, etc. Pays 7¢ to 10¢ a word, on acceptance. Query preferred.

FLORIDA KEYS MAGAZINE—Box 818, 6161 O/S Hwy., Marathon, FL 33040. Address David Ethridge. Articles, 1,000 to 4,000 words, on the Florida Keys: history, environment, natural history, profiles, etc. Fillers, humor. Photos. Pays varying rates, on publication. Query preferred.

FLORIDA SPORTS—Placeo Publishing Corp., Box 18694, Tampa, FL 33679. Bill Chastain, Ed. Profiles of state sports personalities; topical pieces, 1,000 to 1,250 words. Pays $25, on publication.

FLORIDA TREND—Box 611, St. Petersburg, FL 33731. Richard Edmonds, Ed. Articles, to 2,000 words, on Florida business and businesspersons.

THE GEORGETOWNER—P.O. Box 3528, Washington, DC 20007. Articles, 3 to 4 typewritten, double-spaced pages, on subjects of interest to residents of Georgetown. Fiction, same length. Pays $1.50 per column inch, on publication.

GEORGIA JOURNAL—Agee Publishers, Inc., Athens, GA 30603. Jane M. Agee, Ed. Articles, 1,200 words, on people, events, travel, etc. in and around GA. Peotry, to 20 lines. Pays $20 to $25, on acceptance.

GO: THE AUTHENTIC GUIDE TO NEW ORLEANS—1793 Julia St., New Orleans, LA 70113. Katherine Dinker, Ed. Articles, 2,000 words, on local events of interest to visitors. Pays $150, on publication. Query.

GOLD COAST LIFE MAGAZINE—4747 N. Ocean Dr., Ft. Lauderdale, FL 33308. Tina Poveromo, Ed. Articles, from 1,000 words, on life style of southeastern Florida. Pays $50 to $200, on publication

GOLDEN YEARS—233 E. New Haven Ave., Melbourne, FL 32902-0537. Carol Brenner Hittner, Ed. Controlled-circulation monthly for Florida residents over the age of 50. Biographies, celebrity profiles, and pieces on health, nutrition, and travel, 500 words. Cartoons and crossword puzzles. Pays 8¢ a word, on publication.

GULFSHORE LIFE—3620 Tamiami Trail N., Naples, FL 33940. Molly J. Burns, Ed. Articles, 950 to 3,500 words, on personalities, travel, sports, business, investment, humor, nature, on southwestern Florida. Pays $50 to $300. Query.

HIGH COUNTRY NEWS—Box 1090, Paonia, CO 81428. Ed Marston, Managing Ed. Articles on environmental, land management, energy and natural resource issues; profiles of western innovators; pieces on Western politics. Poetry. B & W photos. Pays $2 per column inch, on publication for 750-word roundups and 2,000-word features. Query first.

HONOLULU—36 Merchant St., Honolulu, HI 96813. Brian Nicol, Ed. Features highlighting life in the Hawaiian islands—politics, sports, history, people, events are all subjects of interest. Pays $250 to $400, on acceptance. Columns and department pieces are mostly staff-written. Queries are required.

HUDSON VALLEY MAGAZINE—Box 425, Woodstock, NY 12498. Joanne Michaels, Ed. Profiles, investigative articles, and features on the businesses, arts and resources of the region. Pays $40 to $50, on publication, for features of 1,200 to 1,500 words; queries are required.

ILLINOIS ENTERTAINER—Box 356, Mount Prospect, IL 60056. Guy Arnston, Ed. Articles, 500 to 1,500 words, on local and national entertainment and leisure time activities in the greater Chicago area. Personality profiles; interviews; reviews. Photos. Pays 3¢ to 5¢ a word, on publication. Query preferred.

ILLINOIS TIMES—Box 3524, Springfield, IL 62708. Fletcher Farrar, Jr., Ed. Articles, 1,000 to 2,500 words, on people, places and activities of Illinois, outside the Chicago metropolitan area. Pays 4¢ a word, on publication. Query required.

INDIANAPOLIS MAGAZINE—32 E. Washington St., Indianapolis, IN 46204. Nancy Comiskey, Ed. Articles on almost any topic—health, business, sports, people, etc.—must have a regional tie-in. Lengths vary (to 12 pages). Pays $40 to $300, on publication.

INDIANAPOLIS MONTHLY—701 Broad Ripple Ave., Indianapolis, IN 46230. Deborah Paul, Ed.-in-Chief; Steve Bell, Assoc. Ed. Articles, 1,000 words, on health, sports, politics, business, and Indiana personalities. All material must have a regional focus. Pays varying rates, on publication.

INQUIRER MAGAZINE—*Philadelphia Inquirer,* 400 N. Broad St., Philadelphia, PA 19101. David R. Boldt, Ed. Articles, 1,500 to 2,000 words, and 3,000 to 7,000 words, on politics, science, arts and culture, business, life styles, and entertainment, sports, health, beauty, psychology, education, religion, home and garden, and humor. Short pieces, 200 to 800 words, for "Our Town" department. Pays varying rates. Query preferred.

THE IOWAN MAGAZINE—Mid-America Publishing Corp., 214 9th St., Des Moines, IA 50309. Charles W. Roberts, Ed. Quarterly for educated, older Iowans. Articles, 1,000 to 3,000 words, on the business, arts, people and history of Iowa, with photos, if available. Query first. Pays $100 to $400, on publication.

ISLAND LIFE—P.O. Box X, Sanibel Island, FL 33957. Joan Hooper, Ed. Articles, 500 to 1,200 words, with good color photos, on unique or historical places, wildlife, architecture, on barrier islands off Florida's Gulf Coast. Pays 5¢ a word, $5 per photo, on publication. SASE necessary.

ITHACA—See *Living Publications.*

JACKSONVILLE—P.O. Box 329, Jacksonville, FL 32201. George Wachendorf, Ed. Articles of interest to the Jacksonville business community: strong regional slant a must. Pays $100 to $300, on publication. Query required.

KANSAS!—Kansas Dept. of Economic Development, 503 Kansas Ave., 6th Fl., Topeka, KS 66603. Andrea Glen, Ed. Quarterly. Articles of 5 to 7 typed pages on the people, places, history and events of Kansas. Pays $75 to $150, on acceptance. Query.

KENTUCKY PREMIERE—506 W. Chestnut, Louisville, KY 40202. Frederick Smock, Ed. Articles, 500 to 1,500 words, related to events at the Kentucky Center for the Arts. Pays $100 to $300, on publication. Query.

LAKE SUPERIOR PORT CITIES—325 Lake Ave., S., Meierhoff Bldg., Suite 510, Duluth, MN 55802. Mary Morse, Ed. Articles with unusual twists on regional subjects; historical pieces that highlight the people, places and events that have affected the Lake Superior region. No business or nostalgia pieces. Pays $25 to $200, on publication. Query.

LIVING MAGAZINES—5757 Alpha Rd., Suite 400, Dallas, TX 75240. Chris Caperton, Ed. Man. Articles, 200 to 2,000 words, on home-buying and housing topics. Payments vary. Query with clips required. Published for Dallas, Houston, San Antonio, Austin, Phoenix, Denver, South Florida, and Florida Gulf Coast regional markets.

LIVING PUBLICATIONS—Office Complex, DeWitt Bldg., Ithaca, NY 14850. Jill Hartz, Marina Todd, Eds. Publishes five bimonthly upstate city magazines: *Rochester, Syracuse, Buffalo, Capital District, Ithaca.* Articles, 1,200 to 4,000 words, with black and white or color photos, of interest to urban professionals, including cultural, educational, historical, political, humorous topics. Pays $50 to $400, on publication. Query with bio and writing sample.

LONG ISLAND HERITAGE—132 E. Second St., Mineola, NY 11501. Attn.: Charles Hellmer. Articles, 500 to 700 words, on the history and crafts of Long Island; local artists, collectors, architecture. Pays to $25, on acceptance.

LONG ISLAND'S NIGHTLIFE MAGAZINE—1770 Deer Park Ave., Deer Park, NY 11729. Bill Ervolino, Ed. Articles, 1,000 to 2,500 words, on entertainment, leisure, personalities, 1,000 to 2,000 words. Photos. Pays $50 to $200, on publication. Query preferred.

560

LOS ANGELES MAGAZINE—1888 Century Park E., Los Angeles, CA 90067. Lew Harris, Exec. Ed. Articles, to 3,000 words, of interest to sophisticated, affluent southern Californians, preferably with local focus on a life style topic. Pays from 10¢ a word, on acceptance. Query.

LOS ANGELES READER—8471 Melrose Ave., Los Angeles, CA 90069. James Vowell, Ed. Articles, 1,000 to 3,000 words, on subjects relating to the Los Angeles/Southern California area; special emphasis on entertainment and the arts. Pays $25 to $300, on publication. Query preferred.

LOUISVILLE—One Riverfront Plaza, Louisville, KY 40202. Betty Lou Amster, Ed. Articles, 1,000 to 2,000 words, on community problems and local business success stories, for business leaders of Louisville area. Photos. Pays from $50, on acceptance. Query; articles on assignment only. Limited freelance market.

MAGAZINE OF THE MIDLANDS—*Omaha World-Herald,* World-Herald Sq., Omaha, NE 68102. Tim Anderson, Ed. Profiles and articles on subjects of general interest. All material should have a regional tie-in. Pays $25 to $150, on publication, for articles of 800 to 2,000 words. Photos. Queries are preferred.

MAGNETIC NORTH—P.O. Box 230, Littleton, NH 03561. Articles on history and nature, related to Northern New Hampshire, Western Maine, 1,000 to 2,000 words. Pays $50 to $150, on publication. Queries are required.

MAINELIFE—Box 111, Freedom, ME 04941. George Frangoulis, Ed. Articles, 1,000 to 2,500 words, on home and garden, history, arts and culture, Maine people and business, travel and recreation, energy and environment, wildlife. Photos. Pays $50 per page, on publication.

MARYLAND—Dept of Economic and Community Development, 45 Calvert St., Annapolis, MD 21401. Bonnie Joe Ayers, Ed. Articles, 750 to 2,200 words, on Maryland subjects. Pays varying rates, on acceptance. Query preferred. Guidelines available.

MARYLAND BUSINESS & LIVING MAGAZINE—One E. Chase St., Baltimore, MD 21202. Joni LeSage, Ed. Business/investigative features, 600 to 3,000 words, related to Maryland. Pays $50 to $200, on publication.

MEMPHIS—Towery Press, Box 370, Memphis, TN 38101. Kenneth Neill, Ed. Articles dealing with Memphis and the way it works—politics, business, sports, art, education, profiles, drama, etc. Tough investigative pieces. Pays $75 to $500, on publication, for 1,500- to 5,000-word articles. Queries are preferred. Send SASE for guidelines.

MIAMI/SOUTH FLORIDA MAGAZINE—P.O. Box 34008, Coral Gables, FL 33114. Rick Eyerdam, Managing Ed. Features, 1,500 to 3,000 words, and department pieces, 900 to 1,500 words, with a strong South Florida focus, on personalities, business, media, lifestyle, trends and humor. Short, "bright" items—200 to 400 words—for the "Big Orange" section. Pays $75 to $600, 15 days before publication.

MICHIANA—*The South Bend Tribune,* Colfax at Lafayette, South Bend, IN 46626. Bill Sonneborn, Ed. Articles, 300 to 3,000 words, about the people, places, and events in Northern Indiana and Southern Michigan. Photos. Queries preferred. Pays $50 to $125, on publication.

MICHIGAN BUSINESS—Cranbrook Center, Suite 302, 30161 Southfield Rd., Southfield, MI 48076. Ron Garbinski, Ed. Business news and features, on Michigan businesses. Queries are preferred. Pay varies, on publication.

MICHIGAN LIVING— 17000 Executive Plaza Dr., Dearborn, MI 48126. Len Barnes, Ed. Travel articles, 500 to 1,500 words, on tourist attractions and recreational opportunities in the U.S. and Canada, with emphasis on Michigan: places to go, things to do, costs, etc. Color photos. Pays $100 to $350, extra for photos, on acceptance.

MICHIGAN: THE MAGAZINE OF THE DETROIT NEWS—Evening News Assn., 615 W. Lafayette Blvd., Detroit, MI 48231. Susan Slobojan, Ed. Clifford A. Ridley, Asst. Man. Ed. Articles, from 750 words, on business, politics, arts and culture, science, people, sports and education, etc., with a Michigan slant. Cover articles, to 3,000 words. Some fiction. Pays $150 to $600, on publication. Query preferred.

THE MICHIGAN WOMAN—P.O. Box 1171, Detroit, MI 48012. Marcia Danner, Ed. Articles, 750 words, highlighting the achievements and contributions of Michigan women and helping others enjoy more fulfilling careers and personal lives. Pays 10¢ a word, on publication. Query first.

MILWAUKEE—312 E. Buffalo, Milwaukee, WI 53202. Charles Sykes, Ed. Profiles, investigative articles, and historical pieces, 3,000 to 4,000 words; local tie-in a must. Pays $300 to $500, on publication. Query required.

MISSOURI LIFE—1205 University Ave., Suite 500, Columbia, MO 65201. Douglas Carr, Ed. Articles, 500 to 3,000 words, with photos, on Missouri: history, commerce, culture, people. Photo essays. Pays $50, on publication. Query.

MONTANA MAGAZINE—Box 5630, Helena, MT 59640. Carolyn Cunningham, Ed. Articles covering environmental issues; family-oriented pieces on where to go and what to do in Montana. Articles, averaging 2,000 words, on wildlife, nostalgia, and communities and personalities; columns on wilderness hiking, geology, gardening and photo essays. Queries required. Pays $100 per 1,000 words, on publication.

MONTHLY DETROIT—1400 Woodbridge, Detroit, MI 48207. Steve Spence, Man. Ed. Articles on Detroit people, lifestyles, businesses. Pays negotiable rates, on publication. Query with clips required.

MPLS. ST. PAUL—12 S. 6th St., Ste. 1030, Minneapolis, MN 55402. Marla J. Kinney, Man. Ed. In-depth articles, features, profiles and service pieces, 400 to 3,000 words, with Minneapolis-St. Paul focus. Photo essays. Pays to $500. Query with outline and writing samples.

NEVADA—Capitol Complex, Carson City, NV 89710. Caroline J. Hadley, Ed. Articles, 500 to 700 or 1,500 to 1,800 words, on topics related to Nevada—history, profiles, travel, and places—with photos. Pay varies, on publication.

THE NEVADAN—*The Las Vegas Review-Journal,* Box 70, Las Vegas, NV 89125-0070. A. D. Hopkins, Ed. Articles, about 2,000 words, on history in Nevada, Southwest Utah, Northeast Arizona, and Death Valley area of California. Must be accompanied by B & W photos. Pays $60, extra for photos, on publication. Query preferred.

NEW BEDFORD—5 South Sixth St., New Bedford, MA 02740. Ms. Dee Giles Forsythe, Ed. Upbeat articles, to 3,500 words, historic/nostalgia. Fiction, 1,500 to 2,500 words, and poetry, related to SE Mass./RI area. Pays $50 to $150, on publication. Query preferred.

NEW ENGLAND MONTHLY—P.O. Box 446, Haydenville, MA 01039. Daniel Okrent, Ed. Articles on politics, arts, business, education, crime and nature; a regional angle is a must, and a strong accent on reportage is preferred. Pays, on acceptance, $150 to $200 for short items (600 to 800 words) and from $1,000 for features (3,000 to 4,000 words). Include published clips with query.

NEW HAMPSHIRE PROFILES—109 N. Main Street, Concord, NH 03301. David W. Minnis, Ed. Articles, 500 to 2,000 words, on New Hampshire people, issues, events, and lifestyles. Pays $100 to $300, on publication. Query.

NEW JERSEY LIVING—830 Raymond Rd., RD 4, Princeton, NJ 08540. Marie C. Turi, Asst. Pub. General-interest articles, to 3,000 words, with central New Jersey tie-in. Pays $50, on publication. Query required.

NEW JERSEY MONTHLY—7 Dumont Place, Morristown, NJ 07960. Colleen Katz, Ed. Reportorial and service pieces, 2,000 words, and department pieces, 1,000 words, with a strong regional slant. Some "think" pieces and humor of general interest. Short fillers. Pays $35 to $75 for short pieces, $350 to $1,200 for features, on acceptance. Query first.

NEW JERSEY REPORTER—The Center for Analysis of Public Issues, 16 Vanderventer Ave., Princeton, NJ 08542. Rick Sinding, Ed. Hard-hitting, in-depth articles, 2,000 to 6,000 words, on New Jersey politics and public affairs. Pays $100 to $250, on publication. Queries are required.

NEW MEXICO MAGAZINE—Bataan Memorial Bldg., Santa Fe, NM 87503. Richard Sandoval, Ed. Articles, 250 to 2,000 words, on New Mexico subjects. Pays about 10¢ a word, on publication.

' NEW ORLEANS MAGAZINE—Box 26815, New Orleans, LA 70186. Don Washington, Ed. Articles, 3 to 15 triple-spaced pages, on New Orleans area people and issues. Photos. Pays $50 to $300, extra for photos, on publication. Query.

NEW YORK—755 Second Ave., New York, NY 10017. Edward Kosner, Ed. Laurie Jones, Man. Ed. Feature articles on New York City subjects. Payment negotiated and made on acceptance. Query preferred.

NEW YORK ALIVE—152 Washington Ave., Albany, NY 12210. Mary Grates Stoll, Ed. Articles aimed at developing knowledge of and appreciation for New York State. Features, 3,000 words maximum, on business, lifestyle, education, history and the arts. Department pieces for regular columns, including "Great Escapes" (travel ideas) and "Expressly New York" (unusual places, products or events in New York). Pays $250 to $300 for features, $50 to $100 for departments. Query preferred.

NORTH DAKOTA HORIZONS—P.O. Box 2467, Fargo, ND 58107. Sheldon Green, Ed. Quarterly. Articles, about 3,000 words, on the people, places and events that affect life in North Dakota. Photos. Poetry. Pays $75 to $300, on publication.

NORTHWEST—1320 S.W. Broadway, Portland, OR 97201. Sunday magazine of *The Sunday Oregonian*. Jack R. Hart, Ed. Articles, to 3,000 words, on Pacific Northwest issues and personalities: regional travel, science and business, outdoor recreation, and lifestyle trends. Personal essays. Local angle essential. Pays $75 to $800. Query first.

NORTHWEST EDITION—130 Second Ave. S., Edmonds, WA 98020. Archie Satterfield, Ed. Lively, informative articles, 400 to 1,000 words, on the natural resources of the Northwest: homes, gardens, people, travel, history, etc. Color photos essential. Shorts, 100 to 400 words. Pays $50 to $400, on acceptance. Query required.

OHIO MAGAZINE—40 S. Third St., Columbus, OH 43215. Ellen Stein, Managing Ed. Profiles of the people, cities and towns of Ohio, and short pieces on its institutions (schools, police departments, etc.). Lengths vary; pay varies. Query preferred.

OKLAHOMA TODAY—Box 53384, Oklahoma City, OK 73152. Sue Carter, Ed. Travel articles; profiles, history and arts articles. All material must have regional tie-in. Queries for 1,000- to 2,000-word articles are preferred. Pays $100 to $300, on acceptance. Send SASE for guidelines.

ORANGE COAST—18200 W. McDurmott St., Suite E, Irvine, CA 92714. Katherine Tomlinson, Ed. Articles of interest to educated, affluent Southern Californians. Pieces, 1,000 to 3,000 words, for regular departments: "Profile," "Coasting," (op-ed), "Media", "Business" (hard news about the regional business community), and "Nightlife." Feature articles run 3,000 to 5,000 words. Query. Pays $150 for features, $100 for columns, on acceptance. Guidelines are available.

ORLANDO MAGAZINE—P.O. Box 2207, Orlando, FL 32802. Nancy Long, Features Ed. Articles and profiles, 1,000 to 1,500 words, related to Central Florida. Photos a plus. Pays $50 to $100, on acceptance. Query required.

PD—*St. Louis Post-Dispatcher,* 900 N. Tucker Blvd., St. Louis, MO 63101. Robert W. Duffy, Ed. Profiles, personal-experience pieces and investigative articles, 3,000 to 4,000 words: politics, science, life styles and entertainment, psychology, etc. Humor. Pays $125 to $150, on publication. No unsolicited manuscripts. Query.

PENNSYLVANIA MAGAZINE—Box 576, Camp Hill, PA 17011. Albert E. Holliday, Ed. Quarterly. General-interest features with a Pennsylvania tie-in. Pays 10¢ a word, usually on acceptance. Query preferred.

PHILADELPHIA—1500 Walnut St., Philadelphia, PA 19102. Ben Yagoda, Articles Ed. Articles, 1,000 to 5,000 words, for sophisticated audience, relating to Philadelphia area. No fiction. Pays from $150, on publication. Query.

PHILADELPHIA STYLE—2019 Chancellor St., Philadelphia, PA 19103. Andrea Diehl, Ed. Articles, 500 to 750 words, on travel, leisure, and entertainment. Pays $10, on publication.

PHOENIX BUSINESS JOURNAL—1817 N. 3rd St., Suite 100, Phoenix, AZ 85004. Naaman Nickell, Ed. Articles on leading and innovative businesses and business people in the Phoenix area. Photos. Pays $2.75 to $3.75 per column inch, extra for photos, on publication.

PHOENIX MAGAZINE—4707 N. 12th St., Phoenix, AZ 85014. Fern Stewart Welch, Ed. Dir. Articles, 1,000 to 3,000 words, on topics of special interest to Phoenix-area residents. Pays $75 to $300 for features, on publication. Query.

PITTSBURGH—4802 Fifth Ave., Pittsburgh, PA 15213. Martin Schultz, Ed. Articles, 850 to 3,000 words, with western Pennsylvania slant. 3- to 4-month lead time. Pays on publication.

THE PITTSBURGH PRESS SUNDAY MAGAZINE—*The Pittsburgh Press,* 34 Blvd. of the Allies, Pittsburgh, PA 15230. Ed Wintermantel, Ed. Well-written, well-organized, in-depth articles of local or regional interest, 1,000 to 3,000 words, on issues, trends or personalities. No fiction, hobbies, how-to's or 'timely events' pieces. Pays $100 to $400, extra for photos, on publication. Query.

PITTSBURGH PREVIEW—1112 S. Braddock Ave., Suite 203, Pittsburgh, PA 15218. Kimberly Flaherty, Ed. Career-oriented articles, geared to women, preferably with a local slant. Pays $25 to $300, on publication. Query required.

ROCHESTER—See *Living Publications.*

RURALITE—P.O. Box 557, Forest Grove, OR 97116. Address Editor or Feature Editor. Articles, 1,000 words, of interest to a primarily rural and small-town audience in Oregon, Washington, Idaho, Nevada, and Alaska. Upbeat articles; biographies, local history and celebrations, self-help, etc. Humorous articles, and animal pieces. No fiction or poetry. No sentimental nostalgia. Pays $30 to $100, on acceptance. Queries are preferred.

RURAL LIVING—P.O. Box 15248, Richmond, VA 23227-0648. Richard G. Johnstone, Jr., Ed. Features, 1,000 to 1,500 words, on people, places, historic sites in Virginia and Maryland's Eastern Shore. Family-oriented fiction, 1,000 to 1,500 words. Family humor, 100 to 250 words. Queries are preferred. Pays $150 for articles, on publication.

SACRAMENTO MAGAZINE—P.O. Box 2424, Sacramento, CA 95811. Ann McCully, Managing Ed. Articles, with a regional tie-in, on a broad range of topics: issue-oriented and investigative pieces, profiles, and service articles on dining out and travel. Pieces run about 500 words for "City Lights" column; 1,200 to 1,500 words for departments; 2,500 words for features. Pays average of $200 for features, on acceptance. Query.

SAN ANTONIO MAGAZINE—Chamber of Commerce, P.O. Box 1628, San Antonio, TX 78296. Sandy Brown, Ed. Articles on San Antonio area. Pays $75 to $300, on publication. Query.

SAN DIEGO MAGAZINE—4206 W. Point Loma Blvd., P.O. Box 85409, San Diego, CA 92138. Thomas Shess, Jr., Exec. Ed. Articles, 1,500 to 2,500 words, on local personalities, political figures, life styles, business, history, etc., relating to San Diego area. Photos. Pays $350 to $700, on publication.

SAN DIEGO READER—P.O. Box 80803, San Diego, CA 92138. Jim Mullin, Ed. Articles, 2,500 to 10,000 words, on the San Diego region. Pays $250 to $750, on publication. Query preferred.

SAN FRANCISCO—950 Battery St., San Francisco, CA 94111. Virginia Butterfield, Ed. General-interest articles, 1,000 to 3,000 words, related to the Bay area. Pays from $100 to $500, 30 days after publication.

SAN FRANCISCO FOCUS—500 Eighth St., San Francisco, CA 94103. Mark Powelson, Ed. Service features, profiles of local newsmakers, and investigative pieces on local issues, 2,500 to 3,000 words. Short stories, 1,500 to 2,000 words. Query required. Pays $250 to $400, on publication.

SEATTLE WEEKLY—1931 2nd Ave., Seattle, WA 98101. David Brewster, Ed. Articles, 700 to 4,000 words, with a Northwest perspective. Profiles, investigative pieces. Pays $75 to $800, on publication. Query.

SHREVEPORT—Box 20074, Shreveport, LA 71120. Mary L. Baldwin, Ed. Articles, 800 to 1,500 words, with photos, on business, arts, history, health, travel, events, and profiles. All material must have a tie-in with the Ark-La-Tex area. Pays $75 to $250, on acceptance.

SOUTH CAROLINA WILDLIFE—P.O. Box 167, Columbia, SC 29202. John Davis, Ed. Articles, 1,000 to 3,000 words, with regional outdoors focus:

565

conservation, natural history and wildlife, recreation. Profiles, how-to's. Pays from 10¢ a word.

SOUTH FLORIDA LIVING—700 W. Hillsboro Blvd., Bldg. 3, Ste. 102, Deerfield Beach, FL 33441. Cynthia M. Marusarz, Man. Ed. Articles on developments in the housing industry, home improvements, security, decorating, energy efficiency, etc.; advice on finding, buying, and maintaining a home or condominium in South Florida. Pays 10¢ a word, on acceptance. Query.

SOUTHERN EXPOSURE—P.O. Box 531, Durham, NC 27702. Michael Yellin, Ed. Articles, 500 to 4,000 words, and short stories, 500 to 3,000 words, on political issues, education, land use, and southern people. Fillers, poetry. Pays from $50 to $250, on publication. Query required.

SOUTHERN OUTDOORS—1 Bell Rd., Montgomery, AL 36141. Larry Teague, Ed. How-to articles, 2,000 words, on hunting and fishing for fisherman and hunters in the 16 southern states. Pays 15¢ a word, on acceptance. Queries are preferred.

SOUTHWEST ART—9 Greenway Plaza, Suite 2010, Houston, TX 77219. Susan McGarry, Ed. Articles on the artists, museums, and galleries west of the Mississippi. Particularly interested in representational or figurative arts. Pay rates start at $250, on acceptance, for manuscripts of 1,800 to 2,200 words. Query.

THE STATE: DOWN HOME IN NORTH CAROLINA—P.O. Box 2169, Raleigh, NC 27602. W. B. Wright, Ed. Articles, 600 to 2,000 words, on unusual items about history, travel, people, nostalgia: almost anything related to North Carolina. B & W photos. Short fillers. Pays $15 to $50, on acceptance.

SUBURBIA TODAY—1 Gannett Dr., White Plains, NY 10604. Meryl Harris, Ed. Profiles and articles, 1,500 to 3,000 words, on local arts, travel, history, people, etc. in Westchester, Rockland and Putnam (NY) counties. Pays to $350, on publication. Query required.

SUNDAY—*Chicago Tribune,* 435 N. Michigan Ave., Chicago, IL 60611. John Twohey, Ed. Articles, 2,000 to 3,000 words, on politics, arts, health, travel, etc., for Chicago and Midwestern readers. Pays from $200, on acceptance. Query.

SUNDAY MAGAZINE—*Providence Sunday Journal,* 75 Fountain St., Providence, RI 02902. Mark Silverman, Ed. Profiles, personal-experience pieces, 1,000 to 1,500 words. Pays $75 to $200, on publication.

SUNSET MAGAZINE—80 Willow Rd., Menlo Park, CA 94025. William Marken, Ed. Western regional. Queries considered but not encouraged.

SUNSHINE MAGAZINE—*The News/Sun Sentinel,* P.O. Box 14430, 101 New River Dr. N.E., Ft. Lauderdale, FL 33302. John Parkyn, Ed. Articles, 1,000 to 4,000 words, on topics of interest to South Floridians. Pays to 25¢ a word, on acceptance. Query.

SUSQUEHANNA MONTHLY MAGAZINE—Box 75A, RD 1, Marietta, PA 17547. Richard S. Bromer, Ed. Articles 1,000 to 4,000 words, on regional (SE PA, DE, MD, DC) history, ecology, arts, etc. Pays to $75, on publication. Query with SASE required.

SYRACUSE—See *Living Publications.*

TALLAHASSEE MAGAZINE—P.O. Box 12848, Tallahassee, FL 32317. William L. Needham, Ed. Quarterly. Articles, 800 to 1,100 words, with a positive outlook on the life, people and history of the North Florida area. Some general-interest and humor pieces. Pays 10¢ a word, on publication. Queries are preferred.

TAMPA BAY METRO-MAGAZINE—2502 Rocky Pt. Rd., Suite 295, Tampa, FL 33607. Issues-oriented articles on the development of Tampa Bay metroplex; features on entertainment, arts, politics, sports, 2,000 to 6,000 words. Shorts, 800 to 2,000 words. Pays $100 to $600, within thirty days of publication. Query.

TEXAS HIGHWAYS MAGAZINE—State Dept. of Highways and Transportation, 11th and Brazos, Austin, TX 78701. Frank Lively, Ed. Travel features, 200 to 1,800 words. Pays $150 to $600, on acceptance, extra for photos.

TEXAS WEEKLY—P.O. Box 6192, Pasadena, TX 77506. Dick Nichols, Ed. Sunday supplement of *The Pasadena Citizen.* Articles, 1,000 to 2,000 words, on Gulf Coast related topics. Shorter articles, 500 to 1,500 words. Photos are a plus. Pays $50 to $100, on publication.

THIRD COAST—P.O. Box 592, Austin, TX 78767. Miriam Davidson, Ed. Articles covering the activities of Austin, 1,000 to 1,500 words, on a variety of subjects; urban planning, growth, business, politics and education. Some fiction and poetry. Pays 10¢ a word, on publication. Query first.

TOLEDO MAGAZINE—*The Blade,* Toledo, OH 43660. Sue Stankey, Ed. Articles, to 5,000 words, on Toledo area personalities, news, etc. Pays $50 to $500, on publication. Query.

TORONTO LIFE—59 Front St. E., Toronto, Ont., Canada M5E 1B3. Marq De Villiers, Ed. Articles, 1,000 to 4,500 words, on Toronto. Pays $500 to $2,000, on acceptance. Query.

TROPIC—*The Miami Herald,* One Herald Plaza, Miami, FL 33101. Gene Weingarten, Ed. General-interest articles, 1,500 to 3,000 words, for South Florida readers. Pays $300 to $600, on acceptance.

TULSA—P.O. Box 1620, Tulsa, OK 74101. Lynn Rollins Price, Man. Ed. Factual business-oriented and human interest articles of local interest, 1,000 to 2,500 words. Pays $100 to $250, on publication. Query.

TWIN CITIES READER—100 N. 7th St., Minneapolis, MN 55403. Deborah L. Hopp, Ed.-in-Chief. Articles, 3 to 10 printed pages, on cultural phenomena, city politics, and general-interest subjects, for local readers aged 25 to 44. Pays to $2 per inch, on publication.

ULTRA—2000 Bering Dr., Suite 200, Houston, TX 77057. Barbara L. Dixon, Ed. Articles, 1,000 to 1,500 words, with a regional "good living" focus; arts, personalities, food, health and travel are among the preferred topics. Pays $500 to $1,500, on acceptance. Query.

VALLEY MAGAZINE—16800 Devonshire, Suite 275, Granada Hills, CA 91344. Anne Framroze, Ed. Articles, 1,000 to 3,000 words, on celebrities, issues, education, health, business, dining and entertaining, etc., in the San Fernando Valley. Pays $100 to $500, within 8 weeks of acceptance.

VERMONT LIFE—61 Elm St., Montpelier, VT 05602. Nancy P. Graff, Acting Ed. Articles, 1,500 to 3,000 words, about Vermont subjects only. Photos. Pays 20¢ a word, extra for photos. Query required.

THE VIRGINIAN—P.O. Box 2828, Staunton, VA 24401. Hunter S. Pierce,

IV, Man. Ed. Articles, 2,000 words, relating to Virginia, West Virginia and Maryland.

WASHINGTON MAGAZINE—1500 Eastlake Ave. E., Seattle, WA 98102. Kenneth Gouldthorpe, Ed. Bimonthly. Articles about the people and places of Washington state. Queries are required. Lengths and payment rates vary.

WASHINGTON POST MAGAZINE—*The Washington Post,* 1150 15th St., NW, Washington, DC 20071. Stephen L. Petranek, Man. Ed. Personal-experience essays, profiles and general-interest pieces, to 4,000 words, on business, arts and culture, politics, science, sports, education, children, relationships, behavior, etc. Pays from $100, after acceptance.

THE WASHINGTONIAN—1828 L. St. N.W., Suite 200, Washington, DC 20036. John Limpert, Ed. Helpful, informative, interesting articles, 1,000 to 4,000 words, on Washington-related topics. Pays 20¢ a word, on publication. Query.

WEST MICHIGAN MAGAZINE—7 Ionia S.W., Grand Rapids, MI 49503. Dotti Clune, Ed. Lively, thought-provoking articles offering an inside look at people, places and events in West Michigan. Prime topics: arts, business, dining, entertainment, recreation, travel, and profiles. Payment for manuscripts of 1,500 words varies, on publication.

WESTERN PEOPLE—P.O. Box 2500, Saskatoon, Sask., Canada S7K 2C4. Mary Gilchrist, Managing Ed. Articles on interest to Western Canadians, 2,000 words, on such topics as current events, histor,', and personalities. Pays $20 to $175, extra for photos, on acceptance.

WESTERN SPORTSMAN—P.O. Box 737, Regina, Sask., Canada S4P 3A8. Randy Witte, Ed. Informative articles, to 2,500 words, on outdoor experiences in Alberta and Saskatchewan. How-to's, humor, cartoons. Photos. Pays $40 to $325, on publication.

WISCONSIN—*The Milwaukee Journal Magazine,* Newspapers, Inc., Box 661, Milwaukee, WI 53201. Beth Slocum, Ed. Articles, 500 to 3,000 words, on business, politics, arts, science, personal finance, psychology, entertainment, health, etc. Personal-experience essays and investigative articles. Pays $75 to $500, on publication. Query.

WISCONSIN TRAILS—P.O. Box 5650, Madison, WI 53075. Susan Pigorsch, Managing Ed. Articles, 1,500 to 3,000 words, on history and nostalgia, lifestyle, outdoors, events and happenings. Profiles of artists and craftsmen. Short fillers and fiction related to Wisconsin. Pays $50 to $250, on acceptance and on publication. Query first.

WORCESTER MAGAZINE—P.O. Box 1000, Worcester, MA 01614. Michael C. Bingham, Ed. Articles, to 1,500 words, on arts and entertainment, fashion, education—all with a Worcester County angle. Pays $1.00 to $1.50 per column inch, on publication. Query required.

YANKEE—Main St., Dublin, NH 03444. Articles, 1,500 to 3,000 words, about New England and/or New Englanders, past, present, or future; activities; controversies, if of wide interest, especially the unusual in all events; historical. Humor, folklore, legend, to 2,500 words, related to New England. Pays $25 to $600, on acceptance. Queries or brief outlines preferred. Editorial guidelines available.

YANKEE MAGAZINE'S TRAVEL GUIDE TO NEW ENGLAND—Main St., Dublin, NH 03444. Elizabeth Doyle, Ed. Articles, 500 to 2,000 words, on unusual activities, restaurants, places to visit in New England, for tourists. Photos. Pays $50 to $300, on acceptance. Query with outline and writing samples.

TRAVEL ARTICLES

AAA WORLD—1999 Shepard Rd., St. Paul, MN 55116. George Ashfield, Ed. Articles on automobile and travel concerns, including automotive travel, maintenance and upkeep, 750 to 1,500 words, and other topics of interest to AAA members. Pays $300 to $600, on acceptance. Query preferred.

ACCENT—Box 10010, Ogden, UT 84409. Peggie Bingham, Ed. Articles, 800 to 1,200 words on interesting places, ways to travel, money-saving tips. How-to's; humor. Color photos. Pays 15¢ a word, $35 for photos, on acceptance. Query preferred.

AIRFAIR INTERLINE MAGAZINE—25 W. 39th St., New York, NY 10018. Ratu Kamlani, Ed. Travel articles, 1,000 to 2,500 words, with photos, on shopping, sightseeing, dining, for airline employees. Prices, discount information, and addresses must be included. Pays $75, after publication.

ARIZONA HIGHWAYS—2039 W. Lewis Ave., Phoenix, AZ 85009. Richard G. Stahl, Managing Ed. Informal, well-researched travel articles, 2,000 to 2,500 words, focusing on a specific city or region in Arizona and environs and including anecdotes, historical references, etc. Pays 30¢ to 40¢ a word, on acceptance. Query required. Guidelines available.

CALIFORNIA HIGHWAY PATROLMAN—2030 V St., Sacramento, CA 95818. Travel articles, 1,800 words maximum, focusing on places in California and the West Coast. Humorous travel essays. Pays 2½¢ a word, extra for black and white photos, on publication.

CHARLOTTE OBSERVER—Box 32188, Charlotte, NC 28232. Doug Robouchek, Travel Ed. Travel articles on North and South Carolinas and the Southeast—how-to pieces (what to pack for a trip, etc.), roundup articles (ethnic restaurants of Charlotte, for instance), and destination pieces that focus on specific places or cities in the region. Pay rates start at $25, on publication.

CHARTERING MAGAZINE—P.O. Box 1933, Jensen Beach, FL 33457. Antonia Thomas, Associate Ed. Articles on chartered yacht vacations, 600 to 2,000 words. Query first. Pays varying rates, on publication.

CHEVRON USA—P.O. Box 6227, San Jose, CA 95150. Mark Williams, Ed. Quarterly. Articles, 700 to 1,600 words, on travel and leisure activities in the United States and Canada. Travel anecdotes, 50 to 250 words. Color slides. Pays about 25¢ a word for articles, $25 for anecdotes, on acceptance; extra for slides on publication. Send for free sample copy.

CHICAGO TRIBUNE—Travel Section, 435 N. Michigan Ave., Chicago, IL 60611. Harriet Choice, Exec. Travel Ed. Travel articles, 1,000 to 2,500 words, with photos. Pays $85 to $300, extra for photos, on publication.

COLORADO HOMES & LIFESTYLES—Suite 154, 2550 31st St., Denver, CO 80216. Joseph Kim Bella, Ed. Travel articles on cities, regions, establishments in Colorado; roundups and travel pieces with a how-to focus, 1,200 to 3,000 words. Pays 10¢ to 25¢ a word, on acceptance. Query.

CONNECTICUT TRAVELER—2276 Whitney St., Hamden, CT 06518.

Elke P. Martin, Man. Dir. Articles, 500 to 1,200 words, on travel and tourist attractions in New England. Pays $50 to $175, on publication.

CONNECTIONS—P.O. Box 6117, New York, NY 10150. Jeanine Moss, Ed. Short articles, 250 to 500 words, with first-hand, detail-oriented travel information for women who travel on business to major American cities. Must include credit card, price, distance, time, and related information. Queries are required. Pays $50 to $100, on publication.

COUNTRY MAGAZINE—P.O. Box 246, Alexandria, VA 22313. Philip Hayward, Managing Ed. Travel articles, 1,200 words, on destinations and establishments in the Mid-Atlantic region (VA, MD, DE, WV, NC, NJ, PA); how-to pieces and humorous essays on travel-related subjects, with a regional slant. Pays $3.50 per column inch, on publication. Query.

DIESEL MOTORIST—Diesel Automobile Assn., Box 335, Fort Lee, NJ 07024. Query Editor. Articles, to 1,500 words, on travel, bargains, economy, energy, news, new products, investments, "place reports," "insider reports," etc., related to diesel cars. Photos. Pays $25 to $150, on publication. Query with story outline and SASE.

DISCOVERY—Allstate Motor Club, 3701 W. Lake Ave., Glenview, IL 60025. Mary Kaye Stray, Ed. Articles, 1,000 to 2,500 words, on automotive and travel topics; related consumer-oriented pieces, with photos. Pays $250 to $750, on acceptance. Query required.

EARLY AMERICAN LIFE—Box 8200, Harrisburg, PA 17105. Frances Carnahan, Ed. Travel features about historic sites and country inns, 1,000 to 3,000 words. Pays $50 to $400, on acceptance. Query.

EASY LIVING—1999 Shepard Rd., St. Paul, MN 55116. Jerry Bassett, Ed. Quarterly financial and general lifestyle magazine, with one travel article, 1,200 to 1,800 words, per issue. Photos. Pays $250 to $500, extra for photos, on acceptance.

EUROPE!—408 Main St., Nashua, NH 03060. Carol Grasso, Ed. Quarterly. Travel articles of varying lengths. Especially interested in unusual modes of travel (barge, balloon, bike, horse and wagon, etc.) and out-of-the-way destinations. Include information on hotels, restaurants, shopping, etc. Pays up to $100, on publication.

EUROPEAN TRAVEL AND LIFE—122 E. 42nd St., New York, NY 10166. David R. Breul, Ed.-in-Chief. Articles, 1,500 to 3,500 words, for sophisticated American travelers. Pay starts at $1,000, on acceptance. Queries are required.

FAMILY CIRCLE—488 Madison Ave., New York, NY 10022. Jamie Raab, Travel Ed. Travel articles, to 2,000 words. Destination pieces should appeal to a national audience; preferred are roundups and theme-oriented travel pieces with an emphasis on budget. Pay rates vary, on acceptance. Query first.

FORD TIMES—Ford Motor Co., Room 765, P.O. Box 1899, The American Rd., Dearborn, MI 48121. Arnold S. Hirsch, Ed. Articles to 1,800 words on current subjects, profiles, places of interest, travel, humor, outdoors. Main focus is on North America but some international. Pays from $450, on acceptance. Query with SASE.

FREQUENT FLYER—888 Seventh Ave., New York, NY 10019. Coleman Lollar, Ed. Articles, 1,000 to 3,000 words, on all aspects of frequent business travel, international trade, aviation, T & E, etc. No pleasure travel or personal experience pieces. Pays $100 to $500, on acceptance. Query required.

GULFSHORE LIFE—3620 Tamiami Trail N., Naples, FL 33940. Destination-oriented travel articles, 1,800 to 2,400 words. Payment is negotiable, on publication. Query.

INTERNATIONAL LIVING—824 E. Baltimore St., Baltimore, MD 21202. Elizabeth Philip, Ed. Newsletter. Short pieces and features, 200 to 1,000 words, with useful information on living abroad, investing overseas, and unusual travel bargains. Pays to $200, on acceptance.

ISLANDS—3886 State St., Santa Barbara, CA 93105. Articles on island-related topics—written from a scientific, historical, exploratory, or cultural angle—6,000 words, 2,500 words, or 1,000 words. Pays 25¢ to 50¢ a word, half on acceptance, half on publication. Queries are preferred. Editorial guidelines are available.

MAINELIFE—Box 111, Freedom, ME 04941. Timothy Rice, Ed. Travel articles, 1,500 to 2,500 words or 500 words, about places to see and things to do in Maine. Pays 7¢ a word, extra for black and white or color photos, on publication.

MICHIGAN LIVING—Automobile Club of Michigan, 17000 Executive Plaza Dr., Dearborn, MI 48126. Len Barnes, Ed. Informative travel articles, 500 to 1,500 words, on U.S., Canadian tourist attractions and recreational opportunities; special interest in Michigan. Photos. Pays $100 to $300, extra for photos, on acceptance.

THE MIDWEST MOTORIST—12901 N. Forty Drive, St. Louis, MO 63141. Tim Sitek, Man. Ed. Articles, 1,000 to 1,500 words, with photos, on travel, transportation and consumerism. Pays $50 to $200, on acceptance or publication.

NATIONAL GEOGRAPHIC—17th and M Sts., N.W., Washington, D.C. 20036. Wilbur E. Garrett, Ed. Publishes first-person articles on human geography, exploration, natural history, archeology, and science. Half staff written; half by recognized authorities and published authors. Does not review manuscripts. Query Suggestions Editor.

NATIONAL GEOGRAPHIC TRAVELER—National Geographic Society, 17th and M Sts., NW, Washington, DC 20036. Joan Tapper, Ed. Articles, 1,500 to 4,000 words, that highlight specific places. Query with 1–2 page proposal, resumé, and published clippings required. Pays $1 a word, on acceptance.

NATIONAL MOTORIST—One Market Plaza, Suite 300, San Francisco, CA 94105. Jane Offers, Ed. Illustrated articles, 500 or 1,100 words, for California motorists, on motoring in the West, car care, roads, personalities, places, etc. Photos. Pays from 10¢ a word, extra for photos, on acceptance.

NEW WOMAN—215 Lexington Ave., New York, NY 10016. Armchair travel pieces: personal experience and "what I learned from this experience" pieces, 2,000 to 3,000 words. Pays $500 to $2,000, on acceptance. Query required.

THE NEW YORK TIMES—229 W. 43rd St., New York, NY 10036. Michael J. Leahy, Travel Ed. Considers queries only; include writer's background, description of proposed article. No unsolicited manuscripts or photos. Pays on acceptance.

NORTHWEST—*The Sunday Oregonian Magazine,* 1320 S.W. Broadway, Portland, OR 97201. Travel articles, 800 to 1,000 words, that focus on the central, overall psychological experience—the article should give the reader an idea of what unique experiences he might encounter by taking the trip. All material must pertain to the Northwest (Oregon, Washington, Idaho, and Montana). Include details about where to go, what to see, plans to make, with specific information about reservations, ticket purchases, etc. Pays $150 to $250, on acceptance. Query. Guidelines available.

OFF DUTY MAGAZINE—3303 Harbor Blvd., Suite C-2, Costa Mesa, CA 92626. Bruce Thorstad, U.S. Ed. Travel articles, 1,800 to 2,000 words, for active duty military Americans (aged 20 to 40) and their families, on U.S. regions or cities. Military angle preferable. Pieces with focus on an event or activity, with sidebars telling how-to and where-to. Photos. Pays from 13¢ a word, extra for photos, on acceptance. Query. Send for guidelines. European and Pacific editions. Foreign travel articles for military Americans and their families stationed abroad. Send SASE for guidelines.

OHIO MOTORIST—P.O. Box 6150, Cleveland, OH 44101. F. Jerome Turk, Ed. Articles, 1,500 to 2,500 words, with photos, on domestic (preferably in Ohio) and foreign travel, automotive subjects. Pays $100 to $300, on acceptance.

OKLAHOMA TODAY—Box 53384, Oklahoma City, OK 73152. Kate Lester Jones, Ed. Travel articles, 1,000 to 2,000 words, focusing on a specific place—restaurant, hotel, city, etc.—or roundups of restaurants, shops, etc.; all material must be related to Oklahoma. Pays $200 to $300, on publication. Query required.

THE REGISTER—P.O. Box 11626, 625 N. Grand Ave., Santa Ana, CA 92711. Laura Bly, Travel Ed. Articles, 600 to 1,500 words, with photos, on unique travel destinations and consumer topics. Require "nuts and bolts" sidebar with hotel costs, airfare, etc. Pays from $50, extra for photos, on publication.

SACRAMENTO MAGAZINE—P.O. Box 2424, Sacramento, CA 95811. Cheryl Romo, Ed. Destination-oriented articles in the Sacramento area (or within a six-hour drive), 1,000 to 1,500 words. Pay varies, on acceptance. Query first.

SIGNATURE MAGAZINE—641 Lexington Ave., New York, NY 10022. Barbara Coats, Man. Ed. Articles on travel in U.S. and abroad; features on leisure and entertainment topics: food, wine, sports, the arts, etc. Pays good rates, on acceptance. Query.

TAKEOFF—20 William St., Wellesley, MA 02181. Address Associate Ed. Travel, recreation, and life style magazine for private pilots. Articles of varying lengths on travel and adventure, resorts, and restaurants of interest to men and women who fly for business and recreation. Include information on airports, ground transportation, and hotel accommodations. Photos are a plus. Pays $100 to $350, on publication.

TEXAS HIGHWAYS MAGAZINE—State Dept. of Highways and Transportation, 11th and Brazos, Austin, TX 78701. Frank Lively, Ed. Travel features, 200 to 1,800 words. Pays $150 to $600, on acceptance, extra for photos.

TRANSITIONS—18 Hulst Rd., Box 344, Amherst, MA 01004. Kathleen A. Bemben, Asst. Ed. Articles, to 1,500 words, with B/W photos, for long-stay travelers abroad: work, study, travel. Include practical, first-hand information: travel deals, work and study opportunities, etc. Pays on publication. Send SASE for guidelines.

TRAVEL AGE WEST—100 Grant Ave., San Francisco, CA 94108. Donald

Langley, Man. Ed. Articles, 800 to 1,000 words, with photos, on any aspect of travel useful to travel agents, including names, addresses, prices, etc.; news or trend angle preferred. Pays $1.50 per column inch, after publication.

TRAVEL AND LEARNING ABROAD—P.O. Box 1122, Brattleboro, VT 05301. Douglas I. Grube, Ed. Articles, to 2,500 words, for teachers and advisors who assist students and others planning learning trips abroad. Pays varying rates, on publication. Query.

TRAVEL & LEISURE—1120 Ave. of the Americas, New York, NY 10036. Pamela Fiori, Ed.-in-Chief. Articles, 800 to 2,500 words, on destinations and leisuretime activities. Regional pieces for regional editions. Pays $600 to $2,000, on acceptance. Query; articles on assignment.

TRAVEL HOLIDAY—Travel Bldg., Floral Park, NY 11001. Scott Shane, Ed. Informative, lively features, 1,600 to 1,800 words, on foreign and domestic travel to well-known or little-known places; featurettes, 800 to 1,000 words, on special-interest subjects: museums, shopping, smaller cities or islands, special aspects of destination. Pays from $250 for featurettes, $400 for features, on acceptance. Query with published clips.

TRAVEL SMART—Dobbs Ferry, NY 10522. Short pieces, under 250 words, about interesting, unusual and/or economical places: give specific details on hotels, restaurants, transportation, and costs. Pays $5 to $15.

TRAVEL SMART FOR BUSINESS—Dobbs Ferry, NY 10522. H. J. Teison, Ed. Articles, 200 to 1,000 words, for company executives and business travel managers, on lowering travel costs and increasing travel convenience. Pays on publication.

VISTA/USA—Box 161, Convent Station, NJ 07961. Exxon Travel Club. Patrick Sarver, Ed. Travel articles, 2,000 words, on North America, Hawaii, Mexico and the Caribbean. Pays from $600, on acceptance. Query with writing sample. Limited freelance market.

VOLKSWAGEN'S WORLD—Volkswagen of America, Inc., Troy, MI 48099. Ed Rabinowitz, Ed. Travel articles on unique places to 1,000 words. Pays $150 per printed page, on acceptance. Query.

WESTWAYS—Box 2890, Terminal Annex, Los Angeles, CA 90051. Mary Ann Fisher, Ed. Travel articles on where to go, what to see, and how to get there, 1,500 words. Domestic travel articles are limited to Western U.S. and Canada and Hawaii; foreign travel articles are also of interest. Quality color photos should be available. Pays 20¢ a word, 30 days before publication.

YANKEE MAGAZINE'S TRAVEL GUIDE TO NEW ENGLAND—Main St., Dublin, NH 03444. Elizabeth Doyle, Ed. Articles, 500 to 2,000 words, on unusual activities, restaurants, places to visit in New England, for tourists. Photos. Pays $50 to $300, on acceptance. Query with outline and writing samples.

INFLIGHT MAGAZINES

Inflight magazines are published by commercial airlines for their passengers and use a wide variety of general-interest articles, as well as travel pieces on the airlines' destinations.

AMERICAN WAY—Box 619616, Dallas/Fort Worth Airport, TX 75261-9616. Ann Genett, Ed. American Airlines' in-flight magazine. Features,

1,500 to 1,750 words, on health, business, the arts, etc.; profiles of people and places. Photos. Pays $100 for shorts, from $300 for full-length pieces, on acceptance. Query Articles Editor, Mail Drop, 3D08.

FRONTIER—In-flight Publishing Co., 1637 S. Oakland Ct., Aurora, CO 80012. C. A. Stevens, Ed. and Pub. Frontier Airlines' in-flight magazine. Entertaining articles, 1,500 to 2,500 words, on travel, aviation, and general-interest subjects. Short pieces, 300 to 1,000 words. Photos. Pays $75 to $250, extra for photos, on acceptance and on publication. Query preferred. No recent report.

INFLIGHT—P.O. Box 10010, Ogden, UT 84409. Wayne DeWald, Ed. Articles for male, business-oriented audience, on travel, sports, business. Personality profiles. Photos. Feature length: 1,200 to 1,500 words. Pays 15¢ a word, $35 for color photos, on acceptance. Query with SASE.

NORTHWEST ORIENT—East/West Network, 34 E. 51st St., New York, NY 10022. Northwest Orient's in-flight magazine. Features, 2,000 to 3,000 words, on travel, business, lifestyles, sports, and entertainment. Profiles. Pays from $400 for articles, on acceptance.

OZARK—East/West Network, 5900 Wilshire Blvd., Los Angeles, CA 90036. Laura Doss, Ed. Ozark Arilines in-flight magazine. Uses mostly free-lance material. Query. Same address for Pacific Southwest *PSA Magazine,* Republic Airlines *Republic,* Western Airlines *Western's World,* and Southwest Airlines *Southwest.*

PACE—338 N. Elm St., Greensboro, NC 27401. Leslie Daisy, Man. Ed. Piedmont Airlines in-flight magazine. Articles of interest to business travelers; economic reports, business management and communication. Travel pieces to Piedmont destination cities. Pays varying rates, on acceptance.

PAN AM CLIPPER—East/West Network, 34 E. 51st St., New York, NY 10022. Richard Kagan, Ed. Monthly inflight for Pan Am airlines. Interviews, profiles, and travel pieces on Pam Am destinations, 2,500 words. Very limited free-lance market; queries are required. Pays varying rates, on acceptance.

PSA MAGAZINE—See *Ozark.*

REPUBLIC—See *Ozark.*

SKY—12955 Biscayne Blvd., North Miami, FL 33181. Lidia de Leon, Ed. Delta Air Lines' in-flight magazine. Articles on business, lifestyle, high tech, sports, the arts, etc. Color slides. Pays varying rates, on publication. Query.

SOUTHWEST—See *Ozark.*

UNITED MAGAZINE—East/West Network, 34 E. 51st St., New York, NY 10022. Tom O'Neil, Ed. United Airlines' in-flight magazine. Profiles of unusual or upscale Americans. Travel pieces on United destinations. Interviews. Pays varying rates, 60 days after acceptance. Query.

USAIR—600 Third Ave., Suite 2700, New York, NY 10016. Richard Busch, Ed. In-flight magazine of USAir. Articles, 1,500 to 3,000 words, on travel, business, sports, entertainment, food, health, and other general interest topics. No downbeat or extremely controversial subjects. Pays $350 to $800, on acceptance. Query.

WESTERN'S WORLD—See *Ozark.*

WOMEN'S MAGAZINES

BEAUTY DIGEST—126 Fifth Ave., New York, NY 10011. Diane Robbens, Ed. Reprints of book and magazine pieces, 2,500 to 3,500 words, on beauty, health exercise, self-help, for women. Pays varying rates, on publication.

BRIDE'S—350 Madison Ave., New York, NY 10017. Address Copy and Features Dept. Articles, 1,000 to 3,000 words, for engaged couples or newly-weds, on communication, sex, housing, finances, careers, remarriage, step-parenting, health, babies, religion, in-laws, the marriage relationship. Pays $300 to $600, on acceptance.

CHATELAINE—Maclean Hunter Bldg., 777 Bay St., Toronto, Ont., Canada M5W 1A7. Mildred Istona, Ed. Articles, 3,000 words, on controversial subjects and personalities of interest to Canadian women. Pays $750 for personal-experience pieces, from $1,000 for articles, on acceptance.

COMPLETE WOMAN—1165 N. Clark, Chicago, IL 60610. Suzanne Merry, Assoc. Ed. Positive, upbeat articles, 1,000 to 2,500 words, for 24- to 50-year-old women, on the following: life styles, careers, health/medical, relationships, beauty, psychology, fitness/nutrition, profiles, interviews, investing and financial advice, self improvement. Articles should stimulate, educate, and enhance women's sense of well being in their personal and professional lives. Query first. Pay varies, on publication.

COSMOPOLITAN—224 W. 57th St., New York, NY 10019. Helen Gurley Brown, Ed. Guy Flatley, Managing Ed. Roberta Ashley, Exec. Ed. Articles, to 5,000 words, and features, 2,000 to 3,000 words, on issues affecting young career women. Pays from $1,500 for full-length articles, on acceptance.

ELLE—551 Fifth Ave., New York, NY 10176. Pamela Jablons, Features Ed. Articles for women aged 20 to 50, who are interested in fashion. Subjects of interest include life styles, careers, entertainment, opinion, health, food, fashion, beauty, psychology, consumer issues, fitness and nutrition, travel, and self improvement. Profiles; interviews. Pays good rates, on publication. Query first.

ESSENCE—1500 Broadway, New York, NY 10036. Susan L. Taylor, Ed.-in-Chief. Provocative articles, 1,500 to 3,000 words, about black women in America today: self-help, how-to pieces, celebrity profiles and political issues. Pays varying rates, on acceptance. Query.

THE EXECUTIVE FEMALE—1041 Third Ave., New York, NY 10021. Susan Strecker, Man. Ed. Features, 6 to 12 pages, on investment, money-savers, career advancement, etc., for executive women. Articles, 6 to 8 pages, for "More Money," "Horizons," "Profiles," and "Entrepreneur's Corner." Pays $75 to $250, on acceptance. Limited freelance market.

FAMILY CIRCLE—488 Madison Ave., New York, NY 10022. Margaret Jaworski, Sr. Ed. Susan Ungaro, Articles Ed. Ellen Stoianoff, Eleanore Lewis, Features Eds., Nicole Gregory, Books Ed. Jamie Raab, Fiction and Travel Ed. Articles, 500 to 3,000 words, on career, health, family, child-rearing, fitness and nutrition, social and political issues, humor, self improvement, food, fashion, beauty, education, consumer issues. Send specific proposal, with sample clips and references to other publication credits. Pays $1.00 per word, on acceptance.

FARM WOMAN NEWS—P.O. Box 643, Milwaukee, WI 53201. Ruth C. Benedict, Managing Ed. Articles, to 1,000 words, for farm and ranch women on the following: self improvement, travel and leisure, housekeeping hints, fitness and nutrition, family, education, beauty, fashion, food, and relationships. Pays $40 to $250, on acceptance.

FEELING GREAT—45 W. 34th St., New York, NY 10001. Tim Moriarty, Ed. Articles, 800 or 1,500 to 2,000 words, on health, fitness, self improvement and psychology, for women in their 20's. Pays 25¢ to 50¢ a word, on acceptance. Queries are required.

FLARE—777 Bay St., Toronto, Ont., Canada M5W 1A7. Dianne Rinehart, Man. Ed. Service articles, 1,500 to 3,000 words, on health, careers, relationships, and contemporary problems; articles on home decor, food, and entertaining, for Canadian women aged 18 to 34. Profiles, 750 to 1,500 words, of up-and-coming Canadians. Pays on acceptance. Query.

GLAMOUR—350 Madison Ave., New York, NY 10017. Ruth Whitney, Ed.-in-Chief. Barbara Coffey, Man. Ed. Rona Cherry, Exec. Ed. Janet Chan, Articles Ed. How-to articles, from 1,500 words, on careers, health, psychology, interpersonal relationships, etc., for women aged 18 to 35. Fashion and beauty pieces staff-written. Pays from $1,000.

GOOD HOUSEKEEPING—959 Eighth Ave., New York, NY 10019. Joan Thursh, Articles Ed. Naome Lewis, Fiction Ed. In-depth articles and features on controversial problems, topical social issues; dramatic personal narratives with unusual experiences of average families; new or unusual medical information, 1,200 to 5,000 words. Ideas on subjects of practical interest to women for "Better Way." Pays top rates, on acceptance.

LADIES' HOME JOURNAL—3 Park Ave., New York, NY 10016. Myrna Blyth, Ed.-in-Chief. Address Jan Goodwin or Sondra Forsyth Enos, Exec. Eds. Articles on subjects of interest to women; lengths vary, average 3,500 words. Queries are required. Pay varies, on acceptance.

LADYCOM—1732 Wisconsin Ave., N.W., Washington, DC 20007. Hope Daniels, Ed. Articles, average 1,500 words, for wives of American servicemen in the U.S. and overseas, on lifestyles; pieces on issues of interest to military families. Pays $150 to $600, on publication. Query preferred.

LUTHERAN WOMEN—2900 Queen Ln., Philadelphia, PA 19129. Terry Schutz, Ed. Articles, with photos, on subjects of interest to Christian women. No recipes, homemaking hints. Pays $25 to $50 for articles, on publication.

MCCALL'S—230 Park Ave., New York, NY 10169. Robert Stein, Ed. Human-interest narratives, personal essays and humor pieces, 1,000 to 3,000 words. Always interested in seasonal material; query five to six months in advance. Department pieces: "The Mother's Page" (short humorous, helpful, inspiring, or reassuring items; pays $100 and up); "Vital Signs" (short items on health and medical news; pay varies); "Back Talk" (1,000-word opinion piece; pays $1,000); "Vip-Zip" (short essays—humorous or serious and service-oriented pieces; pay varies). Query for articles; complete manuscript for humor. Pay varies, on acceptance.

MADEMOISELLE—350 Madison Ave., New York, NY 10017. Kate White, Articles Ed. Articles of varying lengths on subjects of interest to women in their mid- to late-twenties: life styles, food, fashion, beauty, fitness, nutrition, self improvement, entertainment, relationships, health and medical. Profiles and interviews. Pays from $750, from $1,750 for features, on acceptance. Query.

THE MICHIGAN WOMAN—P.O. Box 1171, Detroit, MI 48012. Marcia Danner, Ed. Articles, 750 words, that highlight the achievements and contributions of Michigan women, and help others enjoy more fulfilling careers and personal lives. Pays 10¢ a word, on publication. Query first.

MODERN BRIDE—One Park Ave., New York, NY 10016. Mary Ann Cavlin, Man. Ed. Articles, 1,800 to 2,000 words, for bride and groom, on wedding planning, financial planning, juggling career and home, etc. Pays 25¢ a word, on acceptance. Query.

MS. MAGAZINE—119 W. 40th St., New York, NY 10018. Address Manuscript Editor, specify fiction, nonfiction, or poetry. Articles relating to women's roles and changing lifestyles; general interest, self-help, how-to, profiles; fiction. Pays varying rates. Query. Accepts very little free-lance material.

NEW BODY—888 Seventh Ave., New York, NY 10106. Judy Jones, Ed. Lively, readable, service-oriented articles, 1,000 to 2,000 words, by writers with background in health field: exercise, nutrition, and diet pieces for men and women aged 18 to 40. Pays $250 to $500, on publication. Query preferred.

NEW WOMAN—215 Lexington Ave., New York, NY 10016. Pat Miller, Ed./Pub. Address Stephanie von Hirschberg, Senior Ed. Self-help/inspirational articles, 800 to 3,500 words, on psychology, relationships, money, careers. Travel features, with personal discovery angle. Lifestyle, health, and medical features. Profiles of business women. Innovative quizzes. Pays 25¢ to $1 a word, on acceptance. Query.

PIONEER WOMAN—200 Madison Ave., New York, NY 10016. Judith A. Sokoloff, Ed. Articles on Jewish culture, women's issues, social and political topics, and Israel. Queries preferred. Pays 8¢ a word, on publication, for articles of 1,500 to 2,000 words.

PLAYGIRL—3420 Ocean Park Blvd., Santa Monica, CA 90405. Ruth Drizen, Sr. Ed. Solidly-researched, up-to-date articles, 2,500 to 3,000 words, written in an informal, personal style, for contemporary women. Payment negotiable. Query.

REDBOOK—224 W. 57th St., New York, NY 10019. Karen Larsen, Articles Ed. Solidly-researched articles, 1,500 to 3,500 words, for young mothers between the ages of 25 and 44; include clear, substantial quotes from experts and information from reputable studies, surveys, etc. Personal-experience pieces, 1,000 to 2,000 words, on solving problems in marriage, family life, or community, for "Young Mother's Story." Pays $750 to $4,000, on acceptance. Query.

ROMANCE TODAY—575 Madison Ave., New York, NY 10022. Rosemarie Wittman, Ed. Contemporary romance stories (1920–present), with strong, independent heroines, 5,000 to 8,000 words. Query first. Pays on publication.

SAVVY—3 Park Ave., New York, NY 10016. Wendy Reid Crisp, Ed. Service articles for women executives, 500 to 3,000 words, on business politics, finance, entrepreneurs. Pays $300 to $1,000, on acceptance. Query.

SELF—350 Madison Ave., New York, NY 10017. Phyllis Starr Wilson, Ed. Articles, 1,000 to 2,600 words, for women of all ages, with strong how-to slant, on self-development, health, nutrition, psychological issues, money and careers. Pays from $700, on acceptance. Query.

SLIMMER—3420 Ocean Park Blvd., Santa Monica, CA 90405. Lori Berger, Ed. Articles, 2,500 to 3,500 words, and columns, 1,000 words, on nutrition, fitness, beauty, skin care, diet, exercise, fashion, travel, and sports, for women aged 18 to 40. Pays $300 to $500 for features, $100 to $150 for columns, 30 days after acceptance. Query required.

SOMA—2948 NW 60th St., Ft. Lauderdale, FL 33309. Kim G. Weiss, Ed. Nutritionally-oriented articles for women aged 35 to 50, on beauty, health, preventative aging, diet, and fitness. Pays $100 to $150, thirty days after acceptance. Query with published clips.

SUNDAY WOMAN—235 E. 45th St., New York, NY 10017. Merry Clark, Ed. Articles, 1,500 to 2,000 words, for women: health, topical issues, families, lifestyles, relationships, money management, careers, women entrepreneurs, success stories of women in business. Pays from $150 to $500, $50 for reprints, on acceptance. Query.

VIRTUE—P.O. Box 850, Sisters, OR 97759. Becky Durost, Ed. Articles, 1,000 to 1,500 words, on the family, marriage, self-esteem, working mothers, food, decorating; profiles of Christian women. Pays 7¢ per word, on publication. Query required.

VOGUE—350 Madison Ave., New York, NY 10017. Address Features Ed. Articles, to 1,500 words, on women, entertainment and the arts, travel, medicine and health. General features. Rarely buys unsolicited manuscripts. Pays good rates, on acceptance.

WOMAN—1115 Broadway, New York, NY 10010. Sherry Amatenstein, Ed. Personal-experience pieces, to 1,500 words, for single women who want to better their relationships, careers or lifestyles. Short interviews, 800 words, with successful women for "Woman in the News," and "Bravo Woman." Short medical and legal news items for "Let's Put Our Heads Together." Pays 10¢ a word, on acceptance. Query.

WOMAN'S DAY—1515 Broadway, New York, NY 10036. Rebecca Greer, Articles Ed. Human-interest or helpful articles, 1,000 to 2,500 words, on marriage, child-rearing, health, relationships, money management. Dramatic narratives of medical miracles, rescues, etc. Pays top rates, on acceptance. Query.

WOMAN'S WORLD—177 N. Dean St., Englewood, NJ 07631. Janel Bladow, Sen. Ed. Articles, 800 to 2,500 words, of interest to middle-income women between the ages of 18 and 60, on love, romance, careers, medicine, health, psychology, sex, travel, dramatic stories of adventure or crisis. Pays $300 to $1,000, on acceptance. Query.

WOMEN IN BUSINESS—9100 Ward Parkway, Box 8728, Kansas City, MO 64114. Margaret E. Horan, Ed. American Business Women's Assn. Features, 1,000 to 1,500 words, for working women between 35 and 55 years. No profiles. Pays on acceptance. Written query preferred.

WOMEN'S CIRCLE—Box 428, Seabrook, NH 03874. Marjorie Pearl, Ed. Articles on crafts, hobbies, money-saving projects and other subjects of interest to homemakers. Success stories of home business entrepreneurs. Pays varying rates, on acceptance.

WOMEN'S CIRCLE HOME COOKING—Box 1952, Brooksville, FL 33512. Barbara Hall Pedersen, Ed. Food-related articles, to 1,200 words. Pays to 5¢ a word, on publication.

WOMEN'S SPORTS AND FITNESS—310 Town & Country Village, Palo Alto, CA 94301. Martha Nelson, Features Ed. Personality profiles, pieces that encourage involvement in active living (backpacking, aerobic dancing, windsurfing), articles on fitness, nutrition and sports-related issues, strong personal reminiscences and sports-related fiction. Features are 1,500 to 3,500 words. Shorter pieces, to 1,500 words, for departments: "End Zone" (opinions), "Sportif" (nutrition, beauty, health), and "Sports Pages" (short profiles of relatively unknown college and high school athletes and sports-related news items). Pays $200 to $500, on publication, for features; pay varies for shorter pieces.

WORKING MOTHER—230 Park Ave., New York, NY 10169. Vivian Cadden, Ed. Well-thought-out articles, 1,500 to 2,000 words, for working mothers: child care, home management, the work world, single mothers, etc. Pays $500 to $800, on acceptance. Query, with detailed outline.

WORKING WOMAN—342 Madison Ave., New York, NY 10173. Address Julia Kagan. Articles 1,500 to 2,500 words, on business and personal aspects of working women's lives. Pays from $400, on acceptance. Query with published clips required; include daytime phone number.

HOME AND LIFESTYLE PUBLICATIONS

THE AMERICAN ROSE MAGAZINE—P.O. Box 30,000, Shreveport, LA 71130. Harold S. Goldstein, Ed. Articles on home rose gardens: varieties, products, etc. Pays in copies.

AMERICANA—29 W. 38th St., New York, NY 10018. Michael Durham, Ed. Articles, 1,000 to 2,500 words, with historical slant: restoration, crafts, food, antiques, travel, etc. Pays $350 to $600, on acceptance. Query.

BETTER HOMES AND GARDENS—1716 Locust St., Des Moines, IA 50336. Doris Eby, Ed. Dir. Articles, to 2,000 words, on home and family entertainment, money management, health, travel, pets, and cars. Pays top rates, on acceptance. Query.

BON APPETIT—5900 Wilshire Blvd., Los Angeles, CA 90036. Barbara Varnum, Articles Ed. Articles on fine cooking, cooking classes, and kitchens. Query, with samples of published work. Pays varying rates, on acceptance.

CAPPER'S WEEKLY—616 Jefferson St., Topeka, KS 66607. Dorothy Harvey, Ed. Articles, 300 to 500 words: human interest, personal experience, historical. Pays varying rates, on publication.

CHRISTIAN HOME—Box 189, 1908 Grand Ave., Nashville, TN 37202. David Bradley, Ed. Articles on parenting, marriage and devotional life, 1,000 to 1,500 words, for couples and families. Pays 3½¢ to 4½¢ a word, on acceptance.

THE CHRISTIAN SCIENCE MONITOR—One Norway St., Boston, MA 02115. Katherine Fanning, Ed. Marilyn Gardner, Ed., Living/Children's pages. Phyllis Hanes, Food Ed. Articles on lifestyle trends, women's rights, family, parenting, consumerism, fashion, and food. Pays varying rates on acceptance.

THE COOK'S MAGAZINE—Pennington Publishing, 2710 North Ave., Bridgeport, CT 06604. Mary Caldwell, Articles Ed. Articles on trends in home and restaurant cooking, with basic, hands-on, how-to cooking techniques and recipes. Articles for "Science of Cooking" describing how particular aspects of cooking work (the science of ovens; smoked, salted and dried meats, etc.). Short articles, with eight to ten recipes for "Produce" on specific, seasonal ingredient. Short piece, with four or five dessert recipes focused on a particular theme for "Desserts." No unsolicited manuscripts; submit brief query letter, several recipe ideas, recent writing sample, and two original recipes. Guidelines are available. Pays $200 to $375, within 60 days of publication.

COUNTRY JOURNAL—P.O. Box 870, Manchester Center, VT 05255. Tyler Resch, Ed. Broad spectrum of articles dealing with issues and interests of people living in the country—practical how-to advice, concerns about energy and environment, science or natural history or wildlife, concentration on gardening and farming, occasional arts and crafts, and a bit of recreation. No fiction, nostalgia, reminiscence, profiles of "typical" country characters. Pays $400, on acceptance, for articles of 2,500 to 3,000 words. Query preferred.

EARTHTONE—Publication Development, Box 23383, Portland, OR 97223. Pat Jossy, Ed. Feature articles, 1,500 to 2,000 words, on gardening, energy, health, nutrition, home projects, food, recreation, etc. Profiles, interviews. Pays $50 to $300, on publication.

FAMILY CIRCLE—488 Madison Ave., New York, NY 10022. Susan Ungaro, Articles Ed. Articles, to 2,500 words, on child care, consumer affairs, changing lifestyles, health and fitness, jobs, money management, food, travel, gardening; true-life dramas. Query required. Pays on acceptance.

FAMILY CIRCLE GREAT IDEAS—488 Madison Ave., New York, NY 10022. Shari Hartford, Managing Ed. How-to articles on crafts, food, decorating, and remodeling projects. Pay varies, on acceptance. Queries are preferred.

FARM & RANCH LIVING—5400 S. 60th St., Greendale, WI 53129. Bob Ottum, Man. Ed. Articles, 2,000 words, on rural people and situations; nostalgia pieces, profiles of interesting farms and farmers, ranches and ranchers. Pays $15 to $400, on acceptance and on publication.

FARMSTEAD MAGAZINE—Box 111, Freedom, ME 04941. Heidi N. Brugger, Man. Ed. Articles, 700 to 2,500 words, on organic home gardening, country living, livestock and marketing for the small farmer, self-reliant lifestyles, and homestyle recipes. Pays 5¢ a word, on publication. Query preferred.

FLOWER AND GARDEN MAGAZINE—4521 Pennsylvania, Kansas City, MO 64111. Rachel Snyder, Ed.-in-Chief. How-to articles, to 1,200 words, with photos, on indoor and outdoor home gardening. Pays 7¢ a word, on acceptance. Query preferred.

FOOD & WINE—1120 Ave. of the Americas, 9th fl., New York, NY 10036. Warren Picower, Man. Ed. Current culinary or beverage ideas for dining and entertaining at home and out. Submit detailed proposal; no unsolicited manuscripts.

FRIENDLY EXCHANGE—1999 Shephard Rd., St. Paul, MN 55116. Adele Malott, Ed. Articles, 1,000 to 2,500 words, for traditional, home-owning families, on domestic travel, gardening, home decorating, personal finance, sports and the outdoors, consumer interests, etc. with Western U.S. tie-in. Pays $300 to $700 for features. Departments are generated exclusively by reader mail. Pays on acceptance. Query.

GARDEN—The Garden Society, Botanical Garden, Bronx, NY 10458. Ann Botshon, Ed. Articles, 1,000 to 2,500 words, on botany, horticulture, ecology, agriculture. Photos. Pays to $300, on publication. Query.

GARDENS FOR ALL NEWS—180 Flynn Ave., Burlington, VT 05401. Ruth W. Page, Ed. How-to articles on food gardens and orchards, general-interest pieces for gardeners, 300 to 3,000 words. Pays $40 to $300, extra for photos, on acceptance. Query preferred.

THE HERB QUARTERLY—Box 275, Newfane, VT 05345. Articles, 2,000 to 10,000 words, on herbs: practical uses, cultivation, gourmet cooking, landscaping, herb tradition, unique garden designs, profiles of herb garden experts, practical how-to's for the herb businessperson. Include garden design when possible. Pays on publication. Send for writers' guidelines.

HOME MAGAZINE—140 E. 45th St., New York, NY 10017. Olivia Buehl, Ed. Articles of interest to homeowners: remodeling, decorating, how-to, project ideas and instructions, taxes, insurance, conservation and solar energy. Pays varying rates, on acceptance. Query, with 50- to 200-word summary.

THE HOMEOWNER—3 Park Ave., New York, NY 10016. Jim Liston, Ed. Articles, 500 to 1,500 words, with photos, on do-it-yourself home improvement and remodeling projects. Pays $100 to $150 per printed page, on acceptance. Query.

HORTICULTURE—755 Boylston St., Boston, MA 02116. Steven Krauss, Managing Ed. Authoritative, well-written articles, 1,500 to 3,000 words, on all aspects of gardening and horticulture. Pays competitive rates. Query first.

HOUSE & GARDEN—350 Madison Ave., New York, NY 10017. Louis O. Gropp, Ed.-in-Chief. Denise Otis, Martin Filler, Co-Eds. Articles on decorating, architecture, gardening, the arts. No unsolicited articles.

HOUSE BEAUTIFUL—1700 Broadway, New York, NY 10019. Carol Cooper Garey, Dir. Copy/Features. Service articles related to the home. Pieces on design, travel and gardening mostly staff-written. Send for writer's guidelines. Query with detailed outline. SASE required.

HOUSTON HOME & GARDEN—5615 Kirby, Suite 600, P.O. Box 25386, Houston, TX 77265. Gretchen Fallon, Ed. Articles on interior design, regional gardening, cooking, art, architecture, health, fitness, and travel. Limited freelance market. Query.

LOG HOME GUIDE—P.O. Box 40, Fort Irwin, R.R. #1, Haliburton, Ont., Canada K0M 1S0. Articles on building new log homes, especially with solar or alternate heating systems; articles on interesting old log homes and log home decor. Photos essential. Pays 10¢ a word, on publication, extra for photos.

METROPOLITAN HOME—1716 Locust St., Des Moines, IA 50336. Service and informational articles for metropolitan dwellers in apartments, houses, co-ops, lofts and condominiums. Pays varying rates. Query.

THE MOTHER EARTH NEWS—105 Stoney Mt. Rd., Hendersonville, NC 28791. Bruce Woods, Ed. Articles on alternative lifestyles for rural and urban readers: home improvements, how-to's, indoor and outdoor gardening, crafts and projects, etc. Also self-help, health, food-related, ecology, energy, and consumerism pieces; profiles. Pays from $100 per published page, on acceptance. Address Roselyn Edwards, Submissions Ed.

NEW SHELTER—33 E. Minor St., Emmaus, PA 18049. Articles on contemporary home management: how-to, total home design, home improvement, with emphasis on energy efficiency, new products, materials and technologies. Query required.

1001 HOME IDEAS—3 Park Ave., New York, NY 10016. Anne Anderson, Ed.-in-Chief. General-interest articles, 500 to 2,000 words, on home decorating, furnishings, antiques and collectibles, food, household tips, crafts, remodeling, gardening. how-to and problem-solving decorating pieces. Pays varying rates, on acceptance. Query.

RODALE'S ORGANIC GARDENING—33 E. Minor St., Emmaus, PA

18049. M. C. Goldman, Exec. Ed. Articles, to 2,500 words, for organic gardeners: building soil, growing food plants, new developments in horticulture, plant breeding, etc. Pieces on energy conservation and health, for "Organic Living," on food preparation, storage, and equipment, for "Gardener's Kitchen." Photos. Pays $300 to $750, extra for photos, on acceptance. Query.

SELECT HOMES—382 W. Broadway, Vancouver, BC, Canada V5Y 1R2. Pam Miller Withers, Ed. Articles on home improvement, maintenance, decorating, and finance: 1,000-word pieces for "Maintenance and Repair," "Money," "Renovations" (interior and exterior additions, expansions); and "Spaces" (architectural concepts, interior design, storage); short profiles of specific architectural projects for "Architecture" (650 words); articles on recreational or retirement homes for "Cottages" (600 to 1,500 words), on home energy topics for "Energy" (500 to 1,500 words), and home improvement projects for "How-To" (500 to 1,000 words). All material should have a Canadian slant. Pays $50 to $600, half on acceptance, half on publication. Query with two writing samples; enclose international reply coupons.

SMART LIVING—22 E. 29th St., New York, NY 10016. Carol J. Richards, Ed. Articles, 3,000 words, that highlight life in New York City. Pays $150, on publication. No manuscripts will be returned.

WORKBENCH—4251 Pennsylvania, Kansas City, MO 64111. Jay W. Hedden, Ed. Illustrated how-to articles on home improvement and do-it-yourself projects, with detailed instructions, energy conservation and alternatives, manufactured housing. Pays from $125 per printed page, on acceptance. Send SASE for writer's guidelines.

YOUR HOME MAGAZINE—P.O. Box 10010, Ogden, UT 84409. Peggie Bingham, Ed. Upbeat articles, 1,000 to 2,000 words, with color transparencies, for renters and homeowners, on renovating, decorating, remodeling; garden/patio/outdoor articles; profiles of exotic and beautiful houses; short home/garden humor pieces. Bridal section needs bridal etiquette, traditions, fashion, beginning entertaining, etc. Pays 15¢ a word, $35 for color photos, on acceptance. Query with SASE.

SPORTS, OUTDOORS, RECREATION

AERO—P.O. Box 6050, Mission Viejo, CA 92690. Dennis Shattuck, Ed. Articles, 1,000 to 4,000 words, for owners of high performance single- and twin-engine planes, relating to ownership, piloting, and use; pieces on favorite fly-in travel spots. Photos. Pays $75 to $250, on publication.

THE AMATEUR BOXER—P.O. Box 249, Cobalt, CT 06414. Bob Taylor, Ed. Articles on amateur boxing. Fillers. Photos. Pays $10 to $40, extra for photos, on publication. Query preferred.

AMATEUR GOLF REGISTER—2843 Pembroke Rd., Hollywood, FL 33020. Bernard Block, Ed. Articles, 200 to 400 words, on golf, for amateur players. Fillers, 25 to 50 words. Pays $30 a page, $5 a joke, on publication. Query.

THE AMERICAN FIELD—222 W. Adams St., Chicago, IL 60606. William F. Brown, Ed. Yarns about hunting trips, bird-shooting; articles to 1,500 words, on dogs and field trials, emphasizing conservation of game resources. Pays varying rates, on acceptance.

AMERICAN HANDGUNNER—Suite 200, 591 Camino de la Reina, San

Diego, CA 92108. Cameron Hopkins, Ed. Semi-technical articles on shooting sports, gun repair and alteration, handgun matches and tournaments, for lay readers. Pays $100 to $500, on publication. Query.

AMERICAN HUNTER—1600 Rhode Island Ave. N.W., Washington, DC 20036. Mike Hanback, Man. Ed. Articles, 1,400 to 2,000 words, on hunting. Photos. Pays on acceptance.

THE AMERICAN RIFLEMAN—1600 Rhode Island Ave., N.W., Washington, DC 20036. Bill Parkerson, Ed. Factual articles on use and enjoyment of sporting firearms. Pays on acceptance.

ARCHERY WORLD—11812 Wayzata Blvd., Suite 100, Minnetonka, MN 55343. Richard Sapp, Ed. Articles, 1,000 to 2,000 words, on all aspects of bowhunting, with photos. Pays from $100, extra for photos, on publication.

BACKPACKER MAGAZINE—One Park Ave., New York, NY 10016. John A. Delves, Ed. Articles, 250 to 3,000 words, on backpacking, technique, kayaking/canoeing, mountaineering, alpine/nordic skiing, health, natural science. Photos. Pays varying rates. Query.

THE BACKSTRETCH—19363 James Couzens Hwy., Detroit, MI 48235. Ruth LeGrove, Man. Ed. United Thoroughbred Trainers of America. Feature articles, with photos, on persons involved with thoroughbred horses. Pays after publication.

BASEBALL ILLUSTRATED—See *Hockey Illustrated.*

BASKETBALL ANNUAL—See *Hockey Illustrated.*

BASSIN' (formerly *Pro Bass*)—15115 S. 76th Ave. East, Bixby, OK 74008. Andre Hinds, Man. Ed. Articles, 1,500 to 3,000 words, on how and where to bass fish, for the average fisherman. Pays $175 to $225, on acceptance.

BASSMASTER MAGAZINE—B.A.S.S. Publications, P.O. Box 17900, Montgomery, AL 36141. Bob Cobb, Ed. Articles, 1,700 to 2,000 words, with photos, on freshwater black bass and striped bass. "Short Casts" pieces, 400 to 800 words, on news, views, and items of interest. Pays $100 to $350, on acceptance. Query.

BAY & DELTA YACHTSMAN—2019 Clement Ave., Alameda, CA 94501. Dave Preston, Ed. Humorous features, satire and cruising stories. Must have Northern California tie-in. Photos and illustrations. Pays varying rates.

BC OUTDOORS—#202, 1132 Hamilton St., Vancouver, B.C., Canada V6B 2S2. Henry L. Frew, Ed. Articles, to 1,500 words, on fishing, hunting, conservation and all forms of non-competitive outdoor recreation in British Columbia, Alberta, and Yukon. Photos. Pays from 10¢ to 15¢ a word, extra for photos, on acceptance.

BICYCLE GUIDE—128 N. 11th St., Allentown, PA 18102. John Schubert, Ed. Articles, 1,000 to 3,000 words, on all aspects of cycling. Pays from $300.

BICYCLING—33 E. Minor St., Emmaus, PA 18049. James C. McCullagh, Ed. Articles, 500 to 2,500 words, on recreational riding, commuting, equipment, and touring, for serious cyclists. Photos; humor. Pays $25 to $400, on publication. Query. Guidelines available.

BIKEREPORT—Bikecentennial, P.O. Box 8308, Missoula, MT 59807. Daniel D'Ambrosio, Ed. Accounts of bicycle tours in the U.S., interviews, personal-experience pieces, humor and news shorts, 800 to 1,500 words. Pays $25 to $65 per published page. Query.

BIRD WATCHER'S DIGEST—P.O. Box 110, Marietta, OH 45750. Mary B. Bowers, Ed. Articles, 600 to 2,500 words, for bird watchers: first-person accounts; how-to's, pieces on endangered species; profiles. Poetry, cartoons, fillers. Pays to $50 for articles, $25 for reprints, $5 for fillers, $10 for cartoons, $10 for poetry. on publication.

BLUE WATER PADDLER—Box 105032, Anchorage, AK 99510. Doug Van Etten, Ed. Articles, 1,500 words, on topics related to Alaska's coastal environment: fishing, camping, hiking, kayaking, conservation and safety. Related fillers and fiction, 1,500 words. Poetry. Pays on publication. Query.

BOAT PENNSYLVANIA—Pennsylvania Fish Commission, P.O. Box 1673, Harrisburg, PA 17105-1673. Address Editor. Articles, 200 to 2,500 words, with photos, on nonangling boating in Pennsylvania (motorboating, sailing, water skiing, canoeing, kayaking, and rafting). Pays $50 to $200 on acceptance. Must send SASE with all material. Query first.

BOATING—One Park Ave., New York, NY 10016. Roy Attaway, Ed. Illustrated articles, 1,000 to 2,000 words, on power boating. Pays good rates, on acceptance. Query.

BOW & ARROW HUNTING—Box HH, 34249 Camino Capistrano, Capistrano Beach, CA 92624. Roger Combs, Ed. Dir. Articles, 1,200 to 2,500 words, with photos, on bowhunting, profiles and technical pieces. Pays $50 to $200, on acceptance. Same address and requirements for *Gun World*.

BOWHUNTER MAGAZINE—3150 Mallard Cove La., Fort Wayne, IN 46804. M. R. James, Ed. Adventure and how-to articles, 500 to 5,000 words, on bow and arrow hunting. Photos. Pays $25 to $250 and up, on acceptance.

BOWLERS JOURNAL—875 N. Michigan Ave., Chicago, IL 60611. Mort Luby, Ed. Trade and consumer articles, 1,200 to 2,000 words, with photos, on bowling. Pays $75 to $200; on acceptance.

BOWLING—5301 S. 76th St., Greendale, WI 53129. Rory Gillespie, Ed. Articles, to 1,500 words, on amateur league and tournament bowling. Profiles. Pays varying rates, on publication.

CALIFORNIA ANGLER—6200 Yarrow Dr., Carlsbad, CA 92008. Tom Waters, Ed. How-to and where-to articles, 2,000 words, for freshwater and saltwater anglers in California: travel, new products, fishing techniques, profiles. Photos. Pays $50 to $300, on acceptance. Query first.

CASCADES EAST—716 N.E. 4th St., P.O. Box 5784, Bend, OR 97708. Geoff Hill, Ed./Publisher. Articles, 1,000 to 2,000 words, on outdoor activities (fishing, hunting, backpacking, rafting, skiing, snowmobiling, etc.), history, and scenic tours in Cascades region of Oregon. Photos. Pays 3¢ to 7¢ a word, extra for photos, on publication.

CHESAPEAKE BAY MAGAZINE—1819 Bay Ridge Ave., Annapolis, MD 21403. Betty Rigoli, Ed. Technical and how-to articles, to 1,500 words, on boating, fishing, conservation, in Chesapeake Bay. Photos. Pays $65 to $85, extra for cover photos, on publication.

CITY SPORTS MAGAZINE—P.O. Box 3693, San Francisco, CA 94119. Maggie Cloherty, Ed/Northern California. Will Balliett, Ed/Southern California,

1120 Princeton Dr., Marina Del Rey, CA 90291. Articles, 1,700 to 3,000 words, for active Californians. Pays $175 to $325, on publication. Query.

CRUISING WORLD—524 Thames St., Newport, RI 02840. George Day, Ed. Articles on sailing, 1,000 to 3,000 words: technical and personal narratives. No fiction, poetry, or logbook transcripts. 35mm slides. Pays $100 to $1,000, on acceptance. Query.

CYCLIST—20916 Higgins Ct., Torrance, CA 90501. John Francis, Ed. Articles on all aspects of bicycling: touring, travel and equipment.

THE DIVER—P.O. Box 249, Cobalt, CT 06414. Bob Taylor, Ed. Articles on technique, training tips, for coaches, officials, divers. Photos. Pays $15 to $40, extra for photos, $15 to $35 for cartoons, on publication.

DIVER MAGAZINE—8051 River Rd., Richmond, B.C., V6X 1XB, Canada. Neil McDaniel, Ed. Articles, 1,000 to 2,000 words, on aquatic life, diving equipment, technology, dive sites, diving medicine, underwater photography, commercial and scientific diving. Fiction; humor. Photos. Pays $2.50 per column inch, extra for photos, on publication. Query.

EASTERN BASKETBALL—Eastern Basketball Publications, West Hempstead, NY 11552. Rita Napolitano, Man. Ed. Articles on college and high school basketball in the Northeast. Pays $70, on publication. Query.

FIELD & STREAM—1515 Broadway, New York, NY 10036. Duncan Barnes, Ed. Articles, 2,000 to 3,000 words, with photos, on hunting, fishing, camping, conservation. Fillers, 350 to 900 words, for "How It's Done." Cartoons. Pays from $500 for articles with photos, $250 to $350 for fillers, $100 for cartoons, on acceptance. Query on articles.

FINS AND FEATHERS—318 W. Franklin Ave., Minneapolis, MN 55404. Dave Greer, Ed. Articles, 2,000 to 2,500 words, on a wide variety of recreational activities, including hunting, camping, and environmental issues. Pays $100 to $500, on publication. Query.

FISHING WORLD—51 Atlantic Ave., Floral Park, NY 11001. Keith Gardner, Ed. Features, to 2,500 words, with photos, on fishing sites, technique, equipment. Pays $300 for major features, $100 for shorter articles. Query preferred.

THE FLORIDA HORSE—P.O. Box 2106, Ocala, FL 32678. F. J. Audette, Publisher. Articles, 1,500 words, on Florida thoroughbred breeding and racing. Pays $100 to $150, on publication.

FLY FISHERMEN—Box 8200, Harrisburg, PA 17105. John Randolph, Ed. Articles, to 3,000 words, on how to and where to fly fish. Fillers, to 100 words. Pays from $35 to $400, on acceptance. Query.

FLYING MAGAZINE—One Park Ave., New York, NY 10016. Richard Collins, Ed. Articles, 1,500 words, on personal flying experiences. Pays varying rates, on acceptance. Study issues of magazine before submitting. Query.

FOOTBALL DIGEST—Century Publishing Co., 1020 Church St., Evanston, IL 60201. Michael K. Herbert, Ed. Profiles of pro stars, "think" pieces, 1,500 words, aimed at the pro football fan. Pays on publication.

FUR-FISH-GAME—2878 E. Main St., Columbus, OH 43209. Ken Dunwoody, Ed. Illustrated articles, 800 to 2,500 words, preferably with how-to angle, on hunting, fishing, trapping, dogs, camping or other outdoor topics. Some humorous or where-to articles. Pays $40 to $150, on acceptance.

GAME AND FISH PUBLICATIONS—P.O. Box 741, Marietta, GA 30061. Publishes outdoors magazines for thirteen states. Articles, 2,000 to 2,500 words, on hunting and fishing. How-to's, where-to's, and adventure pieces. Profiles of successful hunters and fishermen. No hiking, canoeing, camping, or backpacking pieces. Pays $150 for state specific articles, $250 for general articles, on publication.

GOAL—500 Fifth Ave., 34th fl., New York, NY 10110. Stu Hackel, Ed. Official publication of the National Hockey League. Player profiles, trend stories, 1,000 to 1,800 words, for hockey fans with knowledge of the sport. Pays $100 to $200, before publication. Query.

GOLF DIGEST—495 Westport Ave., Norwalk, CT 06856. Jerry Tarde, Ed. Instructional articles, tournament reports, and features on players, to 2,500 words. Fiction, 1,000 to 4,000 words. Poetry, fillers, humor, photos. Pays varying rates, on acceptance. Query preferred.

GOLF JOURNAL—Golf House, Far Hills, NJ 07931. Robert Sommers, Ed. U.S. Golf Assn. Articles on golf personalities, history, travel. Humor. Photos. Pays varying rates, on publication.

GOLF MAGAZINE—380 Madison Ave., New York, NY 10017. James A. Frank, Exec. Ed. Articles of 1,500 words, with photos, on golf. Shorts, to 500 words. Pays $500 to $1,000 for articles, $75 to $300 for shorts, on publication.

THE GREYHOUND REVIEW—National Greyhound Assn., Box 543, Abilene, KS 67410. Tim Horan, Man. Ed. Articles, 1,000 to 10,000 words, pertaining to the Greyhound dog industry: how to train, historical nostalgia, interviews. Pays $40 to $150, on publication.

GUN DIGEST AND HANDLOADER'S DIGEST—4092 Commercial Ave., Northbrook, IL 60062. Ken Warner, Ed. Well-researched articles, to 5,000 words, on guns and shooting, equipment, etc. Photos. Pays from 10¢ a word, on acceptance. Query.

GUN DOG—P.O. Box 68, Adel, IA 50003. Bob Wilbanks, Man. Ed. Features, 1,000 to 2,500 words, with photos, on bird hunting: how-to's, where-to's, dog training, canine medicine, breeding strategy. Fiction. Humor. Fillers. Pays $25 to $75 for fillers and short articles, $100 to $350 for features, on acceptance.

GUN WORLD—See *Bow & Arrow Hunting.*

GUNS & AMMO—8490 Sunset Blvd., Los Angeles, CA 90069. E. G. Bell, Jr., Ed. Technical and general articles. 1,500 to 3,000 words, on guns, ammunition, and target shooting. Photos, fillers. Pays from $150, on acceptance.

HANDBALL—930 N. Benton Ave., Tucson, AZ 85711. Vern Roberts, Ed. Articles, 1,000 to 2,000 words, on handball and handball players. Photos; fillers, 30 to 40 words. No payment.

HANG GLIDING—U.S. Hang Gliding Assn., P.O. Box 66306, Los Angeles, CA 90066. Gilbert Dodgen, Ed. Articles and fiction, 2 to 3 pages, on hang gliding. Pays to $50, on publication. Query preferred.

HOCKEY ILLUSTRATED—355 Lexington Ave., New York, NY 10017. Stephen Ciacciarelli, Thomas Walsh, Eds. Articles, 2,500 words, on hockey players, teams. Pays $125, on publication. Query. Same address and requirements for *Baseball Illustrated, Wrestling World, Pro Basketball Illustrated, Pro Football Illustrated,* and *Basketball Annual* (college).

HOT BOAT—P.O. Box 1708, Lake Havasu City, AZ 86403. Randy Scott,

Ed. Articles, 850 to 2,500 words, on sporting events, personalities, general-interest, how-to, and technical features. Humor, 600 to 1,500 words. Pays $85 to $400, on publication. Query or send SASE for guidelines.

HUNTING—8490 Sunset Blvd., Los Angeles, CA 90069. Craig Boddington, Ed. How-to articles on practical aspects of hunting. At least 15 photos required with articles. Pays $250 to $400, for articles, extra for color photos, on acceptance.

INSIDE RUNNING & FITNESS—9514 Bristlebrook Dr., Houston, TX 77083. Joanne Schmidt, Ed. Articles, fiction and fillers on running and aerobics in Texas. Photos. Pays $35 to $100, including photos, $5 for fillers, on acceptance.

KITPLANES—P.O. Box 6050, Mission Viejo, CA 92690. Dennis Shattuck, Ed. Articles, geared to the growing market of aircraft built from kits by home craftsmen, on all aspects of design, construction and performance, 1,000 to 4,000 words. Pays $75 to $250, on publication.

LAKELAND BOATING—505 N. Lakeshore Dr., #5704, Chicago, IL 60611. Michael E. Hilts, Ed. Articles, 750 to 2,500 words, for boat owners on the Great Lakes or major inland rivers. Photos, preferably color slides, should accompany manuscript. Pays $75 per page, on publication. Query.

MID-WEST OUTDOORS—111 Shore Dr., Hinsdale, IL 60521. Gene Laulunen, Ed. Articles, 1,500 words, with photos, on where, when and how to fish in the Midwest. Fillers, 200 to 500 words. Pays $15 to $35, on publication.

THE MINOR PRO FOOTBALL NEWS—135 Prospect, Elmhurst, IL 60126. Ronald J. Real, Pub. Minor Pro Football Assn. Lively feature articles, 500 to 2,000 words, with photos, about minor-league and semi-pro football teams. Pays from $15, on publication.

MOTORHOME MAGAZINE—29901 Agoura Rd., Agoura, CA 91301. Bob Livingston, Ed. Articles, to 2,000 words, with color slides, on motorhomes; travel and how-to pieces. Pays to $500, on acceptance.

NATIONAL RACQUETBALL—4350 DiPaolo Center, Dearlove Rd., Glenview, IL 60025. Jason Halloman, Man. Ed. Articles, 800 to 1,200 words, on health and conditioning. How-to's. Profiles. Fiction. Material must relate to racquetball. Pays $25 to $150, on publication.

NAUTICAL QUARTERLY—Pratt St., Essex, CT 06426. Joseph Gribbins, Ed. In-depth articles, 3,000 to 7,000 words, about boats and boating, U.S. and foreign. Pays $500 to $1,000, on acceptance. Query.

NORTHEAST OUTDOORS—P.O. Box 2180, Waterbury, CT 06722-2180. Howard Fielding, Ed. Articles, 500 to 1,800 words, preferably with B/W photos, on camping in Northeast U.S.: recommended private campgrounds, camp cookery, recreational vehicle hints. Stress how-to, where-to. Cartoons. Pays to $80, on publication. Send for guidelines.

NORTHEAST RIDING—209 Whitney St., Hartford, CT 06105. Paul Essenfeld, Pub. Motorcycle-related articles, 500 to 1,000 words, for motorcyclists in the Northeast. Pays negotiable rates, on publication.

OCEAN REALM—6061 Collins Ave., Suite 19C, Miami Beach, FL 33140. S. M. George, Ed. Articles, 1,200 to 1,800 words, on scuba diving and ocean science and technology. Department pieces: adventure; technology/medicine; instruction; photography and marine life. Photos. Short items, 100 to 500 words, for "FYI": up-to-date news items of interest to the diving community. Pays $100 per published page, $5 for FYI, on publication. SASE required.

OFFSHORE—P.O. Box 148, Waban, MA 02168. Daniel Weeks, Man. Ed. Articles, 1,000 to 3,000 words, on boats, people and places along the New England coast. Photos. Pays 5¢ to 10¢ a word, on acceptance.

ON TRACK—17165 Newhope St., "M", Fountain Valley, CA 92708. Steve Nickless, Edit. Dir. Features and race reports, 500 to 2,500 words. Pays $3 per column inch, on publication. Query first.

OUTDOOR LIFE—380 Madison Ave., New York, NY 10017. Clare Conley, Ed. Articles on hunting, fishing and related subjects. Pays top rates, on acceptance. Query.

OUTSIDE—Continental Bank Building, 1165 N. Clark, Chicago, IL 60610. High-quality articles, with photos, on sports, nature, wilderness travel, adventure, etc. Pays varying rates. Query.

PENNSYLVANIA ANGLER—Pennsylvania Fish Commission, P. O. Box 1673, Harrisburg, PA 17105–1673. Address Editor. Articles, 250 to 2,500 words, with photos, on freshwater fishing, boating in Pennsylvania. Pays $50 to $200 on acceptance. Must send SASE with all material. Query first.

PENNSYLVANIA GAME NEWS—Game Commission, Harrisburg, PA 17120. Bob Bell, Ed. Articles, to 2,500 words, with photos, on outdoor subjects, except fishing and boating. Photos. Pays from 5¢ a word, extra for photos, on acceptance.

PGA MAGAZINE—100 Ave. of the Champions, Palm Beach Gardens, FL 33410. Articles, 1,500 to 2,500 words, and humor on golf-related subjects. Pays $200 to $300, on acceptance. Query Editor Bill Burbaum.

PLEASURE BOATING—1995 N.E. 150th St., North Miami, FL 33181. Joe Green, Ed. Articles, 1,000 to 2,000 words, on fishing and recreatinal boating in the South (from Florida to Texas). Fillers, humor, and jokes, to 1,000 words, related to boating. Pays on publication. Query.

POPULAR LURES—15115 S. 76th Ave. East, Bixby, OK 74008. Articles, 1,500 to 3,000 words,on tackle and techniques for catching all freshwater and saltwater fish, primarily bass, trout, catfish, crappie, walleye and salmon. Pays $175 to $225, on acceptance.

POPULAR SCIENCE—380 Madison Ave., New York, NY 10017. Herbert Shuldiner, Exec. Ed. Factual articles, 300 to 2,000 words, with photos and illustrations, on new products for home, car, boat, or outdoor activities. Pays varying rates, on acceptance. Query.

POWERBOAT—15917 Strathern St., Van Nuys, CA 91406. Mark Spencer, Ed. Articles, to 1,500 words, with photos, for powerboat owners, on outstanding achievements, water-skiing, competitions; how-to pieces. Pays about $300, on publication. Query.

PRIVATE PILOT—P. O. Box 6050, Mission Viejo, CA 92690. Dennis Shattuck, Ed. True-experience pieces and technically-based aviation articles, 1,000 to 4,000 words, for aviation enthusiasts. Photos. Pays $75 to $250, on publication. Query.

PRO BASKETBALL ILLUSTRATED—See *Hockey Illustrated*.

PRO BASS—See *Bassin'*.

PRO FOOTBALL ILLUSTRATED—See *Hockey Illustrated*.

THE RUNNER—One Park Ave., New York, NY 10016. Marc Bloom, Ed. Features, 3,000 to 4,000 words, and columns, 900 to 1,500 words, for runners. Pays varying rates, on acceptance.

SAIL—34 Commercial Wharf, Boston, MA 02110. Keith Taylor, Ed. Articles, 1,500 to 3,000 words, with photos, on sailboats, equipment, racing, and cruising. How-to's on navigation, sail, trim, etc. Pays $75 to $1,000 on publication. Writers' guidelines sent on request.

SAILBOARD NEWS—P. O. Box 159, Two S. Park Pl., Fair Haven, VT 05743. Mark Gabriel, Ed. Interviews, articles, and how-to pieces on boardsailing and the boardsailing industry. Photos. Pays from $25, on publication.

SAILING—125 E. Main St., Port Washington, WI 53074. William F. Schanen, III, Ed. Features, 700 to 1,500 words, with photos, on cruising and racing; first-person accounts; profiles of boats and regattas. Query for technical or how-to pieces. Pays varying rates, on publication. Writer's guidelines sent on request.

SAILORS' GAZETTE—337-22nd Ave., Suite 110, St. Petersburg, FL 33704. Alice N. Eachus, Ed. Articles, 500 to 1,500 words, with photos, on Southeastern boating. Emphasis on cruising and how-to's. Pays to 6¢ a word, extra for photos, on publication.

SALMON TROUT STEELHEADER—P O. Box 02112, Portland, OR 97202. Frank W. Amato, Ed. Factual articles, 750 to 2,500 words, with photos, on salmon, trout and steelhead fishing in Western states, Midwest and East coast. Pays to $200, on publication.

SCORE, CANADA'S GOLF MAGAZINE—287 MacPherson Ave., Toronto, Ont., Canada M4V 1A4. Lisa A. Leighton, Man. Ed. Articles, 800 to 3,500 words, on travel, golf equipment, golf history, personality profiles of prominent professionals. Fillers, 25 to 100 words. Pays $10 to $25 for fillers, $125 to $600 for features, on assignment and publication.

SEA KAYAKER—1670 Duranleau St., Vancouver, BC V6H 3S4, Canada. John Dowd, Ed. Articles, 400 to 2,000 words, on ocean kayaking. Fiction. Pays $50 per published page. Query with international reply coupons.

SHOTGUN SPORTS—Box 340, Lake Havasu City, AZ 86403. Frank Kodl, Ed. Articles with photos, on trap and skeet shooting and hunting with shotguns. Pays $25 to $200, on publication.

SKI MAGAZINE—380 Madison Ave., New York, NY 10017. Dick Needham, Ed. Articles, 1,300 to 2,000 words, on skiing. Pays $200, on acceptance. Query.

SKI RACING—Two Bentley Ave., Poultney, VT 05764. Don A. Metivier, Pub./Ed. Interviews, articles, and how-to pieces on national and international alpine and nordic ski competitions. Photos. Pays from $1 per column inch, on publication.

SKIING—One Park Ave., New York, NY 10016. Alfred H. Greenberg, Ed.

589

Personal adventures on skis, from 2,500 words (no first-time-on-skis stories); profiles and interviews, 50 to 300 words. Pays $150 to $300 per printed page, on acceptance.

SKIN DIVER MAGAZINE—8490 Sunset Blvd., Los Angeles, CA 90069. Bonnie J. Cardone, Exec. Ed. Illustrated articles, 500 to 2,000 words, on scuba diving activities, equipment and dive sites. Pays $50 per published page, on publication.

SKYDIVING—P. O. Box 1520, Deland, FL 32721. Michael Truffer, Ed. Timely news articles, 300 to 800 words, relating to sport and military parachuting. Fillers. Photos. Pays $25 to $200, extra for photos, on publication.

SNOWMOBILE—11812 Wayzata Blvd., Suite 100, Minnetonka, MN 55343. Dick Hendricks, Ed. Articles, 700 to 2,000 words, with color photos, related to snowmobiling: races and rallies, trail rides, personalities, travel. How-to's; humor; cartoons. Pays to $450, on publication. Query.

SNOWMOBILE WEST—P. O. Box 981, Idaho Falls, ID 83402. Steve Janes, Ed. Articles, 1,200 words, with photos, on snowmobiling in the western states. Pays to $100, on publication.

SOCCER AMERICA MAGAZINE—P. O. Box 23704, Oakland, CA 94623. Lynn Berling-Manuel, Ed. Articles, to 1,000 words, on soccer; news, profiles, coaching tips. Pays $25 to $100 for features, within 60 days of publication. Query.

SPORT MAGAZINE—119 W. 40th St., New York, NY 10018. Peter Griffin, Man. Ed. Query.

THE SPORTING NEWS—P. O. Box 56, 1212 N. Lindbergh Blvd., St. Louis, MO 63132. Tom Barnidge, Ed.-in-Chief. Articles, 1,000 to 1,500 words, on baseball, football, basketball, hockey, and other sports. Pays $150 to $750, on publication.

SPORTS AFIELD—250 W. 55th St., New York, NY 10010. Tom Paugh, Ed. Articles, 2,000 words, with quality phots, on hunting, fishing, natural history, personal experiences, new hunting/fishing spots. How-to pieces; humor; fiction. Pays top rates, on acceptance.

SPORTS AFIELD SPECIALS—250 W. 55th St.,New York, NY 10019. Well-written, informative fishing and hunting articles, 2,000 to 2,500 words, with photos, with primary focus on how-to techniques: include lively anecdotes, and good sidebars, charts. Pays to $450 for features, on acceptance. Query.

SPORTS ILLUSTRATED—1271 Ave. of the Americas, New York, NY 10020. Articles 1,000 to 1,500 words for regular columns: "Yesterday" (nostalgic recreations of pre-1954 sporting event): "First Person," "Nostalgia," "Reminiscence" (first-person accounts); "On the Scene" and "Perspective" (opinion pieces). Short pieces, 400 to 1,100 words, for: "Footloose" (sports-oriented travel pieces); "Viewpoint"; "Sideline"; "On Deck" (profiles of up-and-coming athletes); "Spotlight" (pieces on excellent athletes in less well-covered sports); "Hot Stove" (off-season analysis); "Reply" and "Update"; "Shopwalk," "Arttalk," and Booktalk" (reviews). Query articles Editor William O. Johnson. Pays $500 to $1,000, on acceptance.

SURFER MAGAZINE—Box 1028, Dana Point, CA 92629. Steve Pezman, Pub. Paul Holmes, Ed. Articles, 500 to 5,000 words, on surfing, surfers, etc. Photos. Pays 10¢ to 15¢ a word, $10 to $600 for photos, on publication.

SURFING—P. O. Box 3010, San Clemente, CA 92672. David Gilovich, Ed. Bill Sharp, Assoc. Ed. First-person travel articles, 1,500 to 2,000 words, on surfing locations; knowledge of sport essential. Pays varying rates, on publication. Query.

TENNIS—P. O. Box 0395, 5520 Park Ave., Trumbull, CT 06611-0395. Shepherd Campbell, Ed. Instructional articles, features, profiles of tennis stars, 500 to 2,000 words. Fillers; humor. Photos. Pays from $100 to $500, from $50 for fillers and humor, on publication. Query.

TENNIS, U.S.A.—3 Park Ave., New York, NY 10016. Grace Lichtenstein, Ed. Articles, 250 to 1,500 words, on local and sectional tennis personalities and news events. Pays $25 to $75, on acceptance. Query; uses very little free-lance material.

TENNIS WEEK—6 E. 39th St., New York, NY 10016. Eugene L. Scott, Pub. David Georgette, Ed. In-depth, researched articles, from 1,000 words, on current issues and personalities in the game. Pays $100, on publication. Query.

TRAILER BOATS—16427 S. Avalon, P. O. Box 2307, Gardena, CA 90248. Jim Youngs, Ed. Technical and how-to articles, 500 to 2,000 words, on boat, trailer or two vehicle maintenance and operation, skiing, fishing, cruising. Fillers; humor. Pays 7¢ to 10¢ a word, on publication. Query.

TRAILER LIFE—29901 Agoura Rd., Agoura, CA 91301. Bill Estes, Ed. Articles, to 2,500 words, with photos, on trailering, truck campers, motorhome, hobbies and RV lifestyle. How-to pieces. Pays to $400, on acceptance. Send for guidelines.

TRI-ATHLETE—6660 Banning Dr., Oakland, CA 94611. William R. Katovsky, Ed. Articles, 1,500 to 3,500 words, on triathlons and training. Pays 5¢ to 10¢ a word, on publication. Query required.

TURF AND SPORT DIGEST—511–13 Oakland Ave., Baltimore, MD 21212. Allen L. Mitzel, Jr., Ed. Articles, 1,500 to 4,000 words, on national turf personalities, racing nostalgia, and handicapping. Pays $75 to $200, on publication. Query.

ULTRASPORT—11 Beacon St., Boston, MA 02108. Chris Bergonzi, Ed. Articles about any participant athletic endeavors; profiles and descriptive pieces; athletics-related fiction, to 3,500 words. Humor, to 1,500 words. Pays $800, on acceptance. Query.

VELO-NEWS—Box 1257, Brattleboro, VT 05301. Barbara George, Ed. Articles, 500 to 2,000 words, on bicycle racing. Photos. Pays $1.75 per column inch, extra for photos, on publication. Query.

WASHINGTON FISHING HOLES—P. O. Box 499, Snohomish, WA 98290. Address Brad Stracener. Detailed articles, with specific maps, 800 to 1,500 words, on fishing holes in Washington. Local Washington fishing how-to's. Photos. Pays on publication. Query. Send SASE for guidelines.

THE WATER SKIER—P O. Box 191, Winter Haven, FL 33882. Duke Cullimore, Ed. Offbeat articles on waterskiing. Pays varying rates, on acceptance.

THE WESTERN BOATMAN—16427 S. Avalon, P. O. Box 2307, Gardena, CA 90248. Ralph Poole, Ed. Articles, to 1,500 words, for boating enthusiasts from Alaska to Mexico, on subjects from waterskiing and salmon fishing to race boats and schooners. Pays 10¢ a word, on publication. Query preferred.

591

WESTERN OUTDOORS—3197-E Airport Loop, Costa Mesa, CA 92626. Timely, factual articles on fishing and hunting, 1,500 to 1,800 words, of interest to western sportsmen. Pays $200 to $300, on acceptance. Query.

WESTERN SALTWATER FISHERMAN—*See California Angler.*

WESTERN SPORTSMAN—P. O. Box 737, Regina, Sask., Canada S4P 3A8. Red Wilkinson, Ed. Articles, to 2,500 words, on outdoor experiences in Alberta and Saskatchewan; how-to pieces. Photos. Pays $75 to $225, on publication.

WIND SURF—P. O. Box 561, Dana Point, CA 92629. Drew Kampion, Ed. Articles on all aspects of windsurfing. Pays 10¢ to 20¢ a word, on publication.

WINDRIDER—P. O. Box 2456, Winter Park, FL 32790. Nancy K. Crowell, Ed. Features, instructional pieces, and tips, by experienced boardsailors. Fast action photos. Pays $50 to $75 for tips, $100 to $250, for features, extra for photos, after publication. Query first.

THE WOMAN BOWLER—5301 S. 76th St., Greendale, WI 53129. Paula McMartin, Ed. Profiles, interviews, and news articles, to 1,000 words, for women bowlers. Pays varying rates, on acceptance. Query with outline.

WOMEN'S SPORTS AND FITNESS—310 Town and Country Village, Palo Alto, CA 94301. Martha Nelson, Features. Ed. How-to's, profiles, and sports reports, 500 to 2,500 words, for active women. Fitness, recreation, adventure-travel, psychology, nutrition and health pieces. Pays from $25, on publication.

WRESTLING WORLD—See *Hockey Illustrated.*

YACHT RACING & CRUISING—23 Leroy Ave., P. O. Box 1700, Darien, CT 06820. John Burnham, Ed. Articles, 8 to 10 typed pages, on sailboat racing and equipment, regatta reports, cruising techniques. Photos. Pays $150 per published page, on publication. Query.

YACHTING—P. O. Box 1200, 5 River Rd., Cos Cob, CT 06807. Deborah Meisels, Assoc. Ed. Articles, 2,000 words, on recreational power and sail boating. How-to and personal-experience pieces. Photos. Pays $250 to $450, on acceptance.

AUTOMOTIVE PUBLICATIONS

AAA WORLD—1999 Shepard Rd., St. Paul, MN 55116. George Ashfield, Ed. Auto safety, driving, consumer and general travel pieces, 750 to 1,500 words. Pays $300 to $600, on acceptance. Query preferred.

AMERICAN MOTORCYCLIST—American Motorcyclist Assn., Box 6114, Westerville, OH 43081-6114. Greg Harrison, Ed. Articles and fiction, to 3,000 words, on motorcycling: news coverage, personalities, tours. Photos. Pays varying rates, on publication. Query.

AUTOBODY AND THE RECONDITIONED CAR—431 Ohio Pike, Suite 300, Cincinnati, OH 45230. Fran Cummins, Assoc. Ed. How-to articles for bodyshop technicians, 1,000 to 2,000 words. Shop tips, 50 to 100 words. Pays $150 to $200 for articles, $10 for tips, on publication. Query.

CAR AND DRIVER—2002 Hogback Rd., Ann Arbor, MI 48104. Don Sherman, Ed. Articles, to 2,500 words, for enthusiasts, on car manufacturers, new developments in cars, etc. Pays to $1,500, on acceptance.

CAR CRAFT—8490 Sunset Blvd., Los Angeles, CA 90069. Jeff Smith, Ed.

Articles and photofeatures on unusual street machines, drag cars, racing events; technical pieces; action photos. Pays from $150 per page, on publication.

CHECKPOINT—P. O. Box 660460, Dallas, TX 75266. T. Pfiffner, Ed. Articles, 400 to 800 words, on automotive and safety topics; how-to's. Pays to 10¢ a word, on publication.

CORVETTE FEVER—Box 55532, Ft. Washington, MD 20744. Pat Stivers, Ed. Articles, 500 to 2,500 words, on Corvette repairs, swap meets, and personalities. Corvette-related fiction, about 700 lines, and fillers. Photos. Pays 10¢ a word, on publication.

CYCLE GUIDE—20916 Higgins Ct., Torrance, CA 90501. Charles Everitt, Ed. Articles on motorcycling. Pays $125 to $2,500, on acceptance. Query required.

CYCLE MAGAZINE—780-A Lakefield Rd., Westlake Village, CA 91361. Allyn Fleming, Man. Ed. Articles, 6 to 20 manuscript pages, on motorcycle races, history, touring, technical pieces; profiles. Photos. Pays on publication. Query.

CYCLE NEWS WEST—2201 Cherry Ave., Box 498, Long Beach, CA 90801. John Ulrich, Ed. Technical articles on motorcycling; race reports; profiles and interviews with motorcycle newsmakers. Pays $2 per column inch, on publication.

CYCLE WORLD—1499 Monrovia Ave., Newport Beach, CA 92663. Paul Dean, Ed. Technical and feature articles, 1,500 to 2,500 words, for motorcycle enthusiasts. Photos. Pays $100 to $200 per page, on publication. Query.

HORSELESS CARRIAGE GAZETTE—P. O. Box 1000, San Gabriel, CA 91776. Bradley Haugaard, Ed. Articles, 1,200 to 2,000 words, on pre-1916 cars, and related topics. Pays $50 to $70. SASE required. Photos essential.

HOT BIKE—2145 W. La Palma, Anaheim, CA 92801. Paul Garson, Ed. Articles, 250 to 2,500 words, with photos, on motorcycles. Event coverage on high performance street sport touring, and tracking motorcycles, with emphasis on Harley-Davidsons. Pays $50 to $100 per printed page, on publication.

HOT ROD—8490 Sunset Blvd., Los Angeles, CA 90069. Leonard Emanuelson, Ed. How-to pieces and articles, 500 to 5,000 words, on auto mechanics, hot rods, track and drag racing. Photo-features on custom or performance-modified cars. Pays to $150 per page, on publication.

KEEPIN' TRACK OF VETTES—P. O. Box 48, Spring Valley, NY 10977. Shelli Finkel, Ed. Articles of any length, with photos, relating to Corvettes. Pays $25 to $200, on publication.

MOTOR TREND—8490 Sunset Blvd., Los Angeles, CA 90069. Tony Swain, Ed. Articles, 250 to 2,000 words, on autos, racing, events; how-to pieces, profiles; photos. Pays $62 per manuscript page, on acceptance. Query.

MOTORCYCLIST—8490 Sunset Blvd., Los Angeles, CA 90069. Art Friedman, Ed. Articles, 1,000 to 3,000 words. Action photos. Pays varying rates, on publication. Query.

RIDER—29901 Agoura Rd., Agoura, CA 91301. Tash Matsuoka, Ed. Articles, to 3,000 words, with emphasis on travel, touring, commuting, and camping motorcyclists. Pays to $450, on publication. Query.

ROAD RIDER MAGAZINE—P. O. Box 6050, Mission Viejo, CA 92690.

Bob Carpenter, Ed. Articles, to 1,500 words, with photos or b&w illustrations, on motorcycle touring. Pays from $100, on publication. Query first.

SPORTS CAR GRAPHIC—8490 Sunset Blvd., Los Angeles, CA 90069. John Hanson, Ed. Articles, 500 to 1,000 words, on modified sports cars; technical how-to pieces. Pays to $500, on acceptance. Guidelines available.

STOCK CAR RACING—P.O. Box 715, Ipswich, MA 01938. Dick Berggren, Ed. Articles, to 6,000 words, on stock-car drivers, races, and vehicles. Photos. Pays to $350, on publication.

THREE WHEELING—Box 2260, Costa Mesa, CA 92628. Bruce Simurda, Ed. Articles, 1,000 to 1,500 words, relating to three- and four-wheel, all-terrain vehicles. Pays $60 per printed page, on publication. Query.

TURBO—9568 Hamilton Ave., P.O. Box 2712, Hamilton Beach, CA 92647. Bud Lane, Ed. Articles, 750 to 2,500 words, related to turbocharged autos. Fillers. Pays about $75 per published page, on publication.

VOLKSWAGEN'S WORLD—Volkswagen of America, Troy, MI 48099. Ed Rabinowitz, Ed. Articles, 1,000 words, related to Volkswagen cars and their owners. Color slides welcome. Pays $150 per printed page, on acceptance. Query first.

FITNESS MAGAZINES

AEROBICS & FITNESS—15250 Ventura Blvd., Suite 802, Sherman Oaks, CA 91403. Peg Angsten, Ed. Articles, 500 to 1,500 words, on fitness, aerobics, sports nutrition, anatomy and physiology. Tips on teaching exercise; profiles; and humor. Opinion pieces for "Fitness Leader Forum." Submit two copies of manuscript. Pays $60 to $160, 30 days after publication.

BRUCE JENNER'S BETTER HEALTH AND LIVING—800 Second Ave., New York, NY 10017. Julie Davis. Ed. Articles, 2 to 35 manuscript pages, dealing with better health. Pays $50 to $1,000, on acceptance and on publication. Query.

CLUB MEMBER—11028 Victory Blvd., Ste. 202, N. Hollywood, CA 91606. Rhonda Wilson, Man. Ed. Features, 3,000 words, and department pieces, 1,500 words, on health, fitness, exercise, sports, and nutrition for health club members. Pays $350 for features, on acceptance. Query.

EXERCISE FOR MEN ONLY—Empire State Bldg., Suite 6204, 350 Fifth Ave., New York, NY 10118. Richard Bennett, Ed. Articles, 2,000 words, on fitness-related subjects: growing, leisure, aerobics, books, sports, etc. Pays varying rates, on publication. Query required.

STRENGTH TRAINING FOR BEAUTY—1400 Stierlin Rd., Mountain View, CA 94043. Laura Dayton, Ed. Articles, 1,500 to 3,00 words, on strength, fitness, sports, and beauty for women body builders. Pays varying rates, on publication. Query.

SUPERFIT—Rodale Press, 33 E. Minor St. Emmaus, PA 18049. Tracy Lynn, Ed. Articles, 1,000 to 1,500 words, on technology and training for the multi-sport, recreational enthusiast. Payment varies, on publication. Query.

TOTAL FITNESS—15115 S. 76th E. Ave., Bixby, OK 74008. Andre Hinds, Man. Ed. Dana Davis, Assistant Ed. Articles, 500–1,000 words, for casual female fitness buffs on diet, fitness and exercise. How-to's. Photos. Pays 10¢ a word, on publication.

WOMEN'S SPORTS AND FITNESS—310 Town and Country Village, Palo Alto, CA 94301. Sports reports and sports fiction; profiles; how-to's, 500 to 2,500 words. Pays from $25, on publication.

WORKOUT—18455 Burbank Blvd., Suite 309, Tarzana, CA 91356. Tim Conaway, Ed. Articles on all aspects of fitness training for athletes involved in a wide variety of sports. Pays varying rates, on acceptance. Query required.

YOGA JOURNAL—2054 University Ave., Berkeley, CA 94704. Stephen Bodian, Ed. Articles, 1,200 to 3,000 words, on holistic health and yoga. Pays $50 to $150, on publication.

CONSUMER/PERSONAL FINANCE

CHANGING TIMES—1729 H St., N.W., Washington, DC 20006. No freelance material.

CONSUMERS DIGEST—5705 N. Lincoln Ave., Chicago, IL 60659. Frank L. Bowers, Ed. Articles, 500 to 3,000 words, on subjects of interest to consumers: products and services, automobiles, travel, health, fitness, consumer legal affairs, family investments and financial management. Photos. Pays from 25¢ a word, extra for photos, on publication. Buys all rights. Query with resumé and samples of writing.

EASY LIVING—1999 Shepard Rd., St. Paul, MN 55116. Articles, 1,000 to 1,800 words, for customers of financial institutions, on personal finance, lifestyle, consumerism, money, and some foreign travel. Pays $250 to $600, on acceptance. Query.

FACT: THE MONEY MANAGEMENT MAGAZINE—305 E. 46th St., New York, NY 10017. Daniel M. Kehrer, Ed.-in-Chief. Carefully researched articles on personal money management and investing, 1,500 to 2,000 words. Pieces, 1,200 to 1,800 words for departments: bonds, funds, real estate, insurance, stocks, etc. Pays from $200 to $500, on acceptance. Query.

FINANCIAL INDEPENDENCE—824 E. Baltimore St., Baltimore, MD 21202. Robert C. Carlson, Ed. Tabloid. Specific, how-to features (up to 800 words) on how to build wealth through self-employment and investing. New business ideas, management advice, and investment strategies. Pays to $100, on acceptance.

MONEY—Time-Life Bldg., New York, NY 10020. Marshall Loeb, Ed. Articles on personal finance: how to earn more money, invest more profitably, spend more intelligently and more pleasurably, save more prudently, and enhance your career. Pays on acceptance and publication. Query.

MONEY MAKER—5705 N. Lincoln Ave., Chicago, IL 60659. John Manos, Ed. Informative jargon-free articles, to 4,000 words, for beginning to sophisticated investors, on investment opportunities, personal finance, and low-priced investments. Pays 20¢ a word, on acceptance. Query for assignment.

THE MONEYPAPER—2 Madison Ave., Larchmont, NY 10538. Vita Nelson, Ed. Financial news and money-saving ideas, especially those of interest to women. Brief, well-researched articles on personal finance, money management: saving, earning, investing, taxes, insurance and related subjects. Features on women's attitudes toward money and personal experiences in solving money management problems. Pays 20¢ a word for articles, on acceptance. Query with resumé and writing sample.

MONEYPLAN MAGAZINE—3500 Western Ave., Highland Park, IL 60035. Margaret Mucklo, Ed. Informative, lively articles, 750 to 1,000 words, on financial topics (taxes, retirement, budget, etc.), for customers of financial institutions. Pays $150 to $200, on acceptance. Query required.

PUBLIC CITIZEN MAGAZINE—P.O. Box 19404, Washington, DC 20036. Bimonthly. Elliot Negin, Ed. Investigative reports and articles of timely political interest, 500 words to feature length, for members of Public Citizen: consumer rights, health and safety, environmental protection, safe energy, tax reform and government and corporate accountability. Photos, illustrations. Pays to $750.

SUCCESS—342 Madison Ave., New York, NY 10175. Scott DeGarmo, Ed.-in-Chief. Profiles of successful individuals, executives; entrepreneurs; psychology, behavior, and motivation articles, 500 to 3,500 words. Columns on personal finance and health. Pays $250, on acceptance. Query.

SYLVIA PORTER'S PERSONAL FINANCE MAGAZINE—380 Lexington Ave., New York, NY 10017. No free-lance material.

WEEKDAY—20 N. Wacker Dr., Chicago, IL 60606. Informative articles, 200 to 1,000 words, on solutions to everyday problems: consumer affairs, legal and community issues, real estate, etc. Pays $20 to $50, on acceptance.

WORLD FINANCIAL REVIEW—824 E. Baltimore St., Baltimore, MD 21202. Elizabeth Philip, Ed. Newsletter. Features and "tips" on investing abroad and business opportunities overseas. Pays on acceptance.

PROFESSIONAL/TRADE PUBLICATIONS

ACCESSORIES MAGAZINE—22 S. Smith St., Norwalk, CT 06855. Reenie Brown, Ed. Dir. Articles, will photos, for handbag, accessory and women's footwear buyers, on store displays, merchandising, retail promotions; profiles. Pays $75 to $100 for short articles, from $100 to $250 for features, on publication. Query.

ADVERTISING WORLD—150 Fifth Ave., New York, NY 10011. Edythe Cudlipp, Ed. Articles, 1,000 to 2,000 words, on international advertising. Pays varying rates, on publication. Query.

ALTERNATIVE ENERGY RETAILER—P.O. Box 2180, Waterbury, CT 06722. John Florian, Ed. Feature articles, 2,000 words, for retailers of alternative energy products—wood, coal and fireplace products and services. Interviews with successful retailers, stressing the how-to. B/W photos. Pays $200, extra for photos, on publication. Query first.

AMERICAN BANKER—One State Street Plaza, New York, NY 10004. William Zimmerman, Ed. Articles, 1,000 to 3,000 words, on banking and financial services industry. Pays varying rates, on publication. Query preferred.

AMERICAN BICYCLIST—80 Eighth Ave., New York, NY 10011. Konstantin Doren, Ed. Articles, 1,500 to 2,800 words, on sales and repair practices of successful bicycle dealers. Photos. Pays from 9¢ a word, extra for photos, on publication. Query.

AMERICAN CLAY EXCHANGE—P.O. Box 2674, La Mesa, CA 92041. Susan M. Cox, Ed. Thoroughly-researched articles to 1,000 words, for collectors and dealers of American-made pottery, with emphasis on antiques and collectibles. Pays $5 for fillers, from $100 on features, on publication.

AMERICAN COIN-OP—500 N. Dearborn St., Chicago, IL 60610. Ben Russell, Ed. Articles, to 2,500 words, with photos, on successful coin-operated laundries and dry-cleaners: promotion, decor, maintenance, etc. Pays from 6¢ a word, $6 per photo, two weeks prior to publication. Query. Send SASE for guidelines.

AMERICAN DEMOGRAPHICS—P.O. Box 68, Ithaca, NY 14851. Cheryl Russell, Ed. Articles, 1,500 to 3,000 words, on demographic trends, business demographics, and health care for strategies in industry, government, and education. Pays $100 to $300, on publication. Query.

AMERICAN FARRIERS JOURNAL—P.O. Box 700, Ayer, MA 01432. Joanne Lowry, Ed. Articles, 800 to 5,000 words, on horse handling, hoof care, tool selection, business practices, maintenance techniques, etc. Pays $50 per published page, on publication. Query.

AMERICAN PAINTING CONTRACTOR—2911 Washington Ave., St. Louis, MO 63103. Rick Hirsch, Ed. Technical articles, to 2,500 words, with photos, on industrial maintenance painting and management of painting business, for contractors and architects.

THE AMERICAN SALESMAN—424 N. Third St., Burlington, IA 52601. D. Ruschill, Ed. Sup. Articles, 900 to 1,200 words, on techniques for increasing sales. Pays 4¢ a word, on publication. Query.

ANTIQUES DEALER—1115 Clifton Ave., Clifton, NJ 07013. Nancy Adams, Ed. Articles, 1,500 words, on national and international trends and news in antiques business. Features by authorities in specific fields. Fillers, 750 words. B/W photos. Pays on publication. Query.

THE APOTHECARY—895 Cherry St., Petaluma, CA 94952. Susan Keller, Man. Ed. Articles, 2,000 to 4,000 words, for pharmacies, on management and marketing techniques, and computer topics. Pays $250, on publication. Query.

ARCHITECTURAL METALS—221 N. La Salle St., Chicago, IL 60601. Don Doherty, Ed. Articles, 1,000 to 2,500 words, on how to design, construct, erect and maintain architectural metal products. Photos, illustrations. Pays varying rates, on publication. Query.

ARCHITECTURE—1735 New York Ave., N.W., Washington, DC 20006. Donald Canty, Ed. Articles, to 3,000 words, on architecture, urban design. Book reviews. Pays $100 to $500, extra for photos. Query.

AREA DEVELOPMENT MAGAZINE—525 Northern Blvd., Great Neck, NY 11021. Tom Bergeron, Ed. Articles for top executives of manufacturing companies, on industrial and office facility planning. Pays $30 per manuscript page. Query.

ART BUSINESS NEWS—60 Ridgeway Plaza, P.O. Box 3837, Stamford, CT 06905. Jo Yanow, Ed. Articles, 1,000 words, for art dealers and framers, on trends and events of national importance to the art industry, and relevant business subjects. Pays $75, on publication. Query preferred.

ART MATERIAL TRADE NEWS—6255 Barfield Rd., Atlanta, GA 30328. Jeffrey Abugel, Ed. Articles, from 800 words, for dealers, wholesalers, and manufacturers of artist materials. Fillers. Pays 10¢ a word, on publication. Query.

AUTOMATION IN HOUSING & MANUFACTURED HOME DEALER— P.O. Box 120, Carpinteria, CA 93013. Don Carlson, Ed. Articles, 500 to 750 words, on various types of home manufacturers and dealers. Query required. Pay $300, on acceptance.

AUTOMOTIVE EXECUTIVE—8400 Westpark Dr., McLean, VA 22102. Gary E. James, Man. Ed. National Automobile Dealers Assn. Articles, 750 to 2,500 words, on management of automobile and heavy-duty truck dealerships and general business and automotive issues. Photos. Pays on acceptance. Query.

BARRISTER—American Bar Assn., 750 N. Lake Shore Dr., Chicago, IL 60611. Anthony Monahan, Ed. Articles, to 3,500 words, on legal and social affairs, for lawyers. Pays $200 to $500, on acceptance.

BARRON'S—22 Cortlandt St., New York, NY 10007. Alan Abelson, Ed. National-interest articles, 1,200 to 2,500 words, on business and finance. Pays from $500, on publication. Query.

BEER WHOLESALER—75 S.E. Fourth Ave., Delray Beach, FL 33444. Kenneth Breslauer, Ed. Articles, 8 to 10 typed pages, on business topics of interest to beer and wine wholesalers; as well as profiles of beer distributors. Pays about $120, on publication.

BETTER BUSINESS—235 East 42nd St., New York, NY 10017. John F. Robinson, Pub. Articles, 10 to 12 double-spaced pages, for the small business/minority business markets, on finance, international trade, technology, etc. Pays on publication. Query.

BLACK ENTERPRISE—130 Fifth Ave., New York, NY 10011. Earl G. Graves, Ed. Articles on money, management, careers, political issues, entrepreneurship, high-technology, and lifestyles for black professionals. Profiles. Pays on acceptance. Query.

BOATING INDUSTRY—850 Third Ave., New York, NY 10022. Olga Badillo, Ed. Articles, 1,000 to 1,500 words, on marine management, manufacturing and selling, for boat dealers. Photos. Pays varying rates, on publication. Query first.

THE BOSTON BUSINESS JOURNAL—393 D. St., Boston, MA 02210. Nancy P. McMillan, Ed. Articles, 500 to 1,200 words, with emphasis on local markets, its people, companies, economy: features, news, commentary. Pays $50 to $150, on publication.

BROADCAST ENGINEERING—P.O. Box 12901, 9221 Quivira Rd., Overland Park, KS 66212. Rhonda Wickham, Man. Ed. Articles, 1,000 to 2,800 words, on engineering and production in commercial AM and FM, educational radio and TV. Items on shortcuts and equipment modification for "Station-to-Station." Pays $150 to $250, $10 to $25 for shorts, on acceptance. Query.

BUILDER—Hanley-Wood, Inc., 655 15th St., N.W., Suite 475, Washington, DC 20005. Frank Anton, Ed. Articles, to 1,500 words, on trends and news in home building: design, marketing, new products, etc. Pays negotiable rates, on acceptance. Query.

BUSINESS AND COMMERCIAL AVIATION—Hangar C-1, Westchester Co. Airport, White Plains, NY 10604. John W. Olcott, Ed. Articles, 2,500 words, with photos, for pilots, on use of private aircraft for business transportation. Pays $100 to $500, on acceptance. Query.

BUSINESS ATLANTA—6255 Barfield Rd., Atlanta, GA 30328. Luann T. Nelson, Ed. Articles, 1,000 to 4,500 words, with Atlanta or "deep South" business angle, strong marketing slant that will be useful to top Atlanta executives and business people. Pays $300 to $800, on publication. Query with clippings.

BUSINESS COMPUTER SYSTEMS—Cahners Publishing Co., 275 Washington St., Newton, MA 02158. Terry Catchpole, Ed. Dir. Nontechnical articles on computer applications for business and corporate readers, 1,000 to 3,000 words. Pays $500 to $1,200, on acceptance. Query.

BUSINESS MARKETING—220 E. 42nd St., New York, NY 10017. Bob Donath, Ed. Articles on selling, advertising, and promoting products and services, for marketing executives. Pays competitive rates, on acceptance. Query only.

BUSINESS SOFTWARE MAGAZINE—M & T Publishing, 2464 Embarcadero Way, Palo Alto, CA 94303. Judy Lee, Man. Ed. Software applications for business-oriented audience; corporate software-user profiles, 1,000 to 2,000 words. No computer jargon. Send for writer's guidelines. Pays varying rates, before publication. Query.

THE BUSINESS TIMES—544 Tolland St., E. Hartford, CT 06108. Deborah Hallberg, Man. Ed. Articles on new products, successful companies, business topics, for Connecticut executives. Pays $1 per column inch, on publication. Query.

BUSINESS TODAY—P.O. Box 10010, 1720 Washington Blvd., Ogden, UT 84409. Brent Israelsen, Ed. Articles, 1,000 to 1,500 words; profiles of corporate executives. Pays 15¢ a word, on acceptance. Query.

BUSINESS VIEW OF SOUTHWEST FLORIDA—P.O. Box 1546, Naples, FL 33939. Ellie Summer, Pub. Innovative articles and columns, 750 to 1,500 words, on business, economics, finance; profiles of business leaders; new trends in technology and advances in management techniques. Real estate and banking trends. Regional angle a must. Pays $75 to $200, on publication. Query.

CALIFORNIA BUSINESS—4221 Wilshire Blvd., Suite 400, Los Angeles, CA 90010. Margaret Hart, Ed. Articles, 1,200 to 1,500 words, on business and econometric issues in California. Pays varying rates, on acceptance. Query.

THE CALIFORNIA HIGHWAY PATROLMAN—2030 V St., Sacramento, CA 95818. Carol Perri, Ed. Articles, 500 to 3,500 words, on traffic safety, recreational vehicle use, consumerism, historic California. Photos. Pays 2½¢ per word, extra for photos, on publication.

CALIFORNIA HORSE REVIEW—P.O. Box 2437, Fair Oaks, CA 95628. Carolee Weber, Ed. Articles, 1,500 to 3,000 words, for professional horsemen, on breeding, training; how-to pieces. Pays $50 to $125, on publication. Query preferred.

CALIFORNIA LAWYER—555 Franklin St., San Francisco, CA 94102. Jonathan R. Maslow, Ed. Articles, 2,500 to 3,000 words, for attorneys in California, on legal subjects (or the legal aspects of a given political or social issue); how-to's on improving techniques in law practice. Pays $250 to $500, on acceptance. Query.

CAMPGROUND MANAGEMENT—500 Hyacinth Pl., Highland Park, IL 60035. Mike Byrnes, Ed. Detailed articles, 500 to 2,000 words, on managing recreational vehicle campgrounds. Photos. Pays $50 to $200, after publication.

CASHFLOW—1807 Glenview, Glenview, IL 60025. Vince DiPaolo, Ed.

Articles, 1,500 to 2,500 words, for treasury managers in public and private institutions: cash management; investments; domestic and international financing; developments in law, economics, and tax. Fillers, to 1,000 words. Pays $9.00 per inch, on publication. Query.

CERAMIC SCOPE—3632 Ashworth N., Seattle, WA 98103. Michael Scott, Ed. Articles, 1,000 to 2,000 words, on retail or wholesale business operations of hobby ceramic studios. Photos. Pays 5¢ a word, extra for photos, on acceptance. Query.

CHEMICAL WEEK—1221 Ave. of the Americas, New York, NY 10020. Patrick P. McCurdy, Ed.-in-Chief. News pieces, to 200 words, on chemical business. Pays $10 per column inch, on acceptance. Query.

CHINA, GLASS & TABLEWARE—P.O. Box 2147, Clifton, NJ 07015. Sue Grisham, Ed. Case histories and interviews, 1,500 to 2,500 words, with photos, on merchandising of china and glassware. Pays $45 per page, on publication. Query.

CHRISTIAN BOOKSELLER—396 E. St. Charles Rd., Wheaton, IL 60188. Karen Tomberg, Ed. Articles, with photos, on all phases of Christian bookstore operation, ideas, news reports, store profiles, industry analyses, audiovisual and music merchandising how-to. Pays $10 to $100, on publication. Query. Send SASE for writer's guidelines.

CHRISTIAN BUSINESS LIFE DIGEST—3108 W. Lake St., Minneapolis, MN 55402. Terry White, Ed. Articles, 500 to 1,200 words, for Christian business and professional people. Fillers; anecdotes. Pays 5¢ a word, on publication. Query for features.

CLEANING MANAGEMENT—15550-D Rockfield, Irvine, CA 92718. R. Daniel Harris, Jr., Pub. Articles, 1,000 to 1,500 words, on managing efficient cleaning and maintenance operations. Photos. Pays 10¢ a word, extra for photos, on publication.

COLLEGE STORE EXECUTIVE—P.O. Box 1500, Westbury, NY 11590. Catherine Orobona, Ed. Articles, 1,000 words, for college store industry only; news; profiles. No general business or how-to articles. Photos. Pays $2 a column inch, extra for photos, on acceptance. Query.

THE COMICS JOURNAL—Fantagraphics, Inc., 707 Camino Manzanas, Thousand Oaks, CA 91360. Gary Groth, Ed. Criticism, essays, personality profiles, 700 to 4,000 words. Pays 1½ a word, on publication.

COMMERCIAL CARRIER JOURNAL—Chilton Way, Radnor, PA 19089. Jerry Standley, Ed. Factual articles on private fleets and for-hire trucking operations. Pays from $50, on acceptance. Query.

COMPUTER CONSULTANT—208 N. Townsend St., Syracuse, NY 13203. Articles, to 2,500 words, on innovative sales techniques, and tips for increasing profitability for computer consultants. Pays varing rates, on publication. Query required.

COMPUTER DECISIONS MAGAZINE—10 Mulholland Dr., Hasbrouck Hgt., NJ 07604. Mel Mandell, Ed. Articles, 800 to 4,000 words, on generic uses of computer systems. Pays $30 to $100 per printed page, on acceptance. Query.

COMPUTER GRAPHICS WORLD—119 Russell St., Littleton, MA 01460. Charles Barrett, Man. Ed. Articles, 1,000 to 5,000 words, on computer graphics technology and its applications. Photos. Pays $50 per printed page, on publication. Query.

COMPUTING FOR BUSINESS (formerly *Interface Age*)—7330 Adams St., Paramount, CA 90723. Les Spindle, Ed. Articles, 1,000 to 5,000 words, on microcomputer applications in the business field. Product reviews. Pays $50 to $80 per published page, on publication.

CONCRETE INTERNATIONAL: DESIGN AND CONSTRUCTION—Box 19150, 22400 W. Seven Mile Rd., Detroit, MI 48219. Robert E. Wilde, Ed. Articles, 6 to 15 double-spaced pages, on concrete construction and design, with drawings and photos. Pays varying rates, on publication. Query.

CONTACTS—Box 407, North Chatham, NY 12132. Joseph Strack, Ed. Articles, 300 to 1,500 words, on management of dental laboratories, lab techniques, and equipment. Pays from 5¢ a word, on acceptance.

CONVENIENCE STORE NEWS—254 W. 31st St., New York, NY 10001. Denise Melinsky, Ed. Features and news items, 500 to 750 words, for convenience store owners, operators, and suppliers. Photos, with captions. Pays $3 per column inch, extra for photos, on publication. Query.

COOKING FOR PROFIT—P.O. Box 367, Fond du Lac, WI 54935. Bill Dittrich, Ed. Practical how-to articles, 1,000 words, on commercial food preparation, managment; case studies, etc. Pays $150 to $250, on publication.

CRAIN'S CHICAGO BUSINESS—740 Rush St., Chicago, IL 60611. Dan Miller, Ed. Business articles about the Midwest exclusively. Pays $9 per column inch, on acceptance.

D & B REPORTS—299 Park Ave., New York, NY 10171. Patricia W. Hamilton, Ed. Articles, 1,500 to 2,500 words, for top management of smaller businesses; government regulations, export opportunities, employee relations; how-to's on cash management, sales, productivity, etc. Pays on acceptance. Query.

DAIRY HERD MANAGEMENT—P.O. Box 67, Minneapolis, MN 55440. Sheila Widmer Wikla, Ed. Articles, 500 to 2,000 words, with photos, on techniques and equipment used in well-managed large and medium dairy operations. Pays $100 to $200, on acceptance. Query.

DAIRY RECORD (formerly *National Dairy News*)—5725 E. River Rd., Chicago, IL 60631. Jerry Dryer, Pub. Articles, to 2,500 words, on innovative dairies, dairy processing operations, marketing successes, and new dairy products, for milk handlers, and makers of cheese, butter, yogurt and ice cream. Fillers, 25 to 150 words. Pays $25 to $300, $5 to $25 for fillers, on publication.

DEALERSCOPE—401 N. Broad St., Philadelphia, PA 19108. Neil Spann, Ed. Articles, 750 to 3,000 words, for dealers, distributors, and manufacturers of audio, video, personal computers, satellite TV, etc., on marketing and finance. Profiles; news items. Pays varying rates, on publication. Query first, with samples.

DENTAL ECONOMICS—P.O. Box 3408, Tulsa, OK 74101. Dick Hale, Ed. Articles 1,200 to 3,500 words, on business side of dental practice, patient and staff communication, personal investments, etc. Pays $100 to $250, on acceptance.

DOMESTIC ENGINEERING—135 Addison St., Elmhurst, IL 60126. Stephen J. Shafer, Ed. Articles, to 3,000 words, on plumbing, heating, air conditioning, and process piping. Photos. Pays $20 to $35 per printed page, on publication.

DRAPERIES & WINDOW COVERINGS—P.O. Box 13079, North Palm Beach, FL 33408. Lynn Mohr, Ed. Articles, 1,000 to 2,000 words, for retailers, wholesalers, designers and manufacturers of draperies and window coverings. Profiles, with photos, of successful businesses in the industry. Pays $150 to $250, after acceptance. Query.

DRUG TOPICS—680 Kinderkamack Rd., Oradell, NJ 07649. Valentine A. Cardinale, Ed. News items, 500 words, with photos, on drug retailers and associations. Merchandising features, 1,000 to 1,500 words. Pays $25 to $50 for news, $50 to $350 for features, on acceptance. Query for features.

DUN'S BUSINESS MONTH—875 Third Ave., New York, NY 10022. Arlene Hershman, Ed. Articles, 1,500 to 2,500 words, on trends in corporation management, the economy, finance, and company performance. Pays from $500, on acceptance.

EARNSHAW'S INFANTS & CHILDREN'S REVIEW—393 Seventh Ave., New York, NY 10001. Christina Gruber, Ed. Articles on retailers, retail promotions, and statistics for children's wear industry. Pays $50 to $150, on publication. Query. Limited market.

EE'S ELECTRONICS DISTRIBUTOR—707 Westchester Ave., White Plains, NY 10604. Edward J. Walter, Ed.-in-Chief. News items for distributors of electronic parts and equipment. Pays $2 per column inch, on publication. Query.

ELECTRICAL CONTRACTOR—7315 Wisconsin Ave., Bethesda, MD 20814. Larry C. Osius, Ed. Articles, 1,000 to 1,500 words, with photos, on construction or management techniques for electrical contractors. Pays $90 per printed page, before publication. Query.

ELECTRONICS WEST—2250 N. 16th St., Suite 105, Phoenix, AZ 85006. Walter J. Schuch, Ed. Articles, 1,000 to 3,000 words, on the electronics industry in the southwest: technological innovations and advances, management techniques, profiles of successful companies, etc. Pays 10¢ a word, on acceptance. Query preferred.

EMPLOYEE SERVICES MANAGMENT—NESRA, 2400 S. Downing, Westchester, IL 60153. June Cramer, Ed. Articles, 800 to 2,500, for human resource, fitness, and employee service professionals. Pays by assignment. Query first.

ENGINEERED SYSTEMS—7314 Hart St., Mentor, OH 44060. Robert L. Schwed, Ed. Articles, case histories, on business management and legal issues related to HVAC engineering systems in large buildings or industrial plants. Pays $125 per page and illustration, on publication. Query.

THE ENGRAVERS JOURNAL—26 Summit St., Box 318, Brighton, MI 48116. Michael J. Davis, Man. Ed. Articles, varying lengths, related to the engraving industry. Photos; drawings. Pays $60 to $175, on acceptance. Query first.

ENTRÉE—7 E. 12th St., New York, NY 10003. Geri Brin, Ed. Articles, 100 to 2,500 words, on trends and people in better housewares industry, both retailers and manufacturers. Pays $200 to $400, on publication. Query.

ENTREPRENEUR—2311 Pontius Ave., Los Angeles, CA 90064. How-to's, 1,500 to 2,500 words, for aspiring and independent business owners, on running a business: advertising, business techniques, and new business ideas. Fillers; columns, 100 to 500 words. Pays 15¢ a word, from $100 for features, $25 for columns, on acceptance. Query.

EXPORT MAGAZINE—386 Park Ave. South, New York, NY 10016. Robert Weingarten, Ed. Articles, 1,000 to 1,500 words, on the export business in foreign countries. Profiles of agents and distributors. Pays $300 to $350, with photos, on acceptance. Query preferred.

FACT: THE MONEY MANAGEMENT MAGAZINE—305 E. 46th St., New York, NY 10017. Daniel M. Kehrer, Ed.-in-Chief. Carefully researched articles on personal money management and investing, 1,500 to 2,000 words. Pieces, 1,200 to 1,800 words for departments: bonds, funds, real estate, insurance, stocks, etc. Pays from $200 to $500, on acceptance. Query required.

FARM BUILDING NEWS—260 Regency Court, Waukesha, WI 53816. Frank Lessiter, Ed. Articles, 500 to 2,000 words, for rural contractors of farm buildings, grain systems confinement equipment and non-farm rural structures. Pays $50 to $175, on publication. Query.

FARM JOURNAL—230 W. Washington Sq., Philadelpia, PA 19105. Practical business articles on growing crops and producing livestock. Pays $50 to $500, on acceptance. Query required.

FENCE INDUSTRY—6255 Barfield Rd., Atlanta, GA 30328. Bill Coker, Ed./Assoc. Pub. Articles on fence industry; interviews with dealer-erectors; on-the-job pieces. Photos. Pays 10¢ a word, extra for photos, on publication. Query.

THE FISH BOAT—P.O. Box 2400, Covington, LA 70434. William A. Sarratt, Ed. Articles on commercial fishing, seafood marketing and processing. Short items on commercial fishing and boats. Pays varying rates, on acceptance. Query.

FITNESS MANAGEMENT—P.O. Box 1198, Solana Beach, CA 92075. Edward H. Pitts, Ed. Authoritative features, 750 to 2,500 words, and news shorts, 100 to 750 words, for owners, managers, and program directors of fitness centers. Content must be in keeping with current medical practice: no fads. Pays 8¢ a word, on publication. Query.

FLORIST—29200 Northwestern Hwy., P.O. Box 2227, Southfield, MI 48037. Susan Nicholas, Man. Ed. Articles, to 2,000 words, with photos, on retail florist business improvement. Photos: Pays 8¢ a word, extra for photos.

FLOWERS &—Teleflora Plaza, Suite 260, 12233 W. Olympic Blvd., Los Angeles, CA 90064. Marcianne Crestani, Exec. Ed. Articles, 1,000 to 2,000 words, with how-to information for retail florists. Pays $400, on acceptance.

FOOD MANAGEMENT—747 Third Ave., New York, NY 10017. Donna Boss, Ed. Articles, on foodservice in healthcare, schools, colleges, prisons, business and industry. Trends and how-to pieces, with management tie-in. Pays to $350. Query.

THE FOREMAN'S LETTER—24 Rope Ferry Rd., Waterford, CT 06386. Carl Thunberg, Ed. Interviews, with photos, with top-notch supervisors and foremen. Pays 8¢ to 12¢ a word, extra for photos, on acceptance.

GARDEN DESIGN—1733 Connecticut Ave., NW, Washington, DC 20009.

Kenneth Druse, Ed. Publication of the Association of American Landscape Architects. Articles, 1,500 to 2,000 words, on classic and contemporary examples of residential landscape, garden, art, history, and design. Interviews. Pays $300, on publication. Query.

GEORGIA BUSINESS—1800 Water Place, Suite 100, Atlanta, GA 30341. Articles, 1,500 to 2,000 words, related to business and Georgia. Pays varying rates, on publication. Query required.

GIFTS & DECORATIVE ACCESSORIES—51 Madison Ave., New York, NY 10010. Phyllis Sweed, Co-Pub./Ed. Articles, 1,500 to 3,000 words, with photos, on promotions, displays, design features of quality retail shops for gifts, tabletop, gourmet, stationery, greeting cards. Color photos. Pays to $150, extra for photos, on publication.

GLASS DIGEST—310 Madison Ave., New York, NY 10017. Oscar S. Glasberg, Ed. Articles, 1,200 to 1,500 words, on building projects and glass/metal dealers, distributors, storefront and glazing contractors. Pays varying rates, on publication.

GLASS NEWS (formerly *The National Glass Budget*)—P. O. Box 7138, Pittsburgh, PA 15213. Liz Scott, Man. Ed. Articles, to 1,500 words, on developments in glass manufacturing, glass factories, types of glass. Personality profiles. Pays 5¢ to 10¢ a word, on publication. Query with SASE.

GOLF SHOP OPERATIONS—P.O. Box 395, Trumbull, CT 06611. Nick Romano, Ed. Articles, 200 to 800 words, with photos, on successful golf shop operations; new ideas for merchandising, display, bookkeeping. Short pieces on golf professionals. Pays $175 to $225, on publication. Query with outline.

THE GOURMET RETAILER—1545 N.E. 123rd St., North Miami, FL 33161. Michael Keighley, Ed. Articles, 2,500 to 3,000 words, for retailers, on products and trends, merchandising, and sales promotion. Pays 5¢ a word, on publication.

GRAPHIC ARTS MONTHLY—875 Third Ave., New York, NY 10022. Roger Ynostroza, Ed. Technical articles, 1,500 to 2,000 words, on printing industry. No profiles. Pays 6¢ to 10¢ a word, on publication. Query.

GREENHOUSE MANAGER—P.O. Box 1868, Fort Worth, TX 76101. Jerry Circelli, Ed. Articles, 2,000 words, accompanied by color slides, of interest to professional greenhouse growers. Pays $100 to $300, on publication. Query required.

HARDWARE AGE—Chilton Way, Radnor, PA 19089. Terry Gallagher, Ed. Articles on merchandising methods in hardware outlets. Photos. Pays on acceptance.

HARDWARE MERCHANDISER—7300 N. Cicero Ave., Chicago, IL 60646. J. W. Stapleton, Ed. Articles, to 1,000 words, with photos, on merchandising in hardware and discount stores. Pays on acceptance.

HARVARD BUSINESS REVIEW—Harvard Graduate School of Business Administration, Soldiers Field Rd., Boston, MA 02163. Query Editors on new ideas about business management, of interest to senior executives. Pays negotiable rates, on publication.

HEALTH FOODS BUSINESS—567 Morris Ave., Elizabeth, NJ 07208. Alan Richman, Ed. Articles, 1,500 words, with photos, on managing health-food stores: security, health cosmetics, advertising. Pays on publication. Query.

HEATING/PIPING/AIR CONDITIONING—2 Illinois Cntr., Chicago, IL

60601. Robert T. Korte, Ed. Articles, to 5,000 words, on heating, piping and air conditioning systems in industrial plants and large buildings; engineering information. Pays $40 per printed page, on publication. Query.

HIGH TECH MARKETING—1460 Post Rd. E., Westport, CT 06880. Phil Maher, Ed. Feature-length articles, 9 to 15 pages, relating to the marketing of high-tech products. Pays 15¢ a word, on acceptance. Query required.

HISPANIC BUSINESS—P.O. Box 6757, Santa Barbara, CA 93160. Jesus Chavarria, Ed./Pub. Features, 2,000 words, on Hispanic business and professional life in U.S. for the Hispanic businesspeople. Articles on culture, education, demographics and career planning. Shorter pieces, 850 words. Pays $250 for features, $75 for shorter pieces, on publication.

HOME FASHIONS TEXTILES—633 Third Ave., New York, NY 10017. Francy Searles, Ed. In-depth features on fashion trends and management; profiles; reports of new products. Photos. Pays varying rates, on acceptance. Query preferred.

HOSPITAL GIFT SHOP MANAGEMENT—7628 Densmore, Van Nuys, CA 91406. Barbara Feiner, Ed. Articles, 750 to 2,500 words, with managerial tips and sales pointers; hospital and merchandise profiles. Pays $10 to $100, on acceptance. Query required.

HOSPITAL SUPERVISOR'S BULLETIN—24 Rope Ferry Rd., Waterford, CT 06386. Susan Rosa, Ed. Interviews, articles with nonmedical hospital supervisors on departmental problem solving. Pays 12¢ a word. Query.

HOSPITALS—211 E. Chicago Ave., Suite 700, Chicago, IL 60611. Frank Sabatino, Man. Ed. Articles, 1,000 to 2,000 words, for hospital administrators. Pays varying rates, on acceptance. Query.

ICP BUSINESS SOFTWARE REVIEW—9000 Keystone Crossing, Indianapolis, IN 46240. Louis W. Harm, Ed. Articles, 300 to 3,000 words, on the computer business, centering on management software: productivity, profitability, return-on-investment. Pays $50 to $500, on publication. Query.

IMPRESSIONS—15400 Knoll Trail Dr., Dallas, TX 75248. Carl Piazza, Ed. Articles for the imprinted sportswear industry, on trends, retail techniques, market information, etc. Pays $50 to $100, on publication. Query.

IN BUSINESS—Box 323, Emmaus, PA 18049. Jerome Goldstein, Ed. Articles on marketing, advertising, and financing, 1,500 to 2,000 words, for people who run small businesses. Profiles of growing small companies. Pays to $200, on publication. Query.

INC.—38 Commercial Wharf, Boston, MA 02110. George Gendron, Ed. Feature articles about how owners and managers of small companies solve common problems. Pays to $1,500 on acceptance. Query.

INCOME OPPORTUNITIES—380 Lexington Ave., New York, NY 10017. Stephen Wagner, Ed. Helpful articles, 2,000 to 3,000 words, on how to make money, how to run a successful business, improve sales, etc. Pays varying rates, on acceptance. Query.

INDUSTRIAL CHEMICAL NEWS—633 Third Ave., New York, NY 10017. Irvin J. Schwartz. Ed. Articles, 500 to 2,000 words, on technical and professional issues of interest to chemists working in industrial labs. Pays $150 to $600, on acceptance. Query.

INDUSTRIAL DESIGN—330 W. 42nd St., New York, NY 10036. Steven Holt, Man. Ed. Articles to 2,000 words, on product development, design management, graphic design, design history, for designers and marketing executives. Profiles of designers and corporations that use design effectively. Pays $250 to $500, on publication.

INFOSYSTEMS—Hitchcock Bldg., Wheaton, IL 60188. Wayne L. Rhodes, Ed. How-to articles, 6 to 8 pages, for managers in the data processing field. Pays negotiable rates, on publication. Query.

INSTANT PRINTER—P.O. Box 368, Northbrook, IL 60065. Dan Witte, Ed. Articles, 5 to 7 typed pages, for owners and/or managers of printing businesses specializing in retail printing: case histories, how-to's, technical pieces, interesting ideas. Opinion pieces, 1 to 2 typed pages. Photos. Pays $150 to $200 ($25 to $50 for opinion pieces), extra for photos, on publication. Query preferred.

INTERFACE AGE—See *Computing for Business.*

JOB SITE—P.O. Box 810, Wayne, MI 48184. Phil Roman, Assoc. Ed. Articles, 1,000 to 4,000 words, for professional surveyors in the construction industry. Photos. Pays $100 to $400, on publication.

KIDS FASHIONS—210 Boylston St., Chestnut Hill, MA 02167. Mary Ann Wood, Man. Ed. Articles, 1,000 to 2,000 words, with photos, on the retailing and merchandising of children's apparel and gift items. Pays from $150, on acceptance.

LOS ANGELES BUSINESS JOURNAL—3345 Wilshire, #207, Los Angeles, CA 90010. David Yochum, Ed. Feature articles on specific industries in the five-county Los Angeles area, stressing the how-to, trends and analysis. Pays on publication.

LOS ANGELES LAWYER—Box 55020, Los Angeles, CA 90055. Susan Pettit, Ed. Journalistic features, 12 to 16 pages, and consumer articles, 8 to 12 pages, on legal topics. Pays $200 to $600, on acceptance. Query required.

LOTUS—1 Broadway, Cambridge, MA 02141. Christopher P. Morgan, Ed. Articles, 1,500 to 2,000 words, for business and professional people using Lotus software. Query with outline required. Payment varies, on acceptance.

LP-GAS MAGAZINE—131 W. First St., Duluth, MN 55802. Zane Chastain, Ed. Articles, 1,500 to 2,500 words, with photos, on LP-Gas dealer operations: marketing, management, etc. Photos. Pays to 15¢ a word, extra for photos, on acceptance. Query.

MADISON AVENUE MAGAZINE—369 Lexington Ave., New York, NY 10017. Stuart Emmrich, Ed. Feature articles on advertising and marketing strategy. Pays $300 to $700.

MAGAZINE DESIGN & PRODUCTION—4551 W. 107th St., Suite 210, Overland Park, KS 66207. Maureen Waters, Asst. Ed. Articles, 6 to 10 types pages, on magazine design and production: printing technology, typesetting, computers, lay out design, etc. Pays $100 to $200, on publication. Query required.

MANAGE—2210 Arbor Blvd., Dayton, OH 45439. Doug Shaw, Ed. Articles, 1,500 to 2,200 words, with photos, on management and supervision for first-line and middle managers. Pays 5¢ a word.

MANUFACTURING SYSTEMS—Hitchcock Bldg., Wheaton, IL 60188. Tom Inglesby, Ed. Articles, 500 to 2,000 words, on computer and information systems for industry executives seeking to increase productivity in manufacturing firms. Pays 10¢ to 20¢ a word, on acceptance. Query required.

MEDICENTER MANAGEMENT—825 S. Barrington Ave., Los Angeles, CA 90049. Dan Barton, Ed. Articles, 2,500 to 3,000 words, on medical/topics. Payment varies, on acceptance. Query required.

MEMPHIS BUSINESS JOURNAL (formerly *Mid-South Business*)—4515 Poplar, Suite 322, Memphis, TN 38117. Barney DuBois, Ed. Articles, to 2,000 words, on business, industry trade, agri-business and finance in the Mid-South trade area. Pays $80 to $200, on acceptance.

MINIATURES DEALER—Clifton House, Clifton, VA 22024. Geraldine Willems, Ed. Articles, about 1,500 words, on advertising, promotion, merchandising of miniatures and dolls and other small business concerns. Pays to $250, on publication.

MIX MAGAZINE—2608 Ninth St., Berkeley, CA 94710. David Schwartz, Ed. Articles, varying lengths, for professionals, on audio, video, music entertainment technology. Pays 10¢ a word, on publication. Query required.

MODERN HEALTHCARE—740 N. Rush St., Chicago, IL 60611. Donald Johnson, Ed. Features on management, finance, building design and construction, and new technology for hospitals, nursing homes, and other health care institutions. Pays $7 per column inch, on publication. Query.

MODERN TILE DEALER—P.O. Box 5417, 110 N. Miller Rd., Akron, OH 44313. Greg Smith, Ed. Merchandising management and service articles, 1,000 to 1,500 words, with photos, on independent tire dealers and retreaders. Pays $200 to $250, on publication.

MONEY MAGAZINE—Time & Life Bldg., New York, NY 10020. Marshall Loeb, Man. Ed. Articles on various aspects of personal finance and investment. Welcomes article suggestions. Pays $2,500 and up for major articles.

MONEY MAKER—5705 N. Lincoln Ave., Chicago, IL 60659. John Manos, Ed. Informative jargon-free articles, to 4,000 words, for beginning to sophisticated investors, on investment opportunities, personal finance, and low-priced investments. Pays 20¢ a word, on acceptance. Query for assignment.

THE MONEYPAPER—2 Madison Ave., Larchmont, NY 10538. Vita Nelson, Ed. Financial news and money-saving ideas, especially those of interest to women. Brief, well-researched articles on personal finance, money management: saving, earning, investing, taxes, insurance and related subjects. Features on women's attitudes toward money and personal experiences in solving money management problems. Pays $75 for articles, on publication. Query with resumé and writing sample.

NATIONAL DAIRY NEWS—See *Dairy Record*.

NATIONAL FISHERMAN—21 Elm St., Camden, ME 04843. James W. Fullilove. Ed. Articles, 200 to 2,000 words, aimed at commercial fishermen and boatbuilders. Pays from $2.50 per inch, extra for photos, on publication. Query.

607

THE NATIONAL GLASS BUDGET—See *Glass News.*

NATION'S BUSINESS—1615 H St., NW, Washington, DC 20062. Lively articles on business-related topics, including management advice and success stories. Pays negotiable rates, after acceptance. Query.

NEW BUSINESS—P.O. Box 3312, Sarasota, FL 33578. Business-related articles of regional/general interest. Pays $75 to $225, on publication. Query.

NEW CAREER WAYS NEWSLETTER—P.O. Box 1142, Haverhill, MA 01830. William J. Bond, Ed. How-to articles, 1,500 to 2,000 words, on new ways to succeed in business careers. Pays varying rates, on publication. Query with outline.

NORTHERN HARDWARE—2965 Broadmoor Valley Rd., Suite B, Colorado Springs, CO 80906. Edward Gonzales, Ed. Articles, 800 to 1,000 words, on unusual hardware stores and promotions in Northwest and Midwest. Photos. Pays 4¢ a word, extra for photos, on publication. Query.

NURSINGWORLD JOURNAL—470 Boston Post Rd., Weston, MA 02193. Ira Alterman, Ed. Articles, 500 to 1,500 words, for nurses and nurse educators, on all aspects of nursing. Photos. Pays from 25¢ per column inch, on publication.

OPPORTUNITY MAGAZINE—6 N. Michigan Ave., Suite 1405, Chicago, IL 60602. Jack Weissman, Ed. Articles, 900 words, on sales psychology, sales techniques, self-improvement. Pays $20 to $40, on publication.

THE OSHA COMPLIANCE LETTER—24 Rope Ferry Rd., Waterford, CT 06386. James Bolger, Ed. Interview-based articles, 800 to 1,250 words, for safety professionals, on solving OSHA-related safety problems. Pays to 12¢ a word, on acceptance, after editing. Query.

PAPERBOARD PACKAGING—7500 Old Oak Blvd., Cleveland, OH 44130. Mark Arzoumanian, Ed. Articles, any length, on corrugated containers, folding cartons and setup boxes. Pays on publication. Query with outline.

PC WEEK—15 Crawford St., Needham, MA 02194. Lois Paul, Exec. Ed. Features, 1,500 to 2,500 words, for large corporate users of PCs; profiles; reviews of PC-related products. Pays $500 to $1,000, on publication. Query required.

PET BUSINESS—7330 N.W. 66th St., Miami, FL 33166. Bob Behme, Pub./ Ed. Articles, 300 to 1,000 words, on all aspects of pet business: success stories, profiles, retail shops, manufacturers, distributors. All material must have a news slant. Photos. Pays to 10¢ a word, extra for photos, on acceptance.

PETS/SUPPLIES/MARKETING—One E. First St., Duluth, MN 55802. David D. Kowalski, Ed. Articles, 1,000 to 1,200 words, with photos, on pet shops, and pet and product merchandising. Pays 10¢ a word, extra for photos. No fiction or news clippings. Query.

PHOENIX BUSINESS JOURNAL—1817 N. 3rd St., Suite 100, Phoenix, AZ 85004. Chambers Williams, Ed. Articles on leading and innovative businesses and business people in Arizona. Photos. Pays $2.75 to $3.50 per column inch, on publication.

PHOTO MARKETING—3000 Picture Pl., Jackson, MI 49201. M. Therese

Wood, Man. Ed. Business articles, 500 words, for owners and managers of camera stores or photo processing labs. Pays 10¢ a word, extra for photos, on publication.

PHYSICIAN'S MANAGEMENT—7500 Old Oak Blvd., Cleveland, OH 44130. Bob Feigenbaum, Ed. Articles, about 2,500 to 3,000 words, on finance, investments, malpractice, and office management for primary care physicians. No clinical pieces. Pays $125 per printed page, on acceptance. Query.

P.O.B.—P.O. Box 810, Wayne, MI 48184. Jeanne M. Helfrick, Assoc. Ed. Technical and business articles, 1,000 to 4,000 words, for professionals and technicians in the surveying and mapping fields. Technical tips on field and office procedures and equipment maintenance. Pays $150 to $400, on publication.

POLICE PRODUCT NEWS—P.O. Box 847, Carlsbad, CA 92008. James Daigh, Ed. Reviews of new products and equipment, and profiles of people in the law enforcement profession, 1,000 to 4,000 words. Fiction. Photos. Pays from $100 to $300, extra for photos, on publication. Writers' guidelines sent on request.

POOL & SPA NEWS—3923 W. Sixth St., Los Angeles, CA 90020. News pieces on swimming pool, spa, and hot tub industry. Photos. Pays 5¢ to 8¢ a word, extra for photos, on publication. Query.

PREMIUM/INCENTIVE BUSINESS—1515 Broadway, New York, NY 10036. Deborah Hauss, Ed. Articles, 2 to 6 typewritten pages, for sales promotion executives and premium buyers, on premium offers, travel, incentive programs, interviews. Pays on publication. Query required.

THE PRESS—302 Grote St., Buffalo, NY 14207. Mary Lou Vogt, Ed. Quarterly. Short profiles, 800 to 1,200 words, on cartoonists and industry and advertising personalities, for advertising executives at newspapers and ad agencies. Pieces on unusual hobbies or occupations. Travel articles. Humor. Pays 10¢ a word, on acceptance.

PRIVATE PRACTICE—Box 12489, Oklahoma City, OK 73157. Shannon Wingrove, Asst. Ed. Articles, 1,500 to 2,000 words, on state or local legislation affecting medical field. Pays $250 to $350, on acceptance.

PROFESSIONAL OFFICE DESIGN—111 Eighth Ave., New York, NY 10011. Tim Robinson, Ed. Articles, to 1,500 words, on space planning and design for offices in the fields of law, medicine, finance, accounting, advertising, and architecture/design. Pays competitive rates, on publication. Query required.

RADIO ELECTRONICS—200 Park Ave., S., New York, NY 10003. Art Kleiman, Ed. Technical articles, 1,500 to 3,000 words, on electronic equipment. Pays $50 to $500, on acceptance.

RESORT & HOTEL MANAGEMENT—P.O. Box A, Del Mar, CA 92014. Articles, 1,000 to 1,500 words, on successful resort and hotel operation and management.

ROBOTICS AGE—174 Concord St., Peterborough, NH 03458. Raymond G. A. Cote, Ed. Technical, tutorial pieces, on robotics technology. Pays varying rates, on publication.

THE ROOFER—P.O. Box 06253, Fort Myers, FL 33906. Karen S. Parker, Ed. Non-technical articles, 500 to 1,000 words, on roofing-related topics: new processes and products, energy savings, roofing concepts, etc., safety and medical pieces; interviews with contractors. Pays negotiable rates, on publication.

RV BUSINESS—29901 Agoura Rd., Agoura, CA 91301. Sheryl Harris, Man. Ed. Articles, 1,500 to 3,000 words, on manufacturing, financing, selling and servicing recreational vehicles. Articles on legislative matters affecting the industry. Pays to $400, on acceptance.

SALES & MARKETING MANAGEMENT—Bill Communications Inc., 633 Third Ave., New York, NY 10017. Robert H. Albert, Ed. Short articles for sales and marketing executives of large corporations. Pays varying rates, on acceptance. Query required.

SATELLITE DEALER—Box 2700, Dept. D., Haily, ID 83333. Ron Rudolph, Ed. Articles, 1,000 to 2,000 words, for retailers of satellite systems. Pays $175 to $300, on publication. Query.

SECURITY MANAGEMENT—1655 N. Ft. Myer Dr., Suite 1200, Arlington, VA 22209. Mary Alice Crawford, Sr. Ed. Articles, 2,500 to 3,000 words, on legislative issues related to security; case studies of innovative security applications; management topics: employee relations, training programs, etc. Pays 10¢ a word, on publication. Query.

SELLING DIRECT—6255 Barfield Rd., Atlanta, GA 30328. Robert Rawls, Ed. Articles, 400 to 1,800 words, for independent salespersons selling to homes, stores, industries, and businesses. Pays 10¢ a word, on publication.

SNACK FOOD MAGAZINE—131 W. First St., Duluth, MN 55802. Jerry Hess, Ed. Articles, 600 to 1,500 words, on trade news, personalities, promotions, production in snack food manufacturing industry. Short pieces; photos. Pays 12¢ to 15¢ a word, extra for photos, on acceptance. Query.

SOFTWARE NEWS—1900 W. Park Dr., Westborough, MA 01581. Edward J. Bride, Ed. Technical features, 1,000 to 1,200 words, for computer literate audience, on how software products can be used. Pays about $150 to $200, on publication. Query preferred.

SOUVENIRS AND NOVELTIES—Suite 226–27, 401 N. Broad St., Philadelphia, PA 19108. Articles, 1,500 words, quoting souvenir shop managers on items that sell, display ideas, problems in selling, industry trends. Photos. Pays from $1 per column inch, extra for photos, on publication.

THE SPORTING GOODS DEALER—1212 N. Lindbergh, St. Louis, MO 63132. Articles, about 500 words, on sporting goods stores. Pays from 2¢ a word, on publication.

SUCCESSFUL FARMING—1716 Locust St., Des Moines, IA 50336. Richard Krumme, Ed. Articles, to 2,000 words, for farming families, on all areas of business farming: money management, marketing, machinery, soils and crops, livestock, and buildings. Pays from $300, on acceptance. Query.

TEXTILE WORLD—4170 Ashford-Dunwoody Rd. N.E., Suite 420, Atlanta, GA 30319. L. A. Christiansen, Ed. Articles, 500 to 2,000 words, with photos, on manufacturing and finishing textiles. Pays varying rates, on acceptance.

TOURIST ATTRACTIONS AND PARKS—Suite 226–27, 401 N. Broad St., Philadelphia, PA 19108. Chuck Tooley, Ed. Articles, 1,500 words, on successful management of parks and leisure attractions. News items, 250 and 500 words. Pays 7¢ a word, on publication. Query.

TRAILER/BODY BUILDERS—1602 Harold St., Houston, TX 77006. Paul Schenck, Ed. Articles on engineering, sales, and management ideas for truck body and truck trailer manufacturers. Pays from $100 per printed page, on acceptance.

TRAINING, THE MAGAZINE OF HUMAN RESOURCES DEVELOP-MENT—50 S. Ninth St., Minneapolis, MN 55402. Jack Gordon, Ed. Articles, 1,500 to 2,000 words, for managers of training and development activities in corporations, government, etc. Pays to 15¢ a word, on acceptance. Query.

THE TRAVEL AGENT—2 W. 46th St., New York, NY 10036. Eric Friedheim, Ed. Articles, 1,500 words, with photos, on travel trade, for travel agents. Pays $50 to $75, on acceptance. Query first.

TRAVEL BUSINESS MANAGER—51 Monroe St., #1501, Rockville, MD 20850. Eleanor Alexander, Ed. Articles and features, 1,000 to 1,800 words, on management and strategic issues in the travel industry. Pays $200 to $500, on publication. Query required. Send SASE for guidelines.

TRAVELAGE—555 N. Birch Rd., Ft. Lauderdale, FL 33304. Marylyn Springer, Ed. Articles, 1,500 to 2,000 words, for travel agents and other travel industry personnel. Interviews. Pays $1.50 per column inch, on publication.

VENDING TIMES—545 Eighth Ave., New York, NY 10018. Arthur E. Yohalem, Ed. Feature and news articles, with photos, on vending machines. Pays varying rates, on acceptance. Query.

VIEW—80 Fifth Ave., New York, NY 10011. Kathy Haley, Ed. Features and short news pieces on the business of television programming (network, syndication, cable and pay). Pays to $600, after publication. Query.

WESTERN INVESTOR—400 S.W. Sixth Ave., Suite 1115, Portland, OR 97204. Business and investment articles, 800 to 1,200 words, about business leaders, trends, products, etc., in the 13 western states. Pays from $50, on publication. Query first.

WESTERN OUTFITTER—5314 Bingle Rd., Houston, TX 77092. Anne DeRuyter, Ed. Articles, to 1,500 words, with photos, on merchandising western and English apparel and supplies. Photos. Pays 10¢ a word, extra for photos, on publication. Query.

WINES & VINES—1800 Lincoln Ave., San Rafael, CA 94901. Philip E. Hiaring, Ed. Articles, 1,000 words, on grape and wine industry, emphasizing marketing and production. Pays 5¢ a word, on acceptance.

WINES OF THE AMERICAS—P.O. Box 498, Geyserville, CA 95441. Articles, 800 to 2,500 words, of interest to wine professionals. Pays 10¢ a word, on publication. Query required: address Mildred Howie.

WISCONSIN BUSINESS JOURNAL—450 N. Sunnyslope Rd., Suite 120, Brookfield, WI 53005. Nancy Aldrich-Ruenzel, Man. Ed. Articles, 1,000 to 6,000 words, on Wisconsin business trends and developments. How-to's for executives on management, finance, marketing and real estate. Profiles of state businesses and executives. Pays negotiable rates, on acceptance. Query.

WOOD 'N ENERGY—P.O. Box 2008, Laconia, NH 03247. Steve Maviglio, Ed. Profiles and interviews, 1,000 to 2,500 words, with retailers and manufacturers of alternative energy equipment. Pays $150 to $250 for articles, on publication. Query.

WORLD OIL—Gulf Publishing Co., P.O. Box 2608, Houston, TX 77001. T. R. Wright, Jr., Ed. Engineering and operations articles, 3,000 to 4,000 words, on petroleum industry exploration, drilling or producing. Photos. Pays from $50 per printed page, on acceptance. Query.

WORLD WASTES—6255 Barfield Rd., Atlanta, GA 30328. Bill Wolpin, Ed. Case studies, 1,000 to 2,000 words, with photos, of refuse haulers, landfill operators, resource recovery operations and transfer stations, with solutions to problems in field. Pays from $100 per printed page, on publication. Query preferred.

ZIP TARGET MARKETING MAGAZINE—North American Publishing Co., 401 N. Broad St., Philadelphia, PA 19108. James McCanney, Ed. Articles, 4 to 6 manuscript pages, for major mailers and mail-order advertisers, on marketing, circulation, mailing operations, fulfillment, mail-order, telemarketing, computer technology, and communications. Pays $200, on publication.

COMPANY PUBLICATIONS

Company publications (also called house magazines or house organs) are excellent, well-paying markets for writers at all levels of experience. Hundreds of these magazines are published, usually by large corporations, to promote good will, familiarize readers with the company's services and products, and interest customers in these products. Always read a house magazine before submitting an article; write to the editor for a sample copy (offering to pay for it) and the editorial guidelines. Stamped, self-addressed envelopes should be enclosed with any query or manuscript.

THE COMPASS—Mobil Sales and Supply Corp., 150 E. 42nd St., New York, NY 10017. R. G. MacKenzie, Ed. Articles, to 3,500 words, on the sea and deep sea trade. Photos. No fiction. Pays to $250, on acceptance. Query.

EXXON U.S.A. MAGAZINE—Exxon Company, U.S.A., P.O. Box 2180, Houston, TX 77252-2180. Downs Matthews, Ed. Articles, 2,000 to 2,500 words, for thought leaders largely outside the oil industry, on Exxon Co.'s public affairs interests and concerns in the U.S.: environmental conservation, business economics, public energy policy, etc. Pays $1,000 to $1,500. Query first.

FRIENDS MAGAZINE—30400 Van Dyke, Warren, MI 48093. Tom Morrisey, Features Ed. Articles on topics of general interest, 800 to 1,200 words, for Chevrolet customers: life styles, sports, travel, food, etc. Must be non-controversial and in good taste. Pays from $300, extra for photos, on acceptance. Query; indicate if photos are available.

THE FURROW—Deere & Company, John Deere Rd., Moline, IL 61265. George R. Sollenberger, Ed.; North America. Articles and humor, to 1,500 words; researched agricultural-technical features; rural social- and economic-trend features. Pays to $1,000, on acceptance.

GO GREYHOUND—Greyhound Tower, Phoenix, AZ 85077. Juanita Soto, Publications Ass't. Human-interest travel articles, 600 to 800 words, with color photos. Pays $350, on publication. Query.

INLAND—Inland Steel Co., 30 W. Monroe, Chicago, IL 60603. Sheldon A. Mix, Man. Ed. Imaginative articles, essays, commentaries, of any length, of special interest in Midwest. Pays varying rates, on acceptance.

THE LOOKOUT—Seamen's Church Institute, 50 Broadway, New York, NY 10004. Carlyle Windley, Ed. Articles, 750 to 1,500 words, relating to merchant marine: oddities, adventure, etc. Graphics, occasional short verse. Pays to $80 for articles with art, extra for black-and-white cover photos, on publication.

THE MODERN WOODMEN—Modern Woodmen of America, Mississippi River at 17th St., Rock Island, IL 61201. Gloria Gergh, Manager, Public Relations. Family- and community-oriented, general-interest articles; some quality fiction. Photos. Pays from $40, on acceptance. Publication not copyrighted.

RAYTHEON MAGAZINE—141 Spring St., Lexington, MA 02173. Robert P. Suarez, Ed. Articles by assignment only. Pays $750 to $1,250, on acceptance, for articles 800 to 1,200 words. Query with writing sample.

SPERRY NEW HOLLAND—Div. of Sperry Corp., New Holland, PA 17557. Gary Martin, Ed. Articles, to 1,000 words, with strong photo support, on production agriculture, research and rural human interest. Pays on acceptance.

ASSOCIATIONS, ORGANIZATIONS

AIR LINE PILOT—Air Line Pilots Association International, 535 Herndon Pkwy., Herndon, VA 22070. C. V. Glines, Ed. Articles, to 3,000 words, on aviation, stressing pilot's point of view; articles on safety and air transport history; profiles of ALPA members. Pays varying rates, on acceptance. Query. Replies only if SASE is provided.

CALIFORNIA HIGHWAY PATROLMAN—2030 V. St., Sacramento, CA 95818. Carol Perri, Ed. Articles, with photos, on transportation safety, California history, travel, topical, consumerism, humor, general items, etc. Photos. Pays 2½¢ a word, extra for black and white photos, on publication.

COLUMBIA—Box 1670, New Haven, CT 06507. Elmer Von Feldt, Ed. Journal of Knights of Columbus. Illustrated articles, 3,000 words, on science, history, sports, current events, religion, education and art. Humorous pieces, to 1,000 words. Pays $200 to $600, on acceptance.

THE ELKS MAGAZINE—425 W. Diversey Pkwy., Chicago, IL 60614. Herbert Gates, Man. Ed. Articles, 3,000 words, on business, sports, and topics of current interest; for non-urban audience with above-average income. Informative or humorous pieces, to 2,500 words. Pays $150 to $500 for articles, on acceptance. Query.

FIREHOUSE—33 Irving Pl., New York, NY 10003. John D. Peige, Exec. Ed. Articles, 500 to 2,000 words, on trends in firefighting equipment and practice and lifestyles of firefighters. Profiles. On-the-scene accounts of fires. Pays $100 to $200, on publication. Query.

THE KIWANIS MAGAZINE—3636 Woodview Trace, Indianapolis, IN

46268. Chuck Jonak, Exec. Ed. Articles, 2,500 to 3,000 words, on home, family, career and community concerns of business and professional men. No travel pieces, interviews, profiles. Pays $250 to $750, on acceptance. Query.

THE LION—300 22nd St., Oak Brook, IL 60570. Robert Kleinfelder, Senior Ed. Official publication of Lions Clubs International. Articles, 800 to 2,000 words, and photo essays, on Club activities. Pays from $50 to $400, including photos, on acceptance. Query.

THE MODERN WOODMEN—Modern Woodmen of America, Mississippi River at 17th St., Rock Island, IL 61201. Gloria Bergh, Manager, Public Relations. Family- and community-oriented, general-interest articles; some quality fiction. Photos. Pays from $40, on acceptance. Publication not copyrighted.

OPTIMIST MAGAZINE—4494 Lindell Blvd., St. Louis, MO 63108. Dennis R. Osterwisch, Ed. Articles, to 1,500 words on general-interest topics of interest to members of civic-service clubs. Pays from $100, on acceptance. Query.

THE ROTARIAN—1600 Ridge Ave., Evanston, IL 60201. Willmon L. White, Ed. Articles, 1,200 to 2,000 words, on international social and economic issues, business and management, human relationships, travel, sports, environment, science and technology; humor. Pays good rates, on acceptance. Query.

TRAVELAGE—555 N. Birch Rd., Fort Lauderdale, FL 33304. Marylyn Springer, Ed. Articles about travel agents, particularly their hobbies, after hours pursuits, former careers and activities, for travel agents and other industry personnel. Regular interviews with travel agents; query first about these. Pays $1.50 per column inch, on publication, for manuscripts of 1,500 to 2,000 words. Publishes four regional editions; distributed free twice a month to travel agents.

WOMEN IN BUSINESS—9100 Ward Parkway, Box 8728, Kansas City, MO 64114. Publication of the American Business Women's Association. Margaret Horan, Ed. Features, 1,000 to 2,000 words, for career women from 45 to 55 years old; no profiles. Pays to $250, on acceptance. Query.

WOODMEN OF THE WORLD MAGAZINE—1700 Farnam St., Omaha, NE 68102. Leland A. Larson, Ed. Publication of the Woodmen of the World Life Insurance Society. Articles on history, travel, sports, do-it-yourself projects, science, etc. Photos. Pays 5¢ a word, extra for photos, on acceptance.

RELIGIOUS AND DENOMINATIONAL

ADVANCE—1445 Boonville Ave., Springfield, MO 65802. Gwen Jones, Ed. Articles, 1,200 words, slanted to ministers, on preaching, doctrine, practice; how-to-do-it features. Pays 2¢ to 4¢ a word, on acceptance.

AGLOW MAGAZINE—P. O. Box 1, Lynnwood, WA 98046-1557. Gwen Weising, Man. Ed. First-person articles and testimonies, 1,000 to 2,000 words, that encourage, instruct, inform or entertain Christian women of all ages, and relate to the work of the Holy Spirit. Should deal with contemporary issues. Pays to 10¢ a word, on acceptance.

AMERICA—106 W. 56 St., New York, NY 10019. George W. Hunt, S.J., Ed. Articles, 1,000 to 2,500 words, on current affairs, family life, literary trends. Pays $75 to $150, on acceptance.

AMERICAN BIBLE SOCIETY RECORD—1865 Broadway, New York, NY

10023. Clifford P. Macdonald, Man. Ed. Material related to work of American Bible Society: translating, publishing, distributing. Pays on acceptance. Query.

AMIT WOMAN—817 Broadway, New York, NY 10003. Micheline Ratzerdorfer, Ed. Articles, 1,000 to 2,000 words, of interest to Jewish women: Middle East, Israel; history, holidays, travel. Pays to $50, on publication.

ANNALS OF ST. ANNE DE BEAUPRÉ—P. O. Box 1000, St. Anne de Beaupré, Quebec, Canada G0A 3C0. Roch Achard, C.Ss.R., Ed. Articles, 1,100 to 1,200 words, on Catholic subjects and on St. Anne. Pays 2¢ to 4¢ a word, on acceptance.

BAPTIST LEADER—American Baptist Churches, USA, P.O. Box 851, Valley Forge, PA 19482-0851. L. Isham, Ed. Practical how-to or thought-provoking articles, 1,200 to 1,600 words, for lay leaders and teachers of local church education. B & W photos a plus. Pays $20 to $70, on acceptance.

THE B'NAI B'RITH INTERNATIONAL JEWISH MONTHLY—1640 Rhode Island Ave., NW, Washington, DC 20036. Marc Silver, Ed. Original, lively articles, 500 to 3,000 words, on trends, politics, personalities, and culture of the Jewish community. Pays 10¢ to 25¢ a word, on publication. Query.

BREAD—6401 The Paseo, Kansas City, MO 64131. Gary Sivewright, Ed. Church of the Nazarene. Devotional, Bible study and Christian guidance articles, to 1,200 words, for teen-agers. Pays from 3¢ a word, on acceptance.

BRIGADE LEADER—Box 150, Wheaton, IL 60189. David R. Leight, Man. Ed. Inspirational articles, 1,000 to 1,800 words, for Christian men who help boys. Pays $60 to $150. Query only.

CATECHIST—2451 E. River Rd., Dayton, OH 45439. Patricia Fischer, Ed. Informational and inspirational articles, 1,200 to 1,500 words, for Catholic teachers, coordinators, and administrators in religious education programs. Pays $25 to $75, on publication.

CATHOLIC DIGEST—P. O. Box 64090, St. Paul, MN 55164. Address Articles Ed. Articles, 2,000 to 2,500 words, on Catholic and general subjects. Fillers, to 300 words, on instances of kindness rewarded, for "Hearts Are Trumps"; accounts of good deeds, for "People Are Like That." Pays from $200 for original articles, $100 for reprints, on acceptance; $4 to $50 for fillers, on publication.

CATHOLIC LIFE—35750 Moravian Dr., Fraser, MI 48026. Robert C. Bayer, Ed. Articles, 600 to 1,200 words, on Catholic missionary work in Hong Kong, India, Latin America, Africa, etc. Photos. No fiction or poetry. Pays 4¢ a word, extra for photos, on publication.

CATHOLIC NEAR EAST MAGAZINE—1011 First Ave., New York, NY 10022. Michael Healy, Ed. Articles, 1,000 to 1,800 words, on places, people, history, ritual, heritage, culture, and traditions of the Near East, especially concerning their religious significance. Special interest in Eastern rites of the church. Photos. Pays 10¢ a word, on publication. Query.

CATHOLIC TWIN CIRCLE—6404 Wilshire Blvd., Suite 900, Los Angeles, CA 90048. Mary Louise Frawley, Ed. Stories and interviews of interest to Catholics, 1,000 to 1,500 words, with photos. Strict attention to Catholic doctrine required. Enclose SASE. Pays 10¢ a word, on publication.

CHARISMA—190 N. Westmonte Dr., Altamonte Springs, FL 32714.

Howard Earl, Sr. Ed. Charismatic Christian articles, 2,000 to 3,500 words, for developing the spiritual life. Photos. Pays varying rates, on publication. Query.

CHESAPEAKE SHALOM—P. O. Box 789, Severna Park, MD 21146. Lee Irwin, Ed. General interest articles, 500 to 1,500 words, on Jewish life and leisure in the Chesapeake Bay region, as well as pieces on Jewish issues and "heartwarming" anecdotes of Jewish-American life. Pays $5 to $15, on publication.

CHRISTIAN BOOKSELLER—396 E. St. Charles Rd., Wheaton, IL 60188. Karen Tornberg, Ed. Articles, 1,500 to 2,000 words, for Christian booksellers, publishers, and suppliers. Interviews with Christian authors and recording artists. Photos with articles only. Pays $20 to $150, on publication. Query.

THE CHRISTIAN CENTURY—407 S. Dearborn St., Chicago, IL 60605. James M. Wall, Ed. Ecumenical. Articles, 1,500 to 2,500 words, with a religious angle, on political and social issues, international affairs, culture, the arts. Photos. Pays about $25 per printed page, extra for photos, on publication.

CHRISTIAN HERALD—Chappaqua, NY 10514. David Kucharsky, Ed. Interdenominational. Articles, personal-experience pieces, to 1,500 words, on biblically-oriented topics. Pays from 10¢ a word for full-length features, from $10 for short pieces, after acceptance. Query first.

CHRISTIAN HOME—Box 189, 1908 Grand Ave., Nashville, TN 37202. Articles, 500 to 1,400 words, on parenting, marriage, and devotional life. Pays 6¢ a word, on acceptance.

CHRISTIAN LIFE MAGAZINE—396 E. St. Charles Rd., Wheaton, IL 60188. Janice Franzen, Exec. Ed. Articles, 1,500 to 2,500 words, on evangelical subjects, Christian living, and Christians in politics, sports, and entertainment. Photos. Pays to $150, on publication.

CHRISTIAN LIVING—850 N. Grove Ave., Elgin, IL 60102. Anne E. Dinnan, Ed. Weekly paper for evangelical and mainline Christian teens. Articles, to 1,200 words, that challenge, interest, and inspire teens to spiritual growth. Taboos: obscenity, sexual scenes, heavy moralizing and preachiness. Pays 6¢ to 9¢ a word, on acceptance.

CHRISTIAN SINGLE—127 Ninth Ave. N., Nashville, TN 37234. Cliff Allbritton, Ed. Articles, 600 to 1,200 words, on leisure activities, inspiring personal experiences, for Christian singles. Humor. Pays 4¢ a word, on acceptance. Query. Send SASE for guidelines.

CHRISTIANITY TODAY—465 Gundersen Dr., Carol Stream, IL 60188. Harold L. Myra, Exec. Ed. Doctrinal, social issues and interpretive essays, 1,500 to 3,000 words, from evangelical Protestant perspective. Pays $300 to $500, on acceptance.

CHURCH ADMINISTRATION—127 Ninth Ave. N., Nashville, TN 37234. Gary Hardin, Ed. Southern Baptist. How-to articles, 750 to 1,500 words, on administrative planning, staffing, organization and financing. Pays 4¢ a word, on acceptance.

CHURCH & STATE—8120 Fenton St., Silver Spring, MD 20910. Joseph L. Conn, Man. Ed. Articles, 600 to 2,600 words, on religious liberty and church-state relations issues. Pays varying rates, on acceptance. Query.

CHURCH EDUCATOR—Educational Ministries, 2861-C Saturn St., Brea, CA 92621. Robert C. Davidson, Ed. Articles, 200 to 3,000 words, with a "person-centered" approach to Christian education. How-to's for adult and juvenile Christian education. Pays from 3¢ to 5¢ a word, on publication.

THE CHURCH HERALD—1324 Lake Drive S. E., Grand Rapids, MI 49506. John Stapert, Ed. Reformed Church in America. Articles, 500 to 1,500 words, on Christianity and culture, politics, marriage and home. Pays 5¢ a word, on acceptance.

THE CHURCH MUSICIAN—127 Ninth Ave. N., Nashville, TN 37234. W. M. Anderson, Ed. Humorous fillers with a musical slant, for southern Baptist music leaders. No clippings. Pays about 4¢ a word, on acceptance. Same address and requirements for *Glory Songs* (for adults), and *Opus One* and *Opus Two* (for teen-agers).

THE CHURCHMAN—1074 23rd Ave. N., St. Petersburg, FL 33704. Edna Ruth Johnson, Ed. Articles, to 1,000 words, which offer humanistic approach to religion, ethics, and education. Pays in copies. Sample copy sent on request.

THE CIRCUIT RIDER—P. O. Box 801, Nashville, TN 37202. Richard Peck, Ed. Articles for United Methodist Pastors, 800 to 1,600 words. Pays $25 to $100, on acceptance. Query, with SASE, preferred.

COLUMBIA—Box 1670, New Haven, CT 06507. Elmer Von Feldt, Ed. Knights of Columbus. Articles, 2,500 to 3,500 words, for Catholic families. Must be accompanied by color photos or transparencies. No fiction. Pays to $750 for articles and photos, on acceptance.

COMMENTARY—165 E. 56th St., New York, NY 10022. Norman Podhoretz, Ed. Articles, 5,000 to 7,000 words, on contemporary issues, Jewish affairs, social sciences, religious thought, culture. Book reviews. Pays on publication.

COMMONWEAL—232 Madison Ave., New York, NY 10016. Peter Steinfels, Ed. Catholic. Articles, to 3,000 words, on political, religious, social and literary subjects. Pays 3¢ a word, on acceptance.

DAILY MEDITATION—Box 2710, San Antonio, TX 78299. Ruth S. Paterson, Ed. Inspirational nonsectarian articles, 650 to 2,000 words. Fillers, to 350 words. Pays ½¢ to 1½¢ a word, on acceptance.

DECISION—Billy Graham Evangelistic Association, 1300 Harmon Pl., Minneapolis, MN 55403. Roger C. Palms, Ed. Articles, Christian testimonials, 1,800 to 2,200 words. Narratives, 200 to 800 words. Pays varying rates, on publication.

THE DISCIPLE—Box 179, St. Louis, MO 63166. James L. Merrell, Ed. Disciples of Christ. Articles on Christian living; devotionals, 150 words. Short humor. Pays $10 to $25 for articles, on publication.

ENGAGE/SOCIAL ACTION MAGAZINE—100 Maryland Ave. N.E., Washington, DC 20002. Lee Ranck, Ed. Articles, 1,500 to 2,000 words, on social issues, for church-oriented audience. Pays $75 to $100, on publication.

THE EPISCOPALIAN—1930 Chestnut St., Philadelphia, PA 19103. Judy Foley, Man. Ed. Articles to 2,000 words, that show Episcopalians solving problems; action stories; profiles. Pays $25 to $100, on publication.

THE EVANGEL—901 College Ave., Winona Lake, IN 46590. Vera Bethel, Ed. Free Methodist. Personal-experience articles, 1,000 words. Short, devotional items, 300 to 500 words. Christian solutions to problems. Pays $25 for articles, on publication. Return postage required.

617

EVANGELICAL BEACON—1515 E. 66th St., Minneapolis, MN 55423. George Keck, Ed. Evangelical Free Church. Articles, 250 to 1,750 words, on religious topics; testimonials; pieces on current issues from an evangelical perspective; short inspirational and evangelistic devotionals. Pays 3¢ a word, on publication. Send SASE for writers' guidelines.

FRIENDS JOURNAL—1501 Cherry St., Philadelphia, PA 19102. Vinton Deming, Editor-Manager. Articles, to 2,500 words. Pays in copies. Query.

THE FUNDAMENTALIST JOURNAL—Langehorn Plaza, Lynchburg, VA 24514. Deborah Huff, Ed. Articles, 800 to 2,500 words, that examine matters of contemporary interest to all Fundamentalists: news articles, profiles, human-interest pieces; moral and religious issues; Bible stories. Pays 10¢ a word, on publication.

GLORY SONGS—See *The Church Musician.*

GOOD NEWS BROADCASTER—Box 82808, Lincoln, NE 68501. Norman A. Olson, Man. Ed. Articles, to 1,500 words, on relating biblical truths to daily living. Photos. Pays 4¢ to 10¢ a word, extra for photos, on acceptance. No simultaneous submissions or reprints. SASE required.

GUIDE—Review and Herald Publishing Co., 55 W. Oak Ridge Dr., Hagerstown, MD 21740. Articles, 1,000 to 2,500 words. Pays 3¢ to 4¢ a word, on acceptance.

GUIDEPOSTS—747 Third Ave., New York, NY 10017. True first-person stories, 250 to 1,500 words, stressing how faith in God helps people cope with life. Anecdotal fillers, to 250 words. Pays $100 to $400, $10 to $25 for fillers, on acceptance.

HIS MAGAZINE—P. O. Box 1450, Downers Grove, IL 60515. Verne Becker, Ed. First-person stories, to 2,000 words, on Christian living in college, for a student audience. Pays 2¢ to 5¢ a word, on acceptance.

HOME LIFE—127 Ninth Ave. N., Nashville, TN 37234. Reuben Herring, Ed. Southern Baptist. Articles, preferably personal-experience, to 2,000 words, on Christian marriage, parenthood, and family relationships. Human-interest pieces, 200 to 500 words. Pays to 4¢ a word, on acceptance.

INSIDE—226 S. 16th St., Philadelphia, PA 19102. Jane Biberman, Ed. Articles, 1,500 to 3,000 words, and fiction, 2,000 to 3,000 words, of interest to Jewish men and women. Pays $100 to $500, on acceptance. Query.

INSIGHT—55 West Oak Ridge Dr., Hagerstown, MD 21740. Dan Fahrbach, Ed. Seventh-day Adventist. Personal-experience narratives, articles and humor, to 1,800 words, for high school and college students. Parables; shorts. Pays 10¢ to 15¢ a word, extra for photos, on acceptance. Query.

INTERACTION—1333 S. Kirkwood Rd., St. Louis, MO 63122. Martha S. Jander, Ed. Articles, 1,500 to 2,000 words, for Lutheran Sunday School teachers. Pays $5 to $35, on publication. Limited free-lance market.

KEY TO CHRISTIAN EDUCATION—8121 Hamilton Ave., Cincinnati, OH 45231. Virginia Beddow, Ed. Articles, on teaching methods, and success stories, for workers in Christian education. Pays varying rates, on acceptance.

LIBERTY MAGAZINE—6840 Eastern Ave. N.W., Washington, DC 20012. Roland R. Hegstad, Ed. Timely articles, to 2,500 words, and photo essays, on religious freedom and church-state relations. Pays 6¢ to 8¢ a word, on acceptance. Query.

LIGHT AND LIFE—901 College Ave., Winona Lake, IN 46590. Lyn Cryderman, Ed. Fresh, lively articles about practical Christian living, and sound treatments of vital issues facing the Evangelical in contemporary society. Pays 4¢ a word, on publication. Query.

LIGUORIAN—Liguori, MO 63057. Rev. Norman J. Muckerman, Ed. Francine O'Connor, Man. Ed. Catholic. Articles and short stories, 1,500 to 2,000 words, on Christian values in modern life. Pays 7¢ to 10¢ a word, on acceptance. Buys all rights.

LIVE—1445 Boonville Ave., Springfield, MO 65802. Kenneth D. Barney, Adult Ed. Sunday school paper for adults. Articles, 1,000 to 1,500 words, on applying Bible principles to everyday living. Pays 2¢ to 3¢ a word, on acceptance. Send SASE for guidelines first.

THE LIVING LIGHT—United States Catholic Conference, Dept. of Education, 1312 Massachusetts Ave. N.W., Washington, DC 20005. Mariella Frye, M.H.S.H., Ed. Theoretical and practical articles, 1,500 to 4,000 words, on religious education, catechesis and pastoral ministry.

LIVING WITH CHILDREN—127 Ninth Ave. N., Nashville, TN 37234. SuAnne Bottoms, Ed. Articles, 800, 1,450 or 2,000 words, on parent-child relationships, told from a Christian perspective. Pays 5¢ a word, after acceptance.

LIVING WITH PRESCHOOLERS—127 Ninth Ave., N., Nashville, TN 37234. SuAnne Bottoms, Ed. Articles, 800, 1,450 or 2,000 words, and fillers, to 300 words, for Christian families. Pays 5¢ a word, on acceptance.

LIVING WITH TEENAGERS—127 Ninth Ave. N., Nashville, TN 37234. Articles, told from a Christian perspective for parents of teenagers, first-person approach preferred. Photos. Pays 5¢ a word, on acceptance.

THE LOOKOUT—8121 Hamilton Ave., Cincinnati, OH 45231. Mark A. Taylor, Ed. Articles, 1,000 to 1,500 words, on families and people overcoming problems by applying Christian principles. Inspirational or humorous shorts, 500 to 800 words. Pays 4¢ to 6¢ a word, on acceptance.

THE LUTHERAN—2900 Queen Ln., Philadelphia, PA 19129. Edgar R. Trexler, Ed. Articles, to 2,000 words, on Christian ideology, personal religious experiences, family life, church and community. Pays $90 to $360, on acceptance. Query.

LUTHERAN STANDARD—426 S. Fifth St., Box 1209, Minneapolis, MN 55440. Lowell G. Almen, Ed. Articles, 500 to 1,000 words, on personal, social, economic and political aspects of church and Christian living; human-interest items; personality profiles. Pays from 10¢ a word, on acceptance.

LUTHERAN WOMEN—2900 Queen Ln., Philadelphia, PA 19129. Terry Schutz, Ed. Articles, preferably with photos, on subjects of interest to Christian women. No recipes, homemaking hints. Pays to $50 for articles, $35 to $40 for fiction, on publication.

MARRIAGE AND FAMILY LIVING—Division of Abbey Press, St. Meinrad, IN 47577. Kass Dotterweich, Man. Ed. Expert advice, personal experience articles, 2,000 to 2,500 words, on marriage and family relationships. Family humor, 1,000 to 2,000 words. Pays 7¢ a word, on acceptance.

MATURE LIVING—127 9th Ave. N. Nashville, TN 37234. Jack Gulledge, Ed. General-interest pieces, travel articles, nostalgia and fiction, under 900 words, for Christian senior adults 60 years and older. Also, profiles recognizing a senior adult for an accomplishment or interesting or unusual experience, 25 lines; must include a B/W action photo. Brief, humorous items for "Cracker Barrel." Pays 5¢ a word, $10 for profiles, $5 for "Cracker Barrel," on acceptance. Buys all rights.

MATURE YEARS—201 Eighth Ave. S., Nashville, TN 37203. Daisy D. Warren, Ed. United Methodist. Articles on retirement or related subjects, 1,500 to 2,000 words. Pays 4¢ a word, on acceptance.

MESSENGER OF THE SACRED HEART—661 Greenwood Ave., Toronto, Ont., Canada M4J 4B3. Write M. Pujolas. Articles, abut 1,500 words, for American and Canadian Catholics. Pays from 2¢ a word, on acceptance.

MIDSTREAM—515 Park Ave., New York, NY 10022. Joel Carmichael, Ed. Jewish-interest articles and book reviews. Pays 5¢ a word, on publication.

MODERN LITURGY—160 E. Virginia St., #290, San Jose, CA 95112. Ken Guentert, Ed. Creative material for Catholic worship services; religious parables, to 1,000 words; how-to's, essays on worship, 750 to 1,600 words. Plays. Pays 3¢ a word, after publication.

MOMENT—462 Boylston St., Boston, MA 02116. Nechama Katz, Managing Ed. Sophisticated articles, 2,000 to 5,000 words, on Jewish topics. Pays $150 to $400, on publication.

MOMENTUM—National Catholic Educational Assn., Suite 100, 1077 30th St., NW, Washington, DC 20007. Patricia Feistritzer, Ed. Articles, 500 to 2,000 words, on outstanding programs, issues and research in education. Book reviews. Pays 2¢ a word, on publication. Query.

MOODY MONTHLY—2101 W. Howard, Chicago, IL 60654. Mike Umlandt, Man. Ed. Articles, 1,200 to 1,800 words, on the Christian experience in school, the home and the workplace. Pays 5¢ to 10¢ a word, on acceptance. Query.

THE NATIONAL CHRISTIAN REPORTER—See *The United Methodist Reporter.*

NEW ERA—50 E. North Temple, Salt Lake City, UT 84150. Brian Kelly, Ed. Articles, 150 to 3,000 words, for young Mormons. Poetry; photos. Pays 5¢ to 10¢ a word, 25¢ a line for poetry, on acceptance. Query.

NEW WORLD OUTLOOK—475 Riverside Dr., Rm. 1351, New York, NY 10115. Arthur J. Moore, Ed. Articles, 1,500 to 2,500 words, on Christian missions, religious issues and public affairs. Pays on publication.

OBLATES MAGAZINE—15 S. 59th St., Belleville, IL 62222. Address Linda Lehr. Articles, 500 to 600 words, for middle-aged Christian Americans, incorporating Gospel values into modern life. Pays $75, on acceptance. Send for free sample copy and guidelines.

OPUS ONE AND OPUS TWO—See *The Church Musician.*

OUR FAMILY—Box 249, Dept. E, Battleford, Sask., Canada S0M 0E0. Albert Lalonde, O.M.I., Ed. Articles, 1,000 to 3,000 words, for Catholic family readers, on modern society, family, marriage, current affairs. Humor, verse. Pays 7¢ to 10¢ a word for articles, on acceptance. Send SASE with Canadian postage for guidelines.

OUR SUNDAY VISITOR—Huntington, IN 46750. Robert Lockwood, Ed.

In-depth features, 1,000 to 1,200 words, on the Catholic Church in America today. Pays $100 to $150, on acceptance.

PARISH FAMILY DIGEST—Noll Plaza, Huntington, IN 46750. Patrick R. Moran, Ed. Articles, to 1,000 words, fillers, and humor, for Catholic families and parishes. Pays 5¢ a word, on acceptance. Query first.

PARTNERSHIP—Christianity Today, Inc., 465 Gunderson Dr., Carol Stream, IL 60188. Ruth Seater, Ed. Articles, 500 to 2,000 words, geared to the needs and interests of women married to men in the Christian ministry. Fillers to 50 words; cartoons. Pays $50 to $300, on acceptance.

THE PENTECOSTAL EVANGEL—1445 Boonville Ave., Springfield, MO 65802. Richard Champion, Ed. Assemblies of God. Religious personal-experience and devotional articles, 500 to 1,000 words. Pays 2¢ to 3¢ a word, on publication.

THE PRESBYTERIAN SURVEY—341 Ponce de Leon Ave., N.E., Atlanta, GA 30365. Vic Jameson, Ed. Articles, to 1,500 words, of interest to members of the Presbyterian Church or ecumenical individuals. Pays to $200, on acceptance. Query.

PRESENT TENSE—165 E. 56th St., New York, NY 10022. Murray Polner, Ed. Serious articles, 2,000 to 3,000 words, with photos, on news concerning Jews throughout the world; first-person encounters and personal-experience pieces. Literary-political reportage. Contemporary themes only. Pays $100 to $200, on publication. Query.

THE PRIEST—200 Noll Plaza, Huntington, IN 46750. Articles, to 2,500 words, on life and ministry of priests, current theological developments, etc., for priests, permanent deacons, and seminarians. Pays $35 to $100, on acceptance.

PURPOSE—616 Walnut Ave., Scottdale, PA 15683–1999. James E. Horsch, Ed. Articles, 350 to 1,200 words, on Christian themes, with good photos; pieces of history, biography, science, hobbies, from a Christian perspective. Pays 5¢ a word, extra for photos, on acceptance.

QUEEN—26 S. Saxon Ave., Bay Shore, NY 11706. James McMillan, S.M.M., Ed. Publication of Montfort Missionaries. Articles, 1,000 to 2,000 words, relating to the Virgin Mary. Pays varying rates on acceptance.

THE RECONSTRUCTIONIST—270 W. 89th St., New York, NY 10024. Dr. Jacob Staub, Ed. Articles, 2,000 to 3,000 words, relating to Judaism. Pays $18 to $36 on publication.

ST. ANTHONY MESSENGER—1615 Republic St., Cincinnati, OH 45210. Norman Perry, O.F.M., Ed. Catholic. Articles, 2,500 to 3,500 words, on personalities, major movements, education, family, and social issues. Human-interest pieces. Humor. Pays from 12¢ a word, on acceptance. Query.

ST. JOSEPH'S MESSENGER—P.O. Box 288, Jersey City, NJ 07303. Sister Ursula Maphet, Ed. Inspirational articles, 500 to 1,000 words. Pays 1¢ a word. Query.

SCOPE—426 S. Fifth St., Box 1209, Minneapolis, MN 55440. Constance Lovaas, Ed. American Lutheran Church Women. Educational and inspirational articles for women in careers, the home, church, and community. Human-interest pieces, 500 to 1,000 words. Fillers. Pays moderate rates, on acceptance.

SEEK—8121 Hamilton Ave., Cincinnati, OH 45231. Eileen H. Wilmot, Ed.

Articles, to 1,200 words, on inspirational and controversial topics and timely religious issues. Christian testimonials. Pays up to 3¢ a word, on acceptance.

SHARING THE VICTORY—8701 Leeds Rd., Kansas City, MO 64129. Skip Stogsdill, Ed. Articles and profiles, to 800 words, for coed Christian athletes and coaches in high school and college. Pays from $25, on publication. Queries required.

SH'MA—Box 567, Port Washington, NY 11050. Eugene B. Borowitz, Ed. Articles, 750 to 2,000 words; analytic, opinion pieces for sophisticated Jewish readers, on ethics, Zionism, and Jewish living. Pays in copies.

SIGNS OF THE TIMES—P.O. Box 7000, Boise, ID 83707. Kenneth J. Holland, Ed. Feature articles on Christians who have performed community services; current issues from a Biblical perspective; health, home, marriage, human-interest pieces; inspirational articles, 500 to 2,000 words. Pays 12¢ to 15¢ a word, on acceptance.

SISTERS TODAY—The Liturgical Press, St. John's Abbey, Collegeville, MN 56231. Sister Mary Anthony Wagner, O.S.B., Ed. Articles, 500 to 3,500 words, on Roman Catholic theology, religious issues for women and the Church. Pays $5 per printed page, on publication. Send articles to Editor at St. Benedict's Convent, St. Joseph, MN 56374.

SOCIAL JUSTICE REVIEW—3835 Westminster Pl., St. Louis, MO 63108. Harvey J. Johnston, Ed. Articles, 2,000 to 3,000 words, on social problems in light of Catholic teaching and current scientific studies. Pays 2¢ a word, on publication.

SPIRITUAL LIFE—2131 Lincoln Rd. N.E., Washington, DC 20002–1199. Christopher Latimer, O.C.D., and Steven Payne, O.C.D., Co-editors. Professional religious journal. Religious essays, 3,000 to 5,000 words, on spirituality in contemporary life. Pays from $50, on acceptance. Guidelines.

SPIRITUALITY TODAY—Aquinas Institute, 3642 Lindell Blvd., St. Louis, MO 63108. Christopher Kiesling, O.P., Ed. Quarterly Biblical, liturgical, theological, ecumenical, historical, and biographical articles of critical, probing kind, 4,000 words, about the challenges of contemporary Christian life. No poetry. Pays from 1¢ a word, on publication. Guidelines available upon request.

STANDARD—6401 The Paseo, Kansas City, MO 64131. Address Ed. Articles, 300 to 2,000 words: true experiences, devotional fillers; with Christian emphasis but not preachy; fillers, cryptograms of Scripture verses or inspiring quotes, cartoons in good taste. Pays 3½¢ a word, on acceptance.

SUNDAY DIGEST—850 N. Grove Ave., Elgin, IL 60120. Judy C. Couchman, Ed. Articles, to 1,500 words, on Christian faith in contemporary life; inspirational and how-to articles. Anecdotes, 500 words. Pays 10¢ a word, on acceptance.

SUNDAY SCHOOL COUNSELOR—1445 Boonville Ave., Springfield, MO 65802. Sylvia Lee, Ed. Articles, 1,000 to 1,500 words, on teaching and Sunday school people, for local Sunday school teachers. Pays 3¢ to 5¢ a word, on acceptance.

SUNSHINE MAGAZINE—Litchfield, IL 62056. Address Ed. Inspirational articles, to 600 words. Short stories, 1,000 words and juveniles, 400 words. No heavily religious material or "born-again" pieces. Pays varying rates, on acceptance.

THEOLOGY TODAY—Box 29, Princeton, NJ 08542. Hugh T. Kerr, Ed. Articles, to 3,500 words, or to 1,500 words, on theology, religion and related social issues. Literary criticism. Pays $35 to $50, on publication.

TODAY'S CHRISTIAN PARENT—8121 Hamilton Ave., Cincinnati, OH 45231. Mildred D. Mast, Ed. Articles, to 1,000 words, on application of Christian principles in child-rearing and aspects of family living; problems and pleasures of parents, grandparents. Serious or humorous fillers. Timely articles on moral issues, social situations, ethical dilemmas; refreshing insights for everyday happenings in the home. Pays to 2½¢ a word, after acceptance. Include SASE.

THE UNITED CHURCH OBSERVER—85 St. Clair Ave. E., Toronto, Ont., Canada M4T 1M8. Factual articles, 1,500 to 2,500 words, on religious trends, human problems, social issues. No poetry. Pays after publication. Query.

UNITED EVANGELICAL ACTION—P.O. Box 28, Wheaton, IL 60189. Don Brown, Ed. National Assn. of Evangelicals. News-oriented expositions and editorials, 750 to 1,000 words, on current events of concern and consequence to the evangelical church. Pays about 7¢ to 10¢ a word, on publication. Query with writing samples.

THE UNITED METHODIST REPORTER—P.O. Box 660275, Dallas, TX 75266-0275. Spurgeon M. Dunnam III, Ed. John Lovelace, Man. Ed. United Methodist. Religious features, to 500 words. Photos. Pays 4¢ a word, on acceptance. Send for guidelines. Same address and requirements for *The National Christian Reporter* (interdenominational).

UNITED SYNAGOGUE REVIEW—155 Fifth Ave., New York, NY 10010. Rabbi Marvin S. Wiener, Ed. Articles, 1,000 to 1,500 words, on synagogue programs and projects, Jewish worship services, rituals, etc. Pays after publication. Query.

UNITY MAGAZINE—Unity School of Christianity, Unity Village, MO 64065. Pamela Yearsley, Ed. Inspirational and metaphysical articles, 500 to 2,500 words. Pays 4¢ to 7¢ a word, on acceptance.

VIRTUE—P.O. Box 850, Sisters, OR 97759. Articles for Christian women. Query only, except for pieces for "One Woman's Journal" and "In My Opinion." Material sent without SASE will not be returned.

VISTA—Box 2000, Marion, IN 46952. Adult fiction, 1,200 to 1,500 words, on Christian living. Devotional and first-person articles. Anecdotes of spiritual significance, 200 to 500 words. Pays 2¢ to 3¢ a word.

WORKING FOR BOYS—St. John's H. S., Main St., Shrewsbury, MA 01545. Brother Alois, C.F.X., Assoc. Ed. Nonfiction, to 1,200 words, for elementary school children, parents: human-interest, how-to, travel, religion, sports. No pictures or puzzles. Pays 4¢ a word, on acceptance. Limited market.

THE YOUNG SALVATIONIST—The Salvation Army, 799 Bloomfield Ave., Verona, NJ 07044. Dorothy Hitzka, Ed. Articles, 1,000 to 1,200 words, teaching the Christian view to everyday living, for teenagers. Short shorts, first-person testimonies, 600 to 800 words. Pays 3¢ to 5¢ a word, on acceptance. SASE required.

THE YOUNG SOLDIER—The Salvation Army, 799 Bloomfield Ave., Verona, NJ 07044. Dorothy Hitzka, Ed. Articles, 600 to 800 words, for children 6 to 12. Must carry a definite Christian message, or teach a Biblical truth. Fillers, puzzles, etc. Pays 3¢ a word, $3 to $5 for fillers, puzzles, on acceptance.

YOUTHWORKER—1224 Greenfield Dr., El Cajon, CA 92021. Noel Becchetti, Ed. Articles, 2,500 to 3,000 words, for ministers of the Christian church who work with teens. Pays $100, on acceptance. Query.

HEALTH

ACCENT ON LIVING—P.O. Box 700, Bloomington, IL 61702. Raymond C. Cheever, Pub./Ed. Articles, 250 to 1,000 words, about physically disabled people—their careers, recreation and sports, self-help devices, and ideas that can make daily routine easier. Good photos a plus. Pays 10¢ a word, on publication. Query.

ALCOHOLISM/THE NATIONAL MAGAZINE—P.O. Box 19519, Seattle, WA 98109. Articles on all aspects of alcoholism: treatment, legislation, education, prevention, and recoverey. Pays 7¢ to 10¢ a word, after publication.

AMERICAN BABY—575 Lexington Ave., New York, NY 10022. Judith Nolte, Ed. Articles, 1,000 to 2,000 words, for new or expectant parents, on prenatal and infant care. Pays varying rates, on acceptance.

AMERICAN FAMILY PHYSICIAN—1740 W. 92nd St., Kansas City, MO 64114. Walter H. Kemp, Man. Publisher. Illustrated articles, 1,600 to 3,200 words, on clinical topics only. Pays from $150, on publication. Query. Most material written by physicians.

AMERICAN HEALTH: FITNESS OF BODY AND MIND—80 Fifth Ave., Suite 302, New York, NY 10011. Address Editorial Dept. Features, 1,000 to 3,000 words, on recent developments in nutrition, exercise, medicine, prevention and psychology. Shorter news items on similar topics: medical advances, consumer health, and life styles. Pays from $125 per manuscript page, on acceptance. Query required.

AMERICAN JOURNAL OF NURSING—555 W. 57th St., New York, NY 10019. Mary B. Mallison, R.N., Ed. Articles, 1,500 to 2,000 words, with photos, on nursing. Pays $20 per printed page, on publication. Query.

BESTWAYS—1501 S. Sutro Terrace, P.O. Box 2028, Carson City, NV 89701. Barbara Bassett, Ed. Articles, 1,500 to 2,000 words, on health, food, life styles, exercise, nutrition. Pays from $75, on publication. Query.

CHILDBIRTH EDUCATOR—575 Lexington Ave., New York, NY 10022. Marsha Rehns, Ed. Articles, 2,000 words, on maternal and fetal health, childcare, child development, and teaching techniques for teachers of childcare and baby care classes. Pays $400, on acceptance. Query with detailed outline.

DANCE EXERCISE TODAY—4501 Mission Bay Dr., Suite 2F, San Diego, CA 92109. Naneene Van Gelder, Ed. Practical articles, 1,000 to 3,000 words, on new programs, business tips, nutrition, sports medicine, and dance exercise techniques; interviews with outstanding professionals. Pays $50 to $125, on acceptance. Query preferred.

EAST WEST JOURNAL—17 Station St., Box 1200, Brookline, MA 02147. Features, 1,500 to 2,500 words, on holistic health, natural foods, the environment, etc. Material for "Body," "Healing," "Family," and "Science," Interviews. Photos. Pays 7¢ to 12¢ a word, extra for photos, on publication.

THE EXCEPTIONAL PARENT—605 Commonwealth Ave., Boston, MA 02215. Maxwell J. Schleifer, Ed. Articles, 600 to 3,000 words, with practical information for parents of disabled children. Pays on publication.

EXPECTING—685 Third Ave., New York, NY 10017. Evelyn A. Podsiadlo, Ed. Articles, 700 to 1,800 words, for expectant mothers. Pays $150 to $350, on acceptance.

HEALTH—3 Park Ave., New York, NY 10016. Articles, 800 to 2,500 words, on medicine, nutrition, fitness, emotional and psychological well-being. Pays $200 to $1,000, on acceptance. Query.

HEALTH LITERATURE REVIEW—True-to-Form Press, 1330 Conwed Tower, St. Paul, MN 55101-2110. Sheila Nauman-Todd, Ed./Pub. Reviews of current and contemporary health literature; articles on health care and trends in health literature and communications. Pays 10¢ a word, for articles, only, on publication. Send for writer's guidelines. Query.

HEALTH PROGRESS—4455 Woodson Rd., St. Louis, MO 63134. Michael F. McCauley, Ed. Journal of the Catholic Health Association. Features, 1,500 to 2,000 words, on hospital management and administration, medical-moral questions, technological developments and their impacts, and financial and human resource management. Pays by arrangement. Query.

HOSPITALS—211 E. Chicago Ave., Chicago, IL 60611. Frank Sabatino, Ed. Articles, 2,000 to 3,000 words, for hospital administrators, on financing, staffing, coordinating, and providing facilities for health care services. Pays varying rates, on acceptance. Query.

LET'S LIVE—444 N. Larchmont Blvd., Los Angeles, CA 90004. Keith Stepru, Man. Ed. Articles, 1,500 to 1,800 words, on preventive medicine and nutrition, alternative medicine, diet, exercise, recipes, and natural beauty. Pays $150, on publication. Query.

NEW BODY—888 Seventh Ave., New York, NY 10106. Norman Zeitchick, Ed. Well-researched, service oriented articles, 1,000 to 2,000 words, on exercise, nutrition, diet and health for men and women aged 18 to 35. Writers should have some background in or knowledge of the health field. Pays $250 to $500, on publication. Query preferred.

NURSING 86—1111 Bethlehem Pike, Springhouse, PA 19477. Jeanmarie Coogan, Ed. Most articles are clinically oriented, and assigned to nursing experts. No poetry. Pays $25 to $350, on publication. Query.

NURSING HOMES—Centaur & Co., 5 Willowbrook Ct., Potomac, MD 20854. William D. Manges, Ed.-in-Chief. Articles, 1,000 to 1,500 words, of interest to administrators, managers, and supervisory personnel in nursing homes; academic and clinical pieces; book reviews, 250–300 words. Pays $100 for articles, $30 for reviews, on acceptance. Photos, graphics welcome.

NURSING LIFE—1111 Bethlehem Pike, Springhouse, PA 19477. Maryanne Wagner, Ed. Dir. Articles, 12 to 15 double-spaced pages, by nurses, lawyers, management consultants, psychologists, with practical advice for staff nurses. Pays negotiable rates, on publication. Query.

NURSINGWORLD JOURNAL—470 Boston Post Rd., Weston, MA 02193. Eileen Devito, Man. Ed. Articles, 500 to 1,500 words, for and by nurses and nurse-educators, on aspects of current nursing issues. Pays from 25¢ per column inch, on publication.

PATIENT CARE—16 Thorndal Circle, Darien, CT 06820. Clayton Raker Hasser, Ed. Articles on medical care, for physicians. Pays varying rates, on publication. Query; all articles assigned.

THE PHYSICIAN AND SPORTSMEDICINE MAGAZINE—4530 W. 77th St. Minneapolis, MN 55435. Gary Legwold, Man. Ed. Articles, 500 to 3,000 words, for physicians who treat athletic injuries. Pays $50 to $900, on acceptance.

RECOVERY—P.O. Box 19519, Seattle, WA 98109. Christina Carlson, Ed. Articles, to 1,500 words, for recovering alcoholics, on how to meet the challenge of sobriety. First-person recovery stories, with helpful how-to's for others, 500 to 1,000 words. Poetry and fillers. Pays $75 to $100 per published page, $15 to $25 for fillers, 45 days after publication.

RN MAGAZINE—Oradell, NJ 07649. Articles, to 2,000 words, preferably by R.N.s, on nursing, clinical care, etc. Pays 10¢ to 15¢ a word, on publication. Query.

RX BEING WELL—800 Second Ave., New York, NY 10017. Mark Deitch, Ed. Articles, 500 to 2,000 words, providing authoritative information on prevention, fitness, nutrition, and current medical topics. No personal-experience pieces. Most articles written or co-authored by doctors. Pays $250 to $750, a few weeks after acceptance. Query with SASE.

RX HOME CARE—825 S. Barrington Ave., Los Angeles, CA 90049. Nancy Greengold, Ed. Articles, 1,000 to 2,000 words, on marketing aspects of home health care and rehabilitation equipment. Pays 10¢ a word, on acceptance. Query first.

TIC—P.O. Box 407, N. Chatham, NY 12132. Joseph Strack, Ed. Articles, 800 to 3,000 words, for dentists; building a practice, improving office procedures, etc. Profiles, with photos, of dentists' achievements in the arts, sports, business, and other fields. Pays on acceptance.

TODAY'S OR NURSE—6900 Grove Rd., Thorofare, NJ 08086. Judith B. Paquet, R.N., Ed. Short humor, 400 to 500 words, for operating room nurses. Pays 10¢ a word, on publication. Query.

VEGETARIAN TIMES—P.O. Box 570, Oak Park, IL 60603. Paul Obis, Ed. Articles, 750 to 3,000 words, on nutrition, exercise and fitness, meatless food, etc. Personal experience and historical pieces, profiles. Pays $25 to $300, on publication.

VIBRANT LIFE (formerly *Your Life and Health*)—55 W. Oak Ridge Dr., Hagerstown, MD 21740. Features, 1,000 to 2,000 words, on nutrition, diet, exercise, fitness and the latest developments in medicine. Seeks upbeat articles on how to live happier and healthier lives, with Christian slant. Pays $100 to $300, on acceptance.

WEIGHT WATCHERS MAGAZINE—360 Lexington Ave., New York, NY 10017. Cheryl Solimini, Sr. Ed. Psychological pieces on weight control; health, fitness, and nutrition; inspirational weight loss stories, 1,200 to 1,500 words. Pays from $250, after acceptance.

EDUCATION

AMERICAN EDUCATION—U.S. Dept. of Education, 400 Maryland Ave. S.W., Washington, D.C. 20202. Beverley P. Blondell, Ed. Articles, 2,000 to

3,000 words, on government policy, opinion, key issues, education programs or activities for all ages.

AMERICAN SCHOOL & UNIVERSITY—401 N. Broad St., Philadelphia, PA 19108. Dorothy Wright, Ed. Articles and case studies, 1,200 to 1,500 words, on design, construction, operation and management of school and college facilities. Payment varies.

CAPSTONE JOURNAL OF EDUCATION—P.O. Box Q, University, AL 35486. Alexia M. Kartis, Asst. Ed. Articles, to 5,000 words, on contemporary ideas in educational research.

CHANGE—4000 Albemarle St. N.W., Suite 500, Washington, D.C. 20016. Reports, 1,500 to 2,000 words, on programs, people and institutions of higher education. Intellectual essays, 3,000 to 5,000 words, on higher education today. Payment varies.

CLASSROOM COMPUTER LEARNING—Peter Li, Inc., 19 Davis Dr., Belmont CA 94002. Holly Brady, Ed. Articles, to 3,000 words, for teachers of grades K–12, related to uses of computers in the classroom; human-interest and philosophical articles, how-to pieces, software reviews, and hands-on ideas. Payment varies, on acceptance.

EDUCATION WEEK—Suite 560, 1333 New Hampshire Ave., Washington, D.C. 20036. M. Matzke, Exec. Ed. Articles covering national elementary and secondary education. Pays 20¢ a word, on publication. Query.

ELECTRONIC EDUCATION—Electronic Communications, 1311 Executive Center Dr., Suite 220, Tallahassee, FL 32301. Sharon Lobello, Ed. Cindy Whaley, Senior Ed. Articles, to 1,000 words, for educators, on uses of technology in education. Fillers. Pays $100 to $200, on publication. Query.

FOUNDATION NEWS—1828 L St. N.W., Washington, D.C. 20036. Arlie W. Schardt, Ed. Articles, to 2,000 words, on national or regional activities supported by, or of interest to, grant makers. Pays to $1,000, on acceptance. Query.

THE HORN BOOK MAGAZINE—Park Sq. Bldg., 31 St. James Ave., Boston, MA 02116. Anita Silvey, Ed. Articles, 600 to 2,600 words, on books for young readers, and related subjects, for librarians, teachers, parents, etc. Pays $20 per printed page, on publication. Query.

INDUSTRIAL EDUCATION—1495 Maple Way, Troy, MI 48084. Andrew Cummins, Ed. Instructional material, projects and how-to pieces, 500 to 1,500 words, with photos and drawings, for industrial arts, vocational and technical education classes. Pays $30 per printed page, on publication.

INSTRUCTOR—545 Fifth Ave., New York, NY 10017. Leanna Landsmann, Ed. How-to articles on elementary classroom teaching, and computers in the classroom, with practical suggestions and project reports. Pays varying rates, on acceptance.

KEY TO CHRISTIAN EDUCATION—8121 Hamilton Ave., Cincinnati, OH 45231. Virginia Beddow, Ed. Articles, 600 to 2,000 words, on Christian education; tips for teachers in the local church. Pays varying rates, on acceptance.

LEARNING 85/86—1111 Bethlehem Pike, Springhouse, PA 19477. Maryanne Wagner, Ed. How-to, why-to, and personal experience articles, to 3,000 words, for teachers of grades K–8. Tested classroom ideas for curriculum roundups, to 600 words. Pays to $300, on acceptance. Query.

MEDIA & METHODS—1511 Walnut St., Philadelphia, PA 19102. Michele Sokoloff, Ed. Articles, 1,200 to 1,500 words, on media, technologies, and methods used to enhance instruction and learning in junior and senior high school classrooms. Pays $25 to $75, on publication. Query.

THE MINORITY ENGINEER—44 Broadway, Greenlawn, NY 11740. James Schneider, Ed. Articles, 1,000 to 3,000 words, for college students, on career opportunities in engineering, scientific and technological fields; techniques of job hunting; developments in and applications of new technologies. Interviews. Profiles. Pays 10¢ a word, on publication. Query. Same address and requirements for *The Woman Engineer.*

PHI DELTA KAPPAN—8th and Union St., Box 789, Bloomington, IN 47402. Robert W. Cole, Jr., Ed. Articles, 1,000 to 4,000 words, on educational research, service, and leadership; issues, trends, and policy. Pays from $100, on publication.

SCHOOL ARTS MAGAZINE—50 Portland St., Worcester, MA 01608. David W. Baker, Ed. Articles, 800 to 1,000 words, on art education with special application to the classroom. Photos. Pays varying rates, on publication.

TEACHER UPDATE—P.O. Box 205, Saddle River, NJ 07458. Nick Roes, Ed. Original suggestions for classroom activities. Each page should have a unifying theme, preferably related to specific monthly issue. Pays $20 per published page, on acceptance. Readers are mostly preschool teachers.

TODAY'S CATHOLIC TEACHER—2451 E. River Rd., Suite 200, Dayton, OH 45439. Ruth A. Matheny, Ed. Articles, 600 to 800 words and 1,200 to 1,500 words, on Catholic education, parent-teacher relationships, innovative teaching, teaching techniques, etc. Pays $15 to $75, on publication.

WILSON LIBRARY BULLETIN—950 University Ave., Bronx, NY 10452. Milo Nelson, Ed. Articles, 1,000 to 3,000 words, on library-related material, education, etc. News reports; opinion pieces, 900 words, for "Vantage Point." Photos. Pays from $100, extra for photos, on acceptance.

THE WOMAN ENGINEER—See *The Minority Engineer.*

FARMING AND AGRICULTURE

AMERICAN BEE JOURNAL—51 N. Second St., Hamilton, IL 62341. Joe M. Graham, Ed. Articles on beekeeping, for professionals. Photos. Pays 75¢ per column inch, extra for photos, on publication.

BEEF—1999 Shepard Rd., St. Paul, MN 55116. Paul D. Andre, Ed. Articles on beef cattle feeding, cowherds, stocker operations, and related phases of the cattle industry. Pays to $300, on acceptance.

BUCKEYE FARM NEWS—Ohio Farm Bureau Federation, 35 E. Chestnut St., Columbus, OH 43216. Keith M. Stimpert, Man. Ed. Articles and humor, to 1,000 words, related to agriculture. Pays on publication. Query.

COUNTRY PEOPLE—5400 S. 60th St., Greendale, WI 53129. Bob Ottum, Man. Ed. Rural/country-related, human-interest features, 300 to 1,000 words, and shorts, one-liners and up, with accent on humor. Pays $25 to $150, on acceptance. Queries preferred.

CRANBERRIES—P.O. Box 249, Cobalt, CT 06414. Bob Taylor, Ed. Articles of interest to cranberry growers, industry processors and agricultural researchers. Pays $15 to $40, extra for photos, on publication. Query.

THE EVENER—P.O. Box 7, 211 W. 6th St., Cedar Falls, IA 50613. Susan Salterberg, Man. Ed. How-to and feature articles, 300 to 2,500 words, related to draft horses, mules and oxen. Pays 3¢ to 10¢ a word, $5 to $25 for photos, on acceptance. Queries preferred.

FARM & RANCH LIVING—5400 S. 60th St., Greendale, WI 53129. Bob Ottum, Man. Ed. Articles, 2,000 words, on rural people and situations, nostalgia pieces; profiles of interesting farms and farmers, ranches and ranchers. Poetry. Pays $15 to $400, on acceptance and on publication.

FARM FUTURES—Plaza East Office Center, 330 E. Kilbourn Ave., Suite 200, Milwaukee, WI 53202. Claudia Waterloo, Ed. Articles, to 1,500 words, on marketing of agricultural commodities, farm business issues, management success stories, and the use of commodity futures and options by agricultural producers. Query with outline.

FARM INDUSTRY NEWS—1999 Shepard Rd., St. Paul, MN 55116. Joe Degnan, Ed. Articles for farmers, on new products, buying, machinery, equipment, chemicals, and seeds. Pays $175 to $400, on acceptance. Query.

FARM JOURNAL—Washington Sq., Philadelphia, PA 19105. Lane Palmer, Ed. Articles, 500 to 1,500 words, with photos, on the business of farming, for farmers. Pays 20¢ to 50¢ a word, on acceptance. Query.

FARM SUPPLIER—Mt. Morris, IL 61054. B. Miller, Ed. Articles, 600 to 1,800 words, preferably with color photos, on retail farm trade products: feed, fertilizer, agricultural chemicals, etc. Photos. Pays about 15¢ to 20¢ a word, on acceptance.

FARMING UNCLE—P.O. Box 91, Liberty, NY 12754. Louis Turo, Ed. Articles, 500 to 700 words, on small stock, poultry, etc. Pays 1¢ a word, on acceptance.

FARMSTEAD MAGAZINE—Box 111, Freedom, ME 04941. Heidi Brugger, Man. Ed. Articles, 500 to 2,500 words, on organic gardening; home, plant, fruit and vegetable varieties, soil building techniques, insects, cash crops, small-scale livestock, equipment, life styles, food, energy, etc. Pays 5¢ a word, on publication. Query preferred.

FLORIDA GROWER & RANCHER—723 E. Colonial Dr., Orlando, FL 32803. Frank H. Abrahamson, Ed. Articles and case histories on farmers, growers and ranchers. Pays on publication. Query; buys little freelance material.

THE FURROW—Deere & Company, John Deere Rd., Moline, IL 61265. George Sollenberger, Exec. Ed. Specialized illustrated articles on farming. Pays to $1,000, on acceptance.

GURNEY'S GARDENING NEWS— Gurney Seed and Nursery Co., 2nd and Capitol, Yankton, SD 57079. Pattie Vargas, Ed. Practical articles on specific gardening topics; gardener profiles. Pays $50 to $375 for articles, 700 to 2,500 words, and $30 to $100 for articles 500 to 1,500 words, on gardening projects for children, and short articles, 300 to 500 words, on gardening tips, hints, methods. Query.

HARROWSMITH—Camden House Publishing, Ltd., Camden East, Ont., Canada K0K 1J0. James H. Lawrence, Ed./Pub. Articles, 100 to 5,000 words, on homesteading, husbandry, organic gardening and alternative energy with a Canadian slant. Pays $25 to $1,000, on acceptance. Query.

NORDEN NEWS—601 W. Cornhusker Hwy., Lincoln, NE 68501. Gary Svatos, Ed. Technical articles, 1,200 to 1,500 words, and clinical features, 500 words, on veterinary medicine. Photos. Pays $200 to $250, $100 for shorter pieces, extra for photos, on publication.

THE OHIO FARMER—1350 W. Fifth Ave., Columbus, OH 43212. Andrew L. Stevens, Ed. Articles on farming, rural living, etc., in Ohio. Pays $20 per column, on publication.

PEANUT FARMER—P.O. Box 95075, Raleigh, NC 27625. Marla Maeder, Ed. Articles, 500 to 1,500 words, on production and management practices in peanut farming. Pays $50 to $350, on publication.

PENNSYLVANIA FARMER—704 Lisburn Rd., Camp Hill, PA 17011. John R. Vogel, Ed. Articles on farmers in PA, NJ, DE, MD and WV; farm operations and successful farm management concepts. Pays $1 per column inch, on publication.

SHEEP! MAGAZINE—Box 329, Jefferson, WI 53549. Dave Thompson, Ed. Articles, to 1,500 words, on successful shepherds, woolcrafts, sheep raising and sheep dogs. B/W photos. Pays $2 per column inch, extra for photos, on publication.

SMALL FARMER'S JOURNAL *(featuring Practical Horse-Farming)*—HC-81, Box 68, Reedsport, OR 97467. How-to's, humor, practical work horse information, livestock and produce marketing, and articles appropriate to the independent family farm. Pays negotiable rates, on publication. Query first.

SUCCESSFUL FARMING—1716 Locust St., Des Moines, IA 50336. Richard Krumme, Ed. Articles on farm management, operations, etc. Helpful hints for farm shops. Pays varying rates, on acceptance.

WALLACES FARMER—#501, 1501 42nd St., W. Des Moines, IA 50265. Monte Sesker, Ed. Features, 600 to 700 words, on farming in Iowa, methods and equipment; interviews with farmers. Pays 4¢ to 5¢ a word, on acceptance. Query.

THE WESTERN PRODUCER—Box 2500, Saskatoon, Saskatchewan, Canada S7K 2C4. Attn. Man. Ed. Articles, to 1,000 words, on agricultural and rural subjects, preferably with a Canadian slant. Photos. Pays from 8¢ a word, $15 for b&w photos and cartoons, on publication.

ENVIRONMENT, CONSERVATION, NATURAL HISTORY

ALASKA OUTDOORS—Box 82222, Fairbanks, AK 99708. Christopher Batin, Ed. Articles, 1,400 to 1,800 words, on outdoor recreational opportunities in Alaska. How-to's, fillers, humor, and investigative pieces on natural resource use. Pays $100 to $200, extra for photos, on acceptance. Query.

AMERICAN FORESTS—1319 18th St., N.W., Washington, DC 20036. Bill Rooney, Ed. Well-documented articles, to 2,000 words, with photos, on outdoors, stressing recreational and commercial uses of forests. Photos. Pays on acceptance.

AMERICAN LAND FORUM—5410 Grovenor Lane, Bethesda, MD 20814. Sara Ebenreck, Exec. Ed. Well-researched fact pieces, 3,500 words, and opinion pieces, 1,000 words, on land use and conservation in the U.S. Pays $150 to $300 for articles, $75 for opinion pieces, on acceptance. Query first.

ANIMAL KINGDOM—New York Zoological Society, Bronx, NY 10460.

Eugene J. Walter, Jr., Ed.-in-Chief. Articles, 1,000 to 2,500 words, with photos, on natural history, ecology and animal behavior, preferably based on original scientific research. No articles on pets. Pays $250 to $750, on acceptance.

THE ATLANTIC SALMON JOURNAL—1435 St. Alexandre, Suite 1030, Montreal, Quebec, Canada H3A 2G4. Joanne Eidinger, Ed. Material related to Atlantic salmon: Conservation, ecology, travel, politics, biology, etc. How-to's, anecdotes, cuisine. Articles, 1,500 to 3,000 words; short fillers and poetry, 50 to 100 words. Pays $100 to $350, on publication.

ENVIRONMENTAL ACTION—1525 New Hampshire Ave., N.W., Washington, D.C. 20036. Articles and features, varying lengths, on a broad range of political and/or environmental topics: energy, toxics, conservation, etc. Pays 7¢ to 10¢ a word, extra for photos, on publication. Query required.

THE JOURNAL OF FRESHWATER—Box 90, 2500 Shadywood Rd., Navarre, MN 55392. Articles on issues and solutions relating to the freshwater environment, for lay readers. Pays $150 to $300, on publication. Query.

MICHIGAN OUT-OF-DOORS—P.O. Box 30235, Lansing, MI 48909. Kenneth S. Lowe, Ed. Features, 1,500 to 2,500 words, on hunting, fishing, camping and conservation in Michigan. Photos. Pays $50 to $150, on acceptance.

NATIONAL PARKS MAGAZINE—1701 18th St., N.W., Washington, DC 20009. Michele Strutin, Ed. Articles, 1,000 to 2,000 words, on natural history, wildlife, outdoors activities, travel and conservation as they relate to national parks: illustrated features on the natural, historic and cultural resources of the National Park System. Pieces about legislation and other issues and events related to the parks. Pays $75 to $200, on acceptance. Query. Send for guidelines.

NATIONAL WILDLIFE AND INTERNATIONAL WILDLIFE—1412 16th St., N.W., Washington, DC 20036. Mark Wexler, Man. Ed., *National Wildlife*. Jon Fisher, Man. Ed., *International Wildlife*. Articles, 1,000 to 2,500 words, on wildlife, conservation, environment; outdoor how-to pieces. Photos. Pays market rates, on acceptance. Query.

OCEANS—Fort Mason Center, Bldg. E., San Francisco, CA 94123. Jake Widman, Ed. Articles, to 5,000 words, with photos, on marine life, oceanography, marine art, undersea exploration, seaports, conservation, fishing, diving, and boating. Pays $100 per printed page, on publication. Query. Guidelines available.

OUTDOOR AMERICA—1701 N. Ft. Myer Dr., Suite 1100, Arlington, VA 22209. Quarterly publication of the Izaak Walton League of America. Articles, 1,500 to 2,000 words, on natural resource conservation issues and outdoor recreation, especially fishing, hunting and camping. Pays from 10¢ a word, for features, on publication. Query Articles Ed. with published clippings.

SIERRA—730 Polk St., San Francisco, CA 94109. James Keogh, Ed. Articles, 1,000 to 2,500 words, on environmental and conservation topics, hiking, backpacking, skiing, rafting, cycling. Book reviews and children's dept. Photos. Pays from $200, extra for photos, on acceptance. Query.

SOUTH CAROLINA WILDLIFE—P.O. Box 167, Columbia, SC 29202. John E. Davis, Ed. Articles, 1,000 to 3,000 words, with regional outdoors focus: conservation, natural history and wildlife, recreation. Profiles, how-to's. Pays on acceptance.

WASHINGTON WILDLIFE—c/o Washington State Game Dept., 600 N.

Capitol Way, Olympia, WA 98504. Wayne Van Zwoll, Ed. Articles, 300 to 2,500 words, on fish and wildlife management and related recreational or environmental topics. Fillers, to 150 words. Photos. Pays in copies. Query.

MEDIA AND THE ARTS

AIRBRUSH ACTION—P.O. Box 73, Lakewood, NJ 08701. Jeff Ressner, Ed. Airbrush and art-related articles, 500 to 3,000 words. Pays $75 to $300, on publication. Query required.

THE AMERICAN ART JOURNAL—40 W. 57th St., 5th Floor, New York, NY 10019. Jane Van N. Turano, Ed. Quarterly. Scholarly articles, 2,000 to 10,000 words, on American art of the 17th through 20th centuries. Photos. Pays $200 to $400, on acceptance.

AMERICAN FILM—The American Film Institute, John F. Kennedy Center, Washington, DC 20566. Peter Biskind, Ed. Feature articles, 2,500 to 4,000 words, on film and television. Profiles; news items; reports. Columns, 100 to 1,500 words. Photos. Pays from $50 to $1,000. Query preferred.

AMERICAN INDIAN ART MAGAZINE—7314 E. Osborn Dr., Scottsdale, AZ 85251. Roanne P. Goldfein, Man. Ed. Detailed, specific articles, 10 typed pages, on American Indian arts—painting, carving, bead work, basketry, textiles, ceramics, jewelry, etc. Pays varying rates for articles, on publication. Query.

AMERICAN THEATRE—355 Lexington Ave., New York, NY 10017. Jim O'Quinn, Ed. Features, 500 to 4,000 words, on the theatre and theatre-related subjects. Payment negotiable, on publication. Query.

ART NEW ENGLAND—353 Washington St., Brighton, MA 02135. Carla Munsat, Stephanie Adelman, Eds. Features, 1,000 to 1,500 words, for artists, curators, gallery directors, collectors. Reviews and art criticism, 500 words. At least 2 photos must accompany article. Pays $10 for short reviews, $50 for longer pieces, on publication. Query.

ARTSATLANTIC—P.O. Box 848, Charlottetown, P.E.I., Canada C1A 7L9. Joseph Sherman, Ed. Articles, 800 to 2,500 words, on visual, performing and literary arts, crafts in Atlantic Canada. Also, "idea and concept" articles of universal appeal. Pays from 10¢ per word, on publication. Query.

ARTSLINE—2518 Western Ave., Seattle, WA 98121. Alice Copp Smith, Ed. Features, 1,800 to 2,400 words, on theatre, dance, and other performing or visual arts in the Northwest or the U.S.; arts-related humor; short pieces, 750 to 1,000 words, pay $75 to $100; longer pieces pay from $200, on acceptance. Query.

BALLET NEWS—The Metropolitan Opera Guild, 1865 Broadway, New York, NY 10023. Robert Jacobson, Ed. Articles, to 2,500 words; profiles of dancers; features on ballet past and present. Pays 12¢ a word, on publication. Query.

BLUEGRASS UNLIMITED—Box 111, Broad Run, VA 22014. Peter V. Kuykendall, Ed. Articles, to 3,500 words, on bluegrass and traditional country music. Photos. Pays 5¢ to 6¢ a word, extra for photos.

BROADCASTER—7 Labatt Ave., Toronto, Ont. Canada M5A 3P2. Barbara Moes, Ed. Articles, 500 to 2,000 words, on communications business in Canada. Pays from $250, on publication. Query.

CHANNELS OF COMMUNICATIONS—19 West 44th St., New York, NY 10036. Les Brown, Ed.-in-Chief. Articles on developments in telecommunications and their impact on society (law, politics, religion, business, education and the arts). No personality profiles or reviews, unless related specifically to their affect on viewers. Pays on publication. Query required.

DANCE MAGAZINE—33 West 60th St., New York, NY 10023. William Como, Ed. Features on dance, personalities, and trends. Photos. Query; limited free-lance market.

DANCE TEACHER NOW—University Mall, Suite 2, 803 Russell Blvd., Davis, CA 95616. Susan M. Wershing, Ed. Articles, 2,500 words, for professional dancers and dance teachers, on practical aspects of a dance teacher's professional life, and political or economic issues related to the dance profession. Profiles on teachers or schools. Must be thoroughly researched. Pays $100 to $300, on acceptance.

DARKROOM PHOTOGRAPHY—One Hallidie Plaza, Suite 600, San Francisco, CA 94102. Richard Senti, Ed. Articles on post-camera photographic techniques, 1,000 to 2,500 words, with photos, for all levels of photographers. Pays $100 to $400. Query.

THE DRAMA REVIEW—School of the Arts, New York Univ., 51 W. Fourth St., New York, NY 10012. Michael Kirby, Articles, with photos, on contemporary, avant-garde theater, theatrical theory and history. Pays 2¢ a word, on publication.

DRAMATICS—3368 Central Pkwy., Cincinnati, OH 45225. S. Ezra Goldstein, Ed. Articles, 1,000 to 3,500 words, on the performing arts: theater, puppetry, dance, mime, one-act plays, etc. Pays $25 to $200, on acceptance.

ELECTRONIC MUSICIAN—P.O. Box 20305, Oklahoma City, OK 73156. Craig Anderton, Ed. Articles that de-mystify the technical aspects of synthesizers and other electronic instruments for working musicians. Pieces on do-it-yourself projects, music-related computer software, music video techniques, cartoons, and tips. Pays $35 per printed page, on publication. Query.

EXHIBIT—Drawer 189, Palm Beach, FL 33480. Mark Adams, Ed. Articles to 800 words, with photos, on fine arts, new movements, techniques, profiles of artists. Query.

FILM QUARTERLY—Univ. of California Press, Berkeley, CA 94720. Ernest Callenbach, Ed. Film reviews, historical and critical articles, production projects, to 5,000 words. Pays on publication. Query.

FRETS—20085 Stevens Creek, Cupertino, CA 95014. Phil Hood, Ed. Articles, 750 to 3,000 words, for musicians, on acoustic string instruments, instrument making and repair, music theory and technique. Covers jazz, folk, bluegrass, classical, etc. Profiles of musicians and instruments. Pays $125 to $300, on acceptance. Query.

FUNCTIONAL PHOTOGRAPHY—101 Crossways Park West, Woodbury, NY 11797. David A. Silverman, Sr. Ed. Articles on use of photography and other image-making processes in science, medicine, research, etc. Photos. Pays varying rates, on publication. Query.

GUITAR PLAYER MAGAZINE—20085 Stevens Creek, Cupertino, CA 95014. Tom Wheeler, Ed. Articles. 1,500 to 5,000 words, on guitarists, guitars, and related subjects. Pays $75 to $300, on acceptance. Buys one-time and reprint rights.

HIGH FIDELITY—825 Seventh Ave., New York, NY 10019. William Tynan, Ed. Articles, 2,500 to 3,000 words, on stereo equipment, video applications, and home-entertainment computer applications. Pays on acceptance. Query.

HORIZON—P.O. Drawer 30. Tuscaloosa, AL 35402. Articles 1,500 to 3,500 words, on art, film, literature, photography, dance, music, theater, and other cultural happenings. Pays from $300 on publication. Query Senior Editor.

INDUSTRIAL PHOTOGRAPHY—50 W. 23rd St., New York, NY 10010. Lynn Roher, Ed. Articles on techniques and trends in current professional photography; audiovisuals, etc. for industrial photographers and executives. Query.

INTERNATIONAL MUSICIAN—1500 Broadway, New York, NY 10036. Kelly L. Castleberry II, Ed. Articles. 1,500 to 2,000 words, for professional musicians. Pays varying rates, on acceptance. Query.

JAZZIZ—P.O. Box 8309, Gainesville, FL 32605. Michael Fagien, Editor-in-Chief. Feature articles on jazz, musicians, instruments, performance, recording and education, 1 to 8 double-spaced typed pages. Reviews, to 2 pages. Pays varying rates, on acceptance. Query.

KEYBOARD MAGAZINE—20085 Stevens Creek, Cupertino, CA 95014. Tom Darter, Ed. Articles, 2,500 to 5,000 words, on keyboard instruments and players. Photos. Pays $125 to $300, on acceptance. Query.

MEDIA HISTORY DIGEST—c/o Editor & Publisher, 11 W. 19th St., New York, NY 10011. Hiley H. Ward, Ed. Articles, 1,500 to 2,000 words on the history of media for wide consumer interest. Puzzles and humor related to media history. Pays varying rates, on publication. Query.

MODERN DRUMMER—870 Pompton Ave., Cedar Grove, NJ 07009. Ronald L. Spagnardi, Ed. Articles, 500 to 2,000 words, on drumming; how-to's, interviews. Pays $50 to $500, on publication.

MODERN PERCUSSIONIST—870 Pompton Ave., Cedar Grove, NJ 07009. Rick Mattingly, Ed. Interviews, 5,000 to 6,000 words, with professional percussionists in all areas of music, for professional musicians. Pays $150 to $350, on publication. Query required.

MODERN RECORDING & MUSIC—1120 Old Country Rd., Plainview, NY 11803. Articles, 5 to 12 double-spaced, typed pages, on recording techniques and other topics of interest to musicians and engineers; interviews with music personalities. Query Sammy Caine, Ed. Pays $150, on publication.

MUSIC MAGAZINE—56 The Esplanade, Suite 202, Toronto, Ont., Canada M5E 1A7. Articles, with photos, on musicians, conductors, and composers, for all classical music buffs. Pays $50 per 1,000 words, on publication. Query.

MUSICAL AMERICA—825 Seventh Ave., New York NY 10019. Shirley Fleming, Ed. Authoritative articles, 1,000 to 1,500 words, on classical music subjects. Pays around 15¢ a word, on acceptance.

NEW ENGLAND ENTERTAINMENT—P.O. Box 735, Marshfield, MA 02050. Paul J. Reale, Ed. News features and reviews on arts and entertainment in New England. Light verse. Pays $10 to $25, $1 to $2 for verse, on publication.

OPERA NEWS—The Metropolitan Opera Guild, 1865 Broadway, New York, NY 10023. Robert Jacobson, Ed. Articles, 600 to 3,500 words, on all aspects of opera; humorous anecdotes. Pays 13¢ a word for articles, on publication. Query.

PERFORMANCE—1020 Currie St., Fort Worth, TX 76207. Don Waitt, Ed. Reports on the touring industry: Concert promoters, booking agents, concert venues and clubs, as well as support services, such as lighting, sound and staging companies. Pays 35¢ per column line, on publication.

PETERSEN'S PHOTOGRAPHIC—8490 Sunset Blvd., Los Angeles, CA 90069. Karen Geller-Shinn, Ed. Articles and how-to pieces, with photos, on still, video, studio and darkroom photography, for beginners and advanced amateurs. Pays $60 per printed page, on publication.

PHOTOMETHODS—One Park Ave., New York, NY 10016. Lief Ericksenn, Ed. Articles, 1,500 to 3,000 words, on innovative techniques in imaging (still, film, video) working situations, and management. Pays from $75, on publication. Query.

PLAYBILL—71 Vanderbilt Ave., New York, NY 10169. Joan Alleman, Ed.-in-Chief. Sophisticated articles, 800 to 2,000 words, with photos, on theater and subjects of interest to theater-goers. Pays $100 to $500, on publication.

POPULAR PHOTOGRAPHY MAGAZINE—One Park Ave., New York, NY 10016. Arthur Goldsmith, Ed. Dir. How-to articles, 500 to 2,000 words, for amateur and professional photographers. Pays $150 to $200 per printed page (including photos). Query with outline and photos.

ROLLING STONE—745 Fifth Ave., New York, NY 10151. Magazine of modern American culture, politics, and art. No fiction. Query; "rarely accepts free-lance material."

SATELLITE DISH MAGAZINE—P.O. Box 8, Memphis, TN 38101. Kathy Ferguson, Ed. Lively entertainment features, 1,000 to 2,000 words, on current or upcoming satellite TV programs; articles on the industry and its people. Pays $100 to $750, within thirty days of publication. Send SASE for writer's guidelines.

SHOW-BOOK WEEK—*Chicago Sun Times,* 401 N. Wabash Ave., Chicago, IL 60611. Henry Kisor, Ed. Articles, interviews and profiles, to 1,000 words, on the lively and fine arts. Pays $50 to $125, on publication.

SOAP OPERA DIGEST—254 W. 31st St., New York, NY 10001. Lynn Davey, Man. Ed. Features, to 1,500 words, for people interested in daytime and nightime soaps. Pays from $200, on acceptance. Query.

SUN TRACKS—Box 2510, Phoenix, AZ 85002. Andy Van De Voorde, Music Ed. Music section of *New Times.* Long and short features, record reviews and interviews. Pays $15 to $150, on publication. Query.

TECHNICAL PHOTOGRAPHY—101 Crossways Park West, Woodbury, NY 11797. David A. Silverman, Sr. Ed. Features, 8 to 10 double-spaced pages, on applications and techniques of image photography for staff image producers. Some material on audio-visuals, film, and video. Pays varying rates, on publication. Query.

THEATRE CRAFTS MAGAZINE—135 Fifth Ave., New York, NY 10010. Patricia MacKay, Ed. Articles, 500 to 2,500 words, for professionals in the business, design, and production of theatre, film, video, and the performing arts. Pays on acceptance. Query.

VIDEO—460 W. 34th St., New York, NY 10001. Doug Garr, Man. Ed. How-to and service articles on video equipment and programming. Interviews and human-interest features related to non-broadcast television, from 800 to 2,500 words. Pays varying rates, on acceptance. Query.

HOBBIES, CRAFTS, COLLECTING

AMERICAN CLAY EXCHANGE—P.O. Box 2674, La Mesa, CA 92041. Susan N. Cox, Ed. Articles, from 400 words, for collectors and/or dealers of American-made pottery, with an emphasis on antiques and collectibles. Photos. Pays from $5 for short items, to $100 for thoroughly-researched articles, on publication. Buys all rights.

ANTIQUE MONTHLY—P.O. Drawer 2, Tuscaloosa, AL 35402. Articles, 750 to 1,200 words, on the exhibition and sales (auctions, antique shops, etc.) of decorative arts and antiques more than 100 years old, with photos or slides. Pays $125, on publication. Query.

THE ANTIQUE TRADER WEEKLY—Box 1050, Dubuque, IA 52001. Kyle D. Husfloen, Ed. Articles, 1,000 to 2,000 words, on all types of antiques and collectors' items. Photos. Pays from $5 to $150, extra for photos, on publication. Query preferred. Buys all rights.

ANTIQUES DEALER—1115 Clifton Ave., Clifton, NJ 07013. Nancy Adams, Ed. Articles, 500 to 2,000 words, on trends, pricing, retailing hints, for antiques trade. Pays $75 to $135; b&w photos. Query.

ANTIQUE WEEK/TRI-STATE TRADER—P.O. Box 90, Knightstown, IN 46148. Tom Hoepf, Ed. Articles, 500 to 1,000 words, on collectors' items; background on antiques, restorations, antique shops, genealogy. Auction and show reports. Photos. Pays from 30¢ an inch, $25 to $50 for in-depth articles on publication. Query.

AOPA PILOT—421 Aviation Way, Frederick, MD 21701. Magazine of the Aircraft Owners and Pilots Assn. Edward G. Tripp, Ed. Articles, to 2,500 words, with photos, on general aviation for beginning and experienced pilots. Pays to $750.

BIRD WATCHER'S DIGEST—P.O. Box 110, Marietta, OH 45740. Mary B. Bowers, Ed. Articles, 600 to 3,000 words, on bird-watching experiences and expeditions; information about rare sightings; updates on endangered species. Pays to $50, on publication.

THE BLADE MAGAZINE—P.O. Box 22007, Chattanooga, TN 37422. I. Bruce Voyles, Ed. Articles, 500 to 3,000 words. Historical pieces on knives and old knife factories, etc.; interviews with knifemakers; how-to pieces. Pays from 5¢ a word, on publication.

CHESS LIFE—186 Route 9W, New Windsor, NY 12550. Larry Parr, Ed. Articles, 500 to 3,000 words, for members of the U.S. Chess Federation, on news, profiles, technical aspects of chess. Features on all aspects of chess— history, humor, puzzles, etc. Fiction, 500 to 2,000 words, related to chess. Photos. Pays varying rates, on acceptance. Query; limited freelane market.

COLLECTOR EDITIONS QUARTERLY—170 Fifth Ave., New York, NY 10010. Krystyna Poray Goddu, Man. Ed. Articles, 750 to 1,500 words, on collectibles: glass, porcelain, *objets d'art,* modern Americana, etc. Pays $150 to $350, on publication. Query.

COUNTRY LIVING—224 W. 57th St., New York, NY 10019. Mary Roby,

Managing Ed. Articles on antiques and collectibles. Pays $200 to $300, on acceptance. Query.

CRAFTS 'N THINGS—14 Main St., Dept. W, Park Ridge, IL 60068. Nancy Tosh, Ed. How-to articles on all kinds of crafts projects, with instructions. Pays $50 to $200 on publication. Send manuscript with instructions and photograph of the finished item.

CREATIVE CRAFTS & MINIATURES MAGAZINE—P.O. Box 700, Newton, NJ 07860. Walter Lankenau, Man. Ed. How-to articles, 200 to 1,500 words, with drawings or photos, on adult handicrafts, miniatures, and collectibles. Pays $50 per page, on publication.

CREATIVE IDEAS FOR LIVING—P.O. Box 2522, Birmingham, AL 35201. Feature articles, 700 to 1,000 words, on good quality creative projects; personality pieces for "Life in Crafts" department; decorating articles. Rates start at $350, after acceptance. Query Ed. Katherine Pearson.

DOLLS, THE COLLECTOR'S MAGAZINE—170 Fifth Ave., New York, NY 10010. Krystyna Poray Goddu, Ed. Articles, 500 to 2,500 words, for knowledgeable doll collectors: sharply focused with a strong collecting angle, with concrete information: value, identification, dollmaking, restoration, etc. Pays $100 to $350, on publication. Query.

FINESCALE MODELER—1027 N. Seventh St., Milwaukee, WI 53233. How-to articles for people who make nonoperating scale models of aircraft, automobiles, boats, figures. Photos and drawings should accompany articles. One-page model-building hints and tips. Pays from $30 per published page, on acceptance. Query preferred.

FRANKLIN MINT ALMANAC—Franklin Center, PA 19091. Well-researched articles, 1,000 to 2,000 words, on noteworthy collectors, collectibles and collections. Pay about $750, on acceptance. Query.

GAMES—515 Madison Ave., New York, NY 10022. Articles on games and puzzles. Short humor. Puzzles, tests, brainteasers, etc. Photos. Pays varying rates on publication. Query preferred.

GEMS AND MINERALS—555 Cajou St., Suite B, Redlands, CA 92373. Jack R. Cox, Ed. Articles, with photos, on collecting, cutting and identifying gems and minerals. How-to pieces on making jewelry. Pays 50¢ per column inch, or $15 per page, on publication. Query.

GLASS CRAFT NEWS—270 Lafayette St., Rm. 1310, New York, NY 10012. David Ostiller, Ed. Practical articles of interest to stained glass hobbyists. No historical articles. Pays $100 to $200, on publication. Query required.

HANDMADE—50 College St., Asheville, NC 28801. Sally Rudich, NB/CL Ed. Service and informational articles related to soft and hard crafts, 100 to 500 words, with visuals. Unique design tidbits, 40 to 100 words. Payment varies, on acceptance. Query required.

THE HOME SHOP MACHINIST—2779 Aero Park Dr., Box 1810, Traverse City, MI 49685. Joe D. Rice, Ed. How-to articles, on precision metalworking and foundry work. Accuracy and attention to detail a must. Pays $40 per published page, extra for photos and illustrations, on publication. Send SASE for writer's guidelines.

HOMEBUILT AIRCRAFT—16200 Ventura Blvd., Suite 201, Encino, CA 91436. Steven Werner, Ed. Articles, to 2,500 words, on building and flying your own plane: pilot reports on specific aircraft; new designs in airplanes and airplane parts; news features; air show coverage; pilot experiences and proficiency. Photos. Pays $150 to $300.

JOEL SATER'S ANTIQUES AND AUCTION NEWS—P.O. Box 500, Mount Joy, PA 17552. Nancy Malloy, Ed. Factual articles, 600 to 1,500 words, on antiques and collecting. Photos. Pays $10 to $20, on publication.

LOOSE CHANGE—Mead Pub. Corp., 21176 S. Alameda St., Long Beach, CA 90810. Sue Boyce, Ed. Cover articles, 3,500 to 12,000 words, for collectors of antique gaming machines, slot machines, gambling as a hobby, modern games, etc. Shorter articles, 900 to 5,000 words, on related subjects. Pays $15 to $250, extra for photos, on acceptance. Buys all rights.

MAKE IT WITH LEATHER—Box 1386, Fort Worth, TX 76101. Earl F. Warren, Ed./Pub. How-to and leathercraft business articles, to 2,000 words, with photos and patterns. Leathercraft-related features. Pays $50 to $300, extra for illustrations and photos, on publication.

METROPOLITAN HOME—750 Third Ave., New York, NY 10017. Barbara Graustark. Articles Ed. Articles, 800 to 1,500 words, for monthly columns "Collecting," and "Wine and Spirits," "Equity Real Estate." Payment varies on acceptance. Query required.

MINIATURE COLLECTOR—170 Fifth Ave., New York, NY 10010. Louise Fecher, Man. Ed. Articles, 500 to 1,200 words, with photos, on outstanding miniatures and the people who make and collect them. Original, illustrated how-to projects for making miniatures. Pays varying rates, on publication. Query.

MODEL RAILROADER—1027 N. Seventh St., Milwaukee, WI 53233. Russ Larson, Ed. Articles, with photos of layout and equipment, on model railroads. Pays $66 per printed page, on acceptance. Query.

NEW SHELTER—33 E. Minor St., Emmaus, PA 18049. Address Articles Ed. Do-it-yourself articles for suburban homeowners, 1,000 to 3,000 words, with photos, on innovative housing, alternative energy, water and resource conservation. Pays from 10¢ a word, extra for photos, on acceptance. Query preferred, with photos.

THE NEW YORK ANTIQUE ALMANAC—Box 335, Lawrence, NY 11559. Carol Nadel, Ed. Articles on antiques, shows, shops, museums, art, investments, collectibles, collecting suggestions, related humor. Photos. Pays $5 to $75, extra for photos, on publication.

PLATE WORLD—6054 W. Touhy Ave., Chicago, IL 60648. Alyson Sulaski Wyckoff, Ed. Articles on artists, collectors, manufacturers, retailers of limited-edition collector's plates. Internationally oriented. Pays varying rates, on acceptance. Query first.

POPULAR MECHANICS—224 W. 57th St., New York, NY 10019. Bill Hartford, Man. Ed. Articles, 300 to 2,000 words, on latest developments in mechanics, industry, science, features on hobbies with a mechanical slant, how-to's on home, shop, and crafts projects. Photos and sketches. Pays to $1,000, $25 to $100 for short pieces, on acceptance. Buys all rights.

THE PROFESSIONAL QUILTER—Oliver Press, Box 4096, St. Paul, MN 55104. Jeannine M. Spears, Ed. Articles, 500 to 1,500 words, for women in small businesses related to the quilting field; business and marketing skills, personality profiles. Graphics, if applicable; no "how-to" quilt articles. Pays $25 to $75, on publication.

RAILROAD MODEL CRAFTSMAN—P.O. Box 700, Newton, NJ 07860. William C. Schaumburg, Man. Ed. How-to articles on scale model railroading; cars, operation, scenery, etc. Pays on publication.

R/C MODELER MAGAZINE—P.O. Box 487, Sierra Madre, CA 91024. Patricia E. Crews, Ed. Technical and semi-technical how-to articles on radio-controlled model aircraft, boats and cars. Pays $25 to $450, 30 days after publication. Query.

THE ROBB REPORT—1 Acton Pl., Acton, MA 01720. Feature articles on investment opportunities, classic and collectible autos, art and antiques, classic and collectible autos, art and antiques, home interiors, boats, travel, etc. Pays on publication. Query with SASE and published clips. Attn: Mary Frakes.

ROCKS AND MINERALS—4000 Albemarle St. N.W., Washington, DC 20016. Marie Huizing, Man. Ed. Articles, 3000 words, on minerals. Pays in copies.

SCALE WOODCRAFT—P.O. Box 510, Georgetown, CT 06829. Richard C. West, Ed. In-depth, how-to articles, varying lengths, for serious scale woodworkers, carvers, modelers. Profiles. Pays varying rates, on publication. Query first.

STITCH 'N SEW—2535 Ridgetop Way, Valrico, FL 33594. Carol R. Pedersen, Ed. How-tos and instructional material for any of the needle arts, to 1,000 words. Fillers, 50 to 100 words. Photos and cartoons. Pays on publication.

WESTART—Box 6868, Auburn, CA 95604. Martha Garcia, Ed. Features, 350 to 700 words, on fine arts and crafts. No hobbies. Photos. Pays 50¢ per column inch, on publication. SASE required.

THE WINE SPECTATOR—Opera Plaza Suite 2040, 601 Van Ness Ave., San Francisco, CA 94102. Harvey Steiman, Man. Ed. Features, 600 to 1,000 words, preferably with photos, on topics and people in the wine industry. Pays from $100, extra for photos on publication. Query required.

WINES OF THE AMERICAS—P.O. Box 498, Geyserville, CA 95441. Mildred Howie, Ed. Articles of interest to wine professionals and connoisseurs, 800 to 2,500 words. Pays 10¢ a word, on publication. Query required.

WOODENBOAT—P.O. Box 78, Brooklin, ME 04616. Jonathan Wilson, Ed. How-to and technical articles, 4,000 words, on construction, repair and maintenance of wooden boats; design, history and use of wooden boats; and profiles of outstanding wooden boats builders and designers. Pays $6 per column inch. Query preferred.

THE WOODWORKER'S JOURNAL—P.O. Box 1629, 517 Litchfield Rd., New Milford, CT 06776. Thomas G. Begnal, Man. Ed. Original plans for woodworking projects, with detailed written instructions and at least one B/W photo of finished product. Pays $80 to $120 per published page, on acceptance.

THE WORKBASKET—4251 Pennsylvania, Kansas City, MO 64111. Roma Jean Rice, Ed. Instructions and models for original knit, crochet, and tat items. How-to's on crafts and gardening, 400 to 1,200 words, with photos. Pays 7¢ a word for articles, extra for photos, on acceptance; negotiable rates for instructional items.

WORKBENCH—4251 Pennsylvania Ave., Kansas City, MO 64111. Jay Hedden, Ed. Articles on do-it-yourself home improvement and maintenance projects and general woodworking articles for beginning and expert craftsmen. Complete working drawings with accurate dimensions, step-by-step instructions, lists of materials, and photos of the finished product must accompany submission. Features on how to reduce energy consumption. Pays from $125 per published page, on acceptance.

YESTERYEAR—P.O. Box 2, Princeton, WI 54968. Michael Jacobi, Ed. Articles on antiques, collectibles, and nostalgia, for readers in Wisconsin, Illinois, Iowa, Minnesota and surrounding states. Photos. Will consider regular columns on collecting or antiques. Pays from $10, on publication.

ZYMURGY—Box 287, Boulder, CO 80306. Charles N. Papazian, Ed. Articles appealing to beer lovers and homebrewers. Pays $25 to $75, for pieces 750 to 2,000 words, on publication. Query.

POPULAR & TECHNICAL SCIENCE; COMPUTERS

ANTIC, THE ATARI RESOURCE—524 2nd St., San Francisco, CA 94107. Nat Friedland, Ed. Programs and information for the Atari computer user/owner. Reviews of hardware and software, original programs, etc., 500 words. Game reviews, 400 words. Pays $50 per review, $60 per published page, on publication. Query.

ASTRONOMY—Box 92788, Milwaukee, WI 53202. Richard Berry, Ed-in-Chief. Articles on astronomy, astrophysics, space travel, research. Hobby pieces on equipment; short news items. Pays varying rates, on publication.

BEYOND—303 N. Glenoaks Blvd., Suite 600, Burbank CA 91502. Charlotte Wolter Ed. College newspaper supplement for technical and engineering schools. Science articles, 1,200 to 2,000 words. Science fiction, 2,000 to 3,500 words. Pays 15¢ a word on publication. Query preferred for non-fiction.

BYTE MAGAZINE—P.O. Box 372, Hancock, NH 03449. Philip Lemmons, Ed. Features on new technology, how-to articles, and reviews of computers and software, varying lengths, for sophisticated users of personal computers. Payment is competitive. Query.

COMPUTE!—P.O. Box 5406, Greensboro, NC 27403. Tom Halfhill, Ed. Timely articles on applications, tutorials, games and programs that address the needs of the consumer computer user. Length: 500 to 6,000 words. Pays on acceptance.

COMPUTER AND SOFTWARE NEWS—425 Park Ave., New York, NY 10022. Charles J. Humphrey, Ed. Newsweekly for hardware and software retailers, distributors and suppliers. News items. Pays 15¢ per published word, on publication.

COMPUTING NOW!—Moorshead Publications, Suite 601, 25 Overlea Blvd., Toronto, Ontario, Canada M4H 1B1. Steve Rimmer, Ed. Articles, from 2,000 to 4,000 words, for large audience, ranging in skill from beginners to business users. Photos and drawings. Pays 8¢ a word, $10 to $50 for drawings, on publication. Query.

DIGITAL REVIEW—160 State St., Boston, MA 02109. Patrick Kenealy, Ed. For users of Digital Equipment (DEC) computers. How-to-articles, profiles, business applications and reviews, to 3,500 words. Pays $500 to $1,500, on acceptance. Include graphics. Query first.

DISCOVERY MAGAZINE—Time & Life Building, Rockefeller Center, New York, NY 10020. Uses staff-written material only.

80 MICRO—ComputerWorld Communications, 80 Pine St., Peterborough, NH 03458. Address Submissions Ed. Technical articles, programs and tutorials for TRS-80 microcomputer; no general-interest articles. Pays $50 to $75 per printed page, on acceptance. Query.

ELECTRONICS WEST—2250 N. 16th St., Suite 105, Phoenix, AZ 85006. Walter J. Schuch, Ed. Profiles, articles on new products and management topics, 1,000 words; news items for high-tech workers. Pays 10¢ a word, on publication.

ENVIRONMENT—4000 Albemarle St. N.W., Washington, DC 20016. Jane Scully, Ed. Factual articles, 2,500 to 5,000 words, on scientific, technological and environmental policy and decision-making issues. Articles must be documented. Pays $100 to $300. Query.

THE FUTURIST—World Future Society, 4916 Elmo Ave., Bethesda, MD 20814. Timothy Willard, Ass't Ed. Features, 1,000 to 5,000 words, on subjects pertaining to the future, environment, education, science, technology, etc. Pays in copies.

GENETIC ENGINEERING NEWS—157 E. 86th St., New York, NY 10028. Joan Graf, Man. Ed. Articles on all aspects of biotechnology; feature articles and news articles. Pays varying rates, on acceptance. Query.

HAM RADIO—Greenville, NH 03048. Rich Rosen, Ed. Articles, to 2,500 words, on amateur radio theory and construction. Pays to $40 per printed page on publication. Query.

HARDCOPY—Box 759, Brea, CA 92621. Leslie Frohoff, Ed. Articles, 2,000 to 3,500 words, for manufacturers, users, and distributors of Digital Equipment Corp. (DEC): how-to pieces on product and system applications, and company profiles. Must have DEC tie-in. Pays $200 to $600, thirty days after acceptance. Query first.

HOT COCO—80 Pine St., Peterborough, NH 03458. Michael Nadeau, Ed. How-to pieces, programs of games, utilities, education, etc., and reviews for Tandy Color Computer users. Pays $50 to $75 per printed page on acceptance, for articles 2 to 15 double-spaced pages. Query.

INCIDER—80 Pine St., Peterborough, NH 03458. Articles for Apple II computer users: applications-oriented, state-of-the-art ready to type in program listings, and how-to pieces, Software and hardware reviews. Pays $100 per printed page, on acceptance. Query preferred.

THE JOURNAL OF FRESHWATER—2500 Shadywood Rd., Box 90, Navarre, MN 55392. Linda Schroeder, Ed. Articles on freshwater environment and science, for lay persons. Photos. Pays $100 to $300, extra for photos, on publication.

LINK-UP—143 Old Marlton Pike, Medford, NJ 08055. Bev Smith, Editor. Feature articles and news stories dealing with online and videotex services for business, personal, and educational use, 500 to 2,000 words. Pays $80 to $200, on publication.

MACWORLD—Editorial Proposals, 555 DeHaro St., San Francisco, CA 94107. How-to articles relating to Macintosh personal computers; varying lengths. Query or send outline with screenshots, if applicable. Pays from $350, on acceptance. Send SASE for writer's guidelines.

MINI-MICRO SYSTEMS—275 Washington St., Newton, MA 02158. George Kotelly, Ed. Technical monthly for computer system users, manufacturers, and integrators. How-to pieces, profiles, news items, etc. Pays $35 to $100 per printed page, on publication. Query.

MODERN ELECTRONICS—76 N. Broadway, Hicksville, NY 10081. Art Salsberg, Ed.-in-Chief. How-to features, tutorials, and construction projects related to latest consumer electronics products and personal computer equipment and software. Lengths vary. Query with outline required. Pays to $150, on acceptance.

NIBBLE—45 Winthrop St., Concord, MA 01742. David P. Szetela, Ed. Programs and programming methods, as well as short articles, reviews and general-interest pieces for Apple Computer and Macintosh users. Send short cover letter and sample program runs with manuscript. Pays $50 to $500 for articles, $20 to $250 for shorter pieces. Send SASE for writer's guidelines.

OMNI—1965 Broadway, New York, NY 10023. Gurney Williams III, Exec. Ed. Articles, 2,500 to 3,500 words, on scientific aspects of the future: space colonies, cloning, machine intelligence, ESP, origin of life, future arts, lifestyles, etc. Pays $800 to $2,500, less for short features, on acceptance. Query.

PC TECH JOURNAL—The World Trade Center, Suite 211, Baltimore, MD 21202. Will Fastie, Ed. How-to pieces and reviews, for technically sophisticated computer professionals. Pays $100 to $1,000 on acceptance. Query required.

POPULAR COMPUTING—70 Main St., Peterborough, NH 03458. Pamela Clark, Ed.-in-Chief. Articles, 1,500 to 3,000 words, on small business and professional uses of personal computers. Pays $150 to $1,000 on acceptance. Query.

POPULAR SCIENCE—380 Madison Ave., New York, NY 10017. C. P. Gilmore, Ed. Articles, to 2,000 words, with photos, on developments in applied science and technology. Short illustrated articles on new inventions and products; photo essays, to 4 pages. Pays from $150 per printed page, on acceptance.

PORTABLE 100/200—Computer Communications, Inc., P.O. Box 250, Camden, ME 04843. Nancy Laite, Man. Ed. Programs and applications for users of TRS-80 Model 100 and Tandy 200 microcomputers, 2,000 to 4,000 words. Product reviews. Pays $100 to $400 for articles, $75 to $200 for reviews, on acceptance. Query.

SCIENCE DIGEST—888 Seventh Ave., New York, NY 10106. Oliver S. Moore, Ed. No unsolicited material.

SCIENCE 86—1333 H St., NW, 11th fl., Washington, DC 20005. Allen Hammond, Ed. Short articles, 500 to 1,200 words, and features, 3,000 to 4,000 words, on developments in the sciences, including social science and economics, medicine and technology. Profiles of scientists. Book reviews. Pays $1,800 to $2,500 for features, $300 to $800 for shorter pieces, on acceptance. Query.

SEA FRONTIERS—3979 Rickenbacker Causeway, Virginia Key, Miami, FL 33149. Jean Bradfisch, Ed. Illustrated articles, 2,000 words, on scientific advances related to the sea, biological, physical, chemical, or geological phenomena, etc., for lay readers. Send SASE for guidelines. Pays $20 to $30 a page, on publication. Query.

SMITHSONIAN—900 Jefferson Dr., Washington, DC 20560. Marlane A. Liddell, Articles Ed. Articles on history, art, natural history, physical science, etc. Query with SASE.

TECHNOLOGY REVIEW—Rm. 10-140 Massachusetts Institute of Technology, Cambridge, MA 02139. John Mattill, Ed. General-interest articles, and more technical features, 1,500 to 5,000 words on technology, the environment and society. Payment varies, on publication. Query.

ANIMALS

ANIMALS—MSPCA, 350 S. Huntington Ave., Boston, MA 02130. Susan Burns, Ed. Journal of the Massachusetts Society for the Prevention of Cruelty to Animals. Articles, to 3,000 words, on animals. Photos. Pays $50 to $75, on acceptance. Query.

CAT FANCY—P.O. Box 6050, Mission Viejo, CA 92690. Linda Lewis, Ed. Articles, from 1,500 to 3,000 words, on cat care, health, grooming, etc. Pays 3¢ to 5¢ a word, on publication.

CATS—P.O. Box 37, Port Orange, FL 32029. Address Eds. Articles, 1,000 to 2,000 words, with illustrations or photos, on cats: unusual anecdotes, medical pieces, humor, articles on cats in art., literature or science. Pays 5¢ a word, extra for illustrations, on publication. Replies in 8 weeks.

THE CHRONICLE OF THE HORSE—Box 46, Middleburg, VA 22117. Peter Winants, Ed. Interviews and how-to articles, 6 to 7 manuscript pages, relating to horses, for sophisticated horsemen. Topics of interest include foxhunting, dressage, training, steeplechase racing, trail riding, equine youth activities; no Western-style pieces. Queries are preferred. Pays $10 to $15 for short, general-interest items of up to 3 pages, on publication. Pays $125 to $200 for articles, on acceptance.

DOG FANCY—P.O. Box 6050, Mission Viejo, CA 92690. Linda Lewis, Ed. Articles, 1,500 to 3,000 words, on dog care, health, grooming, breeds, etc. Photos. Pays 3¢ to 5¢ a word, on publication.

THE FLORIDA HORSE—P. O. Box 2106, Ocala, FL 32678. F. J. Audette, Publisher. Articles, 1,500 words, on Florida thoroughbred breeding and racing. Pays $100 to $150, on publication.

THE GREYHOUND REVIEW—National Greyhound Assn., Box 543, Abilene, KS 67410. Jane E. Allen, Man. Ed. Articles, 1,000 to 10,000 words, pertaining to the Greyhound dog industry: how-to train, historical nostalgia, interviews; satirical fiction. Pays $40 to $150, on publication.

HORSE & RIDER—Box 555, 41919 Moreno Rd., Temecula, CA 92390. Ray Rich, Ed. Articles, 500 to 3,000 words, with photos, on Western riding and general horse care: training, feeding, grooming, etc. Pays varying rates, before publication. Buys all rights.

HORSE ILLUSTRATED—P. O. Box 6050, Mission Viejo, CA 92690. Jill-Marie Jones, Ed. Articles, 1,500 to 3,000 words, on all aspects of owning and caring for horses. Pays 3¢ to 5¢ a word, on publication.

HORSEMAN—5314 Bingle Rd., Houston, TX 77092. David Gaines, Ed. Articles, to 2,500 words, with photos, primarily on western horsemanship. Pays from 10¢ a word, extra for photos, on publication. Query.

HORSEMEN'S YANKEE PEDLAR—785 Southbridge St., Auburn, MA 01501. Nancy L. Khoury, Pub. News and feature-length articles, about horses and horsemen in the Northeast. Photos. Pays $2 per published inch, on publication. Query.

HORSEPLAY—Box 545, Gaithersburg, MD 20877. Cordelia Doucet, Ed. Articles, to 3,000 words, on eventing, show jumping, horse shows, dressage driving, and fox hunting, for horse enthusiasts. Pays 9¢ a word, after publication.

HORSES WEST—Box 537, Station 2, Denver, CO 80206. Articles for horse breeders, horse owners and advertisers in the horse industry, primarily in the Rocky Mountain States. Articles cover the following subjects: regional or national news stories and human-interest features on well-known events or horses and personalities; interviews with successful trainers highlighting techniques and methods; horsekeeping and stable management; veterinary topics; tack and equipment with detailed explanations of their use; showing techniques illustrating new trends; breeding programs. Stories, 1,000 to 2,500 words, with a strong horse angle. Short anecdotes and fiction with a humorous angle. Query first. Feature articles are 1,500 to 2,000 words; news items, horse-keeping tips and how-to pieces are 400 to 1,000 words. Pays 50¢ to $1.00 per column inch, 30 days after publication.

THE MORGAN HORSE—Address Senior Editor, Box 1, Westmoreland, NY 13490. Articles, from 500 to 3,500 words, on equestrian and Morgan topics. Pays 5¢ a word, to $25 for photos, on publication. Query.

PERFORMANCE HORSEMAN—Gum Tree Corner, Unionville, PA 19375. Miranda Lorraine, Articles Ed. Factual how-to pieces for the serious western rider, on training, improving riding skills, all aspects of care and management, etc. Pays from $200, on publication. Query.

PRACTICAL HORSEMAN—Gum Tree Corner, Unionville, PA 19375. Miranda D. Lorraine, Articles Ed. How-to articles on English riding, training, and horse care. Pays on publication. Query.

SPUR MAGAZINE—P. O. Box 85, Middleburg, VA 22117. Address Ed. Dept. Articles, 300 to 5,000 words, on Thoroughbred racing and breeding. Profiles of people and farms. Historical and nostalgia pieces. Pays $50 to $250, on publication. Query. SASE required.

THE WESTERN HORSEMAN—P. O. Box 7980, Colorado Springs, CO 80933. Chan Bergen, Ed. Articles, around 1,500 words, with photos, on care and training of horses. Pays from $150, on acceptance.

CHILD CARE AND DEVELOPMENT

AMERICAN BABY—575 Lexington Ave., New York, NY 10022. Judith Nolte, Ed. Articles, about 1,500 words, for new or expectant parents; pieces on child care. No poetry. Pays on acceptance.

BABY TALK—185 Madison Ave., New York, NY 10016. Patricia Irons, Ed. Articles, 1,500 to 3,000 words, by mother or father, on babies, baby care, etc. Pays varying rates, on acceptance. SASE required.

CHRISTIAN HOME—Box 189, 1908 Grand Ave., Nashville, TN 37202. David Bradley, Ed. Articles on parenting, marriage and devotional life, 1,000 to 1,500 words, for couples and families. Pays 3½¢ to 4½¢ a word, on acceptance.

DAY CARE CENTER—P. O. Box 249, Cobalt, CT 06414. Bob Taylor, Pub./ Ed. Articles of interest to day care center owners, directors, employees, and other experts in early childhood education. Profiles of day care center owners, practical business advice, articles on day care legislation, and pieces about educational and other activities in day care centers. Query first. Pays $15 to $75, extra for photos, illustrations, or cartoons.

THE EXCEPTIONAL PARENT—605 Commonwealth Ave., Boston, MA 02215. Maxwell J. Schleifer, Ed. Articles, 600 to 3,000 words, with practical information for parents of disabled children. Pays on publication.

EXPECTING—685 Third Ave., New York, NY 10017. Evelyn A. Podsiadlo, Ed. Articles, 700 to 1,800 words, for expectant mothers. Pays $150 to $350, on acceptance.

FAMILY JOURNAL—P. O. Box 6024, Columbia, MO 65205. Kathleen Horrigan, Submissions Ed. Practical and anecdotal articles on parenting, from pregnancy through age 8. Pays negotiable rates. Send for guidelines.

GROWING CHILD/GROWING PARENT—22 N. Second St., Lafayette, IN 47902. Nancy Kleckner, Ed. Articles to 1,500 words on subjects of interest to parents of children under 6, with emphasis on the issues, problems, and choices of being a parent. No personal-experience pieces. Pays 8¢ to 15¢ a word, on acceptance. Query.

LIVING WITH CHILDREN—127 Ninth Ave. N., Nashville, TN 37234. SuAnne Bottoms, Ed. Articles, 800, 1,450 or 2,000 words, on parent-child relationships, told from a Christian perspective. Pays 5¢ a word, after acceptance.

LIVING WITH PRESCHOOLERS—127 Ninth Ave., N., Nashville, TN 37234. SuAnne Bottoms, Ed. Articles, 800, 1,450 or 2,000 words, and fillers, to 300 words, for Christian families. Pays 5¢ a word, on acceptance.

LIVING WITH TEENAGERS—127 Ninth Ave. N., Nashville, TN 37234. Articles for parents of teens, told from a Christian perspective; first-person approach preferred. Poetry, 4 to 16 lines. Photos. Pays 5¢ a word, on acceptance.

MARRIAGE & FAMILY LIVING—St. Meinrad, IN 47577. Kass Dotterweich, Man. Ed. Articles, to 2,000 words, on husband-wife and parent-child relationships. Pays 7¢ a word, on acceptance. Query.

PARENTS—685 Third Ave., New York, NY 10017. Elizabeth Crow, Ed.-in-Chief. Articles, 2,000 to 3,000 words, on growth and development of infants, children, teens; family; women's issues; community; current research. Informal style with quotes from experts. Pays from $450, on acceptance. Query.

TODAY'S CHRISTIAN PARENT—8121 Hamilton Ave., Cincinnati, OH 45231. Mildred Mast, Ed. Informative, inspirational or humorous articles, 600 to 1,200 words, on application of Christian principles in marriage, child-rearing, pleasures and problems of parenting, and adult family relationships. Timely articles on relevant issues, from a Christian perspective. Pays varying rates, on acceptance. SASE required.

WORKING MOTHER—230 Park Ave., New York, NY 10169. Vivian Cadden, Ed. Well-thought-out articles, 1,500 to 2,000 words, for working mothers: child care, home management, the work world, single mothers, etc. Pays around $500, on acceptance. Query, with detailed outline.

MILITARY

ARMY MAGAZINE—2425 Wilson Blvd., Arlington, VA 22201. L. James Binder, Ed.-in-Chief. Features, to 5,000 words, on military subjects. Essays, humor, history, news reports, first-person anecdotes. Pays 8¢ to 12¢ a word, $5 to $25 for anecdotes, on publication.

INFANTRY—P. O. Box 2005, Fort Benning, GA 31905-0605. Articles, 2,000 to 5,000 words, on military organization, equipment, tactics, foreign armies, etc., for U.S. infantry personnel. Pays varying rates, on publication; no payment made to U.S. Government employees. Query.

LEATHERNECK—Box 1775, Quantico, VA 22134. William V. H. White, Ed. Articles, to 3,000 words, with photos, on U.S. Marines. Pays $50 to $75 per printed page, on acceptance. Query.

MILITARY REVIEW—U.S. Army Command and General Staff College, Fort Leavenworth, KS 66027. Frederick W. Timmgrman, Ed.-in-Chief. Articles, 2,500 to 4,000 words, on tactics, national defense, military history and any military subject of current interest and importance. Pays $25 to $100, on publication.

NATIONAL GUARD—One Mass. Ave. N.W., Washington, DC 20001. Reid K. Beveridge, Ed. Articles, 2,000 to 4,000 words, with photos, of interest to National Guard members. Pays $200 to $500, on publication.

OFF DUTY—3303 Harbor Blvd., Suite C-2, Costa Mesa, CA 92626. Informative, entertaining and useful articles, 900 to 1,800 words, for military service personnel and their dependents, on making the most of off duty time and getting the most out of service life: military living, travel, personal finance, sports, cars and motorcycles, military people. American trends, etc. Military angle essential. Pays 13¢ to 16¢ a word, on publication. European and Pacific editions also. Guidelines available. Query.

PROCEEDINGS—U.S. Naval Institute, Annapolis, MD 21402. Address Fred H. Rainbow, Ed. Articles, under 4,000 words, on naval and maritime subjects. Pay varies—from $60 to $150 per estimated published page—on acceptance. Editorial guidelines are available.

THE RETIRED OFFICER MAGAZINE—201 N. Washington St., Alexandria, VA 22314. Address Manuscript Ed. Articles, preferably with photos, 1,000 to 2,500 words, of interest to military retirees. Current affairs, contemporary military history and humor, and pieces on travel, hobbies, and second-career job opportunities. Pays to $400, extra for photos, on acceptance. Query preferred. Send for writers guidelines.

THE TIMES MAGAZINE—Army Times Publishing Co., Springfield, VA 22159-0200. Barry Robinson, Ed. Articles, to 3,000 words, on current military life. Photos. Pays $150 to $500, on publication.

VFW MAGAZINE—Broadway at 34th, Kansas City, MO 64111. Magazine for Veterans of Foreign Wars and their families. James K. Anderson, Ed. Articles, 1,000 words, on current issues, solutions to everyday problems, personalities, sports, etc. How-to and historical pieces. Photos. Pays 5¢ to 10¢ a word, extra for photos, on acceptance.

WESTERN

AMERICAN WEST—3033 N. Campbell Ave., Tucson, AZ 85719. Mae Reid-Bills, Man. Ed. Well-researched, illustrated articles, 1,000 to 3,000 words, on western America, past and present, in a lively style appealing to the intelligent general reader. Query required. Pays from $200, on acceptance.

OLD WEST—See *True West.*

PERSIMMON HILL—1700 N.E. 63rd St., Oklahoma City, OK 73111. Sara Dobberteen, Sr. Ed. Articles, 2,000 to 3,000 words, on Western history and art, rodeo, cowboys, ranching, and nature. Profiles, biographies. Pays from $150, on publication.

REAL WEST—Charlton Publications, Inc., Division St., Derby, CT 06418. Ed Doherty, Ed. True stories of the Old West, 1,000 to 4,000 words. Photos. Pays from 3¢ a word, on acceptance.

TRUE WEST/FRONTIER TIMES—P. O. Box 2107, Stillwater, OK 74076. John Joerschke, Ed. True stories, 500 to 4,500 words, with photos, about the Old West to 1930. Some contemporary stories with historical slant. Source list required. Pays 3¢ to 8¢ a word, extra for B&W photos, on acceptance. Same address and requirements for *Old West.*

HISTORICAL

ADIRONDACK LIFE—420 E. Genesee St., Syracuse, NY 13202. William K. Verner, Ed. Features, about 3,000 words, on the history of upstate New York, for general audience. Photos are a plus. Pays $175 to $300, on publication.

AMERICAN HERITAGE—10 Rockefeller Pl., New York, NY 10020. Byron Dobell, Ed. Articles, 750 to 5,000 words, on U.S. history and background of American life and culture. No fiction. Pays from $300 to $1,500, on acceptance. Queries only.

AMERICAN HERITAGE OF INVENTION AND TECHNOLOGY—10 Rockefeller Plaza, New York, NY 10020. Frederick Allen, Managing Ed. Articles, 2,000 to 3,500 words, on the history of technology in America. Query preferred. Pay rates vary, on acceptance.

AMERICAN HISTORY ILLUSTRATED—2245 Kohn Rd., P. O. Box 8200, Harrisburg, PA 17105. Articles, 2,000 to 3,500 words, soundly researched. Style should be popular, not scholarly. Pays $300 to $500, on acceptance. Query with SASE required.

AMERICANA—29 W. 38th St., New York, NY 10018. Michael Durham, Ed. Articles, 1,000 to 2,500 words, with historical slant: restoration, crafts, food, collecting, travel, etc. Pays $400 to $750, on acceptance. Query.

ARIZONA HIGHWAYS—2039 W. Lewis Ave., Phoenix, AZ 85009. Richard G. Stahl, Managing Ed. Articles on Arizona, 2,000 words—history, archaeology, nostalgia. Pays 25¢ to 30¢ a word, on acceptance. Query.

BRITISH HERITAGE—P. O. Box 8200, Harrisburg, PA 17105. Well-researched articles, 1,000 to 2,000 words, blending travel with British history and culture (including the Empire and Commonwealth countries) for readers knowledgeable about Britain. Pays $100 per 1,000 words, on acceptance. Query. Send SASE for guidelines.

CHICAGO HISTORY—Clark St. at North Ave., Chicago, IL 60614. Timothy C. Jacobson, Ed. Articles, to 4,500 words, on urban political, social and cultural history. Pays to $250, on publication. Query.

COBBLESTONE—20 Grove St., Peterborough, NH 03458. Carolyn Yoder,

Ed. Theme-related biographies, and short accounts of historical events, to 1,200 words, for children aged 8 to 14. Pays 10¢ to 15¢ a word, on publication. Send SASE for editorial guidelines with monthly themes.

EARLY AMERICAN LIFE—Box 8200, Harrisburg, PA 17105. Frances Carnahan, Ed. Illustrated articles, 1,000 to 3,000 words, on early American life: arts, crafts, furnishings, architecture; travel features about historic sites and country inns. Pays $50 to $400, on acceptance. Query.

HISTORIC PRESERVATION—1785 Massachusetts Ave., N.W., Washington, DC 20036. Thomas J. Colin, Ed. Articles from published writers, 1,500 to 4,000 words, on historic preservation, maritime preservation and people involved in preservation. High-quality photos. Pays $300 to $850, extra for photos, on acceptance. Query required.

COLLEGE, CAREERS

AMPERSAND—303 N. Glenoaks Blvd., Suite 600, Burbank, CA 91502. Charlotte Wolter, Ed. Articles, 1,000 to 2,000 words, for college students, on careers, academics, recreation, political issues. Short items and humor, 500 words. Pays 15¢ to 20¢ a word, on acceptance. Queries are required.

THE BLACK COLLEGIAN—1240 S. Broad St., New Orleans, LA 70125. James Borders, Ed. Articles, to 2,000 words, on experiences of black students, careers, and how-to subjects. Pays on publication. Query.

CAMPUS VOICE—505 Market St., Knoxville, TN 37902. Lively, irreverent, in-depth articles on issues of interest to 18- to 24-year-old readers. Articles on music and film entertainers, life styles, relationships, and investigative pieces, 2,500 to 3,000 words. Department pieces, 1,500 to 2,000 words, on fitness, job hunting, improving academic performance, college sports. Queries are required; editorial guidelines available. Pays $300 to $2,000, on acceptance.

THE JOURNAL OF CAREER PLANNING AND EMPLOYMENT—College Placement Council, Inc., 62 Highland Ave., Bethlehem, PA 18017. Patricia A. Sinnott, Managing Ed. Quarterly. Articles, 2,000 to 4,000 words, on topics related to career planning, placement, and recruitment, for career development professionals. Pays $200 to $400, on acceptance. Authors' guidelines available. Queries are preferred; include published clips.

ON CAMPUS—Inter-Collegiate Press, 6105 Travis Lane, P.O. Box 10, Shawnee Mission, KS 66201. Ellen Parker, Ed. Articles, 1,000 to 3,500 words, of general interest to college freshman—interviews, profiles, humor, personal experience, how-to, travel, nostalgia, opinion, careers, study guides, financial aid, etc. News briefs, 200 to 400 words. Queries are preferred. Pays $30 to $400, on acceptance. Annual publication.

ALTERNATIVE MAGAZINES

EAST WEST JOURNAL—17 Station St., Box 1200, Brookline, MA 02147. Features, 1,500 to 2,500 words, on holistic health, natural foods, the environment, etc. Material for "Body," "Healing," "Family," and "Science." Interviews. Photos. Pays 7¢ to 12¢ a word, extra for photos, on publication.

FATE—Clark Publishing Co., 500 Hyacinth Pl., Highland Park, IL 60035. Mary M. Fuller, Ed. Documented articles, to 3,000 words, on strange happenings. First-person accounts, to 300 words, of true psychic or unexplained experiences. Pays from 5¢ a word for articles, $10 for short pieces, on publication.

NEW AGE—342 Western Ave., Brighton, MA 02135. Articles, for readers interested in self-development and awareness, on natural foods, holistic health, education, disarmament, etc. Pays from 10¢ a word, on publication. Query.

NEW FRONTIER—129 N. 13th St., Philadelphia, PA 19107. Swami Virato, Ed. New age publication dedicated to the transformation of consciousness on the planet. Articles, 750 to 2,000 words, on parapsychology, hi-tech and consciousness, mind-body-spirit, nutrition, holistic health, Eastern philosophy, sex, yoga, back to nature, peace. Queries are preferred. Pays $30 to $100, on publication.

NEW REALITIES—680 Beach St., San Francisco, CA 94109. James Bolen, Ed. Articles on holistic health, personal growth, parapsychology, alternative lifestyles, new spirituality. Pays to $150, on publication. Query.

PSYCHIC GUIDE—Box 701, Providence, RI 02901. Paul Zuromski, Ed. Articles, to 3,000 words, on metaphysical subjects. Payment is negotiable, on publication.

YOGA JOURNAL—2054 University Ave., Berkeley, CA 94704. Stephan Bodian, Ed. Articles, 1,200 to 3,000 words, on holistic health, spirituality, yoga, and transpersonal psychology; "new age" profiles and interviews. Queries are required. Pays $50 to $150, on publication.

OP-ED MARKETS

Op-ed pages in newspapers—those pages that run opposite the editorials—offer writers an excellent opportunity to air their opinions, views, ideas, and insights on a wide spectrum of subjects and in styles from the highly personal and informal essay to the more serious commentary on politics, foreign affairs, and news events. Humor and nostalgia often find a place here.

THE BALTIMORE SUN—501 N. Calvert St., Baltimore, MD 21278. Stephen Broening, Op-Ed Editor. Articles, 750 to 1,000 words, for Opinion-Commentary page, on a wide range of topics: politics, education, foreign affairs, life styles, science, etc. Humor. Pays $75 to $125, on publication.

BOSTON HERALD—One Herald Sq., Boston, MA 02106. Shelly Cohen, Op-Ed Editor. Pieces, 600 to 800 words, on human-interest, political, regional, life style, and seasonal topics. Pays $50 to $75, on publication.

THE CHICAGO TRIBUNE—435 N. Michigan Ave., Chicago, IL 60611. Pieces, 500 to 800 words, on politics, economics, education, environment, foreign and domestic affairs. Pays $50 to $250, on publication.

THE CHRISTIAN SCIENCE MONITOR—One Norway St., Boston, MA 02115. Susan Sweetnam, Opinion Page Ed. Pieces, 600 to 700 words, for "Opinion and Commentary" page, on politics, domestic and foreign affairs. Humor. Payment varies. Query preferred.

THE CHRONICLE—901 Mission St., San Francisco, CA 94103. Lyle York, "This World" Ed. Articles, 1,500 to 2,000 words, on a wide range of subjects. Pays $50 to $100, on publication.

THE CLEVELAND PLAIN DEALER—1801 Superior Ave., Cleveland OH 44114. William Henson, Deputy Ed. Dir. Pieces, 800 to 1,000 words, on politics, economics, foreign affairs, and regional issues. Pays $50 to $100, on publication.

DALLAS MORNING NEWS—Communications Center, Dallas, TX 75265. Carolyn Barta, "Viewpoints" Ed. Pieces 750 words (1,000 words for Sunday issue), on politics, education, foreign and domestic affairs, seasonal and regional issues. Pays $75 to $100, on publication.

DENVER POST—P.O. Box 1709, Denver, CO 80201. Fred Brown, Asst. Ed. Page Ed. Pieces, 500 to 700 words, on economics, environment, education, law, politics, and science; seasonal and regional issues. Humor. Pays $35 to $50, on publication.

DES MOINES REGISTER—715 Locust St., Des Moines, IA 50312. James Flansburg, "Opinion" Page Ed. Articles, 600 to 800 words, on all topics. Humor. Pays $25 to $250, on publication.

DETROIT FREE PRESS—321 W. Lafayette St., Detroit, MI 48231. Patricia C. Foley, Op-Ed Editor. Articles, 750 to 800 words, on topics of local interest, and opinion pieces. Humor. Pays varying rates, on publication.

THE HARTFORD COURANT—285 Broad St., Hartford, CT 06115. Elissa Papirno, Deputy Ed. Page Editor. Opinionated articles, 750 words (1,000 for Sunday "Commentary" section), on science, environment, politics, economics, law, and domestic and foreign affairs; pieces of regional and season interest. Pays from $40, on publication.

THE LOS ANGELES HERALD EXAMINER—Box 2416, Terminal Annex, Los Angeles, CA 90051-0416. Mike Gordon, Deputy Editor, Editorial Page. Articles, to 800 words, on local topics not covered by syndicated columnists. Humor. Pays $75, on publication.

LOS ANGELES TIMES—Times Mirror Sq., Los Angeles, CA 90053. Commentary pieces, to 800 words, on all subjects. Pays $150 to $250, on publication.

MIAMI HERALD—One Herald Plaza, Miami, FL 33101. Joanna Wragg, Op-Ed Editor. Informed opinion pieces, to 800 words, on all subjects. Pays $35 to $50, on publication.

MILWAUKEE JOURNAL—Box 661, Milwaukee, WI 53201. James P. Cattey, Op-Ed Editor. Pieces, 600 words, on various subjects and humor. Pays $30 to $35, on publication.

THE NEW YORK TIMES—229 W. 43rd St., New York, NY 10036. Robert Semple, Jr., Op-Ed Editor. Pieces, 750 words, on topics not covered by syndicated columnists. Pays $150, on publication.

NEWSDAY—Melville, NY 11747. Ilene Barth, "Viewpoints" Ed. Pieces, 600 to 1,500 words, on foreign and domestic affairs, politics, economics, life styles, law, education, and the environment. Seasonal pieces. Pays $75 to $200, on publication.

THE OAKLAND TRIBUNE—Box 24423, Oakland, CA 94623. Jonathan Marshall, Editorial Page Ed. Articles, 800 words, on any topic. Pays $25 to $75, on publication.

THE OREGONIAN—1320 S. W. Broadway, Portland, OR 97201. David Sarasohn, Forum Ed. Articles, to 800 words, on topics related to the Pacific Northwest, from writers in that area. Humor. Pays $50 to $100, on publication.

THE PHILADELPHIA INQUIRER—400 N. Broad St., Philadelphia, PA 19101. Philip H. Joyce, Op-Ed Editor. All topics, to 800 words. Pieces on offbeat issues, and seasonal topics preferred. Pays $100, on publication.

THE PROVIDENCE JOURNAL—75 Fountain St., Providence, RI 02902. Robert Ranmaker, Commentary Page Ed. Articles, to 750 words, on general interest topics. Pays $25, on publication.

THE REGISTER—625 N. Grand Ave., Santa Ana, CA 92711. Alan W. Bock, Opinion Ed. Opinion pieces, humor and satire; seasonal pieces. Pays $35 to $75, on publication.

THE SACRAMENTO BEE—21st and Q, P. O. Box 15779, Sacramento, CA 95852. Peter Schrag, Editorial Page Editor. Op-ed pieces, to 750 words; topics of regional interest preferred. Pays $75 to $125, on publication. Query.

ST. PETERSBURG TIMES—Box 1211, 490 First Ave., S., St. Petersburg, FL 33731. Robert Pittman, Editorial Page Editor. Authoritative articles, to 2,000 words, on current political, economic, and social issues for "Perspective" section. Payment varies, on publication. Query first.

SEATTLE POST-INTELLIGENCER—6th and Wall Sts., Seattle, WA 98121. John Reistrup, Exec. Ed. Current events articles, 800 to 1,000 words. No humor. Pays $100, on publication.

THE WASHINGTON POST—1150-15th St., NW, Washington, DC 20071. Robert G. Kaizer, "Outlook" Ed. Articles, 800 to 2,500 words, on topics of general interest. Pays $125 to $500, on publication.

ADULT MAGAZINES

CAVALIER—2355 Salzedo St., Coral Gables, FL 33134. Nye Wilden, Man. Ed. Articles with photos, and fiction, 1,500 to 3,000 words, for sophisticated young men. Pays to $400 for articles, to $250 for fiction, on publication. Query for articles.

CHIC—2029 Century Park E., Suite 3800, Los Angeles, CA 90067. Richard Warren Lewis, Articles Ed. Articles, 4,500 words. Pays $750 for articles, on acceptance.

FORUM, THE INTERNATIONAL JOURNAL OF HUMAN RELATIONS—1965 Broadway, New York, NY 10023-5965. Articles, 2,500 words, on sex-related topics, health, lifestyles, personal experiences, etc. Pays $400 to $800, on acceptance. Query.

GALLERY—800 Second Ave., New York, NY 10017. John Bensink, Ed.-in-Chief. Articles, investigative pieces, and fiction, to 4,000 words, for sophisticated men. Short humor, satire, service pieces. Photos. Pays varying rates, half on acceptance, half on publication. Query.

GEM—G&S Publications, 1472 Broadway, New York, NY 10036. Will Martin, Ed. Articles and fiction, 500 to 2,500 words, on sex-related and contemporary topics. No pornographic, obscene, or violent material. Pays varying rates, after acceptance. Same address and requirements for .

GENESIS—770 Lexington Ave., New York, NY 10021. J. J. Kelleher, Ed.-in-Chief. Articles, 2,500 to 3,500 words; celebrity interviews, 2,500 words. Photo essays. Pays 30 days after acceptance. Query.

HARVEY FOR LOVING PEOPLE—Suite 2305, 450 Seventh Ave., New

York, NY 10001. Harvey Shapiro, Ed./Pub. Sexually-oriented articles and fiction, to 2,500 words. Pays to $200, on publication. Query for articles.

HUSTLER—2029 Century Park E., Suite 3800, Los Angeles, CA 90067. Richard Warren Lewis, Articles Ed. Investigative articles and profiles, 5,000 words. Sex Play articles, with educational focus, 1,500 to 2,000 words. Pays from $1,200; from $350 for Sex Play pieces, on acceptance. Query.

OUI—300 W. 43rd St., New York, NY 10036. Attn.: Articles Ed. Articles, 1,200 to 2,500 words, geared to predominantly male audience, age 18–35, college educated. Hard-hitting exposés, new sexual trends, political intrigue. How-to and service articles on new or untapped trends. Query first. Pays to $750.

PENTHOUSE—1965 Broadway, New York, NY 10023. Peter Bloch, Ex. Ed. Kathy Green, Fiction Ed. Bob Hofler, Sr. Ed. General-interest or investigative articles, to 5,000 words. Sophisticated, quality fiction, 3,000 to 6,500 words, with contemporary settings and well-defined characters. Interviews, 5,000 words, with introductions. Satire, humor, and black comedy. Pays to 50¢ a word, on acceptance.

PLAYBOY—919 N. Michigan Ave., Chicago, IL 60611. James Morgan, Articles Ed. Alice K. Turner, Fiction Ed. Articles, 3,500 to 6,000 words, and sophisticated fiction, 1,000 to 8,000 words (6,000 preferred), for urban men. Humor; satire. Science fiction. Pays to $5,000 for articles, to $2,000 for fiction ($1,000 for short-shorts), on acceptance.

PLAYERS—8060 Melrose Ave., Los Angeles, CA 90046. Joe Nazel, Jr., Ed. Leslie Spencer, Assoc. Ed. Articles, 1,000 to 4,000 words, with photos, for black men: travel, business, entertainment, sports; interviews. Fiction. Humor; satire. Pays on publication.

FICTION MARKETS

This list gives the fiction requirements of the general- and special-interest magazines, including those that publish detective and mystery, romance and confession, and science fiction and fantasy stories. Other good markets for short fiction are the little, literary, and college journals (listed on page 674). Though payment is modest—usually in copies here— publication here can help a beginning writer achieve recognition by editors at the larger magazines. Juvenile fiction markets are listed under *Juvenile, Teenage, and Young Adult Magazines.* Publishers of book-length fiction manuscripts are listed under *Book Publishers.*

All manuscripts must be typed double-space and submitted with self-addressed envelopes bearing postage sufficient for the return of the material. Use good white paper; onion skin or erasable bond is not acceptable. Always keep a copy of the manuscript, since occasionally a manuscript is lost in the mails. Magazines may take several weeks—often longer—to read and report on submissions. If an editor has not reported on a manuscript after a reasonable amount of time, write a brief, courteous letter of inquiry.

ALOHA, THE MAGAZINE OF HAWAII—828 Fort Street Mall, Honolulu, HI 96813. Rita Arioyshi, Ed. Fiction to 4,000 words, on Hawaii and its ethnic groups. Pays 10¢ a word on publication. Query.

AMERICAN TRUCKER MAGAZINE—P.O. Box 6366, San Bernadino, CA 92412. Steven Nelson, Man. Ed. Fiction, 1,200 to 2,500 words, for truck drivers and trucking industry personnel. Pays after publication.

ARKANSAS TIMES—Box 34010, Little Rock, AR 72203. Bob Lancaster, Ed. Fiction, to 6,000 words: must have AR slant. Pays $100, on acceptance.

THE ATLANTIC—8 Arlington St., Boston, MA 02116. William Whitworth, Ed. Short stories, 2,000 to 6,000 (occasionally, to 14,000) words, of highest literary quality. Pays on acceptance.

THE ATLANTIC ADVOCATE—P.O. Box 3370, Fredericton, N.B., Canada E3B 5A2. H.P. Wood, Ed. Fiction, 1,000 to 1,500 words, with regional angle. Pays 5¢ to 8¢ a word, on publication.

THE ATLANTIC SALMON JOURNAL—1435 St. Alexandre, Suite 1030, Montreal, Quebec, Canada, H3A 2G4. Joanne Eidinger, Ed. Fiction, 1,500 to 2,500 words, related to the conservation of Atlantic salmon. Pays $100 to $350, on publication.

AUGUSTA SPECTATOR—P.O. Box 3168, Augusta, GA 30904. Fiction to 2,000 words, with Georgia or South Carolina tie-in. Pays $25, plus two copies, on publication.

THE B'NAI B'RITH INTERNATIONAL JEWISH MONTHLY—1640 Rhode Island Ave., NW, Washington, DC 20036. Marc Silver, Ed. Fiction, 1,000 to 4,000 words. Pays 10¢ to 25¢ a word, on publication. Query.

BOYS' LIFE—1325 Walnut Hill La., Irving, TX 75062. Robert E. Hood, Ed. Publication of Boy Scouts of America. Fiction, 1,000 to 3,200 words, for 8- to 18-year-old boys. Two-part serials, to 6,000 words. Pays from $350, on acceptance.

BREAD—6401 The Paseo, Kansas City, MO 64131. Gary Sivewright, Ed. Religious short stories, to 1,500 words, for teenagers. Pays from 3¢ a word, on acceptance.

BUFFALO SPREE MAGAZINE—Box 38, Buffalo, NY 14226. Johanna V. Shotell, Ed. Fiction and humor, to 1,500 words, for readers in the upstate New York region. Pays $75 to $100, on publication.

CAMPUS LIFE—465 Gundersen Dr., Carol Stream, IL 60188. Gregg Lewis, Ed. General fiction and humor reflecting Christian values and worldview (no overtly religious material), for high school and college students. Pays from $150, on acceptance. Limited free-lance market.

CAPPER'S WEEKLY—616 Jefferson Ave., Topeka, KS 66607. Dorothy Harvey, Ed. Novel-length mystery and romance stories: no short stories. Pays $150 to $200. Query.

CAT FANCY—P.O. Box 6050, Mission Viejo, CA 92690. Linda W. Lewis, Ed. Fiction, to 3,000 words, about cats. Pays 3¢ a word, on publication.

CATHOLIC FORESTER—425 W. Shuman Blvd., Naperville, IL 60566. Barbara A. Cunningham, Ed. Official publication of the Catholic Order of Foresters. Fiction, to 3,000 words: no sex or violence. Pays 5¢ a word, on acceptance.

653

CAVALIER—2355 Salzedo St., Coral Gables, FL 33134. Maurice DeWalt, Fiction Ed. Sexually-oriented fiction, to 3,000 words, for sophisticated young men. Pays to $300, on publication.

CHATELAINE—Maclean Hunter Bldg., 777 Bay St., Toronto, Ont., Canada M5W 1A7. Barbara West, Fiction Ed. Fiction, 3,000 to 4,500 words, on issues in contemporary women's lives: relationships, adventure, romance, humor. Canadian setting preferred. Pays from $1,500, on acceptance. Most fiction by Canadian writers.

CHESAPEAKE BAY MAGAZINE—1819 Bay Ridge Ave., Annapolis, MD 21403. Betty Rigoli, Ed. Short stories, to 12 pages; must be related to Chesapeake Bay area. Pays $75 to $85, on publication.

CHICAGO—303 E. Wacker Dr., Chicago, IL 60601. Christine Newman, Fiction Ed. Fiction, 1,000 to 5,000 words. Pays varying rates, on acceptance.

CHRISTIAN HOME—Box 189, 1908 Grand Ave., Nashville, TN 37202. Fiction, 1,000 to 1,500 words. Pays 6¢ a word, on acceptance.

CHRISTIAN LIFE MAGAZINE—396 E. St. Charles Rd., Wheaton, IL 60188. Janice Franzen, Exec. Ed. Fiction, 1,500 to 2,500 words, on problems faced by Christians. Pays to $150, on publication.

CHRISTIAN LIVING—850 N. Grove Ave., Elgin, IL 60102. Anne E. Dinnan, Ed. Short stories, up to 1,200 words, that challenge, interest, and inspire teens to spiritual growth, for Christian teens. Pays 6¢ to 9¢ a word, on acceptance.

CINCINNATI ENTERTAINER—18 E. 4th St., Cincinnati, OH 45202. Susan Conner, Ed. Fiction, 750 words. Pays on publication.

COASTAL JOURNAL—Box 84, Lanesville Sta., Gloucester, MA 01930. Jacqueline Bigford, Ed. Fiction, 1,800 words, relating to the New England Coast—past, present or future—or nautical history. Pays $100, on publication. Limited market.

COBBLESTONE—20 Grove St., Peterborough, NH 03458. Carolyn P. Yoder, Ed. Fiction, 500 to 1,200 words, for children aged 8 to 14 years. Pays 10¢ to 15¢ a word, on publication. Send SASE for editorial guidelines with monthly themes.

COMMENTARY—165 E. 56th St., New York, NY 10022. Marion Magid, Fiction Ed. Fiction, of high quality, on contemporary social or Jewish issues. Pays on publication.

THE COMPASS—Mobil International Aviation and Marine Sales, Inc., 150 E. 42nd St., New York, NY 10017. R. G. MacKenzie, Ed. Short stories, to 3,500 words, on the sea and sea trades. Pays to $250, on acceptance. Query.

CORVETTE FEVER—Box 55532, Ft. Washington, MD 20744. Pat Stivers, Ed. Corvette-related fiction, about 300 lines. Pays 10¢ a word, on publication.

COSMOPOLITAN—224 W. 57th St., New York, NY 10019. Betty Kelly, Fiction and Books Ed. Short shorts, 1,500 to 3,000 words, and short stories, 4,000 to 6,000 words, focusing on contemporary man-woman relationships. Solid, upbeat plots, sharp characterization; female protagonists preferred. Pays $300 to $600 for short shorts, from $1,000 for short stories. Published novels, especially mystery and suspense, accepted for condensing and excerpting. Payment negotiable.

COUNTRY MAGAZINE—P.O. Box 246, Alexandria, VA 22313. Philip Haywood, Ed. Fiction, related to life in the Mid-Atlantic region. Pays on publication. Query with SASE.

CRICKET—Box 100, La Salle, IL 61301. Marianne Carus, Ed.-in-Chief. Fiction, 200 to 1,500 words, for 6- to 12-year-olds. Pays to 25¢ a word, on publication.

DELTA SCENE—P.O. Box B-3, Delta State Univ., Cleveland, MS 38733. Fiction, with Mississippi Delta slant, 1,500 to 2,000 words. Pays $15 to $20, after publication.

DISCOVERIES—6401 The Paseo, Kansas City, MO 64131. Libby Huffman, Ed. Fiction, 800 to 1,000 words, for children grades 3 to 6, defining Christian experiences and values. Pays 3½¢ a word, on acceptance. Query.

DIVER MAGAZINE—8051 River Rd., Richmond, BC, V6X 1X8, Canada. Neil McDaniel, Ed. Fiction, related to diving/diving experiences. Humor. Pays $2.50 per column inch, on publication. Query.

DOG FANCY—P.O. Box 6050, Mission Viejo, CA 92690. Linda W. Lewis, Ed. Fiction, to 3,000 words, about dogs. Pays 3¢ a word, on publication.

EASYRIDERS MAGAZINE—Box 52, Malibu, CA 90265. Lou Kimzey, Ed. Fiction, 3,000 to 5,000 words. Pays from 10¢ a word, on acceptance.

ESQUIRE—2 Park Ave., New York, NY 10016. Rust Hills, Fiction Ed. Literary short stories, 1,000 to 7,000 words, for intelligent adult audience. Pays $1,000 to $1,500, on acceptance.

ESSENCE—1500 Broadway, New York, NY 10036. Susan L. Taylor, Ed.-in-Chief. Fiction, 1,500 to 3,000 words, for largely black, female readership. Pays varying rates, on acceptance. No recent report.

THE EVANGEL—901 College Ave., Winona Lake, IN 46590. Vera Bethel, Ed. Fiction, 1,200 words, on Christian solutions to problems. Pays $35 to $40, on publication.

FAMILY CIRCLE—488 Madison Ave., New York, NY 10022. Jamie Raab, Fiction Ed., Nicole Gregory, Books and Nonfiction Ed. Family-oriented fiction, to 2,500 words, for women; short stories with interesting, romantic, fanciful, or philosophical viewpoints; animal stories. Short shorts, 2 pages. Pays from $500, on acceptance.

FAMILY MAGAZINE—P.O. Box 4993, Walnut Creek, CA 94596. Address Editors. Short stories, to 2,000 words, of interest to high school-educated women between 20 and 35. Pays from $100 to $300, on publication.

FARM WOMAN NEWS—P.O. Box 643, Milwaukee, WI 53201. Ruth C. Benedict, Man. Ed. Fiction, to 1,000 words, of interest to farm and ranch women. Pays $30 to $250, on publication.

GALLERY—800 Second Ave., New York, NY 10017. John Bensink, Ed.-in-Chief. Fiction, to 4,000 words, for sophisticated men. Pays varying rates, half on acceptance, half on publication. Query.

GENTLEMEN'S QUARTERLY (GQ)—350 Madison Ave., New York, NY 10017. Adam Gopnik, Sr. Ed. Fiction, to 3,000 words. Pays on acceptance.

THE GEORGETOWNER—P.O. Box 3528, Washington, DC 20007. Fiction, 3 to 4 typed pages. Pays varying rates, on publication.

GOLF DIGEST—495 Westport Ave., Norwalk, CT 06856. Jerry Tarde, Ed. Unusual or humorous stories, to 2,000 words, about golf; golf "fables," to 1,000 words. Pays 20¢ a word, on acceptance.

GOOD HOUSEKEEPING—959 Eighth Ave., New York, NY 10019. Naome Lewis, Fiction Ed. Short stories, 2,000 to 5,000 words, with strong identification figures for women, by published writers and "beginners with demonstrable talent." Novel condensations or excerpts. Pays top rates, on acceptance.

GUN DOG—P.O. Box 68, Adel, IA 50003. Bob Wilbanks, Man. Ed. Occasional fiction, humor related to gun dogs and bird hunting. Pays $100 to $300, on acceptance.

HANG GLIDING—U.S. Hang Gliding Assn., P.O. Box 66306, Los Angeles, CA 90066. Gilbert Dodgen, Ed. Fiction, 2 to 3 pages, related to hang gliding. Pays to $50. Query preferred.

HICALL—1445 Boonville Ave., Springfield, MO 65802. William P. Campbell, Ed. Fiction, to 1,800 words, for 12- to 19–year-olds with strong evangelical emphasis: believable characters working out their problems according to biblical principles. Pays 3¢ a word for first rights, on acceptance.

HIGHLIGHTS FOR CHILDREN—803 Church St., Honesdale, PA 18431. Kent L. Brown, Jr., Ed. Sports, humor, adventure, mystery, etc., stories, 900 words, for 9- to 12–year-olds. Easy rebus form, 200 to 250 words, and easy-to-read stories, to 600 words, for beginning readers. Pays from 6¢ a word, on acceptance. Buys all rights.

HIS—P.O. Box 1450, Downers Grove, IL 60515. Verne Becker, Ed. Fiction about college students who experience emotional and/or spiritual growth. Pays 2¢ to 5¢ a word, on acceptance.

HOME LIFE—127 Ninth Ave. N., Nashville, TN 37234. Reuben Herring, Ed. Southern Baptist. Fiction, to 2,000 words, on Christian marriage, family relationships. Pays to 4¢ a word, on acceptance.

INSIDE RUNNING—9514 Bristlebrook Dr., Houston, TX 77083. Joanne Schmidt, Ed. Fiction related to running. Pays $35 to $100, on acceptance.

JACK AND JILL—Box 567, Indianapolis, IN 46206. Christine French Clark, Ed. Fiction, to 1,200 words. for 6- to 8–year-olds. Pays about 6¢ a word, on publication.

LADIES' HOME JOURNAL—3 Park Ave., New York, NY 10016. Fiction with strong identification for women. Short stories and full-length manuscripts accepted *through agents only.*

LADYCOM—1732 Wisconsin Ave., NW, Washington DC 20007. Hope Daniels, Ed. Fiction, to 2,000 words, for military wives in the U.S. and overseas. Pays $75 to $200, after acceptance.

LIVE—1445 Boonville Ave., Springfield, MO 65802. Kenneth D. Barney, Adult Ed. Fiction, 1,500 to 2,000 words, on applying Bible principles to everyday living. Send SASE for writers' guidelines. Pays 2¢ to 3¢ a word, on acceptance.

LOLLIPOPS, LADYBUGS AND LUCKY STARS—Good Apple Inc., P.O.

Box 299, Carthage, IL 62321-0299. Cindy Stansbery, Ed. Short stories, to 1,200 words, with educational and/or moral value, for children. Rates vary.

THE LOOKOUT—8121 Hamilton Ave., Cincinnati, OH 45231. Mark A. Taylor, Ed. Fiction for Christian audience. Pays 4¢ to 6¢ a word, on acceptance.

LUTHERAN WOMEN—2900 Queen Lane, Philadelphia, PA 19129. Terry Schutz, Ed. Fiction, 1,000 to 2,000 words, demonstrating character growth and change. Pays $35 to $50, on publication. Include SASE.

McCALL'S—230 Park Ave., New York, NY 10169. Helen DelMonte, Fiction Ed. Short stories, to 3,000 words. Short-shorts, 2,000 words: Contemporary themes with strong identification for intelligent women. Family stories, love stories, humor. Pays from $2,000 for stories, $1,500 for short-shorts, on acceptance.

MADEMOISELLE—350 Madison Ave., New York, NY 10017. Eileen Schnurr, Fiction Ed. Short stories, 2,500 to 4,500 words, of high literary quality. Pays from $1,000, on acceptance.

MATURE LIVING—127 Ninth Ave. N., Nashville, TN 37234. Jack Gulledge, Ed. Zada Malugen, Ass't Ed. Fiction, 900 to 1,475 words, for senior adults. Must be consistent with Christian principles. Pays 5¢ a word, on acceptance.

MATURE YEARS—201 Eighth Ave., S., Nashville, TN 37203. Daisy D. Warren, Ed. United Methodist. Humorous or serious fiction, 1,500 to 2,000 words, for adults. Pays 4¢ a word, on acceptance.

MESSENGER OF THE SACRED HEART—661 Greenwood Ave., Toronto, Ont., Canada M4J 4B3. Write M. Pujolas. Short stories, about 1,500 words, for Catholics. Pays from 2¢ a word, on acceptance.

MICHIGAN, THE MAGAZINE OF THE DETROIT NEWS—615 W. Lafayette Blvd., Detroit, MI 48231. Lisa Velders, Ed. Fiction, with *Michigan* slant, to 3,000 words. Pays $150 to $500 on publication. Query first.

MIDSTREAM—515 Park Ave., New York, NY 10022. Joel Carmichael, Ed. Fiction on Jewish social or political issues. Pays 5¢ a word, on publication.

THE MIRACULOUS MEDAL—475 E. Chelten Ave., Philadelphia, PA 19144. Robert P. Cawley, C.M., Edit. Dir. Catholic. Fiction, to 2,000 words. Pays from 2¢ a word, on acceptance.

MOMENT—462 Boylston St., Boston, MA 02116. Leonard Fein, Ed. Short stories, 2,000 to 4,000 words, on Jewish themes. Pays $150 to $250, on publication.

MS.—119 W. 40th St., New York, NY 10018. Address Ed. Dept. Fiction. Short stories, to 3,000 words, on women's changing self-image and status. Pays varying rates, on acceptance. SASE required.

NATIONAL DOLL WORLD—P.O. Box 1952, Brooksville, FL 33512. Address Karen P. Sherrer. Doll-related fiction, to 1,000 words. Pays to 5¢ a word, on publication.

NATIONAL RACQUETBALL—4350 DiPaolo Center, Glenview, IL 60025. Chuck Leve, Ed. Fiction, related to racquetball. Pays $25 to $150, on publication.

NEW BEDFORD MAGAZINE—5 South Sixth St., New Bedford, MA

02740. Fiction, to 3,000 words, related to southeastern Massachusetts. Short humor. Pays varying rates, on publication.

NEW ERA—50 E. North Temple, Salt Lake City, UT 84150. Brian Kelly, Ed. Fiction, to 3,000 words, for young Mormons. Pays 5¢ to 10¢ a word, on acceptance. Query.

NEW WOMAN—215 Lexington Ave., New York, NY 10016. Pat Miller, Ed. Fiction accepted through agents only.

THE NEW YORKER—25 W. 43rd St., New York, NY 10036. Short stories, humor and satire. Pays varying rates, on acceptance.

NORTHEAST MAGAZINE—*The Hartford Courant,* 285 Broad St., Hartford, CT 06115. Lary Bloom, Ed. Short stories, to 4,000 words; must have Connecticut tie-in, or be universal in theme and have non-specific setting. Pays $300 to $600, on acceptance. SASE required.

OUI—300 W. 43rd St., New York, NY 10036. Barry Janoff, Exec. Ed. Modern, upbeat stories with unusual settings: humorous, science fiction, mystery, etc. Sexual situations or overtones helpful, but not required. Audience: 18–35, mostly but not all male. Length: 1,200 to 2,500 words. Payment varies.

OUR FAMILY—Box 249, Battleford, Sask., Canada S0M 0E0. A. Lalonde, O.M.I. Ed. Fiction, 1,000 to 3,000 words, on the struggle to live the Christian life in the face of modern-day problems. Pays 7¢ to 10¢ a word, on acceptance. Write for guidelines. Enclose *international postal reply coupons* with SAE.

PENTHOUSE—1965 Broadway, New York, NY 10023. Address Fiction Department. Quality fiction, 4,000 to 6,000 words, on contemporary themes. Pays on acceptance. Query. No unsolicited manuscripts.

PILLOW TALK—215 Lexington Ave., New York, NY 10016. I. Catherine Duff, Ed. Short erotic fiction, to 2,000 words, for "Fantasy Forum." Pays from $150, on publication. Query.

PIONEER WOMAN—200 Madison Ave, 18th fl., New York, NY 10016. Judith A. Sokoloff, Ed. Short stories, 2,500 words, with Jewish theme or of interest to women. Pays 8¢ a word, on publication.

PLAYBOY—919 N. Michigan Ave., Chicago, IL 60611. Alice K. Turner, Fiction Ed. Quality fiction, 1,000 to 10,000 words (average 6,000): suspense, mystery, adventure and sports short stories; stories about contemporary relationships; science fiction. Active plots and strong characterization. Pays from $1,000 to $3,000, on acceptance.

PLAYERS—8060 Melrose Ave., Los Angeles, CA 90046. Address Fiction Ed. Offbeat fiction of high literary quality, 1,000 to 5,000 words, for black men. No adventure stories. Pays 10¢ a word for the first 500 words, 2¢ to 8¢ a word thereafter, on publication.

PLAYGIRL—3420 Ocean Park Blvd., Suite 3000, Santa Monica, CA 90405. Mary Ellen Strote, Fiction Ed. Contemporary, romantic fiction, 1,000 to 3,000 words. Pays from $500, after acceptance.

PRIME TIMES—Suite 210, 2802 International Ln., Madison, WI 53704. Journal for the National Assn. for Retired Credit Union People. Joan Donovan, Assoc. Man. Ed. Fiction, 2,500 to 4,000 words. Pays varying rates, on publication. Query.

PURPOSE—616 Walnut Ave., Scottdale, PA 15683-1999. James E. Horsch,

Ed. Fiction, 1,200 words, on Christian problem solving. Pays 5¢ a word, on acceptance.

QUEEN—26 S. Saxon Ave., Bay Shore, NY 11706. James McMillian, S. M.M., Ed. Fiction, 1,000 to 2,000 words, relating to the Virgin Mary. Pays varying rates on acceptance.

RANGER RICK MAGAZINE—1412 16th St. N.W., Washington, DC 20036. Trudy Farrand, Ed. Nature- and conservation-related fiction, for 6- to 12–year-olds. Maximum: 900 words. Pays to $350, on acceptance. Buys all rights.

THE RECONSTRUCTIONIST—270 W. 89th St., New York, NY 10024. Dr. Jacob Staub, Ed. Fiction, 2,000 to 3,000 words, relating to Judaism. Pays $18 to $36, on publication.

REDBOOK—224 W. 57th St., New York, NY 10019. Kathy Sagan, Fiction Ed. Fresh, distinctive short stories, of interest to women, about love and love relationships, being a parent or dealing with one, friendship, careers, or confronting basic problems of contemporary life and women's issues. Pays $850 for short stories (about 9 manuscript pages), from $1,000 for short stories (10 pages, or longer). Allow 6 to 8 weeks for reply. Manuscripts without SASEs will not be returned. No unsolicited novellas or novels accepted.

ROAD KING—P.O. Box 250, Park Forest, IL 60466. George Friend, Ed. Short stories, 1,200 to 1,500 words, for and/or about truck drivers. Pays to $400, on acceptance.

ST. ANTHONY MESSENGER—1615 Republic St., Cincinnati, OH 45210. Norman Perry, Ed. Fiction that makes readers think about issues, lifestyles and values. Pays 12¢ a word, on acceptance. Query.

ST. JOSEPH'S MESSENGER—P.O. Box 288, Jersey City, NJ 07303. Sister Ursula Maphet, Ed. Fiction, 1,000 to 5,000 words. Pays 1¢ a word.

THE SATURDAY EVENING POST—1100 Waterway Blvd., Indianapolis, IN 46202. Rebecca Whitney, Fiction Ed. Upbeat short stories, 500 to 4,000 words, that lend themselves to illustration. Pays varying rates, on publication.

SCHOLASTIC SCOPE—Scholastic, Inc., 730 Broadway, New York, NY 10003. Katherine Robinson, Ed. Fiction for 15- to 18–year-olds, with 4th to 6th grade reading ability. Short stories, 500 to 1,000 words, on teen-age interests and relationships; family, job and school situations. Pays good rates, on acceptance.

SEA KAYAKER—1670 Duranleau St., Vancouver, BC, V6H 3S4 Canada. John Dowd, Ed. Fiction, to 2,000 words, related to ocean kayaking. Pays on publication. Include international reply coupons.

SEEK—8121 Hamilton Ave., Cincinnati, OH 45231. Eileen H. Wilmot, Ed. Fiction, to 1,200 words, on inspirational and controversial topics and timely religious issues. Pays up to 3¢ a word, on acceptance.

SEVENTEEN—850 Third Ave., New York, NY 10022. Bonni Price, Fiction Ed. High-quality fiction for young adults. Pays on acceptance.

SPORTS AFIELD—250 W. 55th St., New York, NY 10019. Tom Paugh, Ed. Fiction, on hunting, fishing, and related topics. Outdoor adventure stories. Humor. Pays top rates, on acceptance.

STANDARD—6401 The Paseo, Kansas City, MO 64131. Address Editor.

Fiction, 800 to 1,700 words, with Christian, emphasis, but not preachy. Pays 3½¢ a word, on acceptance.

STRAIGHT—8121 Hamilton Ave., Cincinnati, OH 45231. Dawn Brettschneider, Ed. Well-constructed fiction, 1,000 to 1,500 words, showing Christian teens using Bible principles in everyday life. Contemporary, realistic teen characters a must. Most interested in school, church, dating and family life stories. Pays about 2¢ a word, on acceptance. Send SASE for guidelines.

SUNDAY DIGEST—850 N. Grove Ave., Elgin, IL 60120. Judy Couchman, Ed. Short shorts (500 words), short stories (1,000 to 1,500 words), and novel excerpts (1,000 to 1,500 words), with religious, evangelical slant. Pays 7¢ to 10¢ a word, on acceptance.

SUNSHINE MAGAZINE—Litchfield, IL 62056. Wholesome fiction, 900 to 1,200 words; short stories for youths, 400 to 700 words. Pays to $100, on acceptance.

SWANK—888 Seventh Ave., New York, NY 10106. Dave Trilby, Fiction Ed. Graphic erotic short stories, to 2,500 words. Pays on publication.

'TEEN—8490 Sunset Blvd., Los Angeles, CA 90069. Address Fiction Dept. Short stories, 2,500 to 4,000 words: mystery, travel, adventure, romance, humor for teens. Pays from $100, on acceptance.

TEENS TODAY—Nazarene Publishing House, 6401 The Paseo, Kansas City, MO 64131. Gary Sivewright, Ed. Short stories, 1,200 to 1,500 words, that deal with teens demonstrating Christian principles in real-life situations; adventure stories. Pays 3½¢ a word, on acceptance.

TORCH ROMANCES—P.O. Box 3307, McLean, VA 22103. Address Fiction Ed. Romantic suspense short stories, 12,000 words, with sensual love scenes; avoid plots that contain murder, drugs and excess violence. Pays flat rate or royalty. Tip sheet.

ULTRASPORT—11 Beacon St., Boston, MA 02108. Chris Bergonzi, Ed. Athletics-related fiction, 3,000 words. Pays $800 to $1,000, on acceptance.

VANITY FAIR—350 Madison Ave., New York, NY 10017. Tina Brown, Ed. Fiction of high literary quality. Pays varying rates. Send manuscript with SASE.

VOGUE—350 Madison Ave., New York, NY 10017. Amy Gross, Features Ed. No unsolicited manuscripts.

THE WASHINGTON POST MAGAZINE—1150 15th St. NW, Washington, DC 20071. Stephen Petranak, Man. Ed. Fiction, 3,000 words: fantasy, humor, mystery, historical, mainstream and science fiction. Pays $200 to $750 on acceptance.

WESTERN PEOPLE—Box 2500, Saskatoon, Sask., Canada S7K 2C4. Short stories, 1,000 to 2,500 words, on subjects or themes of interest to rural readers in Western Canada. Pays $40 to $125, on acceptance. *Enclose international postal reply coupons.*

WILDFOWL—P.O. Box 68, Adel, IA 50003. B. Wilbanks, Man. Ed. Occasional fiction, humor, related to duck hunters and wildfowl. Pays $100 to $300, on acceptance.

WOMAN'S DAY—1515 Broadway, New York, NY 10036. Eileen Herbert Jordan, Fiction Ed. Short fiction, humorous or serious. Pays top rates, on acceptance.

WOMAN'S WORLD—P.O. Box 6700, Englewood, NJ 07631. Elinor Nauen, Fiction Ed. Fast-moving short stories, about 4,500 words, with light romantic theme. Mini-mysteries, 1,500 words, with "whodunit" or "howdunit" theme. No science fiction, fantasy or historical romance. Pays $1,000 for short stories, $500 for mini-mysteries on acceptance. Submit manuscript with SASE.

WOODMEN OF THE WORLD MAGAZINE—1700 Farnam St., Omaha, NE 68102. Leland A. Larson, Ed. Family-oriented fiction. Pays 5¢ a word, on acceptance.

WORKING FOR BOYS—St. John's H.S., Main St., Shrewsbury, MA 01545. Brother Alois, C.F.X., Associate Ed. Fiction, to 1,200 words, for elementary school children, parents. Pays 4¢ a word, on acceptance. Limited market.

WORKING MOTHER—230 Park Ave., New York, NY 10169. Karen Pritzker, Fiction Ed. Realistic short stories, 1,500 to 2,500 words, for working mothers. Pays $500 to $800, on acceptance.

YANKEE—Dublin, NH 03444. Judson Hale, Ed. Deborah Navas, Fiction Ed. High-quality, literary short fiction, to 3,500 words, with setting in or compatible with New England. Pays on acceptance.

YM (formerly *Young Miss*)—685 Third Ave., New York, NY 10017. Deborah Purcell, Fiction Ed. Fiction, to 3,500 words, for young women to age 19: stories must be complex and engaging, with strong characters, plot and dialogue; protagonist may be male or female. Study back issues before submitting. Pays from $350, on acceptance.

YOUNG AMBASSADOR—Box 82808, Lincoln, NE 68501. Nancy Bayne, Man. Ed. Fiction, to 2,000 words, for Christian teens. Pays 4¢ to 10¢ a word, on acceptance.

THE YOUNG SOLDIER—The Salvation Army, 799 Bloomfield Ave., Verona, NJ 07044. Dorothy Hitzka, Ed. Fiction, 600 to 800 words, for Christian children. Pays 3¢ a word, on acceptance.

DETECTIVE AND MYSTERY

ALFRED HITCHCOCK'S MYSTERY MAGAZINE—380 Lexington Ave., New York, NY 10017. Cathleen Jordan, Ed. Well-plotted mystery, detective, suspense and crime fiction, 1,000 to 14,000 words. Submissions by new writers strongly encouraged. Pays 5¢ a word, on acceptance.

ARMCHAIR DETECTIVE—129 W. 56th St., New York, NY 10019. Michael Seidman, Ed. Articles on mystery and detective fiction; biographical sketches, reviews, etc. Pays in copies.

DETECTIVE DRAGNET—1440 St. Catherine W., Suite 625, Montreal, Quebec, Canada H3G 1S2. Dominick A. Merle, Ed. Well-researched true crime stories, 3,500 to 6,000 words, with photos, involving mystery, suspense and lots of human interest. No fiction. Include clippings describing the case, with date, location, and names of victims and suspects. Pays $200 to $300, on acceptance. Same address and requirements for *Detective Cases, Detective Files, Headquarters Detective, Startling Detective,* and *True Police Cases.*

ELLERY QUEEN'S MYSTERY MAGAZINE—380 Lexington Ave., New York, NY 10017. Eleanor Sullivan, Ed. Detective, crime, mystery and spy fiction, 4,000 to 6,000 words. Suspense or straight detective stories. No sex, sadism or sensationalism. Particularly interested in new writers and "first stories." Pays 3¢ to 8¢ a word, on acceptance.

FRONT PAGE DETECTIVE—See *Inside Detective.*

HEADQUARTERS DETECTIVE—See *Detective Dragnet.*

INSIDE DETECTIVE—Reese Communications, Inc., 460 W. 34th St., New York, NY 10001. Rose Mandelsberg, Ed. Timely, true detective stories, 5,000 to 6,000 words. No fiction. Pays $250, extra for photos, on acceptance. Query. Same address and requirements for *Front Page Detective.*

MASTER DETECTIVE—460 W. 34th St., New York, NY 10001. Art Crockett, Ed. Detailed articles, 5,000 to 6,000 words, with photos, on current cases, emphasizing human motivation and detective work. Pays to $250, on acceptance. Query.

OFFICIAL DETECTIVE STORIES—460 W. 34th St., New York, NY 10001. Art Crockett, Ed. True detective stories, 5,000 to 6,000 words, on current investigations, strictly from the investigator's point of view. No fiction. Photos. Pays $250, extra for photos, on acceptance. Query.

STARTLING DETECTIVE—See *Detective Dragnet.*

TRUE DETECTIVE—460 W. 34th St., New York, NY 10001. Art Crockett, Ed. Articles, from 5,000 words, with photos, on current police cases, emphasizing detective work and human motivation. No fiction. Pays $250, extra for photos, on acceptance. Query.

TRUE POLICE CASES—See *Detective Dragnet.*

SCIENCE FICTION AND FANTASY

AMAZING SCIENCE FICTION STORIES—Box 110, Lake Geneva, WI 53147. George Scithers, Ed. Science fiction and fantasy, to 15,000 words. Also general-interest science articles; query first on nonfiction. Pays 4¢ to 6¢ a word, on acceptance.

ANALOG SCIENCE FICTION/SCIENCE FACT—380 Lexington Ave., New York, NY 10017. Stanley Schmidt, Ed. Science fiction, with strong characters in believable future or alien setting: short stories, 2,000 to 7,500 words; novelettes, 10,000 to 20,000 words; serials, to 80,000 words. Also uses future-related articles. Pays to 7¢ a word, on acceptance. Query on serials and articles.

THE ASYMPTOTICAL WORLD—P.O. Box 1372, Williamsport, PA 17703. Michael H. Gerardi, Ed. Psychodramas, fantasy, science fiction, experimental fiction, 1,500 to 2,500 words. Illustrations, photographs. Pays 2¢ a word, on acceptance. Query required.

BIFROST—Southern Circle Press, P.O. Box 1180, Milford, DE 19963. Ann Wilson, Ed. Science fiction and fantasy, varying lengths. No x-rated material. Submit poetry to Cathie Whitehead, 4020 Woolslayer Way, Pittsburgh, PA. 15224. Humor; jokes. Pays in copies. Send SASE for guidelines.

DIFFERENT WORLDS—P.O. Box 6302, Albany, CA 94706. Tadashi Ehara, Ed. Articles, to 5,000 words, on role-playing games; reviews, variants, source materials, etc. Pays 1¢ a word, on publication. Query preferred.

DRAGON MAGAZINE—P. O. Box 110, Lake Geneva, WI 53147. Kim Mohan, Editor-In-Chief. Patrick L. Price, Fiction Ed. Articles 1,500 to 10,000 words, on fantasy and SF role-playing games. Fiction, 1,500 to 8,000 words. Pays 4¢ to 6¢ a word for fiction, slightly lower for articles, on publication. Query.

EMPIRE FOR THE SF WRITER—1025 55th St., Oakland, CA 94608. Millea Kenin, Ed. Articles, 2,000 words preferred, on the craft of writing science fiction and fantasy. Cartoons, illustrations, poetry. Pays negotiable rates, on publication. Query.

FANTASY BOOK—P. O. Box 60126, Pasadena, CA 91106. Nick Smith, Ed. Fantasy short stories, 2,000 to 10,000 words; poetry related to the fantastic. Pays 2½¢ to 4¢ a word, before publication.

FANTASY REVIEW—College of Humanities, Florida Atlantic University, Boca Raton, FL 33431. Robert A. Collins, Ed. Articles and interviews, to 5,000 words. Fantasy and science fiction, poetry. Cartoons, photos, artwork. Pays varying rates. Query preferred.

FOOTSTEPS—Box 63, Westkill, NY 12492. Bill Munster, Ed. Material related to horror, supernatural, or the weird tale: essays, reviews, profiles, fiction, to 3,500 words. Poetry to 40 lines. Pays in copies.

GRIMOIRE—c/o Thomas Wiloch, 8181 Wayne Rd., Apt. H2084, Westland, MI 48185. Thomas Wiloch, Ed. Fiction and poetry, to 2,000 words, on the surreal, macabre and fantastic. Collages, black and white. Query on nonfiction. Pays in copies; SASE.

THE HORROR SHOW—Phantasm Press, Star Route 1, Box 151-T, Oak Run, CA 96069. David B. Silva, Ed. Contemporary horror fiction, to 4,000 words, with a style that keeps the reader's hand trembling as he turns the pages. Pays ½¢ a word, on acceptance. Send SASE for guidelines.

ISAAC ASIMOV'S SCIENCE FICTION MAGAZINE—380 Lexington Ave., New York, NY 10017. Short, character-oriented science fiction and fantasy, to 15,000 words. Pays 4¢ to 7¢ a word, on acceptance. Send SASE for requirements.

THE MAGAZINE OF FANTASY AND SCIENCE FICTION—Box 56, Cornwall, CT 06753. Edward Ferman, Ed. Fantasy and science fiction stories, to 10,000 words. Pays 4¢ to 6¢ a word, on acceptance.

MAGICAL BLEND—Box 11303, San Francisco, CA 94101. Vince Emery, Literary Ed. Positive, uplifting pieces on spiritual exploration, lifestyles, occult, white magic and fantasy. Fiction and features to 5,000 words, poetry, 4 to 40 lines. Pays in copies.

OMNI—1965 Broadway, New York, NY 10023-1965. Ellen Datlow, Ed. Strong, realistic science fiction, 2,000 to 9,000 words, with real people as characters. Some contemporary, hard-edged fantasy. No horror, ghost or sword and sorcery tales. Pays $1,250-$2,000, on acceptance.

ORACLE—21111 Mapleridge, Southfield, MI 48075. Dave Lillard, Ed. Action/adventure science fiction and fantasy, any length. No pornography, heavy violence, horror stories, poems or reviews. Pays 1¢ to 3¢ a word, on acceptance and after publication. Send SASE and 10¢ for guidelines. Query.

OWLFLIGHT—1025 55th St., Oakland, CA 94608. Millea Kenin, Ed. Science fiction and fantasy, to 10,000 words. Science fiction/fantasy poetry, to 100 lines. Photographs, illustrations. Pays 1¢ a word, extra for illustrations, on publication. Query. Send SASE for guidelines.

ROD SERLING'S TWILIGHT ZONE MAGAZINE—800 Second Ave., New York, NY 10017. Michael Blaine, Ed. Fantasy fiction, to 5,000 words: human-centered fantasies of horror, suspense and the supernatural involving "ordinary people in extraordinary events." No sword and sorcery. Avoid genre clichés. Pays about 5¢ a word, half on acceptance, half on publication.

SCIENCE FICTION CHRONICLE—P. O. Box 4175, New York, NY 10163. Andrew Porter, Ed. News items, 100 to 400 words, for SF and fantasy readers, professionals, and collectors. Photos and short articles on authors' signings. Pays 3¢ a word, on publication.

SPACE AND TIME—138 W. 7th St., #4B, New York, NY 10023. Fantasy fiction, to 15,000 words; science fiction, supernatural, sword and sorcery; poetry. Pays ¼¢ a word for fiction, in copies for poetry, on acceptance.

STAR*LINE—P. O. Box 491, Nantucket, MA 02554. Bob Frazier, Ed. Newsletter. Articles, short interviews, on speculative poetry, 500 to 2,500 words. Poetry. Prose poems, 50 to 100 words. Short news items on the world of speculative poetry. Pays $1 to $5 for articles, $1 to $2 for reviews, $1 for ten lines of poetry (5¢ a line thereafter).

THRESHOLD OF FANTASY—P. O. Box 70868, Sunnyvale, CA 94086. Randall D. Larson, Ed. Fiction (fantasy, horror, sci-fi), to 5,000 words; book reviews; interviews to 1,000 words. Pays 5¢ a word for fiction, $20 for interviews, copies for reviews and poetry, on acceptance and on publication.

THRUST: SCIENCE FICTION IN REVIEW—8217 Langport Terrace, Gaithersburg, MD 20877. D. Douglas Fratz, Ed. Articles, interviews, 2,000 to 6,000 words, for readers familiar with SF and related literary and scientific topics. Book reviews, 100 to 800 words. Pays ½¢ to 2¢ a word on publication. Query preferred.

THE TWILIGHT ZONE—See *Rod Serling's Twilight Zone Magazine*.

CONFESSION AND ROMANCE MAGAZINES

INTIMACY—355 Lexington Ave., New York, NY 10017. Robyn L. Guilford, Ed. Fiction, 2,000 to 3,000 words, for women age 18 to 45. Must have interesting plot and contain two descriptive love scenes. Pays $45 to $75, after acceptance. *Jive* geared towards the younger woman seeking adventure and romance.

JIVE—*See Intimacy.*

MODERN ROMANCES—215 Lexington Ave., New York, NY 10016. Jean Sharbel, Ed. Confession stories with reader-identification and strong emotional tone, 1,500 to 7,500 words. Articles for blue-collar, family-oriented women, 300 to 1,000 words. Light, romantic poetry, to 24 lines. Pays 5¢ a word, after publication. Buys all rights.

SECRETS—215 Lexington Ave., New York, NY 10016. Jean Press Silberg, Ed. Realistic, emotional confession stories, 1,500 to 10,000 words, emphasizing family, home, and love relationships. Articles on subjects of interest to blue-collar, family-oriented women. Pays 3¢ a word, on publication. Buys all rights.

TRUE CONFESSIONS—215 Lexington Ave., New York, NY 10016. Barbara J. Brett, Ed. Timely, emotional, first-person stories, 2,000 to 10,000 words, on romance, family life, and problems of today's young blue-collar women.

Love interest and love problems should be stressed. Articles, 300 to 700 words, for young wives and mothers. Pays 5¢ a word, a month after publication.

TRUE EXPERIENCE—215 Lexington Ave., New York, NY 10016. Helene Eccleston, Ed. Realistic first-person stories, 4,000 to 8,000 words (short shorts, to 2,000 words), on family life, love, courtship, health, religion, etc. Pays 3¢ a word, a month after publication.

TRUE LOVE—215 Lexington Ave., New York, NY 10016. Marta Mestrovic, Ed. Fresh, true first-person stories, on young love, marital problems, and topics of current interest. Pays 3¢ a word, a month after publication.

TRUE ROMANCE—215 Lexington Ave., New York, NY 10016. Susan Weiner, Ed. True, romantic first-person stories, 2,000 to 12,000 words. Love poems. Articles, 300 to 700 words, for young wives and singles. Pays 3¢ a word, a month after publication.

TRUE STORY—215 Lexington Ave., New York, NY 10016. Helen Vincent, Ed. First-person true stories, 3,000 to 12,000 words. Pays 5¢ a word, on publication.

POETRY MARKETS

Markets for both serious and light verse are included in the following list of magazines.

Although major magazines pay good rates for poetry, the competition to break into print is very stiff, since editors use only a limited number of poems in each issue. On the other hand, college, little, and literary magazines use a great deal of poetry, and though payment is modest—usually in copies—publication in these journals can establish a beginning poet's reputation, and lead to publication in the major magazines. (The listing of college, literary, and little magazines, which begins on page 674, includes requirements for poetry, fiction, and essays.) Poets will find a number of competitions offering cash awards for unpublished poems in the *Literary Prize Offers* list, beginning on page 753.

Poets should also consider local newspapers as possible verse markets. Although they may not specifically seek poetry from free lancers, newspapers editors often print verse submitted to them, especially on holidays and for special occasions.

The market for book-length collections of poetry is extremely limited. Commercial publishers bring out few volumes of poetry. There are a number of university presses that publish poetry collections, however (see page 748), and many of them sponsor annual competitions. Consult the *Literary Prize Offers* list for more information about these contests.

ACTION—Dept. of Christian Education, 901 College Ave., Winona Lake, IN 46590. Verse for 9- to 11-year olds. Pays $5, on publication.

ALCOHOLISM/THE NATIONAL MAGAZINE—P. O. Box 19519, Seattle, WA 98109. Christina Johnston, Ed. Poetry, 4 to 15 lines, on recovery from alcoholism; humor. Pays $5 to $25, on publication. Guidelines available.

ALIVE! FOR YOUNG TEENS—Christian Board of Publication, Box 179, St. Louis, MO 63166. Short poems, for 12- to 15-year-olds. Pays 25¢ per line, on publication.

ALOHA—828 Fort St. Mall, Honolulu, HI 96813. Rita Ariyoshi, Ed. Poetry relating to Hawaii. Pays $25 per poem, on publication.

AMAZING SCIENCE FICTION STORIES—Box 110, Lake Geneva, WI 53147. George Scithers, Ed. Serious and light verse, with SF/fantasy tie-in. Pays $1.00 per line for short poems, somewhat less for longer ones, on acceptance.

AMERICA—106 W. 56th St., New York, NY 10019. John Moffitt, Poetry Ed. Serious poetry of high quality, preferably in contemporary prose idiom, 10 to 30 lines. Half-rhyme; occasional full rhyme and light verse. Pays $1.40 per line, on publication.

AMERICAN LAND FORUM—5410 Grosvenor Ln., Bethesda, MD 20814. Sara Ebenreck, Ed. Quarterly. Poetry to 50 lines, on American land use and landscape. Pays $15 per poem, on acceptance.

THE AMERICAN LEGION MAGAZINE—P. O. Box 1055, Indianapolis, IN 46206. Ward Beckham, Parting Shots Editor. Humorous verse, to 4 lines. Pays $4.50 a line, on acceptance.

THE AMERICAN SCHOLAR—1811 Q St. N.W., Washington, DC 20009. Joseph Epstein, Ed. Highly original poetry, 10 to 32 lines, for college-educated, intellectual readers. Pays $50, on acceptance.

THE ATLANTIC—8 Arlington St., Boston, MA 02116. Peter Davison, Poetry Ed. Poetry of highest quality. Limited market; only 3 to 4 poems an issue. Interest in young poets. Occasionally uses light verse. Pays excellent rates, on acceptance.

THE ATLANTIC ADVOCATE—P. O. Box 3370, Fredericton, N.B., Canada E3B 5A2. Poetry related to Canada's Atlantic provinces. Pays to $5 per column inch, on publication.

AUGUSTA SPECTATOR—P. O. Box 3168, Augusta, GA 30904. Poetry. Submit to: Jan Cevalina, Poetry Ed., 19 Troon Way, Aiben, SC 29801. Pays in copies.

BIRD WATCHER'S DIGEST—P. O. Box 110, Marietta, OH 45750. Mary B. Bowers, Ed. Poetry, to 30 lines, related to birds or bird watching. Pays to $10, on publication.

BREAD—6401 The Paseo, Kansas City, MO 64131. Gary Sivewright, Ed. Inspirational poetry, to 20 lines, for teenagers. Pays 25¢ a line, on acceptance.

CAPE COD LIFE—P. O. Box 222, Osterville, MA 02655. Brian Shortsleeve, Pub. Poetry, related to Cape Cod, Martha's Vineyard, and Nantucket. Pays on publication.

CAPPER'S WEEKLY—616 Jefferson St., Topeka, KS 66607. Dorothy Harvey, Ed. Traditional poetry and free verse, 4 to 16 lines. Submit up to 6 poems at a time with SASE. Pays $3 to $5, on acceptance.

CHESAPEAKE SHALOM—P. O. Box 789, Severna Park, MD 21146. Lee Irwin, Ed. Poetry for Jewish readers in the Chesapeake Bay region. Pays $2 to $10, on publication.

CHILDREN'S PLAYMATE—P. O. Box 567, Indianapolis, IN 46206. Kathleen B. Mosher, Ed. Poetry for children, 5 to 7 years old, on good health, nutrition, exercise, safety, seasonal and humorous subjects. Pays from $7, on publication. Buys all rights.

THE CHRISTIAN CENTURY—407 S. Dearborn St., Chicago, IL 60605. James M. Wall, Ed. Poetry, to 20 lines. Pays on publication.

CHRISTIAN HERALD—Chappaqua, NY 10514. David E. Kucharsky, Ed. Interdenominational. Short verse on Christian themes. Pays from $5, on acceptance.

THE CHRISTIAN SCIENCE MONITOR—One Norway St., Boston, MA 02115. Roderick Nordell, Ed., The Home Forum. Fresh, vigorous nonreligious poems of high quality, on various subjects. Short poems preferred. Pays varying rates, on acceptance. Submit no more than 5 poems at a time.

CLASS—27 Union Sq. W., New York, NY 10003. W. Franklin Joseph, Ed. Poetry, 8 to 10 lines, related to the Third World population in the U.S. Payment varies, after acceptance.

COBBLESTONE—20 Grove St., Peterborough, NH 03458. Carolyn P. Yoder, Ed. Poetry, to 100 lines, on historical subjects, for 8- to 14-year-olds. Pays varying rates, on publication. Send SASE for guidelines and themes.

COMMONWEAL—232 Madison Ave., New York, NY 10016. Rosemary Deen, Poetry Ed. Catholic. Serious and witty poetry of high quality. Pays 40¢ a line, on publication.

COMPLETE WOMAN—1165 N. Clark St., Chicago, IL 60610. Address Assoc. Ed. Poetry. Pays $10, on publication. SASE necessary for return of material.

COSMOPOLITAN—224 W. 57th St., New York, NY 10019. Karen Burke, Poetry Ed. Poetry about relationships, for young, active career women. Pays from $25, on acceptance.

DAILY MEDITATION—Box 2710, San Antonio, TX 78299. Ruth S. Paterson, Ed. Nonsectarian. Inspirational verse. Pays 14¢ a line to 16 lines, on acceptance.

DECISION—Billy Graham Evangelistic Assn., 1300 Harmon Pl., Minneapolis, MN 55403. Roger C. Palms, Ed. Poems, 5 to 24 lines, on devotional and other subjects; preferably free verse. Pays on publication.

THE DISCIPLE—Box 179, St. Louis, MO 63166. James L. Merrell, Ed. Journal of Disciples of Christ. Poetry, on religious, seasonal, and historical subjects. Pays $2 to $10, on publication.

THE EVANGEL—Dept. of Christian Education, Free Methodist Headquarters, 901 College Ave., Winona Lake, IN 46590. Vera Bethel, Ed. Free Methodist. Devotional or nature poetry, 8 to 16 lines. Pays $5, on publication.

EVANGELICAL BEACON—1515 E. 66th St., Minneapolis, MN 55423. George Keck, Ed. Denominational publication of Evangelical Free Church of America. Some poetry related to Christian faith. Pays 4¢ a word, $2.50 minimum, on publication.

FAMILY CIRCLE—488 Madison Ave., New York, NY 10022. Eleanor Lewis, Poetry Ed. Poetry to 20 lines (occasionally longer), of interest to women and families. Pays from $25, on acceptance. Submit no more than 7 poems at a time with SASE. Query.

FARM AND RANCH LIVING—5400 S. 60th St., Greendale, WI 53129. Bob

Ottum, Ed. Poetry, to 20 lines, on rural people and situations. Photos. Pays $35 to $75, extra for photos, on acceptance and on publication. Query.

FARM WOMAN NEWS—P.O. Box 643, Milwaukee WI 53201. Ruth Benedict, Man. Ed. Traditional rural poetry and light verse, 4 to 30 lines, on rural experiences, for farm and ranch women. Pays $30 to $60, on acceptance.

GEORGIA JOURNAL—Agee Publishers, Athens, GA 30603. Jane M. Agee, Ed. Poetry, to 20 lines, related to GA. Pays on acceptance.

GOLF DIGEST MAGAZINE—495 Westport Ave., Norwalk, CT 06856. Lois Hains, Ass't. Ed. Humorous golf-related verse, 4 to 8 lines, on golf. Pays $20 to $25, on acceptance. Send SASE.

GOOD HOUSEKEEPING—959 Eighth Ave., New York, NY 10010. Serious poetry, of interest to women; send to A. Quarfoot, Poetry Ed. Light, humorous verse; send to Mary Ann Littell, Light Housekeeping Ed. Pays $5 a line, on acceptance.

GRIT—208 W. Third St., Williamsport, PA 17701. Joanne Decker, Assignment Ed. Traditional poetry and light verse, 4 to 16 lines, for readers in smalltown and rural America. Pays $6 for poems up to 4 lines, 50¢ a line for each additional line, on acceptance.

GUIDE—Review and Herald Publishing Co., 55 W. Oak Ridge Dr., Hagerstown, MD 21740. Poetry, to 12 lines, for Christian youth, ages 10 to 15. Pays on acceptance.

HIGH COUNTRY NEWS—Box 1019, Paonia, CO 81428. Ed Marston, Man. Ed. Poetry, related to contemporary western U.S. life styles and issues. Pays on publication.

HOME LIFE—127 Ninth Ave. N., Nashville, TN 37234. Reuben Herring, Ed. Southern Baptist. Short lyrical verse, humorous, marriage and family, seasonal, and inspirational. Pays to $20, on acceptance.

LADIES' HOME JOURNAL—3 Park Ave., New York, NY 10016. No unsolicited poetry; submit through an agent only.

LEATHERNECK—Box 1775, Quantico, VA 22134. Ronald D. Lyons, Ed. Publication of U.S. Marine Corps. Marine-oriented poetry. Pays from $10, on acceptance.

LIVING WITH TEENAGERS—127 Ninth Ave., N., Nashville, TN 37234. Poetry, 4 to 16 lines, for parents of teenagers. Pays on acceptance.

LUTHERAN WOMEN—2900 Queen Ln., Philadelphia, PA 19129. Terry Schutz, Ed. Short poems, for Christian women. Pays on publication. Include SASE.

MCCALL'S MAGAZINE—230 Park Ave., New York, NY 10169. Address Barbara Barton Sloane, Poetry Editor. Poetry and light verse, 4 to 30 lines, of interest to women. Pays $5 a line, on acceptance.

MARRIAGE AND FAMILY LIVING—Abbey Press Publishing Div., St. Meinrad, IN 47577. Kass Dotterweich, Man. Ed. Verse, on marriage and family. Pays $15, on acceptance.

MATURE YEARS—201 Eighth Ave. S., Nashville, TN 37202. Daisy D. Warren, Ed. United Methodist. Poetry, to 14 lines, on pre-retirement, retirement, seasonal subjects, aging. No saccharine poetry. Pays 50¢ to $1.00 per line.

MIDSTREAM—515 Park Ave., New York, NY 10022. Joel Carmichael, Ed. Poetry, of Jewish interest. Pays $25, on publication.

THE MIRACULOUS MEDAL—475 E. Chelten Ave., Philadelphia, PA 19144. Robert P. Cawley, C. M., Ed. Catholic. Religious verse, to 20 lines. Pays 50¢ a line, on acceptance.

MODERN BRIDE—One Park Ave., New York, NY 10016. Mary Ann Cavlin, Man. Ed. Short verse of interest to bride and groom. Pays $25 to $35, on acceptance.

MODERN LITURGY—160 E. Virginia St., #290, San Jose, CA 95112. Ken Guentert, Ed. Poetry for Catholic audience. Pays on publication.

MODERN MATURITY—215 Long Beach Blvd., Long Beach, CA 90801. Ian Ledgerwood, Ed. Short verse, for Americans 55 years and older. Pays from $50, on acceptance.

MODERN ROMANCES—215 Lexington Ave., New York, NY 10016. Jean Sharbel, Ed. Light, romantic poetry, to 24 lines. Pays varying rates, after publication. Buys all rights.

MS.—119 W. 40th St., New York, NY 10018. Address Poetry Ed. Poetry of high quality, on feminist subjects. Pays $75, on acceptance.

THE NATION—72 Fifth Ave., New York, NY 10011. Grace Schulman, Poetry Ed. Poetry of high quality. Pays after publication.

NATIONAL ENQUIRER—Lantana, FL 33464. Jim Allan, Asst. Ed. Short poems of a philosophical or amusing nature. Pays $20, on publication.

NEW AGE—342 Western Ave., Brighton, MA 02135. Patricia Vigderman, Senior Ed. Poetry for readers interested in the natural world and lifelong learning. Pays 10¢ a word, on publication.

NEW ENGLAND ENTERTAINMENT DIGEST—P.O. Box 735, Marshfield, MA 02050. Paul J. Reale, Ed. Light verse, of any length, related to the entertainment field. Pays $1 to $2, on publication.

NEW ERA—50 E. North Temple, Salt Lake City, UT 84150. Brian Kelly, Ed. Poetry for young Mormons. Pays 25¢ a line, on acceptance.

THE NEW REPUBLIC—1220 19th St., N.W., Washington, DC 20036. Robert Pinsky, Poetry Ed. Poetry, of interest to liberal, intellectual readers. Pays $40, after publication.

NEW WORLD OUTLOOK—475 Riverside Dr., New York, NY 10115. Arthur J. Moore, Jr., Ed. United Methodist. Poetry, to 16 lines. Pays on publication.

NEW WOMAN—215 Lexington Ave., New York, NY 10016. Pat Miller, Ed. Poetry. No unsolicited manuscripts. Accepted through agents only.

THE NEW YORKER—25 W. 43rd St., New York, NY 10036. First-rate poetry and light verse. Pays top rates, on acceptance. Include SASE.

OBLATES MAGAZINE—15 S. 59th St., Belleville, IL 62222. Address Linda Lehr. Inspirational poetry, to 16 lines. Pays $25, on acceptance. Send for free sample copy and guidelines.

THE OHIO MOTORIST—P.O. Box 6150, Cleveland, OH 44101. Jerome F. Turk, Ed. Humorous verse, 4 to 6 lines, on automobile and vacation topics. Pays $10 to $15, on acceptance.

OUR FAMILY—Box 249, Dept. E., Battleford, Sask., Canada S0M 0E0. Rev. Albert Lalonde, O.M.I., Catholic. Verse, for family men and women. Pays 75¢ to $1.00 a line, on acceptance. Send self-addressed envelope with international reply coupons for guidelines.

PENTECOSTAL EVANGEL—1445 Boonville, Springfield, MO 65802. Richard G. Champion, Ed. Journal of Assemblies of God. Religious and inspirational verse, 12 to 30 lines. Pays to 40¢ a line, on publication.

PLAYBOY—919 N. Michigan Ave., Chicago, IL 60611. Address Party Jokes Editor. Limericks only. No light or serious verse. Pays $50, on acceptance. Jokes cannot be returned.

PURPOSE—616 Walnut Ave., Scottdale, PA 15683. James E. Horsch, Poetry Ed. Poetry, to 12 lines, with uplifting Christian discipleship angle. Pays to $12, on acceptance.

THE RECONSTRUCTIONIST—270 W. 89th St., New York, NY 10024. Dr. Jacob Staub, Ed. Poetry, relating to Judaism. Pays on publication.

ROLL CALL: THE NEWSPAPER OF CAPITOL HILL—201 Massachusetts Ave. N. E., Washington, DC 20002. Light, humorous satire on Congress or politics. Pays on acceptance.

ST. JOSEPH'S MESSENGER—P.O. Box 288, Jersey City, NJ 07303. Sister Ursula Marie Maphet, Ed. Light verse and traditional poetry, 4 to 40 lines. Pays $5 to $15, on publication.

THE SATURDAY EVENING POST—1100 Waterway Blvd., Indianapolis, IN 46202. Address Post Scripts Ed. Light verse and humor. Pays $15, on publication.

SCOPE—426 S. Fifth St., Box 1209, Minneapolis, MN 55440. Constance Lovaas, Ed. American Lutheran Church Women. Poetry. Pays on acceptance.

SCORE, CANADA'S GOLF MAGAZINE—287 MacPherson Ave., Toronto, Ont., Canada M4V 1A4. Poetry, to 50 words, on the Canadian and U.S. golf scene. Pays to $20, on acceptance.

SEVENTEEN—850 Third Ave., New York, NY 10022. Poetry, to 40 lines, by teens. Submit up to 5 poems. Pays $15, after acceptance.

SHOFAR—43 Northcote Dr., Melville, NY 11747. Poetry, to 50 lines, for Jewish children, aged 8 to 13. Pays to 10¢ a word, on publication.

SISTERS TODAY—The Liturgical Press, St. John's Abbey, Collegeville, MN 56231. Sister Mary Anthony Wagner, O.S.B., Ed. Poetry, to 34 lines, for Roman Catholic audience. Send submissions to Sister Audrey Synnott, R.S.M., 1437 Blossom Rd., Rochester, NY 14610. Pays $10 per poem, on publication.

SOUTHERN EXPOSURE—P.O. Box 531, Durham, NC 27702. Michael Yellin, Ed. Poetry, related to the South. Pays on publication. Include SASE.

STANDARD—6401 The Paseo, Kansas City, MO 64131. Address Editor. Poetry to 20 lines, with Christian emphasis. Pays on acceptance.

THIRD COAST—P.O. Box 592, Austin, TX 78767. Miriam Davidson, Ed. Poetry, with an Austin slant. Pays on publication. Include SASE.

UNITED METHODIST REPORTER—P.O. Box 66027, Dallas, TX 75266. Spurgeon M. Dunnam III, Editor. Religious verse, 4 to 16 lines. Pays $2, on acceptance.

VISTA—Box 2000, Marion, IN 46952. Poetry for Christian readers.

WESTERN PEOPLE—P.O. Box 2500, Saskatoon, Sask., Canada S7K 2C4. Mary Gilchrist, Man. Ed. Short poetry, with Western Canadian themes. Pays on acceptance. Send SAE with International Reply Coupons.

WORKING FOR BOYS—St. John's High School, Main St., Shrewsbury, MA 01545. Verse, to 24 lines. Pays 40¢ a line, on acceptance. Limited market.

YANKEE—Dublin, NH 03444. Jean Burden, Poetry Ed. Serious poetry of high quality, to 30 lines. Pays $35 per poem for all rights, $25 for first rights, on publication.

THE YOUNG SOLDIER—The Salvation Army, 799 Bloomfield Ave., Verona, NJ 07044. Dorothy Hitzka, Ed. Some poetry, for Christian children. Pays on acceptance.

POETRY SERIES

The following university presses publish book-length collections of poetry by writers who have never had a book of poems published. Each has specific rules for submission, so before submitting any material, be sure to write well ahead of the deadline dates for further information. Some organizations sponsor competitions in which prizes are offered for book-length collections of poetry; see *Literary Prize Offers* list on page 753.

THE ALABAMA PRESS POETRY SERIES—Dept. of English, Drawer A1, Univ. of Alabama, University, AL 35486. Address Thomas Rabbitt or Dara Wier. Considers unpublished book-length collections of poetry for publication as part of the Alabama Press Poetry Series. Submissions accepted during the months of September, October, and November only.

UNIVERSITY OF GEORGIA PRESS POETRY SERIES—Athens, GA 30602. Poets who have never had a book of poems published may submit book-length poetry manuscripts for possible publication. Open during the month of September each year. Manuscripts from poets who have published at least one volume of poetry (chapbooks excluded) are considered during the month of January.

WESLEYAN UNIVERSITY PRESS—110 Mt. Vernon St., Middletown, CT 06547. Considers unpublished book-length poetry manuscripts, by poets who have never had a book published, for publication in the Wesleyan New Poets Series. There is no deadline.

GREETING CARD MARKETS

Greeting card companies often have their own specific requirements for submitting ideas, verse, and artwork. The National Association of Greeting Card Publishers, however, gives the following general guidelines for submitting material: Verses and messages should be typed, double-spaced, each one on 3 × 5 or 4 × 6 card. Use only one side of the card, and be sure to put your name and address in the upper left-hand corner. Keep a copy of every verse or idea you send. (It's also advisable to keep a record of what you've submitted to each publisher.) Always enclose a stamped, self-addressed envelope, and do not send out more than ten verses or ideas in a group to any one publisher.

The National Association of Greeting Card Publishers brings out a booklet for free lancers, *Artists and Writers Market List,* with the names, addresses, and editorial guidelines of greeting card companies. This may be obtained by sending a self-addressed, stamped envelope and $1.00 to the Association at 600 Pennsylvania Ave., S.E., Washington, DC 20003.

ABBEY PRESS—St. Meinrad, IN 47577. Attn: P. A. Ledford, Prod. Dir. Long, poetic verses that begin on front of card and continue on inside. All occasions: birthday, friendship, get well, sympathy, congratulations, thank you, etc. Special occasions: Christmas, Easter, Valentine, St. Patrick's, Mother's Day, Father's Day. Pays $30 to $50. Limited market.

AMBERLEY GREETING CARD COMPANY—P.O. Box 36159, Cincinnati, OH 45236. Ned Stern, Ed. Humorous greeting card ideas, for birthday, illness, friendship, congratulations, miss you, thank you, retirement. Risqué and non-risqué humor. No seasonal cards. Pays $40. Buys all rights.

AMERICAN GREETING CORPORATION—10500 American Rd., Cleveland, OH 44144. Kathleen McKay, Free-lance Ed. Studio and light humor. Study catalogue and query before submitting. Limited market.

ARTFORMS CARD CORP.—725 County Line Rd., Deerfield, IL 60015. Attn: Bluma Marder. Verse, suitable for Jewish and general market. Formal for holiday cards and humorous for get well, birthdays, etc. Pays $15 to $25.

BLUE MOUNTAIN ARTS, INC.—P.O. Box 4549, Boulder, CO 80306. Attn: Editorial Staff, Dept. TW. Poetry and prose: inspirational (non-religious) and sensitive; humor. No artwork. No rhymed verse. Query first with SASE. Pays $150, on publication.

BRETT-FORER GREETINGS, INC.—105 E. 73rd St., New York, NY 10021. Ideas and designs for whimsical everyday and Christmas lines. Pays on acceptance.

DRAWING BOARD GREETING CARDS—8200 Carpenter Freeway, Dallas, TX 75222. Jimmie Fitzgerald, Edit. Director. General and studio card ideas. Pays to $80.

FRAN MAR GREETING CARDS, LTD.—587 Main St., New Rochelle, NY 10801. Stationery and party invitations; thank you notes. Pays $25 per idea, within 30 days of acceptance.

FRAVESSI-LAMONT, INC.—11 Edison Pl., Springfield, NJ 07081. Address Editor. Short verse, mostly humorous or sentimental; cards with witty prose. No Christmas material. Pays varying rates, on acceptance.

FREEDOM GREETING CARD COMPANY—P.O. Box 715, Bristol, PA 19007. Submit to Jay Levitt. Verse, traditional, humorous, and love messages. Inspirational poetry for all occasions. Pays $1 a line, on acceptance. Query with SASE.

GALLANT GREETINGS CORPORATION—2654 West Medill, Chicago, IL 60647. Ideas for humorous and serious greeting cards. Pays $30 per idea, in 45 days.

HALLMARK CARDS, INC.—P.O. Box 580, Kansas City, MO 64141. No unsolicited material.

THE KEATING LINE, INC.—27-08 40th Ave., Long Island City, NY 11101. Attn: Arwed H. Baenisch, A.D. Formal verse for all occasions. Everyday and seasonal.

LEANIN' TREE PUBLISHING CO.—Box 9500, Boulder, CO 80301. Address Editorial Assistant. Verse with a western flavor or theme, friendship and inspirational verse, Christian verse for holiday and friendship cards, and short love poems of upbeat, contemporary nature. Pays $35, on publication. Send SASE for guidelines first (required).

THE MAINE LINE COMPANY—P.O. Box 418, Rockport, ME 04856. Attn. Perri Ardman. Untraditional cards for contemporary women. Send SASE with three first class stamps for guidelines. Pays $25 to $50 per card.

ALFRED MAINZER, INC.—27-08 40th Ave., Long Island City, NY 11101. Arwed H. Baenisch, Art Dir. Everyday, Christmas, Mother's Day, Father's Day, Valentine's Day, Easter verses, general and religious occasions. Rates vary. Query.

MARK I—1733 W. Irving Park Rd., Chicago, IL 60613. Overstocked.

OATMEAL STUDIOS—Box 138, Rochester, VT 05767. Attn: Helene Lehrer. Humorous and clever ideas needed for birthday, anniversary, get well, etc., also, Valentine's Day, Christmas, Mother's Day, Father's Day, etc. Query with SASE.

PARAMOUNT CARDS INC.—Box 1225, Pawtucket, RI 02862. Attn: Dolores Riccio. Prose and verse for sensitivity, humorous, and general cards. Send SASE for guidelines. Pays varying rates, on acceptance.

RED FARM STUDIOS—P.O. Box 347, 334 Pleasant St., Pawtucket, RI 02862. Traditional cards, for graduations, weddings, birthdays, get-wells, anniversaries, friendship, new baby, Christmas, and sympathy. No studio humor. Pays varying rates.

REED STARLINE CARD CO.—3331 Sunset Blvd., Los Angeles, CA 90026. Barbara Stevens, Ed. Short humorous studio card copy, conversational in tone, for sophisticated adults; no verse or jingles. Everyday copy, for birthday, friendship, get well, anniversary, thank you, travel, congratulations. Submit material for fall holidays in January; for Valentine's Day and St. Patrick's Day in February; and for Easter, Mother's Day, Father's Day in July. Pays $40 per idea, on acceptance.

ROUSANA CARDS—28 Sager Pl., Hillside, NJ 07205. Attn: Ed Briscoe, Ed. Verse, prose, cutes, and humor for Everyday and all Seasonal lines.

VAGABOND CREATIONS, INC.—2560 Lance Dr., Dayton, OH 45409. George F. Stanley, Jr., Ed. Greeting cards with graphics only on cover (no copy) and short tie-in copy punch line on inside page: birthday, everyday, Valentine, Christmas, and graduation. Mildly risque humor with *double entendre* acceptable. Ideas for humorous buttons and illustrated theme stationery. Pays $15, on acceptance.

WARNER PRESS PUBLISHERS—1200 E. Fifth St., Anderson, IN 46012. Jane Hammond, Product Editor. Prose sensitivity, insp. poems, and verse card ideas, religious themes. Submit Christmas material in June and July. Pays $1 a line, on acceptance. SASE for guidelines.

WILLIAMHOUSE-REGENCY, INC.—28 W. 23rd St., New York, NY 10010. Submit to Nancy Boecker. Captions for wedding invitations. Pays varying rates, on acceptance. Query with SASE.

COLLEGE, LITERARY, AND LITTLE MAGAZINES

FICTION, NONFICTION, POETRY

The thousands of literary journals, little magazines, and college quarterlies being published today welcome work from novices and pros alike; editors are always interested in seeing traditional and experimental fiction, poetry, essays, reviews, short articles, criticism, and satire, and as long as the material is well-written, the fact that a writer is a beginner doesn't adversely affect his chances for acceptance.

Most of these smaller publications have small budgets and staffs, so they may be slow in their reporting time—several months is not unusual. In addition, they usually pay only in copies of the issue in which published work appears and some—particularly college magazines—do not read manuscripts during the summer.

Publication in the literary journals can, however, lead to recognition by editors of large-circulation magazines, who read the little magazines in their search for new talent. There is also the possibility of having one's work chosen for reprinting in one of the prestigious annual collections of work from the little magazines.

Because the requirements of these journals differ widely, it is always important to study recent issues before submitting work to one of them. Copies of magazines may be in large libraries, or a writer may send a postcard to the editor, and ask the price of a sample copy. When submitting a manuscript, always enclose a return envelope, with sufficient postage for its return.

For a complete list of literary and college publications and little magazines, writers may consult such reference works as *The International Directory of Little Magazines and Small Presses,* published annually by Dustbooks (P.O. Box 100, Paradise, CA 95969).

THE AGNI REVIEW—P.O. Box 600, Amherst, MA 01004. Sharon Dunn, Ed. Short stories and poetry. Pays in copies.

ALASKA QUARTERLY REVIEW—Dept. of English, Univ. of Alaska, 3211 Providence Dr., Anchorage, AK 99508. Address Eds. Short stories, novel excerpts, poetry (traditional and unconventional forms). Submit manuscripts between August 15 and May 15. Pays in copies.

THE ALTADENA REVIEW—P.O. Box 212, Altadena, CA 91001. Robin Shectman, Ed. High quality poetry, any form. Interviews, to 3,500 words; reviews, 700 to 1,500 words. Illustrations. Pays in copies.

AMELIA—329 E St., Bakersfield, CA 93304. Poetry, to 100 lines; critical essays, to 2,000 words; reviews to 500 words; belles lettres, to 1,000 words, fiction, to 2,500 words; fine pen and ink sketches; photos. Pays $25 for fiction and criticism, $10 to $25 for other nonfiction and artwork, $2 to $10 for poetry.

THE AMERICAN BOOK REVIEW—P.O. Box 188, Cooper Sta., New York, NY 10003. John Tytell, Ed. Book reviews, 750 to 1,200 words. Pays in copies.

THE AMERICAN POETRY REVIEW—1616 Walnut St., Rm. 405, Philadelphia, PA 19103. Address the Eds. High-quality modern poetry. SASE a must.

AMERICAN QUARTERLY—303 College Hall, Univ. of Pennsylvania, Philadelphia, PA 19104. Richard R. Beeman and Janice Radway, Eds. Scholarly essays, 5,000 to 10,000 words, on any aspect of U.S. culture. Pays in copies.

THE AMERICAN SCHOLAR—1811 Q St. N.W., Washington, DC 20009. Joseph Epstein, Ed. Articles, 3,500 to 4,000 words, on science, politics, literature, the arts, etc. Book reviews. Pays $350 for articles, $100 for reviews, on publication.

AMHERST REVIEW—Box 486, Sta. 2, Amherst, MA 01002. Ruth Abbe, Ed. Fiction, to 8,000 words, and poetry, to 160 lines. Photos and drawings. Pays in copies.

ANOTHER CHICAGO MAGAZINE—Box 11223, Chicago, IL 60611. Fiction, essays on literature, and poetry. Pays $5 to $25, on acceptance.

ANTAEUS—18 W. 30th St., New York, NY 10001. Daniel Halpern, Ed. Short stories, essays, documents, parts-of-novels, poems. Submissions accepted from October 1 to May 1 only. Pays on publication.

THE ANTIGONISH REVIEW—St. Francis Xavier Univ., Antigonish, N.S., Canada. George Sanderson, Ed. Poetry; short stories, essays, book reviews, 1,800 to 2,500 words. Pays in copies.

ANTIOCH REVIEW—P.O. Box 148, Yellow Springs, OH 45387. Robert S. Fogarty, Ed. Timely articles, 2,000 to 8,000 words, on social sciences, literature, and humanities. Quality fiction. Poetry. No inspirational poetry. Pays $10 per printed page, on publication.

APALACHEE QUARTERLY—DDB Press, P.O. Box 20106, Tallahassee, FL 32316. Monica Faeth, Barbara Hamby, and Allen Woodman, Eds. Fiction, to 30 manuscript pages; poems (3 to 5); essays. Pays in copies.

APOCALYPSO—673 Ninth Ave., New York, NY 10036. Articles and fiction, to 3,000 words. Poetry, any length. Pays in copies.

ARIZONA QUARTERLY—Univ. of Arizona, Tucson, AZ 85721. Albert F. Gegenheimer, Ed. Literary essays; regional material; general-interest articles. Fiction, to 3,500 words. Poetry (up to 30 lines)—any form or subject matter. Pays in copies.

AURA LITERARY/ARTS REVIEW—P.O. Box 76, University Center Sta., Birmingham, Al 35294. Fiction and essays on literature, to 6,000 words; poetry; photos and drawings. Pays in copies.

BALL STATE UNIVERSITY FORUM—Ball State Univ., Muncie, IN 47306. Bruce W. Hozeski and Frances Mayhew Rippy, Eds. Short stories and general-interest articles, 500 to 4,000 words. One-act plays. Poetry. Pays in copies.

THE BELLINGHAM REVIEW—412 N. State St., Bellingham, WA 98225. Knute Skinner, Ed. Fiction, to 5,000 words. Poetry of all kinds. Short dramas.

Submit manuscripts between September 15 and June 1. Pays in copies plus subscription. Annual contest.

BELOIT POETRY JOURNAL—RFD 2, Box 154, Ellsworth, ME 04605. First-rate contemporary poetry, of any length or mode. Pays in copies. Send SASE for guidelines.

BERKELEY POETS COOPERATIVE—P.O. Box 459, Berkeley, CA 94701. Charles Entrekin, Ed. Poetry, all forms; no restrictions. Submissions accepted from April 1 to August 1 and from October 1 to February 1. Pays in copies.

BITTERROOT—P.O. Box 489, Spring Glen, NY 12483. Menke Katz, Ed.-in-Chief. Poetry, to 50 lines; B&W camera ready drawings. Pays in copies.

BLACK MARIA—P.O. Box 25187, Chicago, IL 60625. Feminist. Short stories and experimental fiction, to 3,500 words. Poetry of any form. Articles; essays; B & W photos. Pays in copies.

THE BLACK WARRIOR REVIEW—P.O. Box 2936, University, AL 35486. Gabby Hyman, Ed. Serious and imaginative fiction; reviews and essays; poetry (no religious or haiku). Pays per printed page. Annual contest.

THE BLOOMSBURY REVIEW—P.O. Box 8928, Denver, CO 80201. Marilyn Auer, Assoc. Ed.; Carol Arenberg, Senior Ed.; Ray Gonzalez, Poetry Ed. Book reviews, publishing features, interviews, essays, poetry, up to 800 words. Pays $5 to $15, on publication.

BLUELINE—Blue Mountain Lake, NY 12812. Alice Gilborn, Ed. Essays, fiction, to 2,500 words, on Adirondack region or similar areas. Poetry, to 44 lines. No more than 5 poems per submission. Pays in copies.

BOOK FORUM—38 E. 76th St., New York, NY 10021. Essays, 800 to 1,600 words, on books, writers, art, politics, etc. Interviews. Book reviews assigned. Pays $25 to $100, on acceptance. Query.

BOSTON REVIEW—33 Harrison Ave., Boston, MA 02111. Nicholas Bromell, Ed. Reviews and essays, 800 to 3,000 words, on literature, art, music, film, photography. Original fiction, to 5,000 words. Poetry. Pays $40 to $150.

BOTTOMFISH—De Anza College, 21250 Stevens Creek Blvd., Cupertino, CA 95014. Frank Berry, Ed. Short, contemporary fiction, to 3,500 words; poetry, to 100 lines. Pays in copies.

BUCKNELL REVIEW—Bucknell Univ., Lewisburg, PA 17837. Interdisciplinary journal in book form. Scholarly articles on arts, science, and letters. Pays in copies.

CALLIOPE—Creative Writing Program, Roger Williams College, Bristol, RI 02809. Martha Christina, Ed. Short stories, to 2,500 words; poetry (query first to find out about thematic issues). Pays in copies. No submissions April through July.

CALYX, A JOURNAL OF ART & LITERATURE BY WOMEN—P.O. Box B, Corvallis, OR 97339. M. Donnelly, Man. Ed. Fiction, 5,000 words; reviews, 250 to 1,000 words; poetry, to 6 poems; poetry book reviews, to 1,000 words. Pays in copies. Include short bio and SASE.

CANADIAN FICTION MAGAZINE—Box 946, Sta. F., Toronto, Ontario, Canada M4Y 2N9. High-quality short stories, novel excerpts, and experimental fiction, to 5,000 words, by Canadians. Interviews with Canadian authors; translations. Pays $10 per page, on publication.

THE CAPILANO REVIEW—Capilano College, 2055 Purcell Way, North Vancouver, B.C., Canada V7J 3H5. Ann Rosenberg, Ed. Fiction; poetry; drama; visual arts. Pays $10 to $40.

CAROLINA QUARTERLY—Greenlaw Hall 066A, Univ. of North Carolina, Chapel Hill, NC 27514. Mary Titus, Ed. Fiction to 7,000 words, by new or established writers. Poetry (no restrictions on length, though limited space makes inclusion of works of more than 300 lines impractical). Pays $3 per printed page for fiction, $5 per poem, on acceptance.

THE CENTENNIAL REVIEW—110 Morrill Hall, Michigan State Univ., East Lansing, MI 48824-1036. Linda Wagner, Ed. Articles, 3,000 to 5,000 words, on sciences and humanities. Poetry. Pays in copies and subscription.

THE CHARITON REVIEW—Northeast Missouri State Univ., Kirksville, MO 63501. Jim Barnes, Ed. High-quality fiction, to 6,000 words. Modern and contemporary translations. Book reviews. Pays $5 per printed page for fiction and translations.

THE CHICAGO REVIEW—Univ. of Chicago, Chicago, IL 60637. Steve Heminger and Steve Schroer, Eds. Essays; interviews; reviews; fiction; translations, poetry. Pays in copies plus subscription.

CIMARRON REVIEW—Oklahoma State Univ., Stillwater, OK 74078. Jeanne Adams Wray, Man. Ed. Articles, 1,500 to 2,500 words, on history, philosophy, political science, etc. Serious contemporary fiction. Pays in copies.

CINCINNATI POETRY REVIEW—Dept. of English, 069, Univ. of Cincinnati, Cincinnati, OH 45221. Poetry. Pays in copies.

COLORADO-NORTH REVIEW—Univ. Center, Univ. of Northern Colorado, Greeley, CO 80639. Address Ed. Fiction, to 20 typed pages; poetry; graphic art. Include biographical sketch with submission. Pays in copies.

COLORADO STATE REVIEW—English Dept., 322 Eddy, Colorado State Univ., Fort Collins, CO 80523. Fiction submissions accepted from August 1 to December 31; poetry from January 1 to April 30 every year. Poetry, fiction, translation, interviews, reviews, articles. Pays $5 per page.

COLUMBIA, A MAGAZINE OF POETRY & PROSE—404 Dodge, Columbia Univ., New York, NY 10027. Address Eds. Articles and fiction, to 25 typed pages. Poetry. Pays in copies. Annual award.

CONFRONTATION—Dept. of English, C. W. Post of L.I.U., Greenvale, NY 11548. Martin Tucker, Ed. Serious fiction, 750 to 6,000 words. Crafted poetry, 20 to 200 lines. Pays $5 to $40, on publication.

THE CONNECTICUT POETRY REVIEW—P.O. Box 3783, New Haven, CT 06525. J. Claire White and James Chichette, Eds. Poetry, 5 to 40 lines, and reviews, 700 words. Pays $5 per poem, $10 for a review, on acceptance.

COTTON BOLL/THE ATLANTA REVIEW—P.O. Box 76757, Sandy Springs, Atlanta, GA 30358. Mary Hollingworth, Ed. Highly literate short stories, fables, satires, to 5,000 words. Poetry, to 3 typed pages. Pays in copies.

CREATIVE PERSON—1000 Byus Dr., Charleston, WV 25311. Carol Bryan, Ed. Articles, to 2,000 words, and fiction, to 3,000 words, related to the process of creativity. Interviews. Pays $25 or subscription. Query.

CREDENCES—420 Capen Hall, SUNY, Buffalo, NY 14260. Robert

Bertholf, Ed. Interviews; essays; reviews; fiction, to 25 typed pages. Long poems. Pays in copies and cash.

THE CRISIS—N.A.A.C.P., 186 Remsen St., Brooklyn, NY 11201. Maybelle Ward, Ed. Dir. Articles, to 1,500 words, on civil rights, problems and achievements of blacks and other minorities. Pays in copies.

CRITICAL INQUIRY—Univ. of Chicago Press, Wieboldt Hall, 1050 E. 59th St., Chicago, IL 60637. W. J. T. Mitchell, Ed. Critical essays that offer a theoretical perspective on literature, music, visual arts, popular culture, etc. Pays in copies.

CROTON REVIEW—P.O. Box 277, Croton-on-Hudson, NY 10520. Quality short-short fiction (to 14 pages), poetry (to 75 lines), and literary essays. Submissions accepted from September to February only. Pays with copy and honorarium.

CUMBERLAND POETRY REVIEW—P.O. Box 120128, Acklen Sta., Nashville, TN 37212. Address Eds. High-quality poetry and criticism; translations. No restrictions on form, style or subject matter. Pays in copies.

CUTBANK—English Dept., Univ. of Montana, Missoula, MT 59812. Pamela Uschuk, Ed. Essays, reviews (to 1½ pages) short stories, and poetry (3 to 5 at one time). B&W photos; graphics. Pays in copies.

DENVER QUARTERLY—Univ. of Denver, Denver, CO 80208. David Milofsky, Ed. Literary, cultural essays and articles; poetry; book reviews; fiction. Pays $5 per printed page, after publication.

DESCANT—Texas Christian Univ., T.C.U. Sta., Fort Worth, TX 76129. Betsy Colquitt, Ed. Fiction, to 6,000 words. Poetry, to 40 lines. No restriction on form or subject. Pays in copies. Submit manuscripts during academic year only.

THE DEVIL'S MILLHOPPER—Rt. 3, Box 29, Elgin, SC 29045. Jim Peterson, Ed. Poetry, any length. Pays in copies.

EVENT—Kwantlen College, Box 9030, Surrey, B.C., Canada V3T 5H8. Leona Gom, Ed. Short stories; novellas; plays. Pays modest rates, after publication.

FARMER'S MARKET—P.O. Box 1272, Galesburg, IL 61402. Short stories and novel excerpts, to 20 pages, and poetry: must be related to Midwest. Pays in copies. Address The Editors.

FAT TUESDAY—808 3/4 N. Detroit St., Los Angeles, CA 90046. F. M. Cotolo, Ed. Annual. Short fiction, poetry, parts-of-novels, paragraphs, crystal thoughts of any dimension—up to 5 pages. Pays in copies.

FICTION INTERNATIONAL—English Dept., San Diego State Univ., San Diego, CA 92182. Harold Jaffe and Larry McCaffery, Eds. Post-modernist and politically committed fiction and theory. Pays in copies.

THE FIDDLEHEAD—Dept. of English, Univ. of New Brunswick, Fredericton, N.B., Canada E3B 5A3. Serious fiction, 2,500 words, preferably by Canadians. Pays about $10 per printed page, on publication.

FIELD—Rice Hall, Oberlin College, Oberlin, OH 44074. Stuart Friebert, David Young, Eds. Serious poetry, any length, by established and unknown poets; essays on poetics by poets. Translations by qualified translators. Pays $15 to $25 per page, on publication.

FINE MADNESS—P.O. Box 15411, Seattle, WA 98115. Kathryn Mac-Donald, John Marshall, Louis Bergsagel, Eds. Poetry, any length. Pays in copies.

FOOTWORK—Cultural Affairs Office, Passaic County Comm. College, College Blvd., Patterson, NJ 07509. Maria Gillan, Ed. High quality fiction, to 4 pages, and poetry, to 3 pages, any style. Pays in copies.

FORMATIONS—832 Chilton Lane, Wilmette, IL 60091. Jonathan Brent, Ed. Essays and fiction, any length. Pays varying rates, on publication.

FOUR QUARTERS—La Salle College, Philadelphia, PA 19141. John C. Kleis, Ed. Critical articles, 1,500 to 6,000 words, on writers and literary works; "think pieces" on history, politics, the arts. Short stories. Poetry, 8 to 32 lines. Some shorter poems used as fillers. Pays $5 for poems, $25 for fiction and nonfiction, on publication. No submissions in July or August.

THE GAMUT—1216 Rhodes Tower, Cleveland State Univ., Cleveland, OH 44115. Lively articles on general-interest topics concerned with the region or by regional writers, 2,000 to 6,000 words. Photos. Pays $25 to $250, on publication.

GARGOYLE—P.O. Box 3567, Washington, DC 20007. Gretchen Johnsen. Poetry Ed. Poetry, average 10 to 35 lines. Fiction. Pays in copies.

THE GEORGIA REVIEW—Univ. of Georgia, Athens, GA 30602. Stanley W. Lindberg, Ed.; Stephen Corey, Asst. Ed. Short fiction; interdisciplinary essays on arts and the humanities; book reviews; poetry. No submissions in June, July, and August.

GRAIN—Box 1154, Regina, Sask., Canada S4P 3B4. Brenda Riches, Ed. Short stories, to 10 typed pages. Songs, essays, and drama. Poetry (send no more than 6). Pays $30 to $100 for prose; $20 per poem, on publication.

GREAT LAKES REVIEW—Central Michigan Univ., Box 122, Anspach Hall, Mt. Pleasant, MI 48859. Ronald Primeau, Ed. Reviews and scholarly articles, 10 to 15 typed pages, on history, literature, etc., of Midwest. Pays in copies.

GREAT RIVER REVIEW—211 W. 7th St., Winona, MN 55987. Fiction and creative prose, 2,000 to 10,000 words. Quality contemporary poetry; send 4 to 8 poems. Special interest in Midwestern writers and themes.

THE GREENFIELD REVIEW—R.D. 1, Box 80, Greenfield Center, NY 12833. Joseph Bruchac III, Ed. Contemporary poetry, any length, by established and new poets, third world writers. Translations. Pays in copies. No submissions May–Sept.

GREEN'S MAGAZINE—P.O. Box 3236, Regina, Sask., Canada S4P 3H1. David Green, Ed. Fiction, 1,500 to 4,000 words. Poetry, to 40 lines. Pays in copies.

THE GREENSBORO REVIEW—Univ. of North Carolina, Greensboro, NC 27412. Lee Zacharias, Ed. Semi-annual. Poetry and fiction. Submission deadlines: Sept. 15 and Feb. 15. Pays in copies.

THE HARBOR REVIEW—English Dept., UMass-Boston, Boston, MA 02125. Fiction, to 10 pages; poetry, any length. Pays in copies.

HAWAII REVIEW—Dept. of English, Univ. of Hawaii, 1733 Donaghho Rd., Honolulu, HI 96882. Quality fiction, poetry, interviews, and literary criticism reflecting both regional and universal concerns.

HELICON NINE, THE JOURNAL OF WOMEN'S ARTS AND LETTERS—P.O. Box 22412, Kansas City, MO 64113. Poetry and fiction about women. Query preferred.

HOME PLANET NEWS—Box 415, Stuyvesant Sta., New York, NY 10009. Enid Dame, Donald Lev, Eds. Lively, energetic poetry, to 100 lines; shorter poems preferred. Pays in copies and subscriptions.

HUBBUB MAGAZINE—5344 S.E. 38th, Portland, OR 97202. Lisa Steinman, Carlos Reyes, Eds. Poetry. Pays in copies.

IMAGINE, INTERNATIONAL CHICANO POETRY JOURNAL—645 Beacon St., Suite 7, Boston, MA 02215. Tino Villanueva, Ed. Articles, interviews, to 20 pages; reviews; poetry. Pays $7 for articles and interviews, $5 for reviews, and 5¢ a line for poetry.

INDIANA REVIEW—316 N. Jordan Ave., Bloomington, IN 47405. Jane Hilberry, Erin McGraw, Eds. Fiction with an emphasis on style. Poems that are well executed and ambitious. Pays $5 a page for poetry; annual contests.

INLET—Dept. of English, Virginia Wesleyan College, Norfolk, VA 23502. Joseph Harkey, Ed. Short fiction, 500 to 3,000 words (short lengths preferred). Poems of 4 to 40 lines; all forms and themes. Address poetry to H. Rick Hite, Assoc. Ed. Submit between September and March. Pays in copies.

INTERNATIONAL POETRY REVIEW—Box 2047, Greensboro, NC 27402. Evalyn P. Gill, Ed. Contemporary poetry and translations (with original). Pays in copies.

INVISIBLE CITY—P.O. Box 2853, San Francisco, CA 94126. John McBride, Paul Vangelisti, Eds. Reviews, translations, especially contemporary European literature.

THE IOWA REVIEW—EPB 308, Univ. of Iowa, Iowa City, IA 52242. David Hamilton, Ed. Essays, poems, stories, reviews. Pays $10 a page for fiction and nonfiction, $1 a line for poetry, on publication.

JAM TO-DAY—P.O. Box 249, Northfield, VT 05663. Don Stanford and Judith Stanford, Eds. High-quality fiction and poetry, particularly from unknown and little-known writers. Pays $5 per printed page for fiction, $5 per poem, plus copies.

JAPANOPHILE—Box 223, Okemos, MI 48864. Earl R. Snodgrass, Ed. Fiction, to 10,000 words, with a Japanese setting. Each story should have at least one Japanese character and at least one non-Japanese. Pays to $20, on publication. Annual contest.

JOURNAL OF POPULAR CULTURE—Center for the Study of Popular Culture, Bowling Green State Univ., Bowling Green, OH 43403. Ray R. Browne, Ed. Articles. Pays in copies.

KANSAS QUARTERLY—Dept. of English, Kansas State Univ., Manhattan, KS 66506. Literary criticism, art and history. Fiction. Poetry. Pays in copies. Annual awards. Query for articles and special topics.

KARAMU—Dept. of English, Eastern Illinois Univ., Charleston, IL 61920. John Guzlowski, Ed. Traditional or experimental fiction. Poetry. Pays in copies.

LIGHT YEAR—Bits Press, Dept. of English, Case Western Reserve Univ., Cleveland, OH 44106. Robert Wallace, Ed. Annual. "The best funny, witty, or merely levitating verse being written." No restrictions on style or length. Pays

$5 per poem plus 15¢ per line, on publication. Material will not be returned unless accompanied by SASE.

LILITH—250 W. 57th St., New York, NY 10019. Susan Weidman Schneider, Ed. Fiction, 1,500 to 2,000 words, on issues of interest to Jewish women. Pays in copies.

THE LIMBERLOST REVIEW—P.O. Box 771, Hailey, ID 83333. Richard Ardinger, Ed. Poetry, any style or form. Alternate issues devoted to the works of one or two poets in the form of a chapbook. Pays in copies.

LITERARY MAGAZINE REVIEW—English Dept. Kansas State Univ., Manhattan, KS 66506. Reviews and articles concerning literary magazines, 1,000 to 1,500 words, for writers and readers of contemporary literature. Pays modest fees and copies. Query preferred.

THE LITERARY REVIEW—Fairleigh Dickinson Univ., 285 Madison Ave., Madison, NJ 07940. Martin Green, Harry Keyishian, Walter Cummins, Eds. Serious fiction; poetry; translations; reviews; essays on literature. Pays in copies.

THE LITTLE BALKANS REVIEW—601 Grandview Heights Terrace, Pittsburg, KS 66762. Fiction, to 5,000 words; articles, to 6,000 words; and poetry (prefer Kansas slant). Illustrations. Pays in copies.

THE LONG STORY—11 Kingston St., N. Andover, MA 01845. Stories, 8,000 to 20,000 words. Pays $1 a page, on publication. Poetry.

MAGAZINE—P.O. Box 806, Venice, CA 90291. Alexandra Garrett, Jocelyn Fisher, Eds. Contemporary fiction and reviews. Pays in copies.

THE MALAHAT REVIEW—Univ. of Victoria, P.O. Box 1700, Victoria, B.C., Canada V8W 2Y2. Constance Rooke, Ed. Fiction, poetry, and some articles and translations. Pays $12.50 per poem or $30 per 1,000 words of prose, on acceptance.

THE MANHATTAN REVIEW—304 Third Ave., New York, NY 10010. Poetry. Pays in copies.

MASSACHUSETTS REVIEW—Memorial Hall, Univ. of Massachusetts, Amherst, MA 01003. Literary criticism; articles on public affairs, scholarly disciplines. Short fiction. Poetry. No submissions between June and October. Pays modest rates, on publication.

MEMPHIS STATE REVIEW—Dept. of English, Memphis State Univ., Memphis, TN 38152. William Page, Ed. Short stories, novel excerpts, to 4,500 words; poetry, to one page. Pays in copies. Annual award.

MENDOCINO REVIEW—Box 888, Mendocino, CA 95460-0888. Annual. All types of fiction and articles (no reviews), to 2,500 words; poetry. Pays in copies.

METROSPHERE—Metropolitan State College, 1006 11th St., English Dept., Box 32, Denver, CO 80204. Interviews and profiles of writers and artists, 1,200 words; fiction, to 1,500 words; and poetry, to 50 lines. Pays in copies. Query.

MICHIGAN QUARTERLY REVIEW—3032 Rackham Bldg., Univ. of Michigan, Ann Arbor, MI 48109. Laurence Goldstein, Ed. Scholarly essays on all subjects; fiction; poetry. Pays $8 a page, on publication. Annual contest.

THE MICKLE STREET REVIEW—Box 1221, Haddonfield, NJ 08033. Annual. Articles, poems, and artwork related to Walt Whitman. Pays in copies.

MID-AMERICAN REVIEW—Dept. of English, Bowling Green State Univ., Bowling Green, OH 43403. Robert Early, Ed. High-quality fiction, poetry, articles, and reviews of contemporary writing. Fiction to 20,000 words. Reviews, articles, 500 to 2,500 words. Pays to $75, on publication.

MIDWAY REVIEW—SW Area Cultural Arts Council, Suite 134, 3400 W. 111th St., Chicago, IL 60655. Fiction, 2,000 to 4,000 words; reviews and arts-related articles, 500 to 3,000 words; contemporary poetry, any length; one-act plays, 5,000 to 8,000 words. Pays in copies.

MIDWEST QUARTERLY—Pittsburgh State Univ., Pittsburg, KS 66762. James B. Schick, Ed. Scholarly articles, 2,500 to 5,000 words, on contemporary issues. Pays in copies.

MILKWEED CHRONICLE—Box 24303, Minneapolis, MN 55424. Emilie Buchwald, Ed. Poems that reflect a unique voice. No overly religious or political material. Pays $10 per poem, $25 to $50 for essays (750 to 1,500 words), on publication.

THE MINNESOTA REVIEW—Dept. of English, Oregon State Univ., Corvallis, OR 97331. Fred Pfeil, Ed. Poetry, fiction, essays, reviews. Pays in copies.

MISSISSIPPI ARTS AND LETTERS—Box 3510, Persons Publishing, Hattiesburg, MS 39403-3510. Articles, 500 to 8,000 words, on the arts in Mississippi. Reviews, profiles, interviews, contemporary adult fiction, some sci-fi, 1,000 to 8,000 words, by southern authors or with southern settings. Pays $5 to $50, on acceptance. Query.

MISSISSIPPI REVIEW—Center for Writers, Univ. of Southern Mississippi, Southern Sta., Box 5144, Hattiesburg, MS 39406. Serious fiction, poetry, criticism, interviews.

THE MISSISSIPPI VALLEY REVIEW—Dept. of English, Western Illinois Univ., Macomb, IL 61455. Forrest Robinson, Ed. Short fiction, to 20 typed pages. Poetry; send 3 to 5 poems. Pays in copies.

THE MISSOURI REVIEW—Dept. of English, 231 Arts & Science, Univ. of Missouri-Columbia, Columbia, MO 65211. Greg Michalson, Man. Ed. Poems, of any length. Fiction and essays. Pays $5 to $10 per printed page, on publication.

MODERN HAIKU—P.O. Box 1752, Madison, WI 53701. Robert Spiess, Ed. Haiku and articles about haiku. Pays $1 a haiku, $5 a page for articles.

MODERN SENSE—FDR Sta., P.O. Box 426, New York, NY 10105. Contemporary short stories, novel excerpts, small press book reviews, to 15 pages. Pays in copies. Study magazine carefully before submitting.

MONTHLY REVIEW—155 W. 23rd St., New York, NY 10011. Paul M. Sweezy, Harry Magdoff, Eds. Serious articles, 5,000 words, on politics and economics, from independent socialist viewpoint. Pays $50, on publication.

THE MOVEMENT—P.O. Box 19458, Los Angeles, CA 90019. Roberts C. Taylor, Ed. Articles dedicated to spiritual/transformational interests, 1,000 words. Pays in copies. Must include SASE.

MOVING OUT—P.O. Box 21249, Detroit, MI 48221. Quality poetry, fiction, articles and art by women; submit 4 to 6 poems at a time. Pays in copies.

MSS—State Univ. of New York, Binghamton, NY 13901. L. M. Rosenberg,

Joanna Higgins, Eds. Short stories, novellas, essays, poems, illustrations, any length. Tri-quarterly. Pays negotiable rates. No submissions May 1–Aug. 1.

MUNDUS ARTIUM—Univ. of Texas at Dallas, Box 688, Richardson, TX 75080. Rainer Schulte, Ed. Short fiction, poetry, translations, interdisciplinary essays on the humanities. Pays in copies.

NEBO—Dept. of English, Arkansas Tech. Univ., Russellville, AR 72801. Mainstream fiction, to 20 pages; critical essays, to 10 pages; poetry, 5 poems. Pays in copies.

NEGATIVE CAPABILITY—6116 Timberly Rd. N., Mobile, AL 36609. Sue Walker, Ed. Poetry, any length; fiction, essays, art. Pays in copies. Annual Eve of St. Agnes poetry competition.

THE NEW BLACK MASK QUARTERLY—2006 Sumter St., Columbia, SC 29201. Matthew J. Bruccoli, Richard Laymen, Eds. Mystery fiction, 3,000 to 6,000 words. Pays 6¢ to 10¢ a word, on publication.

THE NEW CRITERION—850 Seventh Ave., New York, NY 10019. Robert Richman, Poetry Ed. Poetry.

NEW JERSEY POETRY JOURNAL—Dept. of English, Monmouth College, W. Long Beach, NJ 07764. Poetry. Pays in copies.

NEW MEXICO HUMANITIES REVIEW—Box A, New Mexico Tech, Socorro, NM 87801. Poetry, any length, any themes; southwestern and native American themes welcome. Pays with subscription.

NEW OREGON REVIEW—537 NE Lincoln St., Hillsboro, OR 97124. Steve Dimeo, Ed. Fiction, 3,000 to 5,000 words: literary, suspense, satire, nostalgia, etc.; poetry, to 40 lines. Literary cartoons; B&W photos, graphics. Pays $25 for fiction, $10 for poetry, $10 for photos/graphics. Query required.

NEW ORLEANS REVIEW—Loyola Univ., New Orleans, LA 70118. John Mosier, Ed. Literary or film criticism, to 6,000 words. Serious fiction and poetry.

THE NEW RENAISSANCE—9 Heath Rd., Arlington, MA 02174. Louise T. Reynolds, Ed. Well-crafted short stories (occasionally experimental), excerpts from novels, 3 to 35 pages. Essays, reviews, interviews, 4 to 25 pages; articles, 10 to about 25 pages. Quality poetry, translations. Submit 3 to 6 poems. No haiku. Query for nonfiction. Do not submit in July, August or December. Allow 7 months for reply. Pays from $13, after publication. Query.

THE NEW SOUTHERN LITERARY MESSENGER—400 S. Laurel St., Richmond, VA 23220. Charles Lohmann, Ed. Quarterly. Short stories, satire, contemporary history, 1,000 to 5,000 words. One-act plays and short film scripts. Pays $5 for one-time reprint rights, plus one copy, on publication. Send for guidelines.

NEXUS—Wright State Univ., 006 U.C., Dayton, OH 45431. Nick Adams, Ed. High quality short stories, to 2,000 words; poetry, to 50 lines. Book reviews of recent releases, to 1,500 words.

NIMROD—2210 S. Main St., Tulsa, OK 74114. Quality poetry and fiction, experimental and traditional. Pays in copies. Annual awards for poetry and fiction. Send for guidelines.

THE NORTH AMERICAN REVIEW—University of Northern Iowa, Cedar Falls, IA 50614. Peter Cooley, Poetry Ed. Poetry of high quality. Fiction of highest quality (address Fiction Ed.) Pays 50¢ a line for poetry, $10 per published page for fiction, on acceptance.

NORTH COUNTRY ANVIL—Box 37, Millville, MN 55957. Jim Mullen and Mary Speltz, Literary Eds. Political articles, interviews, criticism, related to productive living, peace and plenitude, and spiritual values in Minnesota. Poetry and fiction. Pays in copies.

THE NORTH DAKOTA QUARTERLY—Box 8237, Univ. of North Dakota, Grand Forks, ND 58202. Nonfiction essays in the humanities. Some fiction, reviews, graphics and poetry. Limited market. Pays in copies.

NORTHWEST MAGAZINE—*The Oregonian,* Portland, OR 97201. Traditional and experimental poetry, by Northwest poets only. Pays $5, on acceptance.

NORTHWEST REVIEW—369 PLC, Univ. of Oregon, Eugene, OR 97403. John Witte, Ed. Serious fiction, comments, and poetry. Reviews. Pays in copies.

OBSIDIAN—Dept. of English, Wayne State Univ., Detroit, MI 48202. Alvin Aubert, Ed. Short fiction, poetry and plays by blacks, interviews, reviews, scholarly articles, on black authors and their work. Pays in copies.

THE OHIO JOURNAL—164 W. 17th Ave., Columbus, OH 43210. William Allen, Ed. Short stories, poetry, book reviews. No submissions during the summer. Pays in copies.

OHIO RENAISSANCE REVIEW—P. O. Box 804, Ironton, OH 45638. James R. Pack, Ed. Science fiction, fantasy, and mystery stories, 400 to 3,000 words. Contemporary, avant-garde poetry, any length. Pays $2.50 per printed column for fiction, 25¢ a line for poetry, on publication.

THE OHIO REVIEW—Ellis Hall, Ohio Univ., Athens, OH 45701. Short stories, poetry, essays, reviews. Pays from $5 per page, plus copies, on publication.

THE ONTARIO REVIEW—9 Honey Brook Dr., Princeton, NJ 08540. Raymond J. Smith, Ed. Poetry and fiction. No unsolicited manuscripts.

ORPHEUS—8812 W. Pico Blvd., #203, Los Angeles, CA 90035. P. Schneider, Ed. Poetry. Pays from $5, on publication.

OTHER VOICES—820 Ridge Rd., Highland Park, IL 60035. Dolores Weinberg, Ed. Short stories and novel excerpts, to 5,000 words. Pays in copies.

OUTERBRIDGE—A-323, College of Staten Island, 715 Ocean Terr., Staten Island, NY 10301. Charlotte Alexander, Ed. Short stories, parts-of-novels, poetry. Special focus issues: urban, rural, Southern, etc. Pays in copies.

PACIFIC REVIEW—Dept. of English and Comp. Lit., San Diego State Univ., San Diego, CA 92182. High quality fiction, essays, reviews, and poetry. Pays in copies.

PANDORA—Empire Books, P.O. Box 625, Murray, KY 42071. Science fiction and speculative fantasy stories, to 5,000 words. Pays 1¢ a word, on acceptance.

PARABOLA—150 Fifth Ave., New York, NY 10011. Lorraine Kisly, Ed. Non-academic articles, 3,000 to 5,000 words, on mythology, comparative religion, the arts, in relation to contemporary life. Book reviews. Some poetry and fiction. Pays varying rates, on publication. Query.

PARIS REVIEW—541 E. 72nd St., New York, NY 10021. Address Fiction and Poetry Eds. Fiction and poetry of high literary quality. Pays on publication.

PARNASSUS—205 W. 89th St., New York, NY 10024. Herbert Leibowitz, Ed. Critical essays and reviews on contemporary poetry. International in scope. Pays in cash and copies.

PARTISAN REVIEW—Boston Univ., 141 Bay State Rd., Boston, MA 02215. William Phillips, Ed. Serious fiction, poetry and essays. Payment varies.

PASSAGES NORTH—William Bonifas Fine Arts Center. Escanaba, MI 49829. Elinor Benedict, Ed. Quality short fiction and contemporary poetry. Pays in copies, occasional prizes and honoraria.

PAVEMENT—Threepenny Poetry, Student Activities Center, Iowa Memorial Union, Univ. of Iowa, Iowa City, IA 52242. Pauline Uchmanowicz, Ed. Poetry. Pays in copies.

THE PENNSYLVANIA REVIEW—Dept. of English, 526 Cathedral of Learning, Univ. of Pittsburg, Pittsburgh, PA 15260. Articles and fiction to 5,000 words, and poetry (to six at one time). Pays in copies.

PERMAFROST—Engl. Dept., UAF, Fairbanks, AK 99701. Poetry, fiction, essays, translations, reviews, b&w art. Pays in copies.

PIEDMONT LITERARY REVIEW—P.O. Box 3656, Danville, VA 24543. Fiction, to 4,000 words. Poems, of any length and style. Special interest in young poets. Pays in copies. Submit up to 5 poems.

PIG IRON—P.O. Box 237, Youngstown, OH 44501. Rose Sayre, Jim Villani, Eds. Fiction and nonfiction, on varying themes, to 8,000 words. Poetry, to 100 lines. Pays $2 per published page, on publication. Query.

PINCHPENNY—4851 Q St., Sacramento, CA 95819. Tom Miner, Elizabeth Goosens, Ed. Prose poems and tiny poems. New writers welcome. Pays in copies.

PLAINS POETRY JOURNAL—Box 2337, Bismarck, ND 58502. Jane Greer, Ed. Traditional poetry; no "greeting card" -type verse. No subject is taboo. Pays in copies.

PLOUGHSHARES—Box 529, Cambridge, MA 02139. Address Fiction or Poetry Ed. Serious fiction, to 7,000 words. Poetry. Pays $10 to $100, on publication. Query.

POEM—c/o English Dept., U.A.H., Huntsville, AL 35899. Robert L. Welker, Ed. Serious poetry, any length. Pays in copies.

POET AND CRITIC—Dept. of English, Iowa State Univ., Ames, IA 50011. Michael Martone, Ed. Poetry, essays on contemporary poetry. Pays in copies.

POET LORE—4000 Albemarle St. N.W., Washington, DC 20016. Susan Davis, Man. Ed. Original poetry, all kinds. Translations, reviews. Pays in copies. Annual contest.

POETIC JUSTICE—8220 Rayford Dr., Los Angeles, CA 90045. Alan C. Engebretsen, Ed. Quarterly. Poetry, 4 to 70 lines. Pays in copies.

POETRY—P.O. Box 4348, 601 S. Morgan St., Chicago, IL 60680. Joseph Parisi, Ed. Poetry of highest quality. Pays $1 a line, on publication.

POETRY NEWSLETTER—Dept. of English, Temple Univ., Philadelphia,

PA 19122. Richard O'Connell, Ed. Quarterly. Poetry and translations. Pays in copies.

THE POETRY REVIEW—The Poetry Society of America, 15 Gramercy Park, New York, NY 10003. Poetry, translations and criticism. Pays $10 per printed page, on publication. Must enclose SASE.

THE PORTABLE LOWER EAST SIDE—110 W. 14th St., 10th fl., New York, NY 10011. Experimental, quality fiction, to 15 pages; poetry, to 3 pages. Articles, related to Lower East Side of New York. Pays in copies.

PRAIRIE SCHOONER—201 Andrew Hall, Univ. of Nebraska, Lincoln, NE 68588. Hugh Luke and Hilda Raz, Eds. Short stories, poetry and essays, to 6,000 words. Pays in copies.

PRIMAVERA—1212 E. 59th St., Chicago, IL 60637. Stories, poems and personal essays, to 30 typed pages, by or about women. Send no more than 6 poems at a time. Pays in copies.

PRISM INTERNATIONAL—E459–1866 Main Hall, Dept. of Creative Writing, Univ. of British Columbia, Vancouver, B.C., Canada V6T 1W5. Michael Pacey, Ed.-in-Chief. Karen Petersen, Fiction Ed. Anne Henderson, Drama Ed. High-quality fiction, poetry, drama, and literature in translation. Pays $15 per published page, on publication. Quarterly.

PROOF ROCK—P.O. Box 607, Halifax, VA 24558. Don Conner, Ed. Fiction, to 2,500 words. Poetry, to 32 lines. Reviews. Pays in copies. Sample copies available.

PUERTO DEL SOL—New Mexico State Univ., Box 3E., Las Cruces, NM 88003. Kevin McIlvoy, Ed. Short stories, to 30 pages; novel excerpts, to 65 pages; articles, to 45 pages, related to the Southwest; and reviews, to 15 pages. Poetry, photos. Pays in copies. Query for articles.

PULPSMITH—5 Beekman St., New York, NY 10038. Harry Smith, General Ed. Literary genre fiction; mainstream, mystery, SF, westerns. Short lyric poems, sonnets, ballads. Essays and articles. Pays $35 to $100 for fiction, $10 to $35 for poetry, on acceptance.

QUEEN'S QUARTERLY—Queens Univ., Kingston, Ont., Canada K7L 3N6. Articles, to 6,000 words, on a wide range of topics, and fiction, to 5,000 words. Poetry: send no more than 6 poems. Pays to $100, on publication.

RACCOON—St. Luke's Press, Suite 401, Mid-Memphis Tower, 1407 Union Ave., Memphis, TN 38104. David Spicer, Ed. Poetry and poetic criticism, varying lengths. Pays in copies.

RAMBUNCTIOUS REVIEW—1221 W. Pratt Blvd., Chicago, IL 60626. Mary Dellutri, Richard Goldman, Nancy Lennon, Eds. Fiction, poetry, short drama. Pays in copies.

RED CEDAR REVIEW—Dept. of English, Morrill Hall, Michigan State Univ., East Lansing, MI 48825. Fiction, 4,000 to 8,000 words. Poetry. Interviews; book reviews. Pays in copies. Query.

RIVERSIDE QUARTERLY—13931 N. Central Expressway #318, Dallas, TX 75243. Science fiction and fantasy, to 3,500 words. Reviews, criticism, poetry. Send fiction to Redd Boggs, Box 1111, Berkeley, CA 94701, and poetry to Sheryl Smith, 40425 Chapel Way, Fremont, CA 94536. Pays in copies.

ROANOKE REVIEW—Roanoke College, Salem, VA 24153. Robert R.

Walter, Ed. Quality short fiction, to 10,000 words, and poetry, to 100 lines. Pays in copies.

SAN FERNANDO POETRY JOURNAL—18301 Halstead St., Northridge, CA 91325. Richard Cloke, Ed. Quality poetry, 20 to 100 lines, with social content; scientific, philosophic and historical themes. Pays in copies.

SAN JOSE STUDIES—San Jose State Univ., 146 Administration Bldg., San Jose, CA 95152. Selma Burkom, Ed. Poetry; fiction. Pays in copies. Annual award.

SANDS—17302 Club Hill Dr., Dallas, TX 75248. Joyce Meier, Ed. Quality fiction with good narrative. Poetry, essays, translations. Pays in copies.

SCANDINAVIAN REVIEW—127 E. 73rd St., New York, NY 10021. Fiction and poetry, translated from Scandinavian languages. Essays on contemporary Scandinavia. Pays to $100, on publication.

SCRIVENER—McGill Univ., Arts B-20, 853 Sherbrooke St. W., Montreal, Quebec, Canada H3A 2T6. Dan Pope, Ed. Biannual. Short stories, 1 to 30 pages; poetry. Pays in copies.

SENECA REVIEW—Hobart & William Smith Colleges, Geneva, NY 14456. Poetry. Pays in copies.

SEVEN—3630 N.W. 22, Oklahoma City, OK 73107. James Neill Northe, Ed. Serious poetry, in any form. Pays $5, on acceptance. Query. Annual contest. Guidelines available.

SEWANEE REVIEW—Sewanee, TN 37375. George Core, Ed. Fiction, to 7,500 words. Serious poetry, to 60 lines, of highest quality. Pays about $10 per printed page for fiction, 60¢ per line for poetry, on publication. Send cover letter and SASE.

SHENANDOAH—Washington and Lee Univ., P.O. Box 722, Lexington, VA 24450. James Boatwright, Ed. Richard Howard, Poetry Ed. Fiction, poetry, and criticism.

SIDEWINDER—Div. of Arts and Humanities, College of the Mainland, Texas City, TX 77591. Thomas Poole, Ed. Fiction and poetry, any length. Pays in copies.

SING HEAVENLY MUSE! WOMEN'S POETRY & PROSE—P.O. Box 13299, Minneapolis, MN 55414. Short stories and essays, to 5,000 words. Poetry. Pays small honorarium, plus copies, on publication.

SINISTER WISDOM—P.O. Box 1023, Rockland, ME 04841. Melanie Kaye-Kantrowitz, Ed. Articles, fiction, poetry, reviews, and plays, from feminist perspective, varying lengths. Pays in copies.

SLIPSTREAM—Box 2071, New Market Sta., Niagara Falls, NY 14301. Fiction, 2 to 25 pages, and contemporary poetry, any length. Pays in copies. Query for themes.

SMALL PRESS REVIEW—Box 100, Paradise, CA 95969. Len Fulton, Ed. News pieces and reviews, to 250 words, about small presses and little magazines. Pays in copies.

SNAPDRAGON—English Dept., Univ. of Idaho, Moscow, ID 83843. Ron McFarland, Ed. Fiction and articles, 2,000 to 4,000 words, and poetry. Pays in copies.

SNOWY EGRET—205 S. Ninth St., Williamsburg, KY 40769. Humphrey A. Olsen, Alan Seaburg, Eds. Poetry to 10,000 words, related to natural history. Fiction and nonfiction, about 3,000 words, related to natural history. Pays $2 per page, on publication. Send fiction and poetry to Alan Seaburg, Ed., 67 Century St., W. Medford, MA 02155.

SONORA REVIEW—Dept. of English, Univ. of Arizona, Tucson, AZ 85721. Richard Cummins and Antonya Nelson, Eds. Fiction, poetry, reviews and short critical articles. Pays in copies. Annual prizes for fiction and poetry.

SOUTH CAROLINA REVIEW—c/o Dept. of English, Clemson Univ. Clemson, SC 29631. Carol Johnston, Man. Ed. Short stories, 3,000 to 5,000 words. Poetry. Criticism. Pays in copies.

SOUTH DAKOTA REVIEW—Box 111, Univ. Exchange, Vermillion, SD 57069. John R. Milton, Ed. Exceptional fiction, 3,000 to 5,000 words, and poetry, 10 to 25 lines. Critical articles, especially on American literature, Western American literature, theory and esthetics, 3,000 to 5,000 words. Pays in copies.

SOUTHERN HUMANITIES REVIEW—9088 Haley Center, Auburn Univ., AL 36849. Thomas L. Wright and Dan R. Latimer, Eds. Short stories, essays, and criticism, 3,500 to 5,000 words; poetry, to 2 pages.

SOUTHERN POETRY REVIEW—Dept. of English, Univ. of North Carolina, Charlotte, NC 28223. Robert W. Grey, Ed. Poems. No restrictions on style, length or content.

SOUTHERN REVIEW—43 Allen Hall, Louisiana State Univ., Baton Rouge, LA 70803. Lewis P. Simpson, James Olney, Eds. Fiction, and essays, 4,000 to 8,000 words. Serious poetry of highest quality. Pays $12 a page for prose, $20 a page for poetry, on publication.

SOUTHWEST REVIEW—Southern Methodist Univ., Dallas, TX 72575. Charlotte T. Whaley, Ed. Short stories, book reviews and articles, 3,000 to 5,000 words. Poetry. Pays on publication.

SOU'WESTER—Dept. of English, Southern Illinois Univ. at Edwardsville, Edwardsville, IL 62026-1001. Dickie Spurgeon, Ed. Fiction, to 10,000 words. Poetry, especially poems over 100 lines. Pays in copies.

SPECTRUM—U.C.S.B., Box 14800, Santa Barbara, CA 93106. Short stories, articles on literature, memoirs. Poetry. Pays in copies and awards. Annual contest.

THE SPIRIT THAT MOVES US—P. O. Box 1585 TW, Iowa City, IA 52244. Morty Sklar, Ed. Biannual. Fiction, poetry, that is expressive rather than formal or sensational. Each issue focuses on a specific theme—query. Pays $10 to $20 for fiction and nonfiction, $5 for poems, on publication.

STONE COUNTRY—P. O. Box 132, Menemsha, MA 02552. Judith Neeld, Ed. High-quality contemporary poetry in all genres. Pays in copies. Semi-annual award.

STONY HILLS: NEWS & REVIEWS OF THE SMALL PRESS—Weeks Mills, New Sharon, ME 04955. Diane Kruchkow, Ed. Reviews of small press books and magazines nationwide, to 500 words. Some short poetry. Pays in copies. Query on nonfiction preferred.

STORY QUARTERLY—P. O. Box 1416, Northbrook, IL 60062. Short stories and interviews. Pays in copies.

STUDIES IN AMERICAN FICTION—English Dept., Northeastern Univ., Boston, MA 02115. James Nagel, Ed. Reviews, 750 words; scholarly essays, 2,500 to 6,500 words, on American fiction. Pays in copies.

SUN DOG—406 Williams Bldg., English Dept., Florida State Univ., Tallahassee, FL 32306. Fiction. Poetry. Awards $100 for best fiction and poems in each issue when funds are available.

SUNRUST—P. O. Box 58, New Wilmington, PA 16142. Keith D. Rowland, Nancy Esther James, Eds. Nonfiction and poetry, to 2,000 words, and poetry to 75 lines, about rural life, nature, memories of the past, and small communities. Pays in copies.

TAR RIVER POETRY—Dept. of English, East Carolina Univ., Greenville, NC 27834. Peter Makuck, Ed. Poems, all styles. Submit between September and May. Pays in copies.

TAURUS—Box 28, Gladstone, OR 97027. Bruce Combs, Ed. Quarterly. Fresh, earnest, and energetic poetry. Pays in copies.

TELESCOPE—15201 Wheeler Lane, Sparks, MD 21152. Jack Stephens, Julia Wendell, Eds. Triannual. Fiction and nonfiction, 10 to 30 pages. Poetry—send no more than 10 poems at a time. Pays 60¢ a line for poetry, $6 a page for prose. Most issues focus on a specific theme; query for details.

TERRA POETICA—Dept. of Modern Languages and Literatures, SUNY at Buffalo, Buffalo, NY 14260. Jorge Guitart, Ed. Poetry: originals and English translations. Pays in copies. Query preferred.

THE TEXAS REVIEW—English Dept., Sam Houston State Univ., Huntsville, TX 77341. Paul Ruffin, Ed. Fiction, poetry, articles, to 20 typed pages. Reviews. Pays in copies.

13TH MOON—Box 309, Cathedral Sta., New York, NY 10025. Marilyn Hacker, Ed. Formal poetry, by women only. Pays in copies. No unsolicited manuscripts May–Sept.

TOUCHSTONE—P. O. Box 42331, Houston, TX 77042. Bill Laufer, Pub. Quarterly. Fiction, 750 to 2,000 words: mainstream, experimental. Interviews, essays, reviews. Poetry, to 40 lines. Pays in copies.

TRANSLATION—The Translation Center, 307A Mathematics Bldg., Columbia Univ., New York, NY 10027. Frank MacShane, Dir. Diane G. H. Cook, Man. Ed. Semiannual. New translations of contemporary foreign poetry and prose.

TRIQUARTERLY—1735 Benson Ave., Northwestern Univ., Evanston, IL 60201. Serious, aesthetically informed and inventive poetry and prose, for an international and literate audience. Pays $10 per page.

THE UNIVERSITY OF PORTLAND REVIEW—Univ. of Portland, Portland, OR 97203. Thompson H. Faller, Ed. Scholarly articles and contemporary fiction, 500 to 2,500 words. Poetry. Book reviews. Pays in copies.

UNIVERSITY OF WINDSOR REVIEW—Dept. of English, Univ. of Windsor, Windsor, Ont., Canada N9B 3P4. Eugene McNamara, Ed. Short stories, poetry, criticism, reviews. Pays $10 to $25, on publication.

THE VILLAGER—135 Midland Ave., Bronxville, NY 10708. Amy Murphy, Ed. Fiction, 900 to 1,500 words: mystery, adventure, humor, romance. Short, preferably seasonal poetry. Pays in copies.

VIRGINIA QUARTERLY REVIEW—One W. Range, Charlottesville, VA 22903. Quality fiction and poetry. Serious essays and articles, 3,000 to 6,000 words, on literature, science, politics, economics, etc. Pays $10 per page for prose, $1 per line for poetry, on publication.

WASCANA REVIEW—c/o Dept. of English, Univ. of Regina, Regina, Sask., Canada S4S 0A2. Joan Givner, Ed. Short stories, 2,000 to 6,000 words; critical articles; poetry. Pays $3 per page, after publication.

WASHINGTON REVIEW—P. O. Box 50132, Washington, DC 20004. Mary Swift, Ed. Poetry; articles on literary, performing and fine arts in the Washington, D.C., area, 1,000 to 2,500 words. Fiction, to 1,000 words. Area writers preferred. Pays in copies.

WAVES—79 Denham Dr., Richmond Hill, Ontario, L4C 6H9 Canada. Short stories, 500 to 5,000 words. Haiku, poetry, to 500 lines. Pays $5 per printed page, on publication. Include international reply coupons.

WEBSTER REVIEW—Webster Univ., Webster Groves, MO 63119. Nancy Schapiro, Ed. Fiction; poetry; interviews; essays; translations. Pays in copies.

WEST BRANCH—English Dept., Bucknell Univ., Lewisburg, PA 17837. Karl Patten, Robert Taylor, Eds. Poetry and fiction. Pays in copies and subscriptions.

WESTERN HUMANITIES REVIEW—Univ. of Utah, Salt Lake City, UT 84112. Jack Garlington, Ed. Articles on the humanities; fiction; poetry; book and film reviews. Pays $150 for fiction, to $50 for poems, on acceptance.

THE WINDLESS ORCHARD—Dept. of English, Indiana-Purdue Univ., Ft. Wayne, IN 46805. Robert Novak, Ed. Contemporary poetry. Pays in copies.

WINEWOOD JOURNAL—P. O. Box 339, Black Hawk, CO 80422. Kate Aiello, Ed. Poetry; short stories; essays; reviews. Pays in copies. Contest.

WISCONSIN REVIEW—Box 276, Dempsey Hall, Univ. of Wisc., Oshkosh, WI 54901. Tom Caylor, Ed. Fiction, to 4,000 words. Quality poems. Pays in copies.

WRITERS FORUM—Univ. of Colorado, Colorado Springs, CO 80933-7150. Alex Blackburn, Ed. Annual. Mainstream and experimental fiction, 1,000 to 10,000 words. Poetry (1 to 5 poems per submission). Send material January through August. Pays in copies.

YALE REVIEW—1902A Yale Sta., New Haven, CT 06520. Kai Erikson, Ed. Serious poetry, to 200 lines, and fiction, 3,000 to 5,000 words. Pays nominal sum.

FILLERS AND SHORT ITEMS

Magazines noted for their excellent filler departments, plus a cross-section of publications using fillers, short items, jokes, quizzes, and cartoons, follow. However, almost all magazines use some type of filler material, and writers can find dozens of markets by studying copies of magazines at a library or newsstand.

Many magazines do not acknowledge or return filler material, and in such cases, writers may assume that after 90 days have passed from the time of submission, a filler may be submitted to another market.

ALASKA OUTDOORS—Box 82222, Fairbanks, AK 99708. Christopher Batin, Ed. Fillers and humor, related to outdoor activities in Alaska. Pays $50, on publication. Query required.

ALCOHOLISM/THE NATIONAL MAGAZINE—P. O. Box 19519, Seattle, WA 98109. "Coffee Break Page": short, true-experience pieces, jokes and anecdotes relating to alcoholism, for professionals in the alcoholism treatment field and recovering alcoholics. Nominal payment.

ALIVE! FOR YOUNG TEENS—Christian Board of Publication, P.O. Box 179, St. Louis, MO 63166. Mike Dixon, Ed. Puzzles, riddles, daffy definitions; poetry, to 20 lines. Pays to $10, 25¢ a line for poetry, on publication.

AMATEUR GOLF REGISTER—Amateur Golfers' Association, 2843 Pembroke Rd., Hollywood, FL 33020. Bernard Block, Managing Ed. Fillers, 25 to 50 words, on golf-related topics. Pays around $15, on publication.

AMERICAN CLAY EXCHANGE—P. O. Box 2674, La Mesa, CA 92041. Short items on American-made pottery. Pays $5, on publication.

THE AMERICAN FIELD—222 W. Adams St., Chicago, IL 60606. W. F. Brown, Ed. Short fact items and anecdotes on hunting dogs, and field trials for bird dogs. Pays varying rates, on acceptance.

THE AMERICAN LEGION MAGAZINE—Box 1055, Indianapolis, IN 46206. Raymond H. Mahon, Parting Shots Ed. Short, funny anecdotes, appealing to military/naval, veterans, older readers; one- or two-line gags; humorous verse, to 4 lines. No sex, religion, or ethnic humor. Pays $15 for anecdotes and gags, $5 a line for verse, on acceptance.

AMPERSAND—303 N. Glenoaks Blvd., Burbank, CA 91502. Short items, 500 words, of interest to college students. Pays 15¢ a word, on acceptance.

ARMY MAGAZINE—2425 Wilson Blvd., Arlington, VA 22201. L. James Binder, Ed.-in-Chief. True anecdotes on military subjects. Pays $10 to $35, on publication.

ARTSLINE—P. O. Box 24287, Seattle, WA 98124. Sophisticated arts-related fillers. Pays on acceptance.

THE ATLANTIC—8 Arlington St., Boston, MA 02116. Some light poetry. Pays from $500 for prose, on acceptance.

ATLANTIC SALMON JOURNAL—1435 St-Alexandre, Suite 1030, Montreal, Quebec, Canada H3A 2G4. Joanne Eidinger, Ed. Fillers, 50 to 100 words, on salmon politics, conservation, and nature. Pays on publication.

BASSMASTER MAGAZINE—B.A.S.S. Publications, Box 17900, Montgomery, AL 36141. Dave Precht, Ed. Anecdotes, short humor and news breaks related to bass fishing, 250 to 500 words. Pays $50 to $100, on acceptance.

BICYCLING—33 E. Minor Rd., Emmaus, PA 18049. Anecdotes and other items for "Open Road" section, 150 to 200 words. Pays $15 to $25, on publication.

691

BIKEREPORT—Bikecentennial, P. O. Box 8308, Missoula, MT 59807. Daniel D'Ambrosio, Ed. News shorts from the bicycling world for "In Bicycle Circles." Pays $5 to $10, on publication.

BIRD WATCHER'S DIGEST—P. O. Box 110, Marietta, OH 45750. Mary Bowers, Ed. Cartoons. Pays $10, on publication.

BOYS' LIFE—1325 Walnut Hill Lane, Irving, TX 75062. Robert Hood, Ed. How-to features, to 400 words, with photos, on hobbies, crafts, science, outdoor skills, etc. Pays from $150.

BUSINESS VIEW OF SOUTHWEST FLORIDA—P. O. Box 1546, Naples, FL 33939. Business- or economic-related shorts, 100 to 300 words. Pays $10 to $25, on publication.

CAPPER'S WEEKLY—616 Jefferson St., Topeka, KS 66607. Dorothy Harvey, Ed. Household hints, recipes, jokes. Pays varying rates, on publication.

CASCADES EAST—716 N.E. 4th St., P. O. Box 5784, Bend, OR 97708. Geoff Hill, Ed. Fillers, related to travel and recreation in Central Oregon. Pays 10¢ a word, on publication.

CASHFLOW—1807 Glenview, Glenview, IL 60025. Vince DiPaolo, Ed. Fillers, to 1,000 words, on varied aspects of treasury financial management, for treasury managers in public and private institutions. Pays on publication. Query.

CATHOLIC DIGEST—P. O. Box 64090, St. Paul, MN 55164. Features, to 300 words, on instances of kindness rewarded, for "Hearts Are Trumps." Stories about conversions, for "Open Door." Reports of tactful remarks or actions, for "The Perfect Assist." Accounts of good deeds, for "People Are Like That." Humorous pieces on parish life, for "In Our Parish." Amusing signs, for "Signs of the Times." Jokes; fillers. Pays $4 to $50, on publication.

CHEVRON USA—P. O. Box 6227, San Jose, CA 95150. Mark Williams, Ed. Quarterly. True, previously unpublished, humorous anecdotes with a travel tie-in, 200 words. Pays $25, on publication.

CHIC—2029 Century Park E., Suite 3800, Los Angeles, CA 90067. Visual fillers, short humor with visuals, 100 to 200 words, for "Odds and Ends" section. Pays on acceptance.

CHICKADEE—59 Front St. E., Toronto, Ont., Canada M5E 1B3. Humorous poetry about animals and nature for children, 10 to 15 lines. Pays on publication.

CHILD LIFE—P. O. Box 567, Indianapolis, IN 46206. Steve Charles, Ed. Puzzles, games, mazes, and rebuses, on health or safety-related subjects, for children 7 to 9 years. Pays $10 to $15, on publication.

CHILDREN'S PLAYMATE—1100 Waterway Blvd., P. O. Box 567, Indianapolis, IN 46206. Kathleen Mosher, Ed. Puzzles, games, mazes for 5- to 7-year-olds, emphasizing health, safety, nutrition. Pays about 6¢ a word (varies on puzzles), on publication.

CHRISTIAN HERALD—40 Overlook Dr., Chappaqua, NY 10514. David Kucharsky, Ed. Poetry and true anecdotes, to 24 lines, on Christian/church themes. Pays $5 to $15, after acceptance.

CHRISTIAN LIFE—396 E. St. Charles Rd., Wheaton, IL 60188. Pat Kampert, News Ed. News items, to 200 words, on trends, ideas, unique personalities/ministries, and events of interest to Christians. Photos. Pays $5 to $15, on publication. Short pieces, 500 to 800 words, of interest to women: handicrafts, recipes, true adventures. Must have some spiritual application. Send to Jan Franzen. Pays $15 to $25.

THE CHURCH MUSICIAN—127 Ninth Ave. N., Nashville, TN 37234. W. M. Anderson, Ed. For Southern Baptist music leaders. Humorous fillers with a music slant. No clippings. Pays around 4¢ a word, on acceptance. Same address and requirements for *Glory Songs* (for adults), and *Opus One* and *Opus Two* (for teen-agers).

CLAVIER MAGAZINE—200 Northfield Rd., Northfield, IL 60093. Barbara Kreader, Ed. Fillers, humor and jokes of interest to keyboard performers and teachers. Pay varies, on publication.

COASTAL JOURNAL—Box 84, Lanesville Sta., Gloucester, MA 01930. Joseph Kaknes, Ed. Fillers. Pays on publication.

COLUMBIA—Box 1670, New Haven, CT 06507. Elmer Von Feldt, Ed. Journal of the Knights of Columbus. Catholic family magazine. Captionless cartoons. Pays $25 for cartoons, on acceptance.

COLUMBIA JOURNALISM REVIEW—700 Journalism Bldg., Columbia Univ., New York, NY 10027. Gloria Cooper, Man. Ed. Amusing mistakes in news stories, headlines, photos, etc. (original clippings required), for "Lower Case." Pays $10, on publication.

COMPUTER CONSULTANT—208 N. Townsend St., Syracuse, NY 13203. Mary McMahon, Ed. Fillers, jokes, cartoons of interest to computer consultants. Pay varies, on publication.

COMPUTER USER'S LEGAL REPORTER—Computer Law Group, 191 Post Rd., W., Westport, CT 06880. Charles P. Lickson, Ed. Fillers and humor, 100 words or less, on "computer law, according to Murphy (what can go wrong with computers will)." Pays $25, on publication.

COUNTRY PEOPLE—5400 S. 60th St., Greendale, WI 53129. Fillers, 50 to 200 words, for rural audience. Pays on publication.

CROSSWORDS GALORE—475 Park Ave. S., New York, NY 10016. Helen Tono, Ed. Crossword puzzles. Payment varies, on publication.

CYCLE WORLD—1499 Monrovia Ave., P. O. Box 1757, Newport Beach, CA 92663. Paul Dean, Ed. News items on motorcycle industry, legislation, trends. Pays on acceptance.

DALLAS CITY (formerly *Westward*)—*The Dallas Times Herald,* 1101 Pacific Ave., Dallas, TX 75202. Humorous essays and life style pieces, 400 to 1,000 words. Photos requested. Pays $50, on publication.

DOWN EAST—Camden, ME 04843. Anecdotes about Maine, to 1,000 words, for "I Remember." Humorous anecdotes, to 300 words, for "It Happened Down East." Pays $10 to $50, on acceptance.

DYNAMIC YEARS—215 Long Beach Blvd., Long Beach, CA 90802. Lorena F. Farrell, Ed. Short items of interest to mid-life readers for "Questions You're Asked," "After Hours," "Personal Notebook," and "Dynamic Americans," 350 words; "Changing Gears," 600 words. Pays $150 to $350, on acceptance. Query first.

EBONY—820 S. Michigan Ave., Chicago, IL 60605. Charles L. Sanders,

Man. Ed. "Speaking of People," short features, to 200 words, on blacks in traditionally non-black jobs. Cartoons. Pays $75 for cartoons, on publication.

ELECTRONIC EDUCATION—Electronic Communications, 1311 Executive Center Dr., Suite 220, Tallahassee, FL 32301. Sharon Lobello, Ed. Fillers of interest to educators. Pays on publication.

ESSENCE—1500 Broadway, New York, NY 10036. Susan L. Taylor, Ed.-in-Chief. Short items, 500 to 750 words, on work and health. Pay varies, on acceptance.

THE EVENER—P. O. Box 7, Cedar Falls, IA 50613. Anecdotes and newsbreaks, 100 to 750 words, related to draft horse, mule and oxen industry. Pays 3¢ to 10¢ a word, on acceptance.

EXPECTING—685 Third Ave., New York, NY 10017. E. Podsiadlo, Ed. Anecdotes about pregnancy, for "Happenings." Pays $10, on publication.

FAMILY CIRCLE—Box 2822, Grand Central Sta., New York, NY 10017. Ideas or suggestions on homemaking, education, and community betterment, for "Readers' Idea Exchange." Pays $50. Unpublished entries cannot be returned or acknowledged. Query.

FARM AND RANCH LIVING—5400 S. 60th St., Greendale, WI 53129. Bob Ottum, Man. Ed. Fillers on rural people and living, 200 words. Pays from $15, on acceptance and on publication.

FARM WOMAN NEWS—P. O. Box 643, Milwaukee, WI 53201. Ruth C. Benedict, Man. Ed. Short verse, 20 to 25 lines, and fillers, to 250 words, on the rural experience. Pays from $40 on publication.

FATE—500 Hyacinth Pl., Highland Park, IL 60035. Mary Margaret Fuller, Ed. Factual fillers, to 300 words, on strange or psychic happenings. True stories, to 300 words, on psychic or mystic personal experiences. Pays $1 to $10.

FIELD & STREAM—1515 Broadway, New York, NY 10036. Duncan Barnes, Ed. Fillers on hunting, camping, fishing. etc., 500 to 1,000 words, for "How It's Done," and "Did You Know?" Cartoons. Pays $250 for "How It's Done," $350 for "Did You Know?," $100 for cartoons, on acceptance.

FLARE—777 Bay St., Toronto, Ont., Canada M5W 1A7. Dianne Rinehart, Man. Ed. Career-related items, graphic puzzles; narrative math problems, etc. Submit seasonal material 6 months in advance. Pays from $35, on acceptance. Query.

FLORIDA KEYS MAGAZINE—Box 818, 6161 O/S Hwy., Marathon, FL 33040. Fillers. Pays on publication.

FRANCHISE MAGAZINE—1044 Hercules, Houston, TX 77058. Jeanne Bishop, Ed. Fillers, humor, jokes of interest to franchise investors; length varies. Pays on acceptance.

GLORY SONGS—See *The Church Musician.*

INSIDE WOMEN'S TENNIS—1604 Union St., San Francisco, CA 94123. Fillers and crossword puzzles with women's tennis data. Pays $25, on publication.

694

THE INTERNATIONAL AMERICAN—201 E. 36th St., New York, NY 10016. Alison R. Lanier, Ed. Short pieces, 200 to 300 words, by writers who have lived abroad, with advice, suggestions, warnings and information for Americans who are now living overseas. No travel tips, no stories of personal interest. Pays $25, on acceptance.

LADIES' HOME JOURNAL—"Last Laughs," Three Park Ave., New York, NY 10016. Brief anecdotes and poems about the funny business of being a woman today. Pays $25. Submissions cannot be acknowledged or returned.

LAUGH FACTORY—400 S. Beverly Dr., #214, Beverly Hills, CA 90212. Jamie Masada, Pub. Quick, snappy, humorous items. Pay varies, on publication.

MANUFACTURING SYSTEMS—Hitchcock Publishing Co., Hitchcock Bldg., Wheaton, IL 60188. Fillers, related to computer industry. Pay varies, on acceptance.

MIAMI/SOUTH FLORIDA MAGAZINE—P. O. Box 34008, Coral Gables, FL 33114. Rick Eyerdam, Managing Ed. Short, "bright" items, 200 to 400 words, for the "Big Orange" section. Pays 15 days before publication.

THE MICHIGAN WOMAN—P. O. Box 1171, Detroit, MI 48012. Fillers, 200 words, of interest to Michigan business and professional women. Pays on publication.

MODERN PHOTOGRAPHY—825 Seventh Ave., New York, NY 10019. Julia Scully, Ed. How-to pieces, 200 to 300 words, with photos, on photography. Pays $50 to $500, on acceptance.

MODERN ROMANCES—215 Lexington Ave., New York, NY 10016. Short items, to 300 words, for "Little Things (That Say 'I Love You')" and "Our Family Tradition." Pays $25, thirty days after month of publication.

NATIONAL ENQUIRER—Lantana, FL 33464. Jim Allan, Asst. Ed. Short, humorous fillers, witticisms, anecdotes, tart comments. Original items preferred, but others considered if source and date given. Short poems of a philosophical or amusing nature. Pay $20, on publication. Self-addressed, stamped envelope required.

NEW ENGLAND MONTHLY—P.O. Box 446, Haydenville, MA 01039. Daniel Okrent, Ed. Shorts, 400 to 1,000 words, on various aspects of life and culture in the six New England states. Pays $75 to $250, on acceptance.

NEW JERSEY MONTHLY—7 Dumont Pl., Morristown, NJ 07960. Larry Marscheck, Man. Ed. Short pieces related to life in New Jersey. Pays $35 to $75, on acceptance.

THE NEW YORKER—25 W. 43rd St., New York, NY 10036. Amusing mistakes in newspapers, books, magazines, etc. Pays from $10, extra for headings and tag lines, on acceptance.

NORTHWEST EDITION—130 Second Ave., S., Edmonds, WA 98020. Archie Satterfield, Ed. Shorts, 100 to 400 words, related to the natural resources of the Northwest. Pays on acceptance.

OHIO FISHERMAN—1570 Fishinger Rd., Columbus, OH 43221. Short, do-it-yourself fishing-related tidbits, 250 to 500 words. Pays varying rates, on acceptance.

OPUS ONE *and* **OPUS TWO**—See *The Church Musician.*

ORBEN'S CURRENT COMEDY—1200 N. Nash St., #1122, Arlington, VA

22209. Robert Orben, Ed. Original material that can be used by speakers and toastmasters (lines for beginning/ending a speech, introducing specific occupations, etc.); material of interest to business speakers (short, sharp comments on business trends, management problems, etc.); and funny, performable one-liners, short jokes and stories related to happenings in the news, trends, fads, etc. Pays $8 per item, on publication. Self-addressed, stamped envelope required.

OUTDOOR LIFE—380 Madison Ave., New York, NY 10017. Clare Conley, Ed. Short instructive items and 1-pagers on hunting, fishing, camping gear, boats, outdoor equipment. Photos. Pays on acceptance.

PARENTS—685 Third Ave., New York, NY 10017. Short items on solutions of child care-related problems for "Parents Exchange." Pays $20, on publication.

PARISH FAMILY DIGEST—200 Noll Plaza, Huntington, IN 46750. Patrick R. Moran, Ed. Family- or parish-oriented humor. Anecdotes, 250 words, of unusual parish experiences, for "Our Parish." Pays $5 to $12.50, on acceptance.

PENCIL HUNT—475 Park Ave. S., New York, NY 10016. Helen Tono, Ed. Word search puzzles. Payment varies, on publication.

PENNYWHISTLE PRESS—Box 500-P, Washington, DC 20044. Anita Sama, Ed. Short fillers, puzzles, word games, humorous stories, for 6- to 12-year-olds. Pays varying rates, on acceptance.

PEOPLE IN ACTION—P.O. Box 10010, Ogden, UT 84409. Profiles, 500 to 700 words, on accomplished cooks, for "Celebrity Chef." Must be accompanied by recipe and color transparency. Query. Pays 15¢ a word, extra for photos, on acceptance.

PLAYBOY—919 N. Michigan Ave., Chicago, IL 60611. Address Party Jokes Editor or After Hours Editor. Jokes; short original material on new trends, lifestyles, personalities; humorous news items. Pays $50 for jokes, on acceptance; $50 to $350 for "After Hours" items, on publication.

PLAYGIRL—3420 Ocean Park Blvd., Suite 3000, Santa Monica, CA 90405. Moe Bryant, Cartoon Ed. Sophisiticated cartoons dealing positively with women and women's issues. Pays $75, on publication.

POPULAR MECHANICS—224 W. 57th St., New York, NY 10019. Bill Hartford, Man. Ed. How-to pieces, from 300 words, with photos and sketches, on home improvement and shop and craft projects. Pays $25 to $100, on acceptance. Buys all rights.

POPULAR SCIENCE MONTHLY—380 Madison Ave., New York, NY 10017. A. W. Lees, Group Ed. One-column fillers, 350 words, with photo or sketch if demo necessary: general workshop ideas, maintenance tips for home and car. Pays from $100; $50 for ideas for "Taking Care of Your Car" and "Wordless Workshop," $200 for "Computer Adventures," $250 for "Adventures in Alternative Energy," on acceptance.

PROCEEDINGS—U.S. Naval Institute, Annapolis, MD 21402. Clayton R. Barrow, Jr., Ed. Short humorous anecdotes for members of Navy, Marine Corps, and Coast Guard profession. Pays $25, on acceptance.

READER'S DIGEST—Pleasantville, NY 10570. Anecdotes for "Life in These United States," "Humor in Uniform," "Campus Comedy" and "All in a

Day's Work." Pays $300, on publication. Short items for "Toward More Picturesque Speech." Pays $50. Anecdotes, fillers, for "Laughter, the Best Medicine," "Personal Glimpses," etc. Pays $20 per two-column line. No submissions acknowledged or returned.

RECOVERY—P.O. Box 19519, Seattle, WA 98109. Poetry and fillers, of interest to recovering alcoholics. Pays $15 to $25, after publication.

ROAD KING—P.O. Box 250, Park Forest, IL 60466. Address Features Ed. Trucking-related cartoons for "Loads of Laughs"; anecdotes to 200 words, for "Trucker's Life." Pays $25 for cartoons, $25 for anecdotes, on publication. SASE required.

RODALE'S ORGANIC GARDENING—33 E. Minor St., Emmaus, PA 18049. Jack Ruttle, Planning Ed. Fillers, 100 to 500 words, on gardening experiences; how-to's, solutions of problems, etc. Photos of lawn art. Cartoons, cartoon ideas. Gardening riddles. Horticultural "bloopers" in local newspapers, etc. Pays $25 to $200, on publication.

ROLL CALL—201 Mass. Ave. N.E., Washington, DC 20002. Sidney Yudain, Ed. Humorous items on Congress; anecdotes, quips. Pays on acceptance.

SACRAMENTO—P.O. Box 2424, Sacramento, CA 95811. "City Lights," interesting and unusual people places, and behind-the-scenes news items, to 250 words. All material must have Sacramento area tie-ins. Pays on acceptance.

THE SATURDAY EVENING POST—1100 Waterway Blvd., Indianapolis, IN 46202. Jack Gramling. Post Scripts Ed. Humor and satire, to 500-words; jokes for "Post Scripts." Pays $15, on publication.

SCHOOL SHOP—Prakken Publications, Inc., Box 8623, 416 Longshore Dr., Ann Arbor, MI 48107. Alan H. Jones, Managing Ed. Puzzles, cartoons of interest to school shop teacher and administrator. Pay varies, on publication.

SCORE, CANADA'S GOLF MAGAZINE—287 MacPherson Ave., Toronto, Ont., Canada M4V 1A4. Lisa A. Leighton, Man. Ed. Fillers, 50 to 100 words, related to Canadian golf scene. Pays $10 to $25, on publication.

SKIING MAGAZINE—One Park Ave., New York, NY 10016. Alfred H. Greenberg, Ed.-in-Chief. Articles, to 600 words, on skiing; humorous vignettes, fillers or skiing oddities. Pays from 15¢ a word, on acceptance.

SLIMMER—3420 Ocean Park Blvd., Suite 3000, Santa Monica, CA 90405. Mark D'Antoni, Art Dir. Sophisticated cartoons dealing with diet and exercise. Pays $50, on publication.

SNOWMOBILE—11812 Wayzata Blvd., Ste. 100, Minnetonka, MN 55343. Dick Hendricks, Ed. Short humor and cartoons on snowmobiling and winter "Personality Plates" sighted. Pays varying rates, on publication.

SOUTH FLORIDA MEDICAL REVIEW—100 N.E. 7th St., Miami, FL 33132. Avram Goldstein, Ed. Short humor, jokes, and puzzles of interest to health care administrators and doctors in Southern Florida. Pays on publication.

SOUTHERN EXPOSURE—P.O. Box 531, Durham, NC 27702. Michael Yellin, Ed. Fillers on civil rights, black politics, nuclear power, utility reform, land use, southern people, etc. Pays from $50, on publication.

SPORTS AFIELD—250 W. 55th St., New York, NY 10019. Unusual, useful tips, 100 to 500 words, for "Almanac" section: hunting, fishing, camping, boating, etc. Photos. Pays $10 per column inch, on publication.

SPUR—Box 85, Middleburg, VA 22117. Anecdotes and short humor, 100 to 500 words, related to the thoroughbred horse industry. Pays $25, on publication.

THE STATE: DOWN HOME IN NORTH CAROLINA—P.O. Box 2169, Raleigh, NC 27602. W. B. Wright, Ed. Short fillers. Pays on acceptance.

SUNDAY DIGEST—850 N. Grove Ave., Elgin, IL 60120. Judy Couchman, Ed. Inspirational anecdotes, short humor (500 words). Writers guidelines on request. Pays 7¢ to 10¢ a word, on acceptance.

TAMPA BAY METRO-MAGAZINE—2502 Rocky Point Rd., Suite 295, Tampa, FL 33607. Shorts, 150 to 1,200 words, on Tampa area. Pays good rates, 30 days after publication. Query.

TEENAGE—P.O. Box 948, Lowell, MA 01853. Jokes and humorous fillers for older teenagers. Categories: "A for Effort," "Excuses, Excuses," "Bloopers and Head Aches," and "Great Moments in High School." Pays from $50, on publication.

THIRD COAST—P.O. Box 592, Austin, TX 78767. Miriam Davidson, Ed. Fillers, related to Austin. Pays 10¢ a word, after publication.

TODAY'S CHRISTIAN PARENT—8121 Hamilton Ave., Cincinnati, OH 45231. Mildred Mast, Ed. Problems and pleasures of parenting; refreshing insights into everyday happenings in the family; short items on Christian living, for "Happenings at Our House." Ideas for family devotions. Appropriate short savings and anecdotes, serious or humorous. Pays varying rates, on acceptance. Self-addressed, stamped envelope required for return of material.

TOUCH—Box 7244, Grand Rapids, MI 49510. Carol Smith, Man. Ed. Fillers, Bible puzzles from NIV version, for Christian girls aged 8 to 14. Pays 2¢ a word, on acceptance.

TRAILER BOATS—P.O. Box 2307, Gardena, CA 90248. Jim Youngs, Ed. Fillers and humor, preferably with illustrations, on boating and related activities. Pays 7¢ to 10¢ a word, on publication.

TRAVEL SMART—Dobbs Ferry, New York 10522. Interesting, unusual, or helpful travel-related tips, to 250 words. Pays $5 to $15, on publication. Query.

TRUE CONFESSIONS—215 Lexington Ave., New York, NY 10016. Barbara J. Brett, Ed. Warm, inspirational first-person fillers, 300 to 700 words, about love, marriage and family life for "The Feminine Side of Things." Pays after publication. Buys all rights.

TURBO—9568 Hamilton Ave., P.O. Box 2712, Hamilton Beach, CA 92647. Bud Lang, Ed. Shorts and good fillers, related to turbo-charged automobiles.

THE VIRGINIAN—P.O. Box 8, New Hope, VA 24469. Hunter S. Pierce, IV, Ed. Dir. Fillers, relating to Virginia and adjacent region of the South. Anecdotes and nostalgic pieces preferred. Pays varying rates, on publication.

VOLKSWAGEN'S WORLD—Volkswagen of America, Troy, MI 48099. Ed Rabinowitz, Ed. Anecdotes, to 100 words, about Volkswagen owners' experiences; cartoons, humorous photos of Volkswagens. Pays from $15, on acceptance.

WESTART—Box 6868, Auburn, CA 95604. Martha Garcia, Ed. Features and current news items, 350 to 500 words, on fine arts. No hobbies. Pays 50¢ per column inch, on publication.

WESTWARD—See *Dallas City.*

WISCONSIN TRAILS—P.O. Box 5650, Madison, WI 53705. Short fillers about Wisconsin: places to go, things to see, etc., 500 words. Pays $100, on publication.

WOMAN—1115 Broadway, New York, NY 10010. Sherry Amatenstein, Ed. Short newsbreaks on medical and legal advances for women for "Let's Put Our Heads Together." Pays on acceptance. Query.

WOMAN'S DAY—1515 Broadway, New York, NY 10036. Short items on personal instructive family experiences and tips, for "Neighbors"; practical suggestions for homemakers. Pays $50, on publication.

WOMEN'S SPORTS AND FITNESS—310 Town and Country Village, Palo Alto, CA 94301. Short pieces, on nutrition, beauty, health, and new products for the active woman; short profiles of up-and-coming female athletes or other female sports figures; book reviews; opinion pieces. Pays from $25, on publication.

YM—685 Third Ave., New York, NY 10017. Deborah Purcell, Articles Ed. First-person, humorous fillers, to 850 words, on any aspect of adolescence: early or late blooming, boy-girl relationships, school, part-time jobs, getting along with siblings, dieting, etc. Serious fillers, to 850 words, on such teen concerns as shyness, loneliness, popularity, self-confidence, etc. Teen quotes. Professional advice. Pays on acceptance.

HUMOR

ACCENT—Box 10010, Ogden, UT 84409. "Just Say" Editor. Occasionally uses humorous pieces, 150 to 300 words. Pays 15¢ a word, on acceptance. Submit complete manuscript.

AEROBICS & FITNESS—15250 Ventura Blvd., Suite 802, Sherman Oaks, CA 91403. Peg Angsten, Ed. Occasionally uses humorous sketches on fitness motivation, 500 to 1,500 words. Pays $60 to $160, after publication. Writer's guidelines available.

ARIZONA HIGHWAYS—2039 W. Lewis Ave., Phoenix, AZ 85009. Don Dedera, Ed. Humor, about 1,500 words, related to Arizona. Pay starts at 25¢ a word, on acceptance. Query first.

THE ATLANTIC—8 Arlington St., Boston, MA 02116. Sophisticated humorous or satirical pieces, 1,000 to 3,000 words. Pays from $500, on acceptance.

BICYCLING—33 E. Minor St., Emmaus, PA 18049. Address Ed Pavelka. Occasional short and snappy humor, 2 to 3 manuscript pages; must be related to cycling. Pays from $25, on publication. Submit complete manuscript.

BIKEREPORT—Bikecentennial, P.O. Box 8308, Missoula, MT 59807. Daniel D'Ambrosio, Ed. Humor, from 1,200 words. Pays $40 to $65, on publication. Submit complete manuscript.

BUCKEYE FARM NEWS—Ohio Farm Bureau Federation, 35 E. Chestnut St., Columbus, OH 43216. Keith M. Stimpert, Managing Ed. Humor, to 1,000 words, related to agriculture. Pays on publication. Query.

THE CALIFORNIA HIGHWAY PATROLMAN—2030 V St., Sacramento,

CA 95818. Carol Perri, Ed. Short humorous pieces; submit complete manuscript. Pays 2½¢ a word, on publication.

CATS—P.O. Box 37, Port Orange, FL 32039. Linda J. Walton, Ed. Occasionally uses humor if it is realistic and not farfetched. Must involve human-cat relationship. Pays $50 per printed page, on publication. Submit complete manuscript.

COLUMBIA—1 Columbus Plaza, New Haven, CT 06507. Publication of the Knights of Columbus. Humor, 1,000 words. Pays $200, on acceptance. Submit complete manuscript or query.

DALLAS CITY—*Dallas Times Herald,* 1101 Pacific Ave., Dallas, TX 75202. Sunday magazine. Address Steven Reddicliffe. Humor, 750 words, by Dallas writers only. Pays $250, on publication. Query.

DALLAS LIFE MAGAZINE—*The Dallas Morning News,* Communications Center, Dallas, TX 75265. Melissa East. Ed. Humorous pieces, 1,000 to 1,500 words, with a strong Dallas angle. Pays $250 to $325, on acceptance. Submit complete manuscript or query.

DETROIT MAGAZINE—Detroit Free Press, 321 W. Lafayette Blvd., Detroit, MI 48231. James G. Cobb, Associate Ed. Funny, clever articles (no clichés), 600 to 1,500 words—the shorter, the better. Pay varies from $100 to $500, on publication. Submit complete manuscript.

THE ELKS MAGAZINE—425 W. Diversey Pkwy., Chicago, IL 60614. Herbert Gates, Ed. Humor and non-political satire, 1,500 words, for a family audience. Pays from 10¢ a word, on acceptance.

FAMILY CIRCLE—488 Madison Ave., New York, NY 10022. Address Jamie Raab. Humorous pieces, up to 1,500 words (the shorter, the better), of interest to women. Pay rates vary, on acceptance. Submit complete manuscripts.

FARM INDUSTRY NEWS—1999 Shepard Rd., St. Paul, MN 55116. Joseph Degan, Ed. Occasionally run humorous articles of interest to Midwestern farmers. Prefers queries. Pays good rates.

FARM WOMAN NEWS—P.O. Box 643, Milwaukee, WI 53201. Ruth C. Benedict, Managing Ed. Humor, 25 to 1,000 words, of interest to farm/ranch/rural women. Pays $25 to $150, on acceptance. Submit query or complete manuscript.

FLORIDA KEYS MAGAZINE—Box 818, 6161 O/S Hwy., Marathon, FL 33040. Address David Ethridge. Humor, up to 1,500 words; must be Keys-related. Pays $4.00 per column inch, on publication. Query.

FORD TIMES—Ford Motor Co., Rm. 765, P.O. Box 1899, The American Rd., Dearborn, MI 48121. Arnold S. Hirsch, Ed. Humor—ranging from vacation/travel/dining anecdotes for "Road Show" to full-length articles or essays—geared to family audience. Pays from $50, on acceptance. Submit complete manuscripts.

FUR-FISH-GAME—2878 E. Main St., Columbus, OH 43209. Ken Dunwoody, Ed. Uses occasional humor pieces, generally 1,500 to 2,200 words, relating to the outdoor experience. Pays $125 to $150, on acceptance. Submit complete manuscript or query.

GOLF DIGEST—495 Westport Ave., Norwalk, CT 06856. Jerry Tarde, Ed.

Humorous articles, 1,200 to 1,500 words, about golf. Pay varies, on acceptance. Submit complete manuscripts.

GOLF JOURNAL—Golf House, Far Hills, NJ 07931. George Eberl, Managing Ed. Intelligent humor, related to golf. Pay varies; about $350 for 1,500 words, after acceptance. Submit complete manuscript.

INQUIRER MAGAZINE—*Philadelphia Inquirer,* 400 N. Broad St., Philadelphia, PA 19101. David R. Boldt, Ed. Humorous pieces, one page. Pay averages $350.

MCCALL'S—2 Park Ave., New York, NY 10169. Address Lucy Sullivan. Humor, 1,000 to 2,500 words. Submit complete manuscripts. Pays top rates, on acceptance.

MAD MAGAZINE—485 Madison Ave., New York, NY 10022. Humorous pieces on a wide variety of topics. No straight text pieces. Query with proposal and SASE. Pays top rates, on acceptance.

NATIONAL REVIEW—150 E. 35th St., New York, NY 10016. William F. Buckley, Ed. Satire, to 900 words. Short, satirical poems. Pays $35 to $100, on publication.

NEW JERSEY MONTHLY—7 Dumont Place, Morristown, NJ 07960. Address Managing Ed. Humorous, people-oriented, New Jersey-oriented articles. Parodies welcome. Pays $200 to $300 for "Exit Ramp" (750 words), more for longer pieces, on acceptance. Query with samples or submit complete manuscript.

NEW YORK ANTIQUE ALMANAC—Box 335, Lawrence, NY 11559. Carol Nadel, Ed. Humorous articles or anecdotes that recall earlier times or recount present-day experiences pertaining to antique collecting, auctions, flea markets, or nostalgic adventures. Pay varies, on publications.

NEW YORK'S NIGHTLIFE MAGAZINE—1770 Deer Park Ave., Deer Park, NY 11729. Bill Ervolino, Ed. Topical humor, 1,000 to 2,000 words, on entertainment, leisure, personalities in New York. Pays from $50, on publication. Query preferred.

OMNI—1965 Broadway, New York, NY 10023. Douglas Colligan, Senior Ed. Humorous and satirical pieces, to 800 words, on aspects of the future: science and technology, the arts, lifestyles. Pays from $500, on acceptance.

OUTDOOR AMERICA—Suite 1100, 1701 N. Ft. Myer Dr., Arlington, VA 22209. Humor, 1,500 words, on natural resource conservation issues. Pays from 10¢ a word, on publication.

PENTHOUSE—1965 Broadway, New York, NY 10023. Peter Bloch, Articles Ed. Kathy Green, Fiction Ed. Satire, humor, black comedy. Pays to 50¢ a word, on acceptance.

PGA MAGAZINE—100 Ave. of the Champions, Palm Beach Gardens, FL 33410. Humorous pieces related to golf, to 1,500 words. Pays to $200, on acceptance.

PLAYBOY—919 N. Michigan Ave., Chicago, IL 60611. James Morgan, Articles Ed. Humor; satire. Pays top rates, on acceptance.

THE ROTARIAN—1600 Ridge Ave., Evanston, IL 60201. Willmon L. White, Ed. Humorous articles, 700 to 1,000 words, appealing to businessmen. Pays $200 to $350, on acceptance. Submit complete manuscript.

SNOWMOBILE—11812 Wayzata Blvd., Suite 100, Minnetonka, MN 55343. Dick Hendricks, Ed. Occasionally uses humor relating to snowmobiling. Pays $150 to $300, on publication. Submit complete manuscript.

SOUTHERN OUTDOORS—1 Bell Rd., Montgomery, AL 36141. Larry Teague, Ed. Publishes one humorous outdoor article in each issue for "*Southern Outdoors* Essay" (1,000 words). All material must have a Southern focus. Query preferred. Pays 15¢ to 20¢ a word, on acceptance. Writer's guidelines available.

TENNIS—5520 Park Ave., P. O. Box 0395, Trumbull, CT 06611. Humor, 750 to 1,000 words, on personal experiences in the game. Pays to $300, on publication.

TODAY'S OR NURSE—6900 Grove Rd., Thorofare, NJ 08086. Judith B. Paquet, R.N., Ed. Short humor, 400 to 500 words, for operating room nurses. Pays 10¢ a word, on publication. Query.

TRAILER BOATS—16427 S. Avalon, P. O. Box 2307, Gardena, CA 90248. Jim Youngs, Ed. Humor, under 1,500 words, on the subject of legally-trailerable boats and related activities. Pays 7¢ to 10¢ a word, on publication. Submit complete manuscript or query.

VIBRANT LIFE—55 W. Oak Ridge Dr., Hagerstown, MD 21740. Ralph Blodgett, Ed. Light tongue-in-cheek pieces on subjects related to the family, home, and health for a Christian audience; no off-color material. Submit complete manuscript. Pays $75 to $125, on acceptance. Writer's guidelines available.

WESTERN SPORTSMAN—P. O. Box 737, Regina, Sask., Canada S4P 3A8. Red Wilkinson, Ed. Humor, to 1,500 words. Pays up to $325, on publication. Query first.

WISCONSIN—*The Milwaukee Journal Magazine,* P. O. Box 661, Milwaukee, WI 53201. Beth Slocum, Ed. Humor, under 1,000 words. Pays $75 to $300, on publication. Submit complete manuscript or query.

WORKING WOMAN—342 Madison Ave., New York, NY 10173. Jacqueline Giambanco, Exec. Ed. Humorous essays, 1,500 words, for career-oriented women. Pays on acceptance. Submit complete manuscript.

JUVENILE, TEENAGE AND YOUNG ADULT MAGAZINES

JUVENILE MAGAZINES

ACTION—Dept. of Christian Education, Free Methodist Headquarters, 901 College Ave., Winona Lake, IN 46590. Vera Bethel, Ed. Stories, 1,000 words, for 9- to 11-year-olds. How-to features, 200 to 500 words. Verse. Seasonal material. Pays $25 for stories, $15 for features with photos or sketch, $5 for poetry, on publication.

CHICKADEE—The Young Naturalist Foundation, 59 Front St., E. Toronto, Ont., Canada M5E 1B3. Janis Nosbakken, Ed. Animal and adventure stories, 200 to 800 words, for children aged 3 to 8. Also, puzzles, activities and observation games, 50 to 300 words. Pays varying rates, on publication. Send complete manuscript and international postal coupons. No outlines.

CHILD LIFE—1100 Waterway Blvd., P.O. Box 567, Indianapolis, IN 46206. Steve Charles, Ed. Articles, 500 to 1,200 words, especially on health and nutrition, safety, and exercise, for 7- to 9-year-olds. General fiction and humor stories, to 1,600 words. Health-related puzzles. Photos. Pays about 6¢ a word, extra for photos, on publication. Buys all rights.

CHILDREN'S DIGEST—1100 Waterway Blvd., P.O. Box 567, Indianapolis, IN 46202. Kathleen B. Mosher, Ed. Health publication for children aged 8 to 10. Informative articles, 500 to 1,200 words, and fiction (especially realistic, adventure, mystery, and humorous), 500 to 1,800 words, with health, safety, exercise, nutrition, or hygiene as theme. Historical and biographical articles. Poetry. Pays 6¢ a word, from $7 for poems, on publication. Buys all rights.

CHILDREN'S PLAYMATE—Editorial Office, 1100 Waterway Blvd., P.O. Box 567, Indianapolis, IN 46206. Kathleen B. Mosher, Ed. Humorous and health-related short stories, 500 to 800 words, for 5-to-7-year-olds. Simple science articles and how-to crafts pieces with brief instructions. "All About" features, about 500 words, on health, nutrition, safety, and exercise. Poems. Pays about 6¢ a word, $7 minimum for poetry, on publication.

CHILD'S PLAY—P.O. Box 1007, Auburn, WA 98071. Regional activities and events guide. Articles, 250 to 750 words, on events, arts, crafts, etc., for children ages 6 to 13. Pay 5¢ a word, on publication.

THE CHRISTIAN SCIENCE MONITOR—One Norway St., Boston, MA 02115. Marilyn Gardner, Ed. "For Children" Page. Feature articles, fiction, and poetry, written by children up to 12 years old. Pays to $25, $5 for short articles and poems.

CLUBHOUSE—Berrien Springs, MI 49103. Elaine Meseraull, Ed. Action-oriented Christian stories: features, 1,000 to 1,200 words; "Story Cubes" and "Thinker Tales" (parables), about 800 words. Children in stories should be wise, brave, funny, kind, etc. Pays to $35 for features, $30 for parables and nonfeatures, on acceptance.

COBBLESTONE—20 Grove St., Peterborough, NH 03458. Carolyn Yoder, Ed. Theme-related biographies, and short accounts of historical events, to 1,200 words, for children aged 8 to 14 years. Fiction, 500 to 1,200 words. Poetry, to 100 lines. Photos. Pays 10¢ to 15¢ a word for prose, varying rates for poetry, on publication. Send SASE for editorial guidelines with monthly themes.

CRICKET—Box 100, La Salle, IL 61301. Marianne Carus, Ed.-in-Chief. Articles and fiction, 200 to 1,500 words, for 6- to 12-year-olds. Poetry, to 30 lines. Pays to 25¢ a word, to $3 a line for poetry, on publication. Send SASE for guidelines. Overstocked.

DASH—Christian Service Brigade, Box 150, Wheaton, IL 60189. Address David Leight. Articles, to 1,500 words, for 8- to 11-year-old boys, on Christian lifestyles, current events. Photo and photo essays. Cartoons. Adventure fiction. Pays 5¢ to 10¢ a word, on publication. Query required.

DISCOVERIES—6401 The Paseo, Kansas City, MO 64131. Libby Huffman,

703

Ed. Stories, 800 to 1,000 words, for 3rd to 6th graders, with Christian emphasis. Poetry, 4 to 20 lines. Cartoons. Pays 3.5¢ a word (2¢ a word for reprints), 25¢ a line for poetry (minimum of $2), on acceptance.

ELECTRIC COMPANY MAGAZINE—See *3-2-1 Contact*.

THE FRIEND—50 E. North Temple, 23rd Fl., Salt Lake City, UT 84150. Vivian Paulsen, Man. Ed. Stories and articles, 1,000 to 1,200 words. "Tiny tot" stories, 300 to 700 words. Pays from 7¢ a word, from 45¢ a line for poetry, on acceptance.

HIGHLIGHTS FOR CHILDREN—803 Church St., Honesdale, PA 18431. Kent L. Brown, Ed. Fiction and articles, to 900 words, for 2- to 12-year-olds. Fiction should have strong plot, believable characters, story that holds reader's interest from beginning to end. No crime or violence. For articles, cite references used and qualifications. Easy rebus-form stories. Easy-to-read stories, 400 to 600 words, with strong plots. Pays from 6¢ a word, on acceptance.

HUMPTY DUMPTY'S MAGAZINE—1100 Waterway Blvd., P.O. Box 567. Indianapolis, IN 46202. Christine French Clark, Ed. Health publication for children ages 4 to 6. Easy-to-read fiction, to 600 words, some with health and nutrition, safety, exercise, or hygiene as theme; humor and light approach preferred. Crafts with clear, brief instructions. Short poems. Stories-in-rhyme. Pays about 6¢ a word, from $7 for poems, on publication. Buys all rights.

JACK AND JILL—Box 567, Indianapolis, IN 46206. Christine French Clark, Ed. Articles, 500 to 1,000 words, for 6- to 8-year-olds, on sports, nature, science, health, safety, exercise. Features 1,000 to 1,200 words, on history, biography, life in other countries, etc. Fiction, to 1,200 words. Short poems, games, puzzles, projects. Photos. Pays about 6¢ a word, extra for photos, varying rates for fillers, on publication.

LOLLIPOPS, LADY BUGS AND LUCKY STARS—Good Apple, Inc., P.O. Box 299, Carthage, IL 62321-0299. Cindy Stansbery, Ed. Short stories, 500 to 1,200 words, for children, preschool to 7. Activities, poetry, fillers, and gameboards. Pays varying rates, on publication. Query.

ODYSSEY—625 E. St. Paul Ave., Milwaukee, WI 53202. Nancy Mack, Ed. Features, 750 to 2,000 words, on astronomy, spacecraft, for 8- to 12-year-olds. Photos. Pays $100, extra for photos, on publication. Query.

ON THE LINE—616 Walnut, Scottdale, PA 15683. Virginia A Hostetler, Ed. Religious articles, 500 to 750 words, for 10- to 14-year-olds. Fiction, 800 to 1,200 words. Poetry, puzzles, cartoons. Pays to 4¢ a word (2¢ a word for reprints), on acceptance.

OUR LITTLE FRIEND—P.O. Box 7000, Boise, ID 83707. Louis Schutter,

Ed. Seventh-day Adventist. Stories, 500 to 1,000 words, for 2- to 6-year-olds. Verse, 8 to 12 lines. Puzzles. Photos. Pays 1¢ a word, 10¢ a line for verse, on acceptance.

OWL—The Young Naturalist Foundation, 59 Front St., E. Toronto, Ont., Canada M5E 1B3. Sylvia Funston, Ed. Articles, 500 to 1,000 words, for children aged 8 to 12, on animals, science, people, places, experiments, etc. Should be informative but not preachy. Pays varying rates, on publication. Send brief outline and international reply coupons.

PENNYWHISTLE PRESS—Box 500-P, Washington, DC 20044. Anita Sama, Ed. Short fiction, 850 words for 8- to 12-year-old children, 400 words for 5- to 8-year-olds. Puzzles and word games. Payments varies, on publication.

PLAYS, THE DRAMA MAGAZINE FOR YOUNG PEOPLE—120 Boylston St., Boston, MA 02116. Elizabeth Preston, Man. Ed. Needs one-act plays, programs, skits, creative dramatic material, suitable for school productions at junior high, middle and lower grade levels. Plays with one set preferred. Uses comedies, dramas, satires, farces, melodramas, dramatized classics, folktales and fairy tales, puppet plays. Pays good rates, on acceptance. Send SASE for manuscript specification sheet. Buys all rights.

PRIMARY TREASURE—P.O. Box 7000, Boise, ID 83707. Louis Schutter, Ed. Seventh-day Adventist. Stories, 600 to 1,200 words, for 7- to 9-year-olds. Verse, 8 to 12 lines, Puzzles. Photos. Pays 1¢ a word, 10¢ a line for verse, on acceptance.

RADAR—8121 Hamilton Ave., Cincinnati, OH 45231. Margaret Williams, Ed. Articles, 400 to 650 words, on nature, hobbies, crafts. Short stories, 900 to 1,100 words: mystery, sports, school, family, with 12-year-old as main character; serials of 2,000 words. Christian emphasis. Poems to 12 lines. Pays to 2¢ a word, to 35¢ a line for poetry, on acceptance. Send SASE for guidelines and sample issue.

RANGER RICK—1412 16th St. N.W., Washington, DC 20036. Trudy Farrand, Ed. Articles, to 900 words, on wildlife, conservation, natural sciences, and nature crafts, for 6- to 12-year-olds. Nature-related fiction welcome. Features on children involved with nature. Games and puzzles. Pays to $350, on acceptance. Buys all rights.

SESAME STREET MAGAZINE—See *3-2-1 Contact.*

SHOFAR—43 Northcote Dr., Melville, NY 11747. Alan A. Kay, Exec. Ed. Short stories, 500 to 750 words; articles, 250 to 750 words; poetry, to 50 lines; and short fillers, games, puzzles, and cartoons, for Jewish children, 8 to 13. All material must have a Jewish theme. Pays 10¢ a word, on publication. Submit holiday pieces at least three months in advance.

STONE SOUP, THE MAGAZINE BY CHILDREN—Box 83, Santa Cruz, CA 95063. Gerry Mandel, Ed. Stories, poems, plays, book reviews by children under 13. Pays in copies.

STORY FRIENDS—Mennonite Publishing House, Scottdale, PA 15683. Marjorie Waybill, Ed. Stories, 350 to 800 words, for 4- to 9-year-olds, on Christian faith and values in everyday experiences. Quizzes, riddles. Poetry. Pays to 5¢ a word, to $5 per poem, on acceptance.

3-2-1 CONTACT—Children's Television Workshop, 1 Lincoln Plaza, New York, NY 10023. Jonathan Rosenbloom, Ed. Entertaining and informative articles, 600 to 1,000 words, for 8- to 12-year-olds, on all aspects of science, scientists, and children who are learning about or practicing science. Pays $75 to $400, on acceptance. No fiction. Also publishes *Electric Company Magazine* and *Sesame Street Magazine*. Query.

TOUCH—Box 7244, Grand Rapids, MI 49510. Carol Smith, Man. Ed. Upbeat fiction and features, 1,000 to 1,500 words, for Christian girls age 8 to 14; personal life, nature, crafts. Poetry; puzzles. Pays 2¢ a word, extra for photos, on acceptance. Query for theme with SASE.

TRAILS—Box 788, Wheaton, IL 60189. Lorraine Mulligan Davis, Ed. Publication of Pioneer Ministries. Christian articles and fiction, to 1,000 words, for 6- to 12-year-old children. Quizzes, games, crafts. Pays about 3¢ a word, on acceptance.

TURTLE MAGAZINE FOR PRESCHOOL KIDS—1100 Waterway Blvd., Box 567, Indianapolis, IN 46206. Beth Wood Thomas, Ed. Stories about safety, exercise, health, and nutrition, for preschoolers. Fiction, 600 words. Simple poems. Stories-in-rhyme; easy-to-read stories, to 500 words, for beginning readers. Pays about 6¢ a word, on publication. Buys all rights. Send SASE for guidelines.

WEE WISDOM—Unity Village, MO 64065. Verle Bell, Ed. Character-building stories, to 800 words, for 6- to 12-year-olds. Pays 3¢ to 4¢ per word, on acceptance.

WONDER TIME—6401 The Paseo, Kansas City, MO 64131. Evelyn J. Beals, Ed. Stories, 200 to 600 words, for 6- to 8-year-olds, with Christian emphasis, to correlate with Sunday School curriculum. Features, to 300 words, on nature, crafts, etc. Poetry, 4 to 12 lines. Pays 3½¢ a word, from 25¢ a line for verse, $2.50 minimum, on acceptance.

YABA WORLD—5301 S. 76th St., Greendale, WI 53129. Paul Bertling, Ed. Articles, 1,500 words, on Young American Bowling Alliance league or tournament bowling. Profiles; how-to's. Photos. Pays $25 to $100, extra for photos, on acceptance. Query preferred.

YOUNG CRUSADER—1730 Chicago Ave., Evanston, IL 60201. Michael Vitucci, Ed. Character-building stories, 600 to 700 words, for 6- to 12-year-olds. Pays ½¢ a word, on publication.

YOUNG JUDAEAN—50 W. 58th St., New York, NY 10019. Mordecai Newman, Ed. Articles, 500 to 1,000 words, with photos, for 9- to 12-year-olds, on Israel, Jewish holidays, Jewish-American life, Jewish history. Fiction, 800 to 1,500 words, on Jewish themes. Poetry, from 8 lines. Fillers, humor, reviews. Pays $10 per printed page.

THE YOUNG SALVATIONIST—The Salvation Army, 799 Bloomfield Ave., Verona, NJ 07044. Capt. Dorothy Hitzka, Ed. Articles, 800 to 1,200 words, with Christian perspective; fiction, 1000 to 1,200 words; short fillers. Young Soldier Section: Fiction, 600 to 800 words; games and puzzles. Pays 3¢ a word, on acceptance.

TEENAGE, YOUNG ADULT MAGAZINES

ALIVE!—Christian Board of Publication, Box 179, St. Louis, MO 63166. Mike Dixon, Ed. Fiction, to 1,200 words, for junior-high-age young people. First-person articles, to 1,200 words, with photos, on interesting youths, projects and activities. Poetry to 16 lines. Cartoons, puzzles, brain-teasers. Pays 3¢ a word, extra for photos, 25¢ a line for poetry, $10 for cartoons, on publication.

ALIVE NOW!—P.O. Box 189, Nashville, TN 37202. Mary Ruth Coffman, Ed. Short essays, 250 to 400 words, with Christian emphasis. Poetry, one page. Photos. Pays $5 to $20, on publication.

AMERICAN NEWSPAPER CARRIER—P.O. Box 15300, Winston-Salem, NC 27103. Marilyn Rollins, Ed. Light fiction, 1,000 words, for teenage newspaper carriers; mystery, adventure, etc. Inspirational articles, editorials. Pays $10 to $25, on acceptance.

BOP—7060 Hollywood Blvd., Suite 720, Hollywood, CA 90028. Julie Laufer, Ed. Interviews and features, 1,000 to 2,000 words, for teenage girls, on stars popular with teenagers. Photos. Pays varying rates, on acceptance. Query preferred.

BOYS' LIFE—1325 Walnut Hill Lane, Irving, TX 75038-3096. Robert E. Hood, Ed. Publication of Boy Scouts of America. Articles, 300 to 1,500 words, and fiction 1,000 or 2,500 to 3,200 words, for 8- to 18-year-old boys. Photos. Pays from $250 for articles, from $350 for fiction, on acceptance. Query for articles.

CAMPUS LIFE—465 Gundersen Dr., Carol Stream, IL 60188. Gregg Lewis, Sr. Ed. Articles reflecting Christian values and world view, for high school and college students. Humor and general fiction. Photo essays, cartoons. Pays from $150, on acceptance. Limited free-lance market.

THE CHRISTIAN ADVENTURER—P.O. Box 850, Joplin, MO 64802. Rosmarie Foreman, Ed. Fiction, 1,500 to 1,800 words, for 13- to 19-year-olds, on Christian living. Fillers. Pays 1.5¢ a word, quarterly.

CIRCLE K MAGAZINE—3636 Woodview Trace, Indianapolis, IN 46268. Karen J. Pyle, Exec. Ed. In-depth features on subjects of interest to service-minded college students, and family-related subjects: communication, housing, nutrition, future jobs, community involvement, etc. B/W photos. Pays $150 to $275, on acceptance. Query preferred.

CURRENT CONSUMER & LIFESTUDIES—3500 Western Ave., Highland Park, IL 60035. Margaret Mucklo, Ed. Practical, well-researched articles, 1,000 to 1,200 words, for high school students, on family living, interpersonal relationships, and consumer topics. Pays $100, on publication. Queries only; no unsolicited manuscripts accepted.

EXPLORING—1325 Walnut Hill Ln., Irving, TX 75062. Scott Daniels, Exec. Ed. Publication of Boy Scouts of America. Articles, 500 to 1,800 words, for 15- to 21-year-olds, on education, careers, Explorer post activities (hiking, canoeing, camping), and program ideas for Explorer post meetings. No controversial subjects. Pays $150 to $400, on acceptance. Query. Send SASE for guidelines.

FREEWAY—Box 632, Glen Ellyn, IL 60138. Cindy Atoji, Ed. First-person true stories, personal experience, how-to's, fillers, and humor, to 1,000 words, with photos, for 13- to 22-year-olds. Christian emphasis. Pays to 8¢ a word.

GRIT—Williamsport, PA 17701. Joanne Decker, National Ed. Articles, 300 to 500 words, with photos, on young people involved in unusual hobbies, occupations, athletic pursuits, and personal adventures. Pays 12¢ a word, extra for photos, on acceptance.

HICALL—1445 Boonville Ave., Springfield, MO 65802. William P. Campbell, Ed. Articles, 500 to 1,000 words, and fiction, to 1,800 words, for 12- to 19-year-olds; strong evangelical emphasis. Pays on acceptance.

IN TOUCH—Box 2000, Marion, IN 46952. Articles, 1,200 to 1,500 words, on contemporary issues, athletes and singers from conservative Christian perspective, for 13- to 18-year-olds. Pays 2¢ to 3¢ a word. Send SASE for guidelines. No queries.

KEYNOTER—3636 Woodview Trace, Indianapolis, IN 46268. David Brill, Exec. Ed. Articles, 1,000 to 2,500 words, for high school leaders: general-interest features; self-help; pieces on contemporary teen-age problems. Photos. Pays $75 to $300, extra for photos, on acceptance. Query preferred.

LIGHTED PATHWAY—922 Montgomery Ave., Cleveland, TN 37311. Marcus V. Hand, Ed. Human-interest and inspirational articles, 1,200 to 1,600 words, for teen-agers. Short pieces, 600 to 800 words. Fiction, 1,500 to 1,800 words. Pays 2¢ to 4¢ a word, on acceptance.

LISTEN MAGAZINE—6830 Laurel St. N.W., Washington, DC 20012. Gary B. Swanson, Ed. Articles, 500 to 1,500 words, on problems of alcohol and drug abuse, for teenagers; personality profiles. Photos. Pays 5¢ to 7¢ a word, extra for photos, on acceptance. Query. Guidelines available.

THE NATIONAL FUTURE FARMER—Box 15160, Alexandria, VA 22309. Michael Wilson, Man. Ed. Articles, to 1,000 words, preferably with photos, for agriculture students aged 14 to 21, on activities of Future Farmers of America, new developments in agriculture, and general-interest subjects. Pays from 6¢ a word, on acceptance. Query.

NEW ERA—50 E. North Temple, Salt Lake City, UT 84150. Brian Kelley, Ed. Articles, 150 to 3,000 words, and fiction, to 3,000 words, for young Mormons. Poetry. Photos. Pays 3¢ to 10¢ a word, 25¢ a line for poetry, on acceptance. Query.

PROBE—1548 Poplar Ave., Memphis, TN 38104. Timothy C. Seanor, Ed. Southern Baptist. Articles, to 1,500 words, for 12- and 17-year-old boys, on teen problems, current events. Photo essays on Baptist sports personalities. Pays 3½¢ a word, extra for photos, on acceptance.

SCHOLASTIC SCOPE—730 Broadway, New York, NY 10003. Katherine Robinson, Ed. For 15- to 18-year-olds with 4th to 6th grade reading ability. Realistic fiction, 400 to 1,200 words, and plays, to 6,000 words, on teen problems. Profiles, 400 to 800 words, of interesting teenagers, with black and white photos. Pays $125 for 500- to 600-word articles and short stories, from $150 for longer pieces, on acceptance.

SEVENTEEN—850 Third Ave., New York, NY 10022. Articles, to 2,500 words, on subjects of interest to teens. Sophisticated, well-written fiction, 2,500 to 3,500 words, for young adults. Poetry, to 15 lines, by teens. Short news and features for "Mini-Mag": general topics for "Lead" (800 words, $250), news items on what's au courant for "What's Doing" (150 to 350 words, $100 to $150), short, instructional features that are practical and interesting—how to mail a package, apply for a credit card, etc.—for "Here's How" (100 to 350 words, $100 to $150). Query first (6 months in advance for seasonal or timely ideas) with SASE and pertinent credits and clips. Payment for articles varies, on acceptance.

SPRINT—850 N. Grove Ave., Elgin, IL 60120. Kevin Miller, Ed. Feature articles, 800 to 1,000 words, for junior high Sunday school students, on teens, current teen problems, and Christian personalities. Fiction, 1000 to 1,200 words, with realistic characters and dialogue. Poetry. Photos. Pays to $100, extra for photos, on acceptance. Submit seasonal material one year in advance. Buys all rights. Query for nonfiction.

STRAIGHT—8121 Hamilton Ave., Cincinnati, OH 45231. Dawn Brett-schneider, Ed. Devotional pieces, features on current situations and issues, humor, for Christian teens. Well-constructed fiction, 1,000 to 1,500 words, showing teens using Christian principles. Poetry, by teenagers. Photos. Pays about 2¢ a word, on acceptance.

'TEEN MAGAZINE—8490 Sunset Blvd., Los Angeles, CA 90069. Over-stocked.

TEENAGE—P.O. Box 948, Lowell, MA 01853. Andrew Calkins, Ed.-in-Chief. Articles, profiles, interviews, short news reports, essays, humor, celebrity interviews, 500 to 2,000 words, on topics of vital interest to sophisticated teens: sex, relationships, college, careers, sports and fitness, dating, health, money, computers, drugs and alcohol, examples of achievement and leadership among peers, advice on "making it" in the adult world. Some preference given to high school and college-age writers; fiction accepted only from students. Pays $25 to $500, on publication.

TEENS TODAY—Nazarene Publishing House, 6401 The Paseo, Kansas City, MO 64131. Gary Sivewright, Ed. Short stories, 1,200 to 1,500 words, dealing with teens demonstrating Christian principles in real-life situations. Adventure stories; stories about relationships and ethics. Pays 3½¢ a word, on acceptance.

TIGER BEAT—105 Union Ave., Cresskill, NJ 07626. Diane Umansky, Ed. Articles, to 4 pages, on young people in show business and music industry. Teen romance fiction, to 1,000 words. Self-help articles. Pays varying rates, on acceptance. Query. Unsolicited manuscripts sent without SASE will not be returned.

TIGER BEAT PRESENTS ROCK!—D.S. Magazines, Inc., 105 Union Ave., Cresskill, NJ 07626. Anne M. Raso, Ed. Articles, to 5½ pages, on well-known pop and rock stars. Pays $50 to $100, on publication. Query with SASE.

VENTURE—Box 150, Wheaton, IL 60189. Address David Leight. Articles, 1,500 words, for 12- to 18-year-old boys, on Christian living, contemporary issues. Adventure fiction, true stories. Photos, photo essays; cartoons. Pays 5¢ to 10¢ a word, on publication. Query, with SASE, required.

WRITING!—3500 Western Ave., Highland Park, IL 60035. Bonnie Bek-ken, Ed. Interviews, 1,200 words, for "Writers at Work" department, for high school students. Pays $100, on publication. Query.

YM—685 Third Ave., New York, NY 10017. Deborah Purcell, Articles/Fiction Ed. Lively articles, 1,500 to 2,500 words, on topics of concern to young women ages 12–18; material should be based on thorough research and interviews with experts, and should strongly represent teenagers' feelings. Fillers, 750 to 1,000 words; short stories, 3,000 to 3,500 words, with romantic themes. Pays from $250 for features, from $350 for fiction, and from $75 for fillers, on acceptance. Query first for articles and fillers.

YOUNG AMBASSADOR—Box 82808, Lincoln, NE 68501. David Lambert, Man. Ed. Articles, to 1,800 words, and honest, well-crafted fiction, to 2,500 words, for conservative Christian teens. B/W photos and color slides. Pays 4¢ to 10¢ a word, extra for photos, on publication.

YOUNG AND ALIVE—4444 S. 52nd St., Lincoln, NE 68506. Richard

Kaiser, Ed. Feature articles and fiction, 800 to 1,400 words, for blind and visually impaired young adults, on adventure, biography, camping, health, hobbies, and travel. Photos. Pays 3¢ to 5¢ a word, extra for photos, on acceptance. Write for guidelines.

YOUTH!—201 Eighth Ave., S., P.O. Box 801, Nashville, TN 37202. Address Ed. Nonfiction and fiction, 700 to 2,000 words, helping teenagers develop Christian identity and live the Christian faith in contemporary culture. Pays 4¢ a word, on acceptance.

THE DRAMA MARKET

REGIONAL AND UNIVERSITY THEATERS

Community, regional and civic theaters and college dramatic groups offer the best opportunities today for playwrights to see their plays produced, whether for staged production, or for dramatic readings. Indeed, aspiring playwrights who can get their work produced by any of these have taken an important step toward breaking into the competitive dramatic field—many well-known playwrights received their first recognition in the regional theaters. Payment is generally not large, but regional and university theaters usually buy only the right to produce a play, and all further rights revert to the author. Since most directors like to work closely with the authors on any revisions necessary, theaters will often pay for the playwright's expenses while in residence during rehearsals. The thrill of seeing your play come to life on the stage is one of the pleasures of being on hand for rehearsals and performances.

Aspiring playwrights should query college and community theaters in their region to find out which ones are interested in seeing original scripts. Dramatic associations of interest to playwrights include the Dramatists Guild (234 W. 44th St., New York, NY 10036), Theatre Communications, Inc. (355 Lexington Ave., New York, NY 10017), which publishes the annual *Dramatists Sourcebook*, and The International Society of Dramatists, publishers of *The Dramatist's Bible* (P.O. Box 3470, Fort Pierce, FL 33448).

Some of the theaters on the following list require that playwrights submit all or some of the following with scripts—cast list, synopsis, resumé, recommendations, return postcard—and with scripts and queries, self-addressed, stamped envelopes (SASE) must *always* be enclosed. Playwrights may also wish to register their material with the U.S. Copyright Office. For additional information about this, write Register of Copyrights, Library of Congress, Washington, DC 20559.

ACADEMY THEATRE—1137 Peachtree St., N.E., Atlanta, GA 30309. Frank Wittow, Artistic Dir. One-act and full-length dramas, and adaptations with new approaches that go beyond the conventions of naturalism; 6 to 8 cast members unless actors can play multiple roles. Simple sets. Pays negotiable rates. Query first.

ACTORS THEATRE OF LOUISVILLE—316 W. Main St., Louisville, KY 40202. Jon Jory, Artistic Dir. One-act dramas and comedies. Send manuscript, cast list, and SASE to "New Play Program." Reports in 6 to 9 months. Pays royalty, on production.

ALASKA REPERTORY THEATRE—705 W. 6th Ave., Suite 201, Anchorage, AK 99501. Robert Farley, Artistic Dir. Full-length dramas, comedies, and adaptations. Queries only; include SASE.

ALLEY THEATRE—615 Texas Ave., Houston, TX 77002. Michael Bigelow Dixon, Lit. Man. No unsolicited manuscripts. Submit synopsis of full-length or one-act comedies, dramas, adaptations, or musicals.

ALLIANCE THEATRE COMPANY—1280 Peachtree St. N.E., Atlanta, GA 30309. Sandra Deer, Lit. Man. No unsolicited manuscripts.

AMERICAN PLACE THEATRE—111 W. 46th St., New York, NY 10036. Chris Breyer, Lit. Man. Full-length plays. Do not prefer commercial comedies; favor plays innovative in both form and content. Send play with SASE. Allow 3 to 5 months for reply.

AMERICAN REPERTORY THEATRE—64 Brattle St., Cambridge, MA 02138. Jonathan Marks, Lit. Man. No unsolicited manuscripts. Submit one-page description of play, 10 page sample, and SASE.

AMERICAN STAGE COMPANY—P.O. Box 1560, St. Petersburg, FL 33731. Victoria Holloway, Artistic Dir. Full-length comedies and dramas. Send synopsis with short description of cast and production requirements with self-addressed postcard. Pays negotiable rates. Submit material September through January.

AMERICAN THEATRE ARTS—6240 Hollywood Blvd., Hollywood, CA 90028. Pamela Bohnert, Dev. Dir. No unsolicited scripts. Submit synopsis, cast list, set requirements, resumé, and SASE. Responds in 8 to 10 weeks.

THE APPLE CORPS.—336 W. 20th St., New York, NY 10011. Bob Del Pazzo, Coordinator. All types of one-act and full-length plays and musicals. Send bound manuscript with SASE. Allow 4 to 6 months for response. Payment varies. No phone calls.

ARENA STAGE—6th and Maine Ave., S.W., Washington, DC 20024. Full-length comedies, dramas, musicals and adaptations. David Copelin, Dir of Play Development. Submit one-page synopsis, 10 pages of dialogue, resumé, and recommendations. No unsolicited manuscripts. Pays varying rates. Workshops and readings offered. Allow 2 to 4 months for reply.

ARIZONA THEATRE COMPANY—P.O. Box 1631, Tucson, AZ 85702. Gary Gisselman, Art. Dir. Walter Schoen, Dir. Full-length comedies, musicals, and dramas. Must include SASE. Pays royalty.

ARKANSAS ARTS CENTER CHILDREN'S THEATRE—Box 2137, Little Rock, AR 72203. Bradley Anderson, Art Dir. Seeks solid, professional (full-length or one-act) scripts. Original, and, particularly, adapted work from contemporary and classic literature. Pays flat rate.

ASOLO STATE THEATRE—P.O. Drawer E., Sarasota, FL 33578. John Ulmer, Artistic Dir. Full-length dramas, comedies, musicals, and children's plays. Small stage. Pays royalty or varying rates. Readings and workshops offered. No unsolicited manuscripts. Submit synopsis and letter of inquiry.

AT THE FOOT OF THE MOUNTAIN—2000 S. 5th St., Minneapolis, MN 55454. Kim Hines, Lit. Man. Full-length and one-act plays of all types, with particular interest in scripts by and about women and women of color. Submit manuscript with synopsis, return postcard, and SASE (best time to submit: early spring). Reports in 4 to 6 months. Pays on royalty basis.

BACK ALLEY THEATRE—15231 Burbank Blvd., Van Nuys, CA 91411. Laura Zucker, Producing Dir. Full-length plays. Submit manuscript with SASE and resumé. Reports in 2–3 months. Pays $500, and travel/expenses for playwright to attend rehearsals.

BARTER THEATER—P.O. Box 867, Abingdon, VA 24210. Rex Partington, Producing Dir. Full-length dramas, comedies, adaptations, musicals and children's plays. Full workshop and reading productions. Allow 6 to 8 months for report. Payment rates negotiable.

BERKELEY REPERTORY THEATRE—2025 Addison St., Berkeley, CA 94704. Sharon Ott, Art. Dir. Amlin Gray, Dramaturg. Besides main season, produces *Playworks*—five staged readings of new plays in second stage. Enclose SASE. Reporting time: 4 months. No sit-coms.

BERKSHIRE THEATRE FESTIVAL—Box 797, Stockbridge, MA 02162. Josephine Abady, Art. Dir. Full-length comedies, musicals and dramas; cast to 8. Query required; submit synopsis and resumé.

BOARSHEAD: MICHIGAN PUBLIC THEATRE—425 S. Grand Ave., Lansing, MI 48933. Nancy-Elizabeth Kammer, Artistic Dir. Full-length comedies and dramas. Midwestern origin/theme preferred. Pays negotiable rates.

CENTER STAGE—700 N. Calvert St., Baltimore, MD 21202. Full-length and one-act comedies, dramas, musicals, adaptations. No unsolicited manuscripts. Send synopsis, resumé, cast list, recommendations and production history, with return postcard and SASE, in late spring. Pays varying rates. Offers workshops and readings. Allow 2 to 6 weeks for reply.

CHOCOLATE BAYOU THEATRE CO.—Box 270363, Houston, TX 77277. Attn. John R. Pearson. Preston Jones New Plays Symposium. Five-week residency to develop work with cast and director. Write for details. Other plays accepted through agents only.

CINCINNATI PLAYHOUSE IN THE PARK—Box 6537, Cincinnati, OH 45206. Michael Burnham, Lit. Man. Full-length comedies, dramas, musicals, adaptations and cabarets. Rarely accepts unsolicited manuscripts. Send synopsis with cast list, resumé, recommendations and return postcard. Pays negotiable rates and travel expenses. Allow 6 months to a year for reply.

CIRCLE REPERTORY COMPANY—161 Ave. of the Americas, New York, NY 10013. Bill Hemmig, Assoc. Lit. Man. Full-length comedies and dramas. Send manuscript, cast list, and SASE.

A CONTEMPORARY THEATRE—100 West Roy St., Seattle, WA 98119. Address Barry Pritchard. Full-length plays of all kinds. Small musicals. Pays on royalty basis.

CROSSROADS THEATRE CO.—320 Memorial Pkwy., New Brunswick, NJ 08901. Lee Richardson, Art. Dir. Full-length and one-act dramas, comedies, musicals and adaptations; experimental pieces; one man/one woman shows. Queries only, with synopsis, cast list, resumé and SASE.

DELAWARE THEATRE COMPANY—P.O. Box 516, Wilmington, DE 19899. Cleveland Morris, Art. Dir. Full-length comedies, dramas, musicals, and adaptations, with cast to 10; prefer single set. Send cast list, synopsis, and SASE. Reports in 6 months. Pays royalty.

DENVER CENTER THEATRE COMPANY—1050 13th St., Denver, CO 80204. Donovan Markey, Art. Dir. Full-length and one-act comedies, dramas, musicals and adaptations. Send manuscript with synopsis, resumé, return postcard and SASE. Pays negotiable rates. Special interest in regional material.

DETROIT REPERTORY THEATRE—13103 Woodrow Wilson Ave., Detroit, MI 48238. Barbara Busby, Lit. Man. Full-length comedies, and dramas. Enclose SASE. Pays royalty. Annual contest.

DORSET THEATRE FESTIVAL—Box 519, Dorset, VT 05251. Jill Charles, Art. Dir. Full-length comedies, musicals, dramas, and adaptations, cast to 8; simple set preferred. Query with synopsis, cast list, 5 to 10 pages of dialogue, resumé and return postcard. No unsolicited manuscripts. Pays varying rates.

EAST WEST PLAYERS—4424 Santa Monica Blvd., Los Angeles, CA 90029. Alberto Isaac, Lit. Man. Full-length comedies, dramas and musicals, dealing with Asian American issues and/or including important roles for Asian actors. Cast up to 15. Send manuscript with synopsis, cast list, resumé and SASE. Pays varying rates. Offers workshops and readings. Allow 3 months for reply.

EMPIRE STATE INSTITUTE FOR THE PERFORMING ARTS—Empire State Plaza, Albany, NY 12223. Barbara R. Maggio, Lit. Man. Full-length and one-act plays and musicals (preferably unproduced) on any subject. Submit manuscript and synopsis. Pays negotiable rates.

THE EMPTY SPACE THEATRE—95 S. Jackson St., Seattle, WA 98104. Tom Creamer, Lit. Man. Unsolicited scripts accepted only from WA, OR, WY, MT, and ID. Annual new play conference for writers from same states: send for brochure. Outside five-state NW region: scripts accepted through agents or established theater groups only.

ENSEMBLE STUDIO THEATRE—549 W. 52nd St., New York, NY 10019. D.S. Moynihan, Lit. Man. Full-length and one-act dramas and comedies, for cast of up to 12; small stage. Send manuscript with cast list, and SASE. Pays $1,000 for full-length, $175 for one-acts.

THE FAMILY—9 Second Ave., New York, NY 10003. Attn. Marvin Felix Camillo, Art. Dir. Full-length dramas and musicals for young people and adults. Submit manuscript with synopsis, resumé, and return postcard. Pays small fee.

FLORIDA STUDIO THEATRE—1241 North Palm Ave., Sarasota, FL 33566. Jeff Mousseau, New Play Development. Full-length comedies, dramas and musicals, preferably with small cast. Query first. Pays varying rates.

FOLGER THEATRE—201 E. Capitol St., S.E., Washington, DC 20003. Bob Stevens, Lit. Man. New versions or adaptations of classics. Payment rates negotiable. Query with SASE.

WILL GEER THEATRICUM BOTANICUM—Box 1222, Topanga, CA 90290. All types of scripts for outdoor theater, with large playing area. Submit manuscript with SASE. Pays varying rates.

GEVA THEATRE—75 Woodbury Blvd., Rochester, NY 14607. Ann Patrice Carrigan, Lit. Dir. Full-length and one-act dramas, comedies and musicals. Submit manuscript with SASE. Pays on percentage basis.

EMMY GIFFORD CHILDREN'S THEATRE—3504 Center St., Omaha, NE 68105. Bill Kirk, Art. Dir. One-act children's plays, especially adaptations from books or classic tales. Include return postcard. Pays $250 to $2,000.

713

THE GOODMAN THEATRE—200 S. Columbus Dr., Chicago, IL 60603. Larry Sloan, Scripts. No unsolicited manuscripts. Query with synopsis, resumé, and SASE only.

THE GROUP THEATRE—3940 Brooklyn NE, Seattle, WA 98105. Attn. Tim Bond. Full-length comedies and dramas, suitable for multi-ethnic casts, of up to 10 players; unit set. Submit synopsis and sample pages of dialogue, with recommendations. Pays negotiable rates. Annual contest.

THE GUTHRIE THEATRE—725 Vineland Pl., Minneapolis, MN 55403. Mark Bly, Lit. Man. Full-length comedies, dramas, and adaptations. Manuscripts accepted only from recognized theatrical agents. Query with detailed synopsis, cast size, resumé, return postcard and recommendations. Pays negotiable rates, and travel/residency expenses. Offers readings. Reports in 1 to 2 months.

HARTFORD STAGE COMPANY—50 Church St., Hartford, CT 06103. Constance Congdon, Lit. Man. Full-length plays of all types, for cast up to 12. No unsolicited manuscripts; submit through agent or send synopsis and 10 pages of sample dialogue. Pays varying rates.

THE HARTMAN THEATER—307 Atlantic St., Stamford, CT 06901. Margaret Booker, Artistic Dir. Full-length comedies, dramas and musicals. No unsolicited manuscripts. Query with synopsis, outline, return postcard and SASE. Reports in 3 to 4 months.

HIPPODROME STATE THEATRE—25 S.E. Second Place, Gainesville, FL 32601. Gregory Hausch, Artistic Director. Full-length plays, with unit sets and casts up to 15. Submit in summer and fall. Enclose return postcard and synopsis.

HOLLYWOOD ACTORS THEATRE—P.O. Box 27429, Los Angeles, CA 90027. Ron Bastone, Art. Dir. Full-length comedies and dramas, for cast of 6 to 15 actors; single or unit set preferred. Send manuscript with synopsis, cast list, resumé, and SASE. Pays 20% of gross receipts.

HONOLULU THEATRE FOR YOUTH—Box 3257, Honolulu, HI 96801. John Kauffman, Art. Dir. Plays, 60 to 90 minutes playing time, for young people/family audiences. Adult casts. Contemporary issues, Pacific themes, etc. Unit sets, small cast. Query or send manuscript with synopsis, cast list and SASE. Royalties negotiable.

ILLINOIS THEATRE CENTER—400 Lakewood Blvd., Park Forest, IL 60466. Steve S. Billig, Artistic Dir. Full-length comedies, dramas, musicals and adaptations, for unit/fragmentary sets, and cast to 8. Send manuscript with recommendations and return postcard. Pays negotiable rates. Workshops and readings offered.

THE ILLUSION THEATER—304 N. Washington Ave., Minneapolis, MN 55401. Michael Robbins, Producing Dir. Seeks writers to collaborate on new plays with the acting company. Submit resumé and synopsis. Pays varying rates.

INVISIBLE THEATRE—1400 N. First Ave., Tucson, AZ 85719. Christine Meissner, Lit. Man. Full-length comedies, dramas, musicals and adaptations, for cast to 10; simple set. Send manuscript with cast list, return postcard and SASE. Pays on percentage basis.

JACKSONVILLE UNIVERSITY THEATRE—Jacksonville Univ., Jacksonville, FL 32211. Davis Sikes, Artistic Dir. Unproduced full-length and one-

714

act dramas and comedies. Send manuscript with synopsis, cast list, return postcard, and SASE. Pays $1,000 and production.

JEWISH REPERTORY THEATRE—344 E. 14th St., New York, NY 10003. Ran Avni, Artistic Dir. Full-length comedies, dramas, musicals, children's plays and adaptations, with cast to 10, relating to the Jewish experience. Pays varying rates. Enclose return postcard.

THE JULIAN THEATRE—953 DeHaro St., San Francisco, CA 94107. Address New Plays. Full-length comedies and dramas with a social statement. Send 5 to 10 page scene, synopsis, cast description, and SASE. Pays on contractual basis. Allow 2 to 9 months for reply. Workshops and readings offered.

LAGUNA MOULTON PLAYHOUSE—606 Laguna Canyon Rd., Laguna Beach, CA 92651. Douglas Rowe, Art. Dir. Children's plays and comedies. Submit manuscript with SASE and return postcard. Payment varies.

LAMB'S PLAYERS THEATRE—500 Plaza Blvd., P.O. Box 26, National City, CA 92050. Address Script Search Committee. All types of full-length plays, for small cast; arena staging. Send manuscript with cast list and synopsis. Pays $500 to $1000.

LITTLE BROADWAY PRODUCTIONS—c/o Jill Shawn, 5240 Genesta Ave., Encino, CA 91316. Musicals and other plays for children; 55 minutes, no intermission. Submit manuscript with synopsis, return postcard, resumé, and SASE. Pays negotiable rates.

LOOKING GLASS THEATRE—175 Matthewson St., Providence, RI 02903. Pamela Messore, Artistic Dir. One-act, participation style children's plays, with cast to 5. Send manuscript with return postcard and SASE. Pays negotiable rates. Allow 6 weeks for reply.

LOS ANGELES THEATRE CENTER—514 S. Spring St., Los Angeles, CA 90013. Mame Hunt, Lit. Man. Full-length comedies, dramas, musicals, and adaptations. Special interest in scripts with social/political content; and by women and ethnic minorities. Query with synopsis, 10 pages of text, and SASE. Pays advance against royalty, on production, and travel and residence expenses.

McCADDEN PLACE THEATRE—1157 N. McCadden Place, Los Angeles, CA 90038. Address Joy Rinaldi, Artistic Dir. Full-length and one-act comedies, dramas and adaptations. Send manuscript with cast list, synopsis, resumé, return postcard and SASE. Pays varying rates.

McCARTER THEATRE COMPANY—91 University Pl., Princeton, NJ 08540. Robert Lanchester, Assoc. Art. Dir. Full-length and one-act comedies, dramas and adaptations. Submit script with SASE, synopsis, resumé, cast list, and recommendations. Pays negotiable rates.

MANHATTAN PUNCH LINE—410 W. 42nd St., New York, NY 10036. Steve Kaplan, Art. Dir. Comedies. Showcase contract. SASE required.

MANHATTAN THEATRE CLUB—321 E. 73rd St., New York, NY 10021. Address Jonathan Alper. Full-length and one-act comedies, dramas and musicals. No unsolicited manuscripts. Send synopsis with cast list, resumé, recommendations and return postcard. Pays negotiable rates. Allow 6 months for reply. Offers workshops and readings.

MEGAW THEATRE, INC.—17601 Saticoy St., Northridge, CA 91325. Address Marcia Steil. Full-length comedies and dramas, with cast of 7 to 10, and unit set. Send manuscripts with synopsis, cast list, resumé, recommendations, return postcard and SASE. Pays on contractual basis. Offers readings.

MIDWEST PLAYLABS—c/o The Playwrights' Center, 2301 Franklin Ave. E., Minneapolis, MN 55406. Full-length previously unproduced scripts (no musicals). Query. Pays stipend, room and board, and travel for 2-week August conference.

MILL MOUNTAIN THEATRE—Center in the Square, One Market Sq., Roanoke, VA 24011. Jo Weinstein, Lit. Man. Full-length and one-act original comedies, dramas, musicals, and adaptations; small casts and simple sets preferred. Submit manuscript with cast list, resumé, return postcard and SASE. Pays varying rates. Readings and workshops.

MILWAUKEE REPERTORY THEATER—929 N. Water St., Milwaukee, WI 53202. John Dillon, Art. Dir. Full-length comedies and dramas. Query with cast list and synopsis. Pays standard royalty.

MISSOURI REPERTORY THEATRE—4949 Cherry St., Kansas City, MO 64110. Felicia Londre, Dramaturg. Full-length comedies and dramas. Query with synopsis, cast list, resumé, and return postcard. Pays standard royalty.

THE NEGRO ENSEMBLE COMPANY—165 W. 46th St., Suite 800, New York, NY 10036. Douglas Turner Ward, Art. Dir. Full-length comedies, dramas, musicals and adaptations pertaining to Black life and the Black experience. Submit March through May. Pays on royalty basis. Enclose return postcard.

NEW DRAMATISTS—424 W. 44th St., New York, NY 10036. Workshop for playwrights. Submit two original, full-length, non-musical scripts, along with resumé, bio, and statement outlining goals. Playwrights from outside New York City may apply only if recommended by theatre professional from a regional theatre. Send for guidelines.

NEW TUNERS/PERFORMANCE COMMUNITY—1225 W. Belmont Ave., Chicago, IL 60657. George H. Gorham, Dramaturg. Full-length musicals only, for cast to 15; no wing/fly space. Send manuscript with cassette tape of score, cast list, resumé and return postcard. Pays on a royalty basis.

NEW YORK SHAKESPEARE FESTIVAL/PUBLIC THEATER—425 Lafayette St., New York, NY 10003. Gail Merrifield, Dir. of Plays and Musicals. Bill Hart, Lit. Man. Plays, musical works for the theater, translations, and adaptations. Submit manuscript, cassette (with musicals), and SASE.

NORTHLIGHT THEATRE—2300 Green Bay Rd., Evanston, IL 60201. Jimmy Bickerstaff, Asst. Art. Dir. Full-length plays, music theatre, translations, and adaptations for cast to 10; small theatre. Synopses only. Royalties, fees and compensations negotiable.

ODYSSEY THEATRE ENSEMBLE—12111 Ohio Ave., Los Angeles, CA 90025. Ron Sossi, Artistic Dir. Full-length comedies, dramas, musicals, and adaptations; provocative subject matter, or plays that stretch and explore the form and possibilities of theatre. Query with synopsis and return postcard. Pays variable rates. Allow 2 to 6 months for reply. Workshops and readings offered.

OLD GLOBE THEATRE—Simon Edison Center for the Performing Arts, Box 2171, San Diego, CA 92112. Address Robert Berlinger. Full-length comedies and dramas. No unsolicited manuscripts. Submit query with synopsis.

ONE ACT THEATRE COMPANY OF SAN FRANCISCO—430 Mason St.,

716

San Francisco, CA 94102. Fredericka Berhardt, Lit. Man. One-act comedies and dramas. Submit manuscript with SASE. Pays negotiable rates.

EUGENE O'NEILL THEATER CENTER—Suite 901, 234 W. 44th St., New York, NY 10036. Annual competition to select new stage and television plays for development at organization's Waterford Ct. location. Submit entries between Sept. 15 and Dec. 1, 1986, for 1987 conference. Send SASE for rules to National Playwright's Conference, c/o above address. Pays stipend, plus travel/living expenses during conference.

PAPER MILL PLAYHOUSE—Brookside Dr., Millburn, NJ 07041. Jeffrey Solis, Dramaturg. Full-length musicals only; simple sets. Submit synopsis and resumé; reports in 6 to 8 weeks. Pays Dramatists Guild contract.

PENGUIN REPERTORY THEATRE—Box 91, Stony Point, NY 10980. Joe Brancato, Art. Dir. Full-length comedies and dramas; cast to 8. Submit manuscript, synopsis, resumé and SASE. Pays varying rates, on production.

PENNSYLVANIA STAGE COMPANY—837 Linden St., Allentown, PA 18101. Pam Pepper, Lit. Man. Full-length plays with cast to 8; one set. Full-length musicals, with unit set and cast to 18. Send manuscript with synopsis, cast list and return postage. Pays negotiable rates. Allow 6 months for reply. Offers readings.

PEOPLE'S LIGHT AND THEATRE COMPANY—39 Conestoga Rd., Malvern, PA 19355. Alda Cortese, Lit. Man. Full-length and one-act comedies and dramas, for cast to 10; unit set preferred. Query before submitting. Pays negotiable rates.

PHILADELPHIA FESTIVAL FOR NEW PLAYS—3700 Chestnut St., Philadelphia, PA 19104. Hilary Missan, Program Coordinator. Full-length and one-act comedies, dramas, and musicals; must be unproduced. Submit script with return postcard, resumé, and SASE, through September 15. Pays varying rates.

PLAYHOUSE ON THE SQUARE—2121 Madison Ave., Memphis, TN 38104. Jackie Nichols, Artistic Dir. Full-length comedies, dramas, and musicals, with unit or single set, and cast to 15. Send manuscript with resumé, return postcard and SASE. Pays $500. Workshops or readings offered.

THE PLAYWRIGHTS FUND OF NORTH CAROLINA, INC.—P.O. Box 646, Greenville, NC 27835-0646. Christine Rusch, Art. Dir. One-act comedies and dramas, especially from SE playwrights. Submit manuscript with SASE. Pays small honorarium. Readings, workshops, and annual contest.

PLAYWRIGHTS HORIZONS—416 W. 42nd St., New York NY 10036. Address Literary Dept. Full-length comedies, dramas and musicals. Send synopsis and SASE. Pays varying rates.

PLAYWRIGHTS' PLATFORM—43 Charles St., Boston, MA 02114. Patrick Flynn, Pres. Script development workshops and public readings for New England playwrights. Full-length and one-act plays of all kinds. Residents of New England send scripts with short synopsis, resumé, return postcard and SASE.

PORTLAND STAGE COMPANY—Box 1458, Portland, ME 04112. Barbara Rosoff, Art. Dir. Full-length comedies, dramas, and musicals, for cast to 8. Send synopsis with return postcard. Pays fee, travel, and board for 4-week residency if play is produced.

THE PUERTO RICAN TRAVELING THEATRE—141 W. 94th St., New

York, NY 10025. Miriam Colon Edgar, Art. Dir. Full-length and one-act comedies, dramas, and musicals; cast to 8; simple sets. Payment negotiable.

RESTON REPERTORY TELEVISION THEATRE—P.O. Box 3615, Reston, VA 22090. Sharon Cohen, Exec. Producer. 30- to 90-minute comedies and dramas, with small cast preferred. Pays on percentage basis. Allow 3 to 4 months for reply. Enclose SASE.

THE ROAD COMPANY—Box 5278, EKS, Johnson City, TN 37603. Robert H. Leonard, Artistic Dir. Full-length and one-act comedies, dramas with social/political relevance to small town audiences. Send synopsis, cast list, and production history, if any. Pays negotiable rates. Reports in 6 to 12 months.

ROUND HOUSE THEATRE—12210 Bushey Dr., Silver Spring, MD 20902. Betty Clark, Production Office Man. Full-length comedies, dramas, musicals, and adaptations; cast to 15; prefer simple set. Submit manuscript, SASE, return postcard, and cassette (if musical). Payment varies.

THE SANTA FE FESTIVAL THEATRE—Box DD, Santa Fe, NM 87502. Thomas Kahn Gardner, Art. Dir. Full-length plays. Query before submitting scripts. Pays percentage, on production.

RICHMOND SHEPARD THEATRE STUDIO—6476 Santa Monica Blvd., Hollywood, CA 90038. Richmond Shepard, Art. Dir. Full-length comedies and dramas; cast to 8; prefer one set. Submit manuscript with SASE. Pays varying rates.

SOCIETY HILL PLAYHOUSE—507 S. 8th St., Philadelphia, PA 19147. Walter Vail, Dramaturg. Full-length and one-act dramas; cast to 10; simple set. Submit synopsis and SASE. Reports in 6 months. Nominal payment.

SOHO REPERTORY THEATRE—80 Varick St., New York, NY 10013. Jerry Engelbach, Artistic Dir. Full-length dramas, musicals, adaptations and mixed media works for thrust stage. No unsolicited manuscripts. Send brief precis, cast list, and resumé. Send for guidelines. Pays $100. Readings offered.

SOUTH COAST REPERTORY—655 Town Center Dr., Box 2197, Costa Mesa, CA 92626-1197. Jerry Patch, Lit. Man. Full-length comedies and dramas. Query with synopsis, resume and return postcard. Pays percent of gross, and travel/living expenses.

SPOKANE INTERPLAYERS ENSEMBLE—P.O. Box 1691, Spokane, WA 99210. Robert A. Welch, Art. Dir. Full-length and one-act comedies, dramas, and adaptations; cast to 10; simple set preferred. Send synopsis, cast list, resume, and return postcard. Payment negotiable.

STAGE ONE: THE LOUISVILLE CHILDREN'S THEATRE—721 W. Main St., Louisville, KY 40202. Moses Goldberg, Artistic Director. Children's plays for adult actors to perform. Pays varying rates. Allow 3 to 4 months for reply. Enclose SASE.

STAGES—709 Franklin St., Houston, TX 77002. Ted Swindley, Art. Dir. Full-length and one-act comedies, dramas, and children's scripts, especially from Texan playwrights; cast to 12; simple set. Submit script, synopsis and resumé. Pays 6% of gross.

STUDIO ARENA THEATRE—710 Main St., Buffalo, NY 14202. Kathryn Long, Dramaturg. Full-length dramas, comedies, and adaptations. Query with synopsis. Pays negotiable rates.

MARK TAPER FORUM—135 N. Grand Ave., Los Angeles, CA 90012.

Plays, preferably full-length, on any subject, for production in thrust theater or flexible theater. Pays on royalty basis. Query first.

THEATRE AMERICANA—Box 245, Altadena, CA 91001. Full-length comedies, dramas, and musicals, preferably with American theme. Send manuscript with cast list and SASE. No payment. Allow 3 to 6 months for reply.

THEATRE BY THE SEA—125 Bow St., Portsmouth, NH 03801. Tom Celli, Art. Dir. Full-length comedies, dramas, musicals, and adaptations, with casts up to 15. Payment rates negotiable. Enclose resumé, cast list, and synopsis.

THEATRE FOR YOUNG PEOPLE—Univ. of North Carolina, Greensboro, NC 27412. Tom Behm, Art. Dir. Full-length children's plays. Submit manuscript with SASE, Dec.-April. Pays $15 to $25 per performance.

THEATRE/TEATRO—Bilingual Foundation for the Arts, 421 N. Ave., #19, Los Angeles, CA 90031. Margarita Galban, Art. Dir. Full-length plays on Hispanic themes or written by Hispanic playwrights; cast to 15. Submit manuscript with return postcard. Pays negotiable rates.

THEATRE THREE—2800 Routh St., Dallas, TX 75201. Address Jimmy Mullen, Festival Coordinator. Full-length comedies and dramas, for New Play Festival. Offers readings.

THEATREWORKS/USA—131 W. 86th St., New York, NY 10024. Barbara Pasternak, Lit. Man. Historical biographies, issue-oriented works, fantasies and adaptations of literary classics for young people; one hour in length; cast to 6 (can double). Include SASE. Pays varying rates.

UNIVERSITY OF ALABAMA THEATRE—115 Music and Speech Bldg., P.O. Box 6386, University, AL 35486. Thomas J. Taylor, Art. Dir. Full-length and one-act comedies, dramas, and musicals. Send manuscript with SASE. Payment varies. Reports in 2 to 3 months. Readings.

LAWRENCE WELK VILLAGE THEATRE—8845 Lawrence Welk Dr., Escondido, CA 92026. Gary Davis, Art. Dir. Full-length comedies, musicals, and musical reviews; cast to 20. Submit manuscript with return postcard and SASE. Pays negotiable rates.

WISDOM BRIDGE THEATRE—1559 W. Howard St., Chicago, IL 60626. Address Douglas Finlayson. Full-length and one-act dramas, comedies, adaptations, and translations. Query with synopsis and SASE. Pays negotiable rates.

WOOLLY MAMMOTH THEATRE COMPANY—1317 G St. N.W., Washington, D.C. 20005. Neil Steyskal, Lit. Man. Innovative scripts for full-length plays; cast to 12. Unusual, small-scale musicals. Submit synopsis with SASE. Pays on performance.

GARY YOUNG MIME THEATRE—9613 Windcroft Way, Rockville, MD 20854. Gary Young, Artistic Director. Mime and comedies, for children and adults, 1 minute to 90 minutes in length; casts of 1 or 2, and portable set. Pays varying rates. Enclose return postcard, resumé, recommendations, cast list and synopsis.

RADIO THEATERS

R. BEAN'S VOICE THEATRE—467 Sidney St., Madison, WI 53703. Gene Becker, Exec. Prod. Radio Theatre. Half-hour radio scripts: mysteries, comedies, adventure, horror, and suspense, etc.; 10- to 15-minute children's scripts. Pays varying rates. Send SASE for "Writers' Format."

CHILDREN'S RADIO THEATRE—1314 14th St., NW, Washington, DC 20005. Joan Bellsey, Art. Dir. Children's radio plays. No unsolicited material. Query with resumé and SASE required.

NATIONAL RADIO THEATRE OF CHICAGO—600 N. McClurg Ct., Suite 502-A, Chicago, IL 60611. Yuri Rasovsky, Producer. Original radio scripts. Write for guidelines.

TIC RADIO THEATRE WORKSHOP—Library Plaza, Marshfield, MA 02050. Radio scripts, 30 minutes, to be aired on a closed-circuit radio service for the visually impaired. Scripts can be in any genre. Pays in copies of master tape. Send SASE for guidelines.

PLAY PUBLISHERS

ART CRAFT PLAY COMPANY—Box 1058, Cedar Rapids, IA 52406. Three-act comedies, mysteries, and farces, and one-act comedies or dramas, with one set, for production by junior and senior high schools. Pays on royalty basis or by outright purchase.

WALTER H. BAKER COMPANY—100 Chauncy St., Boston, MA 02111. Scripts for amateur production: one-act plays for competition, children's plays, musicals, religious drama, full-length plays for high school production. Three-to four-month reading period. Include SASE.

CHILD LIFE MAGAZINE—P.O. Box 567, Indianapolis, IN 46206. Plays, 700 to 1,000 words, for classroom or living-room production by children 8 to 11 years. Pays about 6¢ a word, on publication. Buys all rights.

CHILDREN'S PLAYMATE MAGAZINE—1100 Waterway Blvd., P.O. Box 567, Indianapolis, IN 46206. Kathleen B. Mosher, Ed. Plays, 200 to 600 words, for children aged 5 to 7: special emphasis on health, nutrition, exercise, and safety. Pays about 6¢ a word, on publication.

CONTEMPORARY DRAMA SERVICE—Meriwether Publishing, Ltd., Box 7710, 885 Elkton Dr., Colorado Springs, CO 80933. Arthur Zapel, Ed. Easy-to-stage comedies, skits, one-acts, musicals, puppet scripts, full-length plays for schools and churches. Adaptations of classics, and improvisational material for classroom use. Comedy monologues and duets. Chancel drama for Christmas and Easter church use. Enclose synopsis. Pays by fee arrangement or on royalty basis.

THE DRAMATIC PUBLISHING COMPANY—4150 N. Milwaukee Ave., Chicago, IL 60641. Full-length and one-act plays, musical comedies for amateur, children, and stock groups. Must run at least thirty minutes. Pays on royalty basis. Address Sara Clark. Reports within 10 to 12 weeks.

DRAMATICS—3368 Central Pkwy., Cincinnati, OH 45225. S. Ezra Goldstein, Ed. One-act and full-length plays, for high school production. Pays $40 to $150, on acceptance.

ELDRIDGE PUBLISHING COMPANY—Franklin, OH 45005. Kay Myerly, Edit. Dept. Three-act and one-act plays for schools, churches, community groups, etc., especially comedies. Christmas comedies. Best to submit in summer. Pays varying rates, on acceptance.

SAMUEL FRENCH, INC.—45 W. 25th St., New York, NY 10010. Lawrence R. Harbison, Ed. Full-length plays for dinner, community, stock, college and high school theatres. One-act plays (30 to 45 minutes). Children's plays, 45 to 60 minutes. Pays on royalty basis.

HEUER PUBLISHING COMPANY—Drawer 248, Cedar Rapids, IA 52406. C. Emmett McMullen, Ed. One-act comedies and dramas for contest work; three-act comedies, mysteries or farces, with one interior setting, for high school production. Pays on acceptance.

INSTRUCTOR—545 Fifth Ave., New York, NY 10017. Leanna Landsmann, Ed. Plays, 700 to 2,000 words, for elementary school children. Holiday and seasonal plays only. Send six months in advance. Pays $50 to $100, on acceptance.

PIONEER DRAMA SERVICE—P.O. Box 22555, Denver, CO 80222. Shubert Fendrich, Ed. and Pub. Full-length plays and musicals for the educational market, children's theatre plays to be produced by adults for children, and old-fashioned melodrama. "No unproduced plays, one-acts, or plays which have a largely male cast." Pays on a royalty basis. Buys all rights.

PLAYS, THE DRAMA MAGAZINE FOR YOUNG PEOPLE—120 Boylston St., Boston, MA 02116. Elizabeth Preston, Man. Ed. One-act plays, with simple settings, for production by young people, 7 to 17; holiday plays, comedies, dramas, skits, dramatized classics, farces, puppet plays, melodramas, dramatized folktales, and creative dramatics. Maximum lengths: lower grades, 10 double-spaced pages; middle grades, 15 pages; junior and senior high, 20 pages. Casts may be mixed, all-male or all-female; plays with one act preferred. Manuscript specification sheet available on request. Queries suggested for adaptations. Pays good rates, on acceptance. Buys all rights.

SCHOLASTIC SCOPE—730 Broadway, New York, NY 10003. Katherine Robinson, Ed. For ages 15 to 18 with 4th to 6th grade reading ability. Plays, to 6,000 words, on problems of contemporary teenagers, relationships between people in family, job and school situations. Some mysteries, comedies, and science fiction; plays about minorities. Pays good rates, on acceptance.

THE TELEVISION MARKET

The almost round-the-clock television offerings available for viewers on commercial and educational television stations—greatly expanded by the mushrooming cable TV offerings—may understandably lead free-lance writers to believe that opportunities to sell scripts or program ideas are infinite.

But unfortunately the realities of the television marketplace are generally quite different from this fantasy. With few exceptions, direct submissions of scripts, no matter how good they are, are not considered by producers or programmers, and in general free-lance writers can achieve success in this almost-closed field by concentrating on getting their fiction (short and in novel form) and nonfiction published in magazines or books, combed diligently by television producers for possible adaptations. A large percentage of the material offered over all types of networks (in addition to the motion pictures made in Hollywood or especially for TV) is in the form of adaptations of what has appeared in print.

Writers who want to try their hand at writing directly for this very limited market should be prepared to learn the special techniques and acceptable format of script writing. Also, experience in playwriting and a knowledge of dramatic structure gained through working in amateur, community, or professional theatres can be helpful, though TV is a highly specialized and demanding field, with unique requirements and specifications.

721

This section of the *Handbook* includes the names of TV shows scheduled for broadcast during the 1985–86 season, and names and addresses of the production companies responsible for these shows. The lists should not be considered either complete or permanent. A more complete list of shows and production companies may be found in *Ross Reports Television,* published monthly by Television Index, Inc., 40-29 27th St., Long Island City, NY 11101. The cost is $3.02 ($3.23 for New York residents) prepaid for each issue (including first-class postage).

Because virtually all of the producers of these shows tell us that they will read only scripts (and queries) submitted through recognized agents, we've included a list of agents who have indicated to us that they are willing to read queries from writers about television scripts. The names and addresses of other literary and dramatic agents can be found in *Literary Market Place* (Bowker), available in most libraries. A list of agents can also be obtained by sending a self-addressed, stamped envelope to Society of Authors' Representatives, P.O. Box 650, Old Chelsea Station, New York, NY 10113. Before submitting scripts to producers or to agents, authors should query to learn whether they prefer to see the material in television script form, or as an outline or summary.

Writers may wish to register their story, treatment, series format, or script with the Writers Guild of America. This registration doesn't confer statutory rights, but it does supply evidence of authorship which is effective for five years (and is renewable after that). To register material a writer should send one copy of his work, along with a $10 fee, to the Writers Guild of America Registration Service, 8955 Beverly Blvd., Los Angeles, CA 90048. Writers can also register dramatic material with the U.S. Copyright Office—for further information, write Register of Copyrights, Library of Congress, Washington, DC 20559. The Copyright Office is mainly used for book manuscripts, plays, music or lyrics, which the Writer's Guild will not register.

TELEVISION SHOWS

THE "A" TEAM (NBC)—Stephen J. Cannell Productions.

AIRWOLF (CBS)—Universal Television.

ALL MY CHILDREN (ABC)—ABC Productions.

AMAZING STORIES (NBC)—Amblin Entertainment with Universal Television.

ANOTHER WORLD (ABC)—ABC Productions.

AS THE WORLD TURNS (CBS)—Saatchi & Saatchi Compton Advertising for Proctor and Gamble.

BENSON (ABC)—Witt-Thomas-Harris Productions/Sunset Gower.

GEORGE BURNS COMEDY WEEK (CBS)—40 Share Productions/Universal Television.

CAGNEY & LACEY (CBS)—Barney Rosenzweig Productions/Orion Television.

CHARLIE AND COMPANY (CBS)—Allan Katz/20th Century Fox Television.

CHEERS (NBC)—Paramount Television.

THE COSBY SHOW (NBC)—Carsey-Werner Productions.

CRAZY LIKE A FOX (CBS)—Shulman/Baskin/Schenck/Cardea Productions/Columbia Pictures Television.

DALLAS (CBS)—Lorimar Production.

DAYS OF OUR LIVES (NBC)—Corday Productions.

DIFF'RENT STROKES (ABC)—Tandem Productions, Inc./Sunset Gower Studios.

DYNASTY (ABC)—Richard and Esther Shapiro Productions with Aaron Spelling Productions.

DYNASTY II: THE COLBYS (ABC)—Richard and Esther Shapiro Productions with Aaron Spelling Productions.

THE EQUALIZER (CBS)—Universal Television.

THE FACTS OF LIFE (NBC)—Embassy Television.

FALCON CREST (CBS)—Lorimar Productions.

THE FALL GUY (ABC)—Glen A. Larson Productions/20th Century Fox Television.

FAMILY TIES (NBC)—Paramount Television.

GENERAL HOSPITAL (ABC)—ABC Daytime Programming.

GIMME A BREAK (NBC)—Mort Lachman & Associates with Reeves Entertainment Group.

GOLDEN GIRLS (NBC)—Witt-Thomas-Harris Productions/Sunset-Gower.

GOOD MORNING AMERICA (ABC)—ABC Entertainment.

GROWING PAINS (ABC)—Warner Brothers Television.

THE GUIDING LIGHT (CBS)—Saatchi & Saatchi Compton Advertising for Proctor and Gamble.

HARDCASTLE & MCCORMICK (ABC)—Stephen J. Cannell Productions.

HELL TOWN (NBC)—Breezy Productions.

HIGHWAY TO HEAVEN (NBC)—Michael Landon Productions/MGM-UA Studios.

HILL STREET BLUES (NBC)—MTM Enterprises.

ALFRED HITCHCOCK PRESENTS (NBC)—Universal Television.

HOLLYWOOD BEAT (ABC)—Paramount Television Productions/Stonehedge Productions.

T. J. HOOKER (CBS)—Spelling/Goldberg with Columbia Pictures Television.

HOTEL (ABC)—Aaron Spelling Productions.

HUNTER (NBC)—Stephen J. Cannell Productions.

THE INSIDERS (ABC)—Universal Television.

KATE & ALLIE (CBS)—Mort Lachman with Alan Landsburg Productions.

KNIGHT RIDER (NBC)—Glen A. Larson Productions/Universal Television.

KNOT'S LANDING (CBS)—Lorimar Productions.

THE LOVE BOAT (ABC)—Aaron Spelling Productions with Douglas Cramer.

LOVING (ABC)—Dramatic Creations.

MACGYVER (ABC)—Winkler/Rich Productions/Paramount Television.

MAGNUM P. I. (CBS)—Universal Television.

MIAMI VICE (NBC)—Universal Television.

MISFITS OF SCIENCE (NBC)—Universal/James Parriot.

MR. BELVEDERE (ABC)—Lazy B/F O. B. Productions/20th Century Fox Television.

MOONLIGHTING (ABC)—Picturemaker Productions.

MURDER, SHE WROTE (CBS)—Universal Television.

NBC'S SATURDAY NIGHT LIVE (NBC)—NBC TV.

NEWHART (CBS)—MTM Enterprises.

NIGHT COURT (NBC)—Starry Night Productions/Warner Brothers Television.

ONE LIFE TO LIVE (ABC)—ABC TV.

OUR FAMILY HONOR (ABC)—Lorimar Productions.

RIPLEY'S BELIEVE IT OR NOT (ABC)—Jack Haley Jr./Rastar Productions/Columbia Pictures Television.

RIPTIDE (NBC)—Stephen J. Cannell Productions.

RYAN'S HOPE (ABC)—ABC TV.

ST. ELSEWHERE (NBC)—MTM Enterprises.

SANTA BARBARA (NBC)—Dobson Productions.

SCARECROW AND MRS. KING (CBS)—Warner Brothers Television.

SEARCH FOR TOMORROW (NBC)—Benton & Bowles.

SHADOW CHASERS (ABC)—Warner Brothers Television.

SILVER SPOONS (NBC)—Embassy Television/Sunset-Gower.

SIMON & SIMON (CBS)—Universal Television.

SPENSER: FOR HIRE (ABC)—Nightwatch Productions/Warner Brothers Television.

STIR CRAZY (CBS)—Columbia Pictures Television.

REMINGTON STEELE (NBC)—MTM Enterprises.

TODAY (NBC)—NBC TV.

TRAPPER JOHN, M.D. (CBS)—Don Brinkley Productions/20th Century Fox Television.

TV'S BLOOPERS AND PRACTICAL JOKES (NBC)—Carson Company/Dick Clark Productions.

THE TWILIGHT ZONE (CBS)—CBS Entertainment.

227 (NBC)—Embassy Television.

WEBSTER (ABC)—Georgian Bay, Ltd./Paramount Television.

WHO'S THE BOSS? (ABC)—Embassy Television/Sunset Gower Studios.

THE YOUNG AND THE RESTLESS (CBS)—Columbia Pictures Television.

TELEVISION PRODUCERS

ABC DAYTIME PROGRAMMING—1330 Ave. of the Americas, New York, NY 10019.

ABC ENTERTAINMENT—1965 Broadway, New York, NY 10023.

ABC PRODUCTIONS—101 W. 67th St., New York, NY 10023.

ABC-TV—56 W. 66th St., New York, NY 10023.

BENTON & BOWLES, INC.—909 Third Ave., New York, NY 10022.

STEPHEN J. CANNELL PRODUCTIONS—7083 Hollywood Blvd., Hollywood, CA 90028.

CARSEY-WERNER PRODUCTIONS—NBC Studios, 1268 E. 14th St., Brooklyn, NY 11230.

CARSON PRODUCTIONS—10045 Riverside Dr., Toluca Lake, CA 91602.

CBS ENTERTAINMENT—51 W. 52nd St., New York, NY 10019.

COLUMBIA PICTURES TELEVISION—300 Colgems Sq., Burbank, CA 91505.

CORDAY PRODUCTIONS, INC.—Colgems Sq., Burbank, CA 91505.

DOBSON PRODUCTIONS—NBC Studio 11, 3000 W. Alameda Ave., Burbank, CA 91523.

DRAMATIC CREATIONS —320 W. 66th St., New York, NY 10023.

EMBASSY TELEVISION—1438 N. Gower, Los Angeles, CA 90028.

MORT LACHMAN & ASSOCIATES—Ed Sullivan Studios, 1697 Broadway, New York, NY 10019.

ALAN LANDSBURG PRODUCTIONS—1554 S. Sepulveda Blvd., Los Angeles, CA 90025.

GLEN A. LARSON PRODUCTIONS—10201 W. Pico Blvd., Los Angeles, CA 90064.

LORIMAR PRODUCTIONS—3970 Overland Ave., Culver City, CA 90230.

MGM-UA TELEVISION—10202 W. Washington Blvd., Culver City, CA 90230.

MTM ENTERPRISES—4024 Radford Ave., Studio City, CA 91604.

NBC PRODUCTIONS—NBC Television, 3000 W. Alameda Ave., Burbank, CA 91523.

NBC-TV—30 Rockefeller Plaza, New York, NY 10020.

ORION ENTERPRISES—1875 Century Park East, Los Angeles, CA 90067.

PARAMOUNT TELEVISION—5555 Melrose Ave., Los Angeles, CA 90038.

REEVES ENTERTAINMENT GROUP—11811 Olympic Blvd., Los Angeles, CA 90064.

SAATCHI & SAATCHI COMPTON ADVERTISING, INC.—625 Madison Ave., New York, NY 10022.

AARON SPELLING PRODUCTIONS—1041 N. Formosa Ave., Hollywood, CA 90046.

SUNSET GOWER STUDIOS—1438 N. Gower, Hollywood, CA 90028.

TANDEM PRODUCTIONS—956 Seward St., Los Angeles, CA 90038.

20TH CENTURY-FOX TELEVISION—10201 W. Pico Blvd., Los Angeles, CA 90064.

UNIVERSAL TELEVISION—100 Universal City Plaza, Universal City, CA 91608.

WARNER BROTHERS TELEVISION—4000 Warner Blvd., Burbank, CA 91505.

WITT-THOMAS-HARRIS PRODUCTIONS—1438 Gower, Los Angeles, CA 90028.

TELEVISION SCRIPT AGENTS

ACT 48 MANAGEMENT—Suite #705, 1501 Broadway, New York, NY 10036. Address Literary Department. Reads synopses of scripts for feature films, TV movies and stage plays, accompanied by SASEs.

LEE ALLAN AGENCY—4571 N. 68th St., Milwaukee, WI 53218. TV movies, features; no series or episodes. Reads queries.

HOWARD T. BRODY AGENCY—P.O. Box 291423, Davie, FL 33329. Milton Risblah, Script Consultant. Reads queries and scripts with SASEs.

THE CALDER AGENCY—4150 Riverside Dr., Burbank, CA 91505. Reads queries and synopses for features only; no television material.

BILL COOPER ASSOCIATES—224 W. 49th St., New York, NY 10022. Will look at developed ideas for comedies, dramas for TV, theatre, and motion pictures.

SCOTT C. HUDSON—215 E. 76th St., New York, NY 10021. Reads queries and treatments, with SASEs.

JAFFE REPRESENTATIVES—140 7th Ave., New York, NY 10011. Reads queries and treatments.

WILLIAM KERWIN AGENCY—1605 N. Cahuenga Blvd., #202, Hollywood, CA 90028. Reads queries. No unsolicited manuscripts.

ARCHER KING, LTD.—1440 Broadway, #2100, New York, NY 10018. Reads queries and treatments.

OTTO R. KOZAK LITERARY AGENCY—33 Bay St., East Atlantic Beach, NY 11561. Reads queries.

LUCY R. KROLL AGENCY—390 W. End Ave., New York, NY 10024. Reads queries accompanied by SASE.

L. HARRY LEE LITERARY AGENCY—Box 203, Rocky Point, NY 11778. Reads queries accompanied by SASE only.

HAROLD MATSON CO., INC.—276 Fifth Ave., New York, NY 10001. Reads queries with SASEs.

WILLIAM MORRIS AGENCY—1350 Ave. of the Americas, New York, NY 10019. Reads queries with SASEs.

SUZANNE SHELTON—CNA Associates, 8721 Sunset Blvd., #202, Los Angeles, CA 90069. Reads queries accompanied by SASEs only. No episodic scripts. New series ideas or MFT only.

LONDON STAR PROMOTIONS—7131 Owensmouth Ave., #C116, Canoga Park, CA 91303. Reads queries and synopses.

JACK TANTLEFF—% Hesseltine/Baker Associates, 165 W. 46th St., #409, New York, NY 10036. Reads queries.

VAMP TALENT AGENCY—713 E. La Loma, #1, Somis, CA 93066. Reads queries, treatments and scripts, accompanied by SASE's.

DAN WRIGHT—% Ann Wright Representatives, Inc., 136 E. 57th St., New York, NY 10022. Reads queries. Specializes in motion pictures.

WRITERS & ARTISTS AGENCY—11726 San Vicente Blvd., Los Angeles, CA 90049. Reads queries only; no unsolicited manuscripts accepted.

BOOK PUBLISHERS

Three lists are included here: Hardcover publishers (many of these have paperback subsidiaries as well); publishers of paperback originals; and university presses, which publish a limited number of novels, short fiction and poetry collections, as well as scholarly and specialized books.

Before you submit a complete manuscript to an editor, it is advisable to send a brief query letter describing the proposed book. The letter should also include information about the author's special qualifications for dealing with a particular topic and any previous publication credits. An outline of the book (or a synopsis for fiction) and a sample chapter may also be included.

It is common practice to submit a book manuscript to only one publisher at a time, although it is becoming more and more acceptable for writers, even those without agents, to submit the same query or proposal to more than one editor at the same time.

Book manuscripts may be wrapped in typing paper boxes (available from a stationer) and sent by first-class mail, or, more common and less expensive, by "Special Fourth Class Rate-Manuscript." For rates, details of insurance, and so forth, inquire at your local post office. With any submission to a publisher, be sure to enclose sufficient postage for the manuscript's return.

Royalty rates for hardcover books usually start at 10% of the retail price of the book, and increase after a certain number of copies have been sold. Paperbacks generally have a somewhat lower rate, about 5% to 8%. It is customary for the publishing company to pay the author a cash advance against royalties when the book contract is signed or when the finished manuscript is received. Some publishers pay on a flat fee basis.

HARDCOVER BOOK PUBLISHERS

ABBEY PRESS—St. Meinrad, IN 47577. Rev. Keith McClellan, Pub. Nonfiction Christian materials on marriage and family living. Royalty basis. Query with table of contents and writing sample.

HARRY N. ABRAMS, INC. (Subsidiary of *Times Mirror Co.*)—100 Fifth Ave., New York, NY 10011. Art and other heavily illustrated books. Pays varying rates. Query.

ACADEMIC PRESS, INC. (Subsidiary of *Harcourt Brace Jovanovich*)— HBJ Building, Orlando, FL 32887. Address Erwin V. Cohen, Ed. Dept. Scientific books for professionals; college science texts. Royalty basis. Query.

ACADEMY CHICAGO, PUBLISHERS—425 N. Michigan Ave., Chicago, IL 60601. Anita Miller, Ed. General fiction; mysteries. History; biographies; travel; books by and about women. Royalty basis. Query. SASE required.

ADDISON-WESLEY PUBLISHING CO.—Reading, MA 01867. General Publishing Group: Adult nonfiction on current topics: education, health, psychology, computers, professions, human resources, business, etc. Royalty basis.

ALASKA NORTHWEST PUBLISHING CO.—130 2nd Ave. S., Edmonds, WA 98020. Ethel Dassow, Chief Book Ed. Nonfiction, 10,000 to 100,000 words, with an emphasis on natural resources and history of Alaska, Northwestern Canada, and Pacific Northwest: how-to books; biographies; cookbooks; gardening; humor; nature; guidebooks. *Juveniles:* Picture books, easy-to-read books, and how-to-books, with regional themes. Send query or sample chapters with outline. Limited market.

AMERICAN BOOK COMPANY—See *D.C. Heath.*

ANDERSON WORLD, INC.—1400 Stierlin Rd., Mountain View, CA 94043. Laura Dayton, Book Ed. Books on running, health and fitness subjects, 50,000 to 100,000 words. Query; enclose SASE.

ARBOR HOUSE PUBLISHING CO.—235 E. 45th St., New York, NY 10017. Eden Collinsworth, Pub. Ann Harris, Ed.-in-Chief. General fiction and nonfiction. Royalty basis. Query.

ARCO PUBLISHING, INC.—215 Park Ave. S., New York, NY 10003. William Mlawer, Educational Books; Madelyn Larsen, Consumer Books. Nonfiction, originals and reprints, from 50,000 words. Career guides, test preparation, how-to's, young adult science, needlecraft. No fiction, poetry, humor, history, biography, personal accounts. Pays on royalty basis. Query with outline. Return postage required.

ATHENEUM PUBLISHERS (Subsidiary of *The Scribner Book Companies*)—115 Fifth Ave., New York, NY 10003. Thomas A. Stewart, Vice-President and Ed.-in-Chief. General nonfiction; biography, history, current affairs, belles-lettres; juveniles, from picture books through young-adult. *Argo Books:* science fiction and fantasy for young adults and adults; send complete manuscripts or sample chapters and outline. No unsolicited adult fiction. Royalty basis.

THE ATLANTIC MONTHLY PRESS—8 Arlington St., Boston, MA 02116. Harold Evans, Ed.-in-Chief. Fiction, biography, history, belles-lettres, poetry, general nonfiction, children's books. Royalty basis. Query.

AUGSBURG PUBLISHING HOUSE—Box 1209, 426 S. Fifth St., Minneapolis, MN 55440. Roland Seboldt, Dir. of Book Development. Fiction and nonfiction, for adults, children and teens, on Christian themes. Royalty basis.

BAEN BOOKS—Baen Enterprises, 8 W. 36th St., New York, NY 10018. Elizabeth Mitchell, Sr. Ed. Jim Baen, Pres. High-tech science fiction; innovative fantasy. Query with synopsis and sample chapters. Royalty basis.

BAKER BOOK HOUSE—P. O. Box 6287, Grand Rapids, MI 49506. Daniel Van't Kerkhoff, Ed. Religious nonfiction, academic and popular. Royalty basis.

BEACON PRESS—25 Beacon St., Boston, MA 02108. Joanne Wykoff, Carol Birdsall, Sr. Eds. General nonfiction: world affairs, sociology, psychology, women's studies, political science, art, literature, philosophy, religion. No fiction or poetry. Royalty basis. Query. Return postage required.

BEAUFORT BOOKS—9 E. 40th St., New York, NY 10016. Susan Suffes. Ed. Fiction and nonfiction. Query with outline and sample chapters for nonfiction; complete manuscripts (no first novels) for fiction. Royalty basis.

BEECH TREE BOOKS (Imprint of *William Morrow and Co., Inc.*)—105 Madison Ave., New York, NY 10016. James Landis, Pub. and Ed.-in-Chief. Adult fiction and nonfiction. No unsolicited manuscripts.

BETTER HOMES AND GARDENS BOOKS—See *Meredith Corporation.*

BINFORD & MORT PUBLISHING—1202 N.W. 17th Ave., Portland, OR 97209. J. F. Roberts, Ed. Books on subjects related to the Pacific Coast and the Northwest. Lengths vary. Royalty basis. Query first.

JOHN F. BLAIR, PUBLISHER—1406 Plaza Dr., Winston-Salem, NC 27103. Biography, history, travel and guidebooks, with North Carolina tie-in. Length: at least 75,000 words. Pays on royalty basis. Query Virginia Hege, Editorial Dept.

BLUEJAY BOOKS—130 W. 42nd St., #514, New York, NY 10036. James Frenkel, Ed. Science fiction, fantasy, and related nonfiction. Royalty basis. Query required.

THOMAS BOUREGY & CO., INC.—401 Lafayette St., New York, NY 10003. Rita Brenig, Ed. Light, wholesome, well-plotted romances, modern Gothics, westerns and nurse romances, 50,000 to 60,000 words. Send one-page synopsis. SASE required.

BRADBURY PRESS, INC. (An affiliate of *Macmillan, Inc.*)—866 Third Ave., New York, NY 10022. Norma Jean Sawicki, Exec. Ed. Picture books; juvenile and young adult fiction. Royalty basis.

BRANDEN PRESS—21 Station St., Box 843, Brookline Village, MA 02147.

Adolph Caso, Ed. Novels and biographies, 250 to 350 pages. Query first. Pays on a royalty basis.

GEORGE BRAZILLER, INC.—One Park Ave., New York, NY 10016. Literature, history, philosophy, science, art, social science; fiction. Royalty basis. No unsolicited manuscripts. Query required.

BROADMAN PRESS—127 Ninth Ave. N., Nashville, TN 37234. Harold S. Smith, Supervisor. Religious and inspirational fiction and nonfiction. Royalty basis. Query.

CAROLRHODA BOOKS—241 First Ave. N., Minneapolis, MN 55401. Kendall Morse, Ed. Picture books, fiction, nonfiction for elementary children. Outright purchase. Overstocked.

CARROLL AND GRAF PUBLISHERS, INC.—260 Fifth Ave., New York, NY 10001. Kent E. Carroll, Exec. Ed. General fiction and nonfiction. Royalty basis. Query with SASE.

CBI PUBLISHING CO.—See *Van Nostrand Reinhold Co., Inc.*

CEDARHOUSE PRESS—406 W. 28th St., Bryan, TX 77803. Paul Christensen, Ed. Biographies, books about Texas, experimental novels, collections of short fiction, and poetry collections (modernist technique only). Query with sample chapters and outline. Pays on royalty basis.

CHATHAM PRESS—P.O. Box A, Old Greenwich, CT 06807. Roger H. Lowrie, Man. Dir. Books on the Northeast coast, New England and the ocean. Royalty basis. Query with outline, sample chapters, illustrations and SASE large enough for return of material.

CHILDRENS PRESS—1224 W. Van Buren St., Chicago, IL 60607. Fran Dyra, Ed. Dir. Juvenile nonfiction: science, biography, 10,000 to 25,000 words, for supplementary use in classrooms. Query first. Picture books, 50 to 1,000 words. Royalty basis or outright purchase.

CHILTON BOOK CO.—201 King of Prussia Rd., Radnor, PA 19089. Alan F. Turner, Edit. Dir. Business, and business applications for computers, crafts and hobbies, automotive. Royalty basis. Query with outline, sample chapter, and return postage.

CHRONICLE BOOKS—One Hallidie Plaza, Suite 806, San Francisco, CA 94102. Larry L. Smith, Ed. Nonfiction: West Coast regional recreational guides, regional histories, natural history, art and architecture. Royalty basis.

CITADEL PRESS—See *Lyle Stuart, Inc.*

CLARION BOOKS (Juvenile imprint of *Ticknor & Fields,* a *Houghton Mifflin* company)—52 Vanderbilt Ave., New York, NY 10017. James C. Giblin, Ed. Juvenile fiction and nonfiction, picture books, for ages 4 and up. Royalty basis. Query preferred on manuscripts of more than 20 pages. Publishes approximately 30–35 hardcover titles a year.

COMPUTE! PUBLICATIONS, INC.—324 W. Wendover, Suite 200, Greensboro, NC 27408. How-to computer books; specializes in machine specific publications. Query preferred. Royalty basis.

CONTEMPORARY BOOKS—180 N. Michigan Ave., Chicago, IL 60601. N. Crossman, Exec.Ed. General nonfiction: fitness; self-help; how-to; practical business; nutrition; sports guides. Royalty basis. Query with outline and sample chapter.

DAVID C. COOK PUBLISHING CO.—850 N. Grove Ave., Elgin, IL 60120. Joe Hertel, Book Division Manager; Catherine L. Davis, Man. Ed./Books. Religious children's/juveniles only. Royalty and work-for-hire basis. Query with chapter-by-chapter synopsis and two sample chapters. Unsolicited manuscripts returned unopened. Label envelope "query." SASE required.

COPLEY BOOKS—7776 Ivanhoe Ave., La Jolla, CA 92037. Jean I. Bradford, Ed. Manuscripts, with photos, illustrations, maps, on history of California and the Southwest. Query. Pays on royalty basis.

COWARD, MCCANN (Div. of *Putnam Publishing Group*)—200 Madison Ave., New York, NY 10016. Fiction and nonfiction through agents only.

CRAFTSMAN BOOK COMPANY—6058 Corte del Cedro, P.O. Box 6500, Carlsbad, CA 92008-0992. Laurence D. Jacobs, Ed. How-to construction manuals for builders, 450 pages. Royalty basis. Query.

CREATIVE EDUCATION INC.—1422 W. Lake St., Minneapolis, MN 55408. Ann Redpath, Ed. Nonfiction for children aged 5 to 12. No textbooks. Mostly flat fee basis, some royalty.

THOMAS Y. CROWELL—See *Harper Junior Books Group.*

CROWN PUBLISHERS, INC.—225 Park Ave. S., New York, NY 10003. Betty A. Prashker, Ed.-in-Chief. David Allender, Dir., Children's Books. Fiction and general nonfiction. Royalty basis. Query letters only: Address Ed. Dept.; no unsolicited manuscripts. SASE required.

JONATHAN DAVID PUBLISHERS, INC.—68–22 Eliot Ave., Middle Village, NY 11379. Alfred J. Kolatch, Ed.-in-Chief. General nonfiction—how-to, sports, cooking and food, self-help, etc.—and nonfiction on Judaica. Royalty basis or outright purchase. Query with outline, sample chapter, and resumé.

DELACORTE PRESS (Div. of *Dell Publishing Co., Inc.*)—245 E. 47th St., New York, NY 10017. Jackie Farber, Ed. of adult fiction and nonfiction. George Nicholson, *Books for Young Readers* Ed. General fiction and nonfiction. *Books for Young Readers:* Contemporary fiction for students through secondary school. Royalty basis. Query with outline; no unsolicited manuscripts.

DEMBNER BOOKS—80 Eighth Ave., New York, NY 10011. S. Arthur Dembner, Pres. Self-help, life-style, reference and other nonfiction; good fiction. Royalty basis. Query with outline, sample chapters, and SASE large enough for return of material.

DEVIN-ADAIR PUBLISHERS, INC.—6 N. Water St., Greenwich, CT 06830. C. de la Belle Issue, Pub. J. Andrassi, Ed. Books on conservative affairs, Irish topics, Americana, computers, self-help, health, ecology. Royalty basis. Query with outline, sample chapters, and SASE.

DIAL BOOKS FOR YOUNG READERS (Div. of *E.P. Dutton*)—2 Park Ave., New York, NY 10016. Picture books; Easy-to-Read Books; middle-grade readers; young adult fiction and nonfiction. Submit complete manuscript for fiction; outline and sample chapters for nonfiction. Enclose SASE. Royalty basis.

DILLON PRESS—242 Portland Ave. S., Minneapolis, MN 55415. Uva Dillon, Ed.-in-Chief. Ann-Louise Taylor, Fiction Ed. Juvenile nonfiction; foreign countries, contemporary biographies for elementary and middle grade levels, unusual approaches to science topics for primary grade readers, wildlife, craft/outdoor activities, contemporary issues of interest to young people. Royalty and outright purchase. Query with outline and sample chapter. SASE required. *Gemstone Books:* Fiction for grades K-9: mystery, adventure, romance, science fiction, contemporary problems, historical, girls' sports stories. Royalty and outright purchase.

DODD, MEAD & CO.—79 Madison Ave., New York, NY 10016. Allen Klots, Jerry Gross, Cynthia Vartan, Margaret Norton, Sr. Eds. Joe Ann Daly, Dir., Children's Books. General fiction and nonfiction: biography, history, belles-lettres, travel, mystery, social issues, current events. Juveniles. Royalty basis. Query.

DOUBLEDAY AND CO., INC.—Dept. AA-W, 245 Park Ave., New York, NY 10167. Mystery/suspense fiction, romance, science fiction, 60,000 to 80,000 words. Submit complete manuscript to appropriate editor: Crime Club, Starlight Romance, or Science Fiction. SASE required.

DOWN EAST BOOKS—Box 679, Camden, ME 04843. Nonfiction about New England. Query with sample chapters and outline. Pays on royalty basis.

E.P. DUTTON, INC.—2 Park Ave., New York, NY 10016. General fiction, nonfiction; query with outline and sample chapters. *Lodestar Books,* Virginia Buckley, Ed. Dir. Young adult fiction and nonfiction—submit proposals for nonfiction, complete manuscripts for fiction. Royalty basis. Send queries to Editorial Dept.

EAST WOODS PRESS—429 East Blvd., Charlotte, NC 28203. Sally McMillan, Ed. Outdoor and travel books; cookbooks; self-help and how-to books; sports; trail guides; childcare. Royalty basis. Query with sample chapters.

WM. B. EERDMANS PUBLISHING COMPANY, INC.—255 Jefferson Ave., S.E., Grand Rapids, MI 49503. Jon Pott, Ed.-in-Chief. Protestant theological nonfiction; American history; some fiction. Royalty basis.

EMC CORP.—300 York Ave., St. Paul, MN 55101. Rosemary J. Barry, Ed. Fiction, nonfiction, with high-interest, low vocabulary material. Fiction, to 6,000 words, with a top vocabulary level of 5th grade. Royalty basis. No unsolicited manuscripts accepted.

ENSLOW PUBLISHERS—Bloy St. & Ramsey Ave., Box 777, Hillside, NJ 07205. R. M. Enslow, Jr., Ed./Pub. Specialized nonfiction. Children's nonfiction. Royalty basis. Query first.

PAUL S. ERIKSSON, PUBLISHER—Battell Bldg., Middlebury, VT 05753. General nonfiction; some fiction. Royalty basis. Query with outline and sample chapters.

M. EVANS & CO., INC.—216 E. 49th St., New York, NY 10017. Herbert M. Katz, Ed.-in-Chief. Books on health, self-help, popular psychology, and cookbooks. Commercial fiction for adults. Query with outlines and sample chapters. Royalty basis.

FACTS ON FILE PUBLICATIONS—460 Park Ave. S., New York, NY 10016. John Thornton, Edit. Dir. Reference and trade books on business, science, consumer affairs, the performing arts, etc. Query with outline and sample chapter. Royalty basis.

FARRAR, STRAUS & GIROUX—19 Union Sq. W., New York, NY 10003. General fiction, nonfiction, juveniles. Address queries to Editorial Dept.

FREDERICK FELL PUBLISHERS, INC.—2500 Hollywood Blvd., Suite

302, Hollywood, FL 33020. Nonfiction: business, crafts, health, etc. Royalty basis. Query by letter or with outline and sample chapters. SASE required.

DONALD I. FINE, INC.—128 E. 36th St., New York, NY 10016. Deborah Wilburn, V.P. Literary and commercial fiction. General nonfiction, to 90,000 words. Juveniles. Query with sample chapters. Advance royalty basis. Prefer agent submissions.

FLEET PRESS CORPORATION—160 Fifth Ave., New York, NY 10010. S. Schiff, Ed. General nonfiction; sports and how-to. Royalty basis. Query; no unsolicited manuscripts.

FORTRESS PRESS—2900 Queen Lane, Philadelphia, PA 19129. Harold W. Rast. Th.D., Dir. Serious, nonfiction works, from 100 pages, on theology and religion, for the academic or lay reader. Royalty basis. Query preferred.

FOUR WINDS PRESS (An imprint of *Macmillan Publishing Co.*)—866 Third Ave., New York, NY 10022. Meredith Charpentier, Ed.-in-Chief. Juveniles: picture books, fiction for all ages. Nonfiction for young children. Unsolicited material welcome. Send SASE with all submissions.

THE FREE PRESS—See *Macmillan Publishing Co.*

GARDEN WAY PUBLISHING COMPANY—Storey Communications, Schoolhouse Rd., Pownal, VT 05261. Roger M. Griffith, Ed. How-to books on gardening, cooking, building, etc. Royalty basis or outright purchase. Query with outline and sample chapter.

GEMSTONE BOOKS—See *Dillon Press.*

THE K. S. GINIGER CO., INC.—235 Park Ave. S., New York, NY 10003. General nonfiction; reference and religious. Royalty basis. Query with SASE; no unsolicited manuscripts.

THE GLOBE PEQUOT PRESS—Old Chester Rd., Box Q, Chester, CT 06412. Linda Kennedy, Vice-Pres./Publications Dir. Nonfiction about New England and the Northeast. Travel guidebooks a specialty. Royalty basis. Query with a sample chapter, contents, and one-page synopsis. SASE a must.

GOLDEN PRESS—See *Western Publishing Co., Inc.*

THE STEPHEN GREENE PRESS/THE LEWIS PUBLISHING CO. (A Div. of *Viking/Penguin*)—15 Muzzey St., Lexington, MA 02173. Tom Begner, Pres. General nonfiction; social science, sports, and nature. Royalty basis.

GREENWILLOW BOOKS (An imprint of *William Morrow and Co., Inc.*)—105 Madison Ave., New York, NY 10016. Susan Hirschman, Ed.-in-Chief. Children's books for all ages. Picture books.

GROSSET AND DUNLAP, INC. (Div. of *Putnam Publishing Group*)—51 Madison Ave., New York, NY 10010. Material accepted through agents only.

GROVE PRESS, INC.—196 W. Houston St., New York, NY 10014. Barney Rosset, Ed. General fiction and nonfiction. Royalty basis. Query with outline and sample chapter. SASE required.

HAMMOND INCORPORATED—Maplewood, NY 07040. Dorothy Bacheller, Ed. Nonfiction: reference, travel. Payment varies. Query with outline and sample chapters. SASE required.

HANCOCK HOUSE—1431 Harrison Ave., Blaine, WA 98230. David Hancock, Ed. Nonfiction: cookbooks, gardening, outdoor guides, Western history, American Indians, sports, real estate, and investing. Pays on royalty basis.

HARCOURT BRACE JOVANOVICH—1250 Sixth Ave., San Diego, CA 92101. Adult trade nonfiction and fiction. *Books for Professionals:* test preparation guides and other student self-help materials. *Miller Accounting Publications, Inc.:* professional books for practitioners in accounting and finance; college accounting texts. Juvenile fiction and nonfiction: for beginning readers through young adults, especially contemporary young adult novels and nonfiction with commercial appeal. Query Maria Modugno, Man./Children's Books. Query; unsolicited manuscripts accepted.

HARPER & ROW—10 E. 53rd St., New York, NY 10022. Fiction, nonfiction, biography, economics, etc.: address Trade Dept. College texts: address College Dept. Paperback originals: address Paperback Dept. Religion, theology, etc.: address Religious Books Dept., 1700 Montgomery St., San Francisco, CA 94111. No unsolicited manuscripts; query only. Royalty basis.

HARPER JUNIOR BOOKS GROUP—10 E. 53rd St., New York, NY 10022. Juvenile fiction, nonfiction and picture books imprints include: *Thomas Y. Crowell Co., Publishers:* juveniles, etc.; *J. B. Lippincott Co.:* juveniles, picture books, etc.; *Harper & Row:* juveniles, picture books, etc.; *Trophy Books:* paperback juveniles. All publish from preschool to young adult titles. No unsolicited manuscripts; query only. Royalty basis.

HARVEST HOUSE PUBLISHERS—1075 Arrowsmith, Eugene, OR 97402. Eileen L. Mason, Ed. Nonfiction—how-to's, educational, health—with evangelical theme. No biographies, history or poetry. Query first. SASE required.

HEARST BOOKS—See *William Morrow and Co.*

D. C. HEATH & COMPANY (Incorporating *American Book Company*)— 125 Spring St., Lexington, MA 02173. Textbooks for schools and colleges. Professional books (*Lexington Books* division). Query Bruce Zimmerli, College; Albert Bursma, School; Robert Bovenschulte, Lexington Books.

HERALD PRESS—616 Walnut Ave., Scottdale, PA 15683. Paul M. Schrock, General Book Editor. Christian books for adults and children (age 9 and up): inspiration, Bible study, self-help, devotionals, current issues, peace studies, church history, missions and evangelism, family life. Send one-page summary and sample chapter. Royalty basis.

HOLIDAY HOUSE, INC.—18 E. 53rd St., New York, NY 10022. Margery S. Cuyler, Vice Pres. General juvenile and young-adult fiction and nonfiction. Royalty basis. Query with outline and sample chapter.

HOLT, RINEHART AND WINSTON—521 Fifth Ave., New York, NY 10175. Accepts no unsolicited material.

HOUGHTON MIFFLIN COMPANY—2 Park St., Boston, MA 02108. Linda Glick Conway, Man. Ed. Fiction: literary, mainstream, historical, suspense and science fiction. Nonfiction: history, natural history, biography. Poetry. Query with SASE. Children's Book Division, address Walter Lorraine: picture books, fiction and nonfiction for all ages. Query for nonfiction, complete manuscripts for fiction. Royalty basis.

H. P. BOOKS—P.O. Box 5367, Tucson, AZ 85703. Rick Bailey, Pub. Illustrated how-to's. 50,000 to 80,000 words, on cooking, gardening, photography, etc. Royalty basis. Query.

ICARUS PRESS—P.O. Box 1225, South Bend, IN 46624. Bruce Fingerhut, Ed. General nonfiction; biography; history; sports, travel; regional. Royalty basis or outright purchase. Query preferred.

IDEALS PUBLISHING—11315 Watertown Plank Rd., Milwaukee, WI 53226. Patricia Pingrey, Dir. Children's books, cookbooks. Flat fee basis.

INNER TRADITION/DESTINY BOOKS—377 Park Ave. S., New York, NY 10016. Lisa Sperling, Ed. Nonfiction, on spiritual subjects, astrology, Eastern mysticism, holistic health, diet, nutrition. Cookbooks. Royalty basis. Query required.

KEATS PUBLISHING, INC.—27 Pine St., Box 876, New Canaan, CT 06840. An Keats, Ed. Nonfiction: health, inspiration, how-to. Royalty basis. Query.

ROBERT R. KNAPP, PUBLISHER—Box 7234, San Diego, CA 92107. Professional reference and textbooks in the humanities and social sciences. Royalty basis. Query.

ALFRED A. KNOPF, INC.—201 E. 50th St., New York, NY 10022. Ashbel Green, Vice-Pres. and Senior Ed. Frances Foster, Juvenile Ed. Distinguished fiction and general nonfiction. Juvenile fiction and nonfiction; picture books, 3,000 to 5,000 words. Royalty basis. Query.

LEXINGTON BOOKS—See *D. C. Heath & Company.*

THE LINDEN PRESS (Div. of *Simon & Schuster*)—1230 Ave. of the Americas, New York, NY 10020. Joni Evans, Pub. and Ed.-in-Chief. Marjorie Williams and Allen Peacock, Sr. Eds. Quality fiction and nonfiction, 75,000 to 125,000 words. Royalty basis. Query with a synopsis or outline and writing sample.

J. B. LIPPINCOTT COMPANY—See *Harper Junior Books Group.*

LITTLE BROWN AND COMPANY—34 Beacon St., Boston, MA 02106. Address Ed. Dept., Trade Division or Children's Books, Trade Division. Fiction, general nonfiction, sports books, juveniles; divisions for law, medical and college texts. Royalty basis. Submissions only from authors who have previously published a book or have published in professional or literary journals, newspapers or magazines. Query first.

LIVE OAK PUBLICATIONS—Box 2193, Boulder, CO 80306. Tom Ellison, Ed. How-to books; self-employment, career change, new ways of working, etc. Query required. Pays on flat fee or royalty basis.

LODESTAR BOOKS—See *E. P. Dutton, Inc.*

LOTHROP, LEE & SHEPARD CO. (An imprint of *William Morrow & Co., Inc.*)—105 Madison Ave., New York, NY 10016. Dorothy Briley, Ed.-in-Chief. Juvenile fiction and nonfiction. Royalty basis. Query.

MCGRAW-HILL BOOK CO.—1221 Ave. of the Americas, New York, NY 10020. Fiction and nonfiction. No unsolicited manuscripts. Queries only.

DAVID MCKAY COMPANY—2 Park Ave., New York, NY 10017. James Loutitt, Pres. and Ed. General nonfiction. Unsolicited manuscripts neither acknowledged nor returned.

MACMILLAN PUBLISHING CO., INC.—866 Third Ave., New York, NY 10022. General Books Division: General and genre fiction, general nonfiction—how-to, current affairs, biography, business, religious, juveniles. College texts and professional books in social sciences, humanities, address *The Free Press.* Royalty basis.

MADRONA PUBLISHERS, INC.—P. O. Box 22667, Seattle, WA 98122. Sara Levant, Acquisitions Ed. General-interest nonfiction trade books (no poetry, children's books or fiction). Royalty basis.

MEREDITH CORP., BOOK GROUP *(Better Homes and Gardens Books)*—1716 Locust St., Des Moines, IA 50336. Gerald M. Knox, Ed. Address The Editors. Books on gardening, crafts, health, decorating, etc. Outright purchase. Query with outline and sample chapter.

JULIAN MESSNER (Div. of *Simon & Schuster*)—1230 Ave. of the Americas, New York, NY 10020. Jane Steltenpohl, Exec. Ed. High-interest, curriculum-oriented nonfiction. General nonfiction for junior and senior high, about 30,000 words; Iris Rosoff, Ed.-in-Chief. Royalty basis.

MILLER ACCOUNTING PUBLICATIONS, INC.—See *Harcourt Brace Jovanovich.*

MOREHOUSE-BARLOW CO., INC.—78 Danbury Rd., Wilton, CT 06897. Stephen S. Wilburn, Ed. Dir. Theology, pastoral care, church administration, spirituality, Anglican studies, history of religion, etc. Royalty basis or outright purchase. Query with outline, contents, and sample chapter.

WILLIAM MORROW AND CO., INC.—105 Madison Ave., New York, NY 10016. Sherry Arden, Pub. Adult fiction and nonfiction. No unsolicited manuscripts. *Morrow Junior Books:* David Reuther, Ed.-in-Chief. Children's books for all ages. *Hearst Marine Books:* Paul Larsen, Pub. *Hearst Books:* Joan B. Nagy, Ed. Dir. General nonfiction. No unsolicited manuscripts.

THE MOUNTAINEERS BOOKS—306 Second Ave. W., Seattle, WA 98119. Ann Cleeland, Man. Ed. Nonfiction on mountaineering, backpacking, canoeing, bicycling, skiing. Field guides, regional histories, biographies of mountaineers; accounts of expeditions. Nature books. Royalty basis. Submit sample chapters and outline.

THE MYSTERIOUS PRESS—129 W. 56th St., New York, NY 10019. Dana Groseclose, Man. Ed. Mystery/suspense novels. Query with synopsis. SASE required.

NAL BOOKS (Div. of *New American Library*)—1633 Broadway, New York, NY 10019. Michaela Hamilton, Ed. Dir. Fiction and nonfiction books. Manuscripts and proposals accepted only from agents or upon personal recommendation.

NATUREGRAPH PUBLISHERS—P. O. Box 1075, Happy Camp, CA 96039. Barbara Brown, Gary M. Kunkle, Eds. Nonfiction: natural history, outdoor living, land and gardening, holistic learning and health, Indian lore, crafts and how-to. Royalty basis. Query.

THOMAS NELSON INC.—Nelson Place at Elm Hill Pike, Nashville, TN 37214. Bruce A. Nygren, Exec. Ed. Religious adult nonfiction. Royalty basis. Query with outline and sample chapters.

NEW REPUBLIC BOOKS/HOLT, RINEHART AND WINSTON—1220 19th St., N.W., Washington, DC 20036. Steve Wasserman, Ed.-in-Chief. Books on politics, Washington affairs, culture, the arts. Royalty basis. Query.

NEW YORK GRAPHIC SOCIETY BOOKS/LITTLE, BROWN AND

CO.—34 Beacon St., Boston, MA 02106. Books on fine arts and photography. Query with outline or proposal and vita. Royalty basis.

W.W. NORTON & COMPANY, INC.—500 Fifth Ave., New York, NY 10110. H. Hinzmann, Assoc. Ed. Fiction and nonfiction. Royalty basis. Query with synopsis, 2 to 3 chapters, and resume. SASE required.

OAK TREE PUBLICATIONS—9601 Aero Dr., San Diego, CA 92123. Adult nonfiction: current social, adult and parenting concerns. Juvenile nonfiction, for ages 7 to 11: unique craft, activity, and science books; fiction. Young adult (ages 12 to 16) nonfiction and fiction; no historical biographies or mystery-adventures. Royalty basis. Query with synopsis, outline and credentials. SASE required.

OPEN COURT PUBLISHING COMPANY—Box 599, La Salle, IL 61301. Scholarly books. Elementary textbooks. Royalty basis. Query.

OXFORD UNIVERSITY PRESS—200 Madison Ave., New York, NY 10016. Authoritative books on literature, history, philosophy, etc.; college textbooks, medical, and reference books; paperbacks. Royalty basis. Query.

OXMOOR HOUSE, INC.—Box 2262, Birmingham, AL 35201. John Logue, Ed. Nonfiction: art, photography, gardening, decorating, cooking and crafts. Royalty basis.

PACIFIC SEARCH PRESS—222 Dexter Ave., Seattle, WA 98109. Cookbooks, gardening, health, recreation, crafts and natural history books. How-to books, travel guides and other books with Northwest tie-in. Query or sample chapters and outline should be addressed to Carolyn J. Threadgill, Dir. Pays on royalty basis.

PANTHEON BOOKS (Div. of *Random House*)—201 E. 50th St., New York, NY 10022. Address Daniel Cullen or Helena Franklin. Nonfiction: academic level for general reader on history, political science, sociology, etc.; picture books; folklore. Some fiction. Royalty basis. Query; no unsolicited manuscripts.

PARKER PUBLISHING COMPANY, INC.—West Nyack, NY 10994. James Bradler, Pres. Self-help and how-to books, 65,000 words: health, money opportunities, business, etc. Royalty basis.

PEACHTREE PUBLISHERS, LTD.—494 Armour Circle, N.E., Atlanta, GA 30324. Chuck Perry, Exec. Ed. Fiction and nonfiction of Southern interest. Humor, cooking, gardening, health, how-to, travel, sports and recreation. Query, with sample chapters and an outline for nonfiction, complete manuscript for fiction.

PELICAN PUBLISHING CO., INC.—1101 Monroe St., Gretna, LA 70053. James L. Calhoun, Exec. Ed. General nonfiction: Americana, regional, architecture, how-to, travel, cookbooks, inspirational, motivational, music, parenting, children's, etc. Royalty basis.

PELION PRESS—See *The Rosen Publishing Group.*

PERSEA BOOKS—225 Lafayette St., New York, NY 10012. Address Editorial Dept. Literary fiction; nonfiction; poetry; translation. Royalty basis. Query only.

PHALAROPE BOOKS—Prentice Hall, Inc., Englewood Cliffs, NJ 07632. Mary E. Kennan, Ed. Series in natural history; science. Royalty basis. Submit query with complete manuscript (200 to 300 pages) and SASE.

PHILOMEL BOOKS (Div. of *Putnam Publishing Group*)—51 Madison Ave., New York, NY 10010. Query Christine Grenz. General fiction, nonfiction, picture books for juveniles.

THE PILGRIM PRESS/UNITED CHURCH PRESS—132 W. 31 St., New York, NY 10001. Larry E. Kalp, Pub. Religious and general-interest nonfiction. Royalty basis. Query with outline and sample chapters.

PINEAPPLE PRESS—P. O. Box 314, Englewood, FL 33533. Jane Cussen, Ed. Serious fiction and nonfiction. Books on nature. Length: 60,000 to 125,000 words. Query with sample chapters and outline. Pays on royalty basis.

PLENUM PUBLISHING CORP.—233 Spring St., New York, NY 10013. Linda Greenspan Regan, Ed. Nonfiction, 200 to 300 pages, on scientific and social scientific topics. Royalty basis. Query required.

POSEIDON PRESS (Imprint of *Pocket Books*)—1230 Ave. of the Americas, New York, NY 10020. Ann Patty, V.P. & Pub. General fiction and nonfiction. Royalty basis. Query.

CLARKSON N. POTTER, INC.—One Park Ave., New York, NY 10016. Carol Southern, Ed. Dir. General trade books. Submissions accepted through agents only.

PRAEGER PUBLISHERS (Div. of *CBS Educational and Professional Publishing Group*)—521 Fifth Ave., New York, NY 10175. Ron Chambers, Ed. Dir. General nonfiction; scholarly and reference books. Royalty basis. Query with outline.

PRENTICE-HALL, INC.—Englewood Cliffs, NJ 07632. Lynne A. Lumsden, Vice-President and Editorial Dir., Publishing Division. Nonfiction. Royalty basis. Query first. No unsolicited manuscripts.

PRESIDIO PRESS—31 Pamaron Way, Novato, CA 94947. Fiction with military background; nonfiction: contemporary military history; from 50,000 words. Royalty basis. Query.

PRUETT PUBLISHING COMPANY—2928 Pearl, Boulder, CO 80301. Gerald Keenan, Man. Ed. Nonfiction: railroadiana, Western Americana, recreational guides with Western orientation. Royalty basis. Query.

G. P. PUTNAM'S SONS (Div. of *Putnam Publishing Group*)—200 Madison Ave., New York, NY 10016. General fiction and nonfiction. No unsolicited manuscripts or queries.

RAINTREE PUBLISHERS INC.—330 E. Kilbourn Ave., Milwaukee, WI 53202. Address Ed. Dept. Juveniles: information and reference books; nonfiction and fiction picture books. Outright purchase or royalty basis. Query.

RAND MCNALLY & COMPANY—Editorial Dept., Box 7600, Chicago, IL 60680. Adult nonfiction: travel, geographically related subjects. Juvenile picture books. Royalty basis or outright purchase. Query with SASE (required).

RANDOM HOUSE, INC.—201 E. 50th St., New York, NY 10022. Howard Kaminsky, Pub. Jason Epstein, Ed.-in-Chief. G. Harrison, Exec. V.P. Juvenile Books; Janet Schulman, Ed.-in-Chief, Reference Books. General fiction and nonfiction; reference and college textbooks. Royalty basis. Query with three chapters and outline for nonfiction; complete manuscript for fiction. No unsolicited manuscripts or queries considered at the juvenile department.

RAWSON ASSOCIATES (Div. of *The Scribner Book Cos.*)—115 Fifth Ave.,

New York, NY 10003. Kennett L. Rawson, Pres. General nonfiction. Royalty basis. Query.

REGNERY GATEWAY—940 North Shore Dr., Lake Bluff, IL 60044. Nonfiction, average of 70,000 words in length: politics, business, religion, science, etc. Royalty basis. Query first.

RENAISSANCE HOUSE—541 Oak St., P. O. Box 177, Frederick, CO 80530. Eleanor H. Ayer, Ed. Western Americana, World War II, and Rocky Mountain West; biographies and historical books. Submit outline, two sample chapters, and short bio. Pays on royalty basis.

FLEMING H. REVELL COMPANY—Old Tappan, NJ 07675. Gary A. Sledge, V.P. and Ed.-in-Chief. Inspirational and devotional religious books. Royalty basis. Query.

RODALE PRESS, BOOK DIVISION—33 E. Minor St., Emmaus, PA 18049. Richard Huttner, Pub. Nonfiction: health, nutrition, alternative energy, gardening; etc. Royalty basis or outright purchase. Query.

THE ROSEN PUBLISHING GROUP, INC.—29 E. 21st St., New York, NY 10010. Roger Rosen, Pres. Ruth C. Rosen, Ed. Young adult books, to 40,000 words, on vocational guidance, journalism, theater, etc. *Pelion Press:* music, art, history. Pays varying rates.

RUTLEDGE BOOKS—Balsam Press, Inc., 122 E. 25th St., New York, NY 10010. Barbara Krohn, Exec. Ed. General and graphic-oriented adult nonfiction; cookbooks; sports books. Royalty basis. Query.

ST. MARTIN'S/MAREK—175 Fifth Ave., New York, NY 10010. Fiction: suspense, mystery, historical; general nonfiction: history, political science, biography. Royalty basis. Query before submitting.

SCHOCKEN BOOKS—62 Cooper Sq., New York, NY 10003. Emile Capouya, Exec. V.P. and Dir. General nonfiction: history, Judaica, women's studies, etc. Royalty basis. Query.

SCOTT, FORESMAN & COMPANY—1900 E. Lake Ave., Glenview, IL 60025. Richard T. Morgan, Pres. Elementary, secondary, and college textbooks and materials; lifelong learning, testing electronic material. Royalty basis.

CHARLES SCRIBNER'S SONS—115 Fifth Ave., New York, NY 10003. Christine Pevitt, Ed.-in-Chief. Fiction; general nonfiction, especially science, business, health. Royalty basis. Query first.

SEAVER BOOKS—333 Central Park W., New York, NY 10025. Jeannette W. Seaver, Pub. Trade fiction, nonfiction. Accepts no unsolicited manuscripts. Royalty basis. Query.

SEVEN SEAS PRESS—524 Thames St., Newport, RI 02840. James R. Gilbert, Ed. Books on sailing. Query first. Pays on royalty basis.

SHADOW MOUNTAIN—P. O. Box 30178, Salt Lake City, UT 84130. Jack M. Lyon, Ed. Nonfiction books: psychology, cooking, gardening, hobbies, sports/recreation, women's interests, business, health, parenting, family relations, and self-improvement. Lengths vary. Query with sample chapter and outline.

SIERRA CLUB BOOKS—2034 Fillmore St., San Francisco, CA 94115. Nonfiction: environment, natural history, the sciences; outdoors and regional guidebooks; juvenile fiction and nonfiction. Royalty basis. Query with SASE.

SILVER BURDETT—250 James St., Morristown, NJ 07960. Walter Kossmann, Product Development Ed. Fiction and nonfiction for children, pre-school through twelfth grade. Query required. Royalty basis.

SOS PUBLICATIONS—4223-25 W. Jefferson Blvd., Los Angeles, CA 90016. S. Paul Bradley, Pub. Carla O. Glover, Ed. Novels, mystery, romance, and adventure, 85,000 words, for "Mini-Bound" series. Royalty basis.

STANDARD PUBLISHING—8121 Hamilton Ave., Cincinnati, OH 45231. Address Marge Miller. Fiction: juveniles; based on Bible or with moral tone. Nonfiction: biblical, Christian education. Conservative evangelical. Query preferred.

STANTON & LEE—44 E. Mifflin St., Madison, WI 53703. Regional publishing house: Books on the folkloric, ethnic, and historic aspects of the Upper Midwest. Royalty basis. Query.

STEIN AND DAY—Scarborough House, Briarcliff Manor, NY 10510. Address Editorial Dept. Adult general fiction and nonfiction. Royalty basis. Query with outline and sample chapter for nonfiction; descriptive letter, up to two pages, for fiction. No unsolicited manuscripts. SASE required.

STEMMER HOUSE—2627 Caves Rd., Owings Mills, MD 21117. Barbara Holdridge, Ed. Adult and juvenile fiction and nonfiction. Royalty basis. Query.

STERLING PUBLISHING CO., INC.—2 Park Ave., New York, NY 10016. Burton Hobson, Pres. How-to, self-help, hobby, woodworking, craft, and sports books. Royalty basis or outright purchase. Query with outline, table of contents, sample chapter, and sample of illustration.

STONE WALL PRESS—1241 30th St., N.W., Washington, DC 20007. Nonfiction on hunting, fishing, outdoors, 200 to 300 pages. Pays on royalty basis. Query first.

STRAWBERRY HILL PRESS—2594 15 Ave., San Francisco, CA 94127. Carolyn Soto, Ed. Nonfiction: biography, autobiography, history, cooking, health, how-to, philosophy, performance arts, and Third World. Query first with sample chapters and outline. Pays on royalty basis.

LYLE STUART, INC.—120 Enterprise Ave., Secaucus, NJ 07094. Allan J. Wilson, Ed. General fiction and nonfiction. *Citadel Press* division: biography, film, history, limited fiction. Royalty basis. Query; no unsolicited manuscripts.

SUMMIT BOOKS—1230 Ave. of the Americas, New York, NY 10020. General-interest fiction and nonfiction of high literary quality. No category books. Royalty basis. Query with outline for nonfiction; query with several chapters for fiction.

SWALLOW PRESS—P. O. Box 2080, Chicago, IL 60609. Self-help, history, biography. Contemporary novels. Western Americana. No unsolicited poetry or fiction. Royalty basis.

TAB BOOKS INC.—Blue Ridge Summit, PA 17214. Raymond A. Collins, Vice-Pres., Edit. Dept. Nonfiction: electronics, computer, how-to, aviation, business, solar and energy, science and technology, back to basics, automotive, marine and outdoor life. Royalty basis or outright purchase. Query.

TAPLINGER PUBLISHING CO.—132 W. 22nd St., New York, NY 10011. Bobs Pinkerton, Roy Thomas, Eds. Serious literary fiction. General nonfiction: history, art, etc. Royalty basis.

JEREMY P. TARCHER, INC.—9110 Sunset Blvd., Los Angeles, CA 90069. Jeremy P. Tarcher, Ed.-in-Chief. General nonfiction: psychology, personal development, health and fitness, women's concerns, science for the layperson, etc. Royalty basis. Query with outline, sample chapter and SASE.

TAYLOR PUBLISHING CO.—1550 W. Mockingbird Lane, Dallas, TX 75235. Jim Nelson Black, Edit. Dir. Nonfiction: fine arts, regional, biography, cooking, gardening, sports and recreation, art/photo, and lifestyle. Query with sample chapters and outline required. Pays on royalty basis.

TEXAS MONTHLY PRESS—Box 1569, Austin, TX 78767. Scott Lubeck, Ed. Dir. Fiction, nonfiction, related to Texas or the Southwest: 60,000 words. Royalty basis.

THUNDER'S MOUTH PRESS—Box 780, New York, NY 10025. Neil Ortenberg, Ed. Literary fiction and poetry collections; books on historical and political topics. Query first. Length requirements: poetry, 96 pages; fiction, to 200 pages. Pays on royalty basis.

TICKNOR & FIELDS (Subsidiary of *Houghton Mifflin Company*)—52 Vanderbilt Ave., New York, NY 10017. General nonfiction and fiction. Royalty basis.

TIMES BOOKS (Div. of *Random House, Inc.*)—201 E. 50th St., New York, NY 10022. Jonathan B. Segal, Ed.-in-Chief. General nonfiction and selected fiction. No unsolicited manuscripts or queries accepted.

TOR BOOKS—49 W. 24th St., New York, NY 10010. Beth Meacham, Sr. Ed. Science fiction and fantasy, 60,000 to 100,000 words. Horror novels and thrillers: address Harriet McDougal, Ed. Dir. Query with outline and sample chapters required. Royalty basis.

TROLL ASSOCIATES—320 Rt. 17, Mahwah, NJ 07430. M. Francis, Ed. Juvenile fiction and nonfiction. Royalty basis or outright purchase. Query preferred.

TURNBULL & WILLOUGHBY—1151 W. Webster, Chicago, IL 60614. R. Strobel, Ed. Humor, how-to, hobby books. Query with sample chapter and outline. Pays on royalty basis.

TYNDALE HOUSE—336 Gundersen Dr., Box 80, Wheaton, IL 60187. Wendell Hawley, Ed.-in-Chief. Christian. Juvenile and adult fiction and nonfiction on subjects of concern to Christians. Submit complete manuscripts. Royalty basis.

UNIVERSE BOOKS—381 Park Ave. S., New York, NY 10016. Louis Barron, Vice-Pres. and Ed. Dir. Art, anthropology, ballet, history, music, natural history, biographies, crafts, linguistics, design, social science, etc. Royalty basis. Query with SASE.

VAN NOSTRAND REINHOLD INC. (Incorporating *CBI Publishing Co.*)—115 Fifth Ave., New York, NY 10003. J. Connolly, Pres. Nonfiction: technical, scientific, and reference subjects. Royalty basis.

THE VANGUARD PRESS, INC.—424 Madison Ave., New York, NY 10017. Bernice Woll, Ed. Adult and juvenile fiction and nonfiction. Royalty basis. Query with sample chapters.

VIKING PENGUIN, INC.—40 W. 23rd St., New York, NY 10010. *The Viking Press:* Adult fiction and nonfiction. *Viking Junior Books:* Juveniles. *Penguin Books:* Paperback reprints and originals. *Viking Kestrel:* juveniles.

Puffin: Juvenile paperback reprints and originals. Royalty basis. Query letters only, with SASE.

WALKER AND COMPANY—720 Fifth Ave., New York, NY 10019. Adult and romantic suspense, men's action, especially mysteries. Regency romances, and westerns. Royalty basis. Query with synopsis.

WANDERER BOOKS (Div. of *Simon & Schuster, Inc.*)—1230 Ave. of the Americas, New York, NY 10020. Ron Buehl, Pub. General-interest juveniles, for 8- to 14-year-olds: Nonfiction, series fiction. Flat fee and royalty basis. Query with outline and sample chapter for nonfiction.

FRANKLIN WATTS, INC.—387 Park Ave. S., New York, NY 10016. Jeanne Vestal, Edit. Dir. Juvenile nonfiction. Royalty basis. Query. SASE required.

WESTERN PUBLISHING CO., INC.—850 Third Ave., New York, NY 10022. Doris Duenewald, Pub., Children's Books; Jonathan B. Latimer, Pub., Adult Books; Ronne Peltzmann, Ed.-in-Chief, Children's Books. Adult nonfiction: family-oriented, how-to's, etc. Children's books, fiction and nonfiction: picture books, storybooks, concept books, novelty books. Royalty basis and outright purchase. Query. Same address and requirements for *Golden Press.*

WILDERNESS PRESS—2440 Bancroft Way, Berkeley, CA 94704. Thomas Winnett, Ed. Nonfiction: sports, recreation, and travel in California, Hawaii, Arizona and Oregon. Query required. Pays on royalty basis.

WINCHESTER PRESS—220 Old New Brunswick Rd., CN 1332, Piscataway, NJ 08854. Bob Elman, Consulting Ed. Nonfiction: outdoors, how-to, etc. Royalty basis. Query.

WINGBOW PRESS—2929 Fifth St., Berkeley, CA 94710. Randy Fingland, Ed. Nonfiction: travel/guidebooks for Northern California, San Francisco Bay area, women's interests, health, psychology, how-to. Query or sample chapter and outline preferred. Pays on royalty basis.

WINSTON PRESS—430 Oak Grove, Minneapolis, MN 55403. Janice M. Johnson. Ed.-in-Chief. Trade Books. Nonfiction, from 120 manuscript pages: religion; self-help; popular appeal. Royalty basis. Submit table of contents and one or two sample chapters.

WORKMAN PUBLISHING CO., INC.—1 W. 39th St., New York, NY 10018. General nonfiction. Normal contractual terms based on agreement.

YANKEE BOOKS—Main St., Dublin, NH 03444. Clarissa Silitch, Ed. Books relating to Northeastern U.S. Cooking, crafts, photographs, maritime subjects, travel, gardening, nature, nostalgia, folklore and popular history. No scholarly history, highly technical work, or off-color humor. Regional New England fiction considered. Royalty basis. Query or send complete manuscript.

CHARLOTTE ZOLOTOW BOOKS (Imprint of *Harper & Row*)—10 E. 53rd St., New York, NY 10022. Juvenile fiction and nonfiction "with integrity of purpose, beauty of language, and an out-of-ordinary look at ordinary things." Royalty basis.

THE ZONDERVAN CORPORATION—1415 Lake Dr., S.E., Grand Rapids, MI 49506. Pamela Jewell, Manuscript Review Ed. Nonfiction books with an evangelical Christian viewpoint: self-help; general nonfiction; Bible study; devotional and gift. Fiction, with a religious theme. Royalty basis. Query with outline and sample chapter.

PAPERBACK BOOK PUBLISHERS

ABINGDON PRESS—201 Eighth Ave., S., P.O. Box 801, Nashville, TN 37202. Ronald P. Patterson, Dir. of Pub. Religious nonfiction juveniles.

ACE BOOKS (Imprint of *Berkley Publishing Group*)—200 Madison Ave., New York, NY 10016. Susan Allison, V.P., Ed.-in-Chief. Science fiction and fantasy. Royalty basis or outright purchase. No unsolicited manuscripts.

APPLE BOOKS—See *Scholastic, Inc.*

ARCHWAY PAPERBACKS (Imprint of *Pocket Books*)—1230 Ave. of the Americas, New York, NY 10020. Fiction for ages 8–15, including adventure, suspense, romance, humor, science fiction, fantasy, animals, sports, and young adult novels. Query with outline and SASE. Royalty basis.

ARCSOFT PUBLISHERS—P.O. Box 132, Woodsboro, MD 21798. Anthony Curtis, Pres. Nonfiction hobby books for beginners, personal computing and hobby electronics, for laymen, general and public consumers, beginners and novices. Outright purchase and royalty basis. Query.

AVON BOOKS—1790 Broadway, New York, NY 10019. Susan Jaffe, Ed.-in-Chief. Modern fiction; mysteries, historical romances; general nonfiction, 60,000 to 200,000 words. Science fiction, 75,000 to 100,000 words. Royalty basis. Query with synopsis, sample chapters, and SASE. *Camelot Books:* Ellen Krieger, Ed. Fiction and nonfiction for 5- to 12-year-olds. Pays on royalty basis. Query. *Flare Books:* Ellen Krieger, Ed. Fiction and nonfiction for 12-year-olds and up. Royalty basis. Query.

BACKCOUNTRY PUBLICATIONS, INC.—P.O. Box 175, Woodstock, VT 05091. Christopher Lloyd, Ed. Regional guidebooks, 150 to 300 manuscript pages, on hiking, walking, canoeing, bicycling, and fishing. Royalty basis.

BALLANTINE BOOKS (Incorporating *Fawcett Books Group*)—201 E. 50th St., New York, NY 10022. Leona Nevler, Exec. Ed. Accepts no unsolicited material for general fiction and nonfiction lines.

BANTAM BOOKS, INC.—666 Fifth Ave., New York, NY 10103. Lou Aronica, Coordinator, Science Fiction/Fantasy; Judy Gitenstein, Ed. Dir., Young Readers Books; Carolyn Nichols, *Loveswept;* Steve Rubin, Ed. Dir., Adult Fiction and Nonfiction. General and educational fiction and nonfiction, 75,000 to 100,000 words. No unsolicited manuscripts.

BERKELEY PUBLISHING GROUP—200 Madison Ave., New York, NY 10016. Roger Cooper, Pub. and Ed. Dir. General-interest fiction and nonfiction; science fiction; suspense and espionage novels; romance. Submit through agent only. Publishes both reprints and originals.

BETHANY HOUSE PUBLISHERS—6820 Auto Club Rd., Minneapolis, MN 55438. Address Ed. Dept. Fiction, nonfiction. Religious. Royalty basis. Query required.

CANDLELIGHT ECSTASY ROMANCES (Imprint of *Dell Publishing Co.*)—245 E. 47th St., New York, NY 10017. Lydia E. Paglio, Sr. Ed. Sensuous, realistic contemporary romantic novels, 50,000 to 60,000 words, set in the United States. *Ecstasy Supreme Romances:* 85,000 to 100,000 words, with more complex plots, more fully developed characterizations; not necessarily confined to the United States. Query with 2- to 4-page synopsis only.

CELESTIAL ARTS (Subsidiary of *Ten Speed Press*)—P.O. Box 7327,

Berkeley, CA 94707. Nonfiction, 25,000 to 80,000 words, on all subjects. No fiction or poetry. Query Paul Reed. Royalty basis.

CHARTER BOOKS (Imprint of *Berkley Publishing Group*)—200 Madison Ave., New York, NY 10016. Roger Cooper, Pub. Adventure, espionage and suspense fiction, women's contemporary fiction, family sagas, and historical novels. Westerns, male action/adventure, and cartoon books. No unsolicited manuscripts. Royalty basis or outright purchase.

CLOVERDALE PRESS—133 Fifth Ave., New York, NY 10003. Book packager. Ben Baglio, Ed.: Young adult and juvenile fiction. Popular writing on computers, all age levels. No unsolicited manuscripts. Query with resume. *Moonstone:* Teen-age romantic suspense novels. Query first. Write for tip sheet. Moonstone Books are distributed by Pocket Books, with Pocket imprint.

CONCORDIA PUBLISHING HOUSE—3558 S. Jefferson Ave., St. Louis, MO 63118. Practical nonfiction with moral or religious values. Very little fiction. No poetry. Royalty basis. Query.

THE CROSSING PRESS—P.O. Box 640, Trumansburg, NY 14886. Elaine Gill, John Gill, Pubs. How-to books; feminist; gay; natural food cookbooks. Fiction. Royalty basis.

DAW BOOKS, INC.—1633 Broadway, New York, NY 10019. Donald A. Wollheim, Pub. and Ed. Science fiction and fantasy, 50,000 to 80,000 words. Royalty basis.

DELL PUBLISHING CO., INC.,—245 E. 47th St., New York, NY 10017. *Dell Books:* family sagas, historical romances, sexy modern romances, war action, occult/horror/psychological suspense, true crime, men's adventure. *Delta:* general-interest nonfiction, psychology, feminism, health, nutrition, child care, science. *Juvenile Books: Yearling* (kindergarten through 6th grade; no unsolicited manuscripts); and *Laurel-Leaf* (grades 7 through 12; no unsolicited manuscripts). Submissions policy for *Dell Books:* Send four-page narrative synopsis for fiction, or an outline for nonfiction. Enclose SASE. Don't send any sample chapters, artwork, or manuscripts. Address submissions to the appropriate Dell division and add Editorial Dept.—Book Proposal.

DELTA BOOKS—See *Dell.*

DOUBLEDAY—245 Park Ave., New York, NY 10167. Loretta Barrett, V.P., Exec. Ed. Adult trade books; fiction, sociology, psychology, philosophy, women's, etc. Query.

FAWCETT BOOKS GROUP—See *Ballantine Books.*

THE FEMINIST PRESS—311 E. 94th St., New York, NY 10128. Reprints of significant lost fiction or autobiography by women; reprints of other classic feminist texts; feminist biography; women's studies for classroom adaptation. Royalty basis.

FIRESIDE BOOKS (Imprint of *Simon & Schuster*)—1230 Ave. of the Americas, New York, NY 10020. General nonfiction. Royalty basis or outright purchase. Submit outline and one chapter.

FLARE BOOKS—See *Avon Books.*

GOLD EAGLE BOOKS (Imprint of *Worldwide Library*)—225 Duncan Mill Rd., Don Mills, Ont., Canada M3B 3K9. Mark Howell, Ed. Formula action-adventure novels, adventure fantasy, fantasy, science fiction. "Work for hire" bonus basis. Query with 3 chapters and outline.

HARLEQUIN BOOKS/CANADA—225 Duncan Mill Rd., Don Mills, Ont., Canada M3B 3K9. *Harlequin Romance:* Maryan Gibson, Sr. Ed. Contemporary romance novels, 50,000 to 60,000 words, any setting, ranging in plot from the traditional and gentle to the more sophisticated and sensuous. Query first. *Harlequin Presents:* Maryan Gibson, Sr. Ed. Romantic novels, 50,000 to 60,000 words, any setting. Query first. *Harlequin Superromance:* Laurie Bauman, Sr. Ed. Contemporary romances, 85,000 words, with North American or foreign setting. New writers: query with manuscript and synopsis. Published writers: same, plus copy of published work. *Harlequin Temptation:* Margaret Carney, Sr. Ed. Sensually charged contemporary romantic fantasies, 60,000 to 65,000 words, Send for tip sheets.

HARLEQUIN BOOKS/U.S.—300 E. 42nd St., 6th Fl., New York, NY 10017. *Harlequin American Romance:* Debra Matteucci, Sr. Ed. Contemporary romances, 70,000 to 75,000 words, with American setting and American characters. *Harlequin Gothic Romances:* Reva Kindser, Ed. Modern or period romances, 50,000 to 60,000 words, with element of foreboding or hidden evil. *Harlequin Regency Romances:* Reva Kindser, Ed. Romances, 50,000 to 60,000 words, set in England between 1811 and 1820. Query. *Harlequin Romantic Intrigue:* Reva Kindser, Ed. Contemporary romances, 70,000 to 75,000 words, set against backdrop of suspense and adventure. Query. Send for tip sheet.

JOHNSON BOOKS, INC.—1880 S. 57th Ct., Boulder, CO 80301. Michael McNierney, Ed. Nonfiction: western history and archaeology, how-to, nature, outdoor sports and recreation, regional. Royalty basis. Query.

JOVE BOOKS—200 Madison Ave., New York, NY 10016. Roger Cooper, Ed.-in-Chief. Fiction and nonfiction. No unsolicited manuscripts.

LAUREL-LEAF BOOKS—See *Dell Publishing Co.*

LEISURE BOOKS—Dorchester Publishing Co., 6 E. 39th St., New York, NY 10016. Jane Thornton, Ed. Dir. Historical romance novels, from 100,000 words; contemporary women's fiction, from 90,000 words; horror/occult books, from 90,000 words; adventure/espionage novels, from 80,000 words. Submit query, synopsis, and sample chapters. Royalty or flat fee basis.

LOVESWEPT (Imprint of *Bantam Books*)—666 Fifth Ave., New York, NY 10019. Alicia Condon, Sr. Ed. Highly sensual, adult contemporary romances. Query.

MAGIC MOMENTS (Imprint of *New American Library*)—1633 Broadway, New York, NY 10019. Betty Anne Crawford, Ed. Contemporary teen romances, 45,000 to 50,000 words. No tip sheet. Submit detailed outline and three or more sample chapters. Royalty.

MEADOWBROOK PRESS—18318 Minnetonka Blvd., Deephaven, MN 55391. Marge Hughes, Ed. Dir. Books on infant and child care; maternity; health; travel; consumer interests. Fiction: juvenile mysteries. Royalty basis and outright purchase. Query. SASE required.

MENTOR BOOKS—See *New American Library.*

MOONSTONE—See *Cloverdale Press.*

MORROW QUILL PAPERBACKS (Div. of *William Morrow*)—105 Madison Ave., New York, NY 10016. Alison Brown-Cerier, Man. Ed. Trade paperbacks. Adult fiction and nonfiction. No unsolicited manuscripts.

JOHN MUIR PUBLICATIONS—P.O. Box 613, Santa Fe, NM 87501. Lisa

Cron, Project Coordinator. General nonfiction: gardening, current interest, how-to, travel, auto-related, etc. Fiction: mysteries. Royalty basis. Query with outline and sample chapters.

NEW AMERICAN LIBRARY—1633 Broadway, New York, NY 10019. Pat Taylor, Ed. *Signet Books:* Commercial fiction: historicals, sagas, thrillers, action/adventure. Nonfiction: self-help, how-to, etc. *Plume Books:* Nonfiction: hobbies, business, health, cooking, child care, psychology, etc. *Mentor Books:* Nonfiction originals for high school and college market. Royalty basis. Query with outline and sample chapters.

101 PRODUCTIONS—834 Mission St., San Francisco, CA 94103. Jacqueline Killeen, Ed. Nonfiction: gardening, domestic arts, travel. Royalty basis. Query; no unsolicited manuscripts.

PACER BOOKS FOR YOUNG ADULTS (Imprint of the *Putnam Publishing Group*)—51 Madison Ave., New York, NY 10010. Beverly Horowitz, Ed.-in-Chief. Fiction: adventure, fantasy, humor, non-formula romance novels, 40,000 to 60,000 words. Pays on individual basis. Query with outline or submit complete manuscript.

PENGUIN BOOKS (Div. of *Viking/Penguin, Inc.*)—40 W. 23rd St., New York, NY 10010. Kathryn Court, Edit. Dir. Adult fiction and nonfiction. No original poetry or juveniles. Royalty basis. Query with synopsis and sample chapter.

PLUME BOOKS—See *New American Library.*

POCKET BOOKS (Div. of *Simon & Schuster, Inc.*)—1230 Ave. of the Americas, New York, NY 10020. Address Editorial Department. Some originals. Query with outline. No unsolicited manuscripts.

POINT BOOKS—See *Scholastic, Inc.*

PRICE/STERN/SLOAN PUBLISHERS, INC.—410 N. La Cienega Blvd., Los Angeles, CA 90048. Short, humorous "non-books." Royalty basis or outright purchase. Query.

PUFFIN BOOKS (Div. of *Viking*)—40 W. 23rd St., New York, NY 10010. Juvenile paperbacks. Query letters only, with SASE.

QUEST BOOKS (Imprint of *The Theosophical Publishing House*)—306 W. Geneva Rd., P.O. Box 270, Wheaton, IL 60189-0270. Shirley Nicholson, Senior Ed. Nonfiction books on Eastern and Western religion and philosophy, holism, healing meditation, yoga, astrology. Royalty basis. Query.

REWARD BOOKS (Subsidiary of *Prentice-Hall, Inc.*)—Englewood Cliffs, NJ 07632. Ted Nardin, Manager. Nonfiction: self-help, real estate, selling, business, health, etc. Royalty basis.

SCHOLASTIC, INC.—730 Broadway, New York, NY 10003. *Point:* Brenda Bowen, Ed. Young adult fiction for readers age 12 and up. *Apple Books:* Brenda Bowen, Ed. Fiction for readers ages 9 to 12. Submit complete manuscript with cover letter and SASE. Royalty basis. Romance line for girls 12 to 15 years, 40,000 to 45,000 words, Ann Reit, Ed.: *Wildfire,* realistic problems of girls in first or early relationships; *Sunfire,* American historical romances, 55,000 words. Query with outline and three sample chapters. Write for tip sheets.

SECOND CHANCE AT LOVE (Imprint of *Berkley Publishing Group*)—200 Madison Ave., New York, NY 10016. Ellen Edwards, Sr. Ed. Contemporary category romances, 55,000 words, with mature, experienced heroines, whose previous relationships/marriages have ended and who find true love with their second chance. Originality a must. Humor popular. Royalty basis. Query with synopsis. Tip sheet.

SERENADE and SERENADE/SAGA ROMANCES (Imprints of *Zondervan Publishing House*)—1414 Lake Dr. S.E., Grand Rapids, MI 49506. Anne W. Severance, Ed. Inspirational romances, 60,000 words, for Christian readers. *Serenade:* contemporary. *Serenade/Saga:* historical. Royalty basis. Send sample chapter, outline, synopsis and biographical sketch. Send for tip sheet.

SILHOUETTE BOOKS—300 E. 42nd St., New York, NY 10017. Karen Solem, Ed.-in-Chief. *Silhouette Romances:* Roz Noonan, Ed. Contemporary romances, 53,000 to 58,000 words. *Special Edition:* Mary Clare Kersten, Sr. Ed. Sophisticated contemporary romances, 70,000 to 80,000 words. *Intimate Moments:* Leslie Wainger, Sr. Ed. Sensuous, sophisticated contemporary romances, 80,000 to 85,000 words. *First Love:* Nancy Jackson, Sr. Ed. Contemporary romances for 11- to 16-year-old girls, 45,000 to 50,000 words. Query with synopsis and SASE to appropriate editor. No unsolicited manuscripts.

SPECTRA BOOKS (Imprint of *Bantam Books*)—666 Fifth Ave., New York, NY 10103. Science fiction and fantasy, with emphasis on storytelling and characterization. Query; no unsolicited manuscripts. Advance royalty basis.

SPECTRUM BOOKS (Imprint of *Prentice Hall, Inc.*)—Englewood Cliffs, NJ 07632. Mr. Robin Bartlett, Ed. of Special Projects. Business, finance, self-help, how-to, 50,000 to 60,000 words. Submit proposal, outline, credentials, etc. Royalty basis.

STERLING PAPERBACKS—2 Park Ave., New York, NY 10016. General nonfiction, 50,000 to 90,000 words: how-to, self-help, health, hobbies, etc. Royalty basis or outright purchase. Query with outline and table of contents.

SUNFIRE—See *Scholastic, Inc.*

TEN SPEED PRESS—P.O. Box 7123, Berkeley, CA 94707. Paul Reed, Ed. Self-help and how-to on careers, recreation, etc.; natural science, history, cookbooks. Query with outline and sample chapters. Royalty basis.

TIMBRE BOOKS (Imprint of *Arbor House*)—235 E. 45th St., New York, NY 10017. Address Editorial Dept. Nonfiction: business, sports, humor, health, music, finance, etc. Biographies, essays, reference books. Query with detailed outline or submit complete manuscript. Advance royalty basis.

TROUBADOR PRESS—One Sutter St., Suite 205, San Francisco, CA 94104. Juvenile illustrated games, activity, paper doll, coloring and cut-out books. Royalty basis or outright purchase. Query with outline and SASE.

TURNING POINTS (Imprint of *New American Library*)—1633 Broadway, New York, NY 10019. Teen romances. No unsolicited material accepted.

TWAYNE PUBLISHERS—70 Lincoln St., Boston, MA 02111. Address Editorial Dept. Nonfiction for academic and general readers on women's studies, biography, history, current affairs, literature, and science. Query with chapter outline and one or two sample chapters. Royalty basis.

WARNER BOOKS—666 Fifth Ave., New York, NY 10103. Bernard Shir-Cliff, Ed.-in-Chief. Fiction: historical romance, contemporary women's fiction, unusual big-scale horror and suspense. Nonfiction: business books, health and nutrition, self-help and how-to books. Royalty basis. Query with sample chapters. Also publishes trade paperbacks and hardcover titles.

WILDFIRE—See *Scholastic, Inc.*

WILSHIRE BOOK COMPANY—12015 Sherman Rd., North Hollywood, CA 91605. Specialized nonfiction: Inspirational, self-help: entrepreneurship, business, advertising, mail order, sports, health, horses, etc. Royalty basis. Query with synopsis or outline. SASE required.

WOODBRIDGE PRESS PUBLISHING HOUSE—Box 6189, Santa Barbara, CA 93111. Howard B. Weeks, Ed. Nonfiction: health, gardening, nutrition, humor, cooking. Royalty basis. Query with outline and sample chapter.

YEARLING BOOKS—See *Dell Publishing Co., Inc.*

ZEBRA BOOKS—475 Park Ave., S., New York, NY 10016. Leslie Gelbman, Fiction Ed. Wendy McCurdy, Nonfiction Ed. Biography, how-to, humor, self-help. Fiction: adventure, confessional, gothic, historical, horror, etc. Query required.

UNIVERSITY PRESSES

University presses generally publish books of a scholarly nature or of specialized interest by authorities in a given field. Many publish only a handful of titles a year. Always query first. Do not send any manuscripts until you have been invited to do so by the editor.

BRIGHAM YOUNG UNIVERSITY PRESS—209 University Press Bldg., Provo, UT 84602.

BUCKNELL UNIVERSITY PRESS—Lewisburg, PA 17837.

CAMBRIDGE UNIVERSITY PRESS—32 East 57th St., New York, NY 10022.

THE CATHOLIC UNIVERSITY OF AMERICA PRESS—620 Michigan Ave., N.E., Washington, DC 20064.

COLORADO ASSOCIATED UNIVERSITY PRESS—University of Colorado, 1424 15th St., Boulder, CO 80302.

COLUMBIA UNIVERSITY PRESS—562 West 113th St., New York, NY 10025.

DUKE UNIVERSITY PRESS—Box 6697, College Station, Durham, NC 27708.

DUQUESNE UNIVERSITY PRESS—101 Administration Bldg., Pittsburgh, PA 15219.

FORDHAM UNIVERSITY PRESS—Box L, Bronx, NY 10458.

GEORGIA STATE UNIVERSITY, SCHOOL OF BUSINESS ADMINISTRATION, PUBLISHING SERVICES DIVISION—University Plaza, Atlanta, GA 30303.

HARVARD UNIVERSITY PRESS—79 Garden St., Cambridge, MA 02138.

INDIANA UNIVERSITY PRESS—10th and Morton Sts., Bloomington, IN 47401.

THE JOHNS HOPKINS UNIVERSITY PRESS—Baltimore, MD 21218.

KENT STATE UNIVERSITY PRESS—Kent, OH 44242.

LOUISIANA STATE UNIVERSITY PRESS—Baton Rouge, LA 70803.

LOYOLA UNIVERSITY PRESS—3441 North Ashland Ave., Chicago, IL 60657.

MEMPHIS STATE UNIVERSITY PRESS—Memphis, TN 38152.

MICHIGAN STATE UNIVERSITY PRESS—1405 South Harrison Rd., East Lansing, MI 48824.

THE M.I.T. PRESS—28 Carleton St., Cambridge, MA 02142.

NEW YORK UNIVERSITY PRESS—Washington Sq., New York, NY 10003.

OHIO STATE UNIVERSITY PRESS—Hitchcock Hall, Rm. 316, 2070 Neil Ave., Columbus, OH 43210.

OHIO UNIVERSITY PRESS—Scott Quadrangle, Athens, OH 45701.

OREGON STATE UNIVERSITY PRESS—101 Waldo Hall, Corvallis, OR 97331.

THE PENNSYLVANIA STATE UNIVERSITY PRESS—215 Wagner Bldg., University Park, PA 16802.

PRINCETON UNIVERSITY PRESS—Princeton, NJ 08540.

RUTGERS UNIVERSITY PRESS—30 College Ave., New Brunswick, NJ 08903.

SOUTHERN ILLINOIS UNIVERSITY PRESS—Box 3697, Carbondale, IL 62901.

SOUTHERN METHODIST UNIVERSITY PRESS—Dallas, TX 75275.

STANFORD UNIVERSITY PRESS—Stanford, CA 94305.

STATE UNIVERSITY OF NEW YORK PRESS—State Univ. Plaza, Albany, NY 12246.

SYRACUSE UNIVERSITY PRESS—1011 East Water St., Syracuse, NY 13210.

TEMPLE UNIVERSITY PRESS—Broad and Oxford Sts., Philadelphia, PA 19122.

UNIVERSITY OF ALABAMA PRESS—Drawer 2877, University, AL 35486.

UNIVERSITY OF ARIZONA PRESS—Box 3398, College Station, Tucson, AZ 85722.

UNIVERSITY OF CALIFORNIA PRESS—2223 Fulton St., Berkeley, CA 94720.

UNIVERSITY OF CHICAGO PRESS—5801 Ellis Ave., Chicago, IL 60637.

UNIVERSITY OF GEORGIA PRESS—Athens, GA 30602.

UNIVERSITY OF ILLINOIS PRESS—Urbana, IL 61801.

UNIVERSITY OF MASSACHUSETTS PRESS—Box 429, Amherst, MA 01002.

UNIVERSITY OF MICHIGAN PRESS—Ann Arbor, MI 48106.

UNIVERSITY OF MINNESOTA PRESS—2037 University Ave., S.E., Minneapolis, MN 55455.

UNIVERSITY OF MISSOURI PRESS—107 Swallow Hall, Columbia, MO 65201.

UNIVERSITY OF NEBRASKA PRESS—901 North 17th St., Lincoln, NE 68588.

UNIVERSITY OF NEW MEXICO PRESS—Albuquerque, NM 87131.

UNIVERSITY OF NOTRE DAME PRESS—Notre Dame, IN 46556.

UNIVERSITY OF OKLAHOMA PRESS—1005 Asp Ave., Norman, OK 73019.

UNIVERSITY OF PITTSBURGH PRESS—127 North Bellefield Ave., Pittsburgh, PA 15260.

UNIVERSITY OF SOUTH CAROLINA PRESS—USC Campus, Columbia, SC 29208.

UNIVERSITY OF TENNESSEE PRESS—Communications Bldg., Knoxville, TN 37916.

UNIVERSITY OF UTAH PRESS—Bldg. 513, Salt Lake City, UT 84112.

UNIVERSITY OF WASHINGTON PRESS—Seattle, WA 98195.

UNIVERSITY OF WISCONSIN PRESS—Box 1379, Madison, WI 53701.

THE UNIVERSITY PRESS OF KENTUCKY—Lafferty Hall, Lexington, KY 40506.

UNIVERSITY PRESS OF MISSISSIPPI—3825 Ridgewood Rd., Jackson, MS 39211.

THE UNIVERSITY PRESS OF NEW ENGLAND—Box 979, Hanover, NH 03755.

THE UNIVERSITY PRESS OF VIRGINIA—Box 3608, University Sta., Charlottesville, VA 22903.

THE UNIVERSITY PRESS OF FLORIDA—15 N.W. 15th St., Gainesville, FL 32603.

WAYNE STATE UNIVERSITY PRESS—5959 Woodward Ave., Detroit, MI 48202.

WESLEYAN UNIVERSITY PRESS—55 High Street, Middletown, CT 06457.

YALE UNIVERSITY PRESS—302 Temple St., New Haven, CT 06511.

SYNDICATES

Syndicates are business organizations that publish nothing themselves, but buy material from writers and artists to sell to newspapers all over the country and the world. Authors are paid either a percentage of the gross proceeds or an outright fee.

Of course, features by people well known in their fields have the best chance of being syndicated. In general, syndicates want columns that have been popular in a local newspaper, perhaps, or magazine. Since most syndicated fiction has been published previously in magazines or books, beginning fiction writers should try to sell their stories to magazines before submitting them to syndicates.

Always query syndicates before sending manuscripts—their needs change frequently.

CANADA WIDE FEATURE SERVICE—Box 345, Station A, Toronto, Ontario, M5A 3W7, Canada. Glenn–Stewart Garnett, Ed. Interviews with well-known celebrities and international political figures, 1,500 to 2,000 words with photos. Pays 50% of gross, on publication.

CONTEMPORARY FEATURES SYNDICATE—P.O. Box 1258, Jackson, TN 38301. Lloyd Russell, Ed. Articles, 1,000 to 3,000 words: how-to, back-to-nature, money-savers, travel, business, etc. Self-help pieces, 1,000 to 10,000 words. Pays from $25, on acceptance.

CURIOUS FACTS FEATURES—6B Ridge Ct., Lebanon, OH 45036. Donald Whitacre, Ed. Nonfiction, to 500 words, and fillers to 50 words, for average reader; strange, true and unknown facts and oddities. Pays 50%, on publication.

FICTION NETWORK—Box 5651, San Francisco, CA 94101. Fiction, to 2,500 words. One submission per author; submit manuscript unfolded. SASE required. Pays royalty basis. Allow 12 weeks for response.

HARRIS & ASSOCIATES FEATURES—615 Carla Way, La Jolla, CA 92037. Dick Harris, Ed. Sports and family-oriented features, to 1,200 words; fillers and short humor, 500 to 800 words. Queries preferred. Pays varying rates.

HERITAGE FEATURES SYNDICATE—214 Mass. Ave., NE, Washington, DC 20002. Andrew Seamans, Sr., Man. Ed. Public policy news features; syndicates weekly by-lined columns and editorial cartoons. Query with SASE a must.

HISPANIC LINK NEWS SERVICE—1420 N St., NW, Washington, DC 20005. Hector Ericksen-Mendoza, Ed. Trend articles, general features, Hispanic focus, 650 to 700 words; editorial cartoons. Pay $25 for op/ed column and cartoons, on acceptance. Send SASE for writers' guidelines.

THE HOLLYWOOD INSIDE SYNDICATE—Box 49957, Los Angeles, CA 90049. John Austin, Director. Feature material, 750 to 1,000 words, on TV and motion picture personalities. Story suggestions for 3–part series. Pieces on unusual medical and scientific breakthroughs. Pays on percentage basis for features, negotiated rates for ideas, on acceptance.

INTERNATIONAL MEDICAL TRIBUNE SYNDICATE—600 New Hampshire Ave., Suite 700, NW, Washington, DC 20037. Health and medical news, features, 250 to 1,000 words; technical accuracy and clarity a must. Pays 15¢ to 20¢ a word.

KING FEATURES SYNDICATE—235 E. 45th St., New York, NY 10017. James D. Head, Ed. Columns, comics; most contributions on contract for regular columns. Feature articles for Sunday newspaper supplement "Sunday Woman"; query Merry Clark, Ed.

751

LONGHORN PRODUCTIONS—219 Whitham St., Irving, TX 75060. Michael Davian, Ed., Cindy Gonzalez, Women's Ed. Nationally slanted original features, 1,500 to 3,000 words, and columns, 600 to 1,000 words. Fillers, short humor, trivia, etc. Particularly interested in topical subjects. Pays $5 to $75 per insertion per newspaper, on acceptance for features, on monthly basis for other material. Query required, with SASE.

LOS ANGELES TIMES SYNDICATE—Times Mirror Sq., Los Angeles, CA 90053. Cartoons, comics, features and columns. Query for articles, either one shots or series.

NATIONAL NEWS BUREAU—2019 Chancellor St., Philadelphia, PA 19103. Articles, 500 to 800 words, interviews, consumer news, how-to's, travel pieces, reviews, entertainment pieces, features, etc. Pays on publication.

NEW YORK TIMES SYNDICATION SALES—200 Park Ave., New York, NY 10166. Paula Reichler, V.P./Ed. Dir. Previously published articles only, to 2,000 words. Query with published article or tear sheet. Pays 40%, on publication.

NEWS AMERICA SYNDICATE—1703 Kaiser Ave., Irvine, CA 92714. Leighton McLaughlin, Ed. Columns, comic strips, panel cartoons, serials.

NEWSPAPER ENTERPRISE ASSOCIATION, INC.—200 Park Ave., New York, NY 10166. David Hendin, Sr. Vice Pres. and Ed. Director. Ideas for new concepts in syndicated columns, comic strips, and panels. No single stories or stringers. Payment by contractual arrangement.

OCEANIC PRESS SERVICE—P.O. Box 6538, Buena Park, CA 90622-6538. John R. West, General Manager. Buys reprint rights on previously published novels, self-help, and how-to books; interviews with celebrities; illustrated features on celebrities, family, health, beauty, personal relations, etc.; cartoons, comic strips. Pays on acceptance. Query.

SELECT FEATURES OF NEWS AMERICA SYNDICATE—1703 Kaiser Blvd., P.O. Box 19620, Irvine, CA 92714. Doris Richetti, Man., Select Features. Articles and series dealing with lifestyle trends, psychology, health, beauty, fashion, finance, jobs; personality profiles. Query or send complete manuscript. Pays varying rates, on publication.

SINGER COMMUNICATIONS INC.—3164 W. Tyler Ave., Anaheim, CA 92801. Marian Singer, Ed. U.S. and/or foreign reprint rights to romantic short stories, historical and romantic novels, published during last 25 years. Biography, women's-interest material, all lengths. Home repair, real estate, crosswords. Interviews with celebrities. Illustrated columns, humor, cartoons, comic strips. Pays on percentage basis or by outright purchase.

SPOTLIGHT INTERNATIONAL—157 Passaic Ave., Summit, NJ 07091. Del Rogers, Ed. Dir. Magazine features, with b&w or color slides, on trends; unusual, amazing, or controversial stories; new and exciting inventions; human-interest stories with photos, 500 to 2,000 words. Pays 65% for first rights, 50% for second rights, on publication. Query with SASE preferred.

TRANSWORLD FEATURE SYNDICATE, INC.—373 Park Ave., South, 6th fl., New York, NY 10016. Thelma Brown, Syndication Manager. Feature material for North American and overseas markets. Query required.

TRIBUNE MEDIA SERVICES—720 N. Orange Ave., Orlando, FL 32801. Michael Argirion, Ed. Continuing columns, comic strips, features, electronic data bases.

UNITED FEATURE SYNDICATE—200 Park Ave, New York, NY 10166. David Hendin, Sr. Vice President. Creative, professional columns and comics. No one-shots or series. Payment by contractual arrangement.

UNITED PRESS INTERNATIONAL—1400 Eye St., NW, Washington, DC 20005. Ron Cohen, Man. Ed. Seldom accepts free-lance material.

LITERARY PRIZE OFFERS

Each year many important prize contests are open for free-lance writers. The short summaries given below are intended merely as guides. Closing dates, requirements, and rules are tentative. No manuscript should be submitted to any competition unless the writer has first checked with the Contest Editor and received complete information about a particular contest.

Send a stamped, self-addressed envelope with all requests for contest rules and application forms.

ACADEMY OF AMERICAN POETS—177 E. 87th St., New York, NY 10128. Offers Walt Whitman Award: Publication and $1,000 cash prize for a book-length poetry manuscript by a poet who has not yet published a volume of poetry. Closes in November.

ACTORS THEATRE OF LOUISVILLE—316 W. Main St., Louisville, KY 40202. Conducts the National One-Act Play Contest, with a prize of $1,000 for a one-act, previously unproduced play. Closes in April.

THE AMERICAN ACADEMY AND INSTITUTE OF ARTS AND LETTERS—633 W. 155th St., New York, NY 10032. Offers Richard Rodgers Production Award, which consists of subsidized production in New York City by a non-profit theater for a musical, play with music, thematic review, or any comparable work other than opera. Closes in December.

AMERICAN HEALTH MAGAZINE—80 Fifth Ave., New York, NY 10011. Offers prize of $2,000 for short story about an intense physical experience. Closes in February.

ASSOCIATED WRITING PROGRAMS—Old Dominion University, Norfolk, VA 23508. Conducts Annual Award Series in Short Fiction, the Novel, and Nonfiction. In each category the prize is book publication and a $1,000 honorarium. Closes in December. Offers the Edith Shiffert Prize in Poetry: $1,000 cash prize and publication by the University Press of Virginia for an unpublished book-length collection of poetry. Closes in December.

BEVERLY HILLS THEATRE GUILD—JULIE HARRIS PLAYWRIGHT AWARD—2815 N. Beachwood Dr., Los Angeles, CA 90068. Address Marcella Meharg. Offers prize of $5,000, plus $2,000 for production in Los Angeles area, for a previously unproduced and unpublished full-length play. Closes in November.

THE CALDWELL PLAYHOUSE—P.O. Box 277, Boca Raton, FL 33432. Conducts Playwriting Contest, with prize of $1,000 and production for original, unproduced full-length play. Closes in April of even-numbered years.

CBS INC. AND THE FOUNDATION OF THE DRAMATISTS GUILD— FDG/CBS New Plays Program, The Foundation of the Dramatists Guild, 234 W. 44th St., New York, NY 10036. Sponsor New Plays Program, in which five different theaters select five new plays for production. Winning playwrights also receive prizes of $5,000 each. Closes in September.

CHICAGO MAGAZINE—303 E. Wacker Dr., Chicago, IL 60601. Offers Nelson Algren Award: $5,000, plus publication, for unpublished short story by writer living in the U.S. Closes in January.

COURT THEATRE—The University of Chicago, 5706 S. University Ave., Chicago, IL 60637. Offers Sergel Drama Prize: $1,500 for full-length unpublished and unproduced play. Closes in June of odd-numbered years.

EUGENE V. DEBS FOUNDATION—Dept. of History, Indiana State University, Terre Haute, IN 47809. Offers Bryant Spann Memorial Prize of $750 for published or unpublished article or essay on themes relating to social protest or human equality. Closes in April.

DELACORTE PRESS—Dept. BFYR, 1 Dag Hammarskjold Plaza, New York, NY 10017. Sponsors Delacorte Press Prize for an outstanding first young adult novel. The prize consists of one Delacorte hardcover and Dell paperback contract, an advance of $4,000 on royalties, and a $1,000 cash prize. Closes in December.

FOREST A. ROBERTS-SHIRAS INSTITUTE—Forest Roberts Theatre, Northern Michigan Univ., Marquette, MI 49855. Dr. James A. Panowski, Dir. Conducts annual Playwriting Competition, with prize of $1,000, plus production, for an original, full-length, previously unproduced and unpublished play. Closes in November.

THE FOUNDATION OF THE DRAMATISTS GUILD—234 W. 44th St., New York, NY 10036. Sponsors Young Playwrights Festival. Playwrights under 19 years of age may submit scripts; winning plays will be given full stage productions or staged readings. Closes in July.

HIGHLIGHTS FOR CHILDREN—803 Church St., Honesdale, PA 18431. Conducts Contest for Juvenile Fiction, with cash prizes and publication for short stories. Closes in March.

HONOLULU MAGAZINE—36 Merchant St., Honolulu, HI 96813. Sponsors an annual fiction contest, with a cash prize of $500, plus publication in *Honolulu,* for an unpublished short story with a Hawaiian theme, setting, and/or characters. Closes in September.

HOUGHTON MIFFLIN COMPANY—2 Park St., Boston, MA 02108. Offers Literary Fellowship for fiction or nonfiction project of exceptional literary merit written by American author. Work under consideration must be unpublished and in English. Fellowship consists of $10,000, of which $2,500 is an outright grant and $7,500 is an advance on royalties. There is no deadline.

HUMBOLDT STATE UNIVERSITY—English Dept., Arcata, CA 95521. Sponsors the Raymond Carver Short Story Contest, with a prize of $250, plus publication in the literary journal *Toyon,* for an unpublished short story by a writer living in the U.S. Closes in December.

ILLINOIS STATE UNIVERSITY—Dept. of Theatre, Illinois State Univ., Normal, IL 61761. Address John W. Kirk. Sponsors Fine Arts Competition, with prize of $1,000, plus production, for previously unpublished and unproduced full-length play. Closes in October.

JACKSONVILLE UNIVERSITY—Annual Playwriting Contest, Dept. of Theatre Arts, College of Fine Arts, Jacksonville Univ., Jacksonville, FL 32211. Davis Sikes, Dir. Conducts playwriting contest, with prize of $1,000 and production, for original, previously unproduced script (full-length or one-act). Closes in January.

JEWISH COMMUNITY CENTER THEATRE—3505 Mayfield Rd., Cleveland Heights, OH 44118. Dorothy Silver, Dir. of Cultural Arts. Offers cash award of $1,000 and a staged reading for an original, previously unproduced full-length play on some aspect of the Jewish experience. Closes in December.

CHESTER H. JONES FOUNDATION—P.O. Box 43033, Cleveland, OH 44143. Conducts the National Poetry Competition, with more than $1,800 in cash prizes (including a first prize of $1,000) for original, unpublished poems. Closes in March.

LINCOLN COLLEGE—Lincoln, IL 62656. Address Janet Overton. Offers Billee Murray Denny Poetry Award for original poem by poet who has not previously published a volume of poetry. First prize of $1,000, 2nd prize of $450, and 3rd prize of $200 are offered. Closes in May.

MADEMOISELLE MAGAZINE—350 Madison Ave., New York, NY 10017. Sponsors Fiction Writers Contest, with first prize of $1,000, plus publication, and second prize of $500, for short fiction. Closes in March.

MS. MAGAZINE—119 W. 40th St., New York, NY 10018. Sponsors annual College Fiction Contest for short story by college student. Prize is publication and electronic typewriter. Closes in May.

NATIONAL ENDOWMENT FOR THE ARTS—Washington, DC 20506. Address Director, Literature Program, The National Endowment for the Arts offers fellowships to writers of poetry, fiction, scripts, and other creative prose. Deadlines vary; write for guidelines.

NATIONAL PLAY AWARD—P.O. Box 71011, Los Angeles, CA 90071. National Play Award consists of a $7,500 cash prize, plus $5,000 for production, for an original, previously unproduced play. Sponsored by National Repertory Theatre Foundation. Closes in October of odd-numbered years.

NATIONAL POETRY SERIES—18 W. 30th St., New York, NY 10001. Sponsors Annual Open Competition for unpublished, book-length poetry manuscript. The prize is publication. Closes in February.

THE NEW ENGLAND THEATRE CONFERENCE—50 Exchange St., Waltham, MA 02154. First prize of $500 and second prize of $250 are offered for unpublished and unproduced one-act plays in the John Gassner Memorial Playwriting Award Competition. Closes in April.

O'NEILL THEATER CENTER—234 W. 44th St., Suite 901, New York, NY 10036. Offers stipends, staged readings, and room and board at the National Playwrights Conference, for new stage and television plays. Closes in December.

755

THE PARIS REVIEW—541 E. 72nd St., New York, NY 10021. Sponsors Aga Khan Prize for Fiction: $1,000, plus publication, for previously unpublished short story. Closes in June. Offers Bernard F. Connors Prize: $1,000, plus publication, for previously unpublished poem. Closes in May. Offers John Train Humor Prize: $1,500, plus publication, for unpublished work of humorous fiction, nonfiction, or poetry. Closes in March.

PEN AMERICAN CENTER—568 Broadway, New York, NY 10012. Sponsors PEN/Nelson Algren Award: stipend of $1,000, plus one-month residency at Edward Albee Foundation's summer residence on Long Island, for uncompleted novel or collection of short stories by an American writer who needs assistance to complete the work. Closes in November. Sponsors Renato Poggioli Translation Award: $3,000 grant for a translator working on his or her first book-length translation from Italian into English. Closes in February.

PLAYHOUSE ON THE SQUARE—2121 Madison Ave., Memphis, TN 38104. Address Mr. Jackie Nichols. Conducts Mid-South Playwriting Contest, with stipend for unproduced, full-length play. Southerners are given preference. Closes in April.

POETRY SOCIETY OF AMERICA—15 Gramercy Park, New York, NY 10003. Conducts annual contests—The Celia B. Wagner Memorial Award, the John Masefield Memorial Award, and the Elias Lieberman Student Poetry Award—in which cash prizes are offered for unpublished poems. Contests close in December.

RADIO DRAMA AWARDS—3319 W. Beltline Hwy., Madison, WI 53713. Norman Michie, Exec. Producer. Wisconsin Public Radio conducts annual Radio Drama Awards competition for original scripts by writers in Illinois, Iowa, Michigan, Minnesota, and Wisconsin. Prizes for thirty-minute radio scripts are professional production and cash awards of $500 (first prize), $300 (second), and $200 (third). Closes in January.

REDBOOK MAGAZINE—224 W. 57th St., New York, NY 10019. Conducts Short Story Contest for original fiction. First prize is $1,000, plus publication. Second prize of $500 and third prize of $300 are also offered. Closes in May.

SAN JOSE STATE UNIVERSITY—One Washington Square, San Jose, CA 95192. Address Dr. Howard Burman, Theatre Arts Dept. Sponsors Harold C. Crain Playwriting Contest, with a prize of $500, plus production, for a previously unproduced full-length play. Closes in November.

CHARLES SCRIBNER'S SONS—115 Fifth Ave., New York, NY 10003. Offers Scribner Crime Novel Award: Publication, $3,000, publishing terms to be negotiated, for full-length mystery novel by a writer who has not yet published a novel. Closes in December. Also sponsors the Maxwell Perkins Prize: Publication, $5,000 prize, publishing terms to be negotiated, for a book-length fiction manuscript on some aspect of American life, written by U.S. citizen or resident who has not yet published a novel. Closes in December. Sponsors Scribner Science Writing Prize: Publication, $5,000 advance on royalties, and a $5,000 advertising and promotion guarantee for an unpublished work of nonfiction (full-length treatment or collection of essays) involving natural history, the physical sciences, or the sciences of man. Only writers who are American citizens or permanent residents of the U.S. and who have not previously published a science book for general readers are eligible. Closes in September.

SEVENTEEN MAGAZINE—850 Third Ave., New York, NY 10022. Sponsors short fiction contest for writers between the ages of 13 and 20. Prizes of $2,000, $1,200, $700, and five honorable mentions of $50 are offered. Winning entries may be published in *Seventeen* magazine or publications of Dell Publishing Company. Closes in January.

SIERRA REPERTORY THEATRE—P.O. Box 3030, Sonora, CA 95370. Offers Cummings/Taylor Award of $350, plus production, for original, previously unpublished, unproduced full-length play or musical. Closes in May.

SINCLAIR RESEARCH LTD.—50 Staniford St., Boston, MA 02114. Conducts annual contest for Sinclair Prize for Fiction (5,000 plus publication) for a previously unpublished novel of social or political significance. Write for required entry form; manuscripts must be sent to Sinclair's offices in Great Britain. Closes in July.

SOURCE THEATRE COMPANY—1809 14th St., N.W., Washington, DC 20009. Address Keith Parker, Literary Manager. Conducts National Playwriting Competition for an original, unproduced one-act or full-length play. Cash prize of $250 and production are offered for the winning script. Closes in April.

SUNSET CENTER—P.O. Box 5066, Carmel, CA 93921. Richard Tyler, Director. Offers prize of up to $2,000 for an original, unproduced full-length play in its annual festival of Firsts Playwriting Competition. Closes in August.

SYRACUSE UNIVERSITY PRESS—1600 Jamesville Ave., Syracuse, NY 13210. Address Director. Sponsors John Ben Snow Prize: $1,000, plus publication, for unpublished book-length manuscript about New York State, especially upstate or central New York. Closes in December.

TEXAS WOMAN'S UNIVERSITY—Dept. of Music and Drama, P.O. Box 23865, Denton, TX 76204. Conducts Margo Jones Playwriting Competition, in which a prize of $1,000, plus production, is offered for a full-length, unpublished and unproduced play for and about women. Closes in February.

UNICORN THEATRE—3514 Jefferson, Kansas City, MO 64111. Sponsors National Playwright Competition, with a first prize of $1,000, plus travel and residency while in production, for an original, unpublished and unproduced full-length play. Closes in May.

U.S. NAVAL INSTITUTE—Annapolis, MD 21402. Address Membership Department. Conducts Arleigh Burke Essay Contest, with prizes of $1,500, $1,000, and $750, plus publication, for essays on the advancement of professional, literary, and scientific knowledge in the naval and maritime services, and the advancement of the knowledge of sea power. Closes in December.

UNIVERSITY OF ALABAMA AT BIRMINGHAM—School of Humanities, Dept. of Theatre and Dance, University Sta., Birmingham, AL 35294. Rick J. Plummer, Director. Conducts Ruby Lloyd Apsey Playwriting Competition, with $500 cash prize, plus production and travel expenses, for previously unproduced full-length play. Closes in January.

UNIVERSITY OF CINCINNATI—Elliston Poetry Collection, 646 Central Library, Univ. of Cincinnati, Cincinnati, OH 45221. Offers the George Elliston Poetry Prize, which consists of publication by the Ohio State University Press and a standard royalty contract, for a book-length poetry manuscript by a poet who has not yet published a book. Closes in December.

UNIVERSITY OF HAWAII—Kennedy Theatre, Univ. of Hawaii, 1770 East-West Rd., Honolulu, HI 96822. Conducts annual Kumu Kahua Playwriting Contests with cash prizes for original plays dealing with some aspect of Hawaiian experience. Close in January.

UNIVERSITY OF HAWAII PRESS—2840 Kolowalu St., Honolulu, HI 96822. Sponsors Pacific Poetry Series competition, with prize of publication and royalty contract, for unpublished book-length poetry manuscript by a writer who has not previously published a volume of poetry. Closes in March of odd-numbered years.

UNIVERSITY OF IOWA—Iowa School of Letters Award, Dept. of English, English-Philosophy Bldg., Univ. of Iowa, Iowa City, IA 52242. Offers Iowa School of Letters Award—$1,000, plus publication—for a book-length collection of short stories by writer who has not yet had a book published.

UNIVERSITY OF MASSACHUSETTS PRESS—Juniper Prize, Univ. of Massachusetts Press, c/o Mail Rm., Amherst, MA 01003. Offers Juniper Prize of $1,000, plus publication, for book-length manuscript of poetry. Closes in October.

UNIVERSITY OF MISSOURI PRESS—200 Lewis Hall, Columbia, MO 65211. Breakthrough Editor. Conducts competition for Breakthrough Series: Authors who have not yet published a book are eligible to submit complete manuscripts of poetry, short fiction, or drama; the prize is publication. Closes in March of odd-numbered years.

UNIVERSITY OF PITTSBURGH PRESS—Pittsburgh, PA 15260. Sponsors Drue Heinz Literature Prize—$5,000, plus publication and royalty contract—for unpublished collection of short stories. Closes in August. Also sponsors Agnes Lynch Starrett Poetry Prize—$1,000, plus publication and royalty contract—for book-length collection of poems by poet who has not yet published a volume of poetry. Closes in April.

UNIVERSITY OF WISCONSIN PRESS—Poetry Series, 114 N. Murray St., Madison, WI 53715. Ronald Wallace, Admin. Offers Brittingham Prize in Poetry: $500 plus publication, for unpublished book-length poetry manuscript. Closes in September.

WALT WHITMAN CENTER FOR THE ARTS AND HUMANITIES—2nd and Cooper Sts., Camden, NJ 08102. Sponsors the annual Camden Poetry Award: $1,000, plus publication, for an unpublished book-length collection of poetry. Closes in September.

WORD WORKS—P.O. Box 42164, Washington, DC 20015. Offers the Washington Prize of $1,000 for unpublished poem by American poet. Closes in November.

YALE UNIVERSITY PRESS—Box 92A, Yale Sta., New Haven, CT 06520. Address Editor, Yale Series of Younger Poets. Conducts Yale Series of Younger Poets Competition, in which the prize is publication of a book-length manuscript of poetry, written by a poet under 40 who has not previously published a volume of poems. Closes in February.

WRITERS COLONIES

A writers colony offers isolation and freedom from everyday distractions to writers who want a quiet place to concentrate on their work. Though some colonies are quite small, with space for just three or four writers at a time, others can provide accommodations for as many as thirty or forty. The length of a residency may vary, too—from a couple of weeks to five or six months. These programs have strict admissions policies, and writers must submit a formal application or letter of intent, a resumé, writing samples, and letters of recommendation. Write for application information first, enclosing a stamped, self-addressed envelope (SASE).

CENTRUM FOUNDATION—The Centrum Foundation sponsors residencies of two to three months at Fort Worden State Park, a Victorian fort on the Strait of Juan De Fuca in Washington. Nonfiction, fiction, and poetry writers may apply for residency awards, which include stipend of $600 a month. Application deadline is in early December; send letter explaining the project, short biographical note, and sample of published work. For details, send SASE in fall, to Carol Jane Bangs, Director of Literature Programs, Centrum Foundation, Fort Worden State Park, P.O. Box 1158, Port Townsend, WA 98368.

CUMMINGTON COMMUNITY OF THE ARTS—Residencies of one month or more in the Berkshires. Quarterly deadlines. For more information, send SASE to Cummington Community of the Arts, Cummington, MA 01026.

DORLAND MOUNTAIN COLONY—Novelists, playwrights, and poets may apply for residencies at the Dorland Preserve of the Nature Conservancy in the Palomar Mountains of Southern California. Cottages, firewood, and kerosene are provided. Application deadlines are March 1 and September 1. For further information and application forms, send SASE to Resident Director, Dorland Mountain Colony, P.O. Box 6, Temecula, CA 92390.

DORSET COLONY HOUSE—Writers and playwrights are offered low-cost room with kitchen facilities at the Colony House in Dorset, Vermont. Periods of residency are 3 to 6 weeks, and are available between October 1 and June 1. Application deadlines are September 15, December 15, and February 15 for the periods immediately following the deadlines. For more information, send SASE to John Nassivera, Director, Dorset Colony House, Dorset, VT 05201.

FINE ARTS WORK CENTER IN PROVINCETOWN—Fellowships including living and studio space and monthly stipends at the Fine Arts Work Center on Cape Cod, for writers to work independently. Residencies are for seven months only; apply before the February 1 deadline. For details, send SASE to Jim Potter, Dir., Fine Arts Work Center, P.O. Box 565, 24 Pearl St., Provincetown, MA 02657.

THE HAMBIDGE CENTER—Two-week and two-month residencies are offered to writers at the Hambidge Center in the Northeast Georgia mountains. Send SASE for application form to Director, Residency Program, The Hambidge Center, P.O. Box 33, Rabun Gap, GA 30568.

THE MACDOWELL COLONY—Studios, room and board at the MacDowell Colony of Peterborough, New Hampshire, for writers to work without interruption in semi-rural woodland setting. Selection is competitive. Apply at least six months in advance of season desired; residencies average 5 to 6 weeks. For details and admission forms, send SASE to Admissions Coordinator, The MacDowell Colony, 100 High St., Peterborough, NH 03458.

THE MILLAY COLONY FOR THE ARTS—At Steepletop in Austerlitz, New York—former home of Edna St. Vincent Millay—studios, living quarters, and meals are provided to writers at no cost. Residencies are for one month. Application deadlines are February 1, May 1, and September 1. To apply, send

SASE to The Millay Colony for the Arts, Inc., Steepletop, Austerlitz, NY 12017.

MONTALVO CENTER FOR THE ARTS—Three-month, low-cost residencies at the Villa Montalvo in the foothills of the Santa Cruz Mountains south of San Francisco, for writers working on specific projects. There are a few small fellowships available to writers with demonstrable financial need. Send self-addressed envelope and 37¢ stamp for application forms to Montalvo Residency Program, P.O. Box 158, Saratoga, CA 95070.

UCROSS FOUNDATION—Residencies, two weeks to four months, at the Ucross Foundation in the foothills of the Big Horn Mountains in Wyoming, for writers to concentrate on their work without interruptions. Residencies are available from August through May. The application deadline is October 1; for more information, send SASE to Director, Residency Program, Ucross Foundation, Ucross Route, Box 19, Clearmont, WY 82835.

VIRGINIA CENTER FOR THE CREATIVE ARTS—Residencies of one to three months at the Mt. San Angelo Estate in Sweet Briar, Virginia, for writers to work without distraction. Apply at least three months in advance. A limited amount of financial assistance is available. For more information, send SASE to William Smart, Director, Virginia Center for the Creative Arts, Sweet Briar, VA 24595.

HELENE WURLITZER FOUNDATION OF NEW MEXICO—Rent-free and utility-free studios at the Helene Wurlitzer Foundation in Taos, New Mexico, are offered to creative writers and other artists. Length of residency varies from three to six months. The Foundation is closed from October 1 through March 31 annually. For details, send SASE to Henry A. Sauerwein, Jr., Exec. Dir., The Helene Wurlitzer Foundation of New Mexico, Box 545, Taos, NM 87571.

YADDO—Artists, writers, and composers are invited for short-term residencies at the Yaddo estate in Saratoga Springs, New York. Although there is no fixed charge, voluntary contributions are encouraged. Requests for applications should be sent with SASE before January 15 or August 1 to Curtis Harnack, Exec. Director, Yaddo, Box 395, Saratoga Springs, NY 12866. An application fee of $10.00 is required.

STATE ARTS COUNCILS

State Arts Councils sponsor grants, fellowships, and other programs for writers. To be eligible for funding, a writer *must* be a resident of the state in which he is applying. For more information, write to the addresses listed below.

ALABAMA STATE COUNCIL ON THE ARTS AND HUMANITIES
Albert B. Head, Exec. Director
323 Adams Ave.
Montgomery, AL 36130

ALASKA STATE COUNCIL ON THE ARTS
Jean Palmer, Grants Officer
619 Warehouse Ave., Suite 220
Anchorage, AK 99501

ARIZONA COMMISSION ON THE ARTS
Shelley Cohn, Executive Director
417 W. Roosevelt
Phoenix, AZ 85003

OFFICE OF ARKANSAS STATE ARTS AND HUMANITIES
Amy Aspell, Executive Director
The Heritage Center, Suite 200
225 E. Markham
Little Rock, AR 72201

CALIFORNIA ARTS COUNCIL
Roberta Blagg, Public Information Officer
1901 Broadway, Suite A
Sacramento, CA 95818-2492

COLORADO COUNCIL ON THE ARTS AND HUMANITIES
Ellen Sollod, Executive Director
770 Pennsylvania St.
Denver, CO 80203

CONNECTICUT COMMISSION ON THE ARTS
Address Grant Program
190 Trumbull St.
Hartford, CT 06103

DELAWARE STATE ARTS COUNCIL
Cecelia Fitzgibbon, Administrator
Carvel State Building
820 N. French St.
Wilmington, DE 19801

FLORIDA ARTS COUNCIL
Chris Doolin
Dept. of State
Div. of Cultural Affairs
The Capitol
Tallahassee, FL 32301

GEORGIA COUNCIL FOR THE ARTS
2082 E. Exchange Place, Suite 100
Tucker, GA 30084

HAWAII STATE FOUNDATION ON CULTURE AND THE ARTS
Sarah M. Richards, Executive Director
335 Merchant St., Rm. 202
Honolulu, HI 96813

IDAHO COMMISSION ON THE ARTS
304 W. State St.
Boise, ID 83720

ILLINOIS ARTS COUNCIL
Mary Lee O'Brien, Acting Artists Division Director
State of Illinois Center
100 W. Randolph, Suite 10-500
Chicago, IL 60601

INDIANA ARTS COMMISSION
Geoff Gephart, Program Specialist, Literature
32 E. Washington St., 6th Fl.
Indianapolis, IN 46204

IOWA STATE ARTS COUNCIL
Marilyn Parks, Technical Assistance/Grants Officer
State Capitol Complex
Des Moines, IA 50319

KANSAS ARTS COMMISSION
John Austin Carey, Executive Director
112 West 6th St., Suite 401
Topeka, KS 66603

KENTUCKY ARTS COUNCIL
Roger L. Paige, Director
Berry Hill, Louisville Rd.
Frankfort, KY 40601

LOUISIANA COUNCIL FOR MUSIC AND PERFORMING ARTS, INC.
Literature Program Associate
7524 St. Charles Ave.
New Orleans, LA 70118

MAINE STATE COMMISSION ON THE ARTS AND HUMANITIES
Stuart Kestenbaum
State House, Station 25
Augusta, ME 04330

MARYLAND STATE ARTS COUNCIL
Linda Vlasak, Program Director
Artists-in-Education and Poets-in-the-Schools
15 W. Mulberry St.
Baltimore, MD 21201

MASSACHUSETTS COUNCIL ON THE ARTS AND HUMANITIES
Pat Dixon, Literature Program Director
80 Boylston St., 10th Fl.
Boston, MA 02116

MICHIGAN COUNCIL FOR THE ARTS
Barbara K. Goldman, Executive Director
1200 Sixth Ave., 4th Floor
Detroit, MI 48226

COMPAS: WRITERS IN THE SCHOOLS
Molly LaBerge, Director
308 Landmark Center
75 W. 5th St.
St. Paul, MN 55102

MINNESOTA STATE ARTS BOARD
John Maliga, Program Director
Artist Assistance Program
432 Summit Ave.
St. Paul, MN 55102

762

MISSISSIPPI ARTS COMMISSION
Mrs. Theo Inman, Program Administrator
301 N. Lamar St., Suite 400
Jackson, MS 39201

MISSOURI ARTS COUNCIL
Teresa Goettsch, Program Administrator for Literature
Wainwright Office Complex
111 N. 7th St., Suite 105
St. Louis, MO 63101

MONTANA ARTS COUNCIL
Program Director, Artist Services
35 S. Last Chance Gulch
Helena, MT 59620

NEBRASKA ARTS COUNCIL
Douglas D. Elliott, Associate Director/Programs
1313 Farnam On-the-Mall
Omaha, NE 68102-1873

NEVADA STATE COUNCIL ON THE ARTS
William L. Fox, Executive Director
329 Flint St.
Reno, NV 89501

NEW HAMPSHIRE COMMISSION ON THE ARTS
Phenix Hall, 40 N. Main St.
Concord, NH 03301

NEW JERSEY STATE COUNCIL ON THE ARTS
Noreen M. Tomassi, Literary Arts Coordinator
109 W. State St.
Trenton, NJ 08625

NEW MEXICO ARTS DIVISION
Santa Fe Poets-in-the Schools Program
224 E. Palace Ave.
Santa Fe, NM 87501

NEW YORK STATE COUNCIL ON THE ARTS
Gregory Kolovakos, Director, Literature Program
915 Broadway
New York, NY 10010

NORTH CAROLINA ARTS COUNCIL
Lida Lowrey, Literature Program
Dept. of Cultural Resources
Raleigh, NC 27611

NORTH DAKOTA COUNCIL ON THE ARTS
Donna Evenson, Exec. Director
Black Building, Suite 606
Fargo, ND 58102

OHIO ARTS COUNCIL
727 E. Main St.
Columbus, OH 43205

STATE ARTS COUNCIL OF OKLAHOMA
Ellen Binkley, Assistant Director
Jim Thorpe Bldg., Rm. 640
Oklahoma City, OK 73105

OREGON ARTS COMMISSION
835 Summer St., N.E.
Salem, OR 97301

PENNSYLVANIA COUNCIL ON THE ARTS
Peter Carnahan, Literature and Theatre Programs
Mack Granderson, Artists-in-Education Program
Room 216, Finance Bldg.
Harrisburg, PA 17120

RHODE ISLAND STATE COUNCIL ON THE ARTS
Iona B. Dobbins, Executive Director
312 Wickenden St.
Providence, RI 02903

SOUTH CAROLINA ARTS COMMISSION
Steve Lewis, Director, Literary Arts Program
1800 Gervais St.
Columbia, SC 29201

SOUTH DAKOTA ARTS COUNCIL
Artists-in-Schools Coordinator
108 W. 11th St.
Sioux Falls, SD 57102

TENNESSEE ARTS COMMISSION
320 Sixth Ave. N., Suite 100
Nashville, TN 37219

TEXAS COMMISSION ON THE ARTS
P.O. Box 13406, Capitol Station
Austin, TX 78711

UTAH ARTS COUNCIL
G. Barnes, Literary Arts Coordinator
617 East South Temple
Salt Lake City, UT 84102

VERMONT COUNCIL ON THE ARTS
Geof Hewitt, Grants Coordinator
136 State St.
Montpelier, VT 05602

VIRGINIA COMMISSION FOR THE ARTS
Peggy J. Baggett, Executive Director
James Monroe Bldg., 17th Floor
101 N. 14th St.
Richmond, VA 23219

WASHINGTON STATE ARTS COMMISSION
Lee Bassett, Artists-in-Residence Program
110 9th and Columbia Bldg., MS GH-11
Olympia, WA 98504

WEST VIRGINIA DEPT OF CULTURE AND HISTORY
Arts and Humanities Division
The Cultural Center, Capitol Complex
Charleston, WV 25305

WISCONSIN ARTS BOARD
107 S. Butler St.
Madison, WI 53703

WYOMING COUNCIL ON THE ARTS
Joy Thompson, Executive Director
Capitol Complex
Cheyenne, WY 82001

ORGANIZATIONS FOR WRITERS

AMERICAN MEDICAL WRITERS ASSOCIATION
5272 River Rd., Suite 410
Bethesda, MD 20816
Lillian Sablack, *Executive Director*
   Any person actively interested in or professionally associated with any medium of medical communication is eligible for membership. The annual dues for Active Members are $55.

AMERICAN SOCIETY OF JOURNALISTS AND AUTHORS
1501 Broadway, Suite 1907
New York, NY 10036
Alexandra Cantor, *Executive Secretary*
   Membership is open to qualified professional free-lance writers of nonfiction; qualification of applications are judged by the Membership Committee. Initiation fee is $50 and annual dues are $95.

AMERICAN TRANSLATORS ASSOCIATION
109 Croton Avenue
Ossining, NY 10562
Rosemary Malia, *Staff Administrator*
   Membership is open to any person actively engaged in translating, interpreting, or professionally related work *(Active Member)*, or to any person or organization interested in the objectives of the Association *(Associate Membership)*. Dues for individuals are $50 annually.

THE AUTHORS GUILD, INC.
234 West 44th Street
New York, NY 10036
   A writer who has published a book in the last seven years with an established publisher, or one who has published several magazine pieces with periodicals of general circulation within the last eighteen months, may be eligible for active, voting membership. A new writer—for example, one who has had a contract offer from an established book publisher—may be eligible for

associate membership, on application to the Membership Committee. Dues are $60 a year, which includes membership in The Authors League of America.

THE AUTHORS LEAGUE OF AMERICA, INC.
(Authors Guild and Dramatists Guild)
2343 West 44th St.
New York, NY 10036
The Authors League of America is a national organization of over 12,000 authors and dramatists, representing them on matters of joint concern, such as copyright, taxes, and freedom of expression. Membership in the League is restricted to authors and dramatists who are members of The Authors Guild, Inc. and The Dramatists Guild, Inc. Matters such as contract terms and subsidiary rights are in the province of the two guilds.

THE DRAMATISTS GUILD, INC.
234 West 44th Street
New York, NY 10036
David E. LeVine, *Executive Director*
The Dramatists Guild, the professional association of playwrights, composers, and lyricists, promotes the interests of authors of stage works. It protects their rights in such works and strives to improve the conditions under which they are created. All theater writers (produced or not) are eligible for Active or Associate membership; non-writers interested in the Guild may become Subscribing members.

MYSTERY WRITERS OF AMERICA, INC.
150 Fifth Avenue
New York, NY 10011
Mary A. Frisque, *Executive Secretary*
There are four classifications of membership in MWA: 1) *Active*—for anyone who has made a sale in the field of mystery, suspense, or crime writing (book, magazine, newspaper, motion picture, radio, television). Only *Active* members may vote or hold office. 2) *Associate*—for non-writers who are allied to the mystery field: editors, publishers, critics, literary agents, motion picture, radio or television producers. 3) *Corresponding*—for writers living outside the United States. *Corresponding* members do not need to be American citizens. 4) *Affiliate*—for new writers who have not yet made a sale, or non-writers who are mystery enthusiasts.
Annual dues are $50; $25 for *Corresponding* members.

NATIONAL ASSOCIATION OF SCIENCE WRITERS, INC.
P.O. Box 294
Greenlawn, NY 11740
Anyone who is actively engaged in the dissemination of science information, and has two years or more of experience in this field, is eligible to apply for membership. Active members must be principally engaged in reporting science through newspapers, magazines, television, or other media that reach the public directly. Associate members report science through limited-circulation publications, and other special media. Annual membership dues are $45.

THE NATIONAL WRITERS CLUB
1450 S. Havanna, Suite 620
Aurora, CO 80012
Donald E. Bower, *Director*
The National Writers Club is a nonprofit representative organization of new and established writers, poets, and playwrights, founded in 1937, serving free-lance writers throughout the U.S. and Canada. Membership includes a

subscription to the bimonthly newsletter, *Authorship*. Professional dues are $50 annually, plus a $15 initiation fee.

P.E.N. AMERICAN CENTER
568 Broadway
New York, NY 10012
Karen Kennerly, *Executive Secretary*
P.E.N. American Center is an independent association of writers—poets, playwrights, essayists, editors and novelists—that promotes and maintains intellectual cooperation among men and women of letters in the United States and abroad in the interest of literature, exchange of ideas, freedom of expression, and good will.

The criteria for membership are the publication of two books of literary merit in the United States, and nomination by a P.E.N. member. There are two classifications of dues. Dues: $45 per year (includes invitations to P.E.N. events, auto rental discount, and eligibility for group health insurance).

THE POETRY SOCIETY OF AMERICA
15 Gramercy Park
New York, NY 10003
Dennis Stone, *Administrative Director*
Founded in 1910, The Poetry Society of America seeks through a variety of programs to gain a wider audience for American poetry. The Society offers 17 annual prizes for poetry, and many contests are open to non-members as well as members. Also sponsors workshops, free public poetry readings, publication of the semiannual *The Poetry Review,* and a Newsletter. Dues for all classes of membership are the same—$30 annually.

PRIVATE EYE WRITERS OF AMERICA
1873 Crowley Circle East
Longwood, FL 32779
Robert J. Randisi, *Executive Director*
Writers who have published a work of fiction—short story, novel, television or movie screenplay—with a private eye as the central character are eligible to join the organization as active members. Serious devotees of the P.I. story may become associate members. Dues are $20 for active members, $10 for non-active. Present annual Shamus Award for best in P.I. fictiion.

SCIENCE FICTION WRITERS OF AMERICA
P.O. Box H
Wharton, NJ 07885
Peter D. Pautz, *Executive Secretary*
Any writer who has sold a work of science fiction or fantasy is eligible for membership in the Science Fiction Writers of America. For membership information and applications, writers should apply to the address above. Dues are $50 per year for actives, $35 for affiliates, plus $10 installation fee for new affiliates. Quarterly SFWA Bulletin available to non-members for $10/4 issues.

SOCIETY OF AMERICAN TRAVEL WRITERS
1120 Connecticut Ave., Suite 940
Washington, DC 20036
Ken Fischer, *Administrative Coordinator*
Membership in the Society of American Travel Writers is by invitation. Active Membership is limited to salaried travel editors, writers, broadcasters, or photographers; and to those who are employed as free lancers in any of the above areas and with a sufficient steady volume of published or distributed work about travel to satisfy the Membership Committee. Associate Mem-

bership is open to persons regularly engaged in public relations within the travel industry. Initiation fee for Active members is $150; for Associate members, $300. Annual dues for Active members are $90, for Associate members, $170.

SOCIETY OF CHILDREN'S BOOK WRITERS
P.O. Box 296, MAR Vista Station
Los Angeles, CA 90066
Lin Oliver, *Executive Director*
Full memberships are open to those whose work for children has been published. Associate memberships are open to all those with an interest in children's literature, whether or not they have published. Yearly dues are $30 for both full and associate members.

SOCIETY FOR TECHNICAL COMMUNICATION
815 15th St., N.W.
Washington, DC 20005
William C. Stolgitis, *Executive Director*
The Society for Technical Communication is a professional organization dedicated to the advancement of the theory and practice of technical communication in all media. The membership represents every discipline associated with technical communication, including technical writers and editors, publishers, artists and draftsmen, researchers, educators, and audiovisual specialists. There are about 90 chapters, with 10,000 members, in the United States, Canada, and other countries.

WESTERN WRITERS OF AMERICA, INC.
1753 Victoria
Sheridan, WY 82801
Barbara Ketcham, *Secretary-Treasurer*
Western Writers of America is a non-profit organization of writers of fiction, nonfiction, and poetry pertaining to the traditions, legends, development and history of the American West. Its chief purpose is to promote a more widespread distribution, readership and appreciation of the West and its literature. Dues are $40 a year. Sponsors annual Spur Awards contest.

WRITERS GUILD OF AMERICA, EAST, INC.
555 W. 57th St.
New York, NY 10019
Mona Mangan, *Executive Director*

WRITERS GUILD OF AMERICA, WEST, INC.
8955 Beverly Blvd.
Los Angeles, California 90048
Brian Walton, *Executive Director*
The Writers Guild of America (East and West) represents writers in the fields of radio, television, and motion pictures.

In order to qualify for membership, a writer must fulfill current requirements for employment or sale of material in one of these three fields.

The basic dues are $25 a quarter for the Writers Guild West and $12.50 a quarter for Writers Guild East. In addition, there are quarterly dues based on a percentage of the writer's earnings in any of the fields over which the Guild has jurisdiction. The initiation fee is $1,000 for Writers Guild East and $1,500 for Writers Guild West. Writers living East of the Mississippi join Writers Guild East and West of the Mississippi, Writers Guild West.

AMERICAN LITERARY AGENTS

Most literary agents do not usually accept new writers as clients. Since the agent's only income is a percentage—10% to 20%—of the amount he receives from the sales he makes for his clients, he must have as clients writers who are selling fairly regularly to good markets. Always query an agent first. Do not send any manuscripts until the agent has asked you to do so. The following list is only a partial selection of representative agents. Addresses which include zip codes in parentheses are located in New York City (the majority of agents on this list are in New York). A list of agents can also be obtained by sending a stamped, self-addressed envelope to Society of Authors' Representatives, P. O. Box 650, Old Chelsea Sta., New York, NY 10113 or Independent Literary Agents Assn., Inc., 21 W. 26th St., New York, NY 10010.

BRET ADAMS LTD., 448 W. 44th St. (10036)

JULIAN BACH LITERARY AGENCY, INC., 747 Third Ave. (10017)

LOUIS BERMAN, The Little Theatre Bldg., 240 W. 44th St. (10036)

GEORGES BORCHARDT, INC., 136 E. 57th St. (10022)

BRANDT & BRANDT LITERARY AGENTS, INC., 1501 Broadway (10036)

THE HELEN BRANN AGENCY, INC., 157 W. 57th St. (10019)

CURTIS BROWN, LTD., 10 Astor Place (10003)

KNOX BURGER ASSOCIATES, LTD., 39½ Washington Square South (10012)

COLLIER ASSOCIATES, 875 Sixth Ave., #1003 (10001)

DON CONGDON ASSOCIATES, INC., 177 E. 70th St. (10021)

JOAN DAVES, 59 E. 54th St. (10022)

ANITA DIAMANT, 310 Madison Ave., #1508 (10017)

CANDIDA DONADIO & ASSOCIATES, INC., 231 W. 22nd St. (10011)

THE DORSET GROUP, 820 W. Belmont Ave., Chicago (60657)

ANN ELMO AGENCY, INC., 60 E. 42nd St. (10165)

JOHN FARQUHARSON, LTD., Suite 1914, 250 W. 57th St. (10107)

THE FOX CHASE AGENCY, INC., 419 E. 57th St. (10022)

ROBERT A. FREEDMAN DRAMATIC AGENCY, INC., 1501 Broadway, #2310 (10036)

SAMUEL FRENCH, INC., 45 W. 25th St. (10010)

GRAHAM AGENCY, 311 W. 43rd St. (10036)

BLANCHE C. GREGORY, INC., Two Tudor City Place (10017)

HELEN HARVEY, 410 W. 24th St. (10019)

INTERNATIONAL CREATIVE MANAGEMENT, INC., 40 W. 57th St. (10019)

JCA LITERARY AGENCY, INC., 242 W. 27th St., No. 4A (10001)

LUCY KROLL AGENCY, 390 West End Ave. (10024)

PINDER LANE PRODUCTIONS, LTD., 159 W. 53rd St. (10019)

THE LANTZ OFFICE, 888 Seventh Ave. (10106)

LESCHER & LESCHER, LTD., 155 E. 71st St. (10021)

ELLEN LEVINE LITERARY AGENCY, 432 Park Ave. S., #1205 (10016)

LITERISTIC, LTD., 264 Fifth Ave. (10001)

THE STERLING LORD AGENCY, INC., 660 Madison Ave. (10021)

ELISABETH MARTON, 96 Fifth Ave. (10011)

HAROLD MATSON COMPANY, INC., 276 Fifth Ave. (10001)

GERARD MCCAULEY AGENCY, INC., 141 E. 44th St. #208 (10017)

MCINTOSH & OTIS, INC., 475 Fifth Ave. (10017)

HELEN MERRILL, 337 W. 22nd St. (10011)

WILLIAM MORRIS AGENCY, INC., 1350 Ave. of the Americas (10019)

HAROLD OBER ASSOCIATES, INC., 40 E. 49th St. (10017)

FIFI OSCARD ASSOCIATES, INC., 19 W. 44th St. (10036)

RAINES & RAINES, 71 Park Ave. (10016)

PAUL R. REYNOLDS, INC., 71 W. 23rd St. (10011)

FLORA ROBERTS, INC., Penthouse A, 157 W. 57th St. (10019)

MARIE RODELL-FRANCES COLLIN LITERARY AGENCY, Suite 2004, 110 W. 40th St. (10018)

ROSENSTONE/WENDER, 3 E. 48th St. (10017)

RUSSELL & VOLKENING, INC., 50 W. 29th St. (10001)

GLORIA SAFIER, INC., 244 E. 53rd St. (10022)

JOHN SCHAFFNER ASSOCIATES, INC., 114 E. 28th St. (10016)

JAMES SELIGMANN AGENCY, 175 Fifth Ave., #1101 (10010)

CHARLOTTE SHEEDY LITERARY AGENCY, INC., 145 W. 86th St. (10024)

THE SHUKAT COMPANY, LTD., 340 W. 55th St., #1A (10019)

PHILIP G. SPITZER LITERARY AGENCY, 1465 Third Ave. (10028)

ROSLYN TARG LITERARY AGENCY, INC., 105 W. 13th St., #15E (10011)

WALLACE & SHEIL AGENCY, INC., 177 E. 70th St. (10021)

RHODA WEYR LITERARY AGENCY, 322 Central Park West (10025)

MARY YOST ASSOCIATES, INC., 59 E. 54th St., No. 52 (10022)
ET

INDEX TO MARKETS